Household and Family Religion in Anti

The Ancient World: Comparative Histories

Series Editor: Kurt Raaflaub

Published

War and Peace in the Ancient World
Edited by Kurt Raaflaub

Household and Family Religion in Antiquity
Edited by John Bodel and Saul Olyan

Epic and History
Edited by David Konstan and Kurt A. Raaflaub

Geography and Ethnography: Perceptions of the World in Pre-Modern Societies
Edited by Kurt A. Raaflaub and Richard J. A. Talbert

The Roman Empire in Context: Historical and Comparative Perspectives
Edited by Johann P. Arnason and Kurt A. Raaflaub

Highways, Byways, and Road Systems in the Pre-Modern World
Edited by Susan E. Alcock, John Bodel, and Richard J. A. Talbert

In preparation

Household and Family Religion in Antiquity

Edited by
John Bodel and Saul M. Olyan

A John Wiley & Sons, Ltd., Publication

This paperback edition first published 2012

Edition history: Blackwell Publishing Ltd (hardback, 2008)

Blackwell Publishing was acquired by John Wiley & Sons in February 2007. Blackwell's publishing program has been merged with Wiley's global Scientific, Technical, and Medical business to form Wiley-Blackwell.

Registered Office
John Wiley & Sons Ltd, The Atrium, Southern Gate, Chichester, West Sussex, PO19 8SQ, United Kingdom

Editorial Offices
350 Main Street, Malden, MA 02148-5020, USA
9600 Garsington Road, Oxford, OX4 2DQ, UK
The Atrium, Southern Gate, Chichester, West Sussex, PO19 8SQ, UK

For details of our global editorial offices, for customer services, and for information about how to apply for permission to reuse the copyright material in this book please see our website at www.wiley.com/wiley-blackwell.

Library of Congress Cataloging-in-Publication Data

Household and family religion in antiquity : contextual and comparative perspectives / edited by John Bodel and Saul M. Olyan.
p. cm. – (Ancient world–comparative histories)
Includes bibliographical references and index.
ISBN 978-1-4051-7579-1 (hardcover : alk. paper) ISBN 978-1-118-25533-9 (pbk. : alk. paper) 1. Family–Religious life. 2. Religions. I. Bodel, John P., 1957– II. Olyan, Saul M.
BL625.6.H68 2008
2042.4109014–dc22

2007043652

A catalogue record for this book is available from the British Library.

This book is published in the following electronic formats: ePDFs 9781444302981; Wiley Online Library 9781444302974 ; Mobi 9781444322217

Set in 10/13pt Galliard by Graphicraft Limited, Hong Kong
Printed in Malaysia by Ho Printing (M) Sdn Bhd

1 2012

Contents

List of Figures

Notes on Contributors

Susan Ackerman is the Preston H. Kelsey Professor of Religion and Professor of Women's and Gender Studies at Dartmouth College. She is the author of *Under Every Green Tree: Popular Religion in Sixth-Century Judah* (1992); *Warrior, Dancer, Seductress, Queen: Women in Judges and Biblical Israel* (1998); and *When Heroes Love: The Ambiguity of Eros in the Stories of Gilgamesh and David* (2005).

Rainer Albertz is Professor of Old Testament in the Protestant Theological Faculty of the University of Münster, Germany. He received his Dr theol and *venia legendi* (Habilitation) from the Heidelberg University. His primary area of research is the social and religious history of ancient Israel including the history of its literature. His most recent books are *Elia, ein feuriger Diener Gottes* (2006); *Geschichte und Theologie: Studien zur Exegese des Alten Testaments und zur Religionsgeschichte Israels* (Berlin 2003); *Israel in Exile: The History and Literature of the Sixth Century BCE* (2003; German 2001).

John Bodel is W. Duncan MacMillan II Professor of Classics and Professor of History at Brown University. His main areas of interest in research are the history, literature, archaeology, and epigraphy of the Roman empire. His most recent books are *Dediche sacre nel mondo greco-romano: Diffusione, funzioni, tipologie* (co-edited with Mika Kajava, 2009), *Epigraphic Evidence: Ancient History from Inscriptions* (2001) and (with Stephen Tracy) *Greek and Latin Inscriptions in the USA: A Checklist* (1997).

Deborah Boedeker is Professor Emerita of Classics at Brown University. From 1992 to 2000, she co-directed Harvard's Center for Hellenic Studies. Her books include *Aphrodite's Entry into Greek Epic* (1974) and *Descent from Heaven: Images of Dew in Greek Poetry and Religion* (1984), as well as a number of edited and co-edited volumes, including *Herodotus and the Invention of History* (1987); *Democracy, Empire, and the Arts in Fifth-Century Athens* (1998); and *The New Simonides: Contexts of Praise and Desire* (2001). She is currently working on traditions about the Persian War, Greek poetry and historiography, and the "new Sappho" fragments and their transmission.

Christopher A. Faraone is the Frank C. and Gertrude M. Springer Professor of Classics and Humanities at The University of Chicago. He is co-editor (with D. Dodd) of *Initiation in Ancient Greek Rituals and Narratives: New Critical*

Perspectives (2003) and (with L. McClure) of *Prostitutes and Courtesans in the Ancient World* (2005), and author of *Talismans and Trojan Horses: Guardian Statues in Ancient Greek Myth and Ritual* (1992) and *Ancient Greek Love Magic* (1999). His *The Stanzaic Architecture of Ancient Greek Elegiac Poetry* will appear in 2008.

Daniel E. Fleming is Professor of Assyriology and Hebrew Bible at New York University. His research spans the ancient Near East from Mesopotamia across Syria to Israel, with focus on social and cultural patterns. His most recent books are *Democracy's Ancient Ancestors: Mari and Early Collective Governance* (2004), and *Time at Emar: The Cultic Calendar and the Rituals from the Diviner's Archive* (2000).

Barbara S. Lesko's Egyptological career spans almost fifty years, beginning with degrees from the University of Chicago's Oriental Institute and employment at the University of California, Berkeley and later at Brown University where she was Administrative Research Assistant in the Department of Egyptology from 1982 until her retirement in 2005. Mrs Lesko is the author and co-author of several books, such as *The Great Goddesses of Egypt* (1999) and was collaborating editor, with her husband, of *A Dictionary of Late Egyptian*, 2 vols. (2004). She has contributed numerous articles to anthologies, encyclopedias, and journals, and specializes in lexicography and women's studies.

Theodore J. Lewis (PhD, Harvard University) is Blum-Iwry Professor and Chair of the Department of Near Eastern Studies at The Johns Hopkins University. He is also an academic trustee of the W. F. Albright Institute of Archaeological Research in Jerusalem. His research focuses on the religions of ancient Israel and Syria. He is general editor of the book series Writings from the Ancient World (SBL/Brill), and past editor of the journals *Near Eastern Archaeology* and *Hebrew Annual Review*. He is the author of *Cults of the Dead in Ancient Israel and Ugarit* (1989), and co-author of *Ugaritic Narrative Poetry* (1997). He has recently co-edited (with Gary Beckman) *Text, Artifact, and Image: Revealing Ancient Israelite Religion* (2006). He is currently writing *The Religion of Ancient Israel* for the Anchor Bible.

Saul M. Olyan is Samuel Ungerleider Jr Professor of Judaic Studies and Professor of Religious Studies at Brown University. He received his PhD from Harvard University. His primary areas of research are the history, literature and religion of ancient Israel, and the history of biblical interpretation. His most recent books are *Disability in the Hebrew Bible: Interpreting Mental and Physical Differences* (2008), *Biblical Mourning: Ritual and Social Dimensions* (2004) and *Rites and Rank: Hierarchy in Biblical Representations of Cult* (2000).

Robert K. Ritner is currently Professor of Egyptology at The Oriental Institute of The University of Chicago and was from 1991 to 1996 the first Marilyn M. Simpson Assistant Professor of Egyptology at Yale University. He is the author of the books *The Mechanics of Ancient Egyptian Magical Practice* (1993), *The Libyan Anarchy: Documents from Egypt's Third Intermediate Period* (forthcoming), co-author of *The Literature of Ancient Egypt* (2003), and author of over

100 publications on Egyptian religion, magic, medicine, language and literature, as well as social and political history.

Rüdiger Schmitt is currently research assistant at the University of Münster, Germany. He received his doctorate from Groningen University (1994) and his Habilitation from the University of Münster (2004). His research and teaching *foci* are the history and archaeology of Ancient Israel and the history of ancient Israelite religion. His current project is an investigation of family religion and domestic cult remains. Recent publications include *Alles fauler Zauber?: Zur gegenwärtigen Attraktivität von Magie* (forthcoming), *Magie im Alten Testament* (2004), *Bildhafte Herrschaftsrepräsentation im Alten Israel* (2001).

Stanley K. Stowers is Professor of Religious Studies at Brown University. He received his PhD from Yale University and is the author of *A Rereading of Romans: Justice, Jews and Gentiles* (1994) among other books and articles. Most recently he has published "The Concepts of 'Religion,' and 'Political Religion' in the Study of Nazism," *Journal of Contemporary History* 42.1 (2007) and written a paper, "The Ontology of Religion." He teaches and publishes in the areas of ancient Mediterranean religions, especially early Christianity, and in the theorization of religion.

Karel van der Toorn, a specialist in Israelite and other ancient West Asian religions, is President of the University of Amsterdam. He is author of *Scribal Culture and the Making of the Hebrew Bible* (2007), *Family Religion in Babylonia, Syria and Israel: Continuity and Change in the Forms of Religious Life* (1996), and *Sin and Sanction in Israel and Mesopotamia* (1985), among other books.

Series Editor's Preface

The Ancient World: Comparative Histories

The application of the comparative approach to the ancient world at large has been rare. The new series of which this is the second volume intends to fill this gap. It will pursue important social, political, religious, economic, and intellectual issues through a wide range of ancient societies. "Ancient" will here be understood broadly, encompassing not only societies that are "ancient" within the traditional chronological framework of c. 3000 BCE to c. 600 CE in East, South, and West Asia, the Mediterranean, and Europe, but also later ones that are structurally "ancient" or "early," such as those in pre-modern Japan or in Meso- and South America before the Spanish Conquest. By engaging in comparative studies of the ancient world on a truly global scale, this series will throw light not only on common patterns and marked differences but also illustrate the remarkable variety of responses humankind developed to meet common challenges. Focusing, as it does, on periods that are far removed from our own time and in which modern identities are less immediately engaged, the series will contribute to enhancing our understanding and appreciation of differences among cultures of various traditions and backgrounds. Not least, it will thus illuminate the continuing relevance of the study of the ancient world in helping us to cope with problems of our own multicultural world.

Topics to be dealt with in future volumes include geography, ethnography, and perspectives of the world; recording the past and writing history; and the preservation and transformation of the past in oral poetic traditions.

Kurt A. Raaflaub

Acknowledgments

It is our pleasure to acknowledge the contributions of several colleagues and institutions without whom production of this book would not have been possible. The conference out of which this collection grew took place at Brown University in February 2005. For funding and other assistance with that event, we would like to thank the departments of Classics, Egyptology and Ancient West Asian Studies, and Religious Studies; the programs in Ancient Studies and Judaic Studies; the C. V. Starr Foundation Lectureship Fund; and the Office of the Provost at Brown. We are grateful to our colleagues at Brown, Deborah Boedeker, Barbara Lesko, Leonard Lesko, Kurt Raaflaub, and Stanley Stowers, for help in planning the conference; to Mary Beard, Edward Brovarski, John Gager, Fritz Graf, and Sarah Iles Johnston for participating in the event by invitation; and to Barbara Niekerk of the Program in Judaic Studies for her deft handling of the administrative tasks. To all we extend our sincere thanks for their contributions to this endeavor. Kurt Raaflaub devoted special interest to the project from the beginning and provided careful, detailed comments on each chapter during the evaluation process. We benefited also from the assessment of Blackwell's anonymous referee. The enthusiastic support of Al Bertrand and the responsive help of the production staff at Blackwell, especially Hannah Rolls, have been the more welcome to us for being unobtrusive. Erin Fairburn composed the map and compiled the index with exemplary care. Finally, we are grateful to the Office of the Vice President of Research at Brown for providing funds for indexing.

In the transliteration of Akkadian, Greek, Hebrew, and other languages, we have adopted a simplified system that does not indicate vowel length. Biblical citations follow the original Hebrew, the versification of which sometimes differs from that of Christian translations into English (though not from that of Jewish translations).

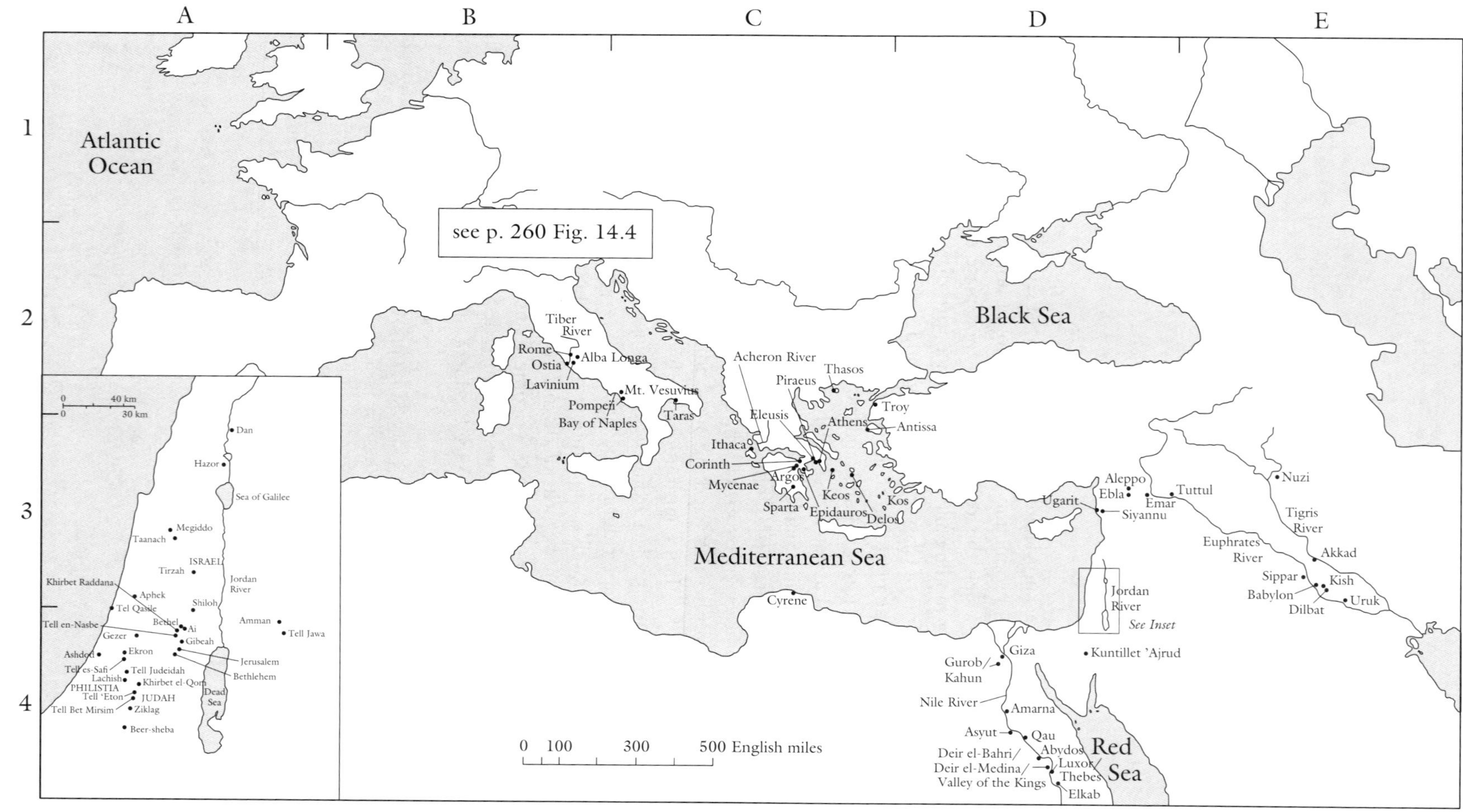

A
B
C
D
E
1
2
3
4
Atlantic Ocean
see p. 260 Fig. 14.4
Black Sea
Mediterranean Sea
Red Sea
Tiber River
Rome
Alba Longa
Ostia
Lavinium
Mt. Vesuvius
Pompeii
Bay of Naples
Taras
Acheron River
Thasos
Piraeus
Troy
Eleusis
Athens
Antissa
Ithaca
Corinth
Mycenae
Argos
Keos
Kos
Sparta
Epidauros
Delos
Cyrene
Aleppo
Ebla
Tuttul
Emar
Ugarit
Siyannu
Nuzi
Tigris River
Euphrates River
Akkad
Sippar
Kish
Babylon
Uruk
Dilbat
Jordan River
See Inset
Giza
Kuntillet 'Ajrud
Gurob/ Kahun
Nile River
Amarna
Asyut
Qau
Abydos
Deir el-Bahri/
Deir el-Medina/
Valley of the Kings
Luxor/
Thebes
Elkab
0 100 300 500 English miles
0 40 km
0 30 km
Dan
Hazor
Sea of Galilee
Megiddo
Taanach
ISRAEL
Tirzah
Jordan River
Khirbet Raddana
Aphek
Tel Qasile
Shiloh
Bethel
Ai
Amman
Tell Jawa
Tell en-Nasbe
Gezer
Gibeah
Ashdod
Ekron
Jerusalem
Bethlehem
Tell es-Safi
Tell Judeidah
Lachish
Khirbet el-Qom
PHILISTIA
Tell 'Eton
JUDAH
Dead Sea
Tell Bet Mirsim
Ziklag
Beer-sheba

BODIES OF WATER

Acheron River	C2
Aegean Sea	C2-C3
Bay of Naples	C2
Euphrates River	E2, E3, E4
Jordan River	D3-D4
Nile River	D4
Red Sea	D4
Tiber River	B2
Tigris River	E2, E3, E4

SITES

Abydos	D4
Ai	Inset-A4
Akkad	D3
Alba Longa	B2
Aleppo	D3
Amarna	D4
Amman	Inset-A4
Antissa	C3
Aphek	Inset-A3
Argos	C3
Ashdod	Inset-A4
Asyut	D4
Athens	C3
Babylon	E3
Beer-sehba	Inset-A4
Bethel	Inset-A4
Bethlehem	Inset-A4
Corinth	C3
Cyrene	C3
Dan	Inset-A3
Deir el-Bahri	D4
Deir el-Medina	D4
Delos	C3
Dilbat	E3
Ebla	D3
Ekron	Inset-A4
Elkab	E4
Eleusis	C3
Emar	D3
Epidauros	C3
Gezer	Inset-A4
Gibeah	Inset-A4
Giza	E4
Gurob	E4
Hazor	Inset-A3
Ithaca	C3
Iulis	See Keos
Jerusalem	Inset-A4
Kahun	E4
Keos	C3
Khirbet Raddana	Inset-A4
Khirbet el-Qom	Inset-A4
Kish	E3
Kos	C3
Kuntillet ‘Ajrud	D4
Lavinium	B2
Luxor	D4
Mari	E3
Megiddo	Inset-A3
Mycenae	C3
Nuzi	E3
Ostia	B2
Piraeus	C3
Pompeii	B2
Qau	D4
Ras Shamra	D3
Rome	B2
Shiloh	Inset-A4
Shuksu	D3
Sippar	E3
Siyannu	D3
Sparta	C3
Taanach	Inset-A3
Taras	C2
Tel el-Miqne	See Ekron
Tel Halif	See Ziklag
Tel Qasile	Inset-A4
Tell Bet Mirsim	Inset-A4
Tell el-Far’ah North	See Tirzah
Tell en-Nasbe	Inset-A4
Tell es-Safi	Inset-A4
Tell ‘Eton	Inset-A4
Tell Jawa	Inset-A4
Tell Judeidah	Inset-A4
Tell Meskene	See Emar
Tell Sukas	See Shuksu
Thasos	C2
Thebes	D4
Tirzah	Inset-A3
Troy	C2
Tuttul	C3
Ugarit	D3
Uruk	E3
Valley of the Kings	D4
Ziklag	Inset-A4

1

Introduction

John Bodel and Saul M. Olyan

This volume grows out of a conference held at Brown University during the winter of 2005. Its purpose, like that of the event which preceded it, is to advance our understanding, both contextually and comparatively, of a distinct and widespread ancient religious phenomenon – household and family religion – within a number of discrete cultural and historical settings of Mediterranean and West Asian antiquity. In order to achieve these goals, we invited a paper, and begin with a chapter, outlining the salient theoretical and methodological issues raised by the study of household and family religion in itself and showing the importance of cross-cultural comparisons for effective theory-formation. A series of essays follows, addressing the phenomenon of household and family religion in a number of different cultural contexts: Second Millennium West Asia (Mesopotamia, Emar, Nuzi, Ugarit); First Millennium West Asia (including Israel); Egypt; Greece; and Rome. A comparative essay by the editors concludes the volume.

Family and household religion is a cutting-edge topic in several of the fields represented here. In some it is just emerging as a distinct subject of interest. In others it has long been studied, but often with a teleologically Christianizing bias that has obscured its essential nature. Past emphasis on religion as manifested in state-sponsored or civic temple cults has tended to give way in several fields to a new recognition that religious expression outside the physical and social contexts of national, regional, or civic worship – expression associated with household, family, and domicile – is also significant and must be investigated in a serious way. Such religious expression might include supplication of a household's patron deities or of spirits associated with the house itself, providing for ancestral spirits, and any number of rituals related to the lifecycle (rites of pregnancy and birth, maturity, old age, and death). And it might occur in a number of different *loci*. For a number of the cultures represented here, the domicile was evidently a central locus for petition of family gods and, in some settings, for contact with dead ancestors. But for some of the cultures of interest to us, the domestic locus hardly exhausts the phenomenon we are calling household and family religion, for the household and family are social units, and the religious activity of their members might also occur in places other than the home, such as at extramural tombs and local sanctuaries. Furthermore, as Stanley Stowers emphasizes in his essay in this volume, the temporal dimensions of household and family religion cannot be ignored. Lifecycle events occur at particular stages of life, in a particular sequence. Thus, any study of household and family religion ought to be shaped by considerations of where a given ritual took place, in the presence or interest of what social group, and when – not only at what time of day (if that is known) but, in certain cases, at what times of year and at what stage in the life of either the participant or the property itself.

Readers might find redundancy in our title and wonder why we have chosen to refer to the phenomenon of interest as "household and family religion" rather than simply "family religion" or "household religion." Because usages within disciplines vary, and because the phenomenon itself takes different forms in different cultural contexts, we did not want to prejudice the issue by imposing a single name, nor did we wish to become overly distracted by debate about nomenclature. Our primary interest is the phenomenon itself, how it was constituted and how it functioned within the cultures under consideration, rather than achieving a consensus regarding terminology. With the goal of approaching the subject from that perspective, we invited our contributors to use whatever terminology they preferred for the phenomenon in question but asked them to justify their usages by explaining the parameters of the territory that each term covered. We asked them, in other words, to begin to theorize the phenomenon for their own fields, thereby providing us with a basis for comparison among cultures.

Most contributors tend to prefer one term or the other, but some are inclined to speak of a "domestic cult" or "popular religion" instead of "family" or "household" religion. Predictably, perhaps, definitions of "household" and "family" vary by cultural and disciplinary context, but most can be broadly classified according to a few basic oppositional categories: families are generally conceived of either broadly, as comprising all descendants of a single male ancestor (a clan), or more narrowly, as constituting a smaller group of closer relatives. Within the latter category, the family can be further defined as either nuclear, having the triadic configuration of mother, father, and offspring, or extended, including also more distant relatives and often spanning several generations. Households, similarly, can be classified as either simple, consisting exclusively of biological kin, or complex, comprising household dependents (principally but not only domestic slaves) as well as blood relatives – in short, all who live within the house (or, more accurately in certain contexts, all who fall within the power of the head of the family). Within these basic categories much variation, of course, is possible – the compositions and configurations of complex households, for example, differed substantially among the cultures under consideration – and practically there is often considerable overlap among them, but fundamentally "family" and "household" characterize different realms, one primarily biological with an important temporal element, the other architectural with an important physical component. The terms chosen for our title may thus be seen to represent two related but essentially different ways by which the phenomenon of interest can be identified and, in a preliminary way, defined.

In addition to textual representations of cultic activity outside of the major sanctuaries, whether epigraphic or literary, relevant materials for reconstructing household and family religion include the material remains of distinct domestic or other loci, related utensils understood to serve cultic purposes, and pictorial representations of cultic acts, deities, or other relevant phenomena. For some cultures, the onomasticon forms another distinct class of pertinent data (e.g., Egypt, Emar, Israel). In some fields, recent archaeological discoveries have increased considerably the material available for study and have stimulated further investigation into the phenomenon. The evidence of Ammonite Tell Jawa, for example, has had considerable impact on discussions of Levantine household and family religion. Our authors draw on various kinds of sources, and their treatments of them are shaped both by the range of evidence available to them and by the questions they ask of it. Some privilege texts in their investigations, others material remains, including visual representations. Still others strive to balance the different classes of evidence. What they share in common is a focus on a distinct religious phenomenon attested cross-culturally and through time.

Why contextual *and* comparative perspectives? Studying family and household religion from the viewpoint of each individual cultural context of interest to us requires little justification. Such a contextual approach has been and remains routine in all of the fields represented in this volume and, what is more important, provides the requisite material for any attempt at comparison. In fact, there can be no worthwhile comparison without a detailed consideration of the phenomenon in each individual context. Thus far, such contextual work has been attempted in only a few of the settings under consideration here (e.g., Second Millennium Babylon, First Millennium Israel, classical Rome). For a number of other cultural contexts, the essays collected in this volume represent a significant initial step, a first attempt at a comprehensive understanding of household and family religion in a particular setting. In contrast to contextual work, which is uncontroversial in itself, being at worst harmlessly antiquarian, comparison has sometimes elicited resistance from scholars in the various fields represented in this volume, as Stowers notes in his essay. Whatever the reasons for such resistance – there are probably more than a few – comparison strikes us as particularly welcome and even necessary when the phenomenon under study, however it is to be more precisely defined, is attested as broadly and cross-culturally as is household and family religion. Comparison has the potential to generate new questions and novel insights; it can lead us to a more nuanced understanding of the category of religious behavior that interests us by revealing points of similarity as well as difference; and it can enable us to distinguish that which is common to a larger Mediterranean and West Asian cultural sphere from that which is particular to one or another cultural setting. First, however, we must explore the nature of the phenomenon in its various manifestations across the region. We therefore begin with a series of studies of household and family religion in individual civilizations, arranged chronologically and consequently moving (roughly) from east to west, in order to gain insight into the phenomenon of interest as it is evidenced in a number of discrete cultural settings over time. These individual studies are followed by an essay in which a preliminary attempt is made at comparison, in the hope of advancing our understanding of the nature of household and family religion across the larger Mediterranean and West Asian world of antiquity.

2

Theorizing the Religion of Ancient Households and Families

STANLEY K. STOWERS

For areas of academic study with deep philological and humanist roots, the title of this volume announces a bold and important venture. The interest in method, and especially in theory and comparison, reflects a growing awareness that even particularistic fields like Classics, Biblical Studies and Egyptology are not self-justifying and autonomous domains of knowledge. Rather, they belong to the universe of knowledge and accountability named in the very concept of a university. I take my task as that of saying something about religion, household, and family in light of the tasks of comparison and theory formation. Although I believe that the principles of domestic religion that I discuss have a broad relevance, I admit up-front that I know almost nothing about many of the cultural areas represented in this volume. I do know a little bit about Greece and Rome and so will use examples from there. I will first make some remarks about family and household and then focus upon religion.

A massive bibliography from several fields exists on the family and household.[1] Those categories are far from unproblematic, but only limited discussion about them is feasible here. Understanding the conjunction of the categories family, household, and religion stands as central to the project of this volume. The difficulty of the task finds illustration in one problem. If religion of the family is defined as the religion that any member of the family might practice, then all religion is religion of the family, since in theory everyone belongs to a family of some sort. Another approach and account is needed to treat religion of the household and family. The vast contemporary literature on the family is a highly political minefield. On one extreme, evolutionary psychologists simply posit that the nuclear family consisting of heterosexual monogamous husband and wife with biologically related children all residing together, and the man working outside the home with the wife tending the hearth and raising the children, is hard-wired in the brain, genetically determined.[2] On the other extreme, some sociologists and cultural anthropologists argue that actual patterns of social relations are so varied that there is no family, but only culturally specific ideologies of the family.[3] Unlike the evolutionary psychologists, at least, the anthropologists have evidence – too much of it.[4] They can point to types of societies in which husbands and wives never live together, or where biological paternity is impossible to know and not taken into account in locating and raising children, and on and on with variations.[5]

In the nineteenth century and the early part of the last century, pan Indo-European evolutionary theories of the family pictured a development from pervasive large extended families in societies based on blood ties toward smaller families in societies based on rational organization finally realized in modernity. These ideas affected writing on Greek and Roman families.[6] After the mid-twentieth century, there was a general reaction against these views and a movement among historians of European and the Mediterranean cultures to show that the nuclear family had always been the norm, including in Greece and Rome.[7] There has been some criticism of this trend, but it still dominates.[8] I find the pioneering work of Andrew Wallace-Hadrill that focuses on various kinds of residences as social places particularly suggestive for thinking about new directions.[9] I will not challenge the consensus about the nuclear family and its focus on "blood ties" except to point to some methodological flaws in the way that the case has been mounted. Noting these flaws will be useful for theorizing the conjunction with religion.

It seems to me that the case for the nuclear family has often been made by using an implicit scheme of analysis that made the husband, wife, and biological children an essence in opposition to slaves, resident workers, freedmen, and other relatives who are treated as non-essential. But, for example, were slaves in Roman households during the later Republic and Empire non-essential? Greece and Rome were cultures that did not even have words for the nuclear family. They were indeed societies in which husbands, wives and their children residing together were important. But making family trump household misses the lesson from the massive work of the anthropologists. The sum and intensity of actual social relations is what counts. Families in which those who make up the supposed nuclear essence have relations and even lifelong emotional attachments to resident slaves, for example, *are* different from the nuclear family. Families in households in which slaves and nurses rather than the nuclear mother do most of the child-rearing *are* different. A household in which there is no distinction between work and home, and in which public and private, insiders and outsiders blur *is* different from the nuclear family that evolutionary psychologists find to be universal. Households in which members of the nuclear family regularly have children with slaves and do not allow slaves to form families *are* different. The examples could be multiplied. The lesson for the task of this volume is that place and residency must be given their due weight. Who lived together and what were their relations? What configuration of relations did the people who lived in that place have with other places? What were the dynamics and cycles of changes in the compositions of those households? Family should not be abstracted from household. Ideologies of household and family should then be analytically distinguished with the awareness that ideology and actual relations affect each other.

Because theory and method have been understood in various ways within and across fields, some comments about my assumptions are in order. I understand theory formation as the activity of critical definition, classification, comparison, and interpretation that aims toward explanation.[10] Explanation is a form of redescription. Most often it involves taking a subject matter described in native, folk, and local terms and redescribing it in terms designed by the researcher to answer the researcher's questions, to broaden the scope of the data, and to understand it systematically, if possible. Theory possesses whatever explanatory power it has by virtue of its difference from the local and native terms of the subject matter. Theory formation is a process that presupposes the fullest possible description and understanding of the local native point-of-view, but is itself a distinct intellectual activity. As Jonathan Z. Smith reminds us with Jorge Luis Borges's parable of the mapmakers, a map is only useful to the extent that it differs from the territory to which it refers.[11] A map that covered every inch of Rhode Island and exactly corresponded to every feature of its topography would be of no use at all. Description and paraphrase are not yet mapmaking. In my estimation, fields like those represented in this conference have wanted too much method without the theory that justifies the method and gives it sense. Someone might teach me the technique of replacing a certain circuit board in my computer but, without the theoretical knowledge of how the computer works, I will never understand why it burned out or the function it performed within the larger system of the computer. Method without theory can be dangerous. Classics and Biblical Studies are replete with examples of literary and social theories that have been imported and turned into methods of reading texts with a loss of the contexts and questions that generated the theories.[12]

The interests and social practices of the scholar make her way of thinking different from the native and local thought, but the scholar's explanation and theory formation is only a specialized version of ordinary human cognitive practices. When Aristophanes said "even the barbarians have gods" (*Birds* 1525) and Herodotus compared the religion of the Greeks to that of the Egyptians and Scythians, they were engaged in rudimentary theory formation about religion. To define and classify, as both Greek writers do, requires comparison. Definition, classification, and comparison are inseparable.[13] Even ordinary folk description involves classification and comparison. The theorist adds a broadened scope, systematic reflexivity, and organized public critique. For Herodotus, the similarity and difference that he described in non-Greek religion required explanation and he provided several. The modern academic adds vastly more data, a potentially universal horizon, and an apparatus of critical reflexivity about those activities that includes the history and state of theory formation across fields of knowledge. Thus comparison is not an extra inquiry that the scholar might want to add to his supposedly more basic practices, but a requirement for anyone who aims at explanation. Indeed, it is fundamental to thought as such. The anti-comparative ethos of some fields is only maintained by a regime of rules and practices that valorize limiting inquiry to descriptive paraphrase so as to strictly control the scope of the data that may be entertained, and the kinds of questions that can be asked.[14] As soon as a scholar seriously considers the thesis that the people in question were not just, say, Greeks or Judeans, but also residents of the ancient eastern Mediterranean region or members of a type of pre-modern society or that they belong to the species *homo sapiens*, then comparison goes hand in hand with such classification.

In my view, the object of study that presents the most difficulties is religion. These difficulties stem not from some special epistemological or ontological status of the object, but from the fact that religion has been treated as special, unique, not subject to the norms of inquiry presupposed for other human activities.[15] That the academic study of religion has only recently and partially been made semi-autonomous from the religious study of religion is one sign of this situation. In the fields that study western antiquity, I am amazed at how rarely writings that treat religion define or in any way specify what the scholar holds religion to be. This means, for one thing, that local intuitive folk assumptions of the scholar about religion often shape studies in ways that cannot easily be the object of critical scrutiny.

One step toward rectifying this problem would be the use of explicit definition. A definition should be a starting point for further work and for revision of the definition. A definition is a theory *in nuce* and thus extremely useful for orienting the writer and the reader. Desiderata for useful theoretical definition include the following. It should specify the ontological status of the phenomenon. In the case of religion, I see it as a human activity, a social/cultural phenomenon. A definition should encompass all or as much as possible of the phenomenon in question. A definition tells one what the researcher, at least initially and tentatively, counts as the limits and boundaries of the phenomenon. A definition should not simply be any particular local perspective. A specification that said religion is belief in the one true god and his son and false variants of sorcery, magic, and heresy might encompass most of the world's religion, but it would represent it from one local perspective. Many of the folk assumptions about religion among scholars who write about antiquity suffer from some, albeit more subtle, form of this problem. Qualifiers such as a system of beliefs, the feeling of awe and reverence, the sacred, transcendence and on and on are examples of attempts to define religion that centrally involve local religious norms about religion. Usually these derive from Christianity and the traditions of nineteenth-century Romanticism.[16] Definitions should be polythetic rather than monothetic.[17] Monothetic is closely related to what people often mean by essentialistic, and involves classification by a single supposedly invariant feature or bounded bundle of features.

I will offer the following definition, by way of illustration and in order to stimulate thinking about the religion of the household and the family. Religions are the often linked and combined practices (i.e., doings and saying) of particular human populations (e.g., imagined as cultures, societies, ethnicities, groups, global movements) that involve the imagined participation of gods or other normally non-observable beings in those practices and social formations, and that shade into many kinds of anthropomorphizing interpretations of the world. Religion is the unfolding activity (including thinking and believing) involving those practices that postulate participation with and make reference to gods, normally non-observable beings and anthropomorphizing interpretations of the world. This definition rests on claims of some reliably generalizable, if not necessarily universal, characteristics of religious activities. Such activities directly or indirectly involve "culturally postulated" beings with human-like agency and other human-like features, especially of human mind.[18] Normally non-observable here should not be taken in a positivistic way. It is not a claim about the reality and epistemological status of these beings, but about a characteristic of native conception. Gods, ancestors and such are typically conceived as not in public view most of the time for various reasons, even if emanations, incarnations, visible instantiations, and representations of the full reality are common.

The beings in this theory can be human-like in a number of ways, but such non-obvious beings usually have attributes of mind such as purposes, will, and intentions.[19] They may have bodies or be bodiless and immaterial. They may be powerful, immortal and beyond every order of existence conceivable to humans or they may be mortal and rather fragile. They may be thought of as agents with whom humans want to communicate and please or they may be conceived as agents that humans want to avoid and keep at a distance. It is a distinctly modern idea to think them supernatural in the sense that there is a split between a natural order of cause and effect by uniform physical laws acting on qualitatively uniform matter versus an entirely other realm of the spiritual. Even the God of the Bible is not beyond the physical and the natural order.[20] The power of the theory, then, comes from, first, allowing for precise discriminations about what is religious and what is not, and, second, from enabling fine discriminations about historical types of religion.

Some reflections on the definition will, I hope, point to its utility. To begin with, religion is a class of practices that involve a broader, species-wide cognitive propensity. This makes it difficult to think of religion as something autonomous in relation to other classes of human activity.[21] This also makes religion a matter of more and less. That religion draws upon the phenomenon of anthropomorphizing allows one to see that there are not clear boundaries at the margins for what is religious and that cases may shade off into areas usually thought of as philosophies of life, folk science, folk psychology, and so on. But why call it a class of practices?[22] Talking of practice provides a way of thinking about the social that avoids the individual/social and thought/action dualisms that have caused so much mischief in our intellectual history. Most of human life unfolds in kinds of activities based on practical skills that the individual did not invent. As such, practices are the primary unit that a culture or society reproduces over time. On this view, a society or culture is not greater than the sum of its parts, but a large number of practical skills assembled and linked in characteristic ways that are passed down from generation to generation. This means that I reject totalizing abstractions like society and social structure in functional analysis.

This way of thinking about religion is polythetic. The human-like beings and characteristics that agents attribute to the world comprise a massive class of thought/action. The class is precisely as complex as human ways of thinking about and acting toward human beings, at least as these can be involved in imagining the non-human world. No single property of the class can apply to all instances of religion, even if characteristic combinations of properties might apply widely across instances.

I will choose the issue of religion's frequently supposed autonomy from other social domains to illustrate this way of theorizing religion for the study of antiquity. Fortunately, there is now wide recognition that religion was organized differently in antiquity as compared to western modernity. A division into semi-autonomous domains such as the economy, politics, high culture, and religion characterizes modernity. It is from this large-scale field and individual life-sphere arrangement of modernity that we get the idea that religion is something essentially separate from areas such as the economy and politics. In antiquity, religion was embedded in a rather seamless social and cultural whole. This means that religion was not a matter of meaning for the individual in a distinct portion of a person's life. It has been typical in modernity to view religion as a sphere of meaning and economy as a sphere of instrumentality, two opposites.

But what happens when we consider the religion of the ancient household and take seriously our way of theorizing it as a class of practices that are continuous with other practices and patterns of human thought? Most economic production in antiquity took place within the household and on land owned and/or worked by members of households, including slaves.[23] Households in the Greek and Roman worlds were organized so that the work of women, children, slaves and other dependents supported the leisure of male heads of households so that they might have freedom for management, cultural (e.g., religion), and political activity. The house was not a place of leisure that one came home to after work at the office, but the center of work and production. Moreover, the domestic economy, based on the idea of non-market exchanges of goods between members of the family, was the ideal model for the outside economy of equals and citizens.[24]

Religious practices and economic practices were intertwined in antiquity and to adequately theorize ancient religions the scholar must understand how practices that made reference to gods and similar beings also involved the economy and politics and so on. It is no accident that the most important religious practices and institutions had to do with land, the wealth from the land and food. The central religious practices in the historical period of the ancient Mediterranean concerned the fruits of the land that landowning heads of households offered back to deities who gave the products and legitimated the ownership and social order. As places of animal, plant and other offerings, temples were centers of massive consumption, redistribution and storage of wealth that competed with households, the other major locus for economy and religion.[25] Scholarship from the social sciences on gift giving, reciprocity and non-market economies are highly relevant, but under-exploited by scholars of antiquity, and especially of religion. One could take art or politics and also show how the practices that comprise these categories of social analysis were also embedded with religious practices.

One central theoretical and methodological lesson from the embeddedness of religious practices is that the analysis of meaning should not be separated from the analysis of power and action. Meaning and power are mutually implicated. The researcher should ask two questions: What were the culture's schemes of classification and how did individuals and groups act with or against those schemes so as to produce and distribute social capital? I will illustrate these two moves with reference to some points at which the theorizing work of two critical heirs of Claude Levi-Strauss, Jonathan Z. Smith and Pierre Bourdieu, touch on domestic religion. Much of Smith's important work on religion has concerned classification and comparison. For a conference that treated an area from Iran to the Aegean and south to Egypt over the course of literate antiquity, Smith was given the unenviable task of making some useful generalizations about religion.[26] He did so by means of a taxonomy of religion from that territory and time span with terms inspired by lines from Dr Seuss's *Green Eggs and Ham*: "I will not eat them here or there; I will not eat them anywhere." Thus his taxonomy took a form particularly appropriate for antiquity, a topography.

The religion of household and family, located primarily in the home and at the family tomb, is the ultimate religion of place. The place of domestic religion is "here" because it is not "there." "There" is the religion of public, civic, and state religion epitomized by the temple. A temple is centrally defined by occupying a separated sacred space in contrast to the home. Put a little differently from Smith's language, "here" is the primary place of human occupation and one crosses over "there" to enter a temple, a place dedicated especially to the occupation of the gods.

One might develop an idea of categories and implicit comparison inherent in Smith's schema with the example of the temple. The temple is a place constructed in such a way that it draws attention to itself as extraordinary over against the ordinariness of the house. Thus in some cultural spheres the temple is explicitly a house for the gods. But even if not explicit, a temple is usually a place with walls or columns, roof, a door or entrance, and so on: in other words, a version of house-building, but very different from any mundane house.[27] This disparity is marked in the archaeological record. While the remains of temple religion are quite striking, traces of domestic religion are difficult to recognize. A household vessel used for libations is likely to be an ordinary cup, while a temple vessel is one made precisely to display its difference from the ordinary household utensil.

The most important form of the religion of "here" was the family or household meal, both every day and for special religious occasions.[28] Codes of hospitality and patterns of inclusion, exclusion, and differentiated participation defined degrees of membership and relatedness to the family. Expressed in an idiom closer to Bourdieu than to Smith, the place, say a dining table and hearth or a courtyard altar, gave structure to practice. The practical skills that those in the household required in order to participate both shaped the participants and gave them capacity for endless elaboration and strategic action within the constraints of the game. Slightly modified versions of food preparation, eating, drinking, serving, pouring, and table talk marked the practices as religious, as involving some relation to gods, ancestors, non-obvious beings, or purpose and value attributed to the non-human world. The religion of "there" in the temple borrowed the everyday practices of "here," but greatly elaborated and exaggerated them to mark them precisely as not everyday. It is not just an everyday dinner, but a sacrificial feast in the house of a god. I will argue that, for the periods and areas in question, both meaning and power involved the mutual opposition and interaction of the "here" and the "there."

Smith writes, "Domestic religion, focused on the extended family, is supremely local. It is concerned with the endurance of the family as a social and biological entity."[29] What I find interesting in this passage is that, although Smith's taxonomy concerns spatial place, he must also speak of, even conflate, spatial place with temporal place.[30] Just as in Greek religion, the sacrifice of an animal at the household hearth in order to introduce a newborn into the household took place at a spatial site, so it also occupied a temporal site in the life of the family, clan and individual in question.[31] Even the title of this volume suggests this key duality of place in speaking of "household and family religion." In the religion both of "here" and "there," ritual had a marked temporal sequence at a marked spatial site, and myth and genealogy coordinated spatial and temporal place.[32] The founder of the city's lineage sprang from this land. The father's father lived and was buried here. I would generalize by saying that a central characteristic of ancient domestic religion was the coordination of spatial and temporal place. Thus the most distinctive rituals of domestic religion in the ancient Mediterranean were rites of passage, of birth, death, and stages of life. Smith points out that the chief threats to the religion of "here" were extinction, dislocation and forgetfulness.[33] Again these involved the conjunction of temporal and spatial place. Extinction is the end of a particular string of connected temporal sites that a group of humans have linked to a story about a spatial place. Forgetfulness is a threat to that activity of genealogical conjunction. Dislocation separates the sites in the life-course of the family and its members from the spatial place to which they are thought intrinsically to belong. Thus the dilemma of the family that is exiled from the burial sites of its ancestors: Reburial and pilgrimage are possible, but will always serve as reminders of a loss of place considered intrinsic to the family. This situation can lead to the creation of a homeland/diaspora culture.

The importance of this conjunction of the spatial and the temporal for the character of domestic religion can be seen by way of contrast with the religion of "anywhere." This is religion that is bound to no place in particular.[34] Examples include many kinds of clubs and associations, wandering religious specialists, religious specialists without official legitimacy, and eventually Christian groups in the first centuries of the Roman Empire. I would argue that this kind of religion typically centers on specialists in books and in writing. The example of Christianity in its first two centuries shows that it is possible for temporal place to entirely trump spatial place. But in domestic religion, the central feature of its practices is that the temporal focus of lifecycle and intergenerational continuity belongs to a place. It is no accident that it took centuries for Christianity to develop rituals of birth, death, and marriage. To some extent, these rituals never do return to the home from the church.

The forms mentioned above represent the dominant and legitimized structure, if not the only religious practice that went on in houses or among members of households. Slaves and others who did not own land either belonged to a household or presumably practiced religion of "anywhere" or religion perhaps ambiguously placed between "the here" and "the anywhere." In some areas, large numbers of people belonged to the households of kings and shared in a religion that conflated the "here" and the "there."[35] Even within ordinary households, members were differentially invested in the central religion of place with gender, age, and freedom or lack of it counting as the key determinants. Thus the deaths of infants and slaves might cause little or no pollution to the house and family and involve little religion.[36] Infants were often even buried within the house area. Contrast the major and threatening pollution of a Greek *kurios*, the male head of the household. Gender is central to the household and much has been written about it. Predominately strategic religious practices, like those included under the category of magic, might not belong to what was considered intrinsic to the house but then characteristically take place there.

The mode of analysis illustrated in Smith's taxonomy belongs in the tradition of Ferdinand de Saussure's linguistic theory and of his heirs such as Levi-Strauss. The analysis works with the idea of meaningful difference. Meaning is the result of placing something in a larger set or system of categories. This approach has had spectacular successes in identifying the patterns of meaning in particular areas of a culture or in, say, describing abstractly how a culture viewed the cosmos or kinship, but it does not help very much in understanding either people's active participation in the world or people's values. By the latter, I mean proportional value, why people value one thing to a greater degree than another.[37] A theory of domestic religion needs a dynamic and historical dimension that goes beyond meaningful difference. It is not an either/or, however, and theorists like Bourdieu who have attempted a theory of practice have usually incorporated structuralist elements.[38] Smith has also been influenced by Bourdieu and others who stress activity.[39] It may be correct that to classify is an act of power but it takes more than schemes of classification to understand the strategic and open-ended quality of human practices. I believe that the structures of thought/language/culture that scholars find ultimately derive from patterns of human activity, from practices.[40]

The oppositions between the religion of "here" and of "there" can be conceived in a reified way, but the relations can also be thought of more dynamically. In Greek and Roman cities, the great threat to the presence and the good will of the gods in the temples was the pollution of the household. Birth, death and sexual activity belonged to the house and family. The pollution of these first two events in the life-course of the family severely contaminated the house and anyone who entered.[41]

That pollution was capable of rendering a temple unfit for the gods. Anyone dying outside of the house must be brought to the house for the extended funeral process. Death pollution must be carefully contained within the house and the dead must be buried outside of the city and away from the house, and its members purified. It is easy to think of this as a fixed, almost natural, system of conceptual oppositions embodied in practice, rules, and law. In the past, scholars tried to explain this pattern by invoking commonsense humanistic western sentiments about the psychological trauma of death. But then striking differences in death practices across history and cultural areas were rendered inexplicable.

In Greek areas, historical and archaeological evidence suggests that the patterns known in archaic and classical times grew out of the political struggles and cultural negotiation involved in the creation of the *polis*, a struggle negotiated in the idiom of place and the gods.[42] On mainland Greece in the Bronze Age, sanctuaries were a part of the houses of rulers.[43] Signs of religion also show up in ordinary houses.[44] A few sites in the tenth century appear in which a sanctuary seems to be completely unconnected with domestic space. In the ninth and especially the eighth century, there was a massive process of building religious spaces that were distinct from domestic spaces. The Greek landscape became populated with temples. Many clues allow us to conclude that these changes took place against the background of assumptions about the gods. The gods belonged to the natural order and were inhabitants of the Greek lands before the Greeks began to vigorously claim and mark space so as to create the *polis*.[45] Thus, for instance, Greeks had a very strong conception of natural temples – places like springs, groves, rivers, caves, high places, and so on that were special to some deity and full of divine presence. Human use of the land required honor and reciprocal relations with the gods based on an economy of gift giving. The idea of a temple became the idea of a place that belonged only to the god, and thus not to any particular family or household. Thus every family, even individual, might relate to the gods at those kinds of temples. Greek religion distinguished itself from other areas to the east and south in that, as seen in Hesiod, cosmogony was not connected with kingship or priestly interests but with a more generalized communal and moral order.[46]

These changes can be mapped by evidence of new patterns of practices regarding pollution and purity. In the late seventh century, water basins for purification started appearing at the entrances to Greek sanctuaries. Within a few decades they were present throughout the Greek Mediterranean.[47] Although evidence varies and is complex, there was a general movement from burials of adults in or near living areas to outside of cities, beginning about 700.[48] This is certainly the case for Athens. A distinct arena of public religion developed in opposition to the pollution of the household and family. Rather than viewing this as a rigid structure, I suggest that we see it as a pattern of contestation between two types and centers of religious power. There were many and constantly changing ways that the religion of the household and family would reach outside into the *polis* and many ways that the religion of the temple and *polis* would reach into the household. Even as a new pattern of symbiosis, this was a dynamic tension, a field of constant negotiation.[49]

Bourdieu's work and other theories of practice based on site ontologies provide ways of theorizing the dynamic temporal dimension of the household and family that is lacking in analyses based only on classification and meaningful difference.[50] Here is the way that I outline such a theoretical approach. The so-called structure, the schemes of meaning that the individual is socialized into and constantly encounters, is located in the projects and practical know-how of individuals and in the natural and humanly modified shape of things at places. An individual's knowledge, beliefs and skills are not systematic but dispersed in sets of practical know-how that correspond to practices in the society. So, for example, most Greeks probably did not have a scheme that rationalized the difference between the Panhellenic Zeus Olympios who evoked the cosmogony of Hesiod and the supremely local Zeus Herkeios, Zeus of the household courtyard, or Zeus Ktesios, Zeus of the household property, sometimes translated as Zeus of the pantry. It took philosophers with specific systematizing practices based on abilities to produce and use texts in order to worry about and "rationalize" such practical differences. But Greeks who attended the great sacrifices of an Olympian festival *knew how* to participate in the practices that evoked beliefs and bits of myths that were embedded in that practical activity. At home, the intensely local culture of the household meant that Greeks imagined those deities as down-to-earth and as close at hand. Zeus of the pantry manifested himself in the form of snakes, animals of the storerooms, and household fields where the grain was grown. Actors inherited the practices, the beliefs, the stories, the language, and so on, but did not simply act on the basis of rules and norms. They also acted strategically on the basis of individual and local interests, especially the interests of household and family. Practical activity takes place in time. Events occur before other events and the actor anticipates objectives and future circumstances. The social norms of gift giving might be rather clear cut, but the actor will both take into account the norms and improvise according to imminent strategic interests and the flow of events.[51] Having received a gift, the actor can make an equal return, or an insultingly or humiliatingly small return, depending on circumstances; he can up the "anti" with a much greater return, reciprocate quickly, slowly, bit by bit, with surprise, predictably, and with endless meanings intended in the nature of the gift. Whatever the social rules and structures, actors with interests in economic gain, prestige, values, and endless varieties of desire can improvise within the possibilities of the practices. Over time, practices can evolve or change due to larger socially shared interests that become orchestrated in practice. To imagine the religion of the family and household means also understanding these processes which add indeterminacy and locality of ends to so-called structure.

Greek religion, a religion of imminent, varied, and intensely human-like deities had an effective fit with a culture of diverse sites of sociality, dispersed power, and competitive social norms. These were not the kind of gods who clearly represented the interests of a king or priesthood. In fact, one of the most salient features of interacting with such deities was uncertainty. As in human gift giving, for example, the god could return or not return the gift or answer the prayer in innumerable ways. Even though philosophers did not like it, the gods acted just as strategically and indeterminately as humans. Moreover, even knowing what the gods meant or wanted required great investment in human interpretive creativity. So we need to ask: What were the kinds of strategic interests that heads of households, wives, sons, daughters, slaves, relatives, and so on brought to the religion of the household? How did patterns of interacting interests shape practice?

In concluding, I come back to comparison. The activity of theory formation thrives off of comparison. I have tried to make some theoretical points using the example of Greek religion. I understand theory formation to be an unending activity of redescription and rectification of earlier redescription in light of new data. The most fruitful form of new data for this theoretical purpose would come not in the form of more data on Greek religion, but from difference, say in the form of another period of time or cultural area. The goal is not identity, but analogies in the sociocultural processes that comprise religion within the context of specific historical circumstances. As Jonathan Z. Smith writes:

> It is axiomatic that comparison is never a matter of identity. Comparison requires the acceptance of difference as the grounds of its being interesting, and a methodological manipulation of that difference to achieve some stated cognitive end. The questions of comparison are questions of judgment with respect to difference: What differences are to be maintained in the interests of comparative inquiry? What differences can be defensively relaxed and relativized in light of the intellectual tasks at hand?[52]

I would add that, for comparison to be both interesting and to achieve intellectual gain, it must spring from theory that frames the purpose and the method. The anthropologist F. J. P. Poole makes the point: "The comparability of phenomena always depends both on the purpose of the comparison and on a theoretically informed analysis . . . What matters in comparison are certain variables that are posited by and cohere in theories and that are aligned with aspects of the phenomena to be compared through some set of correspondence rules."[53]

By organizing a volume that includes ancient West Asia, Egypt, Greece, and Rome and by applying the categories of religion, family, and household across those sets of data, we verge on the possibility of intellectually fruitful comparison. But this, I believe, will only happen as we redescribe each set of data in the ways that this chapter has indicated so as to give a broader human angle to the local and to formulate some of those interesting questions.

Notes

1 For recent discussion and bibliography, see Bonnie J. Fox, *Family Patterns, Gender Relations*, 2nd edn. (New York: Oxford University Press, 2001).

2 For example, David M. Buss, *The Evolution of Desire: Strategies of Human Mating* (New York: Basic Books, 1994).

3 Fox, *Family Patterns*, pp. 25–6.
4 Susan McKinnon, *Neo-Liberal Genetics: The Limits and Moral Tales of Evolutionary Psychology* (Chicago: Prickly Paradigm, 2005).
5 McKinnnon, ibid., and *Family Patterns* are full of such examples.
6 Cynthia B. Patterson, *The Family in Greek History* (Cambridge, Massachusetts: Harvard University Press, 1998), pp. 5–43; Suzanne Dixon, *The Roman Family* (Baltimore: Johns Hopkins University Press, 1992), pp. 19–24.
7 Perhaps most influential for Rome and antiquity have been Richard Saller and Brent Shaw in numerous publications. For a summary of the case and bibliography, see Saller and Peter Garnsey, *The Roman Empire: Economy, Society and Culture* (Berkeley: University of California Press, 1987), pp. 129–41.
8 For important criticisms of the nuclear orthodoxy, see Keith R. Bradley, *Discovering the Roman Family* (New York: Oxford University Press, 1991), especially pp. 4–11; Dale B. Martin, "The Construction of the Ancient Family: Methodological Considerations," *Journal of Roman Studies* 86 (1996): 40–60; "Slave Families and Slaves in Families," in *Early Christian Families in Context*, ed. David L. Balch and Carolyn Osiek (Grand Rapids: Eerdmans, 2003), pp. 207–30.
9 *Houses and Society in Pompeii and Herculaneum* (Princeton: Princeton University Press, 1994); "*Domus* and *Insulae* in Rome: Families and Housefuls," in Balch and Osiek, *Early Christian Families*, pp. 3–18.
10 I adopt and adapt this way of thinking about theory formation from Jonathan Z. Smith, "The End of Comparison: Redescription and Rectification," *A Magic Still Dwells*, ed. Kimberley Patton and Benjamin Ray (Berkeley: University of California), p. 239; Burton Mack, "On Redescribing Christian Origins," *Method and Theory in the Study of Religion* 8 (1996): 256–9.
11 *Relating Religion: Essays in the Study of Religion* (Chicago: University of Chicago Press, 2004), pp. 197–214.
12 Ibid., p. 206.
13 Jonathan Z. Smith, "Classification," and Luther H. Martin, "Comparison," in *Guide to the Study of Religion*," ed. Willi Braun and Russell T. McCutcheon (London: Cassell, 2000), pp. 35–44, 45–56.
14 On paraphrase, see Smith, *Relating Religion*, pp. 30–1, 208–9.
15 See my "The Ontology of Religion," *Introducing Religion: Essays in Honor of Jonathan E. Smith*, ed. Willi Braun and Russell McCutcheon (London: Equinox, 2008). One reaction to the fact that the folk and academic conceptions of religion have a history, often in a post-modernist mood, is to claim either that it is a western category that does not apply more generally or that religion doesn't exist. It is just a folk or scholarly idea. Both tacks are absurd, unless one is a committed idealist. In the first case, all modern concepts of the humanities and social sciences can be traced back to some unacceptable ancestor. This is the originary fallacy. In the second case, if scholarship, including history and anthropology, has shown that a very wide number of societies have social practices that refer to gods, ancestors and such, then it is perfectly legitimate to recognize this as a class of human social activity and cultural production.
16 Hans Penner, "You Don't Read a Myth for Information," in *Radical Interpretation in Religion*, ed. Nancy Frankenberry (Cambridge: Cambridge University Press, 2002), pp. 161–70.

17 On polythetic versus monothetic classification and other useful considerations, see Smith, *Relating Religion*, pp. 22–5; Smith, *Imagining Religion: From Babylon to Jonestown* (Chicago: University of Chicago, 1982), pp. 1–18.

18 I borrow "culturally postulated" from Melford Spiro's famous definition in "Religion: Problems of Definition and Explanation," in *Anthropological Approaches to the Study of Religion*, ed. Michael Banton (London: Tavistock, 1966), p. 96.

19 For discussions of the range of beliefs, see Stewart Guthrie, *Faces in the Clouds: A New Theory of Religion* (New York: Oxford, 1993); Robyn Horton, *Patterns of Thought in Africa and the West* (Cambridge: Cambridge University Press, 1993), pp. 19–49.

20 Stanley Stowers, "What is Pauline Participation in Christ?," *Redefining First-Century Jewish and Christian Identities: Essays in Honor of Ed P. Sanders* (Notre Dame: University of Notre Dame Press, forthcoming).

21 Classes of human activity here need only be analytical categories of the researcher, e.g., the economy.

22 For the claims that follow, Theodore Schatzki, *Social Practices: A Wittgensteinian Approach to Human Activity and the Social* (New York: Cambridge University Press, 1996); *The Site of the Social: A Philosophical Account of the Constitution of Social Life and Change* (University Park, Pennsylvania: University of Pennsylvania Press, 2002); Pierre Bourdieu, *An Outline of a Theory of Practice* (Cambridge: Cambridge University Press, 1977); *The Practice Turn in Contemporary Theory*, ed. Theodore Schatzki, Karin Knorr Cetina, and Eike von Savigny (London; New York: Routledge, 2001).

23 A fact widely acknowledged; e.g., Dixon, *Roman Family*, p. 28. Perhaps surprisingly, though, the economic production of Greek and Roman households is understudied.

24 I think that this is broadly true even for the period after the inundation of Italy with slaves and the creation of the great business estates. The ideology of the purer older Italy with its self-sufficient households so prominent in later writers points to the ideal. On all of this, see Keith Hopkins, *Conquerors and Slaves* (Cambridge: Cambridge University Press, 1978).

25 There is a large and important body of scholarship on so-called sacrifice. For bibliography and issues, see my early effort, "Greeks Who Sacrifice and Those Who Do Not: Toward an Anthropology of Greek Religion," in *The First Christians and Their Social World: Studies in Honor of Wayne A. Meeks*, ed. L. Michael White and Larry O. Yarbrough (Philadelphia: Fortress Press, 1995), pp. 293–333.

26 "Here, There and Anywhere," *Relating Religion*, pp. 323–39; originally published in *Prayer, Magic and the Stars in the Ancient and Late Antique World, Magic in History*, 8, ed. Scott B. Noegel, Joel Walker, and Brannon M. Wheeler (University Park: Pennsylvania State University Press, 2003), pp. 21–36.

27 On this idea of comparative extraordinariness applied to ritual, see Catherine Bell, *Ritual Theory, Ritual Practice* (New York: Oxford University Press, 1992), pp. 74, 90.

28 Smith, *Relating Religion*, p. 327.

29 Ibid., p. 326.

30 Smith's "here, there, and anywhere" is a relational (not absolute) conception of space. It is also a notion of place and space. In other words it is operative in the minds of the participants. For a theorization of the role of things and places as they exist apart from the minds of participants, see Schatzki, *Site of the Social*.

31 For the so-called *amphidromia*, about which we have evidence from classical Athens, see Robert Garland, *The Greek Way of Life: From Conception to Old Age* (Ithaca, New York: Cornell University Press, 1990), pp. 93–7.
32 For an elegant and powerful theorization of ritual/myth in the structuralist mode, see Jonathan Z. Smith, *To Take Place: Toward Theory in Ritual* (Chicago: University of Chicago, 1987).
33 Smith, *Relating Religion*, pp. 326–7.
34 Ibid., pp. 329–34.
35 I am thinking of the Near Eastern kingdoms, Egypt, and Mycenaean Greece in which notable temples were part of the palaces of kings or in the homes of aristocratic rulers.
36 Robert Parker, *Miasma: Pollution and Purification in Early Greek Religion* (Oxford: Oxford University Press, 1983), pp. 41, 72.
37 David Graeber, *Toward an Anthropological Theory of Value* (New York: Palgrave, 2001), pp. 42–3.
38 See Bourdieu in n. 22 above; Bourdieu and Loïc J. D. Wacquant, *An Invitation to Reflexive Sociology* (Chicago: University of Chicago, 1992), pp. 2–139.
39 Smith, *Relating Religion*, p. 53 n. 85.
40 Argued in Graeber, *Theory of Value*. I would add that this is the case, even though these patterns of activity are mediated by language and mind.
41 Parker, *Miasma*, pp. 32–73.
42 François de Polignac, *Cults, Territory, and the Origins of the Greek City-State* (Chicago: University of Chicago, 1995); Susan Guettel Cole, *Landscape, Gender, and Ritual Space: The Ancient Greek Experience* (Berkeley: University of California Press, 2004). I depend on de Polignac, Cole and Morris (below) for the account that follows.
43 Cole, *Landscape*, p. 15.
44 Ian Morris, "Attitudes Toward Death in Archaic Greece," *Classical Antiquity* 8 (1898): 318; *Burial and Ancient Society: The Rise of the Greek City-State* (Cambridge: Cambridge University Press), pp. 189–95.
45 Cole, *Landscape*, p. 37.
46 Ibid., p. 22.
47 Ibid., p. 37 n. 28.
48 Morris, "Cults," pp. 316–17.
49 Patterson (*Family in Greek History*) well emphasizes a dynamic relationship between city and households. Her polemical framework, however, tends to rather simply cast the *oikos* and *polis* as having a mutually positive relationship rather than one of a negotiation of partly different and partly overlapping interests.
50 For site ontologies, see Schatzki, *Site of the Social*.
51 The strategic character of practices is famously developed in Bourdieu, *Outline of a Theory*.
52 *To Take Place*, 13–14; cited in *Relating Religion*, p. 20.
53 "Metaphors and Maps: Toward Comparison in the Anthropology of Religion," *Journal of the American Academy of Religion* 54 (1986): 53 and cited by Jonathan Z. Smith, *Drudgery Divine: On the Comparison of Early Christianities and the Religions of Late Antiquity* (Chicago: University of Chicago, 1990), p. 53.

3

Family Religion in Second Millennium West Asia (Mesopotamia, Emar, Nuzi)

Karel van der Toorn

Introduction

> Considered globally, domestic religion is the most widespread form of religious activity; perhaps due to its very ubiquity, it is also the least studied. This is especially true of domestic religion of the past.[1]

This citation of Jonathan Z. Smith signals the paradoxical position of family religion in ancient Near Eastern studies. The most quotidian religious practices of ordinary men and women tend to escape scholarly attention precisely because they were so common and therefore failed to obtain a prominent place in the written records from the past.

In his comment on the subject, Smith speaks about "domestic religion" where I prefer to use the term "family religion." The difference is one of nuance, but not without importance. The adjective "domestic" implies that the house is the focus of religious activities; the specification "family" throws into relief that the beliefs and practices are tied to the social unit of the family and, more specifically, the extended family. Moreover, the expression family religion emphasizes that this religion is neither "personal," at least in our sense of the term, nor "popular." The one designation is concerned with place, the other with social setting. An inconvenience of the label "domestic" is the suggestion that the religious activities under consideration all take place within the house. Yet while family religion is "supremely local," it is not confined to the house.[2] Most notably, offerings to the family god were usually brought to a local chapel outside the house. "Household religion" might perhaps be a terminological compromise between "domestic" and "family" religion.

My contribution to this volume consists of three sections. I shall first delineate the two components of family religion in Mesopotamia in the second millennium

BCE. They consist of the devotion to the family god, on the one hand, and to the cult of the ancestors, on the other. The investigation into the worship of family gods and the cult of the ancestors will take up the bulk of my contribution. In a third and concluding section, I shall analyze the sociology and psychology of family religion. Whereas the first and second sections use the cuneiform evidence to furnish a description of the historical reality of family religion, the final section is a deliberate step away from the native perspective in order to offer an interpretation from a contemporary western angle.

The topographical focus of my contribution is Mesopotamia. Owing in part to the available evidence, the emphasis will be on Babylonia, that is, southern Mesopotamia. Whenever possible and apposite, I shall broaden the horizon to include data from Western Mesopotamia and Northern Syria: Mari, Nuzi, and Emar. The period we shall be looking at is the second millennium BCE: Most of the data from Babylonia and Mari pertain to its first half; the texts from Nuzi and Emar reflect realities of the second half of the millennium.

The Gods of the Family

Family religion has two facets: it expresses itself in the veneration of a particular god and in the cult of the family ancestors. Let us first consider the god in question. A preliminary issue is one of terminology. The expression "family god" as such does not occur in the Babylonian vernacular. In the texts at our disposal, there is a single reference to the "god(s) of our clan" (dingir *kimtini*) and another one to "the god who knows the house of your father."[3] This is the closest we get to our term "family god." I realize that the Babylonian expression "god of the house" (*il bitim*) could be interpreted as "god of the family," but I believe the evidence indicates that "house" in this expression means just that, namely "house." The usual designation of the family god is "your god" or "the god of your father." When a man is being addressed, the two latter expressions are interchangeable: his god is the god of his father – or, if you prefer, the god of his father is his god as well. To accentuate the privileged relationship between the person and his god, the Babylonians could speak of "the god of your head" – "head" being the idiom for "person", or "self."[4]

The family god is never anonymous. We are not dealing with some unidentified *numen* of the house, but with a named member of the pantheon. His name – family goddesses are in the minority – occurs frequently in legends on cylinder seals and in greeting formulas in letters. The owner of a cylinder seal will often identify himself as "servant of god So-and-so." Letters traditionally contain an opening line in which the sender invokes the blessing of the gods over the addressee; he will normally mention the god of the latter as well as his own god. The systematic collection of these data provides us with an insight into the nature of the family god and some sense of the rationale for the ties of a particular deity with a particular family.

Both minor and major deities occur as family gods. Such little known gods as Shubula, Bel-ṣarbi, Ishar-padan, and Shatwak receive veneration as family gods; but so do widely worshiped Mesopotamian deities such as Adad, Dagan, Enki, Gula, Nergal, and many others. Several patterns emerge from a study of the evidence. Families display a preference for gods that belong to a subordinate level of the pantheon; the greatest gods – such as Anu, Enlil, and Ishtar – ranked too high in the hierarchy for ordinary people to worship them as family gods; only kings and their entourage would dare to approach them as their gods. It was one of the roles of the family gods of ordinary people to intercede with the higher-ups in the divine hierarchy. The popularity of Ninshubur as family god is telling; being the minister of Ishtar, Ninshubur might intercede with the latter goddess.[5] Prayers to the god of the family often refer to his capacity as intercessor.[6]

The primary link between a family and its god was topographical. Normally, the family god had a temple or a shrine in the vicinity of the dwelling-place of the family. For generations, the family of Iddin-Lagamal from the city of Dilbat worshiped the god Lagamal. The underworld deity Lagamal – the name means "Merciless" – was the son of Urash, the city god of Dilbat. Being a son of the city god – presumably a secondary systematization of two local cults – Lagamal had a sanctuary in the city.[7] Urban families did not as a rule venerate the major god of the city as their family god; they tended to worship a local deity with a chapel in the city quarter where they lived.[8] Or used to live – because when a family moved from the one city to another, they would often take the cult of their god along. Migration and deportation were a major factor in the spread of local cults. They explain for instance why the cult of local gods from Uruk – such as Nanaya and Kanisurra – was implanted at Kish.[9]

People with a background in pastoral nomadism tended to worship family gods from tribal sanctuaries in the land of their ancestors. The Amorites are a prime example.[10] They focused their devotion on such Amorite deities as the moon-god Erah (also venerated under the name of Sin, or Sin-Amurrum, "the Amorite moon-god"); Amurrum, also known as "the Amorite god" (^{d}an-mar-tu);[11] Dagan, often in his local manifestations of Dagan-of-Terqa and Dagan-of-Tuttul; and Addu, better known in his Aramean spelling Hadad, usually in the local manifestation of Addu-of-Aleppo. Urbanized Amorites continued to worship their ancestral family gods. If need be, they might adopt a second family god from the city to which they had moved. Pairs of family gods – the one Amorite, the other Babylonian – were not unusual among Amorite families.

On occasion, we find that allegiance to a particular deity was inspired by professional considerations. The one indubitable instance is furnished by the scribes.[12] Without exception, so it seems, scribes worshiped either Nissaba or Nabium, the one the goddess and the other the god associated with the reed stylus and writing. Since the scribal profession was largely hereditary, the worship of these gods was passed on from father to son as well. Scribes would often add a second god to the god of their profession. They referred to themselves as "servant" of Ninshubur (or some other god) and Nabium. A rare case is the occurrence, in the seal of a scribe, of the gods "Nissaba, Ashnan, and Nabium." Professions other than the scribal one did not normally entail devotion to a god associated with them. A chief priest of Shamash, for instance, worshiped Marduk as his family god.[13] In his case, professional devotion and private devotion followed separate tracks.

Because family gods are gods whose sanctuary was in the neighborhood, or in the family's place of origin, their cult took place outside the house. The fact finds an illustration in a humorous text from the first millennium. A doctor from Isin pays a visit to a former client in Nippur, but fails to find him at home. A servant explains:

> "He's not at home, sir."
> "Where has he gone?"
> "He's at the chapel of his god, Shuzianna, making an offering."[14]

The Old Babylonian phenomenon of letter-prayers also implies a distinction between the location of the family house and the location of the chapel of the family god.[15] The cult of the family god was conducted in a sanctuary in the vicinity of the house – unless the family had moved and still regarded a temple in their home territory as the focus of their devotion. Even if some of the more affluent families sponsored local chapels with substantial endowments, these were places of worship outside the privacy of the family quarters.[16]

The relationship between the family god and his devotees is one of mutual interest. By invoking his name, the family promotes the fame of their god; by offering their prayers, they honor their god; by supplying offerings, they feed their god; and by the gift of the annual sacrifice, they keep their god in good cheer.[17] As his part of the deal, the god provides the family with offspring, health, professional success, social esteem, and a happy old age. Each of those points would merit a separate development if it were possible at this juncture. The central idea underlying the theology of family religion is clear, however. Owing to the privileged relation between the family and its god, the latter takes an active interest in the preservation and well-being of that particular family and all its members.

Excursus: The god and goddess of the house

An issue that merits special discussion concerns the cult of domestic gods in the narrow sense of the term. Several Old Babylonian lullabies speak about the unhappy effects of the noise of a crying infant upon "the god of the house" (*il*[*i*] *bitim*) and "the goddess of the house" (*ištar bitim*).[18] They had their abode in the "house sanctuary," known in Akkadian as the *išertum*.[19] Texts from the first millennium attest to the continued veneration of such "house gods."[20] Who are they?

There are three possible identifications of the god and goddess "of the house." (1) The gods "of the house" are identical with the family gods; in other words, the "god of the house" is the same as "the god of the father." The term "house," in this case, could be translated as "family." (2) Alternatively, the gods of the house might be distinct from the family gods, being deities with a special mission to protect the house. In this case they might be either anonymous or specific gods from the Babylonian pantheon. (3) The third possibility is that the gods of the house are not gods in the meaning we usually assign to the term. We know that the Babylonians used the term, too, for cult images and the ghosts of the dead. Thus the "gods of the house" might be the ancestors or ancestor images present in, or connected with, the house. Let us assess the evidence for each of these three interpretations.

The possibility that the god of the house should be identical with the family god finds little to no support in the texts. Terminologically, the "god of the house" and the "god of the father" belong to different categories. Greeting formulas in letters and legends on personal seals – the classic occasions for a reference to the family god – never use the term "the god of my/your house" or "the god of my/your paternal family" (*bit abiya/abika*). The closest parallel to the "god of the house" is the reference to "the god who knows the house of your father" – in which "house" stands for "family" (see above). Texts in which the "god of the house" figures with some frequency – in the Old Babylonian period only the lullabies – never speak of "my god" or "the god of my father." Nor is it possible to establish a definite link between the house sanctuary (*išertum*) and the family god.[21] Normally the house god dwells within the house whereas the family god has his abode outside.

If the house gods are not identical with the family gods, they might be members of the pantheon specializing in house surveillance and health care. This is the position taken by JoAnn Scurlock in a recent article on Mesopotamian house gods.[22] She argues her case on the basis of a first millennium text containing rituals against fungus on the walls of a house. The omen bodes ill: several members of the household might die. To ward off the evil, the house owner is to bring offerings to Ishum, a god and goddess at the doorpost, the Pleiades, and Gula. Scurlock believes that these gods are to be identified as the domestic deities of the average Babylonian household. How strong is her case?

There can be no doubt that many a Babylonian house did indeed contain symbols and representations of deities expected to protect the house and its inhabitants. Kusarikku, the bull-man, occurs in this capacity in the Old Babylonian lullabies; he was represented as a statuette or on a clay plaque.[23] The god Ishum is the herald of Erra, whose powers of protection against pestilence and plagues are celebrated in the *Poem of Erra*. Copies of that text served as house amulets.[24] Gula was a goddess of healing; according to an Old Babylonian text from Nippur, she did indeed receive sacrifice in the domestic sanctuary in the "the house of the father."[25] The Pleiades are gods of the night; their function within the house would be to guarantee its safety at night. It is quite conceivable, in other words, that symbols of Ishum, Gula, and the Pleiades belonged to the furnishings of many a Babylonian house, in a manner comparable to the role of Kusarikkum in the Old Babylonian texts. The crucial question, however, is whether or not they were designated as "the gods of the house."

The Old Babylonian lullabies distinguish between Kusarikkum, on the one hand, and the "god of the house," on the other.[26] Kusarikkum, in other words, is not to be confused with the god of the house. The same holds true of Ishum, Gula, and the

Pleiades. To identify them as the god and goddess of the house would be forcing the evidence.[27] The only pair of deities that might be identical with the god and goddess of the house are the god and goddess near the doorpost (*sippu*). They remain anonymous in the first millennium ritual – unless we interpret ^{d}ištar as a proper name instead of the generic "goddess."[28] Other first millennium texts mention a god and goddess "of the house" (dingir é and ^{d}innin é) located near the gate of the house.[29] Are the god and goddess of the house from the Old Babylonian incantations the same as the god and the goddess near the doorpost from the first millennium ritual? It is difficult to escape that conclusion. It may seem strange that such protective deities were supposed to sleep at night,[30] but the first millennium version of the Old Babylonian lullabies shows that protective gods like Ishtar and Ea were also entitled to sleep.[31] The main difference between the Old Babylonian "god and goddess of the house" and the anonymous god and goddess of the first millennium texts is their location. The Old Babylonian god of the house dwells in the house sanctuary (*išertum*), whereas the god and goddess are located in the gate. However, the difference in location is not sufficient to posit a difference in identity.

The third possibility I adumbrated is that the gods of the house are not gods in the usual sense of the term but images of the ancestors. In an earlier publication I defended this view. Though I would not rule out the possibility, I feel less confident now than I did then. The next section, dedicated to the ancestor cult, will show that the family ancestors were present in the Babylonian house because they were either buried underneath the house or represented by anthropomorphic statuettes. In one case, these images are referred to as "the gods of the house."[32] Since the bulk of the evidence is from the periphery of Babylonia, however, I would hesitate to identify the Old Babylonian house gods with such ancestor images or the remains of the dead in the domestic burial vault. All things considered, the god and goddess "of the house" were not the family gods nor the family ancestors, but protective household deities without a name.

The Cult of the Ancestors

The second component of ancient Near Eastern family religion is the cult of the ancestors. The responsibility for this cult lay with the heir who succeeded the father in the position of paterfamilias. Under normal circumstances, this was the eldest son (*aplum rabum*). He was the *zakir šumim*, literally "invoker of the name," a title based on a central rite of the ancestor cult, that is, the invocation of the names of the dead.

In addition to an oral rite – the calling out of the name – the ancestor cult had a material component in the offering of small substances of food. The act of breaking the bread gave the cult its principal name. It was called the *kispu*, a noun derived from the verb *kasapu*, "to break in small pieces."[33] To Christians, the term might elicit associations with the Lord's Supper. Though there may indeed be a parallel of sorts – is the Eucharist not also an act of commemoration? – the standard offering consisted of a bowl of flour and some water. It was a way of feeding the dead.

The *kispu* was a daily rite performed in conjunction with the meals of the living. According to the ideas of the time, the family shared their food with the ancestors. Once every month the ancestors received more lavish supplies. This occurred during the period between two moons which, for lack of an equivalent in English, we had best refer to with the Latin term *interlunium*. In Babylonian parlance this was the *um bubbuli*, "the day(s) of the disappearance (of the moon)"; it constituted the "beginning of the month" (*reš warḫim*). It was a holiday period of one or two days. Work was suspended and families came together for the occasion. The ancestors received their share in the festive meal. Once every year, moreover, at the end of the fifth month (mid-summer), there was an All Souls' festival at which a vigil was held for the dead.

The texts at our disposal are not very forthcoming about the place of the ancestor cult. Nevertheless, it is possible to infer from attendant indications that the house of the paterfamilias was the center of the cult. We know that the ancestor cult was incumbent, primarily, on the eldest son. Since inheritance texts from Nippur specify that the eldest son always received the "ceremonial table" (*paššur sakke*, banšur zag.gú.la) as his part of the heritage,[34] it is likely that this ceremonial table was linked to the offerings for the ancestors. The Sumerian designation of this table implies that it was located in the house sanctuary known in Akkadian as the *išertum*.[35] We know from deeds of inheritance,[36] the floor plan of a house in Sippar,[37] and administrative documents from Nippur,[38] that the traditional Old Babylonian house did indeed have such a sanctuary.[39] Upon the death of the paterfamilias, this room passed into the possession of the eldest son.[40] It is presumably identical with the é ki.sè.ga (*bit kispim*), "the room of the *kispu*," mentioned in an inheritance text from Nippur,[41] and the é.gal (*ekallu*), "main room," of the inheritance texts from Emar and Nuzi. Other features of the house sanctuary aside from the ceremonial table are the fireplace (*kinunu*)[42] and the lamp (*nuru*).[43]

The ceremonial table of the house sanctuary was used on solemn occasions, such as a wedding, which signified that the activities took place in the presence of the ancestors.[44] The offerings for the dead were placed upon this ceremonial table, as the references to the "chair for the ghost" and the "chair for the family ghosts" imply.[45]

If the ancestor cult took place in the house, this assumes that the ancestors were present there in some form. Their presence could materialize in two ways. In the ideal situation, the Old Babylonian house had a burial vault containing the remains of the family dead.[46] References to this cellar are scarce. A letter refers to a woman who died in an epidemic and is to be buried in the house.[47] Other literary evidence is mostly earlier or later than the Old Babylonian period.[48] There is some archaeological evidence of interment underneath private houses from Old Babylonian Ur. It is clear from archaeological reports, however, that in-house burial was not standard procedure in Babylonia. Domestic offerings to the dead need not imply, then, that the ancestors had their final resting-place under the floor of the family house.

Another way for the dead to be physically present in the house was in the form of images. The references to such images are not unequivocal and mostly in texts originating from the periphery of Babylonia. Texts from Nuzi dealing with inheritance show that the main heir was to perform the cult (*palaḫu*, "to show respect") of the "gods" (dingir.meš, *ilanu*) and the *eṭemmu* of the testator;[49] disinherited kin, on the other hand, forfeited the right to come near "the gods and the *eṭemmu*" of the paterfamilias.[50] The "gods" in question were anthropomorphic images: they could be "made" (*epešu*);[51] some had a big head, others a small one.[52] I am inclined to take the word *eṭemmu* – always in the plural and always written syllabically – in the, perhaps etymological, sense of "bones (of the deceased)."[53] Were the term to denote the disembodied spirits of the dead, there would be no sense in saying that the disinherited were not to approach the *eṭemmu*, since ghosts move about and do not have a fixed abode in the house. The *eṭemmu* must represent the physical remains of the ancestors; the *ilanu*, I would suggest, are their images. The "gods" of the Nuzi inheritance texts, in other words, are ancestor statuettes. That explains why they can be said to receive *kispu*-offerings.[54]

The Nuzi texts have an interesting parallel in the Middle Babylonian texts from Emar. Inheritance texts stipulate that the heir had to invoke (*nubbu*), honor (*palaḫu*), and take care of (*kunnu*) "the gods and the dead" of the paterfamilias. This responsibility is linked to the possession of the main room (é.gal), presumably a designation of the domestic sanctuary,[55] since "the gods" belonged to the paraphernalia of the main room. The term for the "dead" (*metu*, "the dead," *meteya*, "my dead") recalls Hebrew *metim*; it refers to the physical remains of the dead. The *ili*, on the other hand, were images of the dead; they were the focus of the cult of the ancestors. A text from the vicinity of Emar indicates that such images – here referred to as "the gods of the house" (dingir.meš *ša* é-*ti*) – belonged to the family; should the house be sold outside the family, the family retained the right to the images.[56]

The Old Babylonian house sanctuary (*išertum*) was the place of a domestic cult, but this cult was addressed to the ancestors, not the family gods.[57] Aside from the ancestors, other numinous presences in the room are the lamp and the fireplace. Nuzi texts refer to the lamp as divine (^{d}zalag$_2$.meš); first millennium texts also use the divine determinative (^{d}*nuru*). The lamp is the symbol and embodiment of Nusku or Girra. The fireplace (*kinunu*) of the house sanctuary had a comparable significance. The "extinguished brazier" is a standing expression for a family without offspring. The image derives its force from the association between the brazier and the room of the ancestor cult. Though not divine in its own right, the fireplace has a cultic significance that is not to be underestimated.[58]

The ancestors included in the devotion of the living went back as far as the fourth generation, counting back from the oldest family member alive. A prayer to the moon-god enumerates the names of the dead addressed by the living. The list may seem tedious, but is quite illuminating about the extent and the logic of the ancestor cult. It deserves to be quoted in full:

> [S]in, you are the god of heaven and earth.
> [In the mo]rning I am pouring water to you
> [for the f]amily (*kimtum*) of Sin-naṣir, son of Ipqu-Annunitum.
> Release the family of Sin-naṣir, son of Ipqu-Annunitum,
> That they may eat his bread and drink his water –
> Ishme-Ea son of Shamash-naṣir, his wife and his family;
> [Il]tani, naditum of Shamash, his daughter;
> [Sin]-naṣir son of Ishme-Ea;
> *Kasap-Aya, naditum of Shamash, his daughter;
> Sin-iddinam son of Sin-naṣir;
> Iddin-Ea, son of Ishme-Ea;
> Amat-Aya, naditum of Shamash, his daughter;
> Diutubinduga, his son;
> Ebabbar-nu-u'ulshe-hegal, his son;
> Ehursag-mushallim, his son;
> Ipqu-Ea, son of Ishme-Ea;
> Amat-Mamu, naditum of Shamash, his daughter;
> Nidnusha, his son;
> Ibni-Ea, his son;
> Iqish-Ea, son of Ishme-[Ea], his wife and [his] family;
> Ipqu-Aya, son of Ishme-Ea, Abi-mattum his wife [and family?]
> Lamassani, naditum of Shamash, his daughter;
> Ilshu-ibnishu, his son;
> Sin-nadin-shumi, his son;
> Sin-kabit-biltum, son of Sin-nadin-shumi;
> Ikun-pi-Sin son of Ipqu-Aya, whom . . . have struck to death;
> Sin-eribam, son of Ipqu-Aya, asleep in Mashkan-Adad;
> Ipqu-Annunitum, son of Ipqu-Aya, Belessunu, his wife.
> Release the family of Sin-naṣir, son of Ipqu-Annunitum,
> that they may eat his [br]ead and drink his water.[59]

This prayer shows that Sin-naṣir brings offerings to his father, his grandfather, and his great-grandfather. They are his family (*kimtum*); those who preceded them are not mentioned by name (except Shamash-naṣir, the father of his great-grandfather) but included in the general category of the "family" of the ancestors.

The family Sin-naṣir honors is the patrilineal extended family; he includes his uncles and great-uncles; aunts and great-aunts go unmentioned, except for those who had become devotees of Shamash. They had not married, and thus remained within the family. The other women had left the family as a result of marriage. The primacy of the male in the cult is clear from the fact that women are mentioned only as "wife of" one of the ancestors, or – in the case of the *naditum* – as "daughter" of an ancestor. Women were apparently not regarded as ancestors themselves.

Family Religion: Sociology and Psychology

The place of women in the *kispu*-prayer of Sin-naṣir is emblematic of the sociology of Mesopotamian family religion. Family religion implied and reasserted female dependency on the male. A striking illustration of the subordinate position of women is the fact that they did not have a god of their own. When addressing a woman, the Babylonians would speak either of "the god of your father" or "the god of your husband." Women worship the god of the man under whose authority they fall; his god is by definition their god as well. As long as they are unmarried, their devotion is to the god of their father; in wedlock, they worship the god of their husband. Only women outside the jurisdiction of a paterfamilias by virtue of their dedication to a deity have a god of their own. They are in a sense married to the god; he is their god and his divine consort is their goddess.[60]

The place of women in the invocations of the dead confirms their subservient position. When mentioned in the context of the ancestor cult, they are normally referred to as the wife of one of the ancestors. In a number of cases, the invocations do not even give a woman's name; here, she is nothing more than the anonymous "wife of." Daughters do not receive ancestor offerings, except if they were devotees of a god. Such nuns, if the anachronism be permitted, often remained unmarried and thus stayed within the patrilineal family. The *naditu* constitutes the rare case of a woman outside parental control yet provided for in the afterlife by her father's kin group.

In its construction of reality, Mesopotamian family religion creates and legitimizes the chain of authority within the extended family. The son who inherits the paraphernalia of the ancestor cult – the images and the offering table, most notably – succeeds his father in the position of paterfamilias. His authority over the family and his leadership in its religion are indissolubly linked: the ancestors have passed on their authority to him; by honoring them with invocation and offerings, the new male in command proclaims his position.

Within the framework of Mesopotamian family religion, authority is always the attribute of a male, even when the holder of the position of paterfamilias is in fact female. The deceased husband of a widow, who during his lifetime wanted his wife to succeed him as highest authority in the family upon his death, laid down in his will that she receive the legal status of "fatherhood" (*abbutu*).[61] The situation compares to that of the daughter who remained unmarried to take care of her elderly parents. To reward her for her piety, the father might decide to make her "male and female," thus legally empowering her to succeed to the status of "fatherhood" (*abbutu*) in the family. She thereby became the main heir and the principal performer of the ancestor cult.[62] In order to gain her position of authority, the woman first had to be transformed into a man. It is a legal fiction, of course, but one that signifies the patrilineality of the system.

Besides the primacy of the male over the female, Mesopotamian family religion is also characterized by the primacy of the group over the individual. Mesopotamian family religion spells out the primacy of the group by the mere fact that the family god is the god of the group; there is neither individual religion nor a personal god of the individual. Participation in the family religion signifies that one really belongs to the family; disinherited kin are barred from the family rituals. The woman who enters the family through marriage confirms and celebrates her new identity by participating in the religion of her new kin-group. She honors the god of her husband and pledges her piety to his ancestors.

From a psychological point of view, Mesopotamian family religion serves to foster a sense of identity in those who practice it. Through the worship of the family god, all members of the family assert their attachment to a particular place – whether it be the place they came from or where they actually live. That place is part of their identity. Through the cult of the ancestors, they identify with a particular past. The genealogical lists that served in the recitations of the ancestor rituals were also skeletons to be fleshed out by stories about past generations. Family religion provided the Babylonians, then, with both a topographical and an historical sense of place. It made them belong.

Notes

1 Jonathan Z. Smith, *Relating Religion: Essays in the Study of Religion* (Chicago and London: The University of Chicago Press, 2004), p. 325. The quote is from the essay "Here, There, and Anywhere," the opening address at the 2000 conference "Prayer, Magic and the Stars in the Ancient and Late Antique World," University of Washington, published in *Prayer, Magic, and the Stars in the Ancient and Late Antique World*, Magic in History 8, ed. Scott B. Noegel, Joel Walker, and Brannon Wheeler (University Park: Pennsylvania State University Press, 2003), pp. 21–36.

2 See Smith, *Relating Religion*, p. 326: "Domestic religion, focused on an extended family, is supremely local."

3 Stephanie Dalley, C. B. F. Walker and J. D. Hawkins, *The Old Babylonian Tablets from Tell al Rimah* (London: British School of Archaeology in Iraq, 1976), nos. 118: 11; 119: 5.

4 See Van der Toorn, *Family Religion in Babylonia, Syria and Israel: Continuity and Change in the Forms of Religious Life*, Studies in the History and Culture of the Ancient Near East 7 (Leiden: Brill, 1996), pp. 76–7.

5 Brigitte R. M. Groneberg, *Lob der Ishtar: Gebet und Ritual an die altbabylonische Venusgöttin*, Cuneiform Monographs 8 (Groningen: Styx, 1997), pp. 110–11, lines 8–16. For this text, see also Michael P. Streck, "Die Klage 'Ishtar Bagdad' " in *Literatur, Politik und Recht in Mesopotamien: Festschrift für Claus Wilcke,* Orientalia Biblica et Christiana 14, ed. Walther Sallaberger, Konrad Volk, and Annette Zgoll (Wiesbaden: Harrassowitz, 2003), pp. 301–12. On the meaning of the passage about the family god, see also Groneberg, "Eine Einführungsszene in der altbabylonischen Literatur: Bemerkungen zum persönlichen Gott," in *Keilschriftliche Literaturen: Ausgewählte Vorträge der XXXII. Rencontre Assyriologique Internationale*, Berliner Beiträge zum Vorderen Orient 6, ed. Karl Hecker and Walther Sommerfeld (Münster: Dietrich Reimer, 1986), pp. 93–108. On the role of Ninshubur as intercessor, see also Frans

A. M. Wiggermann, "Ninshubur," *Reallexikon der Assyriologie*, ed. Erich Ebeling and Bruno Meissner (Berlin: Walther De Gruyter, 2001) 9: 490–500.

6 See, e.g., Fritz Rudolf Kraus (ed.), *Altbabylonische Briefe in Umschrift und Übersetzung* (Leiden: Brill, 1964–), p. 9 no. 141 ("the god of my father" intercedes with Marduk); p. 12, no. 99: 1–2 (Amurrum intercedes with Shamash); p. 13, no. 164 (Ninmug intercedes with Ishum). See also Van der Toorn, *Family Religion*, pp. 136–8.

7 Van der Toorn, *Family Religion*, pp. 82–3.

8 On neighborhood chapels, see Kathryn Elizabeth Keith, "Cities, Neighborhoods, and Houses: Urban Spatial Organization in Old Babylonian Mesopotamia" (PhD Dissertation, University of Michigan, 1999; UMI Microfilm 9938459), pp. 221–4.

9 See Van der Toorn, "Migration and the Spread of Local Cults," in *Immigration and Emigration Within the Ancient Near East: Festschrift E. Lipinski*, Orientalia lovaniensia analecta 65, ed. Karel Van Lerberghe and Anton Schoors (Leuven: Peeters, 1995), pp. 365–77, esp. pp. 369–70.

10 See Van der Toorn, *Family Religion*, pp. 88–93; Michael P. Streck, *Das amurritische Onomastikon der altbabylonische Zeit. Band 1: Die Amurriter; Die onomastische Forschung; Orthographie und Phonologie; Nominalmorphologie*, Alter Orient und Altes Testament 271 (Münster: Ugarit-Verlag, 2000), pp. 65–7.

11 On the reading and interpretation of an-an-mar-tu, see Thomas Richter, "Die Lesung des Götternamens AN.AN.MAR.TU," in *General Studies and Excavations at Nuzi 10/2*, Studies on the Civilization and Culture of Nuzi and the Hurrians 9, ed. David I. Owen and Gernot Wilhelm (Bethesda, Md.: CDL Press, 1998), pp. 135–7. Richter shows that the Hurrian rendering ^{d}*e-ni a-mur-*[*ri-we*] in an unpublished god-list from Emar supports the traditional understanding of an.an.mar.tu as "the Amorite god." Since the Amorite for "god" (^{d}an) is Il or El (not Anu), the possibility of Amurru being an allomorph of El deserves serious consideration. Note the frequent association of Amurru with his consort Ashratu (better known as Asherah). For this, see Streck, *Onomastikon*, pp. 69–70. The relationship between the characteristics and attributes of Amurru (holding the *gamlu*-stick as an instrument for remitting sins, being "lord of the steppe", thundering, etc.; see Streck, *Onomastikon*, pp. 68–72) and those of El merit further study.

12 See Van der Toorn, *Family Religion*, pp. 81–2.

13 Van der Toorn, *Family Religion*, p. 67.

14 Andrew R. George, "Ninurta-paqidat's Dog Bite, and Notes on Other Comic Tales," *Iraq* 55 (1993): 63–75, esp. 67, lines 29–30.

15 For the so-called letter prayers, see Van der Toorn, *Family Religion*, pp. 130–42, esp. 130 n. 64. Add Piotr Michalowski, "Incantation and Literary Letter Incipits," *Nouvelles assyriologiques brèves et utilitaires* (1991): 48; William W. Hallo, "Two Letter-Prayers to Amurru," in *Boundaries of the Ancient Near Eastern World: A Tribute to Cyrus H. Gordon, Journal for the Study of the Old Testament*, Supplement Series 273, ed. Meir Lubetski, Claire Gottlieb and Sharon Keller (Sheffield: Sheffield Academic Press, 1998), pp. 397–410; Willem H. Ph. Römer, "Miscellanea Sumerologica, V: Bittbrief einer Gelähmten um Genesung an die Göttin Nintinugga," in *Literatur, Politik und Recht in Mesopotamien*, pp. 237–49.

16 Note the dedication of a temple to Hanish-and-Shullat by one Nur-ilishu, who also installed a priest responsible for the sanctuary. See CT 6, 36a, Bu. 91-5-9,704, for which text see Moses Schorr, *Urkunden des altbabylonischen Zivil- und Prozessrechts*,

Vorderasiatische Bibliothek 5 (Leipzig: J. C. Hinrichs, 1913), p. 220; Johannes Renger, "Untersuchungen zum Priestertum in der altbabylonischen Zeit, 2. Teil," *Zeitschrift für Assyriologie* 59 (1969): 104–230, esp. 114–15. See also Marten Stol, "Das Heiligtum einer Familie," in *Literatur, Politik und Recht in Mesopotamie*, pp. 293–300.

17 For a reference to the annual sacrifice, see *Altbabylonische Briefe* 12, 99: 7.

18 Walter Farber, "Zur älteren akkadischen Beschwörungsliteratur," *Zeitschrift für Assyriologie* 71 (1981): 51–72, esp. 63, Obverse, line 13′ *i*$_3$*-lí bi-tim*, line 17′ *il bi-ti-im*; Farber, *Schlaf, Kindchen, Schlaf! Mesopotamische Baby-Beschwörungen und Rituale* (Winona Lake: Eisenbrauns, 1989), pp. 34–5, Vorläufer 1, line 5 *i*$_3$*-lí bi-tim*; pp. 36–7, Vorläufer 2, lines 11, 13 *i-li bi-tim*, *iš-ta-ar bi-tim*.

19 Note the line "She (i.e., Lamashtu) destroyed the *išertum* and the god of the house has left" (*imhaṣma išertam ittaṣi ili bitim*), in Walter Farber, "Zur älteren akkadischen Beschwörungsliteratur," pp. 60–8, esp. 161–3, lines 12′–13′. See also *Cuneiform Texts* 16, Pl. 29: 82–3 *ina ešret il biti la tattananzaz*, "Do not loiter in the sanctuary of the house god . . ." (spoken against a demon; Ignace Gelb et al. (eds.), *Chicago Assyrian Dictionary* [Chicago: Oriental Institute, 1956–2007], vol. A s.v. *aširtu* lexical section). For other references to the house sanctuary in first millennium texts, see Sally M. Freedman, *If a City Is Set on a Height: The Akkadian Omen Series Šumma Alu ina Mele Šakin. Volume 1: Tablets 1–21*, Occasional Publications of the Samuel Noah Kramer Fund 17 (Philadelphia: The University of Pennsylvania Museum, 1998), p. 192: 9: "If there is white fungus in the sanctuary (zag.gar.ra) of a man's house . . ." (*Shumma Alu*, tablet 12).

20 See, e.g., Ronald F. G. Sweet, "An Akkadian Incantation Text," in *Essays on the Ancient Semitic World*, ed. John W. Wevers and Donald B. Redford (Toronto and Buffalo: University of Toronto Press, 1970), pp. 6–11, esp. p. 7, line 5 dingir* é ^{d}innin é (incantation to be recited at the gate of the house); Frans A. M. Wiggermann, *Mesopotamian Protective Spirits: The Ritual Texts*, Cuneiform Monographs 1 (Groningen: Styx and PP Publications, 1992), 134, Text V (building ritual), ii 3′ [dingir] é* ^{d}xv é.

21 The only text that could be invoked to this effect is CBS 1513 mentioned by Johanna Spaey, "Emblems in Rituals in the Old Babylonian Period," in *Ritual and Sacrifice in the Ancient Near East: Proceedings of the International Conference organized by the Katholieke Universiteit Leuven from the 17th to the 20th of April 1991*, Orientalia lovaniensia analecta 55, ed. Jan Quaegebeur (Leuven: Peeters, 1993), pp. 411–20, esp. pp. 418, 420: "After one man cleared the other by means of the weapon of Adad, their deity, in the sanctuary of the house of their father" (*i-na* é *i-še-er-tim ša* é *abišu*[*nu*]). The expression "the house of their father" must be understood as "their family" rather than in a topographical sense. Compare the following references to oath-taking in the sanctuary of the family god(s): (1) "After PN$_1$ cleared PN$_2$ by means of the emblem (šu.nir) of Enlil in the sanctuary of their god" (*i-na e-še-er-tim ša i-li-šu-nu*), T. Pinches, *Cuneiform Texts* 8, Pl. 3a, lines 21–8; (2) "PN$_1$ PN$_2$ and PN$_3$ (. . .) had a lawsuit concerning the heritage. They divided the inheritance in the temple of their city god and their god(s) . . ." (*ina* é dingir *ališunu u ilišunu*), *Cuneiform Texts* 4.9a: 1–7, see also Josef Koehler and Arthur Ungnad, *Hammurabi's Gesetz* (Leipzig: Pfeiffer, 1909), 3.57; Walther Sommerfeld, *Der Aufstieg Marduks*, Alter Orient und Altes Testament 213 (Kevelaer: Butzon & Bercker; Neukirchen-Vluyn: Neukirchener Verlag, 1982), p. 44; Marten Stol, "Das Heiligtum einer Familie," in *Literatur, Politik und Recht in Mesopotamien*, pp. 293–300. All three texts deal with inheritance procedures. The

išertum in question is not a house chapel but a *bit ilim* (é dingir), i.e., a temple, presumably in the vicinity of the house. For the custom of taking an oath in the chapel of the family god, see Stol, "Heiligtum," p. 298.

22 JoAnn Scurlock, "Ancient Mesopotamian House Gods," *Journal of Ancient Near Eastern Religions* 3 (2003): 99–106.

23 See Farber, "Zur älteren akkadischen Beschwörungsliteratur," pp. 51–72, esp. p. 63, Obverse, line 13′. On Kusarikku and his apotropaic functions, see Wiggermann, *Mesopotamian Protective Spirits*, pp. 174–9; Piotr Steinkeller, "Early Semitic Literature and Third Millennium Seals with Mythological Motifs," in *Literature and Literary Language at Ebla*, Quaderni di Semitistica, 18, ed. Pelio Fronzaroli (Florence: University of Florence Department of Linguistics, 1992), pp. 243–83, esp. pp. 260–5.

24 See Erica Reiner, "Plague Amulets and House Blessings," *Journal of Near Eastern Studies* 19 (1960): 148–55.

25 John F. Robertson, "The Internal Political and Economic Structure of Old Babylonian Nippur: The Guennakum and His 'House,'" *Journal of Cuneiform Studies* 36 (1984): 145–190, 172, text CBS 7111:8, and commentary on p. 175. Another text from the archive mentions offerings of grain "relating to Nusku and Ishtar [or "the goddess"?] in the house of the father." See p. 175, text CBS 7670: gir_3 ^{d}nuska gir_3 ^{d}inanna é ad-da-na.

26 See Van der Toorn, *Family Religion*, p. 124.

27 The connection that Scurlock makes between Ishum and the hearth, thus turning him into the functional equivalent of the Roman Vesta, is based entirely on an uncertain etymology that links his name with the word for "fire" (Hebrew *ʾeš*). See Scurlock, "House Gods," p. 103. If there is a Mesopotamian fire god connected with the house, however, it can only be Nusku, god of the torch (*diparu*), the lamp (*nuru*) and the brazier (*kinunu*).

28 Thus Scurlock, "House Gods," p. 103.

29 The incantation to the god and goddess of the house edited by Sweet is to be recited in the gate (ká, *babu*) of the house. See Sweet, "Akkadian Incantation," p. 6. The "house god" to be fashioned in connection with a Standard Babylonian building ritual is to be placed in the outer gate of the house (see Wiggermann, *Protective Spirits*, p. 59).

30 See especially Farber, *Schlaf, Kindchen, Schlaf!*, pp. 36–7, Vorläufer 2, lines 11–14: "Because of your noise the house god cannot sleep, slumber does not take hold of the house goddess" (*ina rigmika ili bitim ul iṣallal ištar bitim ul ihhaz šittum*).

31 Farber, *Schlaf, Kindchen, Schlaf!*, pp. 84–5, line 358: "The Hairy Ones are frightened, sleep does not seize Ishtar in her bed" (^{d}*láh-mu igruru* ^{d}innin *ina uršiša ul iṣabbat šittu*); pp. 94–5, par. 29, line 15; pp. 96–7 par. 31, line 25: "The Hairy Ones are frightened, Ea panics" (*làh-me*(var. *mu*) *igruruma* ^{d}*Ea iggeltu*.

32 See Walther Sallaberger, "Zu einer Urkunde aus Ekalte über die Rückgabe der Hausgötter," *Ugarit Forschungen* 33 (2001): 495–9.

33 On the *kispu* ritual see Akio Tsukimoto, *Untersuchungen zur Totenpflege (kispum) im alten Mesopotamien*, Alter Orient und Altes Testament 216 (Kevelaer: Butzon & Bercker; Neukirchen-Vluyn: Neukirchener Verlag, 1985).

34 E. Prang, "Das Archiv des Imgua," *Zeitschrift für Assyriologie* 66 (1976): 1–44, esp. 16, 28; Prang, "Das Archiv des Bitua," *Zeitschrift für Assyriologie* 67 (1977): 217–34, esp. 224.

35 The term zag.gú.la stands for *sagu*, "sanctuary," a biform of *sakku* and a poetic synonym of *išertum*. In the bilingual lexical list HAR.RA = *hubullu* the banšur zag.gu.la = *paššur sakki* is immediately followed by the banšur zag.gar.ra = *paššur aširti*. See Benno

Landsberger, *The Series HAR-ra = hubullu, Tablets I–IV*, Materials for the Sumerian Lexicon 5 (Rome: Pontificium Institutum Biblicum, 1957), p. 168, lines 198–9. Sumerian zag can be either *sagu* (*sakku*) or *ašírtu*. In a Standard Babylonian prayer to Ishtar, attested in a Middle Babylonian version and probably going back to an Old Babylonian original, the *sagu* stands in parallelism with the *ašírtu*. See Leonard W. King, *The Seven Tablets of Creation* (London: Luzac, 1902), vol. 2, Plate 81, line 75: *šuharrur sage'a šuharrurat aširti*, "deadly silence reigns in my sanctum, deadly silence in my house sanctuary."

36 Charles-F. Jean, *Contrats de Larsa*, Textes cuneiforms du Louvre 11 (Paris: Geuthner, 1926), no. 174, line 14: ha.la *qá-du-um* zag.gar.ra. For a study of this text, see Lubor Matoush, "Les contrats de partage provenant des archives d'Iddin-Amurru," in *Symbolae ad studia orientis pertinentes Frederico Hrozny dedicatae*, Archiv Orientální 17/2, ed. V. Eihar, J. Klima, and L. Matoush (Prague: Czechoslovak Oriental Institute, 1949), pp. 142–73 & Pls. I–II, esp. pp. 164–8.

37 Leonard W. King, *The Letters and Inscriptions of Hammurabi* (London: Luzac and Co., 1900), 2, no. 107. For a discussion of this ground plan of a house in Sippar-Yahrurum, see Ernst Heinrich and Ursula Seidl, "Grundrisszeichnungen aus dem Alten Orient," *Mitteilungen der Deutschen Orient-Gesellschaft* 98 (1967): 24–45, esp. 35–7. The room defined as *e-ši-er-tum* is centrally located in the house; it is adjacent to a pa.pah, *papahum*, "chapel."

38 Robertson, "The Internal Political and Economic Structure of Old Babylonian Nippur," pp. 145–90, 172, text CBS 7111:8, and commentary on p. 175.

39 See also Gábor Kalla, "Das altbabylonische Wohnhaus und seine Struktur nach philologischen Quellen," in *Houses and Households in Ancient Mesopotamia: Papers Read at the 40e Rencontre Assyriologique Internationale*, ed. Klaas R. Veenhof (Istanbul: Nederlands Historisch-Archaeologische Instituut, 1996), pp. 247–56, esp. pp. 250–1. Kalla does not mention the *išertum* but identifies the *papahum*, "chapel," with the é.zag.gar.ra and é.sag.gar.ra. For archaeological investigations of the house sanctuary, see Maria Krafeld-Daugherty, *Wohnen im Alten Orient: Eine Untersuchung zur Verwendung von Räumen in altorientalischen Wohnhäusern*, Altertumskunde des Vorderen Orients 3 (Münster: Ugarit-Verlag, 1994), pp. 66–9, 185–218, 233–5; Laura Battini-Villard, *L'Espace domestique en Mésopotamie de la IIIe dynastie d'Ur à l'époque paléo-babylonienne*, BAR International Series 767 (Oxford: Archeopress, 1999), 1.358–9 (very critical of interpretations of rooms as sanctuaries). For a convenient summary of the evidence, see Kathryn Elizabeth Keith, "Cities, Neighborhoods, and Houses: Urban Spatial Organization in Old Babylonian Mesopotamia" (PhD Dissertation, University of Michigan; UMI Microfilm 9938459), pp. 261–2.

40 See Marten Stol, "Wirtschaft und Gesellschaft in altbabylonischer Zeit," in *Mesopotamien: Die altbabylonische Zeit*, Orbis Biblicus et Orientalis 160/4, ed. Dominique Charpin, Dietz Otto Edzard, and Marten Stol (Fribourg: Academic Press; Göttingen: Vandenhoeck & Ruprecht, 2004), 643–975, esp. 710. Add Jean, *Contrats de Larsa*, no. 174, lines 14–17.

41 Maurice Birot, *Tablettes économiques et administratives d'époque babylonienne ancienne conservées au musée d'art et d'histoire de Genève* (Paris: Geuthner, 1969), no. 37, line 4'. For the interpretation, see Kalla, "Das altbabylonische Wohnhaus," p. 251.

42 See Antoine Cavigneaux and Farouk N. H. Al-Rawi, "Charmes de Sippar et de Nippur," in *Cinquante-deux réflections sur le Proche-Orient ancien offertes en hommage à Léon de*

Meyer, ed. H. Gasche, M. Tanret, C. Janssen, and A. Degraeve (Leuven: Peeters, 1994), pp. 73–89, esp. pp. 85–7, tablet 90648 from the Iraq Museum, line 10: "before the fireplace in the *išertum*" (*ina put kinunim ina išertim*).

43 Note especially the role of the lamp in inheritance texts from Nuzi. On this, see Karlheinz Deller, "Die Hausgötter der Familie Shukrija S. Huja," in *Studies on the Civilization and Culture of Nuzi and the Hurrians in Honor of Ernest R. Lacheman*, Studies on the Civilization and Culture of Nuzi and the Hurrians 1, ed. Martha A. Morrison and David I. Owen (Winona Lake: Eisenbrauns, 1981), pp. 47–76, esp. pp. 62–71.

44 For the use of the *paššur sakke* for the wedding see OB *Gilgamesh*, Pennsylvania tablet, col. iv, 14–18.

45 See Landsberger, *The Series HAR-ra*, 157, tablet IV, line (*kussu eṭimme*); Heinrich Zimmern, *Beiträge zur Kenntnis der babylonischen Religion* (Leipzig: J. C. Hinrichs, 1896), no. 52: 12–14 (chair for the *eṭem kimti*); Van der Toorn, *Family Religion*, p. 52 and note 63; JoAnn Scurlock, "Soul Emplacements in Ancient Mesopotamian Funerary Rituals," in *Magic and Divination in the Ancient World*, Ancient Magic and Divination 2, ed. Leda Ciraolo and Jonathan Seidl (Leiden: Brill/Styx, 2002), pp. 1–6, esp. pp. 2–4.

46 See Stol, "Wirtschaft und Gesellschaft in altbabylonischer Zeit," 643ßß-975, esp. 681.

47 Kraus, *Altbabylonische Briefe* 1, no. 140: 17–25.

48 See Van der Toorn, *Family Religion*, pp. 59–62.

49 YBC 5142, published by Ernest R. Lacheman and David I. Owen, "Texts from Arrapha and from Nuzi in the Yale Babylonian Collection," in *Studies on the Civilization and Culture of Nuzi and the Hurrians*, pp. 377–432, esp. pp. 413, 386–7. The reference is to lines 30–1: [din]gir.meš *ù e-ṭe*$_4$*-em-mì-ya* [*i*]*-pal-la-ah-šu*.

50 See Edward Chiera, *Joint Expedition with the Iraq Museum at Nuzi, V: Mixed Texts*, Publications of the Baghdad School, American Schools of Oriental Research, Texts: Volume V (Philadelphia: University of Pennsylvania Press, 1934), no. 478: 6–8 *i-na* dingir.meš *ù i-na e-ṭe*$_4$*-em-mi* [x] a.šà.meš *ù* é.a.hi.meš (for é.hi.a.meš) *la i-la-ak-ka*$_4$; HSS 19.27:11 *ú-ul* d[ingir.meš]*-ya ú**-[*ul*] *e**-*ṭe*$_4$*-em-mi-ya* . . .

51 Ernest R. Lacheman, *Excavations at Nuzi, 5: Miscellaneous Texts from Nuzi, 2: The Palace and Temple Archives*, Harvard Semitic Studies 14 (Cambridge, Mass.: Harvard University Press, 1950), no. 108: 23–42, discussed by Deller, "Die Hausgötter, pp. 47–76, esp. pp. 73–4.

52 Lacheman, *Excavations at Nuzi, 8: Family Law Documents*, Harvard Semitic Studies 19 (Cambridge, Mass.: Harvard University Press, 1962), no. 5: 10–11, 21; see also Deller, "Hausgötter," p. 52.

53 I tentatively connect Akkadian *eṭemmu* with Hebrew *ʿeṣem*, "bone" which, in the plural, may be used to refer to the bones of the dead (see Num 19: 18; Amos 6: 10 and K.-M. Beyse, "*ʿeṣem*," *Theologisches Wörterbuch zum Alten Testament*, 10 vols., ed. G. J. Botterweck and Helmer Ringgren (Stuttgart: Kohlhammer, 1989), 6: 326–32, esp. p. 330. It should be noted that Akkadian *eṭemmu* often occurs in the plural, even when the reference is to the remains of one dead person. The Sumerogram gidim is calqued on Semitic *qadimu*, appearing in a bilingual list from Ebla as *ga-ti-mu*, translating Sum igi-tùm, connected with Akk *qadmu*, "former" (see Piotr Steinkeller, "The Eblaite Preposition *qidimay* 'Before'," *Oriens Antiquus* 23 [1984]: 33–7, esp. 36–7). I assume a development from **gadim* to gidim, "the former (one)."

54 See Elena Cassin, "Tablettes inédites de Nuzi," *Revue d'Assyriologie* 56 (1962): 57–80, esp. 59–61, text 2, lines 4–5 *a-na* dingir.meš, *ki-ip-sà-ti*. For *kipsu* as a by-form of *kispu*, see also Albert T. Clay, *Legal and Commercial Transactions Dated in the Assyrian, Neo-Babylonian and Persian Periods Chiefly from Nippur*, The Babylonian Expedition of the University of Pennsylvania, Series A: Cuneiform Texts VIII/1 (Philadelphia: Department of Archaeology University of Pennsylvania, 1908), no. 4, line 5 *ina* sag*.du ki-*tim* gidim-*šú li-ṣa-ma-' ki-ip-su*.

55 See Kalla, "Wohnhaus," p. 251 n. 10 for the interpretation of *ekallu* as domestic chapel. See also *Chicago Assyrian Dictionary*, vol. E, s.v. *ekallu*, esp. p. 60b.

56 See Walther Sallaberger, "Zu einer Urkunde," pp. 495–9.

57 Such is essentially also the view developed by Krafeld-Daugherty, *Wohnen im Alten Orient*, pp. 185–218.

58 Note especially the first millennium text *KAR* 300, Rev. 8 [*šumma amelu in*]*a kinunišu išatu ittananpah*: *kur-bi ili ina bitišu sadrat*]: "If a man keeps kindling the fire in his fireplace: the blessing of the god(s) is constantly on his house." For the reading, see Wolfram von Soden, *Akkadisches Handwörterbuch* (Wiesbaden: Harrasowitz, 1965), 1: 510a under *kurbu* and *Chicago Assyrian Dictionary*, vol. K 557a under *kurbu*. The *Shurpu* series mentions the oath "by the torch and the brazier" (*mamit* dizi.gar *u* ki.ne, III 145). For the link between the brazier and Nusku, see the interpretation of "hand of the brazier" (šu ki.ne) as "hand of Nusku," see *Chicago Assyrian Dictionary*, vol. K, 395*b*.

59 Arno Poebel, *Babylonian Legal and Business Documents From the Time of the First Dynasty of Babylon Chiefly from Nippur*, The Babylonian Expedition of the University of Pennsylvania 6/2 (Philadelphia: University Museum, 1909), no. 111: 1–33, studied in detail by Claus Wilcke, "Nachlese zu A. Poebels Babylonian Legal and Business Documents From the Time of the First Dynasty of Babylon Chiefly from Nippur (BE 6/2), Teil 1," *Zeitschrift für Assyriologie* 73 (1983): 48–66, esp. 49–54.

60 See Khaled Nashef, "Zur Frage des Schutzgottes der Frau," *Wiener Zeitschrift für die Kunde des Morgenlandes* 67 (1975): 29–30; Van der Toorn, *Family Religion*, pp. 75–6.

61 See Van der Toorn, "The Domestic Cult at Emar," *Journal of Cuneiform Studies* 47 (1995): 35–49, esp. 40 and note 47.

62 See, e.g., Daniel Arnaud, "La Syrie du moyen-Euphrate sous le protectorat Hittite: contrats de droit privé," *Aula Orientalis* 5 (1987): 211–42, esp. no. 13, lines 4–8. For the reading, see Jean-Marie Durand, "Tombes familiales et culte des ancêtres à Emar," *Nouvelles assyriologiques brèves et utilitaires* (1989): 112. For studies of the phenomenon, see Katarzyna Grosz, "Daughters Adopted as Sons at Nuzi and Emar," in *La femme dans le Proche-Orient antique*, ed. Jean-Marie Durand (Paris: Editions Recherche sur les Civilisations, 1987), pp. 81–6; Zafrira Ben-Barak, "The Legal Status of the Daughter as Heir in Nuzi and Emar," in *Society and Economy in the Eastern Mediterranean*, ed. M. Heltzer and Edward Lipinski (Leuven: Peeters, 1988), pp. 87–97.

4

The Integration of Household and Community Religion in Ancient Syria

DANIEL E. FLEMING

In archaeology and ancient history, the enormous and the magnificent always get the best press: palaces and pyramids, empires and their capitals.[1] Religion is most easily measured by its temples and by its state celebrations, kings at the head. Mesopotamia's great creation myth, the Enuma elish, celebrates the god of the Babylonian kingdom as unquestioned ruler of his divine peers. Real life plays out on a smaller scale, and recent research has produced a countercurrent of attention to the small and unspectacular. In the physical terms of excavation, this is best represented by the house and those who inhabit it. Textual evidence can also illuminate the lives of households and their families, even though the archives of palaces and temples have received first consideration. For the religion of the ancient Near East, few have contributed more to investigation of religion at home than Karel van der Toorn, and it is a pleasure to take part in a discussion that he has done so much to frame.[2]

Rather than respond directly to van der Toorn's portrait, one expression of which is included in this volume, I will focus on the body of evidence for ancient Syrian religion that I know best, the finds from Late Bronze Age Emar. From a variety of mainly textual evidence, I propose one general conclusion. The religion of household and family appears to have been integrated profoundly into the religious life of the larger community. With the discovery of the micro-social perspective, it has become too easy to divide ancient society according to dualities: public versus private spheres, official versus popular ideas and practices. Household or family religion may be treated as a separate system, related only superficially to the values and activities sponsored by the ruling powers. Emar, a merchant town on the elbow of the Euphrates River in western Syria, offers an unusual opportunity to evaluate household and community practices together, and the results show considerable integration of religion in these spheres. The modest cuneiform archives from temples, a small public building, and several houses, all from the fourteenth to twelfth centuries, offer varied evidence for religion in the home as well as in town-wide practice. As always, the information is incomplete, but what we do have suggests provocative connections between public and private affairs. When compared to more modern settings, these connections are perhaps not surprising, but it is nevertheless fruitful to consider their relationships explicitly.

It is tempting to propose that in our evidence from Emar, the religion of the household and the religion of the community are integrated at every level. There are too many gaps in our knowledge to allow certainty but what we have does suggest a pervasive connection. One possible exception may be found in the household domain of women. At least, the specific lines of evidence to be explored here tend to involve the head of household, who is usually a man. I will address the following phenomena:

- Care for the gods and the dead. This is part of the principal heir's inheritance and is mentioned in legal testaments. Sometimes a woman may be specified as heir, but the role is conceptually male in Emar terms. The woman must be declared legally "male and female" in order to take on this responsibility.
- Dagan in public religion and personal names. It may not be possible to assign the task of naming uniquely to father or mother. At least, we cannot restrict naming to the woman's domain.[3]
- Households and public shrines. So far as we can reconstruct the overlapping roles of private residences and public sacred sites, leadership is once again male. The head of household also bears the sacred responsibility.

As we consider the role of households in ancient society and religion, we must beware the false separation suggested by the familiar polarities: public and private, official and popular, associated with palaces and temples on one side and with houses on the other. These are made into distinct social domains, each capable of definition without reference to the other. It strikes me, however, that the household is not in itself a "private" social space. Rather, the household seems to integrate private and public activity in its regular life. The household participates with the larger community both in affairs that are explicitly political and in affairs that are defined by the concerns of each family. There may be some religious acts that pertain to the household without any reference to the larger community. Certainly, the nature of the relationship varied tremendously. Emar's evidence suggests nonetheless that we benefit from asking in every case of household practice how it may be integrated into life outside the individual house and the family that inhabits it.

Stepping back to consider the larger theoretical terrain, we must seek a framework that explains, or even notices, relationships between the rites and religious life of the house and of the community as a whole. It is my impression that few theorists focus on this interaction, natural as the combination may be. Maurice Bloch comes close in his exploration of the ritual of the royal bath among the Merina people of

Madagascar, although he does not address the phenomenon as such. The Merina of his study are Christian, but they retain practices and ideas from before the arrival of Christianity and these belong to deeply embedded social assumptions. Bloch observes in particular "the cult of the blessing," by which an elder invokes the ancestors at the request of an individual; the funerary ritual that attends two stages of temporary interment and then reburial in a communal tomb; and the ritual of the royal bath.[4] In the royal rite, the king sprays his subjects with water, much as heads of household spray their children as part of the ancestor blessing.[5]

Bloch emphasizes both the continuity and the contrasts between royal and everyday household ritual. The impact of the royal act derives in part from what it shares with the people's household life, even as it sets the king apart as preeminent. Merina royal rituals "gain specific meaning through their adoption and adaptation of symbolic forms which organized non-royal life in the Merina culture."[6] I find no specific similarities between modern Madagascar practices and those of ancient Syria. At Emar, the integration of household and community religion takes place more in the realm of collective political life, in the identity of the town as a unit, than at the behest of the king, so far as our evidence permits us a glimpse of some details. Nevertheless, Bloch's search for lines of symbolic connection between public and household religious acts resonates with what I see in this ancient Syrian town.

Emar in the Late Bronze Age

The modest merchant town of Emar occupied the margin of Mesopotamia, bridging the Euphrates drainage and regions further west, toward the Mediterranean sea. In the late third millennium, the city of Ebla dominated this western horizon, supplanted in the early second millennium by Aleppo. By the late second millennium, northwestern power was centered in the Anatolian kingdom of Hatti, replacing the eastern influence of a northern Mesopotamian state called Mittani. Across more than a thousand years, Emar somehow avoided wholesale incorporation into any of these larger polities. Even when the Hittites finally seized Emar outright in the late fourteenth century, the town stood at the fringe of the empire and many features of its political and social life continued without profound change.

One of the most important characteristics of Bronze Age Emar was a persistent commitment to collective governance. The power of individual rulers ebbed and flowed but never properly replaced the tradition of town decision-making by a group of leading peers.[7] At the time of our Late Bronze archives, Emar accepted a newly ambitious family of local kings. Even so, collective political traditions remain prominent, especially through the role of elders in various legal and ritual activities. The visibility of Emar leadership outside the local palace is enhanced by the fact that no palace or palace archive has yet been discovered. By far the largest trove of tablets came from the building M1, a structure that combines the architecture of a large house with that of a classic Syrian temple.[8] This building was occupied by a learned leader who called himself "the diviner of the gods of Emar," and his archives include ritual and administrative texts, scribal and divination lore, and legal documents kept in safe storage for diverse clients. Most of the remaining cuneiform tablets found at Emar are personal legal documents, the majority from houses.[9] Altogether, the written evidence from Emar shows us much about household affairs, especially through legal texts. At the same time, these can be related to public affairs through both internal references and a larger context provided by the ritual and administrative materials.

When we examine the religious life of households represented in legal documents, details suggest deep connections between this sphere and the public sphere of the larger community. The main body of this article will be devoted to exploring the most significant among these details.

Care for the Gods and the Dead

A number of Emar inheritance documents make provision for who will have responsibility to invoke and care for the "gods" and the "dead" of the testator. These "gods" are always nameless and plural, as appear to be the dead, and they accompany the primary house of a well-off family as actual property, physical furnishings. Together, the gods and the dead delimit a family ritual practice that passes from household head to primary heir. If any one element of Emar religion is defined by individual families and their households, this is it.

As a starting point for discussing the religion of family and household at Emar, we must first consider how to interpret this thought-provoking evidence. Immediately, the practice of "invoking" "the dead," placing them in the same category as "the gods," demands a defining role. It is no surprise that families would worship "gods," although it is worth noticing that these seem to be approached in the home, with no reference to any public shrine or temple. Whatever the act involves, it is most often defined as speech, specifically "naming." In family religion, some plural "dead" must receive exactly the same attention, in no way distinguished from "the gods." The dead are also "named," with whatever rites or gifts may accompany the speech. Household religion clearly places front and center the necessity of good relations with the extended family, as represented by the departed. Is any other constituency in view?

Karel van der Toorn has done more than anyone to elucidate the nature of this household religious practice.[10] He has long maintained that the "gods" in this combination also refer to ancestors. Most recently, in his paper for this volume, van der Toorn proposes that "the dead" refer to the physical remains of burial, while "the gods" are images of the dead for use in the cult of the ancestors. Similar documents from Nuzi, slightly earlier and far to the east, combine "the gods" and "the *eṭemmu*" of the testator. The *eṭemmu* is usually rendered "ghost" or "spirit" of the dead, but van der Toorn suggests now that these are literally the "bones" of the deceased.

In spite of some obstacles to the details of this interpretation, van der Toorn's essential perspective strikes me as insightful and persuasive. "The gods" seem to refer to concrete images that are used for the required invocation, while invocation of "the dead" takes a burial site as its point of reference. It remains uncertain whether "the gods" also indicate ancestors. There is no intrinsic barrier to such a conclusion in the terminology itself. In any case, every document that specifies who inherits this responsibility unites them under one action, usually "to invoke" (*nubbu*).[11] Somehow, then, the two nouns must delineate objects that call for separate classification. It does not seem possible, however, that "the dead" represent physical remains or bones. Van der Toorn draws appropriate attention to a parallel between "gods" and "dead" in the Emar testaments and "gods" and *eṭemmus* in similar documents from Nuzi. In order to conclude that "the dead" indicate bones, he must read the *eṭemmu* as essentially the same. To this end, he suggests that *eṭemmu* may be etymologically related to Biblical Hebrew *ʿeṣem*, which may occur in the plural as "bones."

This specific explanation of the inheritance arrangements faces at least two difficulties. First, the *eṭemmu* really does seem to be a spirit, not the bones as physical remains. Human *eṭemmus* properly belong in the underworld, as when Enkidu finds them there in Gilgamesh tablet XII (lines 20–1, 39). Kuta, the great underworld city, is called "the assembly of the *eṭemmus*."[12] A *kudurru* inscription distinguishes the "corpse" that is buried in the "earth" (*erṣetu* = underworld, also) from the *eṭemmu*, which without proper burial of the body is thereby prevented from joining the *eṭemmus* of his ancestral family.[13] The second problem with linking the *eṭemmu* to the Hebrew *ʿeṣem* is that Akkadian already has a more obvious cognate in the word *eṣemtu*, "bone(s)." The singular *eṣemtu* can represent the collective remains of one person,[14] and the plural seems to be reserved for groups of dead people, considered together.[15]

It seems that the *eṭemmu*, and probably Emar's "dead" as well, are ancestors to whom the living family has access through burial and the rites that take place there. If an *eṭemmu* has no burial as a point of contact with the living, it receives no *kispu* (ancestor care), no libations, no mention by name. Neither the *eṭemmu* nor the "dead" are themselves bones or corpses. An *eṭemmu* will roam if not cared for through a burial site, and *eṭemmus* belong in the underworld, into which they enter through the burial of the body in the earth.[16] Van der Toorn's larger interpretation therefore proves persuasive, insofar as both *eṭemmu* and "dead" in the testaments from Nuzi and Emar are defined ritually by approach at the grave site.

This leaves "the gods" to be the other major part of the heir's family religious responsibilities, not defined by the burial place. Van der Toorn observes that "the gods of the house" (DINGIR^{meš} *šá* É-*ti*) follow the family when a house is sold to an outsider in a document from nearby Ekalte. They are mobile, as opposed to a burial. In this connection, Ugarit's *ʾilʾib*, "god of the father" (*ʾilu ʾibi*), or "god-father" (*ʾilu ʾibu*) may offer indirect support for van der Toorn's approach. The term is not rare and appears frequently in lists of offerings to deities. By far the most illuminating usage, however, is found in a repeated description of what a man hopes for in a son, in the tale of Dan'el and Aqhat. As father, Dan'el longs for an heir "to set up the sacred stone of his father's god; in the sanctuary, the votive emblem of his kinsmen."[17] It is important to recognize that these ritual responsibilities do not involve care for the father himself after death. The son must honor the father's *'il'ib* and kin (*'m*) as did the father. The father will go down to dishonor unless his *'il'ib* and his *'m* pass to the care of a son.[18] Care for the *'il'ib* and the *'m* takes place at a "sanctuary" (*qdš*), not identified with any burial language, and a term commonly connected with the worship of major gods in public rites. The Ugaritic tale thus seems to assume the integration of the family religious responsibilities of an heir into public sacred space. The male heir is the same figure designated in legal testaments.

It does therefore seem possible that the essential distinction between "gods" and "dead" or *eṭemmu* spirits in the testaments from Emar and Nuzi has to do with the setting for ritual attention. Only the "dead" or "spirits" are approached by way of burial sites, while all other religious responsibilities to be transferred with an inheritance are understood to warrant definition in terms of "gods." Van der Toorn's idea that these may be associated with physical images makes good sense. The precise bounds of the "god" category for the religious duties of a household head are not certain. There is no reason to exclude ancestral figures from such "gods," but I also see no clear basis for limiting the "gods" of household duty to ancestors alone. The evidence does not allow a secure conclusion.

For all the more eastern Mesopotamian evidence for named individual gods with family interest, there is no sign of these at Emar. Van der Toorn cites letters and seals for the Babylonian situation, but the letters and seals from this Syrian site pass up the opportunity. Greetings in letters usually make no reference to deities, and the only two that I have found both invoke "the gods'" protection generically.[19] Equally generic are the shrines that may be for the "fathers" in certain texts for public ritual.[20]

As the one family religious activity that demands disposition in wills, the invocation of gods and dead seems the quintessence of household religion at Emar. This role must be evaluated with caution. The legal significance does give the activity special weight, even as it perhaps says more about the head of the household than about the family as a whole, especially the women. Invocation of the family deities and dead may belong explicitly to the house but this does not necessarily isolate the family from the larger community. Of course, the very genealogical bonds maintained by remembrance of ancestors reach across individual households to a wider circle of kin. So far as "the dead" may be addressed at a burial site, this grave does not appear to be located inside the house. House sales at Emar are common, and the families of sellers seem to be in no danger of losing contact with their dearly departed. Jean-Claude Margueron, director of the first excavations at Emar, observes that over thirty houses were uncovered at least in part, and he mentions no evidence for burials within them.[21] No communal cemetery has yet been discovered, but the absence of in-house burials suggests the possibility of one or more such sites. One text for public ritual describes a major sacrifice "at the cemetery gate" during a three-day festival for Dagan that has other overtones of underworld interest.[22]

Attention to the dead at Emar must not be considered the solitary interest of separate households, even as the dead provided one essential focus of religious commitment for every family. It is not then surprising that one stock clause in the formulary of inheritance documents combines the statements, "They shall divide my possessions according to the town (custom)," and the qualifier, "The gods belong to the main house."[23] Focus on the location of the gods and focus on who must perform rites for them appear to be mutually exclusive. Only one of the two clauses occurs in any given document. Attribution of the family gods to the primary house and principal heir is somehow the interest of the "town" as a whole, which supports the practice as standard.

Dagan: God of First Resort

In discussion of ancient Near Eastern religion, the stock in trade usually consists of pantheons. Near Eastern religion was constructed from a community of gods, and scholars by habit speak of "the pantheon" worshiped by any given people. One may say that Marduk was the chief god or head of "the pantheon" at Babylon and that Assur led "the pantheon" of the Assyrians. I myself have called Dagan "the head of the pantheon" at Emar, where he dominates more than one domain of religious practice. In retrospect, I find this homogenizing of a religious system to be misleading, and in this evaluation of household life I would like to consider the situation at Emar with more precision.

Realistically, "the pantheon" of Babylon or Assyria is a public construction with political and practical administrative dimensions. At Emar, this public pantheon finds expression in a text that records outlay and procedure for by far the most lavish festival among the several known from the site. According to this long version, in the last year of a seven-year cycle, the people of Emar gather to "give the *zukru* to Dagan," a rite evidently focused on some speech act. During the central week of festivities, all the gods join all the people of Emar outside the fortification walls and donations are made to every temple and shrine, down to the poorest. The list, which has lost some material to breaks, includes 83 sacred sites, divided into three tiers of gods whose status is measured by the size of their allotments. "Dagan Lord of the Offspring" stands at the head of the list, first among 19 major recipients. This is the particular name under which Dagan was worshiped for the *zukru* festival, and the list presents a confusing picture of pantheon priorities. After the Lord of the Offspring comes the storm god (^{d}IŠKUR) and then simple "Dagan," evidently the principal temple of this god. In the hierarchy of *zukru* prestige, the storm god is allowed to step ahead of Dagan, even for a rite that is wholly devoted to Dagan and that offers no active role to the storm god.[24]

Whose pantheon is this? The text was drawn up at the workplace of "the diviner of the gods of Emar," a man charged to oversee ritual defined by the town as such. Politically, it is not completely clear whom the pantheon represents. The diviner seems to serve the collective town under the oversight of the Hittite imperial power, without direct involvement of the local Emar king. Most of the *zukru*'s expenses, however, are borne by the king of Emar. Whatever institution dominates the administrative perspective of the text, the high position of the storm god seems to reflect the influence of one or both public domains. Excavations have shown that the temple of the storm god (Addu or Ba'lu) occupied the western promontory of the town, its highest point.[25] This temple and a parallel neighbor were oriented toward the rising sun, with a pride of place that indicates a public role that we now know goes back to the middle of the second millennium.[26] Since that time, the storm god had looked out over Emar in some dominant public role that is reflected in the *zukru* list.

What then of Dagan? Is he not then the chief god at Emar? This is where it seems that a paradigm of simple unities will fail us. If we set aside the political metaphor of divine kingship, it is not clear how Dagan's position in the middle Euphrates valley should be characterized.[27] Dagan had major temples downstream at Tuttul and Terqa that went back to the third millennium.[28] These do not necessarily make him "head" of a public pantheon there, however.[29] It may be that the model of centralized political authority cannot explain Dagan's importance at Terqa, Tuttul, and Emar. He may still have enjoyed a crucial public status, not ultimately defined or mediated by local kingdoms. Dagan could represent the people as a whole without being tied to individual leadership. Kings could lay claim to Dagan's stature, as at early second-millennium Mari, but this appears to depend on the honor he already enjoyed.[30] This kind of character may account for the continuity between his appearance at Emar in both household affairs and major town-wide ritual. On one side, household recognition of Dagan finds expression in personal names. On the other, the essential *zukru* event belongs entirely to Dagan, and this rite celebrates the unity of the town as such. As a seventh-year bash, it becomes the most important event in Emar's sacred calendar, elevating Dagan to the highest respect – without being king or ruler. In the *zukru* festival text, Dagan is called "father" as well as "Lord of the Offspring," so that he is identified in more familial than political terms.[31] The one other major calendar-based rite that gives Dagan a central role takes place at the end of the fifth and start of the sixth month, overlapping the decline and reappearance of the moon.[32] In general, this is a time of sensitivity to death and the underworld. In the Emar rites, the underworld interest has two direct expressions. The fifth month closes with three days of offerings at *abu* shrines in various public places: temples or structures devoted to named gods, the palace, and a sacred warehouse called the *bit tukli* ("House of Assistance"?). These days are enclosed in a ritual envelope defined by the locking and then opening of unnamed doors. Something is shut away for this dangerous interval. Because the first day incorporates a ceremony "at the cemetery gate," it seems that the doors are somehow shut against the realm of the dead.

What, then, are these *abu* shrines? We cannot be sure from this text alone. Beginning in the early second millennium, Mesopotamian calendars attest a month called Abu, traditionally associated with rites for the dead. This name also has no definite interpretation, although it may somehow relate to a point of access to the underworld.[33] Emar had a shrine for the goddess Ashtartu-of-the-*abu*, and the oldest reference to her renders the name, [^{d}*A*]*š-tar-ti ša ab-bi*, where the doubled *-bb-* marks the plural for "fathers." Even if the larger Mesopotamian *abu* ritual originated in a pit or other entry to the underworld, Emar scribes seem to have interpreted the name from the similar word for "father" or "ancestor," and the Dagan rite thus pertains somehow to care for ancestors.[34] So far as this is so, it is surprising to see such attention to ancestors through this variety of public sites. By their very identification with such institutions, these ancestor shrines must serve the larger community, beyond the bounds of any single household. In this rite, the people of Emar attend to their dead collectively, whatever the individual rites and relationships in play.

Why then is Dagan the lead god of this ritual cluster? He is not an underworld god, never mind its chief, even as he has persistent connections with rites for the dead.[35] It is not enough, however, to say he is involved with the dead because he is "father of the gods" or "the supreme creator god."[36] As "the very father" in the *zukru* festival, Dagan is in some sense "the supreme ancestor," to play on Emar usage of the term. We do not know why "giving the *zukru*" to Dagan became the most important regular ritual at Emar, but perhaps his functions in the *zukru* and in the rites of the *abu* shrines are not entirely separate. Dagan is god of the people themselves, it seems, where the people in turn identify themselves by their people, their ancestors. The living and the dead together define the community, with Dagan the divine point of reference. So far as this hypothesis succeeds, then Dagan was essential to the integration of household and public religion at Emar. Dagan bound the people as an organic whole consisting of household cells, these joined by the idea of a shared community of the living and the dead.

The logic of a community united through its shared ancestry is ultimately tribal. In the evidence from Late Bronze writing, Emar is defined as a town, with no separate tribal identity. It has a powerful political tradition of collective governance, but no population named in a way that reaches beyond those bounds. Nevertheless, it may be that the collective tradition at Emar is rooted in a sense of social organization that assumes a bond of kinship for those who share the same space. No matter the actual origins of Emar residents, they are not finally accepted as citizens based only on their decision to live in this town. In some cases, this may be true in practice, but it is possible that town identity depended on conventions that were profoundly tribal in structure. Dagan was then the "father" of Emar, and worship of him would bridge directly the practices of home and community. When we see Dagan's prominence in the household religious concerns of naming and protecting legal commitments, this prominence must be related somehow to the god's particular role in binding the people into a whole.

Personal Names

Names are a slippery source for historical information because they depend so much on convention. Mesopotamian personal names still carried recognizable meaning, being what Michael O'Connor calls "linguistically transparent."[37] Broad patterns in their popularity offer one view of a religious landscape that centered on the family with each birth. Although Emar personal names have received considerable attention, including now a full monograph, their religious implications remain an open question. As with most ancient Near Eastern onomastica, a large fraction of Emar's personal names invoke some deity. The specific gods mentioned and the range of sentiments expressed can offer some insight into religious traditions attached to naming which gives an enduring identity to the emerging generation.

With any reading of Emar texts that include personal names, one fact immediately stands out. By far the most popular deity is Dagan. I have just argued that Dagan cannot be called "the" head of Emar's pantheon, but along with the storm god (Addu/Ba'lu), he has the highest standing in public ritual. The storm god is the deity invoked second most often in Emar personal names, far behind the frequency found for Dagan. In some way, the pattern suggests that in naming, the sensibilities of public and household religion held much in common.

Comparison of these two gods' appearance in names is nevertheless illuminating. Their use is not obviously predictable from what we know of public ritual at Emar, even with the importance of both gods in both settings. No matter how the names are counted, Dagan comes out far ahead of all others. This issue deserves systematic examination, and I have only undertaken a quick survey.

Technical note: Even with meticulous counting and analysis, no census of personal names in ancient documents can be more precise than any modern population census, and an Emar census will naturally face further obstacles. First, the sample is even less complete and not properly random. In legal texts it is skewed toward people of means, and in Emar's administrative lists toward people who were dependent on public institutions, especially temples. Within the body of attested names, readings are not always certain. Many names have no visible patronym (father's name) or show only the patronym and not the named son. Even where names and patronyms are the same, we cannot always be sure the same person is involved, although this is usually true. In my counts of names borne by individual people, I have culled the clear repeats from the lists, but my final numbers often involve a degree of error, especially with the more common names. Any analysis of the religious implications of personal names is now made tremendously easier by the exhaustive, text-by-text list of every attested name in the CD that accompanies the monograph by Regine Pruzsinszky.[38]

There are two main ways to count: by separate names and by the numbers of individuals bearing a given name. The first is easier, though still not simple. Pruzsinszky's "Akkadian" and "West Semitic" categories are not reliably distinct and are most securely merged as Semitic, by far the largest group at Emar.[39] Out of 425 "theophoric" personal names that are probably Semitic, 175 invoke Dagan and 88 invoke some form of the storm god. No other deity comes close to these numbers.

Technical note: Here, we encounter more barriers to precision. The Dagan names are mostly certain, written in three ways: ^{d}*Da-gan*, ^{d}KUR, and abbreviated as *Da*. Occasional equivalences prove the identifications. The storm god is more difficult, written most often as ^{d}IŠKUR or ^{d}U, and sometimes syllabically as Ba'lu, in various forms. Many names use EN or ^{d}EN, for Ba'lu (West Semitic) and Belu (Akkadian), as "Lord." In names, this title is generally indistinguishable from a major deity. At Ugarit and in much Emar evidence, the title of Haddu/Addu becomes an alternate name for the storm god: Ba'lu (Baal). The problem is that this title also has a deep association with Dagan in the Emar onomasticon and cannot automatically be attached to Addu. A number of names with divine elements occur only with Dagan or "Lord" as the god, and never the storm god. These include: Dagan/EN-tali', Ḫimaši-Dagan/BE, Ia'nu-Dagan/BE, Iaqum-Da/EN, Iarib-Dagan/Da/Ba'lu, Iaṣi-Dagan/EN, Iatur-Dagan/EN, Ibni-Dagan/Da/BE, Iddi'-Dagan/Da/EN, Išbi-Dagan/EN, Itti-Dagan/Da/EN, Itur-Dagan/Da/Ba'lu/EN, Kapi-Dagan/EN, Lami-Dagan/Ba'la, Li'mi-Dagan/Da/Šarru, Ribi-Dagan/EN, Zimri-Dagan/Da/EN.[40] There are other possible examples, but these occur with no other divine representatives. Given this pattern, the storm god numbers may be inflated. I have tended to maximize his figures so as not to overplay Dagan's dominance. Dagan's fraction is impressive enough as it is.

Many of these names appear only once or twice. What happens if we try the trickier task of counting heads, the individuals who bear Dagan and storm god names? Counted this way, Dagan's popularity is even more overwhelming. Fearing false precision, I do not attempt exhaustive totals for Dagan and storm god names. Instead, I offer a sense of scale through the more common examples.

Among names with 10 or more individual bearers, 38 invoke Dagan and only 9 the storm god.[41] With 20 or more bearers, there are 23 for Dagan and only 5 for the storm god. Interestingly, a handful of storm god names are extremely common. Three of five occur with 40 or more individuals, versus 9 for Dagan. The two far most frequent theophoric names invoke the storm god: Zu-Ba'la (c. 124) and Ba'l-malik (c. 100).[42]

Finally, we may count names in individual lists. In this case as well, Dagan leads the storm god by a large margin, even with men who receive bows from the storm god's temple.[43] It is mystifying to find that in all these lists, no matter the provenance, theophoric names are several times more common with the given men in question than with their patronyms. Surely the use of theophoric names was no late fad at Emar. Nothing in the witness lists for the generations of legal documents suggests this. Several possible explanations come to mind, and somehow we must conclude that the full names of fathers are not being provided. We may have clan names in some cases. The patronyms may be abbreviations or nicknames.[44]

If Dagan is the overwhelming favorite in names that invoke the gods, why are the names Zu-Ba'la and Ba'la-malik so popular, far beyond the use of any one Dagan name? One possible explanation is that this reflects indirectly the institutional power of the storm god and his temple. At least one of the two parallel temples at the high-point of the town belonged to the storm god, and there is no evidence that Dagan's temple occupied any such prominent location. Among the 26 tablets and fragments found in the parallel temples (Emar VI.3 42–67), one building preserved three records of the storm god's affairs, along with one for "Ashtartu of the town."[45] One tablet (no. 42) describes king Pilsu-Dagan's dedication of a gold vessel to the storm god in appreciation for his deliverance from a Hurrian enemy.[46] This need not have been the only god who received thanks after this episode, but the specific royal reliance on the storm god in time of crisis is nevertheless noteworthy. The enormous numbers of men named Zu-Ba'la and Ba'la-malik seem to reflect the public stature of the god that is expressed in the physical priority given to his temple. It is not certain what ritual or military activity leads the men listed in text no. 52 to take bows from this establishment, and we cannot assume that full-time service is involved. Even so, there are a striking number of storm-god names in the list, almost all applied to the men given bows, not the patronyms: out of 73 recipients, six named Zu-Ba'la, perhaps two named Ba'la-malik, and one named Ba'la-ma.[47] If there is some military role for worship of the storm god, it is worth noting that the associated goddess Ashtartu takes the title "of Battle" (*ša taḫazi*) for the installation of a major priestess for her temple, the *mašʾartu*. The military interest is by nature public, pertaining to the community as a whole, under threat.

Dagan, meanwhile, enjoys a leading public position as well, as seen in the *zukru* festival alone. Two major Dagan events are included in the consecutive months of rites for "the town" (Emar VI.3 446). Beyond the rites that celebrate Dagan directly, we encounter some sense that he takes first place among the gods of Emar. The feast days of the *mašʾartu* festival, which gives no active role to Dagan, allots individual days of a seven-day feast to major gods. These suggest some sort of ranking, and it is surprising to see the storm god follow Dagan in a rite for Ashtartu. The order includes: Dagan, the storm god, the town god (^{d}NIN.URTA), "the gods," Ea, and a name lost to a break.[48] Dagan also takes a prominent place in the curses offered to guarantee the permanence of a few legal arrangements. Even where the texts record decisions about family affairs, the curses themselves suggest association with the palace. When Dagan is the first god invoked in the curse of a legal document, the king typically leads the witnesses.[49] One document not witnessed by the king offers a similar curse, but with Išhara and the storm god as "Lord of GUR-*x*-[*x*]."[50] It seems that Dagan and the town god ^{d}NIN.URTA, the gods of the *zukru*, perhaps envisioned as father and son like Nippur's Enlil and Ninurta, carry legal force in the royal court.

In spite of these indications of Dagan's formal importance in thirteenth-century Emar, there are hints that this represents a sort of negotiated settlement between the interests of Dagan and the storm god. When we consider the deeper structures of Emar ritual life, Dagan is absent at curious points. He takes no part in the installation of the storm god's priestess (no. 369), a major public rite for the main deity of the western height. In the ritual collection as a whole, Emar supports only two sacred personnel who clearly reside inside a temple and serve there full time: the priestesses of the storm god and of Ashtartu, both women serving at the temple pair of the town's high point. Dagan's priest, like others in town, has no marvelous status, as shown by his modest grain allotment in a long list.[51] Could it be that the western temples were the only Emar temples constructed to house live-in personnel?[52] Otherwise, the building (M1) that yielded the motherload of Emar tablets combines elements of house and temple under the auspices of the man who takes the title, "the diviner of the gods of Emar." This "diviner" actually oversaw much of Emar's ritual life and played a significant administrative role in the affairs of many separate shrines and temples. He inhabited his own sacred center, possibly called "the House of the Gods," again distinct from Dagan.[53]

Can we conclude from this diverse evidence that Dagan was "the head" of Emar's pantheon? Must we imagine a competition for the first place between Dagan and the storm god? It may be that the people of Emar felt no need to settle such questions of hierarchy until their government leaned toward its own hierarchy under Hittite rule. I am inclined to attribute the status of each major god to different social forces and political traditions that coexisted at Emar. Somehow, the storm god laid claim to the best real estate, facing west, toward centers like Aleppo that gave him special honor. Meanwhile, Dagan dominated the popular base, as seen in the proportion of children who carry his name in theirs. So far as the *zukru* celebrates the devotion of the people as a collective town, this may also hint at a different foundation for his special role. Both here and in the curses, Dagan and the god of particular town affairs, written as ^{d}NIN.URTA, combine to represent Emar in terms separate from the storm god. The curses attend the king in his role as traditional town leader, and so the gods of the collective people are invoked. The king thus cloaks his legal authority in a religious power that is not ultimately founded on his own centrality.[54] Against this political backdrop, it should not be surprising that Dagan is the major god who most binds the religious lives of community and household, where the town is conceived as the organic sum of all its household parts.

Households and Public Shrines

By far the largest number of tablets found at Emar come from the building M1, occupied by "the diviner of the gods of Emar." Although this structure has a main room and entrance that fit perfectly the norm for Emar and Syrian temples, three rooms were added along one side. The result is more like a house in total composition.[55] If we begin our analysis of this phenomenon with the assumption that public and private spheres are essentially separate, we may conclude either that the large cella is not truly public or that as a residence the building is not properly private. Both approaches strike me as artificial. The abundant tablet finds from the building M1 show that the diviner who worked there was involved in multiple overlapping activities. He operated a substantial school for apprentices who would earn the title of "diviner," inspired by the technical omen literature that formed one part of their studies. At the same time, the lead diviner himself oversaw much of Emar's "public" ritual life, so far as that adjective may apply. He was responsible for much of what Emar celebrated as a town, with deep involvement in the administration of the individual sacred sites that participated in town-wide ritual. This role took on an inevitable political aspect, as he coordinated the execution of traditional town festivals with the interests of both the local king and the more distant power of the Hittite imperial administration. Through all these activities runs the thread of the diviner's personal interest, reflected especially in private documents that reveal a growing wealth. The diviner's school itself was a family affair, training a new generation to take over from its elders.

The building M1 itself seems to have served a public ritual role, if "the diviner of the gods" himself ran the ubiquitous "House of the Gods." This site is mentioned frequently in ritual texts as a source for supply of offerings, and the installation of Ashtartu's priestess seems to place a sanctuary for "the gods" together in the same category as temples for Dagan, the storm god, and others, where livestock are sacrificed and a feast is held day by day at each location. There is no reason to conclude that the diviner lived anywhere besides his place of work with all its sacred activity.

In this specific case, it is still possible to separate public and household religious practices if we isolate the gods and rites that pertain only to the family. When "the gods" are served or represented through the shrine in the diviner's building M1, they clearly have to do with the religion of Emar as a whole community. This is an important distinction, and the individual family must indeed be considered religiously significant, a unit in its own right. At the same time, however, the building M1 offers one example of how difficult it is at Emar to separate public and private sacred space. We do not know whether the diviner's family had its own family gods of the sort mentioned occasionally in inheritance documents. The testament of the diviner Ba'la-qarrad does not address this question.[56] It appears that in purely physical terms, there was nothing about the diviner's residence that made it profane, inappropriate to the incorporation of a public sanctuary.

In ritual terms, the installation of the storm god's priestess offers a thought-provoking comparison. She goes through a complex rite of passage that accompanies the physical transition from her father's house to a room of her own in the storm god's temple.[57] It now strikes me that this special passage into full identification with the storm god and his abode may not be standard to priests at Emar. Most priests may not have lived in temples that were completely separate from profane structures and supported by institutions capable of paying for full-time staff. The priestesses of the storm god and Ashtartu appear to have been housed in the two prominent western temples, with unique status. Their special preparations to take up residence there suggest that these temples also enjoyed special status as both sacred and physically separate in a way that cannot be assumed for every Emar sanctuary. Certainly each shrine was consecrated, but the sense of separate space requiring special passage need not have been universal.

In concrete terms, it is not obvious that the diviner would have required the same kind of passage rite to prepare him to serve the shrine of the gods that formed part of his own home. Unlike the priestess who had to move from her family's house to the storm god's temple, the diviner may even have been born in the same building where he would eventually serve. Many of the questions related to consecration of persons and space are unanswerable without more evidence. It is possible, however, that we cannot generalize from the portrayal of the storm god's temple and resident priestess.

One more phenomenon adds nuance to the interplay of community and family in supposed public and private domains. A legal document witnessed by an early Emar king guarantees the permanent right of one family to the priesthood of a temple to Nergal.[58] This in itself is no surprise, although the male inheritance of sacred status contrasts with the arrangement for Emar's two priestesses who cannot pass down their offices to daughters. What is intriguing is the fact that the construction of a shrine for public worship of Nergal is not launched in the name of any public authority or institution. A townsman named Pilsu-Dagan (unrelated to the later king) builds the shrine at his own initiative and cost, and he expects to serve as its priest and to benefit from whatever income it generates. The town backs the undertaking, as seen by the presence of both "the elders of Emar" and the king in the document available to us.

Where is the sharp line between public and private religion in this case? The shrine serves the public sphere but it seems to have been created by private entrepreneurship in the financial interest of one family. There is no way to discern the shrine's form and location, although it seems to be separate from Pilsu-Dagan's house. The document envisions the possibility that future interference from outsiders could require the rebuilding of the shrine just as Pilsu-Dagan had made it. Nothing about the transaction suggests that Pilsu-Dagan expected to live in this shrine, and it is simplest to imagine that the family continued its existence as it had been: the same house, the same income from other sources. The religion is public but the institutional framework for it merges public and private, community and family, so that we benefit from an interpretation based on integration of these domains rather than on their isolation.

Religion and Society

I have approached the problem of household and family religion in Mesopotamia through one site, according to the pattern of my larger work. The coherence of a single body of primary evidence can allow a more precise dialogue between actual practice and more general questions. What follows turns back to the problem of how religion relates to social frameworks.

However we conceive of religion's essence, ancient Near Eastern religion was grounded in a "poly" world. Religion linked the human community to what people understood as a much larger society of active wills. Divine activity could take many forms, but the most important expression was willed, the product of minds recognizably like ours. In his piece for this volume, Van der Toorn focuses on the social-psychological role of identity. This is itself embedded in the idea of relationship between beings who impinge on each other's worlds, with needs that mesh and the possibility of mutual commitment. Just as people whose worlds intersect will want or need something from each other, if only to keep the peace, beings classed as "divine" simply enlarged this society of actors to make it more complete.

Identity was then crucial not just for security or comfort but to define a place in this mixed human–divine society. The dimensions of the divine society always overlapped massively with the human: by place, by social level and power, by gender. "The gods" as a whole were not a ruling class – this was only true for the class of ruling gods. As a whole, divine power was unavoidable and untamable, so thus an explanation for the fragility of human life.

Where was the family in all this? Family bonds were the molecular-level glue of every social structure in ancient Syria-Mesopotamia. If tribes and cities represent the two grand social constructions of this world, both go back to villages and camps, built around family ties. Family ties remained the building blocks even of palaces, temples and the specialized professions, though these created the basis for other relations. In social terms, the family and the household were not small-scale alternatives to a separate public domain. Rather, the oldest public social constructions were created of household constituents. In religious terms, we should expect similar organic connections, especially where our evidence is not dominated by the most extreme institutional developments away from these roots. Emar was no major political power or urban center, and the old continuities between households and larger community life remained highly visible.

In the sphere of family religion, I am particularly stumped by the role of the dead. Why are the ancestors so important? Ancestors did not in fact form single strands, straight-line genealogical threads traced back from son to father to grandfather like the name-lists in the book of Genesis. If the care for ancestors was passed down only from firstborn to firstborn, what happened in the households inevitably formed around non-firstborn men? Must we imagine numerous households without family gods or ancestor shrines? All the subordinate households were supposedly placed under a father or a brother, but what of their children? As the population expanded, and the initial circle of paterfamilias roles did not, how could the supply of family, ancestral, and household gods expand to serve all?

This line of thought raises for me another powerful dimension of the ancestors. Ancestors, real or imagined, bind people both into single households and into larger groups made up of multiple households. Tribal identity is founded especially on imagined kinship, and common ancestors are the actual basis for these bonds. Somehow, veneration of ancestors should also contribute to the foundation for whole communities, not just for individual households. Patricia McAnany presents a complex portrait of this phenomenon of attention to ancestors as an expression of current kinship ties in her study of the early Maya. Households must be "contextualized within the larger realm of macrofamily political and economic groupings," which she calls "lineages." She finds that two forces finally shape ancient Maya politics: the centripetal force of divine kingship, which lays claim to central authority, and the centrifugal force of kinship, which produces a panoply of unequal local political actors. "Ancestor veneration" stands at the center of the kinship political force.[59] There is some evidence for such communal rites both from Mesopotamian texts and from other archaeological finds. It is not clear to me how the bridging function of ancestry actually worked at the household level. Somehow, family religion should carry within it not just a straight-line concern for a single strand through time but also an ability to weave the net of shared relationship by which the public sphere took form.

In my extended study of Emar's *zukru* festival, I concluded that the elaborate calendar of the seventh-year rite was ultimately constructed from an event that could occupy a single day. Dagan is brought outside of the town and its fortifications to a shrine of upright stones. The central procession marches him between these stones and back into town, both celebrating his entry into it and acknowledging his connection to the larger land in which it is built. The town "gives the *zukru*" to Dagan, evidently by an act of speech. The verbal root means "to speak, invoke, recall."

At a meeting where I first proposed this idea, Stephen Kaufman wondered in a question whether I would be better off thinking in terms of address to the dead. The ritual text offers no direct clues to support such an interpretation, and I considered the clear town-wide context to count against it. Now I am less certain. Dagan is often associated with rites for the dead, and it now strikes me that an interest in ancestors could be perfectly appropriate for a rite that assembles the whole population of a town to reaffirm its identification as one people, bound under commitment to Dagan. The evidence does not allow a definite answer but the interpretive framework for Emar religion that I endorse here requires that I view the challenge differently. Where the religion of community and household are profoundly integrated, the relationships that define family and town will be intertwined, in part by a shared cast of ancestors. In every expression of household or public religion at Emar and in all ancient Syria, I will be looking for how the one domain assumes the activity of the other.

Notes

1 The ideas in this paper have benefited from conversations with my colleague Anne Porter.
2 See especially his *Family Religion in Babylonia, Syria, and Israel: Continuity and Change in the Forms of Religious Life* (Leiden: Brill, 1996).
3 In Hittite myth, fathers are the ones who name children. See Harry Hoffner, "Name, Namengebung. C. Bei den Hethitern," *Reallexikon der Assyriologie*, ed. Erich Ebeling und Bruno Meissner (Berlin: De Gruyter, 1998), 9: 120. Many biblical stories describe the giving of names, and both women (e.g., Rachel and Leah in Genesis 29–30) and men (e.g., the prophet in Hosea 1) are said to have done so.
4 *From Blessing to Violence: History and Ideology in the Circumcision Ritual of the Merina of Madagascar* (Cambridge: Cambridge University Press, 1986), pp. 39–46.
5 Bloch, "The Ritual of the Royal Bath in Madagascar: The Dissolution of Death, Birth, and Fertility into Authority," in *Rituals of Royalty: Power and Ceremonial in Traditional Societies*, ed. David Cannadine and Simon Price (Cambridge: Cambridge University Press, 1987), p. 286.
6 Ibid., pp. 272–4.
7 I have undertaken an extended study of this phenomenon, with the archives of early second millennium Mari as a point of reference (*Democracy's Ancient Ancestors: Mari and Early Collective Governance* [Cambridge: Cambridge University Press, 2004]). This documentation suggests that Emar (then "Imar") did not even have a king in the Mari period (pp. 212–14).
8 I prefer the analysis of Thomas L. McClellan, "Houses and Households in North Syria during the Late Bronze Age," in *Les maisons dans la Syrie antique du IIIe millénaire aux débuts de l'Islam*, ed. Corinne Castel, Michel al-Maqdissi, and François Villeneuve. (Beirut: Institut Français d'Archéologie du Proche-Orient, 1997), p. 30. For a general discussion of the tablet finds from this building, see my *Time at Emar: The Cultic Calendar and the Rituals from the Diviner's Archive* (Winona Lake: Eisenbrauns, 2000), ch. 2.
9 Texts mentioned in this article come from both the excavations and from unauthorized looting and sales published from private collections. I use the following abbreviations: Emar VI.3: Daniel Arnaud, *Recherches au pays d'Aštata, Tome 3. Textes sumériens et accadiens* (Paris: Éditions Recherche sur les Civilisations, 1986); AuOrS 1: idem., *Textes syriens de l'âge du Bronze Récent* (Barcelona: Editorial AUSA, 1991); RE: Gary M. Beckman, *Texts from the Vicinity of Emar in the Collection of Jonathan Rosen* (Padua: Sargon srl, 1996).
10 See first of all his "Gods and Ancestors at Emar and Nuzi," *Zeitschrift für Assyriologie* 84 (1994): 38–59; and "The Domestic Cult at Emar," *Journal of Cuneiform Studies* 47 (1995): 35–49.
11 Van der Toorn, "Gods and Ancestors," pp. 45–8; "The Domestic Cult," pp. 38–9.
12 LKA 81.3, an incantation.
13 MDP 6 pl. 10 vi 22, *kimtu*. These examples are drawn from the *Chicago Assyrian Dictionary* s.v. *eṭemmu* 1, spirit of the dead.

14 *Chicago Assyrian Dictionary* s.v. *eṣemtu* 1b, "referring to the remains of the dead."

15 The phonological changes necessary to relate Hebrew *ʿeṣem* to Akkadian *eṭemmu* are feasible but not straightforward. Based on Ugaritic, the Hebrew word for "bone" comes from the older consonantal root *ʿẓm*, and Ugaritic attests the possibility of graphic confusion or alteration of *-ṭ-* and *-ẓ-*; Josef Tropper, *Ugaritische Grammatik* (Münster: Ugarit Verlag, 2000), p. 113. The biblical Hebrew segholate *ʿeṣem* would derive from earlier *ʿaṣmu*, which has a different noun formation than *eṭemmu*, with its doubled *-mm-* and internal vowel. The feminine *eṣemtu* is constructed from the absolute form **eṣem-*, from the **eṣmu* base, with a>e under the influence of the lost initial ʻayin.

16 JoAnn Scurlock defines both the *zaqiqu* ("dream soul") and the *eṭemmu* (a body spirit) as "semi-divine, wind-like or shadow-like entities which exist in living beings, survive death, and subsequently receive offerings from the deceased's ancestors at his tomb" ("Soul Emplacements in Ancient Mesopotamian Funerary Rituals," in *Magic and Divination in the Ancient World*, ed. Leda Ciraolo and Jonathan Seidel [Leiden: Brill, 2002], p. 1).

17 The relevant lines (KTU 1.17 i 26–7, etc.) read: (26) *nṣb.skn.ʾilʾibh.bqdš* (27) *ztr.ʿmh.* I follow here certain preferences of Dennis Pardee, in *The Context of Scripture*, ed. William W. Hallo and K. Lawson Younger (Leiden: Brill, 1997), 1: 344. The "father's god" is not taken as a deified ancestor, but the possibility is not excluded. "His kinsmen" are plural, like Hebrew *ʿam* ("people"), although the singular "kinsman" is also feasible. Finally, the "votive emblem" (*ztr*) is based on comparison with Hittite *sittar-* (Matityahu Tsevat, "Traces of Hittite at the Beginning of the Ugaritic Epic of AQHT," *Ugarit Forschungen* 3 [1971]: 351–2). For another translation in the same spirit, with the transliterated text, see Simon Parker (ed.), *Ugaritic Narrative Poetry* (Atlanta: Scholars Press, 1997), pp. 52–3.

18 Because the care for ancestors is addressed in inheritance texts, it is natural to assume that the responsibilities described in the Aqhat tale pertain to the time after the father's death. The last actions of the devoted son, however, apply explicitly to the father's lifetime: fending off assault, supporting him when tipsy, feasting with him (or on his behalf) in the public temples of Baal and El, and keeping his home presentable (see KTU 1.17 i 28–33). This list begins with the *ʾilʾib* and the *ʿm* and then goes on, "to make his smoke go out from the earth; from the dust, the guardian of his place" ([27] *lʾarṣ.mšṣʾu.qṭrh* [28] *lʿpr.dmr.ʾatrh*). I have translated as literally as possible, but choices are inevitable. Pardee (*Context of Scripture*, 1: 344) treats the smoke and "the song of his place" as offerings, an interpretation that requires the verb "to go out" to be rendered as "to send up" and the "earth" to be the land of the living. Earth and dust suggest the realm of the dead, however, and the question is why offering smoke (incense) should leave the earth. I have followed the syntax proposed by Tropper (*Ugaritische Grammatik*, p. 479), even as the real meaning remains obscure. This does sound like some sort of cult of the dead, rather than protection for the living, but I do not understand what is involved. The verb *yṣʾ* may mean "to escape," as in "get out," an action that assumes a starting point in the place to be escaped.

19 Emar VI.3 268; AuOrS 1 96.

20 On the *abu* shrines of Emar VI.3 452: 31–52, see my *Time at Emar*, pp. 184–9. These will be discussed further below.

21 See, for example, his "Architecture et urbanisme," in *Meskéné-Emar: Dix ans de travaux, 1972–1982*, ed. Dominique Beyer (Paris: Éditions Recherche sur les Civilisations, 1982), pp. 35–6.

22 Emar VI.3 452: 34–5; see the discussion of this event in my *Time at Emar*, pp. 184–9.

23 See, e.g., RE 8: 37–39; 28: 32–4; AuOrS 1 46: 9–10; Emar VI.3 184: 11′–12′; 201: 50–1; 203: 3′–4′.

24 I present a new edition of the *zukru* festival text (Emar VI.3 373) in my *Time at Emar*, along with a detailed study of the whole *zukru* tradition (Chapter 3).

25 On the reading of [d]IŠKUR at Emar, see Daniel Schwemer, *Die Wettergottgestalten Mesopotamiens und Nordsyriens im Zeitalter der Keilschriftkulturen* (Wiesbaden: Harrassowitz, 2001), p. 552, etc., for the most thorough and careful analysis.

26 The original excavations led by Margueron produced the texts that identified the southern of the two temples with the storm god during the Late Bronze Age (fourteenth–twelfth centuries). New joint Syrian–German excavations have now identified an earlier and smaller version of this southern temple, without the northern complement, that dates to an older phase of the Late Bronze Age (Uwe Finkbeiner, Hala Attoura, Betina Faist, Uta König, Ferhan Sakal and Frank Starke, "Emar 1999 – Bericht über die 3. Kampagne der syrisch-deutschen Ausgrabungen," *Baghdader Mitteilungen* 32 [2001]: 46). It appears, then, that a solitary storm god temple first gave the site its public prominence, before it was enlarged and joined by the northern temple, perhaps for Ashtartu. During the Early Bronze Age (third millennium), the site was occupied by structures not yet identified by the excavators, but not obviously sacred (Finkbeiner and Ferhan Sakal, "Emar 2002 – Bericht über die 5. Kampagne der syrisch-deutschen Ausgrabungen," *Baghdader Mitteilungen* 34 [2003]: 65–70). So far as the early Late Bronze storm god temple directly overlies Early Bronze use, this western promontory seems not to have seen active use for the several centuries of the Middle Bronze, the time of the Mari textual evidence.

27 According to early second millennium copies of royal inscriptions from Sargon and Naram-Sin, rulers of Agade in the late third millennium, these kings only won victories in the west, up the Euphrates and beyond, because Dagan made them possible. See the discussion and references in Lluís Feliu, *The God Dagan in Bronze Age Syria*, trans. Wilfred G. E. Watson (Leiden: Brill, 2003), pp. 43–4. Dagan's relationship to these Akkadian kings, however, is read through the lens of eastern politics, perhaps even revised to follow the later assumptions of the copyists. For the ground-breaking notion that ancient religious metaphors followed the development of society, including the rise of kingship, see Thorkild Jacobsen, *The Treasures of Darkness: A History of Mesopotamian Religion* (New Haven: Yale University Press, 1976).

28 The evidence for divine lords of Tuttul and Terqa go back to Ebla and Mari of the mid-third millennium, before Agade (Feliu, *The God Dagan*, p. 41). The name Dagan is not written out in either case, but the titles in these old texts match those from the better documented early second millennium.

29 Feliu approaches the question of how to characterize Dagan's role in the Middle Euphrates with appropriate caution. After treatment of the Old Babylonian period (early second millennium), however, he does attribute to him the rank of "principal god" and then "leader within the pantheon of the Middle Euphrates region" and "sovereign" (p. 212). This language may best reflect the perspective of the Mari royal circle, however, and cannot be attributed with confidence to the old traditions of Tuttul and Terqa.

30 Zimri-Lim of Mari gave Dagan's validation first priority in his royal seals (Feliu, *The God Dagan*, pp. 162–3).

31 Dagan receives offerings during the *zukru* festival as "Lord of the Offspring" (*bel bukari*). A separate section of the text elaborates special procedures for sacred processions during the various days of celebration. On the most important day, the full moon of the first month in the seventh year, the god takes part under the name "Dagan the very father" (^{d}KUR *a-bu-ma* [Emar VI.3 373: 190]). For discussion of these titles, see my *Time at Emar*, pp. 88–91.

32 See Emar VI.3 452: 31–52 for the end of the fifth month, there called Abu. The connected rite for the new moon in the following month is presented in Emar VI.3 446: 96–102 (called Ḫalma) and 463: 1–12. For discussion, see *Time at Emar*, pp. 184–95.

33 For further treatment of the problem and its possibilities, beyond my own, see Mark E. Cohen, *The Cultic Calendars of the Ancient Near East* (Bethesda: CDL, 1993), pp. 259–61; Harry A. Hoffner, "Second Millennium Antecedents to the Hebrew *'ob*," *Journal of Biblical Literature* 86 (1976): 385.

34 After careful consideration of Emar VI.3 452, Wayne Pitard concludes that the text is ambiguous, and that the "fathers" may be high officials who are living leaders ("Care of the Dead at Emar," in *Emar: The History, Religion, and Culture of a Syrian Town in the Late Bronze Age*, ed. Mark W. Chavalas (Bethesda: CDL, 1996), p. 136.

35 In this respect I agree with Feliu (*The God Dagan*, pp. 305–6). During the early second millennium, Dagan is associated with both the *kispum* and the *pagra'um* rites in evidence from Mari (ibid., pp. 65–73).

36 Ibid., p. 306.

37 "The Onomastic Evidence for Bronze-Age West Semitic," *Journal of the American Oriental Society* 124 (2004): 446.

38 *Die Personennamen der Texte aus Emar* (Bethesda: CDL, 2003).

39 See my review in the *Journal of the American Oriental Society* 124 (2004): 595–9.

40 For EN (or ^{d}EN) as Ba'lu and Belu, see Pruzsinszky, *Die Personennamen*, pp. 49, 53; for BE with the same meaning, see pp. 142–3. This latter writing goes back in Syria to Ebla in the mid-third millennium.

41 Here I count only the following: Ba'la-kimi (the goddess "Lady"?), Ba'l-beli, Ba'l-malik, Ba'lu-kabar (cf. Belu/EN-kabar, uncertain association), Belu-qarrad (also uncertain), GN (^{d}IŠKUR/^{d}U)-gamil, Ḫinna-Ba'l (^{d}EN/^{d}IŠKUR), Ir'ib-GN (^{d}IŠKUR/^{d}U), and Zu-Ba'la. Only seven of these have a fairly secure attachment to the storm god. I cite these names in the forms given by Pruzsinszky, even where these are sometimes problematic.

42 Here above all, the numbers are imprecise. The most frequent Dagan name in my count is Tura-Dagan, with c. 66 bearers. Zu-Ba'la is usually written syllabically and could be understood to pertain to Dagan, but various hints suggest the storm god. The name is noticeably more common in the two temples associated with the storm god on the western promontory, along with Zu-Aštarti. Only the storm god and Ashtartu have priestesses that are installed as residents in the given temple, with long ritual texts to reflect this.

43 Emar VI.3 52, with 73 entries, five partly broken for the given name, and fourteen missing the patronym. All are men, none identified by title in place of patronym. Among these, 23 men have Dagan names, nine have storm god names, and four are ambiguous "lord" names written with EN/*belu*. The patronyms include five with Dagan and two with the storm god. Two more lists from the diviner's archive in building M1 display the same pattern: no. 279 (barley rations), includes 14 for Dagan, three for the storm god,

and four with ambiguous EN; in patronyms, four for Dagan, one for the storm god, one with EN; no. 336 (names only), includes 32 for Dagan, seven for the storm god, and 4 with EN; in patronyms, four for Dagan, none for the storm god, and one with EN.

44 The relative absence of theophoric personal names as patronyms calls for systematic investigation. In Emar VI.3 336, five of the names that appear as father of father are found elsewhere as simple patronyms: Kutbe (lines 35 and 46), Alal-abi (68 and 80), Ḫalaqi (71 and 29), Qabbari (91 and 15), and Ṭuba (92 and 31). Among these, Kutbe, Ḫalaqi, Qabbari, and Ṭuba occur at Emar only as patronyms (see Pruzsinszky's lists; *Ku-ut-bá* son of Šeḫrapi may then indicate a separate name, the only one with that spelling). Alal-abi, the only theophoric name, has wider use. Note also the father's father Daqqa (no. 52: 33) and Tuqnani (336: 69), both of which occur only as patronyms. Names with this pattern suggest the possibility of a larger clan. In Emar VI.3 336, a number of patronymic names could be read as abbreviations of theophoric names, especially with the god Dagan. Consider Ḫimaši (lines 18, 67, 70, cf. Ḫimaši-Dagan), Pazura (47, cf. Pazuri-Dagan), Išbiya (90, cf. Išbi-Dagan), Milka (95, cf. Milki-Dagan), Zikriya (96, cf. Zikri-Dagan). These short forms show a higher than usual proportion of use as patronyms: Ḫimaši (6 vs. 2 not), Pazura (5 vs. 0), Išbiya (5 vs. 1), Milka (1 vs. 1), and Zikriya (5 vs. 1).

45 Texts 42 (royal dedication to storm god as thanksgiving), 43 (Ashtartu's treasure in precious metals), 45 ("the weapons of the storm god," assigned to named men), 52 (named men who receive bows from the temple of the storm god). None of the tablets from the second building indicates any divine affiliation.

46 This text is one of the few from Emar that describes a political event involving the town as a whole, and it has received considerable attention. For a careful re-edition with notes, see Schwemer, *Wettergottgestalten*, p. 554. The most detailed treatment of Emar VI.3 42, along with other references to a war with the Hurrians, is found in Murray R. Adamthwaite, *Late Hittite Emar: The Chronology, Synchronisms, and Socio-Political Aspects of a Late Bronze Age Fortress Town* (Leuven: Peeters, 2001), pp. 261–70. Pruzsinszky also discusses the event in question (pp. 26–9).

47 Emar VI.3 52: 5, 17, 19, 20, 55, and 70 for Zu-Ba'la; ^{d}IŠKUR-*ma-lik* in line 39 and EN-*ma-lik* in line 38. It is not certain that the writings must distinguish separate names, though this is possible (Adda-malik and Ba'la-malik?). The question is then whether EN-*ma-lik* assumes identification with the storm god rather than Dagan. ^{d}IŠKUR-*ma* appears in line 52.

48 Emar VI.3 370: 45–54, 60–8. See *Time at Emar*, pp. 36–7. Goddesses are not included in the preserved list. "The gods" may indicate the diviner's building M1.

49 These occur in the reigns of Ba'la-kabar I (AuOrS 1 86: 38, Dagan and Shamash), Zu-Aštarti (Emar VI.3 17: 34–6, Dagan, ^{d}NIN.URTA and three others), Pilsu-Dagan (Emar VI.3 125: 37–8, Dagan, ^{d}NIN.URTA, and Išḫara; AuOrS 1 9: 45, Dagan and ^{d}NIN.URTA), and Elli (RE 15: 32, Dagan and ^{d}NIN.URTA). For Emar 17, see the revised readings of Jean-Marie Durand and Lionel Marti, "Chroniques du Moyen-Euphrate. 2. Relecture de documents d'Ekalte, Émar, et Tuttul," *Revue d'Assyriologie* 97 (2003): 142–3.

50 Schwemer (*Die Wettergottgestalten*, p. 561) suggests a plausible reading from a known epithet of the Hurrian storm god Teššub (Tesshub) of Kaḫat, as *bel kurrinni* (here, as *kùr-r*[*i-ni*]). It is not clear what the Hurrian term describes; Schwemer expects some sort of symbol of deity or sanctuary (461).

51 He is first in the long final section of Emar VI.3 279 (line 21), with only 4 *parisu* (per year), well below the amounts of the recipients in the five more exclusive sections ahead of him (up to 30).

52 The storm god's temple was enlarged significantly during the Late Bronze Age. The basic layout of the core structure does not change, but it is possible that one goal was to accommodate a residence that was not already included. No extra rooms are appended to the *in antis* axial form of the main temple, so the lodging would have to be above the main cella, if in the same building, as the installation rite suggests. For the priestess's room, see Emar VI.3 369: 66–75 and my book *The Installation of Baal's High Priestess at Emar: A Window on Ancient Syrian Religion* (Atlanta: Scholars Press, 1992), pp. 186–92. New excavations have elaborated the changing form of the western temples: Uwe Finkbeiner, Hala Attoura, Wendy Eixler, and Ferhan Sakal (eds), "Emar 2001 – Bericht über die 4. Kampagne der syrisch-deutschen Ausgraben," *Baghdader Mitteilungen* 33 (2002): 109–46 and charts, esp. 110–15, Plan 2. Two new rooms have now been discovered for the Late Bronze temple, at the front entrance, showing a new complexity compared to its later form (Finkbeiner and Sakal, "Emar 2002,"), pp. 10–100, esp. pp. 12–13.

53 *Time at Emar*, chapter 2, esp. pp. 35–42.

54 All of the curses come from the thirteenth century, under the royal house of Yaṣi-Dagan, but the tradition that the king leads a list of witnesses goes back to the site's earliest texts which probably reach across much of the fourteenth century. In this earlier period, the leadership of the king is more strongly balanced by the authority of the collective town. See my "Schloen's Patrimonial Pyramid: Explaining Bronze Age Society," *Bulletin of the American Schools of Oriental Research* 328 (2002): 73–80.

55 See especially McClellan, "Houses and Households," p. 30, and my discussion in *Time at Emar*, pp. 4–6.

56 Text no. 7, in Arnaud, "Tablettes de genres divers du Moyen-Euphrate," *Studi micenei ed egeo-anatolici* 30 (1992): 195–245.

57 On the passage from her father's house to the storm god's temple, see my *Installation*, pp. 173–92.

58 AuOrS 1 87.

59 Patricia A. McAnany, *Living with the Ancestors: Kinship and Kingship in Ancient Maya Society* (Austin: University of Texas Press, 1995), esp. pp. 159, 163–4.

5

Family, Household, and Local Religion at Late Bronze Age Ugarit

THEODORE J. LEWIS

> *"Grandma, all the same, burned a candle on the anniversary of Mr. Lausch's death, threw a lump of dough on the coals hen she was baking, as a kind of offering, had incantations over bay teeth and stunts against the evil eye. It was kitchen religion and had nothing to do with the giant God of the Creation who had turned back the waters and exploded Gomorrah, but it was on the side of religion at that."*
>
> Saul Bellow, *The Adventures of Augie March*

Introduction

Over the last century, many historians in the wake of the French *Annales* school turned away from what they saw to be a narrow study of political, military, and diplomatic history (i.e., "traditional event-based narratives") to articulating long-term perspectives (what the French termed *la longue durée*) tied more to geography and climate, economic cycles, large-scale social and cultural factors, even the history of perception ("mentalities"). Archaeologists went from focusing on the material culture of great people and grand events to "the archaeology of society" with its fascination for the mundane and ordinary.[1] Textual scholars "read between the lines" of texts written (and edited) by those who wielded power in order to glimpse the lives of the semi-literate who held less or none at all.[2] In particular, the lives of ancient women started to emerge as scholars willed themselves to look for them.[3] Thus it is that we find ourselves, historians of religion of the present generation, focusing on non-elite (e.g., non-royal, non-priestly) communities that were slighted in the past in favor of the religion of the privileged. Studying the religion of families and households is long overdue.

Four Challenges

Though a desideratum, searching for the lives of the non-elite is fraught with obstacles (one could even say inherently flawed). It is best to acknowledge four challenges we face at the outset lest we read more into the past than prudence allows.

First, it is impossible to tackle all the beliefs and practices that could be listed under the heading "family/household religion." As seen from the present volume, definitions vary as does the scope of treatment. What is "religion" and how ought one to study it?[4] Is family religion centered on cults of ancestors or the religion devoted to a family's patron deity?[5] Or, is family religion that which was practiced by a biologically related group of people (or kinship groups formed by some other means such as marriage or adoption)? Or, should we attend to the place of such activity? Family religion could then be any religious activity occurring in a domestic locale. Having introduced the question of "sacred space," shouldn't one further consider the activities of family groups at local (non-elite) sanctuaries, which in turn presents the notion of community religion?

It would seem that all of the above are necessary to the definition if we take our cue from the terminology of our primary sources. Consider the semantic ranges of the various words for family at Late Bronze Age Ugarit. The story of King Kirta starts out by telling us how his *betu* "family" (lit. "house") had perished.[6] Included in his "house" (*bt*) are his children (*ḥtk, mknt*), his siblings (*'aḫm, bn 'um*), his wife (*'aṯt*), and future descendants (*š́pḥ, yrṯ*),[7] as well as physical space used metonymically to stand for the family (*bt, ṯbt*).[8]

> The house (*bt*) of the king has perished
> that had seven brothers (*'aḫm*),
> eight sons of a mother (*bn 'um*).
> Kirta, his offspring (*ḥtkn*) was crushed
> Kirta, his family line (*mknt*) was sundered . . .
> He married a wife (*'aṯt*), but she departed . . .
> Kirta saw his offspring (*ḥtkh*),
> He saw his offspring (*ḥtkh*) crushed,
> His dwelling (*ṯbth*) utterly sundered.
> Completely did his descendants (*š́pḥ*) perish,
> In their entirety his heirs (*yrṯ*). (KTU 1.14.1.7–15, 21–25)

In addition, ancestors remained a part of one's *betu* ("family") in death much as they did in life. The ancestral dead, many of whom were even buried beneath the family house (see below), could be referred to as "the god of the father" (on which, see below). In KTU 1.161 long-dead ancestors are invoked to participate in a mortuary ritual for a king who has just died. At the end of this text, sacrifices are offered to these ancestral kings of old who are then petitioned to bring blessings (*š́lm*) on the new royal family, i.e., the king, his household,[9] his queen (or kinsmen)[10] and her "house" (*bth*).

When used as a spatial term, *betu* can denote an individual's home, a community drinking house (see *bt mrzḥ* below), the king's home, and the god's home. The modern translations of "palace" and "temple" for the latter two are sensible, yet they strip away the commonality shared horizontally (across social stratification) and vertically (the divine–human encounter). Kings and gods have families (*betu*) as do commoners; so too all three groups have physical houses (*betu*) in which they eat, drink, interact, and sleep with their families. While their physical *betu* are common in many respects (e.g., architecturally and symbolically), they are equally uncommon. The scale, ornamentation, and symbolical nature of royal or divine homes (i.e., palaces and temples), when compared with the homes of commoners, would reinforce the subservient role of the non-elite.

The second barrier is the nature of our sources. Searching out the religion of the family from elite (e.g., royal, priestly, legal) texts necessarily skews the portrait. Negligible literacy rates underscore that the texts from which we are mining our data were not produced or read by the majority of the population. Even the texts we find in private residences are often those of high-ranking officials (e.g., the archives found in the so-called "House of Rašapabu" and "House of Rapanu," both located in the residential quarter of the city).[11] K. van der Toorn has articulated well the constraints by which we must go about our work: "It is only on the assumption that dynastic religion is the royal version of family religion that the insights obtained from the Ugaritic texts can be given a wider application . . . [we cannot] be sure that the concepts and practices from these realms are representative of the general population of Ugarit."[12]

According to G. del Olmo Lete, even the elite version that we read in texts such as the story about King Kirta might be "rhetorical hyperbole" where what is stated for one king's royal ideology (especially the exaltation of an eponymous ancestor) may not apply to all kings.[13] Yet like van der Toorn, del Olmo Lete concludes that we can nonetheless go about our work because the texts still "provide interesting, if fleeting, glimpses of the social institutions of Ugarit and its ideology."[14] What is required is caution in how we extrapolate from our elite texts. There is no need to be overly pessimistic. For example, when an average Ugaritian heard of how Ilu intervened on King Kirta's behalf in providing him with a longed-for son or healing him from dire illness, he could easily see how the gods are intimately involved in meeting the daily needs of mortals. For an analogy closer to home, one need only consider how a Jew or Christian today might appropriate the royal psalms from Iron Age Israel to address his or her personal needs.

Third, archaeology is a necessity. Simply put, one *cannot* fully articulate non-elite religion without relying on what material culture offers. By its very nature, archaeology can uncover so much of what escapes the purview of elite texts. I have written elsewhere on the advantages and limitations of text and object as well as the desideratum to interface the worlds of philologians and archaeologists in a complementary fashion.[15] When it comes to Ugarit, all textual specialists thank the Mission de Ras Shamra for its ongoing and tireless efforts to bring the Late Bronze kingdom of Ugarit to life. Marvelous resources such as those found in the RSO series are simply indispensable.[16] Yet at the same time, one must lament that many of our resources for unpacking family religion remain under the ground or unpublished. Thus a full study of family religion at Ugarit must await a future time when a collaborative study of the latest findings may be undertaken.

Fourth, we must acknowledge at the outset that even our best synthetic efforts present only a schematic picture. Due to the brevity of our material (both in space and time), we are prone to generalize the data we have into a whole that never existed. Granted, there are many aspects of family religion that resist periodization and would fit neatly into a Braudelian *longue durée* framework. Yet rarely do we sufficiently apply the discount factor to our data necessitated by variation within space and time. The family religion we depict at one locale at a given time may be different from the religion practiced some years prior or later, as well as being distinct from the religion of a different locale some miles away even if it is located in the general vicinity.

Overall, the Late Bronze Age city (kingdom) of Ugarit with its strategic location was quite successful economically with thriving commerce and industry. In the words of M. Yon, it enjoyed "spectacular prosperity."[17] Though small, it was a cosmopolitan city with an international presence. With its resident royalty, priesthood, merchants, and scribes, it enjoyed the benefits of arts and literature as well as the structure of administrative oversight. Even those on the lower rungs of society shared in benefits of urban life and international trade. It would be a mistake then to extrapolate from this narrow portrait a romanticized panorama about village life across rural Syria in the Late Bronze and Iron Ages.

The Religion Practiced by the Family Household

The religion I am focusing on in this chapter is that practiced by local family (non-elite) households. Kings, high-ranking officials, elite merchants, and priests certainly shared certain familial concerns with commoners. All alike petitioned the gods for personal health and prosperity, for safe births, fit children and sturdy livestock, for snakebite remedies and sexual potency, for good weather, adequate water, and abundant crops. The overlap between elite and non-elite religious concerns was likely quite large. Yet elite religion was occupied with obtaining, securing, and bequeathing power (e.g., the throne, the temple economy) via divine and human diplomacy more than the transitions of life (birth, marriage, death) that characterized the religion practiced in the common household.[18]

Viewing the Gods as Family

Language of the family (father, mother, husband, wife, son, daughter, brother, sister, in-law) permeates the Ugaritic pantheon at every turn. Ba'lu, for example, is the son of Dagan, the father to three daughters (Pidray, Tallay, and Arsay) and the brother of Anatu if not also her husband.[19] Ba'lu invites his brothers//his kinsmen//the seventy sons of the mother goddess Athiratu to a family feast in his house (built by permission of his father Ilu through the intervention of Athiratu, Ilu's wife; KTU 1.4.6.38–59).

According to M. Smith (building on D. Schloen's significant work on the patrimonial household),[20]

> the notion of the family [in the Ugaritic pantheon provides] a cohesive vision of religious reality . . . It is evident from the language of family relations that the model of the patriarchal household is central to the Ugaritic texts' presentation of divinity . . . Equally fundamental to the family unit is the language of parentage . . . The social metaphors for chief deities overwhelmingly reflected the patriarchal experience in households nonroyal and royal alike.[21]

Though family language is attested throughout the pantheon, a brief look at the two most prominent family deities (Ilu and Athiratu) will serve to illustrate the point. Ilu was portrayed in text and iconography with grey hair and beard, apt depictions for "the father of years" (*'ab šnm*). He was understood to be "father" to gods (see *'ab bn 'il* passim in KTU 1.40) and humans (*'ab 'adm*) alike. Family metaphors (*bn 'il, dr 'il, dr bn 'il*) are used to describe deities and humans as his children.[22] In a text celebrating his sexual prowess, women cry out to him "father, father," "mother, mother" (*'ad 'ad//'um 'um* KTU 1.23). In this same text, he impregnates (the same?) women/wives who cry out to him as "husband, husband" (*mt mt*). In turn, they bear him two children (the gods Shaḥru and Shalimu).

Known for his wisdom (KTU 1.4.4.41–3; 1.4.5.3–4) and benevolence (*lṭpn'il d p'id*), we find Ilu beseeched by gods and humans looking for his blessings, especially the granting of children. In response to a request from Ba'lu, Ilu blesses Danilu with a son in the tale of Aqhatu (see below). In the Kirta Epic, Ilu blesses King Kirta, himself the "son of Ilu," (*bnm 'il//špḥ* KTU 1.16.1.10) with a wife and children (KTU 1.14.1.26ff; 1.15.2.12ff). The same story also tells of Ilu's beneficence in healing an ailing Kirta (KTU 1.16.5.10ff).[23] Time and time again Ilimilku, the scribe of this text, underscores Ilu's divine parentage of the king.

The goddess Athiratu was referred to as the mother of the seventy minor gods referred to as her "sons" (*šb'm bn 'aṯrt*; KTU 1.4.6.46). She suckles newborn gods in KTU 1.23.24, 59, 61. She may also suckle King Kirta's heir (KTU 1.15.2.26–8), yet the reading of this text is now debatable.[24] Iconography such as the ivory panel of a winged goddess suckling two (royal?) individuals may lend support to her nurturing role though this relief is uninscribed and thus the goddess in question is unclear.[25]

Athiratu is commonly referred to as *rbt*, "the Great One," a designation used also of the wives of human kings in the Akkadian texts from Ugarit.[26] There are strong hints that Athiratu played a similar role along side of Ilu. Thus Ba'lu and Anatu in their quest to secure a house for Ba'lu (because all of Athiratu's other sons have houses) approach Athiratu first rather than going to Ilu directly. Athiratu then approaches her husband Ilu with her request that he then grants. Later in the same story, Athiratu is sought out by Ilu to choose one of her sons as heir to sit on the throne succeeding Ba'lu (who at this point in the story is in the underworld).

Because Athiratu is Queen *Mother*, she is approachable by royalty such as King Kirta who makes a vow to offer her gifts of silver and gold in exchange for her assistance (along with father Ilu's aid earlier in the story) in obtaining Hurraya as his wife (KTU 1.14.4.34–43). While we have no text that explicitly says so, it is possible that non-elite persons (having heard the famous story) may have dreamed that they too could be favored with Athiratu's assistance in obtaining a spouse. We can conjecture that similar vows were enacted within family religion. Compare the betrothal of the gods Yarikh and Nikkal-Ib in KTU 1.24, a text that was then used in human wedding ceremonies to assure mortals of a divinely blessed union.

Elsewhere in a very interesting section in the Ba'lu Myth, Athiratu, though *rbt*, is described as even more approachable as she goes about common domestic chores. Her activities are remarkable for their non-elite character. Every Ugaritic woman could fully relate to Athiratu's working with a spindle, washing laundry, and setting pots on top of fire and coals (KTU 1.4.2.2–11).[27] Thus, even though Athiratu's maternal nature is primarily focused on gods and royal children,[28] non-elite persons would have felt a special affinity for her much as Catholic parishioners hold Mary to be their mother even though her royal status is that of *Theotokos.*

Cultic Activities Related to Family/Life Cycles

One way to define family religion is by describing the religious/cultic activities in which common (non-elite) families engaged. Not having the rights, privileges, and access to temple culture that the elite had, we may assume that many of their activities took place within the domestic and local sphere. In addition, in contrast to the religious activities a monarch would use to secure his reign or those cultic actions a hierarchical priesthood (or scribal class) would employ for power and influence, family religion centers on life transitions, issues pertaining to birth, marriage, and death and the related concerns of filial piety, adoption, illness, and inheritance. (It goes without saying that such matters would be of concern to the elite as well.)

Various literary genres provide avenues into these spheres of activities. Consider, for example, what can be gleaned from onomastica, prayers, letters, and even elite tales such as the famous Aqhatu story.

Onomastica

Onomastic evidence (often a key indicator of non-elite religion) can mark an individual's identity by various means including place, occupation, and social group. The onomastic evidence at Ugarit reveals that a large percentage of personal names include a marker of family relationship, again underscoring the importance of the household. These include "son of," "daughter of," "brother of," "relative of," "household of," "husband of," "wife of," as well as references to inheritance that can refer to adoption.[29] D. Pardee and P. Bordreuil summarize:

> Generally speaking, the Ugaritians seem to have considered the patronym the most important element to be stated when identifying a person, for it is usually given and

> may indeed function as the only identifier (CTA 105), both masculine (*bn* PN "son of PN") and feminine (*bt* X "daughter of X"). Long lists, such as CTA 102, rarely omit the patronym.[30]

G. del Olmo Lete has also written insightfully of how

> in everyday life, the giving of a name is one of the few ways by which we can learn about how personal and family piety was expressed, inasmuch as it tells us which gods were actually vital in the religious feeling of the ordinary faithful and the kinds of relationship they had with them and what they hoped to gain from them.[31]

In his catalogue of divine descriptors, familial and other intimate terms are attributed to the god Ilu. They include references to "father," "lover," "friend," "benevolent." As seen above through the mythological texts, here too Ilu is one who "creates" and "grants," a "fertile" god whose worshipers are portrayed as his "children."[32]

Prayer

On the individual level, prayer would be at the heart of each and every ritual activity where one would beseech the gods for succor. Regrettably, individual prayers from the non-elite spheres of society are by their very nature absent from our textual evidence. In fact, there are precious few prayers overall in the texts that have been preserved for us from Ugarit. The most famous prayer (KTU 1.119.26′–36′) prays for Baʿlu's help when the city is under attack.[33] We read of vows, sacrifice, various offerings, and a procession to Baʿlu's temple that give ritual expression to pleas for divine assistance. Such actions could easily be envisioned as part of any family's worship at a time "when the strong enemy attacks your (pl.) gates and city walls." Yet the first part of the text depicts a regularly prescribed series of rites including cultic obligations on the part of the king. Thus we can only guess at what degree if any of such actions and words would have been known by the average family.[34]

A similarly opaque text is KTU 1.65, the genre of which has been categorized in various ways (e.g., prayer, eulogy, deity list).[35] What is noteworthy is how family language is used in addressing one's attention to the gods:

> Ilu, the sons of Ilu
> the family of the sons of Ilu
> assembly of the sons of Ilu
> Tukamuna and Shunama [= two of Ilu's sons]
> Ilu and Athiratu.

What follows next is either an appeal to Ilu for favor (*ḥnn*), help (*nṣbt*) and prosperity (*šlm*) or an assertion that Ilu has the qualities of grace, solidity and well-being.[36] M. Smith notes how the vocabulary to describe the structure of the divine family is precisely the vocabulary used in administrative texts that list the various members that made up human families (e.g., KTU 4.360).[37]

Letters

Everyday letters are more apt than other genres to provide a window into the religious life of the household. Regrettably, our corpus at Ugarit is small in number (approximately 100 letters in Ugaritic and 150 in Akkadian) and elite in nature (the Ugaritic letters contain mostly the correspondence of the royal family; the Akkadian letters reflect international diplomacy). Thus only rarely do they open a door into the private life of families such as when a certain official named Iriritharuma expresses concern about putting his wife and children in peril (KTU 2.33.28).

Granted, opening greetings in epistolary texts regularly use religious vocabulary (even on a personal level), yet they are so tightly formulaic that it would be a mistake to read too much personal piety into them.[38] G. del Olmo Lete is optimistic in using letters "to enter the sphere of personal and everyday attitudes." He argues that "in spite of their stereotyped nature, . . . these formulae permit a glimpse of the widespread trust that the personal piety of the Ugaritic faithful had in the power and will of their gods to intervene in their favor and guarantee the basics of existence: well-being, health, and a long life."[39] One can certainly hope that there was heart-felt belief behind the standardized words Azzi'iltu (the son of the famous Urtenu) used to write his parents: "May it be well with you. May the gods guard your well-being, may they keep you well." In the same text, he addresses his sister similarly: "May it be well with you. [May] the gods keep (you) well, may they guard you, may they [keep] you [wh]ole."[40]

Consider too how the gods of one's family can be included in such greeting formulas as the givers of blessings:

> Peace be upon you
> May the gods of the land of Tibat
> and the gods of the lands of Ugarit,
> and all the gods of our family (dingir-meš *bit ab[ini]*),
> keep you in good health,
> and give you favor
> and satiate you with old age
> before the gods of [our] family (dingir-meš *bit ab[ini]*), – forever.[41]

Perhaps del Olmo Lete is correct, that such formulae provide us with a "glimpse" of the general ethos of Ugaritic society. Yet in the final analysis, one is forced to admit that stereotyped formulae can be mechanical as easily as they can be sincere.

The Tale of Aqhatu

One narrative poem (the tale of Aqhatu) is particularly striking in the many issues of family religion that it addresses. Granted, the tale is an elite one and thus extrapolating from it for non-elite religion runs rewards and risks.[42]

As the story opens,[43] we hear of a legendary patriarch named Danilu, known for defending the claims and needs of widows and orphans (KTU 1.17.5.4–8), those members of the local community most likely to be in financial distress and lacking a voice among the elite. Day after day, Danilu, motivated by the most desperate of needs, presents food and drink offerings to the gods. Six days pass before we learn that his longing is for a son. The childless Danilu, robed in specific garments,[44] engages in prostration rituals at night, prompting some scholars to interpret the text as an incubation scene. The god Baʿlu compassionately intercedes on Danilu's behalf with the benevolent Ilu (*ʾil d pʾid*), the father of humanity. Ilu grants his request, blessing Danilu and his wife with conception, recognized as a divine gift in this text and elsewhere at Ugarit (KTU 1.15.2.16–28; KTU 1.24.5–7) just as much as Judeans recognized it in their traditions (e.g., Genesis 16:11; Isaiah 7:14).

Divine visitation follows. The Kathiratu (goddesses of conception and wedlock)[45] come to Danilu's house. There he holds a six-day feast in their honor. Note the simple fact that the feast is held in the home. No pilgrimage to a temple (with a specialized priesthood and cult) is necessary for family religion. The divine can be immanent in daily life and daily surroundings. Because the gods too have families who eat, drink, and sleep in houses (*betu*), it is proper for a petitioner to show them hospitality in his own house (*betu*). While the occasion (divinely inspired conception) is indeed special, the notion itself of having gods over for dinner is unremarkable; for family religion, it is understood. With their work of conception accomplished, the Kathiratu goddesses leave on the seventh day (perhaps to return as midwives at the birth of the child).[46]

Over a hundred lines are missing at this point in the narrative.[47] They most likely described the hoped-for piety of the son to be born (later named Aqhatu) and his early years. Yet we are not at a loss when it comes to filial piety for it was highlighted at the beginning of the story in the type of son requested by Baʿlu and granted by Ilu. In four refrains, we read of the duties of an ideal son.[48] The following text (KTU 1.17.1.25–34) contains the words of Baʿlu's intercession. These same words are then found in the mouths of Ilu as he grants the request (KTU 1.17.1.43–8), a messenger as he delivers the birth announcement to Danilu (KTU 1.17.2.1–8), and finally Danilu as he rejoices in the good fortune bestowed upon him by the gods (KTU 1.17.2.12–23).

(25) w ykn . bnh . b bt .	Let there be a son in his house,
šrš . b qrb (26) hklh .	A descendant in his palace;
nṣb . skn . ʾilʾibh .	One who sets up the stela of his divine ancestor,[49]
b qdš (27) ztr . ʿmh .	In the sanctuary, the marker of his clansman;

l 'arṣ . mšṣ'u . qṭrh	One who delivers his life from the Underworld,
(28) l ʿpr . d̲mr . 'at̲rh .	One who guards his footsteps from the Dust;
ṭbq . lḥt (29)n'iṣh .	One who squelches his detractors' slander,
g̮rš . d . ʿšy . lnh	One who drives away those who act against him;
(30) 'aḫd . ydh . bškrn .	One who holds his hand when he is drunk,
mʿmsh (31) [k]šbʿ yn .	One who supports him when he is full of wine;
sp'u . ksmh . bt . bʿl	One who eats his grain offering in the temple of Baʿlu,
(32) [w]mnth . bt .' il .	His portion in the temple of Ilu;
ṭḫ . g̮g̮h . b ym (33) [t̲'i]ṭ .	One who patches his roof on a rainy (lit. "muddy") day,
rḥṣ . npṣh . b ym . rt̲	One who washes his clothes on a mucky day.

That the six filial duties listed above combine mundane and cultic activities suggests that the Ugaritians might not have been as quick as we are to categorize activities as "religious" or "secular." The cultic duty of setting up a stela for one's Ilu-ibi, i.e., one's divine ancestor (or one's ancestor's god) underscores a central tenet of family religion. Elsewhere we read of sacrifices being offered to one's Ilu-ibi.[50] That the deity Ilu-ibi is the first god mentioned in the Ugaritic deity lists (the so-called "pantheon lists") is even more striking.[51] Scholars are divided as to whether Ilu-ibi refers to one's deified ancestor or the patron god of one's ancestor, yet the importance of this deity should not be lost in the debate.

The interpretation to which the present author holds is that the text refers to the devotion to one's deceased ancestor as a god.[52] K. van der Toorn has written eloquently on how "the dead were included in the community of the living." Commemoration rituals fostered "cohesion" by endowing "the living with a family identity that is anchored in the past."[53] In royal religion, we know from a mortuary text (KTU 1.161) that deceased kings were sought to grant blessings on the current monarchy.

Elsewhere we read of the Inashu-Ilima who "receive sacrifices as a collective entity."[54] In D. Pardee's words, they are "perhaps 'men (who have become) divine,' a designation of the dead, either limited to royalty or inclusive of the entire population."[55] We do not know to what degree commoners sought favors from their deceased relatives. The passage above gives no indication of the motive underlying setting up a stela or marker for one's divine ancestor. At the least, it is a ritual of commemoration that would have reinforced the familial bond between the living and the dead as would the frequent practice at Ugarit of locating the family tomb immediately beneath one's house. What is clear is that strengthening clan solidarity past and present was central to family religion.

When it comes to the sacred space mentioned in lines 26b–27a by the word *qdš*, it seems that it is the *local* sanctuary to which reference is made. It makes more sense to see the erection of a stela to one's deified ancestor (*skn 'il'ibh*) or marker of one's clansman (*ztr ʿmh*) in a local sanctuary rather than in one of the two acropolis temples. (On the presence of local sanctuaries, see below.)

An alternate interpretation of Ilu-ibi argues that solidarity with one's ancestors is being expressed (and physically enacted) by the succeeding generations' worship of the same deity. (Here, compare the biblical "god of my/your/their father" or "the god of Abraham/Isaac/Jacob.") The sense of communion and belonging that one has with his/her family (present and past) is reinforced as each generation reaffirms, practices, and hands down the same faith as one's parents, grandparents, and great-grandparents.[56] That the deity of one's ancestor is ranked first in the ritual pantheon would be a powerful testimony to the importance of a family's ongoing confession.

The other specifically cultic duty entails eating a sacrificial meal on behalf of one's father (lines 32b–33a). The two temples mentioned (one to Baʿlu, the other to Ilu) may correspond to the two temples on the acropolis at Tell Ras Shamra.[57] Here the good son carries on his father's ritual duties. Implied is that the son embraces his father's gods as his own and stands in his father's stead presumably because the father is unable to do so. The act of eating one's father's meal before (and with) the gods is yet another example of how family religion strengthens bonds both vertical (family to deity) and horizontal (family member to family member).

There may be other cultic acts in this narrative yet the text is too difficult to allow certainty. The word *qṭr* in line 27 could refer to incense, and the drinking described in lines 30–31a could easily be seen in the context of a ritual banquet.[58] Drinking assuredly had stronger religious connotations than we might first assume. In the ancient Near East it was understood, to borrow the words from Judges 9:13, that wine cheers the hearts of both gods and humans (*tirošî hamešammeaḥ ʾelohim waʾanašim*).

When we resume the Aqhatu narrative (after the aforementioned large break in the text), we find Danilu advocating at the city gate for widows and orphans, people whose family support structure has been shattered. Ugaritians realized what the biblical prophet Amos would later make famous, that the words justice and righteousness were parallel terms (cf. Amos 5:24 where *mišpaṭ//ṣedaqah*). Perhaps the original teller of the tale desired to underscore this feature when he chose Danilu's name and that of his wife Danataya, both of which are derived from the root meaning "to judge."

Next we hear of a second feast in Danilu's home, again one fit for the gods. This time the divine visitor is Kotharu-wa-Hasisu, the artisan deity sometimes referred to in the plural (see immediately below) due to his double name. Whereas Danilu served the first feast, his wife Danataya is the central character preparing a lamb for Kotharu-wa-Hasisu. She "dines and wines the gods, serves and honors them" (KTU 1.17.5.21–31). Again, note in family religion how the deity visits the home (rather than the petitioner traveling to a temple to have his visit mediated by specialists). The artisan deity bears a gift for the new son, a bow and arrows of exquisite craftsmanship.

The text again breaks off. Scholars assume from the few words preserved that Danilu is either presenting the bow and arrows to his son Aqhatu and/or training him how to hunt. That there is a broken mention of "game in his temple/palace" (*ṣd bhk[lh]*) reminds us of many cultures where hunting rituals are of a religious nature as are the prayers of thanksgiving to the gods for wild game on the dinner table.

The dominant theme in what follows is the murder of Aqhatu by the goddess Anatu, a huntress who is desirous of Aqhatu's gift.[59] It is hard to envision how such an action fits a story filled with family piety.[60] Yet S. B. Parker, following G. del Olmo Lete, notes how in the story of Aqhatu overall:

> social roles and duties seem to receive supreme attention, judged by the number of such that are referred to, the extent to which they are described, and the frequency with which they are reinforced by repetition. . . . All of this speaks specifically of *familial* piety – a piety built on the assumption of the solidarity and indispensability of the family, including its past and future members. For this piety, the greatest tragedy and the greatest challenge is the loss of a son (cf. Gen 22). Danel's pious family thus faces the worst life can bring. Yet the poem shows that piety steadily, persistently, and apparently successfully copes with that worst.[61]

Indeed, the rest of the story of Aqhatu that is preserved brings us back to the family. The story that started with the womb ends at the tomb. For this final stage of the lifecycle, we read of mourning rituals by Danilu attended now by his daughter Pugatu who acts out her own faithful duties toward her father. When the news of Aqhatu's death reaches Danilu, he searches for his son's remains to afford him proper burial. Amidst wailing and cursing, a father buries his son. When Danilu returns to his home, the community (notably women) joins him in his house and in public with a display of weeping and wailing. Men add expressions of grief through bloodletting rituals of skin laceration. The mourning lasts "for days, for months; for months, for years; even for seven years." At the end of seven years, Danilu sends the mourning women and men away and offers sacrifices with incense to the gods. We last read of a daughter (Pugatu) seeking her father's blessing (*brk*) as she seeks revenge for the killing of her brother.[62] The patriarch gives his blessings, using the same idiom the father-god Ilu used at the outset of the story to bless Danilu with a full life.[63]

There is much more going on in this famous tale. Yet for our purposes, it is instructive to see how an elite tale can preserve references to religion taking place at the family level and within family space. It would be dangerous to draw detailed inferences about ritual practice from a literary poem such as this that may have been a "purely aesthetic . . . satisfying portrayal of life in an idealised past era."[64] We could easily mis- and over-interpret some items (e.g., that it was common practice for professional mourners to stay in one's home for a full seven years!) while mis- and under-interpreting other items (no mention is made of burial underneath the home as attested archaeologically at Tell Ras Shamra). Yet scholarly sobriety is equally dangerous if our exactitude leads to us missing one of the story's central tenets: the importance of the religion that took place within the home. When juxtaposed with the royal story of King Kirta (where he too longed for progeny), one cannot fail to see how concerns about preserving the royal dynasty dominate the royal poem whereas they are absent in the life story of Danilu, his wife Danataya, and their children Aqhatu and Pugatu.

Religion at the Local/Community Level

While family religion focuses inward on the cultic life played out within the domestic sphere, it must be stressed that many lifecycle events may have involved participants beyond immediate family members. Celebration rituals over births and weddings as well as mourning rites at burials would entail the gathering of the local community in larger venues. Certain concerns (e.g., illness) may have necessitated turning to religious specialists with the appropriate skills. Some of their procedures may have been done in private, even in the home, while others would have been done in dedicated local spaces. In many respects then, family religion is intertwined with community religion.

Rough estimates put the size of Late Bronze Age Ugarit at between 6,000 and 8,000 people living in approximately 1,000 houses.[65] The densely populated city constituted approximately 25 percent of the population of the entire kingdom that included some 150 towns and villages in the area. Thus local practices of religion made up the lion's share of the kingdom's religious experience.

Much has been written on the social organization and social stratification of Ugarit and its environs and the various models by which they may be understood.[66] Our information about the non-elite is only minimally reflected in our texts. They included farmers, herders, sailors, soldiers, conscripts, low-skilled workers involved in service industries, unskilled laborers, servants as a result of debt, and slaves. As far as local religion within the city of Ugarit is concerned, there was a mixture of elite and non-elite living in close proximity. (This contrasts with the two areas where space was restricted to the elite: the palace area and the acropolis with its two major temples and House of the High Priest.[67]) M. Yon has documented "clear social overlapping" in the archaeology of the residential area. "The large houses of the rich, small, simple habitations, and urban craft activities coexisted in the same blocks."[68] As for village life, the positions of father and elders were pre-eminent. This fact needs to be underscored if one aims to appreciate the importance of family religion on the local/community level. Nevertheless, as within the city, the position of the king – his control and involvement – permeated village life.

Local Sanctuaries

The existence of local sanctuaries within the kingdom of Ugarit can be documented through text and archaeology. The best example of a local sanctuary positioned in the heart of the domestic sections of the city is the so-called Rhyton Sanctuary (see section below on archaeology).

Yet our texts are not altogether silent. KTU 1.17 (see full discussion above) refers to a sacred locale (*qdš*) where a dutiful son was to set up a stela for his divine ancestor (*ʾilʾib*), or a marker for his clansman. In KTU 1.109.11–13 and KTU 1.130.12[69] we read specifically of sacrifices to Ilu-ibi offered "at the temple of Baʿlu of Ugarit" (*bbt bʿl ʾugrt*). While it is possible that the *qdš* in KTU 1.17 also refers to one of the acropolis temples, it is also possible (more likely?) that it refers to a local sanctuary, many of which are preserved in the archaeological record (see below). The acropolis temples would have been proper places for the offering of blood sacrifices. Yet the erection of an ancestral stela would not have necessitated the presence of an altar and a system of blood disposal.

Two texts (KTU 1.79, 1.80) refer to local sanctuaries in villages outside of the city of Ugarit.[70] In particular, they mention three named *gittu*-farm complexes,[71] which were rural agricultural communities often under control of the king.[72] One specific *gittu* (Gittu-Ilištami[73]) is mentioned in both texts. Reference is also made to two "houses" (*bt*) within these *gittu* communities where the cult took place. The word *betu* here surely refers to domestic or local sanctuaries. One "house" is that of an individual (Ubbinniyana in 1.80.2) while the other house involves a local assembly of some sort (*bt qbṣ* in 1.79.8).[74] Both texts describe a religious officiant by the name of Ṣitqanu. In one text he sacrifices (*dbḥ*) seemingly a kid (*gdy*) to the god Rashpu (1.79.8) while in the other text he slaughters (*tbḫ*) a ewe and a ram, yet without mention of any deity as recipient.

Rashpu is named in the deity lists (in various manifestations and even in the plural *ršpm*) and is a regular recipient of offerings (e.g., ewes, rams, cows) in the ritual texts. He is usually thought to be a god of pestilence and a lord of the underworld due to his equation with Nergal in the deity lists and his mention as Shapshu's "gatekeeper," presumably opening the gates of the netherworld for the sun goddess to enter when she sets in the evening (KTU 1.78). The story about King Kirta's family dying from disease and sword (referenced at the beginning of this chapter) mentions how Rashpu and Yamm were also responsible (KTU 1.14.1.16–21; cf. 1.103.39–40). Thus perhaps Ṣitqanu's offering on behalf of these rural farms was for the health and/or productivity of livestock. In fact, KTU 1.80 describes the slaughtering of the ram to be done "throughout shearing-time" (*qb kl ygz ṭ!<b>ḫ*[75] *šḫ*).

Another text that may be relevant (KTU 4.15) was found on the acropolis in the house of the grand priest in 1929. Though brief, KTU 4.15 contains what seems to be a heading (*bt . ʾil*) followed by a list with nine references to *bt* that are then specified further by personal names.[76] In addition, the word *bʿl* precedes each entry.

1 *bt . ʾil*
2 *bʿl . bt . a<u>d</u>m*ny
3 *bʿl . bt . pdy*
4 *bʿl . bt . nqly*
5 *bʿl . bt . ʿlr*
6 *bʿl . bt . ssl*

7 *b‘l . bt . ṯrn*
8 *b‘l . bt . ktm*n
9 *[b‘]l . bt . ndbd*
10 *[–] . ṣnr*
11 *[b‘]l . bt . bsn*
12 *ẓr(?)[. . .]*
13 *b[. . .]*

Due to the multivalent meanings of the word *betu* (see above), there is no consensus on the interpretation of this term in KTU 4.15 with some scholars preferring to see a patronymic list while others see a list of sanctuaries. Clemens states that "there is a broad (but by no means universal) consensus that [*bt* . *'il*] in line 1 does in fact mean 'temple of Ilu.'"[77] Taking this as his cue, he concludes that "the most probable" interpretation "relates the text specifically to the cult and temple of Ilu."[78] The word *b‘l* then may refer to laborers of specific families who would have worked within the temple. This is certainly a viable option. Alternatively, in light of the reference to the *betu* Ubbinniyana in KTU1.80.2 (see too *bt qbṣ* in KTU 1.79.8 and *bt šbn* in KTU 4.16.1), perhaps we have references to named local sanctuaries at *gittu*-farm communities that were under the supervision of the crown and/or temple of Ilu.[79] Thus, just as KTU 1.79 and 1.80 were found in the royal palace (due to royal administrative control of some kind), so too the find spot of KTU 4.15 in the house of the grand priest may not be a coincidence.

Drinking as Religious Activity: Local Drinking Clubs

Another type of "household" or community-based religion is the institution known as the *marziḫu*. While attested over nearly two millennia throughout the Levant,[80] our discussion here will be limited to the *marziḫu* organization at Ugarit where it is mentioned in four Akkadian texts (RS 14.16; RS 15.70; RS 15.88; RS 18.01) and five alphabetic Ugaritic texts (KTU 1.21, 1.114, 3.9, 4.399, 4.642). (On the archaeology of the *marziḫu*, see below).

The *marziḫu* has been treated by many researchers including this author.[81] Recent studies include works by J. McLaughlin, B. Schmidt, M. Smith, D. Pardee, C. Maier and E. M. Dörruß, D. M. Clemens, M. Bietak and K. M. McGeough.[82] Thus the relevant data are readily available. My conclusions stated previously were as follows:

> What can be said about the *marziḫu* strictly from the Ugaritic evidence? It seems that the term *marziḫu* designated a socio-religious organization whose leader was called a *rb* and whose members were called *mt mrzḥ* = *LÚ.MEŠ mar-zi-i* (KTU 3.9). KTU 1.114 (*'il yṯb bmrzḥh*) suggests that the term *marziḫu* could also function as a designation for a place, evidently a shortened form of *bêtu marziḫi*. But in the majority of texts *marziḫu* seems to refer to an organization (guild?) of some kind. RS 15.70 and RS 15.88 indicate that a member's ownership in the society's holdings was passed on

> to his sons. The property of the *marziḫu* organization included vineyards, fields, storerooms, and most notably a "house." This *bêtu marziḫi* occurs in almost every text and seems to designate the meeting-place for the organization. It was presumably owned by the organization and paid for out of membership dues (but cf. also KTU 3.9 which attests that the *bêtu* could be leased).
>
> Drinking seems to have been a primary activity to judge from Ilu's behavior in KTU 1.114 and the organization's ownership of vineyards (RS 18.01; KTU 4.642). In other respects, the various *marziḫu* organizations seemed to have engaged in normal contractual agreements. They could grow quite powerful as evidenced by their participation in large transactions requiring many witnesses (RS14.16) and their property-owning status. J. C. Greenfield has noted that the *marziḫu* "had state sanction since the king transferred and confirmed ownership of *marziḫu* property." The *marziḫu* phenomenon seems to have been widespread and could occur in even relatively small cities (RS 18.01). A phrase from RS 18.01 referring to "the *marziḫu* of city X" (*be-ri LÚ.MEŠ mar-zi-i ša* ^uru^*A-ri ù be-ri LÚ.MEŠ mar-zi-i ša* ^uru^*Sí-ia-ni*) might even signify that there was only one *marziḫu* organization per city. (Of course, such a reference could be due simply to the small size of these cities.)
>
> The most notable religious feature is the association of the *marziḫu* organizations with a particular patron deity (see Šatrana in RS 15.70; Hurrian Ištar in RS 18.01; and most likely Anatu in KTU 4.642) . . . Finally, the *marziḫu* is associated with the *rp'm* in KTU 1.21.[83]

If we use definitions derived from our primary sources, then the *marziḫu* with its emphasis on activities under divine patronage performed within its *betu* does indeed constitute a type of "household" religion. One text (KTU 3.9) even mentions how a certain individual established a *marziḫu* "in *his* house."[84] Anthropological studies have underscored the religious nature of many drinking rituals. Even biblical culture notes how wine gladdens gods and men alike (Judges 9:13). Yet because the religious activity of the *marziḫu* organizations did not entail sacrifice, D. Pardee concludes that "the absence of this most characteristic feature of West Semitic cultic activity leads one to believe that the primary characteristic of the *marziḫu* was not cultic."[85] Perhaps this is splitting hairs over the definition of "cultic," but such a statement underscores the need for nuancing our descriptions of the religious activities of local communities. Activities need not be centralized within a temple complex (with the altar as the focal point of its sacred space and rites) to be religious in nature. Community and family religion often escape notice precisely because their activities were, for the most part, not sacrificial in nature (but see KTU 1.79 and 1.80 above) nor took place within royal/priestly sacred space.

Rather than concentrating on family units, the "house" referred to in the *marziḫu* texts was centered around elective social affinity groups within the local community (though "sons" are mentioned in RS 15.70 and RS 15.88).[86] J. C. Greenfield's observations about the elite nature of the organization (see above) have been echoed in recent research. K. M. McGeough, reaffirms the conclusions of J. McLaughlin: "the findspots of the tablets relating to *marziḫu*, the kinds and amounts of land owned by the group or its members, and the quantities of money involved in the *marziḫu* texts at Ugarit indicate that members of the group were elite inhabitants of the city."[87] Thus once again we are faced with the dilemma of teasing out non-elite religion from elite sources. (We should expect as much from the archaeological landscape – compare Yon's above-mentioned remarks about the "social overlapping" of elite and non-elite space even within the residential areas.) One text (RS 18.01) is particularly helpful in this regard. In this text we read of two *marziḫu* organizations located in southern border villages far away from the city of Ugarit itself. One *marziḫu* group was located in the village of Aru on the Ugarit side of the border, the other in an unnamed village on the Siyannu side of the border.[88] These two groups disputed the ownership of a vineyard located in Shuksu (Tell Sukas located within Siyannu) dedicated to Hurrian Ishtar.

Though royalty (Padiya, the king of the small state of Siyannu[89]) had a hand in resolving the dispute between these two *marziḫu* organizations, it is clear that we are dealing with border villages far smaller than the urban center of Ugarit. Thus one can conjecture that some of the *marziḫu* organizations were much smaller than others and may have included members who were not at all as wealthy or elite as those of their urban counterparts.

Religious Specialists Working at the Community Level

It is common to find treatments of the elite religious personnel at Ugarit, whether they are royal, priestly or scribal. The king's prominent role in the royal cult is well known (especially through the ritual texts).[90] That the queen is associated with sacrifice in some respect (*bdbḥ mlkt*; KTU 4.149.14–15; cf. KTU 1.170) and royal sons and daughters with processional rituals (*bn mlk wbn[t] mlk tʿln pʾamt šbʿ*; KTU 1.112.6–7) gives clear evidence for the religious involvement of the entire royal family. Elite cultic personnel are well attested in the persons of Attanu-purulini (diviner?),[91] the chief priest (*rb khnm*) who was also the chief of the cultic herdsmen (*rb nqdm*; KTU 1.6.6.55–6), Ḫuraṣanu, the chief priest (*ḫrṣn rb khnm*; KTU 6.10),[92] and Agaptharri, a diviner mentioned in liver models used for divination (KTU 1.141; RS 24.325).[93] As for the religious training of scribes, there is no better example than that of Ilimilku, who records his credentials as follows in a colophon at the end of the Baʿlu myth: "The scribe (*spr*): Ilimilku the Shubbanite, disciple (*lmd*) of Attanu-purulini, (who is) chief of the priests, chief of the cultic herdsmen; *ṯaʿiyu*-official of Niqmaddu, (who is) king of Ugarit" (KTU 1.6.6.53–7).[94]

Other religious personnel, due to their specialized skills, would also fall under the elite category although some were certainly of lower rank than others. Various offices include: *khnm* ("priests"; cf. "circle of priests," *dr khnm*), *qdšm* ("holy" personnel whose cultic role is debated), *ṯaʿiyu*-officials who would have performed the *ṯaʿu* sacrifice (yet see too the exorcism in KTU 1.169.3), *nqdm* (animal providers?), *mḫllm* ("purifiers"), *mlḫš* ("charmer"), *šʾib mqdš* ("water-drawer of the sanctuary"), *šrm* ("singers"), and *mṣlm* ("cymbalists"). It is difficult to describe the roles of the above functionaries with any degree of specificity due (surprisingly) to their near absence in the ritual texts that describe some of the very actions they performed.[95] (Compare the frequent attestations to such functionaries in the administrative and economic texts, yet without mention of cultic functions.) The reason, one may assume, is the attention given to the king, the omnipresent religious officiant in these texts.

Due to the nature of our source material, scholars have been unable to articulate when and how the non-elite may have come in contact with elite functionaries. We can guess that commoners may have viewed certain public rituals such as divine images led in procession by elite personnel including the king (cf. KTU 1.43, 1.112).[96] It is obvious from economic texts that unskilled workmen (*bʿlm*) operated within elite sacred space on a regular basis. It is also clear from KTU 1.79 and 1.80 (see above) that certain religious functionaries such as Ṣitqanu were intimately involved with the lives of villagers.

It is logical to assume that certain royal rituals were public in nature and thus observed by the general population. Compare especially the national sacrificial ritual attested in KTU 1.40 which, although mentioning King Niqmaddu, presumably his queen (*ʾaṯt*) and various foreigners, also mentions the citizenry of Ugarit, differentiating male (*bn ʾugrt*) and female participants (*bt ʾugrt*). According to D. Pardee, "the rite may have been to promote communion, both between the social groups named in the text and between humans and deities honored (ʾIlu and his family)."[97] The ideology presented in the story of King Kirta (KTU 1.16.6.45–50; cf. KTU 1.17.5.4–8) also underscores that the king's role (religious and otherwise) was precisely to champion the case of the non-elite (the widow, the poor, the oppressed, the orphan).

As noted above, there were also occasions in the life of families where religious specialists would have been consulted depending on one's resources and connections, thus again blurring the lines between elite and non-elite religion. Our extant texts (surely revealing just the tip of the iceberg) refer to all sorts of occasions requiring religious expertise that would have concerned all inhabitants of Ugarit regardless of class: weddings (KTU 1.24), marriage and divorce (RS 15.092; RS 16.141; RS 16.158; RS 16.143), adoption and inheritance (RS 21.230; RS 16.344; RS 15.092), mourning rituals (KTU 1.19.4.9–11, 20–2), divination (e.g., KTU 1.127; 1.140), dream interpretation (KTU 1.86), treating snakebites (KTU 1.100), hangovers (KTU 1.114), sexual dysfunction (KTU 1.169), and the power of the evil eye (KTU 1.96).

The Archaeology of Family Religion

Archaeology is the primary way that we can counter the nature of our textual evidence that, for the most part, evinces an elite perspective. For ancient Syria, one

Figure 5.1 Terracotta imprints of children's feet when they were sold into servitude to the chief diviner and scribe Ba'al-malik. From Temple M1 at Tell Meskene (Emar)

of the best examples of archaeology uncovering the lives of the non-elite comes from Tell Meskene (ancient Emar). Here where we have found in the Late Bronze Age Temple M1 the actual imprints (in terra cotta) of the feet of children who were sold by their parents into slavery to satisfy a debt (see Figure 5.1). As we view their individualized footprints (made all the more personal by their inscribed names), we become connected personally to the plight of this non-elite family who faced such economic desperation. Three of four children are named: Ba'la-bia, a two-year-old girl and her twin brothers, Ba'al-belu and Ishma'-Dagan, each one year old. The parents (Zadamma and his wife Ku'e) themselves pressed each foot in the clay. A sales contract reveals that the purchaser of these slave children was none other than an elite religious officiant, a chief diviner and scribe by the name of Ba'al-malik.[98] At least for the two boys the story has a happier ending. Y. Cohen has documented (through colophons found in Temple M1) how they were educated by Ba'al-malik who trained them to be scribes.[99] Thus we have rare documentation of specific non-elite persons gaining specialized skills within the religious sphere.

Sadly, the majority of the non-elite go unnoticed. We rarely read of their names or the specifics of their daily activities whether sacred or profane. Our data force us to talk about them in generalities. Thankfully, the Mission de Ras Shamra has dedicated significant time and energy to uncovering the domestic areas of Ugarit. These include: the Residential Quarter (*Quartier Résidentiel*), the City Center (*Centre de la ville*), the South City Trench (*Tranchée Ville Sud*), and the Lower City (*Ville Basse*). Though not fully published, the literature on these areas is substantial and readers are directed there for detailed discussions.[100] M. Yon, the director of the

Mission de Ras Shamra's excavations from 1978–98, has summarized the relevant material for our present study:

> Cult places are identified across the city's habitation areas (religious activities were omnipresent). These sanctuaries integrated into the insulae opened directly onto the public streets or belong to blocks otherwise occupied by residential buildings. Their sacral character is recognized in their architectural organization (the Rhyton Temple in the City Center) and/or, when the plan of an area is poorly preserved or difficult to interpret, in the furnishing discovered (ceremonial rhytons, cultic furniture, incense burners, statuettes and stelae), and objects tied to the practice of divination such as inscribed liver and lung models. Domestic cults, which are a manifestation of the popular religion, are attested by the number and dispersion across the inhabited areas of small idols (pendants in precious metal, terracotta figurines).[101]

Elsewhere, Yon adds:

> The existence of these places of worship found *throughout* the city is evidence of the presence of religious activities among *all* the inhabited areas, and not just the areas reserved for it. One cannot exclude either the existence of *domestic cults*, a manifestation of popular religion *side by side with frequentation of the great temples*, to judge by the number and dispersion in *all* areas of the site of small figurines, whether it be pendants in precious metal or the effigy of the goddess (Astarte?) or more humble figurines modeled in terracotta.[102] (emphasis mine)

As noted in the introduction above, a full analysis of family religion must await a future time when textual studies can be integrated with a synthesis of the archaeological material. Yet from Yon's remarks it is clear that we have just scratched the surface of unpacking domestic religion at Ugarit. For example, tombs located under family dwellings underscore the rich kinship Ugaritians shared with their ancestors whose remains needed to be kept close to the living.[103] Figurines could represent "prayers in clay"[104] of those who could not afford bronze statuary (see Figure 5.2). Anchors found in wells, springs, and tombs (as well as in the elite precincts of the Temple of Baʿlu) show how commoners (sailors and other seafarers) left behind physical signs of their attempts to secure protection as they sailed the seas.[105]

Particular attention needs to be given to the so-called "Rhyton Sanctuary" (referenced above by Yon[106]), one of the best examples in the ancient Near Eastern world of community religion. Excavations between 1978 and 1982 revealed a local sanctuary situated in the City Center. The religious activities practiced within this residential cult complex (that included an oil press) were thriving at the same time as those taking place within the two acropolis temples, the palace, and the royal sacred space known as the "Hurrian" temple. Yet, as M. Yon underscores, the rhyton "temple did not have the status of those of the acropolis: this can be observed both in the mediocre quality of the architecture and the common quality of the offerings and furnishings found associated with it. There are no royal

Figure 5.2 Terracotta figurine of a nude from the City Center (Ugarit). M. Yon, *The City of Ugarit*, p. 155, notes how "the presence of these figurines in houses reflects the domestic cult"

aspects." Yon further suggests that the sanctuary (with its 17 rhytons) was a meeting place for a *marziḫu* organization (cf. K. M. McGeough who thinks a better candidate would be the *Bâtiment au vase de Pierre* in the Residential Quarter).[107]

Conclusion

The four challenges presented at the outset of this paper are not to be minimized. Describing the religion of families and households at Ugarit remains a daunting enterprise. In addition, as we have seen above, the porous boundaries between non-elite and elite religion make such a study murky. Nonetheless, one conclusion is firm: the religion of the family (*betu*) was of paramount importance at Late Bronze Age Ugarit among humans of all social standings, especially the non-elite.

Notes

1 See T. Levy (ed.), *The Archaeology of Society in the Holy Land* (New York: Facts on File, 1995).

2 See, for example, Rainer Albertz's groundbreaking work on popular religion: *Persönliche Frömmigkeit und offizielle Religion: religionsinterner Pluralismus in Israel und Babylon* (Stuttgart: Calwer Verlag, 1978).

3 C. Meyers has boldly critiqued the way archaeological data are recovered and published. "Gender archaeology," she writes, "should be incorporated into the conceptual framework of all projects. Anything less represents a bias that should be deemed as ethically intolerable as tossing away the remains of periods that do not interest the excavator." See C. Meyers, "Engendering Syro-Palestinian Archaeology: Reasons and Resources," *Near Eastern Archaeology* 66 (2003): 185–97, esp. 189.

4 Scholars teaching in departments of religious studies have long wrestled with problems of definition in theory (substantive vs. functional) and approach (e.g., historical studies vs. philosophy of religion vs. cultural studies) as well as in practice (e.g., what type of curriculum to offer to students or the area of the discipline to fill with any faculty opening). See D. L. Pals, *Eight Theories of Religion*, 2nd edn. (New York: Oxford University Press, 2006).

5 K. van der Toorn includes each of these in his *Family Religion in Babylonia, Syria and Israel* (Leiden: Brill, 1996), p. 153ff.

6 On the motif of the loss of family group in the ancient Near East as well as the interpretation of the story of King Kirta, see S. B. Parker, *The Pre-biblical Narrative Tradition: Essays on the Ugaritic Poems Keret and Aqhat* (Atlanta: Scholars Press, 1989), pp. 146–216.

7 Compare the Hebrew cognate *mišpaḥah* which includes nuances of the extended family and the larger clan. Perhaps by having his offspring die so too did Kirta's hope for a family legacy. On the other hand, it may be that *špḥ* here designates simply his immediate offspring. Cf. its use in KTU 1.14.3.48–9 parallel to *ǵlm* (Manfried Dietrich et al., *Die Keilalphabetischen Texte aus Ugarit*, Alter Orient und Altes Testament 24 [Kevelaer: Butzon & Bercker; Neukirchen-Vluyn: Neukirchener, 1976]). See D. Pardee, "The Kirta Epic," in *The Context of Scripture*, ed. W. W. Hallo and K. L. Younger (Leiden: Brill, 1997) 1: 333 n. 11.

8 See Wyatt, *Religious Texts from Ugarit: The Words of Ilimilku and his Colleagues* (Sheffield: Sheffield Academic Press, 1998), p. 182 n. 22.

9 The text actually reads *ba(!)h* but has been restored by most scholars to either *bth*, "his household" or *bnh*, "his sons."

10 The text is broken *[x]ry[x]* and has been restored to read queen [Tha]rye[lli] as well as *['a]ry[h]*, "[his ki]nsmen."

11 M. Yon, *The City of Ugarit at Tell Ras Shamra* (Winona Lake, Ind: Eisenbrauns, 2006), pp. 72–6.

12 van der Toorn, *Family Religion in Babylonia, Syria and Israel*, pp. 153, 169.

13 G. del Olmo Lete, *Canaanite Religion According to the Liturgical Texts of Ugarit* (Bethesda, MD: CDL Press, 2004), p. 328.

14 del Olmo Lete, *Canaanite Religion*, p. 327.

15 See T. J. Lewis, "How Far Can Texts Take Us? Evaluating Textual Sources for Reconstructing Ancient Israelite Beliefs about the Dead," in *Sacred Time, Sacred Space: Archaeology and the Religion of Israel*, ed. B. M. Gittlen (Eisenbrauns: Winona Lake, 2002), pp. 169–217.

16 For domestic religion, see below, note 100.

17 M. Yon, "Ugarit," *The Oxford Encyclopedia of Archaeology in the Near East* (New York: Oxford University Press, 1997), 5: 258.

18 It is not my intention to minimize the importance of securing an heir for the kingdom at large. Certainly commoners would have been impacted by the stability/instability of the monarchy.

19 See M. Smith, *The Origins of Biblical Monotheism* (Oxford: Oxford University Press, 2001), pp. 56–7 on the debate surrounding recent suggestions (e.g., by P. Day and N. Walls) that Anatu is not the spouse of Ba'lu.

20 J. D. Schloen, *The House of the Father as Fact and Symbol: Patrimonialism in Ugarit and the Ancient Near East* (Winona Lake, Ind.: Eisenbrauns, 2001).

21 Smith, *The Origins of Biblical Monotheism*, pp. 54–60.

22 For the language of family applied to Ugaritic conceptions of the divine, see M. C. A. Korpel, *A Rift in the Clouds* (Münster: Ugarit-Verlag, 1990), pp. 232–64. For foundational works on family relations at Ugarit, see A. van Selms, *Marriage and Family Life in Ugaritic Literature* (London: Luzac, 1954) and A. Rainey, "Family Relationships at Ugarit," *Orientalia* 34 (1965): 10–22. The latter work was based on Rainey's more extensive 1962 Brandeis dissertation, "The Social Stratification of Ugarit."

23 This is corroborated by the presence of Ilu's name at the head of twelve deities invoked in a therapeutic text dealing with snakebites (KTU 1.100). Yet in this text Ilu does not provide the necessary remedy (incantation) which comes from another deity, Horanu, more skilled in such matters. See too KTU 1.107.38, another snakebite text, where Ilu and Horanu are paired.

24 In KTU 1.15.2.27, E. Greenstein (*Ugaritic Narrative Poetry*, ed. S. B. Parker [Atlanta: Scholars Press, 1997], pp. 25, 45 n. 66) now reads 'Aṯtartu rather than 'Athiratu. D. Pardee has the latter in "The Kirta Epic," p. 337.

25 For a picture of the ivory panel, see Lewis, "Syro-Palestinian Iconography and Divine Images," in *Cult Image and Divine Representation in the Ancient Near East*, ed. N. H. Walls (Boston: American Schools of Oriental Research, 2005), pp. 98–9 and fig. 4.32.

26 See Smith, *The Origins of Biblical Monotheism*, 45, p. 221 n. 44 (with bibliography) and G. J. Brooke, "The Textual, Formal and Historical Significance of Ugaritic Letter RS 34.124 (KTU 2.72)," *Ugarit Forschungen* 11 (1979): 69–87.

27 A balanced summary of the numerous interpretations of this passage can be found in S. Wiggins, *A Reassessment of "Asherah": A Study According to the Textual Sources of the First Two Millennia* BCE., Alter Orient und Altes Testament 235 (Kevelaer: Butzon & Bercker; Neukirchen-Vluyn: Neukirchener Verlag, 1993), pp. 44–8.

28 See Wiggins's (ibid.) conclusion on p. 71.

29 For an introduction to the onomastic evidence, see R. Hess's overview, "The Onomastics of Ugarit" in *Handbook of Ugaritic Studies*, ed. W. G. E. Watson and

N. Wyatt (Leiden: E. J. Brill, 1999), pp. 499–528. This work includes a full bibliography. Note in particular the works by D. Pardee, D. Sivan, W. H. van Soldt, and W. G. E. Watson.

30 D. Pardee and P. Bordreuil, "Ugarit: Texts and Literature" in *The Anchor Bible Dictionary*, ed. D. N. Freedman (New York: Doubleday, 1992), 6: 713.

31 del Olmo Lete, *Canaanite Religion*, p. 338.

32 Ibid., p. 339.

33 Convenient translations can be found in Wyatt, *Religious Texts from Ugarit*, pp. 416–22; del Olmo Lete, *Canaanite Religion*, pp. 304–5, 341; Pardee, *Ritual and Cult at Ugarit* (Atlanta: Society of Biblical Literature, 2002), pp. 50–3, 149–50.

34 Wyatt (*Religious Texts from Ugarit*, p. 416) speaks of the "pride in citizenship" and "corporate identity" in relation to this text. del Olmo Lete (*Canaanite Religion*, p. 305) sees the king taking part "in a communal liturgy in the interest of the whole of Ugarit."

35 Convenient translations can be found in Wyatt, *Religious Texts from Ugarit*, pp. 363–5; del Olmo Lete, *Canaanite Religion*, 340–3; Pardee, *Ritual and Cult at Ugarit*, pp. 21–3.

36 Compare and contrast, for example, the translations of del Olmo Lete (*Canaanite Religion*, pp. 341–2), Pardee (*Ritual and Cult at Ugarit*, pp. 22–3) and Wyatt (*Religious Texts from Ugarit*, pp. 363–5).

37 Smith, *The Origins of Biblical Monotheism*, pp. 58–9.

38 Even servants use such religious formula when writing their masters. See Pardee, "'Anantēnu to His Master Ḫid̲miratu," in *The Context of Scripture. Vol. III. Archival Documents from the Biblical World*, ed. W. W. Hallo and K. L. Younger (Leiden: Brill, 2002), p. 112.

39 del Olmo Lete, *Canaanite Religion*, pp. 336–7.

40 This is the translation of Pardee, "Double Letter, from 'Azzī'iltu to his Parents, From Same to his Sister," in *The Context of Scripture. Vol. III*, p. 112.

41 This letter (RS 20.178 = Ugaritica V, #55) is one of the Akkadian texts found in the private residences of Ugarit's upper classes. It was written by a high government official by the name of Rap'anu to his sister. The translation here is that of van der Toorn (*Family Religion in Babylonia, Syria and Israel*, p. 168) to whom I am indebted for bringing my attention to this passage.

42 The tablets were found in the so-called high priest's house near the two temples on the acropolis. The elite status is also underscored by the colophon on the left edge of KTU 1.17 mentioning the name of the prominent scribe Ilimilku. See the astute comments of Parker (*The Pre-biblical Narrative Tradition*, pp. 142–3) as to "why this work elevating traditional, family responsibilities [was] recorded by the scribe laureate of Ugarit, and kept in the residence of the high priest of Ugarit."

43 About ten lines are missing from the beginning of the story.

44 See Wyatt's (*Religious Texts from Ugarit*, p. 251 n. 6) discussion of the history of scholarship on these garments. Wyatt notes that "the garments Danel wears (*ṣt, mizrt*) [are] presumably a ritual one appropriate to the occasion and an undergarment." For further difficulties with this passage, see Pardee, "The 'Aqhatu Legend," in *The Context of Scripture. Vol. I. Canonical Compositions from the Biblical World*, ed. W. W. Hallo and K. L. Younger (Leiden: Brill, 1997), p. 343 n. 2.

45 For further on the Kathiratu (or Kotharatu), see Pardee, "Kosharoth" in *Dictionary of Deities and Demons in the Bible*, 2nd edn., ed. Karel van der Toorn, Bob Becking, and Pieter W. Van der Horst (Leiden: Brill, 1999), pp. 491–2.

46 Our texts are broken at this point in the story.

47 Pardee, "The 'Aqhatu Legend," p. 345 n. 23.

48 Note that our text is gendered in two respects. No mention is made of the duties of the ideal daughter. The filial piety here is moreover what the son does for his father, not his mother.

49 Or "his father's god." See below.

50 E.g. KTU 1.41.35; KTU 1.91.2–9; KTU 1.109.12, 15, 19, 35; KTU 1.130.12; KTU 1.148.1, 10, 23; 1.164.3, 6. These are royal texts but one may assume that commoners also sacrificed to their Ilu-ibi.

51 The deity lists are KTU 1.47. 1.65, 1.74, 1.102, 1.118, 1.148 and RS 20.24. See Pardee, *Les textes rituels*, Ras Shamra-Ougarit 12 (Paris: Éditions Recherche sur les Civilisations, 2000), vol. 1; idem, *Ritual and Cult at Ugarit*, pp. 11–24 and Wyatt, *Religious Texts from Ugarit*, pp. 360–2.

52 See van der Toorn, "Ilib and the 'God of the Father'," *Ugarit Forschungen* 25 (1993): 379–87; idem, *Family Religion in Babylonia, Syria and Israel*, pp. 154–68. KTU 1.113 also shows how deceased kings were deified. We do not know if the average Ugaritian thought that only the royal dead were accorded such deification or if people of lesser rank could also achieve preternatural status. On KTU 1.113, see Pardee, *Ritual and Cult at Ugarit*, pp. 195–202; Lewis, *Cults of the Dead in Ancient Israel and Ugarit*, Harvard Semitic Monographs 39 (Atlanta: Scholars Press, 1989), pp. 47–52.

53 van der Toorn, *Family Religion in Babylonia, Syria and Israel*, pp. 48, 52.

54 Pardee, *Ritual and Cult at Ugarit*, p. 280. See below on how one's deified ancestors were sought to intervene in healing rituals.

55 Pardee, *Ritual and Cult at Ugarit*, p. 280.

56 When a king would sacrifice to his ancestor's god (e.g., *'id ydbḥ mlk l'il'ib* in KTU 1.164) he would be strengthening the royal dynasty and his position within it.

57 Ritual texts refer to a "temple of Ilu" (*bt 'il*, e.g. KTU 1.119.14; see too *qdš 'il* in 1.119.6) and it may be that the acropolis temple usually designated "the temple of Dagan" (based on the nearby discovery of the Dagan stela; see KTU 6.13, 6.14) was in reality Ilu's. See note 79 below.

58 See Lewis, *Cults of the Dead in Ancient Israel and Ugarit*, pp. 53–71.

59 On the nature of Anatu as a huntress, see P. Day, "Anat: Ugarit's 'Mistress of Animals,'" *Journal of Near Eastern Studies* 51 (1992): 181–90.

60 Some scholars have seen a marriage proposal in Anatu's words "Listen, valiant [Aqhatu], You are my brother, I am your si[ster]" in KTU 1.18.1.19–25. Yet this is unlikely and the broken state of the text rules out any confidence in any interpretation. See the judicious comments of Neal H. Walls, *The Goddess Anat in Ugaritic Myth*, SBL Dissertation Series 135 (Atlanta: Scholars Press, 1992), pp. 193–4.

61 Parker, *The Pre-biblical Narrative Tradition*, pp. 142–3.

62 Though our sources at Ugarit are limited, vengeance too can be filled with religious connotations as easily seen in the Hebrew Bible's *go'el haddam* passages.

63 Astutely pointed out by Pardee, "The 'Aqhatu Legend," p. 355 n. 127.

64 Parker, *The Pre-biblical Narrative Tradition*, p. 143.

65 See M. Heltzer, *The Rural Community in Ancient Ugarit* (Wiesbaden: Reichert, 1976), pp. 103–12; M. Liverani, "Ras Shamra, histoire," *Supplément au Dictionnaire de la Bible*, (Paris: Letouzey et Ané, 1979), 9: 1319–20; Yon, "Ugarit: The Urban Habitat – The Present State of the Archaeological Picture," *Bulletin of the American*

Schools of Oriental Research 286 (1992): 19–20; W. H. van Soldt, "Ugarit: A Second Millennium Kingdom on the Mediterranean Coast," in *Civilizations of the Ancient Near East*, ed. Jack M. Sasson et al. (New York: Scribner, 1995), 2: 1258; Yon, "Ugarit," p. 260; J.-P. Vita, "The Society of Ugarit," in *Handbook of Ugaritic Studies*, p. 455.

66 The literature here is vast. For a sampling, see Heltzer, *The Internal Organization of the Kingdom of Ugarit* (Wiesbaden: Reicher Verlag, 1982); idem., "The Late Bronze Age Service System and Its Decline," in *Society and Economy in the Eastern Mediterranean*, ed. M. Heltzer and E. Lipiński (Leuven: Peeters, 1988), pp. 7–18; E. Lipiński, "The Socio-Economic Condition of the Clergy in the Kingdom of Ugarit," in *Society and Economy in the Eastern Mediterranean*, pp. 125–50; P. Vargyas, "Stratification Sociale à Ugarit," in *Society and Economy in the Eastern Mediterranean*, pp. 111–23; van Soldt, "Ugarit: A Second Millennium Kingdom," pp. 1260–4; Vita, "The Society of Ugarit," pp. 455–98; Schloen, *The House of the Father*; W. G. E. Watson, "Daily Life in Ancient Ugarit (Syria)," in *Life and Culture in the Ancient Near East*, ed. R. E. Averbeck, M. W. Chavalas, D. B. Weisberg (Bethesda, MD: CDL Press, 2003), pp. 130–9.

67 Granted, there is a large residential area to the south of the temples (excavated in 1935–6), yet its character has yet to be defined. Elite objects such as an Egyptian basalt statue of Princess Chnumet, a highly decorated gold bowl, and a gold cup depicting a (royal?) hunt come from this area. See Yon, *The City of Ugarit*, pp. 106–7, 114, 130–1 fig. 12, 164–5 figs. 56–7.

68 Yon, "Ugarit," p. 260.

69 See conveniently Pardee, *Ritual and Cult at Ugarit*, pp. 31, 33.

70 For the most complete study of these texts, see Pardee, *Les textes rituels*, pp. 428–38.

71 On the meaning of *gt*, see Schloen, *The House of the Father*, pp. 232–5; Pardee, *Ritual and Cult at Ugarit*, p. 122 n. 9.

72 KTU 1.79 and 1.80 were both found in the Royal Palace.

73 See van Soldt, *The Topography of the City-State of Ugarit* (Münster: Ugarit-Verlag, 2005), p. 9.

74 Alternatively, *qbṣ* could be a personal name similar to Ubbinniyana in KTU1.80.2. See, *Les textes rituels*, p. 433. Compare also *bt šbn* in KTU 4.16.1.

75 Following the restoration by Pardee, *Les textes rituels*, 435 and *Ritual and Cult at Ugarit*, p. 122 n. 9.

76 Heltzer (*The Rural Community in Ancient Ugarit*, pp. 72–3) had earlier understood most of these terms to be deity names with a few terms referring to Ugaritic villages. See the critique in D. M. Clemens, *Sources for Ugaritic Ritual and Sacrifice*, Alter Orient und Altes Testament 284 (Münster: Ugarit-Verlag, 2001), pp. 286–7.

77 Clemens, *Sources for Ugaritic Ritual and Sacrifice*, p. 281.

78 Ibid., p. 283.

79 There are multiple references to the temple of Ilu in our textual sources (see above, note 57). One would expect as much for the head of the pantheon. As noted above, the acropolis temple commonly referred to as the Temple of Dagan may have been Ilu's. This is very appealing when one compares the more prominent role of Ilu in our textual and iconographic sources. See Lewis, "Syro-Palestinian Iconography and Divine Images," figs. 4.12, 4.18, 4.19.

80 In addition to its presence at Ugarit, it is also attested in biblical texts (Amos and Jeremiah), Phoenician texts from Carthage and Piraeus, Aramaic texts from

Elephantine, Palmyra and Nabatea, rabbinic references by both the Tannaim and Amoraim, and the mosaic map at Madeba (6th c. CE).

81 Lewis, *Cults of the Dead in Ancient Israel and Ugarit*, pp. 80–94.

82 Complete bibliographies may be found in Clemens, *Sources for Ugaritic Ritual and Sacrifice*, pp. 269–70 n. 645 and K. M. McGeough ("Locating the Marziḥu Archaeologically," *Ugarit Forschungen* 35 [2003]: 418–20).

83 Lewis, *Cults of the Dead in Ancient Israel and Ugarit*, pp. 83–4.

84 Yet note the difficulty of the reading *btw* where one would expect *bth*. Due to repeated graphic missteps with the letter *h* in this text, Pardee (*Ritual and Cult at Ugarit*, p. 220 n. 14) "wonders if the scribe was simply having a bad day."

85 Pardee, "*Marziḥu*, *Kispu* and the Ugaritic Funerary Cult: A Minimalist View," in *Ugarit, Religion and Culture*, ed. N. Wyatt, W. G. E. Watson, and J. Lloyd (Münster: Ugarit Verlag, 1996), p. 278. Elsewhere (*Ritual and Cult at Ugarit*, p. 217), he refers to "the essentially noncultic nature of the [*marziḥu*] institution." He also comments: "though each *marziḥu* appears to be devoted to a particular deity, and though cultic personnel could be members, the institution itself was neither cultic nor located in a holy place" (*Ritual and Cult at Ugarit*, p. 184 n. 2). McGeough ("Locating the Marziḥu Archaeologically," pp. 411, 414) concludes similarly about the "non-cultic" nature of the *marziḥu* in his attempt to dissociate it from the Rhyton Sanctuary.

86 See M. O'Connor, "Northwest Semitic Designations for Elective Social Affinities," *Journal of the Ancient Near Eastern Society* 18 (1986): 67–80.

87 McGeough ("Locating the Marziḥu Archaeologically," p. 410) summarizing the conclusions of J. McLaughlin (*The Marzeaḥ in the Prophetic Literature* [Leiden: Brill, 2001], pp. 66–70).

88 See the van Soldt, *The Topography of the City-State of Ugarit*, pp. 69–71.

89 On Siyannu and Ushnatu, see van Soldt, ibid., pp. 64, 68–71.

90 See Pardee, *Les textes rituels* and *Ritual and Cult at Ugarit*. The literature on royal cult is vast. See, for example, J.-M. de Tarragon, *Le culte à Ugarit* (Paris: J. Gabalda, 1980), pp. 79–129; P. Merlo and P. Xella, "The Ugaritic Cultic Texts," in *Handbook of Ugaritic Studies*, pp. 296–300. Even the sacrifice by a foreign king is mentioned in KTU 2.40.14–17. See Clemens, *Sources for Ugaritic Ritual and Sacrifice*, pp. 223–3.

91 On the meaning of *prln* as "diviner" corresponding to Akkadian *baru*, see van Soldt, "*'Atn Prln*, ''Attā/ēnu the Diviner'," *Ugarit Forschungen* 21 (1989): 367–8 and the bibliography in Clemens, *Sources for Ugaritic Ritual and Sacrifice*, pp. 876–7. On Attanu-purulini, see further Lipiński, "The Clergy at Ugarit," pp. 131–3.

92 For the history of scholarship on the term *ḫrṣn*, now taken by most scholars to be a personal name, see Lipiński, "The Clergy at Ugarit," pp. 126–313 and Clemens, *Sources for Ugaritic Ritual and Sacrifice*, pp. 489–91.

93 See Lipiński, ibid., pp. 133–7.

94 Numerous translations of this passage exist reflecting various and nuanced interpretations of each of the terms for cultic personnel. This translation is that of Pardee, "The Baʿlu Myth," in *The Context of Scripture, Vol. 1*, p. 273. On the *ṯaʿiyu*-official, see D. Fleming, "The Voice of the Ugaritic Incantation Priest," *Ugarit Forschungen* 23 (1991): 146–8 and van Soldt, "Babylonian Lexical, Religious and Literary Texts and Scribal Education at Ugarit and its Implications for the Alphabetic Literary Texts," in *Ugarit: Ein ostmediterranes Kulturzentrum im Alten Orient*, ed. M Dietrich and O. Loretz (Münster: Ugarit-Verlag, 1995), p. 189.

95 This is not the proper venue to treat the many theories about the status and functions of such personnel. Readers are directed to the secondary literature on the topic that includes: de Tarragon, *Le culte à Ugarit*, pp. 131–44; Heltzer, *The Internal Organization of the Kingdom of Ugarit*, pp. 131–9; Lipiński, "The Socio-Economic Condition of the Clergy in the Kingdom of Ugarit," in *Society and Economy in the Eastern Mediterranean*, pp. 125–50; Vargyas, "Stratification Sociale à Ugarit," in *Society and Economy in the Eastern Mediterranean*, pp. 111–23; Heltzer, "The Economy of Ugarit," in *Handbook of Ugaritic Studies*, pp. 433–6; M. Dijkstra "The List of *qdšm* in KTU 4.412 +ii 8ff.," *Aula Orientalis* 17–18 (1999–2000): 81–9; Vita, "The Society of Ugarit," pp. 455–98; Clemens, *Sources for Ugaritic Ritual and Sacrifice*, pp. 319–26, 330–1, 448–50, 1085–9; Pardee, *Ritual and Cult at Ugarit*, pp. 239–40; Watson, "Daily Life in Ancient Ugarit," pp. 140–2; McGeough, "Exchange Relationships at Ugarit: A Study of the Economic Texts," (PhD Dissertation, University of Pennsylvania, 2005) Ch. 3, 5.

96 Pardee notes Mari parallels where the divine statue traveled from rural sanctuaries into the city. See *Les textes rituels*, p. 222 n. 21, *Ritual and Cult at Ugarit*, p. 69.

97 Pardee, *Ritual and Cult at Ugarit*, p. 78.

98 C. Zaccagnini, "Feet of Clay at Emar and Elsewhere," *Orientalia* 63 (1994): 1–4; J.-M. Durand, review of D. Arnaud, *Recherches au Pays d'Aštata, Emar VI*, *Revue d'Assyriologie* 84 (1990): 74–5. I owe these references to Y. Cohen (see n. 99).

99 Y. Cohen, "Feet of Clay at Emar: A Happy End?" (forthcoming). I am indebted to Cohen for sharing this manuscript with me prior to publication.

100 J. C. Courtois, "L'Architecture Domestique à Ugarit au Bronze Récent," *Ugarit Forschungen* 11 (1979): 105–34; O. Callot, *Une Maison à Ougarit: Études d'architecture domestique*, Ras Shamra-Ougarit 1 (Paris: Éditions Recherche sur les Civilisations, 1983); M. Yon, P. Lombard, and M. Reniso, "L'organisation de l'Habitat: Les Maisons A, B, et E," in *Le Centre de la ville, 38–44e (1978–1984)*, Ras Shamra-Ougarit 3, ed. Marguerite Yon and Olivier Callot (Paris: Éditions Recherche de la Civilisation, 1987), pp. 11–128; M. Yon, "Ugarit: The Urban Habitat," pp. 19–34; Callot, *La Tranchée "ville sud": Études d'architecture domestique*, Ras Shamra-Ougarit 10 (Paris: Éditions Recherche sur les Civilisations, 1994); Yon, *La cité d'Ougarit sur le tell de Ras Shamra* (Paris: Éditions Recherche sur les Civilisations. 1997); Callot, "A Visit to a Home," *Near Eastern Archaeology* 63 (2000): 202–4; Callot and Y. Calvet, "Le 'Bâtiment au Vase de Pierre' du 'Quartier Residentiel' d'Ougarit (fouille 1966)," in *Études Ougaritiques: I. Travaux 1985–1995*, Ras Shamra-Ougarit 14, ed. M. Yon and D. Arnaud (Paris: Éditions Recherche sur les Civilisations, 2001), pp. 65–82; C. Castel, "Naissance et Développement d'une Maison dans la 'Ville Basse' orientale d'Ougarit (fouille 1936)," in *Études Ougaritiques: I. Travaux 1985–1995*, pp. 41–64; J. Mallet and V. Matoïan, "Une Maison au Sud du 'Temple aux Rhytons' (fouilles 1979–1999)," in *Études Ougaritiques: I. Travaux 1985–1995*, Ras Shamra-Ougarit 14, ed. M. Yon and D. Arnaud (Paris: Éditions Recherche sur les Civilisations, 2001), pp. 83–190; Yon, *The City of Ugarit at Tell Ras Shamra*; McGeough, "The Material Remains of the Ugaritic Economy," in *Exchange Relationships at Ugarit*, pp. 417–51.

101 Yon, "Ugarit," p. 260.

102 Yon, "Ugarit: History and Archaeology," in *The Anchor Bible Dictionary*, ed. D. N. Freedman (New York: Doubleday, 1992), 6: 704.

103 S. Marchegay ("The Tombs," *Near Eastern Archaeology* 63 [2000]: 208–9) has tabulated 16 tombs in the Residential Quarter with its large houses, 14 in the South City Trench, over 20 in the South Acropolis Trench, and 31 in the Lower City. She concludes: "the more dense the housing in a quarter, the more tombs it possesses."

104 For this designation, see Z. Zevit, *The Religions of Ancient Israel: A Synthesis of Parallactic Approaches* (London: Continuum, 2001), p. 274 followed by W. G. Dever, *Did God Have a Wife? Archaeology and Folk Religion in Ancient Israel* (Grand Rapids: Eerdmans, 2005), pp. 58, 185. The interpretation of figurines remains very uncertain. For additional material from Syria, see A. A. Petty, "Anthropoinorphic Figurines from Umm el-Marra, Syria: Chronology, Visual Analysis and Function," PhD disst., Johns Hopkins University, 2005.

105 See H. Frost, "Anchors Sacred and Profane," in *Arts et Industries de la Pierre*, Ras Shamra-Ougarit 6, ed. Marguerite Yon and Annie Caubet (Paris: Éditions Recherche sur les Civilisations, 1991), pp. 355–410; Wyatt, "The Religion of Ugarit: An Overview," in *Handbook of Ugaritic Studies*, p. 583; and A. Brody, *"Each Man Cried Out To His God": The Specialized Religion of Canaanite and Phoenician Seafarers* (Atlanta: Scholars Press, 1998).

106 See, too, Yon's fuller treatment: "The Temple of the Rhytons at Ugarit," in *Ugarit, Religion and Culture*, ed. N. Wyatt, W. G. E. Watson, and J. Lloyd (Münster: Ugarit-Verlag, 1996), pp. 405–22.

107 McGeough, "Locating the Marziḫu Archaeologically," pp. 407–20.

6

Family Religion in Ancient Israel and its Surroundings

Rainer Albertz

When I investigated what I called "personal piety" in ancient Israelite families about 30 years ago in Heidelberg for my *Habilitationsschrift*,[1] there were very few Old Testament scholars who were aware that such a phenomenon as "family religion" existed.[2] Slowly, the situation has changed remarkably. With my differentiation between "personal piety" and "official religion" in mind, Karel van der Toorn wrote his detailed study *Family Religion in Babylonia, Syria, and Israel* (1996).[3] I myself tried to describe the development of family religion through the course of the history of ancient Israelite religion (1992/94);[4] and Erhard S. Gerstenberger conceptualized the first Old Testament Theology that demonstrates an appropriate appreciation for family religion (2001).[5] This aspect of religion was incorporated in the latest book on families in ancient Israel, edited by Leo G. Perdue (1997).[6] Moreover, at the end of 2004, the first comprehensive guide to ancient Mediterranean and Near Eastern religions was published. Among other topics, it deals with the "Religious Practices of the Individual and the Family" in each of the civilizations under consideration.[7]

Terms and Concepts

To distinguish a family religion within a given religion requires recognition of a kind of religious pluralism. Among Old Testament scholarship there is still a high degree of uncertainty as to how to deal properly with the obvious pluralism within Israelite religion. Three main concepts are in use and sometimes mixed together: the concept of syncretism, the concept of popular religion, and the concept of internal religious pluralism. I would like to present a short survey of these three terms and concepts in order to clarify the theoretical framework within which family religion can be studied properly.[8]

Syncretism

In the older research, the differences in beliefs and rites of pre-exilic Israelite religion are often explained by the assumption that a Mosaic Yhwh-religion was heavily influenced and partly modified by Canaanite religion. According to their degree of syncretism, H. Ringgren identified several diverging tendencies that existed in Israelite religion, e.g., the official religion of the Jerusalem temple and the kingdom, a syncretistic folk religion, the religion of the great prophets, and the religion of the Deuteronomistic circle.[9]

Generally speaking, we can acknowledge that influence or borrowing from outside can cause differences within a religion. But in the case of Israel, we have to face many difficulties concerning this hypothesis. First, we do not know whether there ever existed a specific Canaanite religion nor do we know what it was like assuming it existed. Often, when the prophet Hosea or the Deuteronomic theologians claim a Canaanite origin for a particular practice, they only inveigh against a ritual or belief which they do not want to tolerate any longer, though it may have been a part of Israelite religion for a long time.[10] Second, it is not generally true that the beliefs and rites of the ordinary people are more shaped by syncretism than the official state cult; the temple and kingship theology of Jerusalem was nothing other than a syncretistic construction.[11] Third, it must be remembered that syncretism is a process and not a state. When it is successful, the foreign elements are accepted as part of the borrowing religion and no longer seen as alien; other-wise they are removed. So the explanation that a certain religious or cultic element was of syncretistic origin one hundred or five hundred years earlier often does not explain its significance in the present religion. For example, the archaeologist Seymour Gitin, who excavated the Philistine town Ekron, observed that, of the seventeen small stone altars found there, only six were found in the auxiliary buildings of the city temple, but nine were found in the industrial zone and two in the domestic area. Twelve of the altars he classified as portable.[12] Gitin concluded correctly from these data that there existed a "form of decentralized worship system" in contrast to the centralized worship in the city temple, but he offered the following explanation: "No doubt, this dual worship system was a result of Ekron's exposure to multiple ethnic cultic traditions when it became an international olive-oil production centre in the 7th century BCE."[13] This may be the case, although I have my doubts, but Gitin overlooked the functional explanation: Those nine altars clearly attest to a more private form of worship apart from the central temple and constitute good evidence for the existence of a domestic cult or a workplace cult in seventh-century Ekron. Thus, a focus on the concept of syncretism can impede the discovery of family religion.

Popular Religion

The division between official and popular religion or *Volksfrömmigkeit* is very popular among Old Testament scholars,[14] but only a few are aware that it was derived from the *Volkskunde* of the nineteenth century and was developed to analyze customs of the people in Christian, mainly Catholic, societies.[15] In this context, the term "popular religion" denotes a phenomenon in which laymen take elements of orthodox Catholic beliefs, rites and symbols and redefine them and reuse them for their own religious purposes, e.g., crosses with the Corpus Christi erected on fields as apotropaic and fertility symbols. Thus, popular religion in this original sense is a kind of degenerate subtype of official religion. It presupposes the establishment of orthodoxy, a clear stratification between a priestly elite and an unprofessional laity, and a claimed priestly monopoly over all goods of salvation.[16]

Therefore we must ask critically whether such conditions ever existed in the ancient world or when comparable structures emerged.[17] We can be sure that in Israel the first attempts at establishing some kind of orthodoxy were not made before the late seventh century BCE. Thus, Old Testament scholars normally use the term "popular religion" in a more unspecific sense for popular ideas concerning God's action in the lives of the individual, the community, and in nature,[18] which differ from what is seen as "official" in scripture. In this usage "popular religion" can mean very different things: For J. B. Segal, "popular religion" means ideas and practices concerning women, magic and magical practitioners;[19] for Martin Rose, it denotes the religious views of the opponents, who were attacked by the Deuteronomic theologians or the prophet Jeremiah. It can even be the Zion theology Jeremiah attacked in his temple sermon (Jer 7:4), which clearly belonged to the official state religion of Judah.[20] So the term is more confusing than clarifying. I agree for the most part with the fundamental criticism of Jacques Berlinerblau, who recommended that we lessen our reliance on the term "popular religion," and pleaded for a more sociologically precise methodology in order to "delineate religiosity among particular Israelite groups."[21]

Internal Religious Pluralism

The third explanation for religious and ritual diversity is a sociological one. Since all higher societies are subdivided into different types of groups, the religious symbols and practices, which are closely related to the needs of those groups, differ more or less, too. In traditional societies we can distinguish at least three levels of societal groups: the family, the local community, and the whole people, be it organized into a tribe or a state, which in pre-modern times constituted – although interrelated – more separated spheres of life than they do today. Since ancient Israel was such a traditional society, I propose to distinguish at least two or three levels of Israelite religion: the personal piety related to the family, the official religion related to the whole people,[22] and in between – not as clearly to be described as the other two – the local religion related to the village or town.[23] The two or three levels of religion differ from one another in respect to their target group, their supporters, their religious ideas and practices, their functions, and their degree of institutionalization. Following the former *Religionswissenschaftler* Günter Lanczkowski of Heidelberg, who described similar phenomena in the Greek, Chinese and Maya religion, I call this "internal religious pluralism."[24] It is defined as structural pluralism, which is related to the substructures of society. And it must be distinguished from those differences that result from social stratification, religious and political institutions, local traditions, and interest groups. These can lead to subdivisions within the three structural levels (e.g., official theology of the temple and that of the court; personal piety of the rich and that of the poor).

There are still some problems left as to the terminology. Instead of "personal piety," one can use the term "family religion" as long as one is aware that the personal faith of the family members is included. Instead of "official religion," one can speak of "tribe" or "state religion" as well. I still use the term "official religion" because this type of religion includes more than the religion of state institutions. Moreover, the form of political organization changed several times in the history of ancient Israel. But the term "official" must not be misunderstood as the religion that is valid for the whole society, but only what claims to be or become valid for it. Therefore not only the state religion of kings and priests but also the opposing preaching of the prophets belongs to the "official religion" in my paradigm, since they both are related to the fate of the whole society. Unfortunately, the term "folk religion," that would go nicely with "family religion," is fixed with a different meaning by the *Volkskunde*.

I think the concept of internal religious pluralism offers a good opportunity to describe on the one hand family religion as a subject of its own, and on the other hand the possible interrelations with local and state religion. I would like to draw the focus a little bit more on ancient Israelite families: These families were relatively independent economic and cultural units and were defined by the *bet 'ab*, "the house of the father." Therefore, the target group of Israelite family religion was that face-to-face community that lived together in the house of the family head, the center of its everyday life. Supporters of the family religion were the members of the household, to which belonged not only the father, the mother and their children, but which could also include some other relatives and non-related persons (alien workers and slaves).[25] Family religion aimed at serving the survival of the family and its members and the fostering of their identity. The degree of institutionalization in family religion was very low. Seldom was there need of a religious expert; in most cases the father or the mother carried out the ritual functions.

Depending on the level of education and the wealth of the families in question, the shape of family religion could vary. Thus, in the post-exilic period we can distinguish a personal theology of the wealthy (pious wisdom), which had a higher degree of reflection,[26] from the piety of the poor (psalms of the poor).[27] In the course of development, elements of the official religion were included (e.g., Torah piety).[28]

Nevertheless, such different kinds of piety or personal theology remained a religion of private matters focused on the needs of the family and its individual members.

Because of their fundamental functional orientation towards the needs of families, which were similar among the peoples of the ancient Near Eastern cultures, the family religions of that region are less different than the religions of the nations to which family members belonged. Since family religion was less separated from and more open to the larger religious environment, it often appears syncretistic, but it is not of syncretistic origin.

Methodological Design

Accessing family religion is a challenge, for normally it left few written sources and inconspicuous archaeological remains. In many cases, the literary and archaeological evidence for official religion is much more prominent; that is the reason why family religion was often overlooked. This observation is as true for ancient Israel as for its neighbors.

Literary sources

In Palestine, the conditions conducive to the preservation of literary sources are rather bad, since in this area mainly papyrus sheets were used for writing and these were rarely preserved, given the wet climate. Thus, the evidence of individual and family religion that we have in other places, such as private letters, short prayers, vows, instructions for family rituals, and incantations, did not usually survive. Only a few inscriptions on pottery shards, stone and seals, which can more or less be assigned to family religion, have been discovered thus far.[29] For the ancient neighbors of Israel, we are nearly completely limited to archaeological evidence. For ancient Israel itself we are – apart from archaeological artifacts – still mostly restricted to the Hebrew Bible. This source is full of religious and cultic information, but, although its authors made use of older traditions that reflected the lives of ordinary people more than any other literati of the ancient Near East, they selected, shaped, and revised the material according to the standpoint of the official Israelite religion and to the needs of the whole people, mainly during the Persian period. In short, we have to be aware that this source is biased, often shaped by an all-Israel perspective and in its final form comparatively late. Therefore, the information about religious and cultic activities of the family in the Hebrew Bible must be read critically, and its reliability must be proven in every case.

The theophoric personal names of the Hebrew Bible are a good source for reconstructing family religion,[30] and these can be amplified by many seals and inscriptions. They are not biased by the official view and permit an overview of the symbolic world of family religion, the gods who are venerated, and their important functions. A group of texts of great value are the individual *Gattungen* in the Psalms (laments, thanksgivings and oracles of salvation), although they are often already influenced by the official religion. A lot of information on family religion is also preserved in the Patriarchal narratives (Genesis 12–50) and in the Former Prophets (Judges–2 Kings). At least several legal prohibitions in the Pentateuch (Exodus–Deuteronomy) reflect the religious practices of family religion. For the later development of family religion, the Psalms, Proverbs, Job, Kohelet, and Ben Sira are important.

Archaeological findings

Since the literary evidence pertaining to family religion is so rare or problematic, the archaeological evidence is of crucial importance. Unfortunately, the archaeologists who excavated many sites in Palestine were mainly interested in monumental architecture and spectacular finds.[31] Thus, only a few domestic areas were thoroughly excavated (e.g., in Tell Bet Mirsim, Beer Sheba, Tell en-Nasbe, Megiddo, and Hazor), and, unfortunately, these were often badly documented. Since many excavators were not aware of the probable existence of a family religion, they often misinterpreted those findings that could have pointed to the existence of a domestic cult,[32] or even overlooked relevant evidence as we have seen in the case of Ekron.[33] Therefore, a thorough and systematic archaeological examination of family religion has not yet been carried out,[34] and available evidence is still meager and ambiguous.

The categorization of cult places remains unclear: John S. Holladay divided fundamentally between an "established worship" and a "tolerated nonconformist worship"; the former he subdivided into "the town or national level" and "the neighbourhood level", to which he attributed manifestations of local nonconformist worship such as Jerusalem cave 1,[35] and the domestic cult.[36] These subdivisions correspond roughly to the levels of state religion, local religion and family religion according to my model, but because of the category of "nonconformist worship" taken from the popular religion model – defined by the occurrence of figurines – Holladay introduces a pejorative contrast which stands in tension with his sociological and local categories. Should we really characterize all family religion as "nonconformist"?

Z. Zevit endeavors to offer more objective categories. First, he uses the terms "cult room," "cult corner," "cult cave," "cult complex," "cult center," "temple," "temple complex," and "shrine" in a defined sense with the intent of describing the different cult sites more exactly.[37] Second, he tries to divide all the cult places into two classes: those "whose construction is well integrated into a much larger plan attributable to centralized planning or control,"[38] and "those, whose construction does not demonstrate this feature" (Figure 6.1).[39] Class 1 has its basis in a suitable criterion and corresponds to what I call official or state religion; more problematic is class 2, which includes all that does not look like what is under official control, e.g., a local open air cult complex (*bamah*) such as the "Bull Site," a cave such as that from Tel 'Eton, or a cult corner such as Megiddo locus 2081, which might have

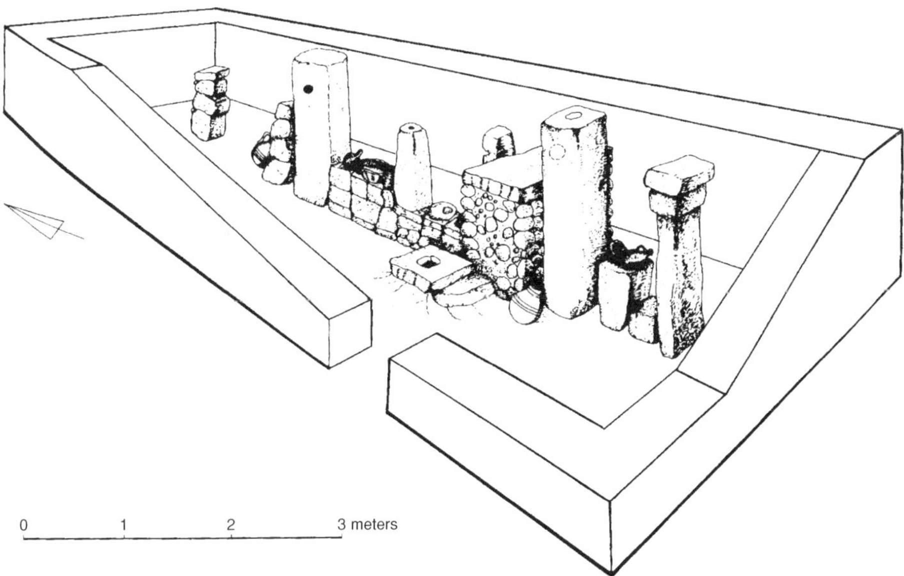

Figure 6.1 Reconstruction of cult room 340 within the tenth-century BCE building 338 at Megiddo. From Zevit, *The Religions of Ancient Israel*, p. 229, Fig. 3.60

been a site of the domestic cult. Even more problematic is that Zevit does not integrate the domestic cult into his scheme; it seems to be too unimportant to get its own class.[40]

At all events, J. S. Holladay and Z. Zevit both see some archaeological evidence for a domestic cult in ancient Israel. Holladay gives a rough statistical analysis of the artifacts with cultic connotation such as female figurines, cult stands, animal figurines, model chairs, and rattles which were found in the domestic areas of Tell Bet Mirsim (level A) and Beer Sheba (strata III–II). According to him, about 50 percent of all houses exhibit signs of cultic activity; among these finds, the pillar-based figurines play a dominant role. From the temporal distribution of these artifacts in Hazor, he demonstrates that there was an impressive floruit of familial cult activity during the second half of the eighth century.[41] Because of the bad standard of publication, Z. Zevit rejects the material from Tell Bet Mirsim and accepts only three sets of evidence for the domestic cult in ancient Israel: houses 25 and 430 in Beer Sheba and house 440 in Tirzah.[42] He also considers the possibility of Philistine domestic and workplace cult sites in Ekron[43] because of the distribution of limestone altars over the domestic and industrial zones, as mentioned above.[44] To this we can now add another clear piece of evidence from Tel Halif (Ziklag).[45] The disputed "cultic structure" in Taanach is best interpreted as two workplace cults.[46]

The most extensive evidence of domestic cult in ancient Palestine comes from Tell Jawa near Amman in Transjordan.[47] Since 1992, nine domestic buildings of the period Iron II were excavated, and in all of them the excavators found larger or smaller collections of cultic artifacts varying from two to forty-three pieces. In this Ammonite settlement, the assemblage for the family cult differs in some items from that in ancient Israel. On the one hand, the limestone altars and the Judean style pillar figurines are lacking; on the other, there are more male figurines and tripod cups than there are in Judah.[48] In many cases the same or similar artifacts are as common in Transjordan as in Cisjordan. In Tell Jawa, the cultic activities of the families seem to have taken place generally on the roof or upper storey of the houses as in Mesopotamia and often in Israel after the eighth century.[49] From these rich finds, the excavator Paulette M. Michèle Daviau tried to define an assemblage of artifacts which can be seen as typical for the domestic cult and this may help to identify the domestic cult in contexts with less clear finds in the future. The assemblage consists of female, male, and zoomorphic figurines, anthropomorphic and zoomorphic vessels, model shrines, decorated chalices, one-handled cups, tripod cups perforated and unperforated,[50] lamps, gaming objects, libation tables, and basalt bowls, along with small vessels, miniature vessels, and high status vessels. The divine presence could also be symbolized by a stone baetyl.[51]

As far as I can see, Daviau is the first biblical archaeologist to be aware of the significance of family religion and the concept of internal religious pluralism; she never refers to me, but at least she refers to Karel van der Toorn.[52] I hope that her approach will help to bring the archaeological exploration of family religion to the fore during the next decades. Even now, in my view, it gives us two new insights.

First, since in the domestic cult of Tell Jawa male and female figurines were used side by side (with a ratio of 8:4), as is typical in Semitic religions, and one of the male figurines (TJ 100) carries the *Atef* crown,[53] a clear symbol of divinity, we have additional evidence that the masses of female figurines in Judah, which were also used in domestic cultic contexts but mostly lack a clear divine indicator, nevertheless represent a divine being, probably Asherah, the mother goddess, as many scholars guessed before.[54] The one-sided preference for a goddess in the Judean domestic cult, which cannot be sufficiently explained by the importance of woman on the level of family worship, since that would be similar among the Ammonites, has probably to do, as Karel van der Toorn has suggested recently,[55] with the fact that in Judah Asherah played an important role as mediatrix of Yhwh, as we can see from the inscription of Khirbet el-Qom.[56]

Second, in his important study on family religion, Karel van der Toorn vacillates about whether we should attribute family religion to the nuclear family or better to the wider clan. Concerning the domestic cult he states: "There is neither archaeological nor literary evidence for a domestic cult performed by single nuclear families. Related families constituted one cultic body . . ."[57] I think that the archaeological evidence of Tell Jawa has made it clear that the domestic cult was actually performed by the nuclear family, plus those relatives and aliens who lived in the same house.

To conclude, for the domestic cult we have seven sets of archaeological evidence from ancient Israel and Judah (tenth–eighth century BCE), nine from Ammonite

Tell Jawa (eighth century), and two from Philistine Ekron (seventh century).[58] I think this evidence could be amplified considerably if one investigates systematically the assemblages of cultic artifacts which were found in domestic areas during all past and present excavations by using the assemblage found in Tell Jawa as a rough guide, assuming slight variation from region to region.[59] The fact that 30 percent of Judean pillar figurines (79 of 255) were found in houses, as Raz Kletter pointed out,[60] gives a good impression of how far the domestic cult was probably spread.

Religious Practices and Beliefs of the Israelite Family in the Pre-exilic Time

Up to the seventh century, the members of Israelite families lived in their own religious sphere that was not much influenced by the official religion of the Israelite and Judean states. There were some minor changes, especially under the cultural influence of Assyrian domination beginning in the second half of the eighth century, but during the pre-Josianic period Israelite family religion essentially remained constant.[61]

Religious practices

The most private religious practices performed by the members of the family took place in the dwelling of the family, where the cultic paraphernalia were installed, whether in a niche of the court, in an inner room or on the upper floor. There, the so-called "model shrines" served as little shrines to house divine figurines.[62] From the cult utensils found in the dwellings, we can conclude roughly what the domestic cult looked like. What P. M. M. Daviau has described for Tell Jawa – it "comprises the setting up of a figurine or symbolic stone in a particular area . . . , food and drink offerings, use of scenting materials, lighting lamps, sprinkling the figurine, the baetyl, or the sacred area itself, offerings in small or miniature vessels, casting of lots or divination, and libations"[63] – is nearly true for the Israelite family cult. There, we also have plenty of evidence for incense offerings (perforated tripod cups and jars). The remains of a burnt grain offering are attested in Megiddo locus 2081, where it was probably offered on the bigger one of the two four horn altars (Figure 6.2). And jugs and juglets were used for libations (Figure 6.3). Slaughtered offerings and ceremonial meals (*zebaḥ*), which took place in the local sanctuary (see 1 Sam 9:12ff.), were excluded from the domestic cult.[64]

One important motivation for the domestic cult was probably the case of illness or distress of a family member. At such times, the ceremony of lament was performed by the father, a man of God or a prophet (1 Kgs 17:7–24; 2 Kgs 4:32–7).[65] It was accompanied by offerings, magical rites, and exorcism (Isa 38:21) and found its climax in the recitation of a psalm of lament, probably spoken by the liturgist line

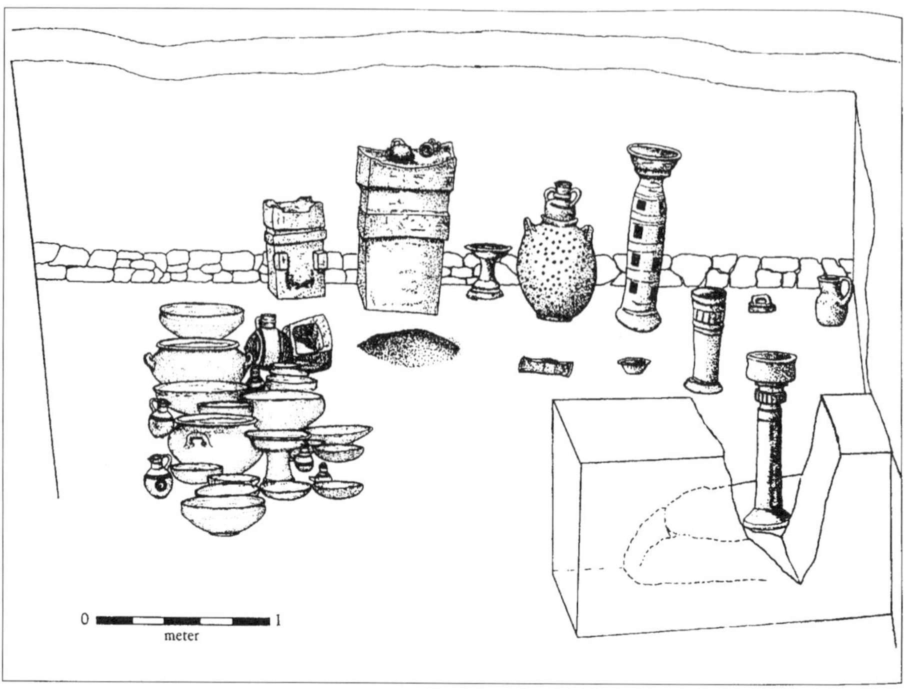

Figure 6.2 Reconstruction of the cult corner, locus 2081, at Megiddo. From Zevit, *The Religions of Ancient Israel*, p. 224, Fig. 3.55

by line, to be repeated by the sick person. After that the liturgist could give the sick person a positive answer from God, the oracle of salvation. Perhaps lot casting, for which we have some archaeological (gaming vessels)[66] and literary evidence (ephod in Judg 17:5), was done with this ceremony.

Similar rituals took place in connection with the distress of infertility, pregnancy, and birth; here the mother of the house stood at the center of the domestic cult. The naked figure of the mother-goddess Asherah, whose fertility is emphasized by the size of her breasts, the way in which she holds her body, or the presence of a child,[67] functioned especially in this case as a representation of the mediatrix who would intercede with Yhwh on behalf of the sufferer that he might give her his help. The woman who had given birth to a child praised God by giving her baby a name indicating thanksgiving. Probably thankful offerings were connected with this; likewise with the feast of weaning (Gen 21:8). The lament of the childless woman (1 Sam 1:10; Isa 54:1f.) and the promise of childbirth (Gen 18:10, 14; Judg 13:3, 10; 2 Kgs 4:16) belonged to the deepest female religious experiences in the horizon of family religion. Thus the domestic cult centrally aimed at the protection of all family members and the survival of the family group.

Finally, ancestor worship, which was performed daily and monthly, might have taken place at the domestic shrine,[68] since the teraphim, which seem to have been figurines of the deified ancestors (Gen 31:19, 30–5), belonged to the house chapel,

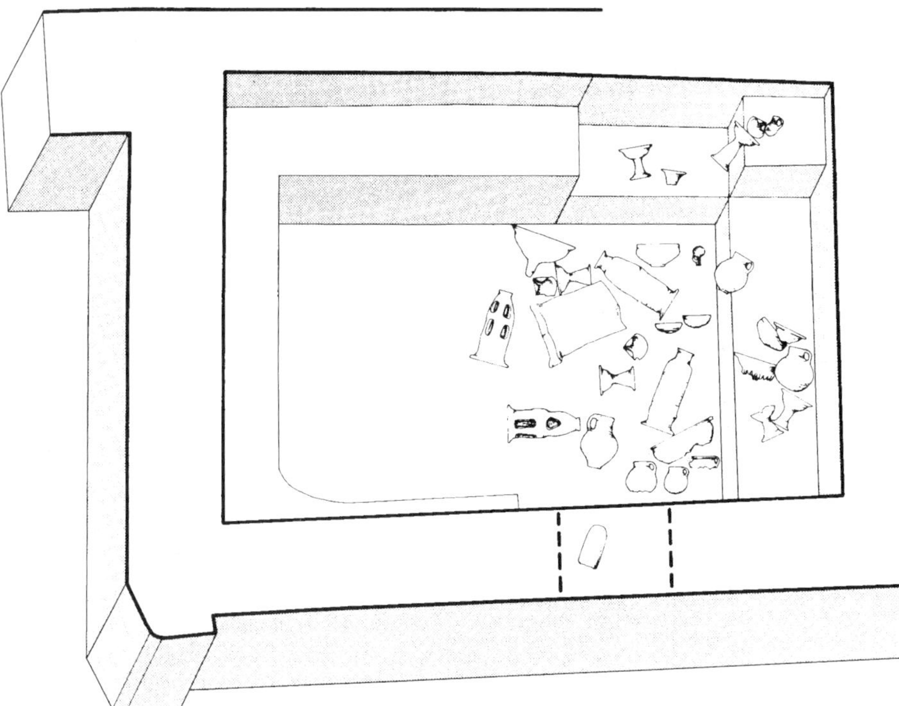

Figure 6.3 Cult room 49 at Lachish. From Aharoni, *Investigations at Lachish: The Sanctuary and the Residency (Lachish V)*, p. 28, Fig. 6. Courtesy of the Institute of Archaeology, Tel Aviv University

according to Judg 17:5. The ancestors were fed with vegetable offerings (Deut 26:14) in order to insure their protection of the family. These rituals might have played a major role in strengthening the identity of the nuclear family.

Other ritual practices of the Israelite family draw upon a wider social circle for participants than does the domestic cult. In cases of acute emergency, e.g., before a birth which was proving to be difficult (Gen 25:22) or when a child was seriously ill (1 Kings 14) and therefore the possibilities of family divination came to an end, families could make requests to God through a man of God or a prophet in order to obtain a prognosis. Solemn requests to Yhwh (*daraš*) were a form of intuitive manticism, in which a human being functioned as a medium (2 Kgs 8:7ff.; cf. Isa 38; 2 Kings 5). He or she was paid by the family (1 Kgs 14:3; 2 Kgs 8:9). Requests, however, could be made not only to Yhwh, but also to other gods of a region, who, like Baal of Ekron, were famous for their oracles (2 Kings 1). Even the spirits of the dead could be implored (1 Samuel 28). Against a common view, I believe that necromancy, unlike the ancestor cult, was not part of family religion itself. Basing our statement on the parallels in Babylon, we can be sure that the obtaining of a divine oracle was often preceded by a ceremony of petition.

Another sort of familial practice, in this case including relatives and neighbors, took place at the local sanctuary, which was generally situated outside the settlement (*bamah*).[69] All such rites involved ceremonial meals (*zebaḥim*), for which cultic purity and a bigger altar than the one available at home were needed. If a family member had been healed or rescued, the family would perform a thanksgiving ceremony (*zebaḥ hattodah*, Lev 7:12; cf. Ps 66:15–20). With the assistance of a priest or a seer, the father slaughtered a sheep or a goat, parts of it were dedicated to God, but most of it was consumed by the family itself and the invited relatives, neighbors, and friends (1 Samuel 9–10). During the festive meal the person who had been healed spoke of his distress, his lamentation, and his rescue by God and recited a song of thanksgiving in the assembly (Psalms 30, 40, 41). Through the shared feast, he was fully accepted again into the village community.

Such a ceremonial meal could also take place as a result of a vow (*neder*) made by a family member in distress.[70] The vow was an urgent form of prayer, which could be uttered anywhere in time of need, including at the domestic shrine, of course, but it usually had to be fulfilled at a public sanctuary. The fact that Absalom, having fled to distant Syria, vowed a meal offering to Yhwh-in-Hebron indicates that he felt particularly drawn to the local cult of the place in which he had been born and brought up (2 Sam 15:8). That means that family ceremonial meals established a special relationship between the families and quite specific sanctuaries and that as a result the family cult took on a regional coloring. 1 Samuel 1 reports how Samuel's family used to make a pilgrimage to the sanctuary of Shiloh every year, evidently to fulfill the vows made the year before. This family sacrificial feast at which women and children took part was called the *zebaḥ hayyamim* ("annual sacrifice", 1 Sam 1:21; 2:19).

The same name *zebaḥ hayyamim* is given to a sacrificial feast (1 Sam 20:6), because of which David's whole clan met once a year in Bethlehem at the time of a new moon; therefore it is also called *zebaḥ mišpaḥah* (v. 29). On the basis of the evidence from Mesopotamia, Karel van der Toorn has convincingly shown that this feast must be understood as the annual ancestor festival in which all the clan members were required to participate.[71] It is likely that this ceremonial meal of the whole clan took place at the local sanctuary. Commemorating the dead of the year and the deified ancestors of the lineage, the common identity of the related families was strengthened.

Passover was also a family ritual until the seventh century BCE. Possibly, after it had been slaughtered and roasted in the local sanctuary, each family's sheep was eaten by the family at home, together with unleavened bread and bitter herbs (Exod 12:1–13). Perhaps rooted in an old nomadic ritual, originally celebrated before the herd was transferred from the winter to the summer pasture (note the staff and sandals in 12:11),[72] the Passover retained a clearly apotropaic function: the sheep's blood smeared on the lintel and on the two doorposts of the entrance to each house was intended to protect the family against a child-killing demon (12:21–24).

Individual family members could protect themselves against demons, sorcery and the evil eye by amulets, which are frequently attested by archaeology.[73] They were heavily influenced by an Egyptian style and could have the form of scarabs, seals, anthropomorphic figures showing Egyptian gods and goddesses (Anat, Isis, Sachmet, Theoris, Bes, Pataeke), objects (Horus-eye, moon, Djed-pillar), and animals (lion, sow, sow with piglets). In the Hebrew Bible those amulets were called *ḥotam*, "seal" (an Egyptian loanword), *leḥašim*, "conjuring amulets" (Isa 3:20), *saharonim*, "little moons", or *šebisim*, "little suns" (Isa 3:18); by the prophet Ezekiel they were denounced as *gillulim*, "dung pellets" (Ezek 14:3; 20:7). The apotropaic function of the amulets was based on imitative magic; the luxury silver amulets of Ketef Hinnom worked with blessings.[74] In heavy conflicts family members could make use of magical experts, often women, who manufactured special amulets and other magic tools (Ezek 13:17–23), or formulated incantations against their enemy; the ostracon from the seventh century BCE found at Horvat 'Uzza in the eastern Negev seems to have been such a private incantation.[75] Harmful magic of sorceresses was not officially forbidden in Judah before the late eighth century BCE (Exod 22:17).

Family cult and official cult came into contact during the offering of the first fruits. On the one hand, these sacrifices of the year's first harvest were firmly related to the family's agricultural produce and thus its economy; on the other hand, the first fruits of barley and wheat were offered during the main annual feasts, the period from the feast of Unleavened Bread to the feast of Weeks, which were celebrated with sacrifices and ceremonial meals at the local or regional sanctuary. The harvest of fruits and grapes was celebrated by families during the feast of Succoth. But even in this larger cultic framework the first fruit offerings were partly consumed within the family group (Deut 16:11). The firstborn offerings of animals, which applied to sheep, goats, and oxen (Exod 34:19), were sacrificed on the eighth day after birth (22:28–9) at the local sanctuary outside the festival season. Thus, all of this cultic activity concerning familial agriculture and breeding primarily aimed at the securing of blessing. Apart from that, during the feast of Unleavened Bread the families also commemorated the exodus (Exod 23:15; 34:18). Before the seventh century, that was the only occasion in the year that Israelite families were involved in the people's official history.

In addition to the practices already described above, families had to observe several taboos. It was not allowed to interbreed different kinds of beasts or to mingle different kinds of seed or to put on garments woven with different kinds of yarn (Lev 19:19). During the harvest, families were not to reap into the edges of their field (19:9) nor completely strip their vineyards or glean the fallen grapes (19:10). In cases when new fruit-bearing trees were planted, it was forbidden to use their fruit for a period of three years; not before the family had donated the fruits of the fourth year for a sacred use were they permitted to make use of them from the fifth year on (19:23–5). Every seventh day, the families had to keep a day of rest in order to let their domestic animals and their slaves refresh (Exod 23:12), and every seventh year they had to allow their fields to lie fallow (23:10–11). Behind all these rites stands the awareness that human beings should not be allowed to muddle the order of creation or exploit other creatures for their own benefit, but respect the needs of plants, animals, and poor people.

There were probably many other religious practices performed by the family that we do not know of. But compared with modern families in industrial societies, we can only wonder about the richness of rites and rituals which accompanied daily life and the agricultural production of ancient Israelite families. Admittedly, they did not live isolated from the religious and cultic sphere of their region and their state. They needed the local and regional sanctuaries for their ceremonial meals and offerings, and they enlisted the help of religious experts to manage their crises, but they independently and autonomously organized their religious life to a high degree without any major control.

Religious beliefs

Ancient Israelite families not only had their own religious practices, but also their own beliefs, which in spite of many correspondences differed considerably from those of contemporary official Israelite religion. A good survey of the symbolic world of Israelite family religion is provided by theophoric names. If one investigates all of the predicates of Israelite personal names mentioned in the Hebrew Bible or in seals and inscriptions, one will find many statements of thanksgiving or confession that one can find also in expressions of the official cult, e.g., that Yhwh has heard and seen the needy in their distress, taken pity on them, and rescued them. But one will likewise notice considerable differences: In all of these names there is scarcely a reference to any of the central beliefs of Israel's official religion, e.g., the exodus, the revelation at Sinai, the wanderings in the desert, or the occupation of the land; nor is there any hint of the official theology of national temples such as that of Shiloh, Jerusalem, and Bethel, or the theology of kingship.[76] That this is no chance result seems evident from the fact that the same lack of concern with the central issues of official religion appears in older wisdom materials, which are also concerned with the leading of everyday life. Thus, for families, as far as day-to-day life was concerned, the central issues of state religion were of minor importance.

Instead, issues such as pregnancy and childbirth are central, with names expressing beliefs about the process itself and Yhwh's role in it, e.g., the divine blessing, mercy, assistance, protection, help, rescue, and deliverance experienced by the mother and her whole family during the dramatic events surrounding pregnancy and birth.[77] But this kind of personal piety derived from theophoric personal names is not restricted to the situation of pregnancy and childbirth. One finds a considerable correspondence between the semantic field of the names and that of the individual psalms of lament and thanksgiving, including the oracles of salvation, which cover a much wider range of situations in which distress and relief might be relevant. More than fifty percent of all verbs and nouns used in personal names also occur in those psalm genres; and more than sixty percent of all verbs and nouns used in the petitions and confessions and thanksgivings of the individual psalms also turn up in the personal names.[78] Thus we can conclude, on the one hand, that the ritual psalm prayers, although they were composed by religious experts and are often late in their given form, were still heavily influenced by the piety of families. On the other hand, we can also conclude that the religious beliefs expressed in the names emerged from a wider religious experience within families treating distress and relief.

Moving to the individual psalms of lament, where the official traditions of Israelite religion are also lacking,[79] we recognize that family religion is strongly shaped by a close personal relationship of the individual with the divine. The god imagined here is a personal god, invoked as "my god"[80] or confessed as "my help," "my protection," "my trust," or "my hope".[81] This close relationship of personal trust can be shown to have been established by the divine creation of every individual:

> But you are he who drew me from the womb,
> who instilled confidence into me at my mother's breast.
> Upon you I was cast from the day of my birth;
> from my mother's womb you have been my god.[82]
>
> Ps 22:9–10

Since his god created him, everybody, since the date of his birth, stands in a close relationship of personal trust to his god as long as he lives. That means that the faith of the members of Israelite families did not depend upon Yhwh's founding and saving acts according to the official religion, be it Israel's deliverance from Egypt, or Jerusalem's election for Yhwh's dwelling, or the choice of the Davidic monarchy. Rather, it was based on natural grounds, not on history; it was unconditional, not dependent on ritual or ethical behavior; and it was generally indissoluble and indestructible during one's life, independent from human decision. It can be demonstrated that in all of these specific features, the symbolic world of family religion was constructed according to the personal relations of the family members themselves, especially the mutual relations between children and their parents, which are generally unconditional, indissoluble, and indestructible in a similar way. What is said about confidence, protection, and security in relation to the personal god corresponds to the ideal experiences of every infant with respect to his mother or his father.[83] Thus, the beliefs of family religion are heavily shaped by basic relations and experiences within the family group.

Turning to the theophoric elements in personal names, it becomes clear that Israelite families could choose gods other than Yhwh to be their family god. In Hebrew personal names taken from the Hebrew Bible, from seals, or inscriptions, several different kinds of theophoric element are mentioned:

- first, old nomadic (?) family gods such as Shadday and Ṣur;
- second, divinized designations of kinship such as *ʾab* "father", *ʾaḥ* "brother", *ʿam* "paternal uncle", and *ḥam* "father-in-law"; they are widespread in the

Semitic nomenclature from an early period; whether they denote the family god or refer to the ancestors, is disputed;[84]

- third, the Syrian Canaanite god El, who is attested by the Ugaritic texts of the second millennium BCE as the king and the father of gods, but functions in the first millennium not only in Israel, but also in southern Syria and Ammon, as personal guardian deity;[85]
- fourth, old Canaanite epithets for gods, or gods who arise from them, such as *melek* "king," *'adon* "lord," *ba'al* "lord," *gad* "fortune," or Canaanite gods such as Shalem, Mot, or Egyptian deities such as Horus, Isis and Bes;
- fifth, national gods such as Yhwh, the Phoenician Baal, or the Edomite Qaus;[86]
- the family god could be named "god of my/your/his father" (Gen 31:5, 29, 42; 49:25; 50:17), or "god of a certain forefather" (Gen 31:42, 53) in order to emphasize a longer lasting personal relationship to a certain god, who was inherited from the father.

Concerning the Hebrew names, we can observe a development from pluralism to conformity, and from polylatry to monolatry: For the early monarchic period, the Hebrew Bible attests to 61 different theophoric names, from which 32 percent contain a divinity identified as a relative, 19 percent El, 19 percent Yhwh, 6.5 percent Baal, and 3 percent old epithets as theophoric elements. In the late monarchic period these findings have changed considerably: From 57 different theophoric names, only 2 percent contain a divinity identified as a relative, 14 percent El, 5 percent old epithets, but 78 percent Yhwh. Also in the seals coming mostly from the eighth to the fifth centuries Yhwh names reach a total of 62 percent.[87] Thus, it took about three or four centuries until a majority of Israelite families accepted their national god Yhwh also as their family god. In any case, it was still possible in the late seventh century for the prophet Jeremiah to accuse Judeans of turning to foreign deities for their private needs, while calling Yhwh for help in case of national distress (Jer 2:27); even during the early sixth century the veneration of the Queen of Heaven seems to have been very popular among the Judean families, especially their female members (Jer 7:17f.; 44:15–23). Thus, in most of the pre-exilic period, Israelite families could venerate other deities instead of or besides Yhwh in their household cults. During this period, internal religious pluralism could have the wide range of a manifest polytheism.

A Brief Look Forward

For the further development of Israelite family religion, only a brief look forward can be given here. Until the seventh century, nobody seemed to have been worried about the fact that the beliefs and cultic practices of Israelite families differed widely from those of the state and temple religion. The polemic of Jeremiah in Jer 2:27 suggests that in the late seventh century, members of Judean families were still not aware of having done anything wrong when they trusted in gods other than

Yhwh for their private needs. It was probably only the foreign cultural and religious influences affecting family religion in Judah under the long Assyrian rule, much more than the Judean state religion (Molech cult, astral symbols, Queen of Heaven),[88] that made the differences obvious, differences which those who felt responsible for religious affairs were no longer prepared to tolerate. Beginning with Josiah's reform in 622 BCE, several efforts were made to link family religion more closely to Israel's official religion. All family sacrifices traditionally offered at the local shrines had to be taken to the temple of Jerusalem, where they could be better controlled (Deut 12:12–18). The Passover ritual was withdrawn from the family cult; it became a pilgrimage feast celebrated in the central sanctuary and focused on the historical event of the exodus (16:1–8). During every offering of the first fruits, the father had to recite Israel's official salvation history (26:1–12). The worship of any other god than Yhwh was strictly forbidden (6:4). Family members were even told to report and kill their relatives who worshiped other gods (13:7–12).[89] On the one hand, the national religion was provided with the personal intimacy of family religion (6:5); on the other hand, new household rites were invented to implant the beliefs of the official religion into the everyday life of all families (6:6–9, 20–5).[90]

Prepared by the Josianic reform, Judean families were able to become the main tradents of Israelite religion during the Babylonian exile, after the official institutions, the Jerusalem temple and the Davidic kingdom, had collapsed in 587 BCE. New or reformed family rites and customs such as circumcision, observance of the Sabbath, and dietary rules now became clearly defined signs of religious identity, which enabled Judaism to survive the crisis.[91] After the exile, due to the failure of state restoration and the lasting Diaspora communities, official and familial religion came closer together with the result that early Judaism looked like a religion in which families constituted, apart from the temple and the Torah, one of the load-bearing pillars.

Notes

1 Rainer Albertz, *Persönliche Frömmigkeit und offizielle Religion* (Stuttgart: Calwer Verlag, 1978).

2 See Otto Eißfeldt, "'Mein Gott' im Alten Testament," *Zeitschrift für die alttestamentliche Wissenschaft* 61 (1945–8): 3–16; Hermann Vorländer, *Mein Gott* (Neukirchen-Vluyn: Neukirchener Verlag, 1975).

3 Karel van der Toorn, *Family Religion in Babylonia, Syria, and Israel* (Leiden: Brill, 1996), pp. 181–372; the part concerning ancient Israel is titled "From Family Religion to Personal Devotion" and deals with family religion of the Northern State during the pre-exilic period. The same author has now offered an interesting scenario of family and local religion of a presumed Israelite Iron I village: idem, "Nine Months Among the Peasants in the Palestinian Highlands," in *Symbiosis, Symbolism, and the Powers of the Past*, ed. William G. Dever and Seymour Gitin (Winona Lake: Eisenbrauns, 2003), pp. 393–423.

4 Albertz, *A History of Israelite Religion in the Old Testament Period*, 2 vols. (Louisville: Westminster, 1994), 1:23–39, 94–103, 177–80, 186–95, 2:399–411, 507–22, 556–63; see also the overview in idem, "Religious Practices of the Individual and Family," in *Religions of the Ancient World: A Guide*, ed. Sarah I. Johnston (Cambridge: Belknap Press, 2004), pp. 429–30.

5 Erhard S. Gerstenberger, *Theologien im Alten Testament* (Stuttgart: Kohlhammer 2001), pp. 26–77. That he labels Israelite family religion sometimes as *Familientheologie* seems a little bit problematic to me, since it lacks nearly all theological reflection for most of the pre-exilic period.

6 See Joseph Blenkinsopp, "The Family in First Temple Israel," in *Families in Ancient Israel*, ed. Leo G. Perdue (Louisville: Westminster, 1997), pp. 48–103; Leo G. Perdue, "The Israelite and Early Jewish Family," ibid., pp. 163–222.

7 Johnston, *Religions of the Ancient World*, pp. 423–37.

8 For the following, see Albertz, "Wieviel Pluralismus kann sich eine Religion leisten?" in *Pluralismus und Identität*, ed. Joachim Mehlhausen (Gütersloh: Bertelsmann, 1995), pp. 193–200.

9 Helmer Ringgren, *Israelitische Religion* (Stuttgart: Kohlhammer, 1982), pp. 50–1.

10 See the several examples which I discuss in *A History of Israelite Religion*, 1: 172–3; 210–11.

11 Ibid., 1: 114–38.

12 Gitin, "Israelite and Philistine Cult and the Archaeological Record in Iron Age II," in *Symbiosis, Symbolism, and the Powers of the Past*, pp. 289–91.

13 Ibid., p. 289.

14 See, among many others, Eduard Meyer, *Der Papyrusfund von Elephantine* (Leipzig: J. C. Hinrich'sche Buchhandlung, 1912), pp. 38–67; Anton Jirku, *Materialien zur Volksreligion Israels* (Leipzig: Deichert'sche Verlagsbuchhandlung, 1914); Vorländer, *Mein Gott*; Martin Rose, *Der Ausschließlichkeitsanspruch Jahwes* (Stuttgart: Kohlhammer, 1975); Judah B. Segal, "Popular Religion in Ancient Israel," *Journal of Semitic Studies* 27 (1976): 1–22; Othmar Keel and Christroph Uehlinger, *Göttinnen, Götter und Gottessymbole*, 4th edn. (Freiburg: Herder 1999); Wolfgang Zwickel, "Religionsgeschichte Israels," in *Religionsgeschichte Israels*, ed. Bernd Janowski and Matthias Köckert (Gütersloh: Bertelsmann 1999), pp. 9–56.

15 See Michael N. Ebertz and Frank Schultheis (eds.), *Volksfrömmigkeit in Europa* (München: Kaiser, 1986), pp. 11–52; Pieter H. Vrijhof and Jacques Waardenburg (eds.), *Official and Popular Religion* (The Hague: Mouton, 1979), pp. 1–6, 668–704.

16 See Ebertz and Schultheis, *Volksfrömmigkeit in Europa*, p. 25. They define "Volksfrömmigkeit" as follows: "Unter 'popularer Religiosität' sind spezifische Konfigurationen religiöser Vorstellung und Praktiken zu verstehen, die sich infolge einer Monopolisierung der Definition von und der Verfügbarkeit über die 'Heilsgüter' bzw. das 'religiöse Kapital' bei den von der Definition von und der Verfügbarkeit über diese Heilsgüter Ausgeschlossenen herausbilden."

17 Cf. the similar criticism of Ziony Zevit, *The Religions of Ancient Israel* (London: Continuum, 2001), pp. 662–3.

18 So Vorländer, *Mein Gott*, p. 63.

19 Segal, "Popular Religion in Ancient Israel," p. 22.

20 Rose, *Der Ausschließlichkeitsanspruch Jahwes*, pp. 213–51. Likewise Susan Ackerman, *Under Every Green Tree* (Atlanta: Scholars Press, 1992), regards "popular religion" as those practices which were criticized by the prophets, e.g., the veneration of the Queen

of Heaven (Jeremiah 7; 44), the wailing for Tammuz (Ezekiel 8), or the Moloch cult (Isaiah 57). William G. Dever, *What Did the Biblical Writers Know and When Did They Know It?* (Grand Rapids: B. Eerdmans, 2001), p. 196, defines "popular religion" only in a negative way; according to him it "is an alternate, nonorthodox, nonconformist mode of religious expression. It is largely noncentralized, noninstitutional, lying outside state priests or state sponsorship."

21 Jacques Berlinerblau, "The 'Popular Religion' Paradigm in Old Testament Research," *Journal for the Study of the Old Testament* 60 (1993): 18. Cf. my similar older criticism of the "popular religion" paradigm in Albertz, *Persönliche Frömmigkeit und offizielle Religion*, pp. 14–18. Berlinerblau stresses the biased view of the elite literati in texts of the Hebrew Bible and therefore considers "popular religious groups" to be a mere construction of the biblical literati (ibid., pp. 12–15, 18), but I think we can evaluate the historical reality behind the polemics. Berlinerblau still thinks that the term "popular religion" can be used "as a sort of conceptual umbrella under which the investigation of women, heterodox elements, the non-privileged classes . . . among others, would serve as the . . . primary objects of scholarly scrutiny" (p. 19). But even then it would confuse very different realities: the religiosity of women plays an important role in family religion and has little to do with heterodoxy and under-classes.

22 Albertz, *Persönliche Frömmigkeit und offizielle Religion*, pp. 2–3; 11–13; idem, *A History of Israelite Religion*, 1: 18–21; idem, "Wieviel Pluralismus kann sich eine Religion leisten?," pp. 197–200.

23 This third level I have borrowed from Bernhard Lang, "Persönlicher Gott und Ortsgott," in *Fontes atque Pontes*, ed. Manfred Görg (Wiesbaden: Harrassowitz, 1983), pp. 271–301, and Manfred Weippert, "Synkretismus und Monotheismus," in idem, *Jahwe und die anderen Götter*, (Tübingen: Mohr Siebeck, 1997), pp. 11–19, but I have not developed it in detail.

24 Günter Lanczkowski, *Begegnung und Wandel der Religionen* (Darmstadt: Wissenschaftliche Buchgesellschaft, 1981), pp. 50–5.

25 Lawrence E. Stager, "The Archaeology of the Family in Ancient Israel," *Bulletin of the American Schools of Oriental Research* 260 (1985): 17–18, has convincingly shown that the so called "four-room-house" generally has to be seen as the dwelling of a nuclear family (6–8 persons). In any case, as the compounds of several houses demonstrate, often extended families of different sizes (10–30 persons) could dwell and work together (ibid., pp. 18–23). Thus, the *bet 'ab* can consist of a single house or a compound of houses and includes the nuclear and the extended family.

26 See for more details Albertz, *A History of Israelite Religion*, 2: 511–17.

27 See for more details, ibid., 2: 518–22.

28 See for more details, ibid., 2: 556–63.

29 See the blessings formulated on the pithoi from Kuntillet Ajrud and in the burial inscription from Khirbet el-Qom (Johannes Renz and Wolfgang Röllig, *Handbuch der Althebräischen Epigraphik*, 3 vols. [Darmstadt: Wissenschaftliche Buchgesellschaft, 1995], I/1: pp. 59–64, 202–11); greetings, wishes, and oaths in several letters on ostraca from Arad and Lachish (ibid., pp. 145–8; 379–430); apotropaic blessings, strongly influenced by Jerusalem theology, on two silver amulets from Ketef Hinnom (ibid., pp. 447–56); a possible incantation from Horvat Uzza (Itzaq Beit-Arieh, "A literary Ostracon from Horvat 'Uza," *Tel Aviv* 20 [1993]: pp. 55–65); and a vow on an Ammonite seal (Jacques Berlinerblau, "The Israelite Vow," *Biblica* 72 [1991]: 551–2).

30 This methodological assessment is explicitly shared by Hans Rechenmacher, *Personennamen als theologische Aussagen* (St. Ottilien: Eos, 1997), pp. 3–4, and by most of the contributors of Michael P. Streck and Stefan Weninger (eds.), *Altorientalische und semitische Onomastik* (Münster: Ugarit Verlag, 2002), in some way.

31 For example Wolfgang Zwickel, *Der Tempelkult in Kanaan und Israel* (Tübingen: Mohr Siebeck, 1994), p. 9, excluded the "Privatkult" explicitly, without referring to any religious-historical model of internal pluralism.

32 See, for example, the endless discussions on Megiddo locus 2081 and the "cultic structure" of Taanach, both of which were interpreted as temples. The first biblical archaeologist, as far as I see, who explicitly faced the problem of cultic artifacts in a secular context, was Ora Negbi, "Israelite Cult Elements in Secular Contexts of 10th Century BCE" in *Biblical Archaeology Today 1990*, ed. Avraham Biran and Joseph Aviram (Jerusalem: Israel Exploration Society, 1993), pp. 221–30.

33 See above p. 90.

34 After referring to my book *Persönliche Frömmigkeit*, Wolfgang Zwickel, *Räucherkult und Räuchergeräte* (Fribourg: Universitätsverlag, 1990), 38 n. 137, stated: "Eine archäologische Aufarbeitung des Themas steht bislang leider aus." Unfortunately his statement is still true.

35 Holladay, "Religion in Israel and Judah under the Monarchy," in *Ancient Israelite Religion*, ed. Patrick D. Miller Jr, Paul D. Hanson, and S. Dean McBride (Philadelphia: Fortress Press, 1987), 270–1, understood it to be a cult place, as did Zevit, *The Religions of Ancient Israel*, pp. 206–10. But cf. Dever's suggestions, see below, p. 112 n. 89.

36 See Holladay, ibid., pp. 268–81.

37 *The Religions of Ancient Israel*, pp. 123–4.

38 To this group, he attributes Kuntillet 'Ajrud, Arad, Dan, Hazor, Jerusalem, Lachish (room 49), and Megiddo (room 340).

39 E.g., Ai, Bet Lei, "Bull Site", Ebal, Jerusalem (cave), Megiddo (locus 2081), and the cave of Tel 'Eton. See ibid., p. 654.

40 In his conclusions (ibid., pp. 265–6). Zevit describes the cult places he discusses as "an extremely heterogeneous collection." Concluding that the cult places "indicate that the religion was practiced differently in home, village, sanctuary, urban temple, and extra-urban sanctuary," Zevit came close to my model of internal religious pluralism, but he fails to integrate his primary local division of cult places into a sociological concept.

41 "Religion of Israel and Judah under the Monarchy," pp. 275–82. Unfortunately, Holladay did not go into details. His study "Archaeology and the Religion of Israel" announced in note 106 seems not to be published thus far.

42 See Zevit, *The Religions of Ancient Israel*, pp. 172, 175–6 (see esp. note 91), 241, 652.

43 See ibid., pp. 132, 138–9. One can add also two chalices; one was found in the domestic zone (next to one of the altars), the other in the industrial zone. See Gitin, "Seventh Century BCE: Cultic Elements at Ekron," in *Biblical Archaeology Today 1990*, pp. 253–4. Meanwhile forty-five of those limestone altars have been found, twenty-two of them in Israel and Judah. See Gitin, "The Four-Horned Altar and Sacred Space," in *Sacred Time, Sacred Place*, ed. Barry M. Gittlen (Winona Lake: Eisenbrauns, 2002), p. 109. Because this type of altar is also used in temples (e.g., Arad, Ekron), it constitutes no clear reference to family religion.

44 See above, p. 90.

45 See Paul F. Jacobs and Oded Borowski, "Tell Halif 1992," *Israel Exploration Journal* 43 (1993): 66–7.

46 See similarly Zevit, *The Religions of Ancient Israel*, pp. 235–7. The pottery found in the cistern nearby shows close parallels to that of domestic cults at Megiddo, locus 2081 and building 10. For discussion, see Walter E. Rast, *Taanach I* (Cambridge: American Schools of Oriental Research, 1978), pp. 27–35. Zwickel, *Der Tempelkult in Kanaan und Israel*, p. 244, attributes the finds to the area of personal piety.
47 See the final report in Paulette M. Michèle Daviau, *Excavations at Tall Jawa*, 2 vols. (Leiden: Brill 2002–3).
48 Daviau, "Family Religion, " in *The World of the Aramaeans*, 2 vols., ed. eadem, John W. Wevers, and Michael Weigl (Sheffield: Sheffield Academic Press, 2001), 2: p. 203.
49 Ibid., 201, and 2 Kings 23:12; Jer 19:13; 32:29; 48:38; Zeph 1:5.
50 That the censer cups can be attributed to the "Privatkult" was already seen by Zwickel, *Räucherkult und Räuchergeräte*, p. 38; the same is true for the later censer boxes (ibid., p. 88).
51 See Daviau, "Family Religion," pp. 222–3. The assemblage of room 303 of house 300 can be seen in eadem, "The Fifth Season of Excavation at Tall Jawa (1994)," *Annual of the Department of Antiquities of Jordan* 40 (1996): 88.
52 See ibid., pp. 216–17, 221 and 223–4.
53 Similar heads of male figurines are found in Amman Citadel, Tell el 'Umeiri, Tell el-Jalul, and Bethsaida. See Christoph Uehlinger, "Anthropomorphic Cult Statuary in Iron Age Palestine and the Search for Yahweh's Cult Images," in *The Image and the Book*, ed. Karel van der Toorn (Leuven: Peeters, 1997), p. 121; they seem to represent the Ammonite God Milkom/El.
54 For example, Zevit, *The Religions of Ancient Israel*, pp. 271–3; Dever, "Women's Popular Religion," *Biblical Archaeology Review* 17 (1991): 64–5; Dever mingles the concept of popular religion with the concept of internal religious pluralism. His conclusion that the household rites were performed mainly by women is misleading. See the more balanced view of Carol L. Meyers, "From Household to the House of Yahweh," in *Congress Volume Basel 2001*, ed. André Lemaire (Leiden: Brill, 2002), pp. 277–303.
55 Van der Toorn, "Israelite Figurines," in *Sacred Time, Sacred Place*, p. 61.
56 See lines 2–3: "Blessed was Uriyahu by Yhwh; and from his enemies through his Asherah he has rescued him" (Renz and Röllig, *Handbuch der Althebräischen Epigraphik* I/1: 208–10). See already Asherah's interceding role in Ugarit (*KTU* 1.4 IV–V, 1–97 [Manfried Dietrich, Oswald Loretz, and Joaquin SanMartin, (eds.), *Die keilalphabetischen Texte aus Ugarit* (Kevalaer: Butzon & Bercker; Neukirchen-Vluyn: Neukirchener, 1976)]).
57 See van der Toorn, *Family Religion in Babylonia, Syria, and Israel*, p. 254, referring to the "Bull Site" as being a suitable cult place for such a clan religion. But since this open-air cult complex seems to have served as a sanctuary for five villages in the neighborhood, this classification is highly questionable. The location of domestic cult niches on the upper floor of the private houses in Tell Jawa suggests strongly their use by households rather than larger social bodies such as clans.
58 The assemblage of a shrine model, three tripod cups, an animal rhyton, and two painted miniature vessels, which are said to have been found in the vicinity of Mount Nebo, are probably the remains of a Moabite domestic shrine. See Saul S. Weinberg, "A Moabite Shrine Group," *Muse* 12 (1978): 30–48. Since they were obtained in the antiquities trade, their origin remains unclear.
59 For example, see three additional pieces of evidence that are recorded in James B. Pritchard, *Tell es-Sa'idiyeh* (Philadelphia: University of Pennsylvania, 1985), pp. 9–10,

21–2, 25–6, from a site in the middle Jordan valley (ninth and eighth century BCE): house 64 (stratum VII), house 9, and house 16 (stratum V). Since there is a similarity to the pottery in Samaria and Tirzah, it can be taken as an Israelite settlement, although the identification of the site (Zaphon?) is still uncertain.

60 Raz Kletter, *The Judean Pillar-Figurines and the Archaeology of Asherah* (Oxford: Hadrian Books, 1996), p. 105.

61 Zwickel, "Religionsgeschichte Israels," p. 27 note 54, questions this assessment and refers to changes in the equipment of the domestic cult such as the introduction of censer cups in Palestine after the late eleventh century BCE, or the distribution of pillar figurines after the eighth century. But one must be careful not to conclude too quickly that changes among artifacts reflect changes in ritual practices, since artifacts of the domestic cult are often substituted by another type of artifact without a change in function (e.g., censer cups, incense altars, incense boxes or plaque figurines, pillar figurines).

62 See Joachim Bretschneider, *Architekturmodelle in Vorderasien* (Neukirchen-Vluyn: Neukirchener Verlag, 1991), pp. 101–43, 162–6. Model shrines were used in both the official and the domestic cults (p. 169). See Uehlinger, "Anthropomorphic Cult Statuary and the Search for Yahweh's Cult Image," pp. 106–8, 114–15.

63 "Family Cult," p. 221.

64 Ibid., p. 223.

65 See Erhard S. Gerstenberger, *Der bittende Mensch* (Neukirchen-Vluyn: Neukirchener Verlag, 1980), pp. 147–60; idem, *Theologien im Alten Testament*, pp. 40–1.

66 Daviau, "Family Religion," pp. 217–18.

67 See Keel and Uehlinger, *Göttinnen, Götter und Gottessymbole*, numbers 320, 321, 323–8; Uehlinger, "Anthropomorphic Cult Statuary," numbers 12–14, 26–7, 32–41 and pp. 109–10, 119.

68 Van der Toorn, *Family Religion in Babylonia, Syria, and Israel*, pp. 206–35, has convinced me that the ancestor cult played a more important role in Israelite family religion than I had acknowledged earlier (Albertz, *A History of Israelite Religion in the Old Testament Period*, 1: 37–9). That we should distinguish between a daily, monthly and yearly type of ancestor veneration is what I took from his investigations of the ancestor cult in Mesopotamia (ibid., pp. 42–65).

69 See the "Bull Site" in the Samarian hill country, Tumulus 5 west of Jerusalem, or the Edomite cult complex in Horvat Qitmit. Whereas the "Bull Site" and Tumulus 5 only consist of a temenos wall around the burning place, the latter also has adjoining buildings for the cultic equipment and the sacrificial meals. See further Zevit, *The Religions of Ancient Israel*, pp. 142–9, 176–80, 303–5.

70 See Berlinerblau, *The Vow and "Popular Religious Groups" of Ancient Israel* (Sheffield: Sheffield Academic Press, 1996); Hubert Tita, *Gelübde als Bekenntnis* (Fribourg: Universitätsverlag, 2001).

71 *Family Religion in Babylonia, Syria, and Israel*, pp. 50–2, 211–14.

72 So the old hypothesis of Leonard Rost, "Weidewechsel und alttestamentlicher Festkalender," in idem, *Das Kleine Credo und andere Studien zum Alten Testament* (Heidelberg: Quelle und Meyer, 1965), pp. 101–12.

73 See Christian Herrmann, *Ägyptische Amulette aus Palästina/Israel* (Fribourg: Universitätsverlag, 1994). He counted 232 amulets from Iron Age I, 525 from Iron Age II.

74 Ibid., pp. 417–22; and Renz and Röllig, *Handbuch der Althebräischen Epigraphik* I/1: 447–56.

75 See Beit-Arieh, "A Literary Ostracon from Horvat 'Uza,"; Meindert Dijkstra, "Woman and Religion in the Old Testament" in *Only One God?*, ed. Bob Becking, Meindert Dijkstra, Marjo C. A. Korpel, and Karel J. H. Vriezen. (Sheffield: Continuum, 2001), pp. 168–9.

76 See Albertz, *Persönliche Frömmigkeit und offizielle Religion*, pp. 56–8. There are only a few exceptions such as the post-exilic name Shekanyah "Yhwh hast taken up (his) dwelling" (Neh 3:9; 6:18; Esr 8:2, 5), which probably refers to the reconstruction of the temple of Jerusalem (515 BCE), or the symbolic name Ikabod, "Where is the glory?," given to Eli's son after the ark was lost (1 Sam 4:21). The name Elyashib, "Yhwh has brought back", which Martin Noth, *Die israelitischen Personennamen im Rahmen der gemeinsemitischen Namengebung* (Stuttgart: Kohlhammer, 1928), p. 213, applied to the return from exile, is to be understood as a name of compensation: "Yhwh has brought back (the dead son)." On this, see Johannes J. Stamm, "Hebräische Ersatznamen," in *Studies in Honor of Benno Landsberger on His Seventy-Fifth Birthday, April 1965*, Assyriological Studies 16 (Chicago: University of Chicago Press, 1965), pp. 416, 423; this accords with the fact that the name is now likewise found on Arad ostraca written before the exile (Renz and Röllig, *Handbuch der Althebräischen Epigraphik* I/1: 362 passim).

77 Albertz, *Persönliche Frömmigkeit und offizielle Religion*, pp. 49–50; cf. pp. 61–71.

78 Ibid., p. 61ff. In my investigation I dealt mainly with the names mentioned in the Bible, but the result would not change considerably if one were to include all of the recent epigraphic evidence.

79 The only possible exceptions are Ps 22:4–6; 77:14–21; 143:5; they can be explained by a later revision (cf. Ps 22:24–7) or later developments. On this, see Albertz, *Persönliche Frömmigkeit und offizielle Religion*, pp. 30–2, 178–201.

80 The epithet "my god" (*'eli, 'elohay*) appears 29 times in the 39 individual laments (e.g., Ps 22:2, 11; 3:8; 5:3; 7:2, 4), and 19 times in individual thanksgivings, psalms of confidence and related texts (e.g., Ps 18:3; 30:13; 91:2). Including related expressions such as "my savior god", we have 59 pieces of evidence in the individual prayers. On this, see also Vorländer, *Mein Gott*.

81 See Ps 18:3; 27:1; 31:4; 38:16; 40:18; 54:6; 59:17f.; 62:3, 7; 71:5–7; 94:22; 140:8, etc.

82 See Ps 119:73; 138:8; Job 10:3, 8–13; 35:10; cf. Ps 139:13; Jer 2:27; Jes 64:7 and the corresponding oracles of salvation. See Isa 43:1; 44:2, 21, 24; 49:5; 54:5; cf. Job 14:15 and Albertz, *Weltschöpfung und Menschenschöpfung* (Stuttgart: Calwer Verlag, 1974), pp. 7–51; see also the personal names, which contain six different verbs of creation (e.g., Bera'iah, Asa'el, Elkanah, Benaiah, Jehoiachin, Yeser; ibid., p. 156).

83 See the Verb *hsh* "to seek shelter" in the confessions of confidence (Ps 7:2; 11; 25:20; 31:2 etc.), which is clearly taken from childhood experience, and the reflection in Ps 27:10 (Albertz, *Persönliche Frömmigkeit und offizielle Religion*, p. 94).

84 Van der Toorn, "Ancestors and Anthroponyms," *Zeitschrift für die alttestamentliche Wissenschaft* p. 108 (1996), pp. 1–11, argues strongly for ancestors.

85 See especially Ingo Kottsieper, "El – ferner oder naher Gott?," in *Religion und Gesellschaft*, ed. Rainer Albertz (Münster: Ugaritverlag, 1997), pp. 27–41, who refers not only to the personal names in southern Syria and Ammon, but also to the Ahikar proverbs.

86 See Albertz, *A History of Israelite Religion*, 1: 97–8.

87 The high degree of names containing Yhwh as theophoric element in the seals proves according to Jeffry H. Tigay, "Israelite Religion" in *Ancient Israelite Religion*, ed.

Patrick D. Miller Jr, Paul D. Hanson, and S. Dean Bride (Philadelphia: Fortress Press, 1987), p. 177, an "overwhelmingly Yahwistic society in the heartland of the Israelite settlement." But this is an apologetic conclusion that is unconvincing because it is based on only a limited data set (names). An apologetic tendency can be also noticed in the study of Jeaneane D. Fowler, *Theophoric Personal Names in Ancient Hebrew* (Sheffield: Sheffield Academic Press, 1988). Presupposing the monotheistic shape of ancient Israelite religion, she ignores the internal plurality and overstates the differences between old Hebrew names and other Semitic onomastica.

88 For more details, see Albertz, *A History of Israelite Religion*, 1: 186–95, and Keel and Uehlinger, *Göttinnen, Götter und Gottessymbole*, pp. 322–69.

89 Dever, "Women's Popular Religion," p. 64, has reasonably guessed that the hoard of broken cult figurines found in Cave 1 of Jerusalem should be taken as evidence for Josiah's reform.

90 For more details, see Albertz, *A History of Israelite Religion*, 1: 210–16.

91 For more details, see ibid., 2: 399–411.

7

Family Religion in Israel and the Wider Levant of the First Millennium BCE

Saul M. Olyan

Family religion is becoming a topic of growing interest in biblical studies and cognate fields, and recent monographs, articles, reference works, and symposia attest to its popularity as an area of research.[1] The term, used with increasing frequency in scholarship, competes with other contemporary scholarly terms such as popular religion, domestic cult, household religion, and individual piety to describe a constellation of religious practices not primarily associated with the sanctuaries and ideologies of official cult. Often, family religion is contrasted with official religion. Yet much about first-millennium Israelite and Levantine family religion remains to be elucidated. The family unit in question must be delineated clearly, and the full range of loci where family religion was practiced must be identified. The nature of the relationship of family religion to the official cult demands clarification, and the role played by non-family members in family religion warrants examination. Finally, a preference for the term "family religion" over competing terms such as "popular religion" or "individual piety" requires justification. This chapter represents an initial attempt to theorize some aspects of first-millennium family religion in Israel, with attention to its wider Levantine context. Drawing upon archaeological evidence as well as texts, I shall assess the understandings of family religion current in the field, at the same time developing my own perspectives. I shall engage primarily the work of Rainer Albertz and Karel van der Toorn, the two leading specialists in first-millennium Levantine family religion.

Albertz, who contrasted "personal piety" with "official religion" in his pioneering 1978 monograph *Persönliche Frömmigkeit und offizielle Religion*, now prefers to speak of two or three "levels" of Israelite religion: "family religion" or "the personal piety related to the family"; the official religion of the people Israel; and in between, possibly the local religion of town or village.[2] These "differ from one another," he states, "in respect to their target group, to their supporters, their religious ideas and practices, their functions, and their degree of institutionalization."[3] For Albertz, family religion's focus was the immediate needs of family members and the survival of the family as a unit; the official cult, in contrast, was normative in its claims, concerning itself with dynastic and national interests, and focusing on the people as a whole; little is said by Albertz about the local religion of village and town, and how it might be distinct from both family religion and the official cult.[4] Albertz defines the "family" as the household (*bet 'ab* in Hebrew, "the house of the father"), best understood in my view as an extended or joint family living together in a single domicile under a male head that might take the form of a nuclear family much of the time, as J. David Schloen has recently suggested.[5] Family religion is therefore the religious activity of the household, which takes place primarily in the domicile but, at times, also in the local sanctuary (e.g., for sacrifices). In contrast, Karel van der Toorn has emphasized the importance of the clan/village as the focus of family religion rather than the individual household.[6] Where Albertz accents the domicile as the primary locus of family devotion to patron deity and ancestors – two central components of family religion – while also acknowledging a role for the local shrine, van der Toorn suggests that it is the local shrine that is central, rather than the domicile, both for the worship of the patron god and for devotion to deified ancestors.[7]

Was the single household rather than the clan the social unit at the center of first-millennium Levantine family religion, as Albertz claims, and as he believes the recent evidence from Tell Jawa in Jordan indicates?[8] Or was the clan the primary social unit of interest, as van der Toorn has argued? Moreover, was the primary locus for family religion the domicile (Albertz) or the local sanctuary (van der Toorn)? Certainly the Ammonite cultic assemblages found in individual Tell Jawa houses, along with those previously identified at sites such as Beersheba and Tell Halif in Judah and Tell el-Far'ah North (Tirzah) in Israel, suggest that the household/domicile cannot be ignored or devalued as social context/locus, in explorations of first-millennium Israelite/Judean/Ammonite family religion, for evidently rites could occur in individual domiciles, presumably conducted by members of the household for their own benefit.[9] Thus, it seems fair to speak of a domestic cult of sorts involving the household, though how widespread it was remains unclear; certainly it was only one aspect of family religion, which in Israel/Judah also manifested itself at local sanctuaries at various times in the year, including the "annual sacrifice" or "sacrifice of the clan" (e.g., 1 Sam 20:6, 29).[10] This yearly observance which van der Toorn has argued is a clan-based ancestor feast on the basis of Mesopotamian analogies – an argument now accepted by Albertz – raises the issue of a clan-oriented dimension to Israelite and Judean family religion.[11] It seems that family religion in Israel/Judah, as evidenced in extant archaeological and textual sources, could have both a domestic and sanctuary locus, and could involve either the household alone or the household in direct interaction with the rest of the clan of which it was a part.

Another way of stating my point: Albertz is correct to draw our attention to the household and domicile, while van der Toorn is equally correct not to allow us to neglect the clan and local sanctuary. Neither, however, acknowledges sufficiently the evident importance of both social groups and both loci as components of family religion in Israel/Judah. A third and, I believe, equally important locus for the practice of family religion, and one that I wish to bring into relief, was the family tomb, located on patrimonial property, or, for urban dwellers, on the outskirts of town.[12] Burial rites had the tomb as their focus; this was also probably true of at least some aspects of the ancestor cult. (I shall have more to say about both ahead.) Given the extant evidence, it is unclear whether burial and ancestral cultic rites at the tomb involved the household alone or a larger social unit such as the clan. It is possible that this varied through time and space, given that some tombs were probably shared by a number of related households, while others apparently were not, and given that textual representations of burial rites sometimes include the participation of family members beyond the household, and sometimes they do not (e.g., Judg 16:31 describes the burial of Samson by "his brothers and all the house of his father"; 2 Sam 2:32 suggests that Asahel was buried by his brothers, David, and others).[13]

In addition to the tomb as a locus of family religion, I would also suggest that we consider the regional sanctuary. Van der Toorn and Albertz speak of local sanctuaries as loci for the practice of family religion, yet a number of texts describe or allude to pilgrimages of the household (or a portion of it) to non-local sanctuaries having a regional and even a national significance, some of which enjoyed state sponsorship (e.g., 1 Sam 1:3; 1 Kgs 12:26–30; Hos 4:15; Amos 4:4–5; 5:4–5; 8:14).[14] Excavations also suggest the presence of regional sanctuaries in various periods, and some examples from Iron II probably reflect the involvement of the state.[15] When we speak of the range of loci of family rites, we ought to include not only the local sanctuary, but the regional sanctuary as well.

Thus, from my perspective, "family religion" is a useful descriptive and analytical term for the study of first-millennium Israelite cult. It encompasses the religious practices of distinct, interrelated social units (household *and* clan) in a number of different loci (domicile, local and regional sanctuary, family tomb). In terms of its ability to describe evidenced phenomena, it is superior to competing terms such as "domestic cult" or "household religion," due to the ambiguity of the English word "family," which can point both to household and to clan, and due to the fact that use of the term "family religion" does not restrict us to a single locus, as does a term such as "domestic cult." "Household religion" strikes me as a less attractive term, since it does not communicate the larger, clan dimension of first-millennium Israelite family religion. "Individual piety," as others have noted, is a rather unhelpful term in an ancient context in which "individuals were first and foremost members of a group, the principal one being the family."[16] As for another competing term, "popular religion," I agree with Albertz that it is ill-defined and used inconsistently by scholars in the field, and that it is "more confusing than clarifying."[17] This is due to the fact that it communicates nothing about any specific social group or cultic locus. (I might also add parenthetically that the term "popular religion" has an unfortunate history of pejorative use in the biblical field.[18]) Our choice of terminology must ultimately be determined by the evidenced phenomenon we wish to describe and analyze, and the effectiveness of our chosen term in describing and analyzing it. Given this desideratum, the term "family religion" is far preferable to its competitors when discussing family-centered cult in Israel and the wider Levant of the first millennium.

What was the nature of the relationship of family religion to the official cult? The issue of continuity or discontinuity with the practices and ideologies of the official cult has divided specialists. Albertz has treated the issue in some depth, emphasizing the discontinuities that he believes existed between family religion and the official cult in Israel and Judah, particularly for the period before the establishment of Deuteronomistic cultic reforms in the late seventh century BCE, a move that he views as – at least in part – an attempt to bring family religion into the orbit of official religion. Eventually, after Jerusalem's destruction and the exile of much of Judah's elite to Babylon, elements of the official cult were incorporated into family piety, but the pre-exilic norm for Albertz is, for all intents and purposes, mainly discontinuity between family and official religion.[19] In contrast, van der Toorn has emphasized continuity between family religion and the official cult, arguing recently that family religion "functions within, and presupposes, the wider context of the official religion. Also, its practices . . . are informed by notions and ideas adopted from the doctrines of the reigning religion."[20] Although van der Toorn is convinced that most manifestations of family religion are to be found in local sanctuaries rather than individual houses, I believe his argument for continuity finds support nonetheless in extant evidence of first-millennium family religion as practiced in the domicile.[21]

Albertz has made several strong points in favor of discontinuity. Certainly he is correct to highlight what might well have been the foci of family religion as it was practiced domestically, e.g., concerns such as fertility, successful childbirth and weaning, and cure of illness, not at all issues central to the official cult.[22] It is also the case that slaughter of sacrificial animals and attendant rites such as the burning of fat and organ meat and the manipulation of blood are nowhere evidenced materially for the domestic expression of first-millennium Levantine family religion, much in contrast to the rites of sanctuaries, where they were central.[23] And Albertz's argument that families "independently and autonomously organized their religious life to a high degree without any major control" from religious authorities appears to be sound, at least for family rites that occurred away from the sanctuary.[24] Yet extant evidence suggests that Albertz has overemphasized discontinuity with the official cult in his reconstruction. Domestic cultic assemblages not infrequently include one or more model shrines, the presence of which suggests some kind of sanctuary orientation even for domestic religious ritual, as Ziony Zevit has noted.[25] Why else would one have a model of a sanctuary in the home if not to recall the modeled sanctuary during domestic cultic rites? The same observation may be made about other cultic miniatures such as cooking pots, lamps, or incense altars, which appear to model the full-sized examples characteristic of sanctuaries.[26] Model shrines and other cultic miniatures have been found in sanctuaries, underscoring an apparent continuity between family religious practices in the domicile and sanctuary cult.[27] Which particular sanctuary or sanctuary-type a model shrine is intended to represent remains, however, unclear.[28] Albertz notes the existence of model shrines in domestic cultic assemblages in passing, without exploring the implications of their presence for his thesis of general discontinuity.[29] If anything, the presence of model shrines and cultic miniatures in domestic cultic assemblages signals a significant degree of continuity with sanctuary practice and ideology. And aside from modeling, rites such as the offering of libations and incense and the kindling of lamps likely occurred in domestic cultic contexts, just as they did in sanctuaries.[30]

The big question, of course, is to what extent the modeled sanctuaries and their rites represent official cult. The degree to which official ideologies would have spread to local sanctuaries is unclear, though it seems highly likely that such ideologies would be manifest at regional, state-sponsored cultic centers such as Bethel, Dan, Beersheba, Arad, and Jerusalem, which, as noted previously, were apparently magnets for pilgrims who were not locals. In fact, Amos 7:10–17 describes Bethel as "a sanctuary of the king" and "a temple of the kingdom." Thus, if the rites and architecture of regional, state-sponsored sanctuaries are modeled in domestic cultic settings, we can speak with some justification of evidence of continuity between family domestic rites and the official cult. Such modeling seems likely, given architectural features such as elaborate pillars/capitals and facades at the entryway of some models, hardly what one would expect to find in the architecture of modest, local sanctuaries. Rather, these are more likely characteristic of wealthier sanctuaries with regional significance and state sponsorship.[31]

Other alleged evidence for disjunction between family and official religion should also be reconsidered in my view. Though Albertz is correct to suggest that the vast majority of Israelite and Judean names lack allusion to the national story (e.g., covenant, exodus-conquest), and, in the case of Judah, to the Davidic royal ideology and the Zion theology, all elements central to the ideology of official cult, it does not necessarily follow that the onomasticon suggests that official, normative ideology had little impact in the lives of common people, as Albertz has argued.[32] Rather, it may be simply that naming is most frequently focused on the deity's characteristics (Joram – "Yhwh is exalted"), what s/he has done for the parents personally (Jonathan – "Yhwh has given") or how s/he relates to them (Joab – "Yhwh is father"), instead of on other, less personal issues such as those central to official cult. Even extant royal and priestly names follow this pattern: they are almost entirely lacking in allusion to larger, national concerns, though the royal establishment and the priestly lineages of central sanctuaries were themselves the creators and purveyors of official ideologies![33] It remains unclear to what degree official ideologies had an impact on the quotidian lives of Israelites, Judeans, and others in the Levant of the first millennium. Certainly, names, given their characteristic form and content, cannot be used convincingly to demonstrate that they did not.

Further developing his discontinuity theme, Albertz has also drawn upon the onomasticon to argue that for much of the Iron II period, a majority of Israelite families did not accept the national deity Yhwh as their family god. He bases this argument on the assumption that El and Yhwh are separate gods, and that divine epithets such as "father" (*'ab*), "paternal uncle" (*'am*), "rock" (*ṣur*), "lord" (*'adon*), or "master" (*ba'al*), refer to deities other than Yhwh. Thus, for Albertz, personal names with El, Baal, Adon, Ab, or Am as theophoric element attest to deities other than Yhwh as family gods in Israel.[34] The problem with this argument is that it is not at all clear that these theophoric elements refer to deities other than Yhwh. F. M. Cross has made a fairly compelling case that Yhwh was, from the beginning, a distinct manifestation of El with storm characteristics, not an entirely separate deity; at all events, by Iron II, the period of most of our names, Yhwh and El are clearly identified as the same god in biblical texts.[35] Furthermore, Yhwh himself is called by the other epithets in question (e.g., Ahiyah, "Yhwh is my brother"); even Baal ("master") was used as an epithet of Yhwh in the eighth century according to Hos 2:18, and probably earlier (see the etiology for the place name Baal Perazim in 2 Sam 5:20, and the personal name Baalyah, "Yhwh is master," a hero of David in 1 Chr 12:5). As Jeffrey Tigay notes, the use of Baal as an epithet of Yhwh is attested in the Murashu archive from Nippur, suggesting that the practice persisted in at least some circles into the fifth century.[36] Therefore, if someone bears a name compounded with Baal, El, "father," "brother," or "paternal uncle," that person's parents could as easily be worshipers of Yhwh as of another god. And if the family genealogy has names compounded with Yhwh as well as names containing these ambiguous epithets, and the name of no other identifiable deity is present, it is likely that the epithets themselves refer to Yhwh. Saul's genealogy in 1 Chr 8:33–6 is a case in point. Most of the names are either ambiguous hypocoristica (e.g., Saul, Micah, Ahaz) or full names compounded with ambiguous epithets (e.g., Abinadab, Eshbaal, Meribbaal, Malkishua). The one deity clearly present in the genealogy is Yhwh (Yonathan, Yehoaddah), suggesting that the ambiguous epithets probably also refer to him.[37]

Thus, though there is certainly evidence for some disjunction between family religion as manifest in the domicile and the practices of the official cult (e.g., a lack of animal sacrifice in the domicile's shrine), there is also evidence suggesting continuity (e.g., the likely modeling of the regional, state-sponsored sanctuary and its cult in the domicile),[38] and some alleged evidence for discontinuity ought to be reconsidered (e.g., the onomasticon).[39] When the pilgrimage dimension of family religion is considered, the potential for continuity between family religion and the official cult is brought into relief: It appears that households sometimes transported themselves from the domicile to a regional, state-sponsored sanctuary, and participated in that sanctuary's rites: sacrificial meals were taken, vows fulfilled, petitions offered. The regional, state-sponsored sanctuary thus became a context for the pursuit of personal concerns as well as – presumably – the locus par excellence for the promulgation of official ideology. As mentioned, the rites of the local sanctuary may also have been shaped to some degree by official ideologies, though we do not know enough to say anything about this at this point in time.

Though the family tomb deserves attention as a central locus of family religion, it is rarely mentioned in other treatments, which tend to focus on the domicile or the local shrine. Burial rites culminated in interment in the family tomb, and there is evidence that the tomb probably functioned as one of several loci for the ancestral cult. Though few texts describe burial rites in detail, the familial dimension of interment is undisputed by scholars.[40] Texts suggest that burial rites probably began at the home of the deceased, or another domicile (Num 19:14; Am 6:10), and culminated at the tomb to which a procession of mourners transported the corpse (e.g., 2 Sam 3:31–7). The heir and other male family members were obligated to bury the dead (e.g., Gen 35:29; 50:5, 12, 14); both male and female family members mourned the dead, and were joined by close associates of the family who took up the role of "comforter" (*menaḥem*). Evidence from Judean tombs and other burials of the Iron II period analyzed by Elizabeth Bloch-Smith suggests that the deceased were typically supplied at the time of burial with food and other items thought to be useful in the afterlife.[41] The heir and other male kin were probably those charged with maintaining the family tomb (e.g., with performing secondary burial rites).[42] Some evidence indicates that family members and close friends/allies also sought to protect the physical integrity of the corpse until burial was possible (e.g., 2 Samuel 21). Mesopotamian parallels suggest that the widely attested concern that the dead be buried, preferably by family members, without physical mutilation, and with appropriate honors in the family tomb, stems from concern for how the dead will fare in the afterlife.[43] It is also possible that as in Mesopotamia, survivors sought to secure blessings from the dead and avoid their wrath through these actions, though this remains unclear.

Observance of ancestral rites after burial, perhaps at regular intervals, may also have been motivated at least in part by these concerns. Though evidence for ancestral rites is sparse for Israel in particular and first-millennium Syria-Canaan generally, it does seem that in Israel they included at minimum food offerings to the dead, perhaps at regular intervals (Deut 26:14; Tob 4:17; Sir 30:18). The erection of a memorial stela by the heir and his ritual invocation of the name of the deceased are also evidenced (2 Sam 18:18). Texts suggest that such a stela might have been erected in any one of several loci.[44] Unhappily, it is not clear how often invocation of the name occurred or how frequently offerings to the dead were presented. As mentioned, van der Toorn has argued for a yearly sacrifice for the family dead at the sanctuary, and Albertz has accepted this view. More frequent offerings may well have been the rule. Albertz believes that the domicile's shrine might also have been the context for regular ancestral rites, given the presence of teraphim – probably ancestor figurines, as argued by van der Toorn and Theodore Lewis – in domestic settings according to some biblical texts (1 Sam 19:13, 16).[45] This may well be the case, but I would also add the tomb as a probable locus for some ancestral rites, given the texts (admittedly late) tying feeding the dead to the tomb (Tob 4:17; Sir 30:18), given passages that suggest a memorial stela could stand at the tomb (Gen 35:20), and given the possibility that at least some of the food offerings and other items found in Iron II Judean family tombs were placed there after burial, for the benefit of the deceased. We still know too little about ancestral observances to say very much with confidence, but it does seem probable that such rites occurred in a variety of contexts (sanctuary, domicile, tomb), perhaps at set times in each locus.

We must also keep in mind that patterns of observance almost certainly varied through time and space, and between the cultures of the first-millennium Levant, though extant evidence allows us to say little about this. In any case, our understanding of family religion can only be enriched by careful study of the tomb as a ritual locus.

Another intriguing aspect of Israelite family religion that warrants our attention is the role that non-family members apparently played in at least some family-centered rites. Albertz and van der Toorn have noted the presence of slaves and clients/resident aliens in households, and considered their role in family religion.[46] But texts suggest that associates outside of the household and the clan could also play a part in family rites. As I mentioned in my discussion of burial, close friends and allies were obligated to play the role of comforter to mourning family members at times of death; they played a similar role at times of personal or corporate calamity or petition. Comforters enacted mourning, thereby bringing into relief and perpetuating their positive social relationships with mourning family members and, in death contexts, possibly with the deceased as well.[47] At least one text (Psalm 35) suggests that at times of petition of the deity due to illness, friends were expected to enact mourning (presumably along with family members), likely in order to increase the petition's chances of success: "As for me," says the Psalmist, complaining about disloyal friends, "when they [i.e., friends] were sick, my clothes were sackcloth, I afflicted myself with fasting . . . I walked around like one mourning his mother," meaning that he enacted petitionary mourning rites on behalf of suffering friends (vv 13–14). Other passages in the psalms of individual complaint suggest that friends were expected to support the petitioner during a time of trouble. In Psalm 38, a sick supplicant mourns while entreating the deity (v 7), and notes how his friends, including those with formal ties, stood at a distance, refusing to approach him: "My intimates and friends stand apart from my affliction, my neighbors stand at a distance" (v 12).[48]

Thus, difficult family situations such as illness or death had a significant non-familial dimension that we must acknowledge when we seek to describe and analyze family religion fully. It may well be that other aspects of family religion, such as fertility and birth-related petitions and feasts, also included a significant non-familial, non-household component among participants, though about this we can only speculate. The non-familial dimensions of family religion bring into relief the larger social networks of families, underscoring the importance of non-kinship-based social relationships even in societies in which ties of blood and marriage are paramount. The degree to which these observations about the participation of non-family members in family rites might apply to first-millennium Levantine family religion outside of Israel remains unclear, due to a lack of evidence, though it seems likely that there were at least some common practices, if not many.

In conclusion, Israelite family religion can be analyzed in terms of both the social units involved in family rites and the loci of those rites. I have argued that a number of primary social units (the household and the clan) and loci (domicile, local sanctuary, regional, state-sponsored sanctuary, family tomb) are central to our understanding of Israelite family religion. In order to develop the broadest possible perspective on our subject, I believe it is best to avoid playing down one social unit in favor of another, or privileging one locus over another, given that each social unit and locus is relevant to our analysis. In addition, the evidence that non-family members played a role in family rites must be incorporated into our analysis if we hope to develop a more nuanced understanding of family religion.

On the question of continuity/discontinuity with the official cult, I believe that the situation is more complex than Albertz has suggested. Although Albertz is certainly correct to identify several elements of discontinuity (e.g., lack of animal sacrifice and its attendant rites in the domestic expression of family religion; focus on family-specific concerns such as childbirth, weaning, and healing from disease), there may be more elements of continuity than he acknowledges (e.g., the likely modeling of the regional, state-sponsored sanctuary and its rites in the home) and some of his evidence for discontinuity is open to alternative interpretations (e.g., the onomasticon). Thus, extant evidence suggests that family religion in Israel stands in a complex relationship with the official cult, departing from its rites (e.g., lack of domestic animal sacrifice), alluding to them (e.g, modeling the processing of sacrificial meat through the presence of miniature cooking pots in domestic shrines) and probably sharing some of them (e.g., libations, incense offerings in the home). One need not posit a nearly complete disjunction between family religion and the official cult in order to speak of internal religious pluralism in Israelite religion, for family religion and official cult remain distinct phenomena, even when their shared characteristics are acknowledged.

Though extant evidence of first-millennium Levantine family religion comes mainly from Israel, some comparisons are possible between Israelite evidence and that of Israel's neighbors. Evidence suggests that the domestic expression of family cult in Israel and Judah, and domestic family religion at Tell Jawa in Ammon shared a number of characteristics, including modeling sanctuary cult through model shrines and cultic miniatures, and through ritual acts such as kindling lamps and the presentation of libations and possibly incense or other aromatics. Differences in cultic assemblages between those of Tell Jawa and what one typically finds at Israelite and Judean sites include the absence of Judean-type pillar figurines from Tell Jawa and a greater proportion of male figurines there than one would expect to find in Israel/Judah.[49] These continuities and differences are precisely what one would expect of related, contiguous though distinct cultures.

Notes

1 See, e.g., the articles under the rubric "Religious Practices of the Individual and Family," in *Religions of the Ancient World: A Guide*, ed. Sarah Iles Johnston (Cambridge and London: Harvard University Press, 2004), pp. 423–37; and Manfred Hutter (ed.), *Offizielle Religion, locale Kulte und individuelle Religiosität: Akten des religionsgeschichtlichen Symposiums "Kleinasien und angrenzende Gebiete vom Beginn des 2. bis*

zur Mitte des 1. Jahrtausends v. Chr.": (Bonn, 20.–22. February 2003), Alter Orient und Altes Testament 318 (Münster: Ugarit-Verlag, 2004).

2 "Family Religion in Ancient Israel and its Surroundings," pp. 91–2. *A History of Israelite Religion in the Old Testament Period*, 2 vols., Old Testament Library (Louisville: Westminster/John Knox, 1994), 1: 19; *Persönliche Frömmigkeit und offizielle Religion: Religionsinterner Pluralismus in Israel und Babylon* (Stuttgart: Calwer, 1978). Local religion, Albertz notes, is more difficult to describe than the other two types. In *Persönliche Frömmigkeit*, Albertz had considered using "family religion" instead of "personal piety," but had decided at the time that "personal piety" was the more appropriate expression (*Persönliche Frömmigkeit*, 11). On this, see further n. 16.

3 "Family Religion in Ancient Israel and its Surroundings," p. 92. *A History of Israelite Religion*, 1: 19.

4 Though Albertz now incorporates local/village religion into his original binary model as a third, intermediate level of religion, acknowledging the influence of Manfred Weippert and Bernhard Lang on his thinking, he does not develop the tripartite model in any depth, as he himself acknowledges ("Family Religion in Ancient Israel and its Surroundings," p. 107 n. 23. *A History of Israelite Religion*, 1:248 n. 78), and speaks about it with a degree of ambivalence ("Alongside [family religion and official religion] we can *in part* also distinguish a third level, the local level, that of the village community, which is situated between the level of the family and that of the people or state" [*A History of Israelite Religion*, 1: 19; italics mine]), due to the difficulty one encounters in attempting to describe it as a distinct entity.

5 *The House of the Father as Fact and Symbol: Patrimonialism in Ugarit and the Ancient Near East*, Studies in the Archaeology and History of the Levant 2 (Winona Lake, IN.: Eisenbrauns, 2001), pp. 135–6, 150–1.

6 See, most recently, "Religious Practices of the Individual and Family: Introduction," in *Religions of the Ancient World*, pp. 423–4. See also *Family Religion in Babylonia, Syria & Israel: Continuity & Change in the Forms of Religious Life*, Studies in the History and Culture of the Ancient Near East 7 (Leiden: Brill, 1996), p. 3. Van der Toorn prefers to distinguish only two levels in ancient religions: family religion, whose focus is the village/clan, and the official cult.

7 *Family Religion*, pp. 241–2. Van der Toorn does, however, acknowledge the possibility of ancestor veneration in the domicile. Elsewhere, he notes the general evidence for domestic cult (ibid., pp. 245–6).

8 "Family Religion in Ancient Israel and its Surroundings," pp. 92, 96. On domestic cult at Tell Jawa, see P. M. Michèle Daviau, "Family Religion: Evidence for the Paraphernalia of the Domestic Cult," in *The World of the Aramaeans II: Studies in History and Archaeology in Honour of Paul-Eugène Dion*, ed. P. M. Michèle Daviau, John W. Wevers, and Michael Weigl (Sheffield: Sheffield Academic Press, 2001), pp. 199–229.

9 On the domestic assemblages of Tell Jawa, which include items such as model shrines, miniature vessels, and zoomorphic figurines, see Daviau, "Family Religion"; for the assemblages found at Beersheba and Tell el-Far'ah North (Tirzah), see Ziony Zevit, *The Religions of Ancient Israel: A Synthesis of Parallactic Approaches* (London and New York: Continuum, 2001), pp. 175–6, 241; for domestic cultic items from Tell Halif, see Oded Borowski, "Hezekiah's Reforms and the Revolt against Assyria," *Biblical Archaeologist* 58 (1995): 151–2.

10 Unfortunately, we know virtually nothing about Ammonite family religion outside of the domicile, and the same is true for other non-Israelite Levantine societies of the first millennium. Daviau notes that we have yet to discover any kind of Ammonite temple, and so we cannot even speak of Ammonite official religion or, I might add, the rites of local sanctuaries ("Family Religion," p. 223). Van der Toorn's several treatments of first-millennium Syrian family religion are completely dependent on royal evidence such as the Hadad inscription from Zinjirli, as he acknowledges himself ("Religious Practices of the Individual and Family: Syria-Canaan," in *Religions of the Ancient World*, pp. 427–9; *Family Religion*, pp. 153–77).

11 Van der Toorn, *Family Religion*, pp. 211–18. Albertz has accepted van der Toorn's understanding of the "annual sacrifice" or "sacrifice of the clan," in "Family Religion in Ancient Israel and its Surroundings," p. 100.

12 First-millennium Judean tombs are treated in depth by Elizabeth Bloch-Smith, *Judahite Burial Practices and Beliefs About the Dead*, Journal for the Study of the Old Testament Supplements 123 (Sheffield: Sheffield Academic Press, 1992).

13 On the likelihood that related households shared aggregate tombs, see the discussion of Bloch-Smith, ibid., p. 148. In addition, note Schloen, *House of the Father*, p. 346, who argues that at least some intramural tombs found at Ugarit were shared by urban clans.

14 Obligatory pilgrimages of male members of the household to a sanctuary (Exod 23:17; 34:23; Deut 16:16) are as relevant to our understanding of family religion as domestic cultic rites that may have involved mainly or exclusively women (e.g., birth-related rites). We must admit, however, that we know very little about the gender dimensions of Levantine family religion. Relevant texts are difficult to interpret (e.g., Deuteronomy 16, which calls for the obligatory pilgrimages of all males three times a year [v 16] but alludes to the presence of women as well [vv 11, 14]), as is material data. Nonetheless, the subject is worthy of a thorough treatment, which I intend to provide in a future publication.

15 E.g., the "Bull Site" and Shiloh for the Iron I period, and Dan, Megiddo 338 and 2081, Beersheba and Arad for Iron II. See, conveniently, the summaries of Beth Alpert Nakhai, as well as her argument that evidence of uniformity in structure and content (e.g., standardization of ritual objects) suggests state involvement in the cult (*Archaeology and the Religions of Canaan and Israel* [Boston: American Schools of Oriental Research, 2001], pp. 170–1, 177–8, 182–3, 184–5, 186–7, 193).

16 Van der Toorn, *Family Religion*, p. 3. Van der Toorn also provides a trenchant critique of the related terms "personal religion" and "private religion" (ibid., pp. 3–4). Albertz has always believed that the individual must be considered in the context of the family (*Persönliche Frömmigkeit*, p. 11: "[Die Familie] ist der wesentliche Lebensraum des Einzelnen und damit auch der Raum der persönliche Frömmigkeit"; *A History of Israelite Religion*, 1: 19: ". . . as yet there was no such thing as the individual detached from the family . . ."; see most recently "Family Religion in Ancient Israel and its Surroundings," p. 91), but preferred in *Persönliche Frömmigkeit* to make use of the expression "personal piety" for the piety of the individual in the family context, apparently to draw attention to what he believes are the truly personal dimensions of family religion: "Man könnte auch von 'Familienreligion' sprechen, doch wird durch diesen Begriff suggeriert, als müsse die Familie in jedem Fall als ganze religiös tätig werden. Das braucht aber nicht so zu sein: die Klage der kinderlosen Frau ist ihre eigene Klage, dennoch geht es in ihr um den Bestand der Familie als ganzer" (*Persönliche Frömmigkeit*, p. 11). Today, Albertz does indeed speak of family religion, though he

understands it as "personal piety related to the family," thereby acknowledging individual piety to some degree, while focusing attention largely on the family unit ("Family Religion in Ancient Israel and its Surroundings," p. 92).

17 "Family Religion in Ancient Israel and its Surroundings," p. 91. See similarly *A History of Israelite Religion*, 1:248 n. 80.

18 Examples of scholars who associate "popular religion" with concepts such as "heterodoxy," "paganism," "foreignness," and "syncretism" may be found in Mark S. Smith, *The Early History of God: Yahweh and the Other Deities in Ancient Israel* (New York: HarperCollins, 1990), pp. xx–xxi, who provides a critique. See also the similar observations of van der Toorn, "Religious Practices of the Individual and Family: Introduction," in *Religions of the Ancient World*, p. 423, from the larger perspective of the history of religions.

19 "Family Religion in Ancient Israel and its Surroundings," p. 105; "Religious Practices of the Individual and Family: Israel," in *Religions of the Ancient World*, pp. 429–30; *A History of Israelite Religion*, 1: 186–95, 210–16; 2: 399–411.

20 "Religious Practices of the Individual and Family: Introduction," in *Religions of the Ancient World*, p. 423. See also *Family Religion*, p. 38 on Babylonia. In *Family Religion*, van der Toorn argued that the Israelite official cult, initiated in his view by Saul in the late eleventh century, came to co-opt and absorb family religion to a great degree during the following centuries of the monarchy.

21 I must point out that van der Toorn would certainly not agree with some of my positions in the following analysis, such as the original identity of Yhwh and El, or my interpretation of many if not most Israelite theophoric names compounded with Baal as referring not to the Canaanite storm god, but to Yhwh. On these points, see the discussion ahead.

22 See "Family Religion in Ancient Israel and its Surroundings," pp. 97–9, and *A History of Israelite Religion*, 1: 33–4, 187 on the central concerns of family religion.

23 Albertz, "Family Religion in Ancient Israel and its Surroundings," p. 97, *A History of Israelite Religion*, 1:100. As Albertz notes, Daviau makes a similar observation for Tell Jawa ("Family Religion," pp. 221–3). Note, however, that a number of biblical texts locate the Passover offering in a domestic context (e.g., Exod 12:1–13).

24 "Family Religion in Ancient Israel and its Surroundings," p. 102.

25 *Religions of Ancient Israel*, p. 340. On model shrines, see further Zevit, ibid., pp. 328–43; Christoph Uehlinger, "Anthropomorphic Cult Statuary in Iron Age Palestine and the Search for Yahweh's Cult Images," in *The Image and the Book: Iconic Cults, Aniconism, and the Rise of Book Religion in Israel and the Ancient Near East*, ed. Karel van der Toorn (Leuven: Peeters, 1997), pp. 106–7, 114–15; Joachim Bretschneider, *Architekturmodelle in Vorderasien und der östlichen Ägäis vom Neolithikum bis in das 1. Jahrtausend*, Alter Orient und Altes Testament 229 (Neukirchen-Vluyn: Neukirchener; Kevelaer: Butzon & Bercker, 1991), pp. 101–43.

26 On these miniatures, see the recent discussion of Daviau, "Family Religion," pp. 213–14.

27 On the model shrine found in the sanctuary of LB Kamid el-Loz in Lebanon, see the discussion of Zevit, *Religions of Ancient Israel*, pp. 330–2; on that of the Jerusalem "cult cave," see ibid., pp. 338–9. (The "cult cave" in Jerusalem may or may not be a sanctuary.) For the model shrines found in Megiddo 338 (tenth century), see Nakhai, *Archaeology*, p. 177. Cultic miniatures have also been found in sanctuaries such as the Hazor Orthostat Temple and in the Jerusalem "cult cave." On this, see Daviau, ibid., p. 214.

28 I do not accept Zevit's argument that model shrines represent wayside chapels rather than sanctuaries (*Religions of Ancient Israel*, pp. 339–40). As he himself acknowledges, no such chapel has ever been identified through excavation. Furthermore, characteristics of model shrines are shared with sanctuaries (e.g., pillars at entryway; throne room inside). However, as is often acknowledged, it is no simple task to identify the particular sanctuary represented by each model shrine.

29 "Family Religion in Ancient Israel and its Surroundings," p. 96.

30 Though lamps and juglets are relatively common in domestic cultic assemblages, evidence for the burning of incense remains unclear. It is possible that aromatic items were mainly presented rather than burned in domestic settings, at least in some places, though about this we cannot be sure. See further Zevit, *Religions of Ancient Israel*, p. 139, on the evidence from Ekron specifically. On the problem of identifying tripod cups as censers, and the mostly unstained tripod cups discovered at Tell Jawa, see the discussion of Daviau, "Family Religion," pp. 207–8.

31 On the characteristics of excavated state-sponsored regional cultic centers such as Dan and Megiddo, see Nakhai, *Archaeology*, pp. 177, 184–5. These include use of ashlar, pillars with capitals, privileged siting and complex ceramic assemblages.

32 "Family Religion in Ancient Israel and its Surroundings," pp. 103–4; *A History of Israelite Religion*, 1: 95–9; *Persönliche Frömmigkeit*, pp. 49–77.

33 Of all Judean royal names, only one, Manasseh, is obviously political. The rest resemble typical Judean names (e.g., Yedidyah, Abiyah, Rehabam, Yehoshaphat, Yehoram, Uzziah, Amaziah, Yotam, Ahaz, Yoshiah, Zedekiah). Priestly names are no different, as the genealogy of Zadok suggests (1 Chr 5:34–41).

34 "Family Religion in Ancient Israel and its Surroundings," pp. 103–4; *A History of Israelite Religion*, 1: 95–9.

35 For Cross's argument, see *Canaanite Myth and Hebrew Epic* (Cambridge, MA.: Harvard University Press, 1973), pp. 44–75.

36 *You Shall Have No Other Gods: Israelite Religion in the Light of Hebrew Inscriptions*, Harvard Semitic Studies 31 (Atlanta: Scholars Press, 1986), p. 68 n. 23.

37 Contrast Albertz's analysis of the same genealogy, in which he argues that the various epithets suggest multiple family gods, only one of which was Yhwh (*A History of Israelite Religion*, 1: 97–8). Van der Toorn, among others, argues that the familial epithets in these names refer not to Yhwh or other high gods, but to dead ancestors (*Family Religion*, pp. 228–31). This seems unlikely, given frequently attested names such as Abiyah/Yoab (Yhwh is [my] father) and Ahiyah/Yoah (Yhwh is [my] brother), which tie Yhwh directly to familial relations with the worshiper. Even a name such as Rehabam has its parallel Rehabyahu, suggesting that the kinsman (Am) in question in the name Rehabam is Yhwh.

38 Given the lack of evidence for animal sacrifice in domestic cultic settings, it is intriguing to note the presence of miniature cooking pots among domestic cultic assemblages. One miniature pot from Tell Jawa even shows evidence of soot staining (Daviau, "Family Religion," p. 214).

39 Some might be tempted to suggest goddess worship as another potential point of discontinuity, yet the fact that shrine models and other cultic items often appear to have goddess associations does not necessarily suggest disjunction, given the evidence for the place of Asherah and other goddesses in non-Deuteronomistic forms of official cult. On this, see further Saul M. Olyan, *Asherah and the Cult of Yhwh in Israel*, Society of

Biblical Literature Monograph Series 34 (Atlanta: Scholars Press, 1988); on the apparent goddess associations of model shrines, see, e.g., Uehlinger, "Anthropomorphic Cult Statuary," p. 107.

40 What remains unclear, as noted earlier, is whether burial rites and ancestral rites at the tomb involved the household alone, or the household in conjunction with the larger clan. This may well have varied through time and space.

41 *Judahite Burial Practices*, p. 105.

42 On secondary burials in Judean tombs, see Bloch-Smith, ibid., pp. 36–7, 42–3 and the older survey of Eric Meyers, "Secondary Burials in Palestine," *Biblical Archaeologist* 33 (1970): 2–29, especially 10–17.

43 Gilgamesh XII.151 in Andrew R. George, *The Babylonian Gilgamesh Epic: Introduction, Critical Edition and Cuneiform Texts*, 2 vols. (Oxford: Oxford University Press, 2003), 1: 734; Ashurbanipal and tombs of the kings of Elam, in Maximilian Streck (ed.), *Assurbanipal und die letzten assyrischen Könige bis zum Untergange Nineveh's*, 3 vols. (Leipzig: J. C. Hinrichs, 1916), 2: 56 (lines 74–6); Esarhaddon's succession treaty in Simo Parpola and Kazuko Watanabe, *Neo-Assyrian Treaties and Loyalty Oaths*, State Archives of Assyria 2 (Helsinki: Helsinki University Press, 1988), p. 57 (6.638–40).

44 Though 2 Sam 18:18 mentions the Valley of the King (?) as the location of Absalom's memorial stela, Isa 56:5 may suggest that such a stela could stand in a sanctuary. The ancestral narrative in Gen 35:20 mentions the erection of such a stela at the tomb itself. Note that Gen 35:20 suggests that a husband could erect a memorial stela for his dead wife.

45 Albertz, "Family Religion in Ancient Israel and its Surroundings," pp. 98–9; van der Toorn and Lewis, "Teraphim," in *Theologisches Wörterbuch zum Alten Testament*, 10 vols.,
ed. G. J. Botterweck & Helmer Ringgren (Stuttgart: Kohlhammer, 1995), 8: 765–78. See also van der Toorn, *Family Religion*, pp. 218–25.

46 Albertz, "Family Religion in Ancient Israel and its Surroundings," p. 92; van der Toorn, *Family Religion*, p. 212.

47 On comforting the mourner, see Saul M. Olyan, *Biblical Mourning: Ritual and Social Dimensions* (Oxford: Oxford University Press, 2004), pp. 46–9, 88–9.

48 I take Hebrew *'ohabim*, literally "lovers," which I have translated "intimates," to be indicative of a formal relationship, given the use of the same term in covenant settings such as 1 Sam 18:16 and 1 Kgs 5:15. Unsupportive friends and allies are a topos of the psalms of individual complaint. For another example, see Ps 88:19 ("You kept far from me intimate and friend").

49 As noted by Daviau, "Family Religion," p. 203.

8

Household Religion, Family Religion, and Women's Religion in Ancient Israel

Susan Ackerman

For scholars of some societies of the ancient Near Eastern and eastern Mediterranean worlds, the terms family and household seem basically to function as synonyms, by which I mean, first, that both "family" and "household" tend to be defined by reference to persons – the composite group of individuals who make up the family and/or household unit (this in contrast to the definitions we will explore shortly, in which the term household tends to be defined by reference to space) – and, second, that the body of individuals in question tends to be seen as one and the same, with those who make up the collective known as the family (which is most typically defined in terms of biological or marital kinship) understood as identical to those who make up the household. It follows that in this conceptualization, the terms family religion and household religion are likewise taken as basically synonymous, and that family/household religion is defined primarily, like "family" and "household," in terms of persons; family/household religion is thus the religious practices undertaken together and beliefs professed jointly by the group of individuals that constitutes the family/household unit, and this regardless of the space – a home, a tomb, a local sanctuary, a major temple – in which the religious activities of this aggregate body of individuals might take place. Because both the terms family and household, that is, are defined according to this paradigm by reference to people, not place, family/household religion is understood as that which the people who make up the family/household collective do to give expression to their religious convictions, divorced from any considerations of location.

As I have already intimated, however, scholars of some of the other societies of the ancient Near East and eastern Mediterranean tend to see the terms "family" and "household," and thus the terms "family religion" and "household religion," operating somewhat differently in the cultures that they study, so that while family – as in the definition above – still refers to a collective of persons (typically described, also as above, as a group of individuals who are biologically or maritally related), household is defined in spatial terms, as the domestic environment inhabited by the community of individuals who make up the family unit. It follows that in this sort of understanding, in which family and household are not synonymous, family religion and household religion are likewise not synonymous entities, so while family religion – again as above – remains defined as that which the biologically- and maritally-related individuals who constitute a family unit do together to give expression to their collective's religious convictions, whatever the location, household religion – because the term household is spatially construed – is defined as those religious activities that the family members who co-inhabit a domestic space undertake jointly within that locale.

This latter description, which distinguishes between the terms family and household and thus between family religion – the religious beliefs jointly expressed and religious practices jointly undertaken by a biologically- and maritally-bonded group – and household religion – the religious activities engaged in by this biologically- and maritally-bonded group within its own home – seems to me more accurately to describe the ancient society of the Near Eastern and Mediterranean worlds that I know best, the society of ancient Israel during the period of the Iron Age (c. 1200–586 BCE). Still, in order to describe accurately ancient Israelite households and thus ancient Israelite household religion, which is the topic to which I will turn initially in this essay, we need to introduce some important specifications. We need, for example, to specify carefully the precise nature of ancient Israelite household space, for as archaeological analyses of the past twenty or so years have compellingly demonstrated, the typical household space in Israelite culture – and especially the typical household space within the villages of the ancient Israelite countryside, in which, it is estimated, 80 to 90 percent of the population lived[1] – seems not to have been the single-family, free-standing domicile we moderns might most readily envision when we think of a "house." Rather, an ancient Israelite household was a multi-building compound, comprised primarily of closely adjacent or, more commonly, contiguous houses (and sometimes also, as we will see below, other structures) that all opened onto a common courtyard and that were separated from similar multi-building compounds that stood within the same village by streets, paths, or stone enclosure walls (Figures 8.1a, 8.1b and 8.2).[2]

The inhabitants of these multi-building household compounds, moreover, could include individuals other than biologically- and maritally-related members of a family. To be sure, because ancient Israelite society was overwhelmingly kinship-based, we are almost certainly to understand that the various domiciles within ancient Israelite household compounds were occupied by members of different generations of an extended family, one in which the sons of an original family patriarch had built homes near or contiguous to their father's original house as they came of age, married, and had children of their own (and here we need to note not just the kin-based nature of ancient Israelite society, but in addition its insistence on patrilineal descent and patrilocal marriage). Indeed, as suggested by Lawrence E. Stager, whose 1985 article "The Archaeology of the Family in Ancient Israel" remains the premier

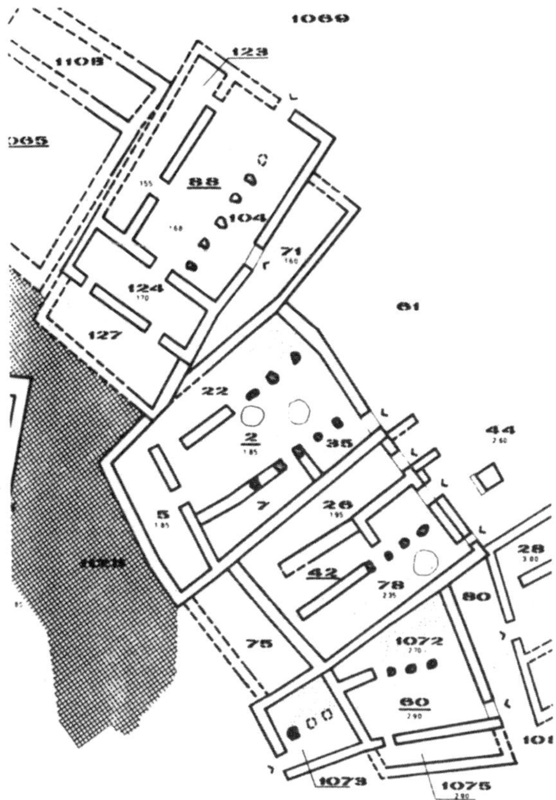

Figure 8.1a Site plan showing individual houses clustered in larger household compounds at Tel Masos. From Fritz and Kempinski, *Ergebnisse*, Plate 3

presentation of this reconstruction, we likely see in the archaeological remains of these multi-generational clusters of homes that make up a household compound the reflex of what is described in the Hebrew Bible as the *bet 'ab*, the so-called "house of the father," also alluded to more metaphorically in Jesus' claim in the New Testament that "in my father's house(hold), there are many houses" (John 14:2).[3] Still, despite the kin-based language that these biblical texts evoke to describe ancient Israel's household compounds, our evidence suggests that the members of the "house of the father" could in fact include individuals who were not related to the compound's patriarch through biology or marriage: slaves, the *ger*, or "sojourner," and others who were affiliated with and served the family.

Biblical "clues to this residential pattern," Stager correctly writes, "can be found in the description of the *bet* Micah [or "house of Micah"] in Judges 17–18."[4] Indeed, repeatedly within this text – in Judg 17:4, 8, 12; 18:2, 3, 13, 15, 18, 22, 25, and 26 – we find references to the household (*bet*) of a man named Micah, a member of the tribe of Ephraim, according to Judg 17:1, who lived during "the days of the judges," or during the premonarchical or tribal period of ancient

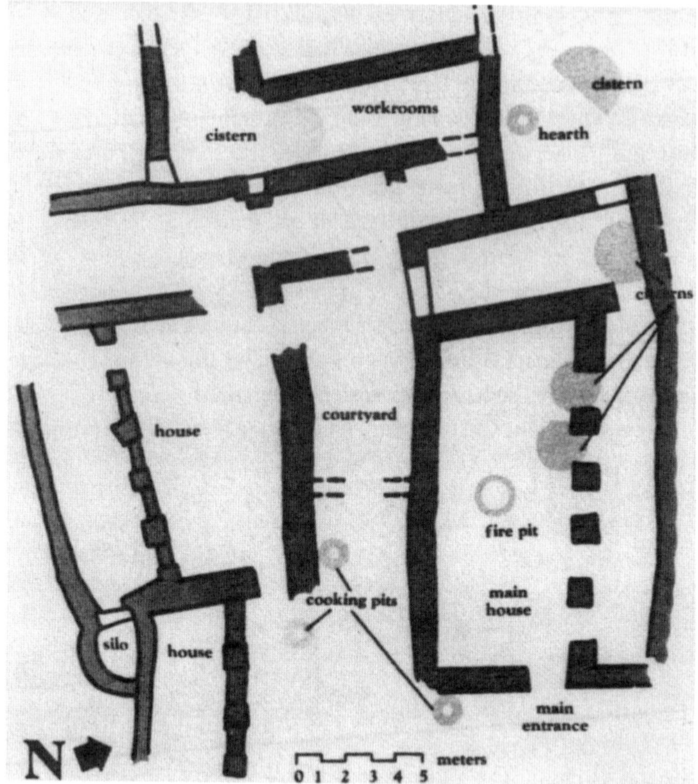

Figure 8.1b Site plan showing individual houses clustered in larger household compounds at Khirbet Raddana. From Callaway, "A Visit with Ahilud," p. 47

Israelite history (Iron Age I; c. 1200–1000 BCE), at just the time – not coincidentally – when the extended household compound as the primary architectural configuration of Israelite domestic space begins to appear in the archaeological record. Micah's household, according to our Judges text, includes, at least, Micah's mother (who is presumably widowed, given that her husband is never mentioned in our story and, more important, that the story's household is consistently identified using the name of her son, who has seemingly taken over the role of paterfamilias from his deceased father) and Micah's son, whom we are told in 17:5 was installed by his father as the household's priest. According to Judg 17:7–13,[5] moreover, this household grows to include a young Levite – a group generally depicted in the biblical tradition as ancient Israel's priestly caste – who had been sojourning in the Judahite town of Bethlehem but who relocates to Ephraim to find a place for himself, as, in the Bible's understanding, the members of the landless levitical community were generally expected to do. This Levite apparently succeeds Micah's son as the household's priest, probably because his priestly credentials are more culturally recognized and acknowledged than are those of Micah's biological son,

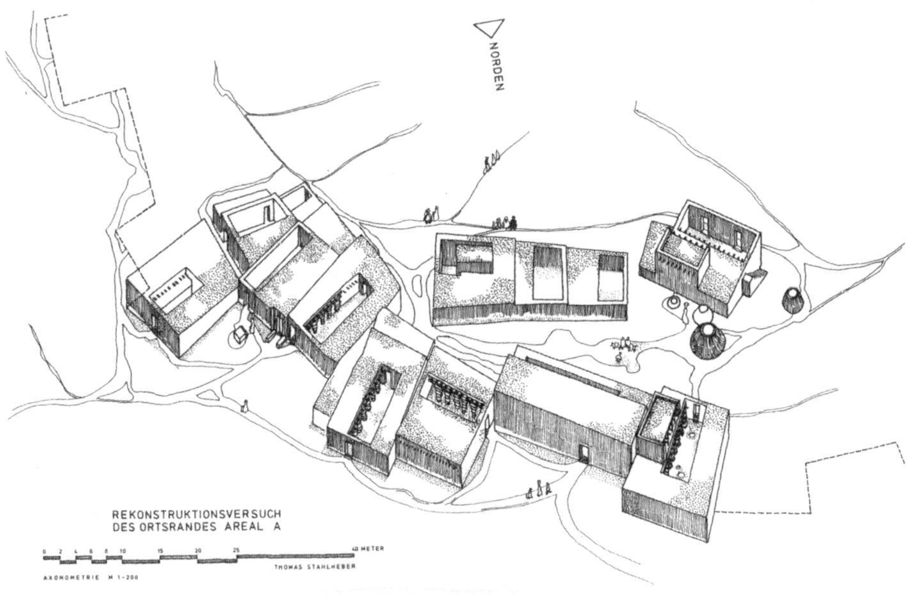

Figure 8.2 Artist's reconstruction showing several multi-house compounds within a typical ancient Israelite village. From Fritz and Kempinski, *Ergebnisse,* Vol. 1, Figure 2

and thus he brings a measure of prestige to his position within Micah's household that Micah's less formally qualified offspring has been unable to provide. Certainly, Micah's words in 17:13, "*Now* I know that Yhwh [the God of Israel] will make things go well for me, because the Levite has become my priest" (emphasis mine), suggest this.

This Levite priest, we are told in the immediately preceding verse (17:12), was therefore installed "in the house of Micah" (*bebet mikah*), an indication – as noted above – that the ancient Israelite household could include individuals beyond the family patriarch's biological and marital kin group. As we read on, our Judges text also indicates – again, as noted above – that "the house of Micah" (*bet mikah*) was made up of more than a single home. In Judg 18:3, for example, we read that five members of the tribe of Dan – who have come north from their temporary encampment in the southwest to scout out possible territory for their tribesmen to settle permanently – are staying in the house of Micah (*bet mikah*) when they overhear the voice of Micah's Levite priest and then "turn aside" (*sur*) to speak to him "there" (*šam*), that is, in a space that is seemingly other than Micah's home. Yet as we have seen, the Levite is said in Judg 17:12 to be in the house of Micah (*bet mikah*). How to explain this seeming contradiction? I would interpret by suggesting that the Levite was indeed in the "house of Micah" in the sense that he was resident in one of the several buildings that made up Micah's household compound and that it was there that Micah's Danite visitors encountered him when they turned aside from the actual "house of Micah" – meaning Micah's personal domicile – to speak to him. I would interpret similarly the grammatically difficult passage found in 18:15, in which a company of six hundred men from Dan – who are on their way to the far north to capture the site of Laish, which by this point in the story has been identified as a potential home for Dan by the five original Danite scouts – turns aside, on the advice of the scouts, toward the *bet-hanna'ar hallewi bet mikah*, literally "the house of the young Levite, the house of Micah." Because this phrase approaches the nonsensical, some commentators delete the second half of it, the reference to "the house of Micah," as an extraneous gloss that was secondarily added to the text.[6] But I think we might better imagine a point in the scribal transmission of this verse in which a *be*, meaning "in," that preceded the phrase *bet mikah*, or "house of Micah," was mistakenly dropped.[7] If so, then the original text would be rendered *bet-hanna'ar hallewi bebet mikah*, "the house of the young Levite that was in the house of Micah," and it would suggest that Micah's "house" needs to be understood precisely according to the paradigm of the multi-building complex that I described above, with the Levite priest of Micah's household living in some structure within the patriarch's extended compound other than the home of Micah himself.

That the *bet mikah*, or "house of Micah," is comprised of multiple buildings is also suggested by Judg 18:13–14, in which we are told that the reason the six hundred Danites who are passing by *bet mikah* (v 13), or the "house of Micah" (singular), are advised by the five advance scouts who are among their company to turn aside is that there were precious religious objects that might be stolen located *babbattim ha'elleh* (v 14), literally "in these *houses*" (plural), or, more idiomatically, at least as I would interpret, "in these buildings" that make up the extended household compound that is the "house of Micah." After the Danites do indeed steal Micah's religious treasures, moreover, they are pursued by "the men who were in the houses that were with the house of Micah" (*ha'anašim 'ašer babbattim 'ašer 'im-bet mikah*; Judg 18:22), or, more idiomatically (at least, again, as I would interpret), "the men whose homes were within the household compound of Micah":[8] that is, Micah's sons, possibly his grandsons, and possibly unrelated servants, slaves, and other sojourners – although *not* the Levite, who has been persuaded by the Danites to flee with them, having become convinced that it would profit him more to serve as priest for an entire tribe than it has serving as priest for only Micah's household.[9]

But rather than focus on this issue of the Levite's fortunes after joining with the men of Dan, let us return to the matter of the building in which the Levite was housed within the many buildings that, according to Judg 18:3, 13–14, 15, and 22, made up Micah's extended household compound, for it is implied in Judg 18:17 that it is this structure that the Danites entered in order to steal Micah's religious treasures. We are told further in this verse that these religious treasures include (although the text of 18:17 is somewhat corrupted and therefore confused) teraphim (most likely ancestor figurines used in rituals of necromancy),[10] an ephod (also a ritual object – most likely, some sort of priestly garment – that, like the teraphim, was used for purposes of divination),[11] and a figurine of cast metal (Hebrew *pesel umassekah*).[12] These precious objects are mentioned at several other points in the story as well – in 17:4–5; 18:14, 18 and 20, for example – and, at least in 17:4–5 and 18:14, 20 in an uncorrupted and thus clearer form.[13] In addition, according to 17:5, the ephod and teraphim seem to have been housed within a "shrine" (*bet 'elohim*) that belonged to Micah, and 17:4, by virtue of juxtaposition, suggests that the figurine of cast metal stood there too. The structure within Micah's residential compound, that is, within which the Levite was housed according to 18:3, 15, and probably 18:17 seems to have been – as 17:5 would have it – a dedicated shrine building in which precious religious objects were placed. From at least one premonarchical Israelite village, moreover, early twelfth- through mideleventh-century BCE Ai (et-Tell), we have archaeological evidence of a similar dedicated shrine room that was associated with a complex of clustered-together houses and that housed religiously precious objects.

The room in question at Ai (Room 65) is among the domestic buildings found in Area D of the site, which is in Ai's northeast corner (Figure 8.3). Although

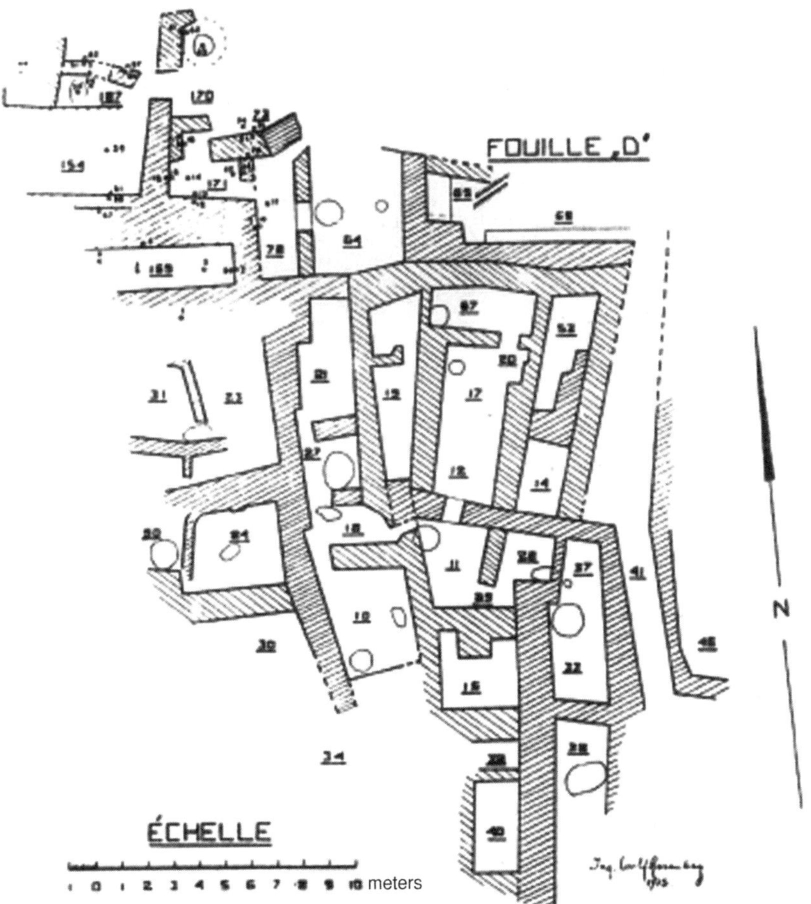

Figure 8.3 Plan showing the location of Room 65 at Ai. From Marquet-Krause, *Fouilles de 'Ay (et-Tell)*, Pl. XCVII

excavated by the French archaeologist Judith Marquet-Krause in the 1930s and labeled by her as a cult room ("un lieu saint"),[14] this room's religious character has only recently been thoroughly analyzed, especially by Ziony Zevit in his 2001 study of Israelite religion.[15] In support of the identification of this space as a shrine, Zevit – and also Beth Alpert Nakhai, in her archaeological survey of Canaanite and Israelite cultic sites – cites several factors. First, the room itself, which is 8.5 by 3 meters,[16] is somewhat larger than the others found at Ai,[17] which suggests a special role for it. More important, two walls of the room (the western and southern) are benched,[18] which indicates that the special role of the space was religious, given that narrow benches on which worshipers could place dedicatory offerings are otherwise known to be a distinctive feature of ancient Israelite religious architecture (they are found, for example, in the two gate shrines that flank the entry of the West Building [or Building A] at the mid-ninth to mid-eighth-century BCE site of Kuntillet 'Ajrud [Figure 8.4]).[19]

The contents of Room 65 at Ai further suggest the religious nature of the space. They include an unusually tall fenestrated offering stand with feet (human? lion?) encircling its base,[20] which Ruth Amiran, who excavated at Ai with Marquet-Krause, recalls was found on the shrine's western bench (Figures 8.5 and 8.6).[21] Also among the room's contents were a large bowl with stubby protuberances and a large funnel-shaped chalice designed to fit atop a (different?) offering stand; both of these seem to have stood on the floor in front of the western bench.[22] One to two animal figurines and jewelry were found in Room 65 as well.[23] According to Joseph Callaway, who conducted excavations at Ai in the 1960s, eleventh-century BCE Ai had a population of about 150 to 300 people,[24] who would have been grouped into

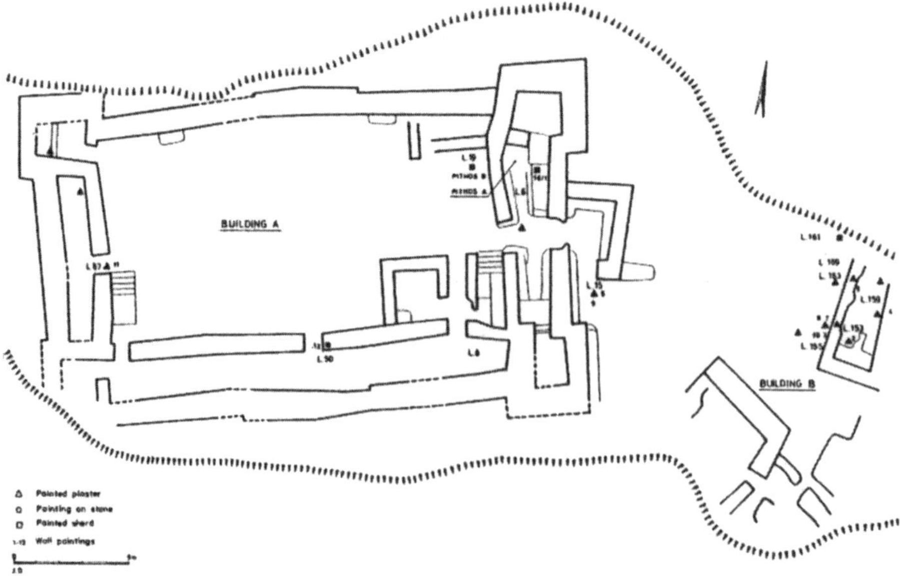

Figure 8.4 Plan showing the benched gate shrines that flank the entry of Building A at the site of Kuntillet 'Ajrud. From Meshel, *Kuntillet 'Ajrud*

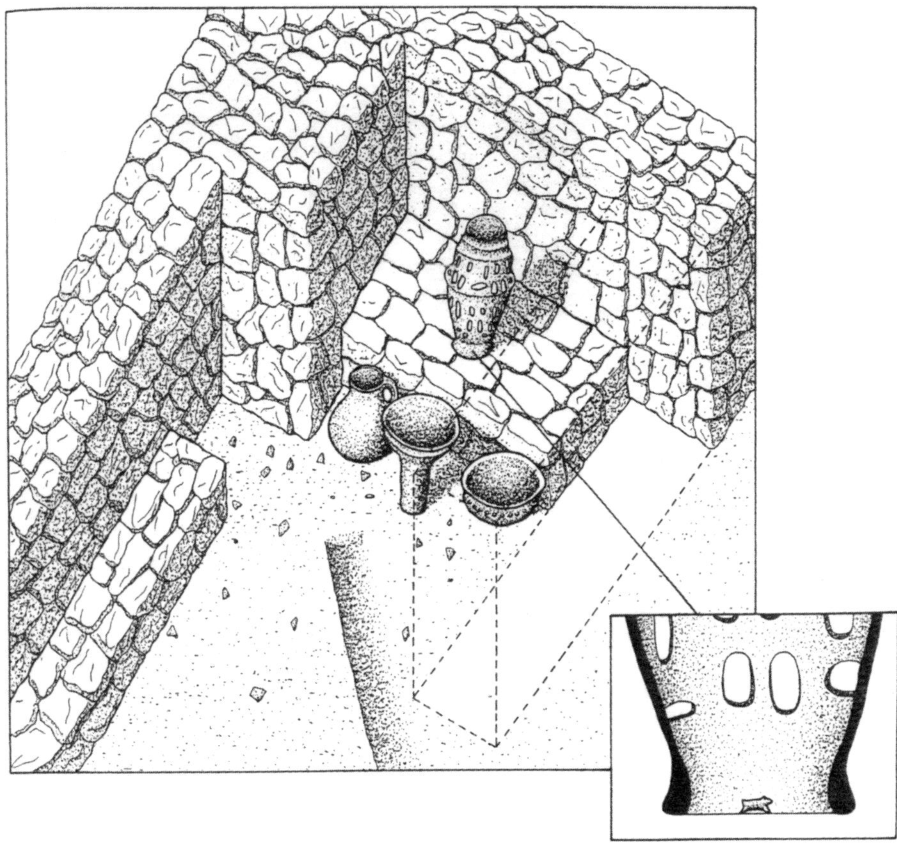

Figure 8.5 Artist's reconstruction of Room 65 at Ai, showing the fenestrated offering stand atop the western bench and other cult vessels on the floor below. From Zevit, *The Religions of Ancient Israel*, p. 155, Fig. 3.16

perhaps ten to twenty household compounds,[25] each of which, as we have already discussed in relation to our Judges 17–18 text, was presumably occupied by members of a multi-generational kin group and this group's affiliates (Figure 8.7). Room 65 could have easily served as a shrine for one of these household groups. More specifically, Room 65 would have been a space within one group's household compound where compound members could engage in what the archaeological data (and biblical texts such as Jer 7:16–20 and 44:15–19, 25, as we will see below) imply are the fundamental rituals of ancient Israelite household religion: the making of food, drink, or other dedicatory offerings, the burning of incense, and the pouring out of libations – and with regard to libations, we should note that Room 65 had a channel that appears to have drained the floor area in front of the western bench, a feature not found in any of the nearby buildings.[26]

Considering this room at Ai in tandem with Judges 17–18, moreover, suggests that it may be wealthy households in particular (more on this below) that could

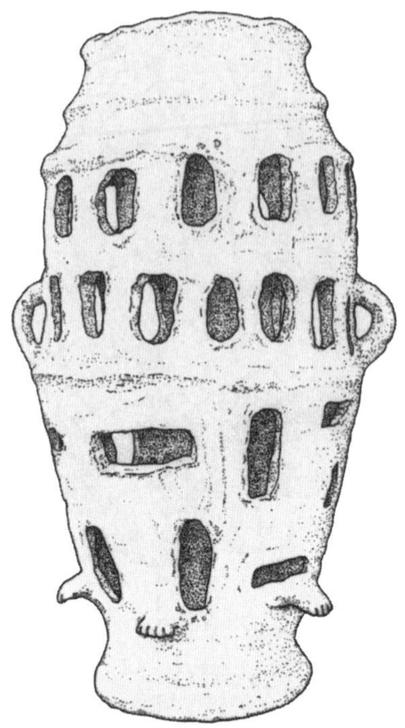

Figure 8.6 Fenestrated offering stand from Ai. From Dever, *Did God Have a Wife?* p. 112

include within their multi-building compounds a dedicated shrine building or room and that could furnish this dedicated sanctuary space with especially precious religious objects: elaborate offering stands, other pottery vessels, animal figurines, and jewelry, as at Ai; teraphim, an ephod, and a figurine of cast metal, as in the Judges account. Our Judges text also allows us to suggest that a wealthy household could hire a priest (Micah's Levite is said to be given room, board, clothing, and ten pieces of silver a year in exchange for his priestly service; Judg 17:10) to serve and have oversight of its dedicated sacred space. In addition, Judg 17:1–4, in which the origins of the cast-metal figurine that seems to have sat in Micah's shrine building are described, invites speculation regarding the degree to which a household's women members may have been involved in the furnishing of their compound's sanctuary space.

According to Judg 17:1–4, Micah's mother had a hoard of eleven hundred pieces of silver (which is, like Micah's ability to hire a Levite priest, a key indicator of her household's wealth); this silver Micah, for unspecified reasons, stole. In Judg 17:2, the mother, evidently unaware that her son was the thief, utters an oath, which, although her precise words are not quoted, has been plausibly linked by Josef Scharbert to the sort of "audible curse oath" mentioned in Lev 5:1, whereby a "person who has been wronged" (by, for example, theft) pronounces an imprecation,

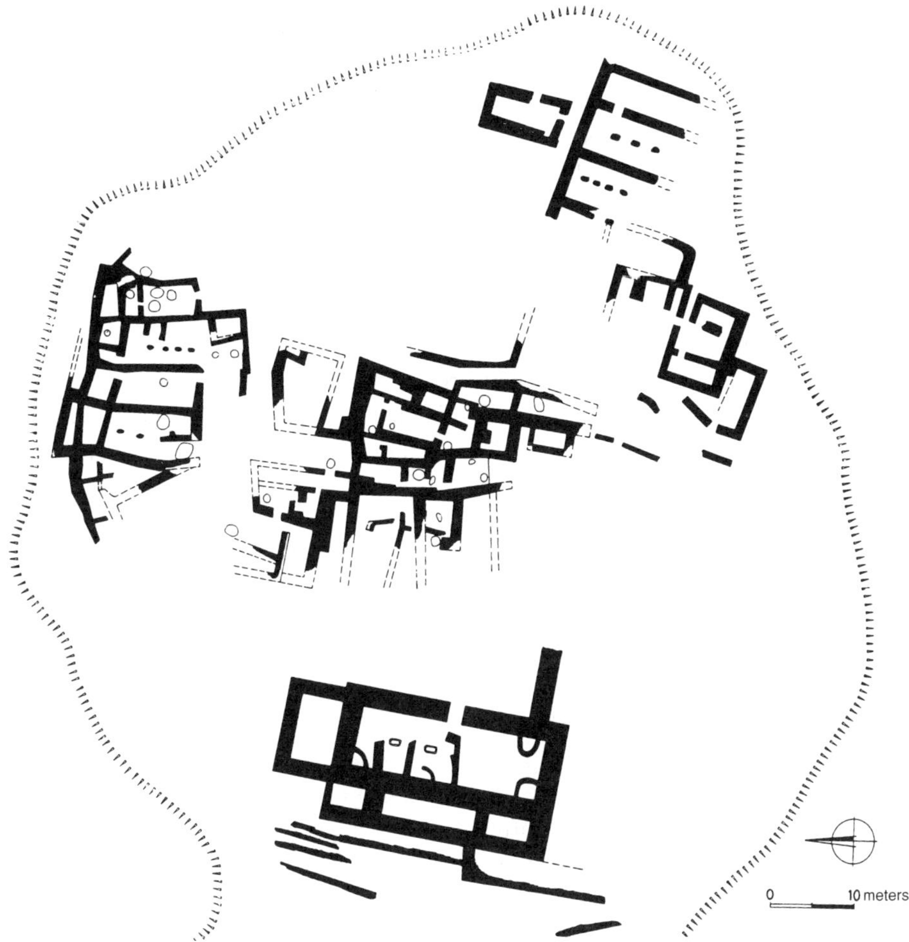

Figure 8.7 Plan of twelfth-century BCE Ai showing multiple clusters of houses (the monumental building to the south dates from the Early Bronze Age). From Kempinski and Reich, *The Architecture of Ancient Israel*, p. 235

with the assumption that, once this curse has been "pronounced publicly or made known openly,"[27] it becomes incumbent on the wrongdoer – or, indeed, on any accomplice of the wrongdoer or any witness of the crime – to come forward and testify.[28] Thus, according to Judg 17:2, Micah responds as required by confessing his guilt, and his mother further rejoins by uttering a blessing to nullify her original curse (see similarly 1 Kgs 2:45, where Solomon's blessing neutralizes Shimei's curse of 2 Sam 16:5–8, and 2 Sam 21:1–3, where David seeks a blessing from the Gibeonites to reverse their earlier curse).[29] Reflected here is the ancient Israelite belief in the near magical power of words to produce real outcomes, meaning that a curse oath is no idle threat but an actual guarantor that harm will come to its recipient; likewise, blessings are not simply expressions of good wishes but genuine warrants of good fortune. This is because Yhwh is the agent who is called upon to execute these utterances, just as it was Yhwh who was called on in Judg 17:2 to bless Micah after he confessed his guilt, as well as, presumably, to curse him as the thief who stole his mother's silver.

In fact, Scharbert describes curses such as the one found in Judg 17:2 as essentially "prayers to Yahweh that he would bring calamity on the evildoer and thus call him to account"; Sheldon H. Blank likewise describes curses as "imprecatory prayer[s], a type of religious expression."[30] In Judg 17:2, notably for the purposes of our inquiry, these religious expressions are put in the mouth of a woman. Rather astonishingly, this is one of the very few times in the entire Hebrew Bible that a woman is identified as offering up a prayer: see only (1) Gen 25:22, in which Rebekah "inquires" – *daraš* – of Yhwh, an activity that we might plausibly assume involved prayer; (2) 1 Sam 1:10, in which Hannah is said to pray to Yhwh (*wattit-pallel*) and to continue praying in 1:12; (3) 1 Sam 1:26–7, in which Hannah alludes back to her earlier prayer; (4) 1 Sam 2:1, in which Hannah is said to pray again; and (5) Psalm 131, in which the prayer addressed to Yhwh may be uttered by a woman.[31] More noteworthy still, however, is the fact that the author(s) and/or redactor(s) of Judges 17–18 do nothing to indicate that Micah's mother's oath and curse prayers are anything out of the ordinary. This suggests that it was fully the norm for ancient Israelite women to pray as part of, at least, their household-based religious devotions and simply a coincidence (albeit one that belies the heavily androcentric focus of the biblical text) that so few women in the Hebrew Bible are said to do so.[32] Moreover, Judg 17:2 seems rather emphatically to indicate that Micah's mother's prayers of cursing and blessing in the name of Yhwh are as authoritative as the curses and blessings uttered by any man and that they thus must be respected and responded to appropriately and with alacrity to secure the son's well-being before God. Micah's mother's uttering of a curse and then a blessing within the walls of her household compound, that is, can be taken as evidence of this woman's ability – and, by implication, all women's ability – to act as a powerful cultic agent within the context of ancient Israelite household religion.

In addition, in Judg 17:3, Micah's mother decrees that she will dedicate two hundred pieces of the silver that her son returns to her to Yhwh, to be used by a metallurgist or refiner (Hebrew *ṣorep*) to make a figurine of cast metal. Despite the fact that the use of images in the worship of Yhwh is something that elsewhere in the Bible is condemned, we are arguably to understand this particular figurine as somehow representing the Israelite god Yhwh: as I have just noted, the silver is specifically said by the mother in Judg 17:3 to be consecrated to Yhwh; Yhwh is also the deity who is called upon in 17:2 to bless Micah after he returns his mother's stolen silver and presumably to curse him before he confessed his guilt; Yhwh is moreover the only deity mentioned elsewhere in both the larger Judg 17:1–4 pericope and the larger still Judges 17–18 text of which Judg 17:1–4 is a part. Arguably as well we are to envision this representation of Yhwh as a small figurine – possibly anthropomorphic, possibly theriomorphic[33] – that was cast in bronze and then covered with silver overlay,[34] as similar small-scale bronze figurines covered with silver and/or gold have been found by archaeologists at several Syro-Palestinian sites of the Middle Bronze, Late Bronze, and early Iron Ages (c. 2000–1550 BCE, 1550–1200 BCE, and 1200–1000 BCE, respectively).[35] Silver- and gold-covered images are mentioned too by the eighth-century BCE prophet Isaiah in Isa 30:22 (*ṣippuy pesile kesep* and *ʾapuddat massekat zahab*).

Furthermore, if I have been correct in suggesting above that Judg 17:4, 17:5, and 18:17, when taken in tandem, are meant to imply that the figurine that Micah's mother is said to have commissioned stood in the *bet ʾelohim*, or the household shrine of Micah, and if I have also been correct in suggesting that Judg 18:3, 15, and probably 18:17 indicate that this household shrine was a distinct and dedicated space within Micah's multi-building household compound, similar to Room 65 at Ai, then I think the text allows us to conclude that ancient Israelite women could play an important role in helping furnish shrines such as the Judges 17–18 and Ai cult spaces. Indeed, I think Judges 17–18 allows us to conclude that an Israelite woman like Micah's mother could be imagined as contributing to household shrines such as the one alluded to in Judg 17:5 and the one found at Ai the objects that were those sanctuaries' *most valuable* furnishings, given our understanding that the figurine Micah's mother commissioned was made of bronze and silver, both of which were, like all metals, relatively scarce in ancient Israel and hence remarkably precious.

Indeed, we might surmise that an exceptionally valuable object of the sort Micah's mother is said to have commissioned would have served as the focal point of the shrine in which it was located, analogous to the role as focal point that seems to have been assumed by the fenestrated cult stand with feet that stood atop the western bench in Room 65 at Ai. Crucial to note here is the suggestion of William G. Dever that the fenestrated cult stand at Ai is meant to represent a temple of the Israelite god, Yhwh, with the feet that ring the stand's base indicating symbolically that Yhwh is "at home" in his sanctuary.[36] Moreover, we can note comparative ethnographic data that indicate that women would have made ancient Israel's household pottery (although it must be admitted that some of our archaeological evidence and some later biblical texts – Jer 18:1–3 and 1 Chr 4:23 – point to the presence of pottery workshops in ancient Israel staffed by male professionals).[37] Still, we can argue that it is at least possible that a woman made the fenestrated offering stand from the small village of Ai that represented Yhwh resident in his temple and that served as the focal point of that site's twelfth-/eleventh-century BCE household shrine, just as Micah's mother commissioned a figurine that was meant somehow to represent Yhwh, who stood "at home" in and as the focal point of Micah's household shrine in Judges 17–18. Judges 17–18 thus correlates with our archaeological evidence to suggest that an ancient Israelite woman like Micah's mother could take responsibility for producing or commissioning a precious icon that represented the god Yhwh who was venerated in her household's shrine and could further expect to see that image revered as her household shrine's most sacred object. Such a woman therefore could – and should – be understood as her household shrine's primary patron, an extraordinary indication of the powerful role women might play within the religious lives of ancient Israelite household compounds.

Still, as is so often the case in the Bible, the biblical writers, even when suggesting a powerful role for women within ancient Israelite tradition, refuse to affirm this absolutely. We see this, for example, in the failure of Judg 17:1–4 to assign to Micah's mother a name, instead referring to her only as *ʾimmo*, "his [Micah's] mother," six times in the space of three verses (17:2–4).[38] This is significant, for the giving of names in the Bible – especially the giving of names to women – is often an important marker of those women's autonomy and authority. Conversely, to deny a woman a name is often to mark her as powerless and someone easily victimized within a male-dominated culture.[39] This is especially true in the book of Judges, where the text's many powerful women are most typically named (for example, Achsah [Judg 1:11–15], Deborah [Judg 4:4–16; 5:1–23], Jael [Judg 4:17–22, 5:24–7], and Delilah [Judg 16:4–22]), whereas those who fall victim to androcentric agendas or traditions most often remain nameless: Sisera's mother, who waits helplessly and ultimately in vain for her son to return victorious from battle (Judg 5:28–30); Jephthah's daughter, who is killed to fulfill her father's foolish vow to sacrifice whomever or whatever (the Hebrew *ʾăšer* is ambiguous) first comes forth from his house when he returns from war (Judg 11:29–40);[40] Samson's Timnite wife, who is abandoned by her husband seven days after they were wed and then murdered by her own countrymen (Judg 14:1–15:6); and the Levite's concubine, who is thrust by her husband out of the house in which they have lodged for the night to be raped and killed by the Benjaminites of Gibeah (Judg 19:1–30). To be sure, there are some exceptions within Judges, as both the woman of Thebez, who crushes the skull of the royal pretender Abimelech and so brings an end to the civil strife that has consumed her land (Judg 9:50–7), and Samson's mother, who outshines her husband Manoah in the story of Samson's birth (Judg 13:2–24), remain unnamed.[41] Nevertheless, biblical convention would lead us to expect that a woman like Micah's mother, who plays such a leadership role in her household's cult, would be identified by name. The effect of the biblical writers' failing to do so is to downplay the importance of this otherwise powerful woman.

Also in the concluding verses of the Judges 17–18, the text moves to obscure any indication of Micah's mother's contribution to her household's shrine. Thus, in 18:31, we are told that the Danites "maintained for themselves Micah's image that he had made" throughout the time that Yhwh's sanctuary stood in Shiloh. This reference to Yhwh's sanctuary that stood and then, as our text implies, ceased to stand in Shiloh perhaps alludes to the destruction of Shiloh and the sanctuary that presumably stood there in the second half of the eighth century BCE by the Assyrians, or perhaps to the destruction of Shiloh and its presumed sanctuary in c. 1050 BCE by the Philistines: the archaeological evidence has been interpreted in both ways.[42] But "*Micah's image* that *he* had made": what does the text refer to here? It might be the ephod or the teraphim, both of which Micah is said to have made in 17:5. Yet as I have noted above, the term ephod in the Bible most commonly refers to some sort of religious garment and not to any sort of divine representation.[43] Moreover, while teraphim does seem to refer to some sort of sacred figurines, the images in question, as I noted above as well, are most probably representations of family ancestors, and it seems unlikely that representations of an *Ephraimite's* family ancestors would interest the *Danites* as the object of their primary religious veneration. Furthermore, the Hebrew term used for Micah's image in 18:31 is *pesel*, a word that elsewhere in Judges 17–18 is used exclusively to describe the image Micah's mother commissioned according to Judg 17:3 (see Judg 17:3, 4; 18:14, 20; and even 18:17, 18, in which, although the Hebrew is somewhat ambiguous, the *pesel* is clearly distinguished from the ephod and the teraphim).[44] One is left to conclude that the *pesel* that is credited to Micah in 18:31 is the one Micah's mother is said to have made in 17:4, meaning that in 18:31, the text erases Micah's mother from her own story, ignoring her contribution to the furnishing of her household's shrine and assigning that honor to her son instead. I am reminded of Exod 15:1–18, 20–1, in which the victory hymn that, according to 15:20–1, was sung by Miriam after Yhwh's miraculous triumph over Pharaoh and his Egyptian army at the Reed (more traditionally "Red")[45] Sea was reassigned to Moses in Exod 15:1,[46] or Judges 4–5, where the role described for Deborah as war leader in the Israelite tribes' holy war against a coalition of Canaanite kings led by Sisera in Judges 5, especially in vv 7, 12, 15, was reassigned in the later prose retelling of this tale in Judges 4 to her male counterpart, Barak (see especially Judg 4:6–16).[47]

Indeed, the redactors of the Judges 17–18 story so completely erase Micah's mother from the text that she is not mentioned again after 17:4, immediately following the story of her commissioning of the religious figurine. In this way, not only do this passage's editors move to obscure the role that a woman like Micah's mother could play in furnishing her household's shrine, even serving as that shrine's principle patron, they also deny us information regarding women's continuing roles in the life of such a sanctuary. Did women, for example, after providing some of a household shrine's furnishings, continue to visit the objects they had given and make offerings to the deity to whom their gifts had been consecrated? Common sense, it seems to me, suggests that they would, but our text is mute. Fortunately, however, we can make up somewhat for the silence of Judges 17–18 on this point by considering the two other texts in the Hebrew Bible that illuminate women's role in ancient Israelite household religion, Jer 7:16–20 and the related Jer 44:15–19, 25.

Jeremiah 7:16–20 is a part of a long diatribe (Jer 7:1–8:3) that is attributed to the prophet Jeremiah and set in Jerusalem during the waning years of the pre-exilic period (c. 609–586 BCE).[48] In it, Jeremiah condemns Jerusalem's late seventh- and early sixth-century BCE inhabitants for all sorts of behaviors he considers either religiously misinformed (such as the people's trusting that Yhwh will not allow the foreign powers to which the Southern Kingdom of Judah has become vassal – Egypt and then the Babylonian Empire – to destroy the national temple in Jerusalem) or utterly apostate (such as rituals of child sacrifice or the worship of the sun, the moon, and the host of heaven). Included in this harangue is Jeremiah's censure of Judahites who are participating in the worship of a goddess known only as the Queen of Heaven, probably a syncretistic deity who incorporates elements in her character of both the west Semitic goddess Astarte and the east Semitic goddess Ishtar.[49] In Jer 44:15–29, 25, Jeremiah similarly denounces his fellow Judahites for the worship of the Queen of Heaven, both the worship of the Queen of Heaven in which these particular Judahites, who were part of a group that had fled to Egypt in the aftermath of the Babylonian destruction of Jerusalem in 586 BCE, were currently engaging and the worship of the Queen of Heaven by these same Judahites, and others, in the decades before their nation's fall. We are further told, in Jer 44:17, that among these "others" who had worshiped the Queen of Heaven prior to 586 BCE were the ancestors of the fugitive group addressed in that text and their "kings" (*melakim*) and "princes" or "officials" (*śarim*). From this last remark, we might deduce that at least one site where the Queen of Heaven was worshiped prior to the fall of Jerusalem was in shrines within the palaces and other monumental state buildings that were the domains of these kings and officials. Although they predate the Jeremiah passages by a little more than three centuries, archaeological analogies might be provided by Cult Corner 2081 and Cult Room 340 in Building 338 from tenth-century BCE Megiddo, both of which are small installations that seem to have been used for religious purposes that are located within large administrative buildings (Figure 8.8).[50]

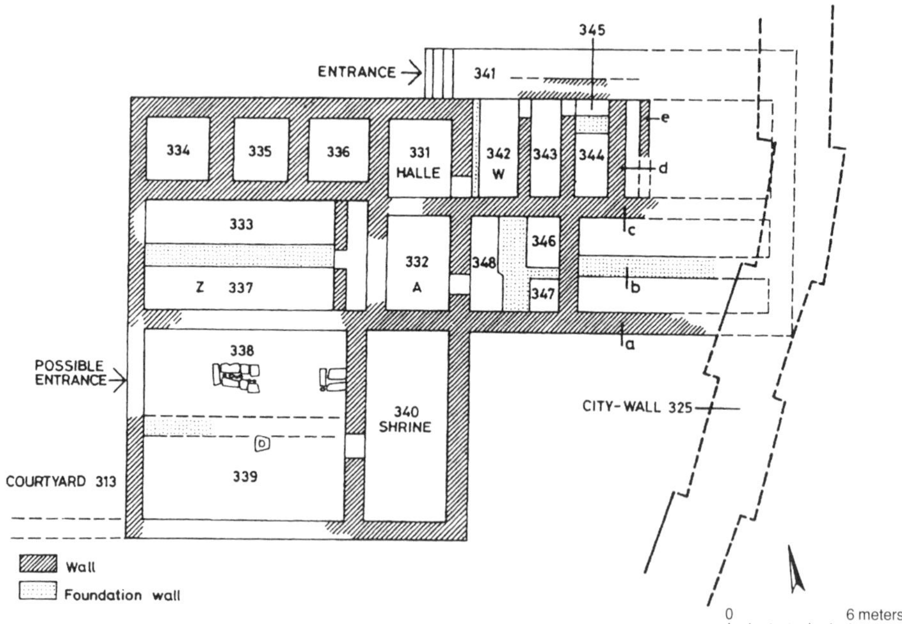

Figure 8.8 Site plan showing the location of Cult Room 340 within the tenth-century BCE Building 338 at Megiddo. From David Ussishkin, "Schumacher's Shrine", p. 157, Fig. 4

The real stress in Jer 7:16–20 and 44:15–19, 25, however, is not on the Queen of Heaven's worshipers among members of the Judaean officialdom, but on her worshipers among Judah's non-elites. Certainly, in Jer 44:15–19, 25, it is non-elites whom Jeremiah censures for their participation in the Queen of Heaven's cult, particularly the husbands and wives among the company of fugitives that had fled to Egypt. Likewise, in Jer 7:16–20, it is husbands, wives, and also children of pre-destruction Judah and Jerusalem who are the particular object of the prophet's scorn: "the children gather wood," we are told, "the fathers kindle fire, and the women knead dough to make cakes for the Queen of Heaven" (Jer 7:18). The location, moreover, where these children's, fathers', and women's cakemaking activities most logically would have taken place was within these individuals' households, for it was within households that the grain and other foodstuffs that would have been needed to make the Queen's bread cakes would have been stored, within households that this grain would most plausibly have been ground into flour and the bread dough prepared, and within households that the oven or *tabun* needed to bake the bread cakes would have been located. We might further propose that not only were the cakes that were to be offered to the Queen of Heaven prepared within the household, but that the actual offerings were presented there, perhaps within distinct and dedicated shrine rooms such as Room 65 at Ai that I discussed in conjunction with my analysis of Judges 17–18 above, but also perhaps within smaller "cult corners" or shrine spaces that were located within individual homes. Certainly, these sorts of "cult corners" or shrine spaces within homes are well attested in the archaeological record, in remains, for example, from twelfth- and eleventh century BCE Khirbet Raddana; tenth-century BCE Megiddo; tenth- or ninth-century BCE Tell el-Far'ah North (probably biblical Tirzah);[51] and ninth- and eighth-century BCE Beersheba.[52]

I would in addition suggest that in this household-based cult of the Queen of Heaven, women played a particularly significant role.[53] For example, the role of the woman in kneading the dough for the Queen of Heaven's offering cakes in Jer 7:18, and presumably baking them, was surely more important to the ritual than the children's gathering of wood or the father's kindling of fire. Women are also specifically identified in Jer 44:19 and 25 as having burned incense and poured out libations to the Queen of Heaven in the past and as intending to do so in the future. We should recall, moreover, that the making of food, drink, and incense offerings – what the great historian of Mesopotamian civilization A. Leo Oppenheim has famously described as "the care and feeding of the gods"[54] – are precisely the rituals that our archaeological evidence from Ai's Room 65 indicated were central to ancient Israelite household religion, as they were in fact central to ancient Israelite religion generally and to all ancient Near Eastern worship. This has enormous implications for understanding the place of women within the household cult of the Queen of Heaven and within ancient Israelite household religion more generally, for if women are as crucially involved as Jer 7:16–20 and 44:15–29, 25 suggest in preparing and apportioning to their households' god or gods the food and drink offerings that are the essence of ancient Israelite worship, then women must be seen as utterly critical actors within Israelite household cult.

It is furthermore important to realize that it is not just coincidental that women are described as performing the most critical of the ritual acts of household religion alluded to in Jer 7:16–20 and 44:15–29, 25: making the Queen of Heaven's cakes, pouring out to her libations, and burning incense in her honor. Rather, the archaeological and related anthropological analyses that in recent years have revealed to us so much about the nature of ancient Israelite households in general have also made clear that many of the activities of the household were gender specific, especially within the rural household compounds in which the vast majority of the Israelite population, as I noted above, lived. The primary economy of these rural households was agrarian, and within them, men undertook tasks such as the physically quite demanding chore of developing new land for cultivation (both by clearing previously forested tracts of trees and stones to create fields and by building the walls that transformed the slopes of the central hill country – the heart of ancient Israelite settlement – into artificially flat terraces that were used for cultivating olive trees and grape vines). Men probably did the work as well of plowing and otherwise tending the fields they had created (see, for example, 1 Sam 8:12), which were used primarily for growing grain; of hewing cisterns; of building homes; and of ferrying harvested grain to these homes (which were typically located on non-agriculturally productive land, often on hilltops that might have been as much as a mile or two climb from the fields in the valleys below).[55]

Women, however, as I have already noted, probably took primary responsibility for domestic pottery production and also for the work of textile production, as is indicated, according to Carol Meyers, by the several biblical texts that associate women with spinning and weaving – for example, Josh 2:6; Judg 16:13–14; Ezek 13:17–18, and most famously, Prov 31:10–31 – and in addition by a 1973 ethnographic survey that determined that women do the work of weaving and spinning in 84 percent and 87 percent, respectively, of the 185 worldwide societies from which data on human labor patterns were collected.[56] This same survey further determined that women do the work of food production in all but three or four of the societies that were surveyed,[57] and several biblical texts likewise associate women with bread-making and with cooking more generally (for example, Lev 26:26; 1 Sam 8:13 and 28:24; Eccl 12:3; and, of course, Jer 7:16–20). Meyers has argued, moreover, that, as a consequence of their responsibilities with regard to food production, women controlled food distribution, determining how the food and drink they had prepared should be allocated to their households' members.[58] These particular obligations, Meyers has additionally intimated, might reasonably be expected to carry beyond the mundane sphere and into the supernatural, so that women would assume not only the tasks of preparing food for their households and allocating it to household members, but the tasks of preparing food and drink offerings and apportioning them to their households' god or gods.[59] The Queen of Heaven texts from Jeremiah confirm that this is so. Because women generally assumed responsibilities within their households for food processing and distribution, it was women in Jer 7:16–20 and 44:15–19, 25, who took charge of preparing food and drink offerings for the goddess venerated in their households, the Queen of Heaven, and then presenting these foodstuffs to her.

This responsibility assumed by women as a part of ancient Israelite household religion – preparing food and drink for the god or gods venerated within their households and then presenting these offerings – is a role that arguably carries over into the sphere of family religion, which I defined, recall, at the beginning of this paper as differentiated from household religion both in terms of space and of participants: household religion being the religious activities the members of a household – both that household's biologically- and maritally-related members and its affiliates – jointly undertake within their domestic compound, whereas family religion is that which the biologically- and maritally-related individuals who constitute a family unit do together to give expression to their collective's religious convictions, whatever the location. Such a location, I suggested, might actually be the home, but also could be a tomb, a local sanctuary, or a major temple. Indeed, women's role in preparing and allocating food and drink offerings within family religion is best illustrated, in my opinion, by a Hebrew Bible text – 1 Samuel 1–2 – that is arguably set at a local sanctuary, the shrine of Shiloh, that seems to lie 15 or so miles from the hometown of a man named Elkanah and his family.[60]

According to 1 Sam 1:3, 7, 21, and 2:19, Elkanah and his family journey annually to Shiloh to offer sacrifice at the sanctuary of Yhwh there. The familial context here – Elkanah is typically accompanied by his two wives Peninnah and Hannah, by Peninnah's sons and daughters, and, at least on one occasion (more on this below), by Hannah's son Samuel, before he is given to serve Yhwh at the Shiloh sanctuary – clearly suggests that we should examine this story within the context of family religion; in fact, according to some commentators, the annual occasion of Elkanah's family's journey to Shiloh is a family or clan sacrifice such as is alluded to in 1 Sam 20:6.[61] My own preference, however, would be to suggest that it is the fall harvest festival of Succoth that is the occasion of the family's annual journey: I think this is suggested literarily by the juxtaposition of 1 Samuel 1–2 with the story that immediate precedes it in the Hebrew Bible, Judges 21, which commentators unanimously agree concerns the fall harvest festival of Succoth;[62] I further think understanding the festival of 1 Sam 1–2 as the fall harvest festival, which involved, among other things, copious drinking in celebration of the pressing of the new wine, well explains an otherwise peculiar detail in 1 Sam 1:14, where the priest Eli, when he sees Hannah praying silently, rather suddenly jumps to the conclusion that she is drunk.[63] Yet even though I would not take the setting of 1 Samuel 1–2 as a family or clan sacrifice, I would still, as I have already intimated, suggest it offers an important window into family religion and, especially, women's roles within the family cult.

Let us consider, for example, 1 Sam 1:21–8. In this text, we are told that Hannah, whose prayer as described in 1:10–18, in which she asked God to reverse her barrenness so that she might bear a son, has, in fact, borne her miracle child

Samuel; thus, she proposes to abstain from making her family's annual journey to Shiloh until the boy is weaned (a process that make have taken as long as three years).[64] After the boy is weaned, however, Hannah does return to Shiloh, to give him – as she has vowed to do in the course of her prayer in 1 Sam 1:10–18 – as a Nazirite dedicated to the service of Yhwh for all his life. According to some scholars, this return journey, which is described in 1:24–8, may have entailed a trip to the Shiloh sanctuary separate from the journey Elkanah's family customarily made every year;[65] for others (and I include myself here), the journey in question was the usual annual pilgrimage. This is, at least, how the ancient Greek Codex Vaticanus, the Lucianic group of Greek miniscules, and probably the Dead Sea Scroll recounting of this story interpret.[66] For these traditions, that is – and I believe most obviously for the Masoretic tradition as well, although the Masoretic text does not make this point explicitly – the journey to Shiloh described in 1 Sam 1:24–8 is one and the same as the customary journey made annually to sacrifice, although this particular journey also includes the additional activity of dedicating Samuel to Yhwh's service.

The text's description of this particular journey in addition includes details that are not specified elsewhere concerning what foodstuffs, precisely, are brought to sacrifice: these are, according to 1:24, a three-year old bull (reading here with the Greek tradition, as opposed to the Masoretic text, which has three bulls being brought to Shiloh),[67] an ephah of flour (somewhere between three-eighths and two-thirds of a bushel),[68] and a skin of wine. The text, moreover, explicitly states that it was *Hannah* who brought these things – "And she [Hannah] went up with him [Samuel] to Shiloh, with a three-year-old bull, and bread, and an ephah of flour, and a skin of wine" – and this even though Elkanah was present (he appears by the end of v 24 in the Greek and probably the Dead Sea Scroll traditions and by v 25 in the Masoretic text). For some commentators, the focus on Hannah as delivering her family's offerings to Shiloh is therefore unexpected and can only be explained by the fact that on this particular occasion, *her* vow to give her son Samuel as a Nazirite dedicated to Yhwh's service is to be fulfilled and so she atypically upstages her husband. Our discussion of Jer 7:16–20 and 44:15–19, 25, however, suggests a very different conclusion: that Hannah quite reasonably is identified as the member of her family who has the responsibility for delivering her family's offerings to the Shiloh sanctuary, given that it was women who had primary responsibility for the allocation of a household's food resources in ancient Israel, including food resources that were to be dedicated to some god or gods. It makes perfect sense, that is, for Hannah in her role as manager of her household's foodstuffs to be identified as accountable for delivering her family's sacrificial offerings to Shiloh. And in the years Hannah stayed home and was unable to fulfill her duty in this regard, Elkanah's other wife, Peninnah, may be envisioned as taking on this womanly task. Certainly, 1 Sam 1:21–2, which speaks of Elkanah and "all his household" minus Hannah going to Shiloh while Samuel was nursing, suggests Peninnah would have made this trip and thus could have assumed the obligation of conveying the foodstuffs for her family's offerings to the shrine.

Hannah and Peninnah should surely also be envisioned as assuming the obligation for manufacturing the ephah of flour that was a part of the offerings described in 1 Sam 1:24, for as I noted as well in discussing Jer 7:16–20, 44:15–19, 25, women had primary responsibility within Israelite households not only for allocating food resources but for food production generally and for the tasks associated with bread-making more specifically. Indeed, Carol Meyers estimates that ancient Israelite women would have spent as much as two hours every day grinding grain (wheat, but occasionally barley) into first a rough meal and then the flour (according to one scholar's estimate, one liter per person for day)[69] that would have been used for their households' bread and in addition, as 1 Sam 1:24 shows us, for dedicatory offerings.[70] Moreover, the fact that women assumed primary responsibility for food production within their households may well mean that, if the grain offering Hannah brought on her family's behalf to Shiloh was transformed into sacrificial loaves (see Judg 6:19, where an ephah of flour is used to make offering cakes), either by being baked in an oven, or toasted on a griddle, or pan-fried (all these methods are described in Lev 2:4–7), rather that just being mixed with oil and burned on the altar (as in Lev 2:1–2), then we should probably envision Hannah and Peninnah as playing a critical role in this bread-making process, as did the women who baked bread cakes for the Queen of Heaven in Jer 7:16–20 and 44:15–19, 25. And most likely Hannah and Peninnah, as the principal agents of food production within their households, should also be envisioned as crucially engaged in the cooking of the sacrificial meat that was eaten by Elkanah's family after the bull that was brought to Shiloh had been slaughtered (and we should note in this regard that the annual sacrifice in question in 1 Samuel 1–2 was clearly the *šelamim* offering, in which the participants boiled and then ate the slaughtered animal's meat while the fat was burned as an offering to Yhwh, this as opposed to *ʿolah* offerings, in which the entire animal was burned on the altar to Yhwh).[71] Certainly, we have no indication in 1 Samuel 1–2 that anyone outside the family took on the task of cooking the sacrificial animal's meat; indeed, 1 Sam 2:13–15, which describes the priest's servant coming to the Israelites to claim the priestly portion as the sacrificial meals are being prepared, makes clear that neither this servant, nor the priests he serves, nor any other cultic representative was responsible for cooking the sacrificial flesh. Instead, this was a family responsibility, and who else within the family would have undertaken it but the women?[72]

Another task for which ancient Israelite women assumed primary responsibility within their families, as I noted above, was the production of textiles, and it is significant in this regard that in 1 Sam 2:19, Hannah is said to make for Samuel a "little robe" and take it to him every year when she went to Shiloh with Elkanah to sacrifice. Furthermore, I would argue that, like the foodstuffs Hannah takes charge of bringing on these yearly journeys, this robe she makes for Samuel should be seen as dedicated for *religious* purposes. Crucial to note here is the notice in the previous verse that Samuel by this point in the story is "ministering before Yhwh" and wearing in this capacity a linen ephod, which we will remember is a part of the priestly vestments. The robe Hannah brings to Shiloh each year is, by implication, also a part of Samuel's priestly apparel and hence an item that she should be seen as dedicating towards the upkeep of Shiloh's religious community. Still, Hannah is not said to bring to Shiloh robes or other garments for any members of Shiloh's priestly community other than her son, which indicates her act of bringing Samuel a robe can still be seen within the context of family religion. It is an action, to return to the definition of family religion I offered above, that one family member does on behalf of a biological relation to give expression to a religious conviction they share.

There is much more that could be said about Hannah's role in this story and what it says about women's place in family religion: that she is repeatedly said to pray, for example, one of the few times in the Bible (as we have already seen) that a woman is said to do so; that she is said to offer a vow, again, one of the few times in the Bible that a woman is said to do so; that she is said, in 1:25, to stand alongside her husband Elkanah as he offers sacrifice at Yhwh's altar (and even, according to the Masoretic tradition, although it is probably corrupt, to wield the sacrificial knife jointly with her husband); that she is said, according to the Greek and probably Dead Sea Scrolls versions of 1:26–8, which probably preserve the better reading, to go alone to the priest Eli to dedicate her son as a Nazirite who will serve Yhwh forever; that she herself may undertake temporarily, as she seeks to bear her Nazirite-son-to-be, the strictures imposed by the Nazirite vow.[73] In the interest of space, however, I will not elaborate on these issues here, but rather close with one final observation about Hannah's role in family religion: that in praying fervently that her barrenness might be reversed to that she could give birth to a son, she no doubt gives voice to what is one of the primary concerns of ancient Israelite family religion – if not the primary concern – human reproduction generally and the bearing of sons in particular, for it is only through the bearing of sons that a family could perpetuate itself in ancient Israel's system of patrilineal descent.

I would compare, moreover, the way in which the women of Jer 44:15–19, 25, might likewise be described as giving voice to some of the major concerns of ancient Israelite household religion: when they had previously worshipped the Queen of Heaven before the fall of Judah and Jerusalem, they claim, "we had plenty of food, and it went well with us, and we saw no evil." Yet, they go on to say that since they have left off worship of the goddess (in response, perhaps, to Jeremiah's castigations as found in Jer 7:16–20?), "we have lacked everything, and we have been consumed by the sword and by famine." The women of Jer 44:15–19, 25, that is, are described both as performing the primary ritual acts of ancient Israelite household religion – the making of food and drink offerings to a household's patron god or gods – and as articulating the presuppositions that drive these acts, the securing for their households' inhabitants the agricultural fecundity and the security from both natural disasters and human attackers that they needed in order to survive. Somewhat similarly, Hannah is described in 1 Samuel 1–2 as having an integral role in the central rites of her family's religion – the bringing of the family's food and drink offerings to Yhwh's shrine at Shiloh – and as articulating one of any family's central religious concerns, the procuring of sons. In this way, women may be understood not only as critical actors within the practice of ancient Israelite household and family religion, but also as the theologians who give voice to some of household and family religion's most constitutive beliefs.

Notes

1 I take these population estimates from William G. Dever, *Did God Have a Wife? Archaeology and Folk Religion in Ancient Israel* (Grand Rapids, MI, and Cambridge, UK: Eerdmans, 2005), p. 18; Philip J. King and Lawrence E. Stager, *Life in Biblical Israel*, Library of Ancient Israel (Louisville and London: Westminster/John Knox, 2001), p. 21; Paula McNutt, *Reconstructing the Society of Ancient Israel*, Library of Ancient Israel (Louisville: Westminster/John Knox; London: SPCK, 1999), p. 152. Cf., however, Oded Borowski, *Daily Life in Biblical Times* (Atlanta: Society of Biblical Literature, 2003), pp. 9, 13, who estimates that only 66 percent of the Israelite population, at least during the Iron II period (c. 1000–586 BCE), lived in rural locations.

2 These household compounds of ancient Israel have now been described by many different scholars: I have found most helpful Borowski, *Daily Life in Biblical Times*, pp. 13–21; William G. Dever, *Who Were the Early Israelites and Where Did They Come From?* (Grand Rapids, MI, and Cambridge, UK: Eerdmans, 2003), pp. 102–7; idem, *Did God Have a Wife?*, pp. 18–29; King and Stager, *Life in Biblical Israel*, pp. 9–19, 28–43; Carol Meyers, *Discovering Eve: Ancient Israelite Women in Context* (New York and Oxford: Oxford University Press, 1988), pp. 128–38; Lawrence E. Stager, "The Archaeology of the Family in Ancient Israel," *Bulletin of the American Schools of Oriental Research* 260 (1985): 1–35.

3 Stager, "Archaeology of the Family," pp. 20, 22; on the translation of John 14:2, see further King and Stager, *Life in Biblical Israel*, p. 12.

4 Stager, "Archaeology of the Family," p. 22.

5 According to several scholars, Judg 17:1–4 was originally separate from the story that follows in Judg 17:7–13: this is particularly indicated by the fact that Micah's name is rendered differently in Judg 17:1–4 and in Judg 17:7–13 (*mikayehu* in Judg 17:1 and 4 versus *mikah* in Judg 17:8, 9, 10, 12, and 13). Judg 17:5–6, according to this reconstruction, was added by a redactor to bring 17:1–4 and 7–13 together, as these two verses set the stage for Micah's appointment of a levitical priest to serve his household in 17:7–13 by indicating that Micah had a shrine and sacred objects in his house – teraphim and an ephod (on which see further below, nn. 10, 11, and 13) – that required the service of a religious specialist (first Micah's son and then the Levite). See further Robert G. Boling, *Judges: A New Translation with Introduction and Commentary*, Anchor Bible 6A (Garden City, NY: Doubleday, 1975), pp. 258–9, and Karel van der Toorn, *Family Religion in Babylonia, Syria and Israel: Continuity and Change in the Forms of Religious Life* (Leiden, New York, Köln: Brill, 1996), p. 247; also, the somewhat similar proposal advanced by Victor H. Matthews, *Judges and Ruth*, New Cambridge Biblical Commentary (Cambridge, UK: Cambridge University Press, 2004), pp. 168, 170.

6 So, e.g., the editors of the Biblia Hebraica Stuttgartensia, note on Judg 18:15; James D. Martin, *The Book of Judges*, Cambridge Biblical Commentary (Cambridge, UK: Cambridge University Press, 1975), p. 193; George F. Moore, *A Critical and*

Exegetical Commentary on Judges, 2nd edn., International Critical Commentary (Edinburgh: T. & T. Clark, 1903), p. 397.

7 This emendation is also suggested by Boling, *Judges*, p. 264, although his overall understanding of what is meant by *bet mikah* differs significantly from mine.

8 See similarly Stager, "Archaeology of the Family," p. 22; van der Toorn, *Family Religion*, pp. 197–8; Carol Meyers, "The Family in Early Israel," in *Families in Ancient Israel*, ed. Leo Purdue et al. (Louisville, KY: Westminster John Knox, 1997), p. 17; and Ziony Zevit, *The Religions of Ancient Israel: A Synthesis of Parallactic Approaches* (London and New York: Continuum, 2001), p. 626.

9 As Marc Brettler somewhat colloquially but aptly states, the Levite opts "to become a 'big shot' in Dan rather than remain a 'hick priest' in Ephraim." See Marc Brettler, "The Book of Judges: Literature as Politics," *Journal of Biblical Literature* 108 (1989): 409.

10 The most up-to-date and persuasive work on the teraphim and their function is Karel van der Toorn and Theodore J. Lewis, "*terapim*," *Theologisches Wörterbuch zum alten Testament*, ed. G. J. Botterweck and H. Ringgren (Stuttgart: W. Kohlhammer, 1995), 8: 765–78; see also Karel van der Toorn, "The Nature of the Biblical Teraphim in the Light of the Cuneiform Evidence," *Catholic Biblical Quarterly* 52 (1990): 203–23; idem, *Family Religion*, pp. 218–25.

11 Although some scholars have suggested the term ephod in Judg 17:5 refers to a garment that clothed one of Micah's teraphim or some other cult statue (the practice of clothing cult statues was well known in Israel and more generally in the ancient Near East; see, e.g., Ezek 16:16–18; Jer 10:5, 9; Ep Jer 6:9, 11–13, 20, 33, 72) or to a divine representation itself, as the term ephod possibly means in 1 Sam 21:9 and in Judg 8:27, where Gideon and his family bow down to the ephod he has made (see van der Toorn, *Family Religion*, p. 250; Karel van der Toorn and Cees Houtman, "David and the Ark," *Journal of Biblical Literature* 113 [1994]: 230), most commonly in the Bible, ephod is understood as an overgarment, often elaborately woven, that is part of the priestly vestments. See further Menahem Haran, *Temples and Temple Service in Ancient Israel* (Oxford: Clarendon, 1978), pp. 166–8; King and Stager, *Life in Biblical Israel*, p. 10; Carol Meyers, "Ephod," *Anchor Bible Dictionary*, ed. D. N. Freedman (New York: Doubleday, 1992) 2: 550a–b; Patrick D. Miller, *The Religion of Ancient Israel*, Library of Ancient Israel (London: SPCK; Louisville, KY: Westminster John Knox, 2000), p. 56.

12 Grammatically, the phrase *pesel umassekah* is a hendiadys, whereby two nouns (*pesel*, "image," and *massekah*, "molten image") connected by "and" indicate a single concept. Cf., however, David M. Gunn, *Judges*, Blackwell Bible Commentaries (Oxford: Blackwell Publishing, 2005), p. 231; Lillian Klein, *The Triumph of Irony in the Book of Judges*, Journal for the Study of the Old Testament Supplement Series 68, Bible and Literature Series 14 (Sheffield, UK: Almond, 1988), p. 150.

13 Boling, *Judges*, 256, takes the teraphim in to be synonymous with the figurine of cast metal, whereas C. A. Faraone, B. Garnand, and C. López-Ruiz, "Micah's Mother (Judg 17:1–4) and a Curse from Carthage (*KAI* 89): Canaanite Precedents for Greek and Latin Curses against Thieves?" *Journal of Near Eastern Studies* 64 (2005): 164 n. 13, argue the phrase *'epod uterapim* as a whole should be taken as referring to the figurine of cast metal, with *terapim* referring specifically to the image proper and *'epod* to its molten plating. Somewhat similarly, van der Toorn, *Family Religion*, p. 250, argues that the phrase *'epod uterapim* should be read as a hendiadys (above, n. 12), meaning

"an ancestor image" or "ancestor images" (see n. 11 on the possible meaning of *ʾepod* as image), and he also seems to indicate that he takes this "ancestor image" or these "images" to be equivalent to our story's cast-metal image. His reasons for suggesting this, however, are unclear and thus unpersuasive to me, as are Boling's reasons for suggesting that the teraphim of Judges 17–18 and the text's cast-metal figurine are to be equated. Moreover, I am not compelled by van der Toorn's arguments for *ʾepod uterapim* as a hendiadys, nor am I compelled by Faraone's, Garnand's, and López-Ruiz's argument that 17:1–4 and 17:5–6 should be read as variants of the same story and so the image(s) of 17:4 (the cast-metal figurine) and of 17:5 (*ʾepod uterapim*) should be read as one and the same. Rather, it seems to me the plainest meaning of the text – and certainly the one embraced by the overall redactor of Judges 17–18 (see 18:17, 18, and 20) – is to see the cast-metal figurine, the *ʾepod*, and the *terapim* as distinct objects. See further Rainer Albertz, *A History of Israelite Religion in the Old Testament Period*, Old Testament Library (Louisville, KY: Westminster/John Knox Press, 1992), 1:37: "the teraphim . . . are here [in Judges 17–18] distinguished clearly from a cultic image of the god proper [i.e., the *pesel umassekah*]" and "teraphim appear alongside . . . ephod."

14 Judith Marquet-Krause, *Les fouilles de ʿAy (et-Tell), 1933–35*, Bibliothèque archéologique et historique 45 (Paris: Geuthner, 1949), p. 23; this reference brought to my attention by Beth Alpert Nakhai, *Archaeology and the Religions of Canaan and Israel*, American Schools of Oriental Research Books 7 (Boston: American Schools of Oriental Research, 2001), p. 173.

15 Zevit, *The Religions of Ancient Israel*, pp. 153–6; see also the brief discussions of Dever, *Did God Have a Wife?*, p. 113, and Nakhai, *Archaeology and the Religions of Canaan and Israel*, p. 173.

16 Zevit, *The Religions of Ancient Israel*, p. 153.

17 Nakhai, *Archaeology and the Religions of Canaan and Israel*, p. 173.

18 Zevit, *The Religions of Ancient Israel*, p. 153.

19 For the most recent discussion, see Dever, *Did God Have a Wife?*, pp. 160–2.

20 The feet were originally called leonine by Marquet-Krause, *Les fouilles de ʿAy*, p. 23, and this identification was subsequently adopted by Joseph A. Callaway, "Ai," in *The New Encyclopedia of Archaeological Excavation in the Holy Land*, ed. E. Stern (Jerusalem: Israel Exploration Society and Carta, 1993), 1: 45, and Nakhai, *Archaeology and the Religions of Canaan and Israel*, 173. Dever, *Did God Have a Wife?*, p. 113, interprets the feet as human.

21 As reported in Zevit, *The Religions of Ancient Israel*, p. 153.

22 Ibid., pp. 153, 155.

23 Ibid., p. 153, reports that a single "primitively-formed animal figurine, a horse or a dog," was found inside the fenestrated offering stand; Nakhai, *Archaeology and the Religions of Canaan and Israel*, p. 173, citing Callaway, "Ai," p. 45, reports that two animal figurines were found in Room 65.

24 Joseph A. Callaway, "Ai," in *Anchor Bible Dictionary*, 1: 130a.

25 In *Who Were the Early Israelites?*, p. 78, Dever estimates that as many as ten to fifteen people lived in each of the individual houses of the two- to three-household compounds found at twelfth-century BCE Tel Masos, but in his more recent *Did God Have a Wife?*, pp. 18–19, he numbers the occupants of a multi-home household compound at fifteen to twenty. In their *Life in Biblical Israel*, p. 12, King and Stager seem to assume there were approximately 12.5 people per household compound (they suggest that a village of

250 people would have had 20 compounds, with 17 people occupying the largest compound of this hypothetical site). Meyers, in "The Family in Early Israel," p. 19, writes that "a family size [by which she means the extended family of a multi-household compound and its affiliated members] would rarely exceed fifteen"; van der Toorn, in *Family Religion*, p. 197, also assumes an average of about fifteen people per household compound.

26 Zevit, *The Religions of Ancient Israel*, pp. 154, 156.

27 Josef Scharbert, "*'alah*," in *Theological Dictionary of the Old Testament* 1: 262; see also Carol Meyers, "Judg 17:1–4, Mother of Micah," in *Women in Scripture: A Dictionary of Named and Unnamed Women in the Hebrew Bible, the Apocryphal/Deuterocanonical Books, and the New Testament*, ed. C. Meyers, with T. Craven and R. S. Kraemer (Boston: Houghton Mifflin, 2000), p. 248.

28 As pointed out by Sheldon H. Blank, "The Curse, Blasphemy, the Spell, and the Oath," *Hebrew Union College Annual* 23 (1950/51): 94 n. 62, Lev 19:14 prohibits cursing the deaf, precisely because they cannot be expected to have heard the curse and to thus be compelled to respond or face the consequences the curse has set forward.

29 These examples brought to my attention by Blank, "The Curse, Blasphemy, the Spell, and the Oath," p. 94.

30 Scharbert, "*'alah*," p. 265; Blank, "The Curse, Blasphemy, the Spell, and the Oath," p. 95.

31 Patrick D. Miller, "Things Too Wonderful: Prayers of Women in the Old Testament," in *Biblische Theologie und gesellschaftlicher Wandel: Für Norbert Lohfink SJ*, ed. G. Braulik, W. Gross, and S. McEvenue (Freiburg, Basel, and Wien: Herder, 1993), p. 237, identifies what he describes as ten or eleven instances of women praying in the Hebrew Bible (although he then lists thirteen): Gen 21:16–17; 25:22; 29:35; 30:24; Exod 15:21; Judg 5:1–31; Ruth 1:8–9; 4:14; 1 Sam 1:10, 12–15, 2:1–10; 1 Kgs 10:9; and Psalm 131; see also idem, *They Cried to the Lord: The Form and Theology of Biblical Prayer* (Minneapolis: Fortress, 1994), n. 2 on p. 413. But I have reservations concerning Miller's sense of what should be classified as prayer, which I would define more narrowly than he, limiting the category of prayer to moments in which an individual or a community speaks directly to God. I would thus not, *contra* Miller, see Gen 21:16–17 as prayer, since there is no indication that Hagar's words in this verse are directed to God; similarly, I would argue that Leah's words in Gen 29:35 and Rachel's words in Gen 30:24, which are spoken as part of wordplays that gloss the names of their sons, Judah and Joseph, are addressed not directly to God but to the family members and others (e.g., midwives) who might attend these women at birth. Naomi's words in Ruth 1:8–9 likewise seem to me words that are really addressed to her daughters-in-law, rather than words of a prayer per se, and Exod 15:21 and Judg 5:1–31, although addressed to Yhwh, are *hymns* of thanksgiving, a genre I would differentiate from prayer. Somewhat similarly, I would categorize the Bethlehemite women's words in Ruth 4:14 and the Queen of Sheba's words in 1 Kgs 10:9 as words of benediction, not prayer, whose intended audience, moreover, is really not the deity but those to whom these blessings are spoken. Brettler also raises concerns about Miller's understanding of Psalm 131: see Marc Zvi Brettler, "Women and Psalms: Toward an Understanding of the Role of Women's Prayer in the Israelite Cult," in *Gender and Law in the Hebrew Bible and the Ancient Near East*, Journal for the Study of the Old Testament Supplement Series 262, ed. V. H. Matthews, B. M. Levinson, and T. Frymer-Kensky (Sheffield, UK: Sheffield

Academic Press, 1998), p. 39, and, idem, "Mother of Psalmist (God's Serving Girl): Pss 22:9–10; 27:10; 35:14; 50:20; 51:5; 71:6; 86:16; 109:14; 116:16; 131:2; 139:13," in *Women in Scripture*, p. 297.

32 Certainly, later tradition seems to assume female prayer as a given, as can be seen in both deuterocanonical and New Testament texts. The heroine Judith prays to God, for example, in the second-century BCE deuterocanonical book that bears her name, before she undertakes to kill her people's enemy, the Assyrian general Holofernes (Judith 12:8); Esther prays in the so-called Greek Additions to Esther that are found in the Septuagint version of that book (GEsther 4:30 [or in the citation system used in Jerome's Latin translation, Esther 14:3–19]); and in the fourth- or third-century BCE book of Tobit, Sarah, the future wife of Tobit's son Tobias, prays to God that she might die rather than face the reproach to which she has been subject, which is the result of circumstances beyond her control (Tobit 3:10, 11). She is then exhorted to pray again in 6:18 and 8:4 and does so in 8:4. New Testament references to women's prayer include (1) Acts 1:14, where the eleven disciples who remain after Jesus' death are said to be constantly devoting themselves to prayer, along with "certain women," including Jesus' mother Mary; and (2) 1 Cor 11:13, in which, although women are forbidden to pray with their heads uncovered, no other strictures on women's ability or right to pray are presumed.

33 Anthropomorphized images of gods and goddesses were a common part of the Canaanite religious culture of the Late Bronze Age (c. 1550–1200 BCE), but archaeologists have discovered precious few images from Iron Age Israel (c. 1200–586 BCE) that might be taken as anthropomorphic representations of Yhwh: only, for example, (1) a seated bronze figurine from eleventh-century BCE Hazor (for a line drawing, see Othmar Keel and Christoph Uehlinger, *Gods, Goddesses, and Images of God in Ancient Israel* [Minneapolis: Fortress, 1998], Fig. 141 on p. 117, or Miller, *The Religion of Ancient Israel*, Fig. 5 on p. 18; for a photograph, see James B. Pritchard, *The Ancient Near East in Pictures Relating to the Old Testament*, 2nd edn., with supplement [Princeton: Princeton University Press, 1969], #833, or Ora Negbi, *Canaanite Gods in Metal: An Archaeological Study of Ancient Syro-Palestinian Figurines* [Tel Aviv: Tel Aviv University Institute of Archaeology, 1976], Pl. 34, #1454); and (2) a stick figure carved into a limestone altar from eleventh-century BCE Gezer (for a line drawing, see again Miller, *The Religion of Ancient Israel*, p. 19). A twelfth-century BCE bull figurine found at the site of an open-air sanctuary near Dothan might represent Yhwh in theriomorphic form, but this is not at all clear: the bull could also represent a Canaanite god, such as El or Baal, or it could represent a pedestal atop which Yhwh was understood invisibly to stand, in the same way Yhwh was understood to sit invisibly enthroned atop the cherubim throne of the ark of the covenant. See Amihai Mazar, "The 'Bull Site' – An Iron Age I Open Cult Place," *Bulletin of the American Schools of Oriental Research* 247 (1982): 27–32.

34 As is suggested by C. Dohmen, "*massekah*," *Theological Dictionary of the Old Testament* 8:432 (this reference brought to my attention by Faraone, Garnand, and López-Ruiz, "Micah's Mother," 164 n. 13); King and Stager, *Life in Biblical Israel*, p. 9.

35 For discussion of this sort of image, see further Negbi, *Canaanite Gods in Metal*, 2 and *passim*; for representative examples, see Keel and Uehlinger, *Gods, Goddesses, and Images of God*, Fig. 56 on p. 59 (= Pritchard, *Ancient Near East in Pictures*, #497), a bronze statue of an enthroned god with gold overlay, from Late Bronze Age Megiddo,

and Fig. 139 on p. 117 (= Pritchard, *Ancient Near East in Pictures*, #494), a bronze statue of the god Reshef [?] with overlay, from early Iron Age Megiddo); King and Stager, *Life in Biblical Israel*, Ill. 84 on p. 173, a bronze calf with silver overlay, from Middle Bronze Age Ashkelon; Miller, *The Religion of Ancient Israel*, Fig. 2 on p. 4 (= Pritchard, *Ancient Near East in Pictures*, #826), a bronze statue of the Canaanite god El with gold overlay, from Late Bronze Age Ugarit, and Fig. 3 on p. 15 (= Pritchard, *Ancient Near East in Pictures*, #481), a bronze statue of a warrior god [Baal?], with the head and headdress covered in gold and the body in silver, from Late Bronze Age Syria.

36 Dever, *Did God Have a Wife?*, p. 121.

37 On women as the manufacturers of ancient Israelite household pottery, see ibid., 86; Meyers, *Discovering Eve*, 148; eadem, "The Family in Early Israel," pp. 25–6; Bryant G. Wood, *The Sociology of Pottery in Ancient Palestine: The Ceramic Industry and the Diffusion of Ceramic Style in the Bronze and Iron Ages*, Journal for the Study of the Old Testament Supplement Series 103 (Sheffield: JSOT Press, 1990), p. 24, who cites D. E. Arnold, *Ceramic Theory and Cultural Process* (Cambridge: Cambridge University Press, 1985), pp. 100–5, and S. E. van der Leeuw, "Towards a Study of the Economy of Pottery Making," in *Ex Horreo*, ed. B. L. van Beek, R. W. Brandt, and W. Groenman-van Waateringe (Amsterdam: Universiteit van Amsterdam, 1977), pp. 70–2. On the archaeological data that points to a class of male professional potters in ancient Israel, see Wood, *The Sociology of Pottery*, pp. 15–50; on the biblical data, see Meyers, *Discovering Eve*, p. 148.

38 In addition to my discussion here, see E. Aydeet Mueller, *The Micah Story: A Morality Tale in the Book of Judges*, Studies in Biblical Literature 34 (New York: Peter Lang, 2001), 54, and n. 18 on p. 88, who correctly notes that, in contrast to other female protagonists in Judges, Micah's mother's anonymity has generally been unnoticed by scholars.

39 See Carol Meyers, "The Hannah Narrative in Feminist Perspective," in *Go to the Land I Will Show You: Studies in Honor of Dwight W. Young*, ed. J. Coleson and V. Matthews (Winona Lake, IN: Eisenbrauns, 1996), pp. 120–2 (= "Hannah and her Sacrifice: Reclaiming Female Agency," in *A Feminist Companion to Samuel and Kings*, The Feminist Companion to the Bible 5, ed. A. Brenner [Sheffield: Sheffield Academic Press, 1994], pp. 96–9), but note the important cautions offered by Adele Reinhartz, *"Why Ask My Name?" Anonymity and Identity in Biblical Narrative* (New York and Oxford: Oxford University Press, 1998), passim.

40 On the characterization of this vow as foolish, see especially Phyllis Trible, "A Meditation in Mourning: The Sacrifice of the Daughter of Jephthah," *Union Seminary Quarterly Review* 36 (1981): 61; eadem, "The Daughter of Jephthah: An Inhuman Sacrifice," in *Texts of Terror: Literary Feminist Readings of Biblical Narratives*, Overtures to Biblical Theology 13 (Philadelphia: Fortress, 1984), p. 96; eadem, "A Daughter's Death: Feminism, Literary Criticism, and the Bible," in *Backgrounds for the Bible*, ed. M. P. O'Connor and D. N. Freedman (Winona Lake, IN: Eisenbrauns, 1987), p. 4.

41 For this characterization of Samson's mother, see J. Cheryl Exum, "Promise and Fulfillment: Narrative Art in Judges 13," *Journal of Biblical Literature* 99 (1980): 43–59; eadem, "'Mother in Israel': A Familiar Figure Reconsidered," in *Feminist Interpretation of the Bible*, ed. L. M. Russell (Philadelphia: Westminster, 1985), pp. 82–4; eadem, "Samson's Women," in *Fragmented Women: Feminist (Sub)versions of Biblical Narratives* (Valley Forge, PA: Trinity Press International, 1993), pp. 61–93,

especially pp. 63–8; eadem, "Feminist Criticism: Whose Interests are Being Served?" in *Judges and Method: New Approaches in Biblical Studies*, ed. G. A. Yee (Minneapolis: Fortress, 1995), p. 79; Adele Reinhartz, "Samson's Mother: An Unnamed Protagonist," *Journal for the Study of the Old Testament* 55 (1992): 25–37.

42 According to Danish archaeological excavations of Shiloh in 1926, 1929, 1932, and, especially, 1963, the site was destroyed during the Assyrian invasions of the second half of the eighth century BCE. According to the most recent excavator of the site, Israel Finkelstein, however, Shiloh was destroyed already in c. 1050 BCE, perhaps by the Philistines. Finkelstein further argues, contra the Danes, that there was no significant resettlement after this destruction. See further Marie-Louise Buhl and Svend Holm-Nielsen, *Shiloh, The Danish Excavations at Tell Sailun, Palestine, in 1926, 1929, 1932 and 1963* (Copenhagen: National Museum of Denmark, 1969), and Israel Finkelstein, "The History and Archaeology of Shiloh from the Middle Bronze Age II to Iron Age II," in *Shiloh: The Archaeology of a Biblical Site*, ed. I. Finkelstein et al. (Tel Aviv: Monograph Series of Tel Aviv University, 1993), pp. 388–9; Leslie Watkins (based on material submitted by Israel Finkelstein), "Shiloh," in *The Oxford Encyclopedia of Archaeology in the Near East*, ed. E. M. Meyers (New York and Oxford: Oxford University Press, 1997), 5: 29.

43 See further above, n. 11.

44 See further above, n. 13.

45 English versions traditionally render Hebrew *yam-sup* as "Red Sea" based on its translation in the Latin Vulgate as *Mare Rubrum*. Yet, while Hebrew *yam* is correctly translated as "sea," the word *sup* means not "red" but "reed." It is generally regarded to be a loanword from Egyptian *ṯwf*, "papyrus plant."

46 Most scholars presume that the Exod 15:20–1 pericope that attributes the victory hymn to Miriam is the older ascription, for it is easy to see how, over time, tradition would have changed from assigning the song to Miriam and attributed it to her more famous brother. It is difficult to imagine, conversely, that a song originally ascribed to Moses would have later been accredited to a more minor character. See Frank M. Cross and David Noel Freedman, "The Song of Miriam," *Journal of Near Eastern Studies* 14 (1955): 237, who write, "It is easy to understand the ascription of the hymn to the great leader. It would be more difficult to explain the association of Miriam with the song as a secondary development"; also Phyllis Trible, "Bringing Miriam out of the Shadows," *Bible Review* 5/1 (February 1989): 34 n. 5.

47 Susan Ackerman, *Warrior, Dancer, Seductress, Queen: Women in Judges and Biblical Israel*, Anchor Bible Reference Library 17 (New York: Doubleday, 1998), pp. 31–2.

48 On issues of the date of Jer 7:1–8:3, and its attribution to the prophet Jeremiah, see Susan Ackerman, *Under Every Green Tree: Popular Religion in Sixth-Century Judah*, Harvard Semitic Monographs 46 (Atlanta, GA: Scholars Press, 1992), pp. 5–8.

49 Ackerman, *Under Every Green Tree*, pp. 8–34, especially pp. 20–34, eadem, "'And the Women Knead Dough': The Worship of the Queen of Heaven in Sixth-Century Judah," in *Gender and Difference in Ancient Israel*, ed. P. L. Day (Minneapolis: Fortress, 1989), pp. 109–24 (= pp. 21–32 in *Women in the Hebrew Bible: A Reader*, ed. A. Bach [New York and London: Routledge, 1999]).

50 For discussion, see Nakhai, *Archaeology and the Religions of Canaan and Israel*, pp. 177–8, and, much more thoroughly, Zevit, *The Religions of Ancient Israel*, pp. 220–5, 227–31.

51 The remains of domestic cult from Tell el-Far'ah North are dated to the tenth century BCE by Dever, *Did God Have a Wife?*, pp. 115, 117, and by Elizabeth A. Willett, "Women and Household Shrines in Ancient Israel" (PhD dissertation, University of Arizona, 1999), p. 118, but to the ninth-century BCE by Zevit, *The Religions of Ancient Israel*, p. 241.

52 On the remains of shrine spaces within homes from twelfth- and eleventh-century BCE Khirbet Raddana, see Dever, *Did God Have a Wife?*, p. 115, and Nakhai, *Archaeology and the Religions of Canaan and Israel*, pp. 173–4; on the similar remains from tenth-century BCE Megiddo, see again Nakhai, *Archaeology and the Religions of Canaan and Israel*, p. 177, who cites as well Yigael Shiloh, "Iron Age Sanctuaries and Cult Elements in Palestine," in *Symposia Celebrating the Seventy-Fifth Anniversary of the Founding of the American Schools of Oriental Research (1900–1975)*, ed. F. M. Cross (Cambridge, MA: American Schools of Oriental Research, 1979), p. 149; on household shrine remains from Tell el Far'ah North, see Willett, *Women and Household Shrines*, pp. 118–33, and Zevit, *The Religions of Ancient Israel*, pp. 241 and 337–8; on the ninth- and eighth-century BCE materials from Beersheba, see John S. Holladay, Jr., "Religion in Israel and Judah Under the Monarchy: An Explicitly Archaeological Approach," in *Ancient Israelite Religion: Essays in Honor of Frank Moore Cross*, ed. P. D. Miller, P. D. Hanson, and S. D. McBride (Philadelphia: Fortress, 1987), pp. 275–6; Willett, *Women and Household Shrines in Ancient Israel*, pp. 134–53; Zevit, *The Religions of Ancient Israel*, pp. 175–6.

53 See similarly Zevit, *The Religions of Ancient Israel*, pp. 541, 555.

54 A. Leo Oppenheim, *Ancient Mesopotamia: Portrait of a Dead Civilization*, rev. edn. (Chicago and London: University of Chicago Press, 1977), p. 183.

55 Borowski, *Daily Life in Biblical Times*, pp. 14, 22, 114–16; Dever, *Did God Have a Wife?*, pp. 26–7; King and Stager, *Life in Biblical Israel*, p. 16; Meyers, *Discovering Eve*, p. 148; eadem, "The Family in Early Israel," p. 24.

56 Carol Meyers, "Material Remains and Social Relations: Women's Culture in Agrarian Households of the Iron Age," in *Symbiosis, Symbolism, and the Power of the Past: Canaan, Ancient Israel, and Their Neighbors from the Late Bronze Age through Roman Palaestina. Proceedings of the Centennial Symposium, W. F. Albright Institute of Archaeological Research and American Schools of Oriental Research, Jerusalem, May 29 – May 31, 2000*, ed. William G. Dever and Seymour Gitin (Winona Lake, IN: Eisenbrauns, 2003), p. 433; see also Borowski, *Daily Life in Biblical Times*, pp. 113–14, 123–5.

57 Meyers, "Material Remains and Social Relations," p. 431; see also Borowski, *Daily Life*, pp. 113–14, 123–5.

58 Meyers, *Discovering Eve*, pp. 146–7.

59 Ibid., p. 163.

60 There is some question here regarding the name and precise location of the hometown of Elkanah and his family. First, Samuel 1:1 suggests a village Ramathaim in the hill country of Ephraim, which the church historian Eusebius long ago identified with New Testament Arimathea (Matt 27:57; John 19:38), or modern Rentis, a site about 17 miles west and a little south of Shiloh. Somewhat later in the text (1:19), however, Elqanah's family is described as coming from Ramah, a hill-country town that lay in the tribal territory of Benjamin, about five miles north of Jerusalem, near the Benjaminite–Ephraimite border. Benjaminite Ramah, moreover, is identified as the hometown of Elkanah and his son Samuel at several other points in 1 Samuel: 1 Sam

2:11; 7:17; 8:4; 15:34; 16:13; 19:18; 25:1; and 28:3. Most scholars thus prefer to equate the Ramathaim of 1 Sam 1:1 with Ramah of Benjamin, about 14 miles due south of Shiloh (see further the relevant articles in any standard Bible dictionary: e.g., Patrick M. Arnold, "Ramah," in *Anchor Bible Dictionary*, 5:613b; Stephen R. Miller, "Ramah," in *Eerdman's Dictionary of the Bible*, ed. D. N. Freedman [Grand Rapids, MI: Eerdmans, 2000], 1108a–b). The issue is not one that need overly concern us here: our interest is the role of the sanctuary of Shiloh as a local shrine that lies about 15 miles or so from Elkanah's family's hometown, regardless of whether that hometown is taken to be Ephraimite Ramathaim or Benjaminite Ramah.

61 Menahem Haran, "Ze<u>b</u>aḥ Hayyamim," *Vetus Testamentum* 19 (1969): 12 n. 2; C. L. Seow, *Myth, Drama, and the Politics of David's Dance*, Harvard Semitic Monographs 44 (Atlanta: Scholars Press, 1989), pp. 23–5.

62 Unfortunately, this juxtaposition is obscured in Christian Bibles, in which the book of Ruth has secondarily been inserted between Judges and 1 Samuel.

63 See further my discussion in *Warrior, Dancer, Seductress, Queen*, pp. 113 and 258; also, David J. A. Clines, "The Evidence for an Autumnal New Year in Pre-Exilic Israel Reconsidered," *Journal of Biblical Literature* 93 (1974): 28.

64 See 2 Macc 7:27; Mayer I. Gruber, "Breast-Feeding Practices in Biblical Israel and in Old Babylonian Mesopotamia," in *The Motherhood of God and Other Studies*, South Florida Studies in the History of Judaism 57 (Atlanta: Scholars Press, 1992), p. 72, citing Hilma Granqvist, *Child Problems Among the Arabs* (Helsingfors, Söderström, 1950), p. 79; Meyers, *Discovering Eve*, p. 151, citing Roland de Vaux, *Ancient Israel* (New York: McGraw-Hill, 1961), p. 43; and Hans W. Wolff, *Anthropology of the Old Testament* (Philadelphia: Fortress, 1974), pp. 121, 178; also the references assembled by Jacques Berlinerblau, *The Vow and the 'Popular Religious Groups' of Ancient Israel: A Philological and Sociological Inquiry*, Journal for the Study of the Old Testament Supplement Series 210 (Sheffield, UK: Sheffield Academic Press, 1996), p. 109 n. 37.

65 This suggestion goes back to Julius Wellhausen, *Der Text der Bücher Samuelis untersucht* (Göttingen: Vandenhoeck & Ruprecht, 1871), p. 41; see further Stanley D. Walters, "Hannah and Anna: The Greek and Hebrew Texts of 1 Samuel 1," *Journal of Biblical Literature* 107 (1988): 400–1 and n. 25 on p. 401.

66 See P. Kyle McCarter, *I Samuel: A New Translation with Introduction and Commentary*, Anchor Bible 8 (Garden City, NY: Doubleday, 1980), p. 57; Andrew Fincke, *The Samuel Scroll from Qumran: 4QSam[a] restored and compared to the Septuagint and 4QSam[c]* (Leiden, Boston, Köln: Brill, 2001), pp. 9 and 30, note on Col. II, lines 9–10.

67 As McCarter (among others) points out, the Masoretic text has suffered a simple corruption here, as the *m* of the original reading *bpr mšlš*, a "three-year old bull," has been mistakenly repositioned to yield *bprm šlš*, "three bulls." See McCarter, *I Samuel*, pp. 56–7.

68 On ephah, see Carol Meyers, "An Ethnoarchaeological Analysis of Hannah's Sacrifice," in *Pomegranates and Golden Bells: Studies in Biblical, Jewish, and Near Eastern Ritual, Law, and Literature in Honor of Jacob Milgrom*, ed. D. P. Wright, D. N. Freedman, and A. Hurvitz (Winona Lake, IN: Eisenbrauns, 1995), p. 84.

69 See Borowski, *Daily Life in Biblical Times*, p. 72, who cites Klaas A. D. Smelik, *Writings from Ancient Israel: A Handbook of Historical and Religious Documents* (Louisville, KY: Westminster/John Knox, 1991), p. 106.

70 Carol Meyers, "Everyday Life: Women in the Period of the Hebrew Bible," in *The Women's Bible Commentary, Expanded Edition, with the Apocrypha*, ed. C. A. Newsom and S. Ringe (London: SPCK; Louisville, KY: Westminster/John Knox, 1998), p. 254.

71 We are told in 1 Sam 1:3, 21; 2:19, for example, that the reason the household of Elkanah goes annually to Shiloh is *lizboaḥ*, which means, literally, "to slaughter [an animal] as a *šelamim* offering." See Gary A. Anderson, "Sacrifice and Sacrificial Offerings (OT)," in *Anchor Bible Dictionary* 5: 878b.

72 Phyllis Bird, "The Place of Women in the Israelite Cultus," in *Ancient Israelite Religion*, p. 417 n. 37; eadem, "Women's Religion in Ancient Israel," in *Women's Earliest Records, from Ancient Egypt and Western Asia, Proceedings of the Conference on Women in the Ancient Near East, Brown University, Providence, Rhode Island, November 5–7, 1987*, Brown Judaic Studies 166, ed. B. S. Lesko (Atlanta: Scholars Press, 1989), p. 293.

73 Ackerman, *Warrior, Dancer, Seductress, Queen*, pp. 113–14.

9

Ashdod and the Material Remains of Domestic Cults in the Philistine Coastal Plain

Rüdiger Schmitt

Family Religion and the Archaeology of Palestine

Scholarly interest in the topic of family religion in Israel and its ancient Near Eastern environment has increased notably during the past few decades.[1] However, scholarly work has focused mainly on the literary evidence; the archaeological material has only been explored in part,[2] though recent studies have demonstrated the crucial importance of archaeological finds for the reconstruction of family religion in Ancient Israel/Palestine.[3] Therefore, the archaeological features of family religion are still a question for research.[4] The aim of this case study is to determine archaeological features that point to religious activities in the household or in the neighborhood and to refine the typology of cult places and cultic activities at Iron Age living quarters.

General Problems of Philistine Material Culture

The arrival in the Coastal Plain of a new ethnic group from the Aegean, the Philistines, is marked for the majority of scholars by the arrival of a new pottery type, the locally produced Mycenean ware represented in Ashdod Stratum XIIIa and Tel Miqne/Ekron Stratum VII in the first third of the twelfth century BCE.[5] This kind of pottery was replaced by the bichrome ware at Ashdod Stratum XII and Tel Miqne Stratum VI in the middle of the twelfth century which flourished until the end of the eleventh century BCE. The ethnic significance of the pottery has been questioned by several scholars, because (a) the total amount of Philistine pottery in central Philistine cities such as Ashdod and Tel Miqne is only about c. 27 percent of the total; and (b) the forms of Philistine pottery closely resemble older local Canaanite types. J. F. Brug states therefore:

> Our distribution studies confirm that the heartland of the so-called Philistine Ware is indeed the coastal plain which the literary texts associate with the Philistines. Philistine Ware does occur at sites which are not Philistine, but the consistency and percentage of its occurrence diminishes sharply as one gets further away from the Philistine heartland . . . It is, therefore, virtually certain that this pottery was manufactured by inhabitants of Philistia and used by Philistines.

But "This does not mean that Philistine Ware must be an indicator of the time of arrival of the Philistines, nor that it is a sure indicator of their ethnic background."[6] Also, the production of the typical Philistine terracotta figurines in Ashdod does not begin parallel to the monochrome ware but with the introduction of the bichrome ware. Only in Ekron can two objects, a Ψ-type figurine and an Ashdoda-type head, be dated to the initial phase of Philistine pottery production, marked by the monochrome Mycenean IIIC 1:b-ware. All in all, "Philistine" terracotta figurines are indeed typical for Philistine material culture, but they cannot serve as an indicator of the arrival of a new ethnicity. The main problem concerning the terracotta figurines is whether they reflect Aegean or Mycenean cult practices or neither. The relatively late appearence of the terracotta figurines, especially their flourishing until Iron Age II B/C and the typological differences between them and their Aegean "sisters" show that they were developed in Palestine during the Early Iron Age. Therefore, they are not relevant for determining the question of ethnicity, although the objects are distinctive for the material culture of the Philistines in the Iron Age I and II.[7]

The Typology of the Figurines

The corpus of Philistine terracotta figurines consists of seven main types with several subtypes (Figure 9.1):

Type I: Ψ figurines
Type II: mourning figurines
Type III: chair figurines, so called "Ashdodas"
Type IV: male "snow man" figurines
Type V: "snow man" figurines of musicians
Type VI: pillar figurine/Ψ-type mixed style
Type VII: female "snow man" figurines[8]

The majority of Philistine figurines are represented by a unique type of figurine in the form of a chair with four legs and a highly stylized head in form of a *kalathos* on a long neck, nicknamed "Ashdoda." This type is present at Ashdod and Tel

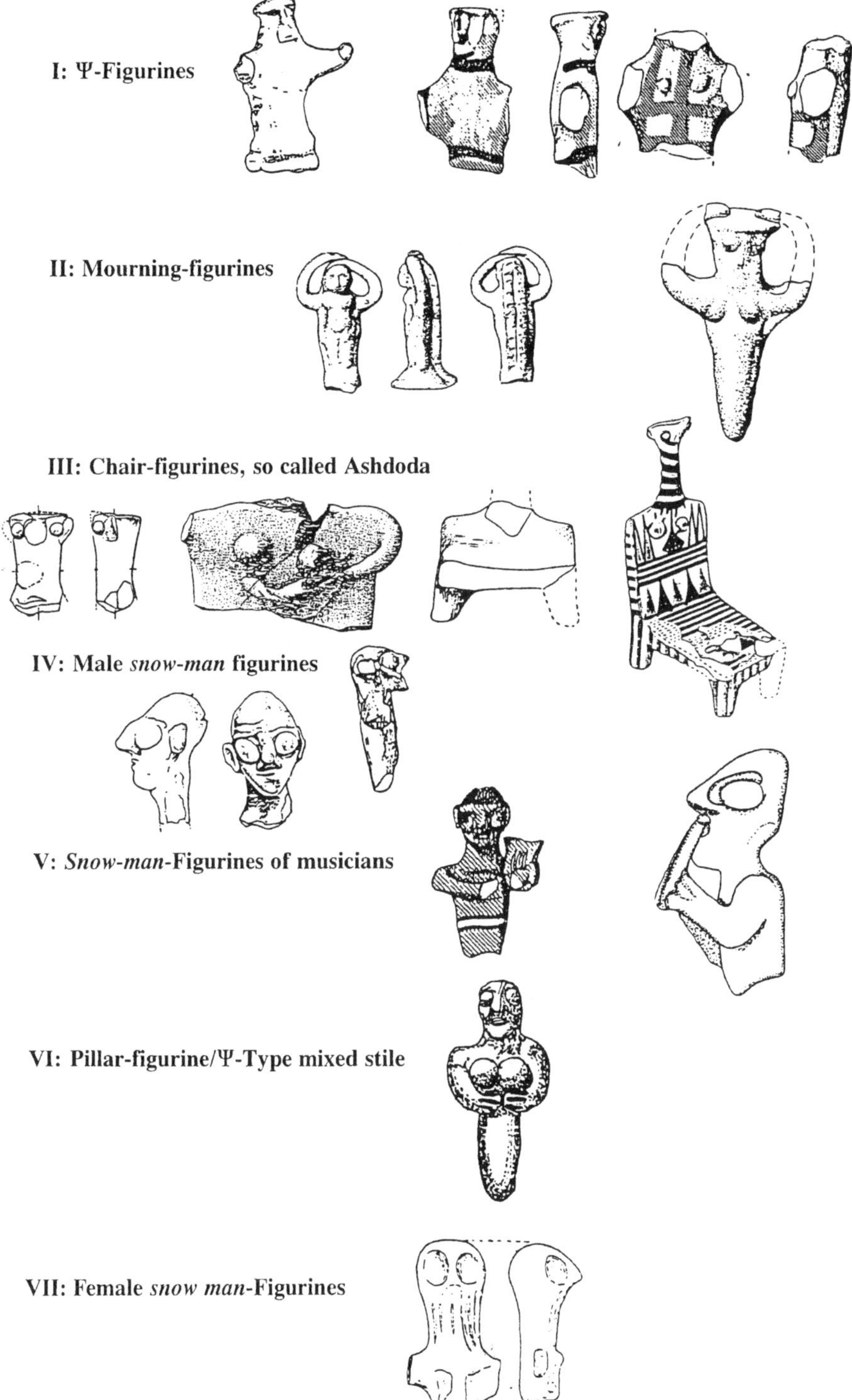

Figure 9.1 Typological chart of Philistine terracotta figurines

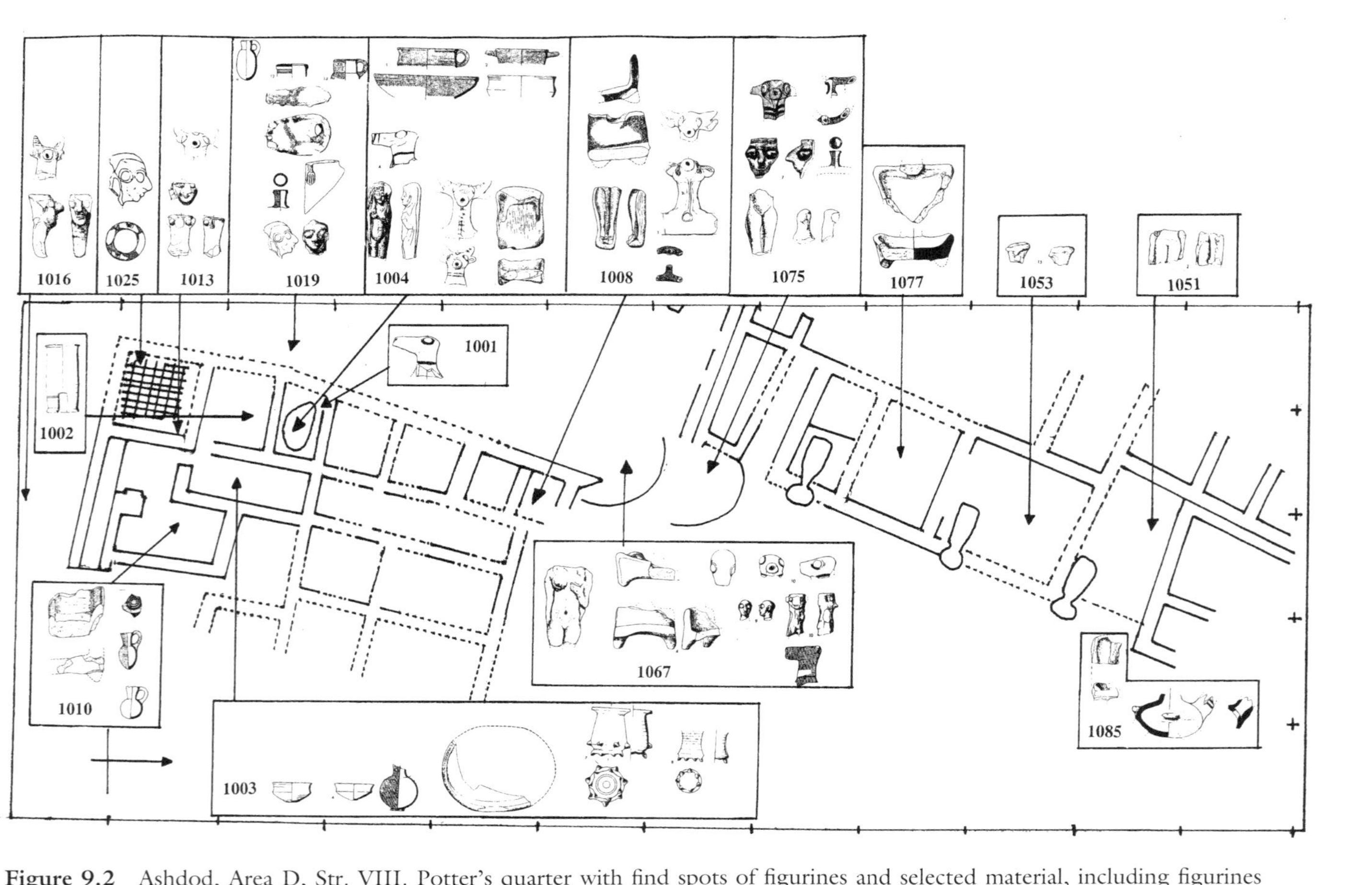

Figure 9.2 Ashdod, Area D, Str. VIII. Potter's quarter with find spots of figurines and selected material, including figurines found in Strata VII–VI workshop. Redrawn and compiled by the author after Dothan, *Ashdod, II/III*, Plan 8 and Figs. 38–47

Qasile and, as several head fragments indicate, also at Tel Miqne, Tell es-Safi, Aphek and Tell Judeideh. Only one figurine from Ashdod is fully preserved; the vast majority of the group consists of fragments of neck, head, or chair. Some of the chairs have applied breasts on the back-rest. From the iconographic point of view, it is quite obvious that these figurines represent the image of an enthroned female deity. Twenty-three chair fragments and twenty Ashdoda-like heads dating from Iron Age I B to Iron Age II C were found at Ashdod. The greatest number belong to Iron Age II B. Besides the Ashdoda fragments, eleven male heads and two male torsi were found at Ashdod, which probably belong to a standing nude male figurine. These figurines lack any iconographical indication that they represent a divine being (e.g., crown, weapons, or other divine attributes). Unfortunately, there is as yet insufficient evidence to identify the goddess represented by the Ashdoda figurines with the Asherah mentioned in an inscription on a storage jar from Tel Miqne/Ekron,[9] or with the deity *pt[g]yh* – possibly an original Philistine goddess – mentioned in a seventh century BCE dedicatory inscription from the same city,[10] though the Ashdoda clearly represents a kind of mother goddess. The male heads and figurines without divine emblems are most probably representations of ancestors.[11]

A Potter's Sanctuary at Ashdod

The archaeological contexts of these figurines is highly significant. Most of them were found in the so-called potters' quarter and adjacent living-areas in Area D. The potters' quarter of Ashdod Stratum VIII (= Stratum D 3) was most probably destroyed at the end of the eighth century during the conquest of Sargon II.[12] A great number of figurines came from pits in which they were buried together with other pottery remains.[13] A building complex in the south of Area D has been interpreted as a small temple by the excavators[14] (Figure 9.2). The installations in room 1010 consist of a small platform (Locus 1022) with three courses of brick of about 1.35m to 1.15m and a bench running along the southeast wall (W1013). The installations were covered with a white wash. In the northwest corner of room 1010 there is a room paved with pebbles of about 3–4m (1009); in the southeast corner a second room of about 3m by 3m, paved with mudbrick, was excavated (1025). Just one Ashdoda fragment has been found in room 1010 itself.[15] The mudbrick room yielded one male head.[16] In the debris of room 1010 one jug, two juglets and one bowl were found.[17] The adjacent room 1003, together with 1006 and 1045, forms most probably a long corridor leading to room 1010. Room 1003 contains two knob-footed cups of unclear use (maybe incense-burners), two jugs, one store jar, a loom-weight, four bowls, one cooking pot, one jar, and a unique terracotta basin.[18]

Three more Ashdoda fragments, two Astarte plaques and two male heads, were found in the adjacent rooms of the building and its vicinity. Another assemblage of probable cultic objects and vessels was found in Locus 1019, an open space either belonging to the older Iron II B Stratum IX (= Stratum D 4) or to Stratum VIII (= Stratum D 3): The assemblage consists of one Ashdoda fragment and one head of a male figurine, a zoomorphic libation vessel, six craters, a stand, a fragment of a kernos ring bowl, five bowls, among them a miniaturized form, a juglet and a jug, and two jars.[19] It is possible that the Stratum VIII (= Stratum D 3b) pit 1004, containing a similar assemblage, including various pottery,[20] another Ashdoda fragment,[21] a plaque-figurine and four zoomorphic kernos ring spouts,[22] can be associated with Locus 1019.

Some scholars, especially Wolfgang Zwickel and myself, discussed the problem of the cultic character of Area D and came to the conclusion that the structures have no explicit cultic meaning, because most of the objects do not form any kind of cultic assemblage. We concluded this because (a) they were not closely associated with the proposed cultic installations; (b) most of the pottery is of non-cultic types (bowls, craters, cooking pots, jars); and (c) the whole character of Area D, the potters' quarter, points to an industrial and commercial use.[23] The finds from Tell Jawa, especially the domestic cult assemblages consisting of terracotta figurines, various types of small vessels, libation vessels, etc.,[24] have led me to reconsider my proposal from ten years ago. However, the few finds in the proposed cultic room 1010 remain problematic, especially since the achitecture is not comparable to any other temple in Iron Age Palestine. But the mixed utilitarian and non-utilitarian character of the pottery assemblage in the building leads me to the conclusion that some kind of cultic use is possible. Perhaps the cultic use of room 1010 was occasional, while the utensils for the cult were stored in the other rooms, usually serving as store rooms. Also, the similar mix of utilitarian and non-utilitarian assemblages of Locus 1019 and Pit 1004 suggests an occasional cultic use for these loci as well. The figurines accompanied by libation vessels, jugs and craters point to a kind of libation and/or meal ritual for the goddess represented by the Ashdoda figurines. Moreover, it is likely that these cultic activities had something to do with the process of pottery production. The finds from the potters' workshop itself indicate that the production of pottery was accompanied by cultic activities. The Ashdoda and the other types of figurines found in the area of the workshop, which was still in use in Stratum VII, could have been used to insure the success of the production process through their display near the kilns.[25] A great number of broken figurines and kernos fragments, most probably originating from the workshop, were found in pit 1067 (Figure 9.3).[26] Therefore, it seems quite possible that the assemblages, including Ashdoda figurines and male ancestor figurines, were used in cultic activities associated with the craftsmen's work, in particular to insure the success of the problematic process of firing the kilns and producing the pottery. If this was the case, the assemblages point to a kind of group or guild cult, which includes the persons involved in the production process. The occasional use of industrial buildings for cultic purposes is also present in seventh-century Ekron, where a great number of limestone altars point to cultic practices associated with the olive oil industry.[27]

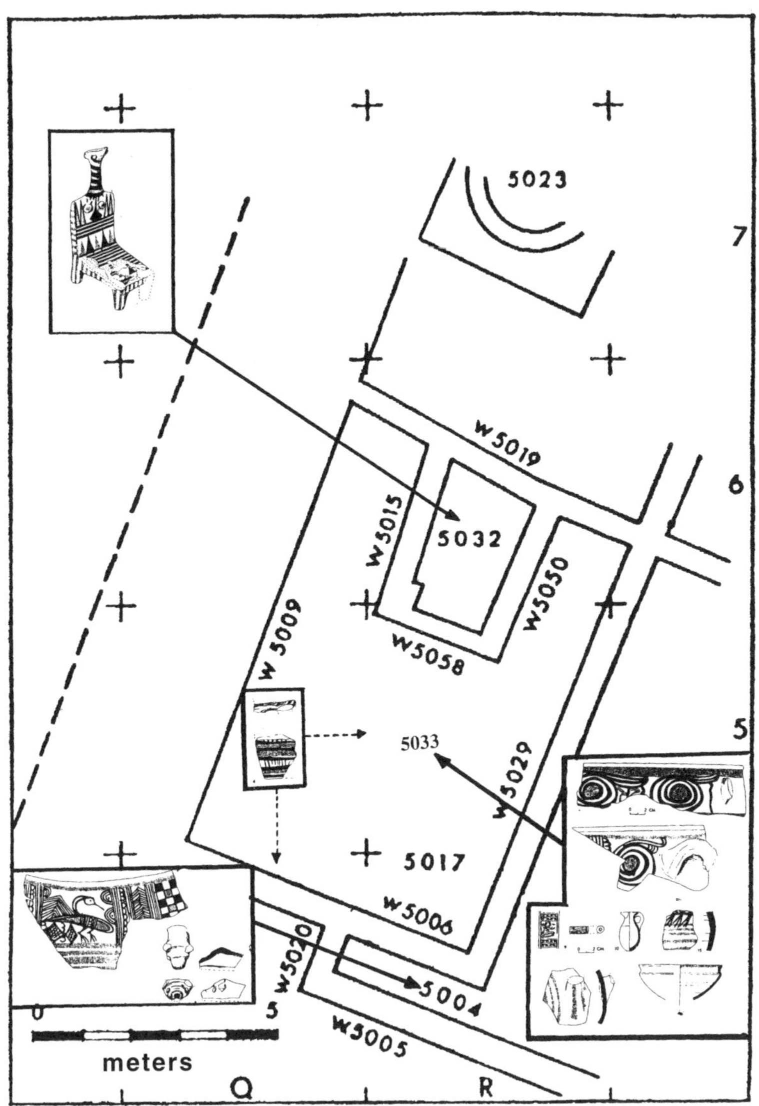

Figure 9.3 Ashdod, Area H, Stratum XI. Find spots of figurines and selected pottery items. Compilation of Rüdiger Schmitt after Dothan, *Ashdod II/III*, Plan 21 and Figs. 86, 87, 91, 92

Material Remains of Domestic Cult

The Ashdoda figurines and their relatives must also have been widely used in the domestic cult at Ashdod. The problem is that the great majority of terracotta figurines came from pits in or outside of the houses, so that nothing can be said about the exact place and context of their original use, though it is clear that they were used in cultic activities in the housing areas in some way. Of special

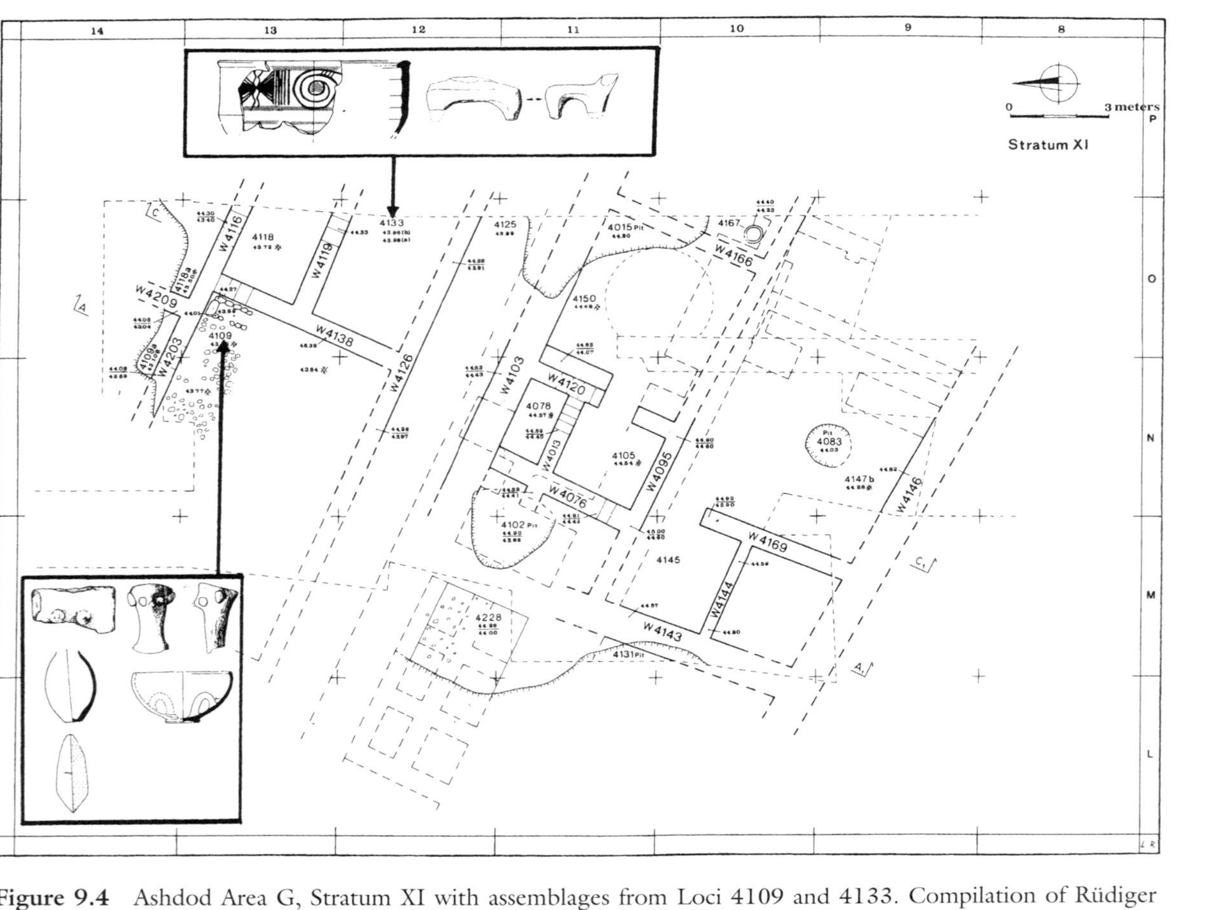

Figure 9.4 Ashdod Area G, Stratum XI with assemblages from Loci 4109 and 4133. Compilation of Rüdiger Schmitt after Dothan/Porath, *Ashdod V*, Plan 12 and Figs. 40, 42

interest is the content of a Stratum XI (4b/Iron I B) building in area H. The building's remains and the artifacts excavated in the building itself indicate a prosperous domicile.[28] The famous, complete bichrome-painted Ashdoda figurine[29] was uncovered in room 5032, but – unfortunately – in a secondary context, as part of a large heap of rubble and broken pottery fill in the room.[30] However, the complete Ashdoda, another fragment of a similar figurine,[31] a fragment of a bird figurine and a zoomorphic kernos ring spout (most probably the head of a dog)[32] can be associated with the rich contemporary bichrome Philistine pottery of the building[33] (Figure 9.4).

In the residential area G, Stratum XI (Iron Age II A), room 4133 yielded an Ashdoda chair fragment together with a crater[34]; the adjacent yard (Locus 4109) yielded an Ashdoda back-rest fragment and the head of another Ashdoda together with a so called "spinning bowl", a bone spatula, and a juglet[35] (plan 3). Here too, the findings point to cultic activities as well in the rooms and in the courtyard of the building.

Although the finds mostly form no coherent assemblage from a single find-spot, it is clear that luxury and non-utilitarian pottery objects and the Ashdoda figurines point to forms of domestic cult consisting of the worship of the goddess represented by the figurine and the male ancestors represented by the male figurine fragments with libations and meal-offerings. The findings in the Tell Qasile houses, especially an Ashdoda fragment from one of the dwellings,[36] confirm the obervations from Ashdod, that cultic practices with figurines had their place in the domestic cult.

Conclusions

The assemblages of terracotta figurines, non-utilitarian objects of pottery such as kernos rings, and utilitarian pottery, mostly of luxury types, at Ashdod, were likely used in cultic activities of the family and the workmen of the potters' workshop. Such activities consisted of drink and meal offerings to the goddess represented by the Ashdoda figurines, and to the ancestors. The cult assemblages from Ashdod are quite similar to those of the superimposed phases (319, 200 and 131, Strata XII–X) of the temple at Tell Qasile, which is a village shrine. The assemblages of the shrine include terracotta figurines and a small terracotta naos, together with non-utilitarian pottery such as kernos rings, other forms of libation vessels and stands, as well as utilitarian luxury-types such as a lion-shaped rhyton and small bowls.[37] The difference between the remains of the domestic cult and the potters' cult on the one hand, and those of the shrines on the other, is that the shrines contain a slightly greater amount of specialized objects such as the small model shrine (naos), anthropomorphic vessels, and stands. Therefore, the cult assemblages in Ashdod (and Tell Qasile) enable us to differentiate between village shrines, guild cults which were practiced occasionally in or near industrial areas, and domestic cult, on the basis of the composition of the assemblages themselves and the character of related installations.

In comparison, evidence from Beersheba[38] and many other sites suggests similar cultic features, e.g., cultic assemblages with figurines, votive objects, luxury and non-utilitarian vessels and incense altars, often associated with food processing and production installations.[39] Thus, the evidence from Ashdod and from domestic units in Israelite and Judean settlements shows that the cultic assemblages and the practices associated with them are quite similar in Philistia and in Judah/Israel. Furthermore, the Israelite and Judean household cult assemblages do not indicate a permanent "holy corner" or continuously used sacred space in the profane context of the dwellings. Like in the Ashdod dwellings, the ritual objects – mostly easily portable – could be used in different spaces of the household and could have been stored when not in use. Additional evidence from the excavations at Tell Jawa in Ammon, which yielded several cultic assemblages in the dwellings (mostly from the basement, but also in some cases from the upper story), with a similar content of figurines, luxury and non-utilitarian vessels, suggests the same picture. Thus, the archaeological evidence provides additional proof for the observations of Rainer Albertz and Karel van der Toorn concerning the international character of family religion in the Ancient Near East.[40]

Notes

1 Rainer Albertz, *Persönliche Frömmigkeit und offizielle Religion: Religionsinterner Pluralismus in Israel und Babylon* (Stuttgart: Calver, 1978); ibid., "Wieviel Pluralismus kann sich eine Religion leisten? Zum religionsinternen Pluralismus in alten Israel," in *Pluralismus und Identität*, Veröffentlichung der Wissenschaftlichen Gesellschaft für Theologie 8, ed. Joachim Mehlhausen (Gütersloh: Gütersloher Verlagshaus, 1995), pp. 193–213; ibid., *Religionsgeschichte Israels in alttestamentlicher Zeit*, Grundrisse zum Alten Testament 8, 2nd edn. (Göttingen: Vandenhoeck & Ruprecht, 1996–1997), pp. 45–68, 143–57, 291–304, 327–37; ibid., "Religious Practices of the Individual and Family: Israel," in *Religions of the Ancient World: A Guide*, ed. Sarah I. Johnston (Cambridge and London: Harvard University Press, 2004), pp. 429–30; Karel van der Toorn, *Family Religion in Babylonia, Syria and Israel: Continuity and Change in the Forms of Religious Life*, Studies in the History and Culture of the Ancient Near East 7 (Leiden, New York, Cologne: Brill, 1996); Erhard Gerstenberger, *Theologien im Alten Testament: Pluralität und Synkretismus alttestamentlichen Gottesglaubens* (Stuttgart: Kohlhammer, 2001), pp. 26–77; Bernhard Lang, *Jahwe, der biblische Gott: Ein Porträt* (Darmstadt: Wissenschaftliche Buchgesellschaft, 2002), pp. 137–72; Joseph Blenkinsopp, "The Family in First Temple Israel," in *Families in Ancient Israel: The Family, Religion, and Culture*, ed. Leo G. Perdue (Louisville: Westminster John Knox Press, 1997), pp. 48–103.

2 See Urs Winter, *Frau und Göttin*, Orbis Biblicus et Orientalis 53 (Fribourg: Universitätsverlag; Göttingen: Vandenhoeck & Ruprecht, 1983), pp. 127–134; Wolfgang Zwickel, *Räucherkult und Räuchergeräte*, Orbis Biblicus et Orientalis 97 (Fribourg: Universitätsverlag; Göttingen: Vandenhoeck & Ruprecht, 1990), p. 38; Susan Ackerman, *Under Every Green Tree: Popular Religion in Sixth-Century Judah*, Harvard Semitic Monographs 46 (Atlanta: Scholars Press, 1992); Carol Meyers, "From

Household to House of Yahweh: Women's Religious Culture in Ancient Israel," in *Congress Volume, Basel 2001*, ed. André Lemaire (Leiden and Boston: Brill, 2002), pp. 277–303.

3 Paulette M. Michèle Daviau, "Family Religion: Evidence for the Paraphernalia of the Domestic Cult," in *The World of the Aramaeans II: Studies in History and Archaeology in Honour of Paul-Eugène Dion*, ed. P. M. Michèle Daviau, John W. Wevers, and Michael Weigl, Journal for the Study of the Old Testament, Supplement Series (Sheffield: Sheffield Academic Press, 2001), pp. 199–229.

4 See Wolfgang Zwickel, *Räucherkult und Räuchergerüte*, p. 38 n. 137.

5 See, for example, Trude Dothan, *The Philistines and their Material Culture* (New Haven: Yale University Press, 1982), p. 94.

6 John F. Brug, *A Literary and Archaeological Study of the Philistines*, BAR International Series 265 (Oxford: Biblical Archaeology Review, 1985), p. 106.

7 Rüdiger Schmitt, "Philistäische Terrakottafigurinen", *Ugarit-Forschungen 31* (1999): 641–43.

8 Ibid., pp. 579–80.

9 Seymour Gitin, "Ekron of the Philistines Part II: Olive-Oil Suppliers to the World," *Biblical Archaeology Review* 16 (1990): 232 n. 18.

10 Seymour Gitin, Trude Dothan, and Joseph Naveh, "A Royal Dedicatory Inscription from Ekron," *Israel Exploration Journal* 47 (1997): 1–16; Ingo Kottsieper, "Eine Tempelbauinschrift aus Ekron," in *Texte aus der Umwelt des Alten Testaments Ergänzungslieferung*, ed. Otto Kaiser (Gütersloh: Gütersloher Verlagshaus, 2001), pp. 189–90.

11 Schmitt, "Terrakotttafigurinen", p. 635.

12 Moshe Dothan, "Ashdod", in *The New Encyclopedia of Archaeological Excavations in the Holy Land*, ed. Ephraim Stern (Jerusalem: Israel Exploration Society), 1: 100.

13 Moshe Dothan, *Ashdod II/III: The Second and Third Season of Excavations, 1963, 1965, Soundings in 1967*, ATIQOT 9/10 (Jerusalem: Central Press, 1971), pp. 88–105; Rachel Hachlili, "Figurines and Kernoi," in Moshe Dothan, *Ashdod II/III*, pp. 125–6.

14 Moshe Dothan and David Noel Freedman, *Ashdod I: The First Season of Excavations*, ATIQOT 7 (Jerusalem: Central Press, 1967), 133–4; Hachlili, "Figurines and Kernoi," pp. 125 and 135.

15 Dothan and Freedman, *Ashdod I*, Fig. 43.6 = Schmitt, "Terrakottafigurinen", Cat. No. 24.

16 Schmitt, "Terrakottafigurinen," Cat. No. 69.

17 Dothan and Freedman, *Ashdod I*, Fig. 37.15 (bowl), 22 (jug), 24.25 (juglets).

18 Ibid., Fig. 38.7–8; Fig. 37.2–3, 11–12, 16, 19; Fig. 39.1, 3.

19 Ibid., Fig. 42.18; Fig. 43.1; Fig. 42.19; Fig. 39.10; Fig. 42.3–7; Fig. 39.8, 10; Fig. 42.1, 2, 8, 15, 16; Fig. 42.9, 13; Fig. 42.11, 12.

20 Ibid., p. 148; Fig. 36: four bowls, three craters, flask handle, lamp.

21 Schmitt, "Terrakottafigurinen", Cat. No. 25.

22 Dothan and Freedman, *Ashdod I*, Fig. 43.4; Fig. 44.1–2; 45.4.

23 Zwickel, *Der Tempelkult in Kanaan und Israel*. Forschungen zum Alten Testament 10 (Tübingen: J. C. B. Mohr, 1994), 247; Schmitt, "Terrakottafigurinen", pp. 582–3.

24 See Daviau, "Family Religion," pp. 199–229.

25 Schmitt, "Terrakottafigurinen", Cat. No. 54 (near kiln 1164, under Hellenistic kiln 1053); Cat. No. 33 (between kilns 1088 and 1164); Cat. No. 31 (C/4, Locus 1085 near kiln 1169); Astarte-Plaque near kiln 1168 (Locus 1051; Dothan, *Ashdod II/III*, Fig. 64.2).

26 Kernoi: Dothan, *Ashdod II/III*, Fig. 66.2; 68.1. Figurines: Fig. 62.9; 62.10; Fig. 63.4 (= Schmitt, "Terrakottafigurinen", Cat. No. 30); 63.6 (= Schmitt, "Terrakottafigurinen", Cat. No. 34); 64.1 (Astarte plaque); 64.10 (female head). Male heads/figurines: Fig. 62.9 (= Schmitt, "Terrakottfigurinen", Cat. No. 77); 62.10 (= Schmitt, "Terrakottafigurinen", Kat. No. 93).

27 See Gitin, "Seventh Century BCE. Cultic Elements at Ekron" in *Biblical Archaeology Today 1990*, ed. Avraham Biram and Joseph Naveh (Jerusalem: Israel Exploration Society, 1993), pp. 248–58.

28 Dothan, *Ashdod II/III*, 162; Moshe Dothan and Trude Dothan, *People of the Sea: The Search for the Philistines* (New York: Macmillan, 1992), pp. 152–3.

29 Schmitt, "Terrakottafigurinen", Cat. No. 19 (= Dothan, *Ashdod II/III*, Fig. 91.1).

30 Dothan, *Ashdod II/III*, p. 161.

31 Schmitt, "Terrakottafigurinen", Cat. No. 21 (= Dothan, *Ashdod II/III*, Fig. 91.4).

32 Dothan, *Ashdod II/III*, Fig. 92.5, p. 8.

33 See Dothan, *Ashdod II/III*, Figs. 86, 87.

34 Moshe Dothan and Yosef Porath, *Ashdod V: The Fourth–Sixth Seasons of Excavations 1968–1970*, ATIQOT 13 (Jerusalem: Israel Antiquities Authority, 1993), Fig. 42.8 (= Schmitt, "Terrakottafigurinen" Cat. No. 27); 40.3.

35 Dothan and Porath, *Ashdod V*, 42.3 (= Schmitt, "Terrakottafigurinen", Cat. No. 23); 42.5 (= Schmitt, "Terrakottafigurinen", Cat. No. 58); Fig. 42.1 (spinning bowl); 41.9 (juglet).

36 Schmitt, "Terrakottafigurinen", Kat. Nr. 22 and p. 589 (= Amihai Mazar, "Excavations at Tell Qasile 1982–1984, Preliminary Report," *Israel Exploration Journal 36* [1986]: Pl. 3a, Fig. 6.1).

37 Amihai Mazar, *Excavations at Tell Qasile I*. QEDEM 12 (Jerusalem: Institute of Archaeology, Hebrew University, 1980), p. 120.

38 Yohanan Aharoni, *Beer-Sheba I: Excavations at Tel Beer-Sheba 1969–1971 Seasons* (Tel Aviv: Institute of Archaeology, 1973), Loci 844, 859, 808: Pl. 22–5.

39 See Albertz and Schmitt, *Family Religion in Ancient Israel* (Winona Lake, IN: Eisenbrauns, forthcoming).

40 Albertz, *Religionsgeschichte Israels*, p. 413; van der Toorn, *Family Religion*, p. 374.

10

Household Religion in Ancient Egypt

Robert K. Ritner

The famous assessment by Herodotus that the Egyptians were "religious beyond measure, more than any other people" (II.37) is supported both by an abundance of relevant artifacts and by a correspondingly prodigious history of scholarly publication. Yet despite a plethora of studies both general and specific on Egyptian religion, the term "household religion" is conspicuously absent from the field of Egyptology. It is ignored or avoided in titles of volumes and articles, and no such lemma may be found either individually or within the general treatment of "religion" in common references such as the *Lexikon der Ägyptologie* or *The Oxford Encyclopedia of Egyptology*.[1] The reasons for this absence are not hard to discover and become apparent when one consults the necessarily brief entries on "house" in the same reference works.[2] A selection of remarks by Felix Arnold suffices to sketch the problem, as each historical paragraph begins on a disparaging note. Regarding prehistoric houses, "evidence for the origins of Egyptian architecture is still scanty."[3] "The domestic architecture of the Old Kingdom has been little studied."[4] "In the 1980s, the most progress was made in the study of the domestic architecture of the Middle Kingdom . . . all . . . reflect the architecture designed and employed by the state."[5] "The house of the New Kingdom as known from Tell el-Amarna is the best documented of all Egyptian house types."[6] "Domestic architecture of the Third Intermediate Period and the Late period has met little interest among Egyptologists."[7]

With ancient domestic architecture typically located beneath modern settlements while temples, tombs, and palaces remain accessible at the desert edge or beyond, Egyptian geography and scholarly interest have joined to favor state and funerary practices over "household" concerns. Exceptions to this rule are usually either state "towns" adjoining pyramids or forts, or aberrant settlements like the utopian Amarna of Akhenaton (with often "revolutionary" household cult) or the restricted

– and again state-sponsored – artisans' village of Deir el-Medina. Further diminishing the perceived role of the household is the relatively restricted nature of Egyptian notions of "family." In sharp contrast to the kinship-based ("tribal") societies that surrounded it, Egyptian culture was based on the "nuclear family" composed of a father, mother, children and perhaps a widowed mother and unmarried sisters of the husband.[8] A range of Egyptian terms for "family" (*3b.t, mhw.t, wḥy.t, h3w, hnw*) can in certain contexts include servants and associates, but real or fictive extended families played no official role in indigenous social organization.[9] To explain the extended kinship relations of their neighbors, Egyptians employed their own terminology (*mhw.t, wḥy.t*), sometimes adding a throwstick determinative to stigmatize "tribe" as an alien concept.[10]

In spite of these rather severe limitations, evidence for religious practices within the home does survive in the form of artifacts and features from excavated houses themselves, from textual sources recovered from village dumps in addition to references in official literary, administrative and theological compositions, and in scenes, biographical texts and objects found within tombs. While such sources might seem to justify a special focus on family religion, the close relationship of this material to general community practices, including festivals, pilgrimages, votive offerings and amuletic use, as well as the stark imbalance in Egyptian evidence between the state and private sphere, has shifted the categories of analysis.

For Egyptology, all discussion of household or family religion is but a minor facet subsumed within a broader classification termed "popular" or "personal" religion, or far less accurately, "the religion of the poor."[11] An illustrative example of the relatively diminished interest accorded the household is provided by the 1987 study by Ashraf Sadek entitled *Popular Religion in Egypt during the New Kingdom*, which opens by noting that "the focus of personal worship is multiple: at home, in minor shrines and cult-places (whether in desert, countryside or town streets), and at the outer fringes of the great official temples."[12] Aside from this initial mention of "at home," the house and its religious role are cited on only five additional pages within the 296 page volume.[13] Sadek's expressed justification for this seeming disparity is the reasonable recognition that the bulk of our information derives from the single site of Deir el-Medina, whose material has been "reviewed at length" by the excavator Bruyère in a volume dedicated to the subject.[14] Nevertheless, it is possible to expand upon the conclusions of Bruyère and to extend the discussion well beyond New Kingdom Deir el-Medina, both geographically and temporally.

Before attempting to survey the evidence itself, it is useful to consider the likely subcategories of household religion that are to be expected in an Egyptian context. My own suggestions largely parallel the biographical model offered by Baines for his survey of Egyptian "practical religion," yet one more expression for "popular religion" that he understands as "religion in an everyday context"[15] but which I would consider a better description of magical acts for practical ends.[16] Egyptian theology does not contrast religion with magic, and by either definition "practical religion" is certainly a feature of domestic practice, which employs both simple veneration in household shrines and performative "magical" images and acts to ensure security through both the natural transitions of life and intrusive episodes of illness, danger, and misfortune.[17] Kemp has even equated domestic cult with "magic," but that term must be applied carefully, as the private rituals of bedroom protection that he cites are paralleled in state cult and do not exhaust the range of household religious expression.[18] Domestic traditions could be expected with the transitional stages of birth, puberty, marriage, fertility/pregnancy, and death, including as well further prophylactic measures to secure health and other benefactions. In fact, the evidence is highly skewed, with issues of fertility and general health best documented, while household religious activities with some transitional "rites of passage" are attested poorly if at all.

Marriage, for example, has no known religious component, and beyond the exchange of "bridal gift" or dowry, texts speak only of a generically-phrased celebration: "spending a happy day" (*ir hrw nfr*) with the household and guests.[19] One supposed reference to an official, religious oath required to solemnize marriage is far more likely evidence of legal action regarding divorce and property claims and is in any case a court matter outside the sphere of domestic ritual.[20] Similarly, household activities regarding death are poorly attested. Herodotus records certain conventions regarding death (II.85), and his remarks are amplified by tomb depictions of all periods.[21] As in modern Egyptian funerals, men and women mourn separately,[22] but, contra Herodotus, who notes this only for women, both sexes rend their hair and clothing, casting dirt upon their heads. As described by Lane in 1842, however, the custom survived antiquity only among "mourning women of the lower classes."[23] In some New Kingdom scenes, women wear blue headbands, the probable antecedent of a further custom that survived into the nineteenth century to distinguish the immediate household of the deceased.[24] On the basis of a unique funerary scene of a princess in the royal tomb at Amarna, the embalmed corpse was probably laid out in the home.[25]

This necessary recourse to a royal scene raises broader theoretical issues of the degree to which royal and private households are fundamentally distinct, and thus whether the scholarly dichotomy of state vs. private – or palace vs. household – religion might mask as much as it reveals. Amarna art might be considered a viable exception, as it is typically defined as "revolutionary" not only for its suppression of traditional gods, but for a "naturalistic" tendency allowing domestic scenes previously against decorum. Yet royal families faced the same transitional phases and afflictions as commoners, and following the Eighteenth Dynasty ruling families of non-royal ancestry may employ religious practices of common origin.[26] As summarized by Baines, "the élite and the rest may be united by everyday religious practices that are not part of official ideology and are concerned with problems of comprehending, accepting, and responding to the world, to loss, and to suffering that are treated in religious terms by very many cultures."[27] In particular, images concerning fertility – the best attested form of household religion – appear in both royal and private contexts, so that it has been suggested that "folkbeliefs relating to fertility were to be found at the highest levels of Egyptian society and were integrated with the state religion, even though they did not occupy a central position in it."[28] At the

New Kingdom royal "harim community" of Gurob, fertility figurines recovered by Petrie are indistinguishable from others found in private contexts and blur all proposed divisions, as they may be elite, common, daily life or funerary.[29]

The funeral itself is known to leave from the house of the deceased, but thereafter funerary ritual shifts to the tomb, and additional household rituals are largely unknown. As a result, authors have often excluded funerary cult from the broader category of "popular religion." As noted again by Sadek, "conventional funerary religion, centered upon burial-customs, does not come within the purview of everyday religion in its concern with this life rather than the afterlife. Only at certain very limited points will any cult of the dead impinge on 'popular religion' . . . as studied in this book."[30] For household practice, Sadek cites only the presence of a "limited ancestor-cult" in private houses, but other points of intersection are significant and will be discussed below.

Birth

Given the high mortality rate for both mother and child in pre-modern times, it is not surprising that a large number of household religious practices are concerned with issues of birth.[31] These range from preparatory acts designed to ensure safe delivery to a variety of protective measures for the newborn child. Medical papyri contain several simple tests to determine the outcome of pregnancy,[32] and while these may derive from home "folklore" (and they certainly become folk practice outside of Egypt), their surviving Egyptian context is in the formal, state-supported scriptorium – again perhaps blurring the distinction between elite and common ("household") practice.

As a possible example of preparatory ritual for birth, one may consider a passage in the literary Papyrus Westcar (col. 10/2), in which gods transformed into midwives visit the home of a non-royal but elite woman pregnant with children destined to become kings. They reach the home of the father, Ra-user, and "they find him standing with kilt upside down."[33] The grammatical form actually stresses the special context in which he is found, and early commentators assumed that Ra-user's attire was aberrant and that the description humorously indicated the future father's confusion. In 1970, E. Staehelin reconsidered the passage in light of Egyptian and other birth rituals and considered the disordered attire typical, stressing the need to eliminate all knots in the household that might constrain birth. For Staehlin, the "disordered kilt" meant a kilt untied.[34] The practice is to be compared with the disordered and intentionally unbraided hair shown on images of women in confinement for delivery (see, for instance, Figs. 10.1 and 10.2).[35] Other practices for adult fertility and the achievement of pregnancy will be discussed in a subsequent section.

The physical presence of divine midwives in the Westcar tale finds a practical household substitute in the decoration of a birth-brick recovered from the mayor's residence at Wah-sut, a Middle Kingdom pyramid town in modern South Abydos.[36]

Figure 10.1 Hieroglyphic determinative indicating the disheveled hair of a woman giving birth; Courtesy of The Oriental Institute, The University of Chicago

Figure 10.2 Hieroglyphic determinative indicating the disheveled hair of a woman giving birth; Courtesy of The Oriental Institute, The University of Chicago

Hieroglyphic, relief, and literary evidence attest to the use of bricks as a support during birth, and one of the goddesses of personal fate, Meskhenet, was personified as a birth-brick, a true goddess in a household context.[37] The sole surviving, identifiable object of its kind, the Wah-sut birth-brick of circa 1750 to 1650 BCE was decorated on all six sides, of which five are preserved. Emblems of the goddess Hathor flank a scene of the mother holding her child between female attendants, while other sides display files of defensive animals, a defeated enemy and the protective goddess Beset. The imagery offers the mother and child the immediate presence of Egypt's most prominent "mother goddess," with divine emissaries and a slaughter scene to repel all threatening forces during birth. The social setting for the painted brick, it should be noted, is an elite household.

Immediately at birth, the child received a name. Although this was typically given by the mother, and often pronounced at the moment of birth (e.g., Wersu "He's big," Mersure "May Re love him"), both literary texts (Papyrus Westcar) and onomastica indicate that fathers, siblings, and midwives might also provide names.[38] The high percentage of personal names incorporating divinities and divine epithets – even among commoners – is a clear indication of family religiosity and cult allegiances even in the absence of other household devotional evidence.[39]

Beginning in the Third Intermediate Period (c. 1000 BCE), common names of the form "The god NN has said that he will live" attest to new oracular procedures that guaranteed health to newborns. While this oracle occurred at a temple setting, the resulting declaration of itemized protections offered by the god was copied onto papyrus and taken home to be worn as a phylactery in a tubular case at the neck.[40] Amulets of all varieties are, of course, the most common attestation of personal or household devotion, and their usage spans all classes and all categories: transitional phases, generic health and fortune, combating specific disease, and benefits and protection after death. Here we can acknowledge the individual's earliest use of amulets at birth and not repeat the point at every subsequent stage.[41]

One supposed household rite for the newly born has been connected with Coptic and Arabic ceremonies involving a sieve, used either to support the mother in labor (Coptic) or in a ritual of the seventh day after birth (Arabic), when the child is placed by a wise woman (*daya*) in a sieve with grain and vegetables, surrounded by candles and turned to the cardinal directions.[42] Suggested Egyptian antecedents in birth temples (mammisis), however, entail no actual sieve, but rather Anubis offering the lunar disc (and its cyclical rebirth) to a divine child and goddesses with tambourines.[43]

The continued health of the neonate and mother was assured by a variety of objects that display animal files parallel to those found on the Wah-sut birth-brick. A baby's feeding cup (3.5 cm by 8.0 cm), now in the Metropolitan Museum of New York, is contemporary with the Middle Kingdom birth-brick. Composed of blue faience, the ovoid cup is decorated with an addorsed frieze of apotropaic animals, the pregnancy goddess Taweret with double knives and the god Bes holding snakes, all leading toward the spout.[44] The feeding cup was found in a basket with a crocodile amulet in surface debris in a cemetery, unassociated with a burial. In its elaborate decoration, it differs from plain pottery "daily life" examples found in child burials, so that it has been suggested to be either an elaborate burial object or a specialized pediatrician's cup.[45] This reasoning, however, actually inverts the evidence, with burial examples considered the only legitimate "daily use" objects and the unburied example a probable "burial object." More likely, the Met feeding cup represents a high status version of a common product, with imagery reinforcing spells recited in the nursery.

The existence of home nursery spells is proved by Papyrus Berlin 3027, a Middle Kingdom collection of "Magical Spells for Mother and Child" said to be recited by the male "lector priest."[46] Included spells contain recitations against specific illnesses and demons, for security of the birth-bricks, for safeguarding mother's milk, for knotting a child's amulet, and a regimen of protective spells uttered at dawn, sunset, the following sunrise and sunset. One of the spells against demons (C, cols. 1/9–2/6) repels the dead who might come with vampiric kiss to injure the baby. Directions accompanying the spells recommend knots, garlic, and "honey which is sweet to men, but bitter to those who are in the beyond" (col. 2/4–5). The written text is a scriptorium product, with parallels in other temple-directed magical papyri, and the setting is again an elite household, with a male magician on staff. A further male title, "magician of the nursery" (*ḥk3y n k3p*), reveals the prominence of male practitioners even within female spaces, but one tomb relief may preserve evidence of multiple female magicians in the home.

On the rear wall of the Eighteenth Dynasty tomb of Bebi at el-Kab, six females attend dual representations of the seated tomb owners. Designated simply as "nurse" (*ḫnmt.t*), two figures at the left edge each raise an amuletic knife while three extend both a knife and a serpent staff toward the seated couple. A similar female figure holds a serpent wand and knife at the opposite end of the banquet scene.[47]

Such knives and wands are known as instruments to protect the bed, and here they ensure rebirth for Bebi and his family.

Although "amuletic knives" traditionally have been conflated with the category of "wands," both their material and form prove them to be distinct.[48] The objects are engraved with a series of animal spirits holding knives, occasionally accompanied by texts declaring that the figures offer protection by night and day. An explicit link to motherhood is provided by images of the hippopotamus goddess of pregnancy, Taweret, and the preferred material for their manufacture: a hippopotamus tusk. The shape of the piece, while determined by its material, is probably intended to represent a knife, comparable to those held by the figures depicted upon it. Unmistakable signs of wear suggest that they were used to delineate protective circles around a child's bed. Secondarily, the knives appear in funerary contexts where they ensure the rebirth of their deceased owner (as in the case of Bebi). In the New Kingdom, even cultic statuary might be protected by this means.

The decoration of these knives parallels that on the faience feeding cup and also on what may be true wands, the so-called "amuletic rods" made of rectangular faience segments, whose sides have relief images of the standard protective animals. Like the amuletic knives, they are found in both settlements and cemeteries, employed (perhaps during recitations) for the living and the dead.[49]

The true wands that do accompany "amuletic knives" in relief scenes have no such decoration, but are themselves often shown in the hands of the divine figures depicted on the knives. These wands are the serpent staves made famous by the polemical episode of Exodus 7:8–12, in which both Egyptian magicians and Aaron transform their rods into snakes. Since I have recently dedicated an extensive article to the history and use of serpent wands,[50] I shall not belabor the issue here. Wands or staves in the form of snakes have an extensive tradition in Egypt, serving as the emblem of choice both for Heka, the god of magic, and his priestly practitioners. The appearance of such wands in the hands of family nurses in the tomb of Bebi demonstrates once more the continuity between "private" and "state" imagery. The bedchamber is the certain locus of serpent imagery in private houses, as will be discussed under the category of general adult protections, and the pairing of bedchamber knives and serpent wands in the tomb of Bebi is thus reasonable; the tomb is not merely the house but the bedroom of the dead.

Puberty

The transition from child to youth at puberty was accompanied by two formal rites that are explicitly noted in texts and depictions. Most commonly mentioned is a change in hairstyle, the cutting of the sidelock of youth. While these sidelocks – on an otherwise shaved head – were worn by both male and female children, the skewed biographical evidence presents only the male version of events. With the removal of the sidelock, the full head of hair was now allowed to grow so that it would require a headband. The act of "tying the fillet" (*ṯs mḏḥ*) marked the entrance to adulthood for males, an Egyptian counterpart to the "first beard" emblematic of manhood in Greek and other cultures. Tomb biographies may thus sketch the initial career of the author by stating that "he was a child who tied the fillet" in a specific reign or region.[51] It is unclear, however, to what extent this transitional act was marked by either household or public celebration. Greek documents from Hellenistic Egypt record undeniably public "coming-of-age" festivals called, depending upon textual restoration, either *Mallokouria*, "the occasion of cutting the hair lock," or *Mellokouria*, "the occasion of becoming a youth." In either case, the event is celebrated in a state temple at a formal dinner. This so-called "obscure festival" could represent imported Greek custom, adopted Egyptian custom, or a fusion of the two.[52]

If the individual who "tied the fillet" was until that moment a "child" (*ẖrd*), the youth who experienced the next puberty rite, circumcision, could be described as a "man" (*s*). Young men without sidelocks are shown undergoing circumcision in relief scenes from the Old Kingdom tomb of Ankhmahor, so that the respective order of the practices is clear. As the act of "tying the fillet" is the preferred expression for attaining manhood, while the act of circumcision is most explicitly connected with true sexual maturity, the rites must have followed one another closely.[53] Household celebrations may be presumed, but the communal character of Egyptian circumcision is not in doubt, at least for the decentralized First Intermediate Period. Oriental Institute Stela 16956 relates the virtues of a regional prince named Weha, including his fortitude during a group circumcision (ll. 4–5): "I was circumcised together with 120 men (*s*). There was none whom I struck and none who struck me among them. There was none whom I scratched and none who scratched me among them."[54]

When one considers the lack of obvious anesthetic and the surgeon's instructions on the Old Kingdom relief to his assistant ("Hold him fast. Don't let him faint."), Weha's pride is comprehensible. Though a unique personal testimony, it is not the only reference to group circumcision.[55] Male circumcision was seemingly obligatory for royalty and the priesthood,[56] and the rite continued to be a legal necessity for priests in the Ptolemaic and Roman periods. As such, it remained a matter of more than household concern.[57]

The religious character of the ritual is not in doubt. Theological glosses incorporated within Book of the Dead Chapter 17 provide the divine origin for the practice: "What is that? It means that drops of blood dripped from Re's phallus when he set about cutting himself. Then (they) became the gods that are in the presence of Re. They are Authority and Perception."[58] A formal circumcision scene appears among the Dynasty 25 reliefs celebrating the divine birth of kings in the Mut temple in Thebes,[59] and at the beginning of the same dynasty, Pharaoh Piye had refused to meet personally with uncircumcised Libyan rulers from the Delta as they were ritually unclean.[60] Piye's reaction to such "impurity" echoes earlier mistreatment of Libyan soldiers for the same offense to Egyptian mores.[61]

Puberty rituals for women are poorly known for both household and public contexts. Votive offerings to temples of Hathor may represent gifts at the time of a menarche rituals but this cannot be proved. A few Roman-era dinner invitations for a *Therapeuteria* on behalf of unmarried daughters might represent a post-menarche family festival, or a celebration following female circumcision. Evidence for either is mixed, with classical sources the primary evidence for genital mutilation among Egyptian women. Surviving female mummies do not display the modifications now questionably called "Pharaonic circumcision."[62]

Fertility/Pregnancy

If male rituals dominate public celebrations of puberty, it is unquestionably female fertility that dominates adult ritual within a household setting. This is to be expected, given the family need to produce healthy children and the primary role of the wife as "Lady of the House" (*nb.t pr*).[63] Artifacts regarding aspects of adult female sexuality and reproduction are the most elaborate and best studied of all household religious products and range from prominent architectural features to small amuletic figures.

In the standardized, four-room homes of Ramesside Deir el-Medina, the first two rooms served general functions and were followed by the private bedroom and kitchen. The first, and thus the most public, room commonly featured a secluded, raised brick platform less than a meter wide, placed in a corner, and approached by three or four narrow steps. Termed *lit clos* or "box-bed" by the excavator Bruyère, these platforms were screened by walls either partial or reaching to the ceiling (see Figure 10.3). Where preserved, the walls are whitewashed and sometimes decorated with paintings of Bes and women dancing, at toilette or playing instruments.[64] The choice of deity suggests a direct link to childbirth, as does the common appearance of the convolvulus vine in scenes with women. This vine is otherwise depicted in paintings and on ostraca as an integral feature of outdoor constructions usually accepted as "birth-arbors."[65] In the crowded urban setting of Deir el-Medina, outdoor arbors were unfeasible, and so these architectural elements have been assumed to be the conjugal bed or the very place "on which the birth took place."[66] Such interpretations are unlikely, however, given the excessively narrow dimensions of the supposed "beds" and the certain use of freestanding brick birthstools. The religious connotations of the paintings are nonetheless clear and invite comparisons with examples found in the workmen's village at Amarna.

Official religious hostility at Amarna may have discouraged the construction of such raised platforms in private houses except where they served the worship of the royal family,[67] but in three published instances paintings were later added to interior walls of the first or second room. The fragmentary images are directly comparable to the later examples at Deir el-Medina, with dancing Bes figures before Taweret and a series of female figures who appear to be dancing with heels not touching the

Figure 10.3 "Box-bed" at Deir el-Medina. Photo by Robert K. Ritner

ground. Broken images of the convolvulus vine recovered from street debris may indicate an additional, but now lost example.[68] The religious focus of the public rooms was thus not dependent upon the presence of the supposed bed, even if fertility imagery remains dominant. A possible counterpart to the *lit clos* is the so-called "bin," a much smaller plastered feature appearing in the first room or kitchen of six Amarna houses. Kemp has suggested this to be a household offering table or altar.[69] If true, this interpretation would be paralleled by unambiguous altars in Deir el-Medina kitchens, and more importantly, it would identify the true function of the supposed "box-beds."

Indeed, Valbelle, following an alternate suggestion by Bruyère, has now reidentified the *lit clos* as an altar with reference to the Amarna evidence, and my former student Leslie Warden has reminded me of the similarity in design between these household altars and the stepped sanctuaries of chapels at both Amarna and Deir el-Medina.[70] Side walls and short staircases typify both undisputed naoi in public shrines and the "bed-altars" of Deir el-Medina. The find of an actual offering table before the *lit clos* of Deir el-Medina house NE XI, together with a female statuette and a divine *atef*-crown fragment on the platform itself, should settle the matter.[71] The fact that Deir el-Medina brick platforms are *not* maternity beds is further confirmed by textual evidence from the same site that unambiguously mentions "beds for women" in the context of "protection for birth." In these hieratic ostraca recording the sale and decoration of such beds, the material is explicitly said to be of *wood*, not brick.[72] The front room construction is thus the most elaborate of various household shrines to be discussed below. The associations with fertility derive not from the architectural design, but from family priorities.

In this regard, it is important to note that the worship of fertility deities is not confined to one room. Small household shrines in the form of wall niches may appear throughout the house, and these do include Hathor and Taweret honored by stelae and offering basins.[73] The prominence of fertility deities in home shrines long predated the New Kingdom. The few artifacts of domestic cult from the Middle Kingdom town site of Kahun feature not only a Taweret figure, but two stone offering stands depicting bowls supported by dwarves – surely antecedents of the god Bes in later shrines.[74]

While altars celebrating fertility are preserved only exceptionally, feminine figurines for the same purpose are abundantly attested at multiple sites and in contexts ranging from home to temple to tomb.[75] Long known and now studied in detail, the typically nude figurines are made of various materials (stone, wood, ivory, faience or simple clay) and exhibit a wide range of artistic quality. The most recent examination posits six distinct classes, but as a group they are united by an explicit representation of female sexuality either by emphasizing the pubic triangle even at the expense of representational legs or faces, by adding tattoos otherwise shown on naked dancers, or by placing the nude woman on a bed (never a *lit clos*). Wigs considered "seductive" are a regular feature, children may accompany the women, the tattoos include Bes, and the convolvulus vine occasionally appears as further decoration.[76] Once classed simply as "concubines of the dead," the objects appear as votive offerings in Hathor shrines, as objects of domestic cult and as tomb offerings even for women, so that "fertility figurine" has become the preferred designation.[77] Since, however, the figurines can be found in male graves, those examples accord well with Egyptian notions that deceased males retain sexual potency in the next world.[78] For these cases the older term is accurate, so that one must qualify statements that they "are not to be called concubines."[79] In any case, they are sufficiently clear in their details that in the domestic context they cannot be confused as "toys."[80]

At Amarna, female figurines were recovered throughout the residential area of the workmen's village, and one find in particular is of interest for later domestic practice. In a small room beneath the stairs of "an ordinary house" (N49.21), excavators found a group including one figurine, two model beds and a stela depicting a woman and girl worshiping Taweret.[81] This "space under the stairs" is the specific area reserved for women during menstruation in Demotic, Coptic, Egyptian Aramaic and Greco-Egyptian contracts, and the term may survive in colloquial Upper Egyptian Arabic as ẖarara, an expression for bathroom. The practice of segregating menstruating women is further signaled by the expression "the place of women" in Ostracon OIM 13512 from Deir el-Medina.[82] While the Deir el-Medina location is said to have accommodated eight women, and is thus presumably outside the home, the Amarna example establishes a feminine link with this domestic space as early as the New Kingdom. As noted by the excavators, the space "has more the appearance of a little shrine than of a structural staircase."[83] Female figurines continue in use until the Coptic period, and so similar are they in their simplified style that the Musée Guimet catalogue lists them as "figurines of prehistoric type deriving from Coptic houses."[84]

The fact that many of these female figurines have been found broken or discarded should not lead to confusion with a distinct category of female (and male) figures used in public and private execration rites.[85] In contrast to the fertility figurines, the cursing images are usually depicted as bound captives and were deposited within abandoned cemeteries after elaborate ritual abuse. The discarding of fertility images is more easily explained, as their value declines with the prospective parents' age and desire for pregnancy. At length, they might even be considered undesirable, so that intentional breakage and disposal become logical.

Two final classes of objects that may be associated with female fertility have distinctly medical links. So-called "pregnancy vases" (*Gravidenflasche*) in the form of rotund women with hybrid human and hippopotamus characteristics create a visual link between the expectant mother and Taweret, goddess of pregnancy. Unguents taken from the body of the representational vase thus become the "transubstantiated" healing fluids of the goddess herself and were used, it has been suggested, to heal stretch marks. Since other figural vases for healing fluids of Isis and Hathor are associated with the medical and priestly establishment, it is doubtful that "pregnancy vases" are explicitly items of domestic "cult" rather than medical paraphernalia in domestic space. In contrast, figural vases of Bes, popular from the late Nineteenth Dynasty into Roman times, are less likely to be temple products before the Late Period, so that vessels in deity shape cannot be rigidly classified as "professional" vs. "domestic" utensils. Like other objects of "daily life," figural vases of all types have been recovered from graves.[86]

In Roman-era Egypt, gemstones worn on rings served as specialized amulets to regulate the opening of the uterus for menstruation, conception, and birth. Displaying clear links to earlier Egyptian iconography and medical theory, these gemstones are distinct from generically protective amulets.[87]

One might wonder at the absence of cultic fertility imagery for men, but ancient concepts and bias can readily account for this. From biological observation, male responsibility for infertility could only be based on true impotence, with the woman held responsible for all other aspects of sterility. Serial marriage, not male enhancing ritual, was the norm. Excavated Hathor shrines do reveal (relatively rare) examples of stone or wooden votive phalli perhaps dedicated to relieve this situation – unless they are intended to ensure the general fecundity of family, crops, and animals. No such "votive phalli" have been found in homes. In Hellenistic times, ithyphallic clay and faience figures of Bes and the young Horus were in vogue as domestic items, but whether these were intended to stimulate male or female readiness is unclear.[88]

Death

The use of female figures as tomb offerings provides yet a further link between domestic and funerary cult, a bond already noted with respect to amuletic knives and serpent wands. One female figurine in Berlin (Inv. no. 14517) illustrates this link quite clearly by the addition of a carved inscription that addresses the male tomb owner: "May a birth be given to your daughter, Seh."[89] Here a family member has made a direct appeal to a deceased ancestor, invoking the powers of sexual potency noted above. The supposed "concubine" and child represented by the figure may in fact be Seh and her desired child, but the image and text should be understood as individual manifestations of a pervasive system of "necromancy" in Egypt, a system that so permeates Egyptian religion that it has typically gone unnoticed.[90] Communication with the dead, whether for blessing, advice, information, healing or protection, is a central feature of state-sponsored literature, public veneration and oracles, funerary spells, private correspondence, and domestic cult. In the home, the primary locus for such interaction is a household shrine, again best attested at Deir el-Medina.

Evidence for such veneration is generally termed the "ancestor cult," although Egyptian references stress the solar powers of the venerated deceased as an *3ḫ iqr n Rˁ* "excellent spirit of Re."[91] Wall niches in the first two rooms, like those for the worship of major deities, are provided with stelae and offering tables. Limestone flower bouquets accompanied more perishable offerings on these tables. Rather than a cult statuette, however, a small bust represented the family member. Examples are not confined to Deir el-Medina and also appear, for example, at Gurob and 13 other sites.[92] Averaging 10 to 25 cm high, the approximately 150 examples are usually uninscribed and often now of disputed gender, though the preferred red coloration suggests males.[93] An attempt to identify many as female or even Hathor on the basis of (unisex) wigs and a secondary inscription has been refuted.[94] If in isolation it is unclear whether the busts represent individual ancestors, different ancestors through reuse over time, or a collectivity of the departed, it should be remembered that the busts were often accompanied or even replaced on the altar by inscribed stelae.

Such stelae are again prominent at Deir el-Medina, but are also distributed throughout Egypt and appear even at Aniba in Nubia.[95] Only seven female dedicatees are attested.[96] The stelae are usually dedicated to one, or occasionally two, deceased men who can be identified as fathers, brothers, cousins, husbands, or sons of the male or female dedicator. The known relationships suggest that the recipients of the ancestor cult are individuals only recently deceased and still considered potentially active – or at least interested – in family matters. The relief scenes on the stelae conform to standard funerary images of the deceased before an offering table, and the obvious link to the funerary cult is strengthened by the find spots of the stelae and associated materials. All features of the "domestic" ancestor cult (busts, stelae, offering tables) are equally found in tomb chapels, with busts and stelae recovered also from community shrines, temples to divinities, royal mortuary monuments, the Valley of the Kings, and even the royal palace in Memphis. As summarized by Friedman, "it appears that the domestic, votive, and funerary functions of these objects flowed easily into one another in village life without sharp distinctions."[97] At Deir el-Medina, the close proximity of the village to the tombs of the residents and their royal work sites surely facilitated this interaction.

At the household shrine, common communication ("prayers") between the living and the dead will have left no written record, but in the tombs themselves this form of "necromancy" could be supplemented by more formal "letters to the dead," attested from the Old Kingdom until the second half of the seventh century BCE.[98] Thereafter, the practice changes species, evolving directly into "letters to deceased animal deities" left at popular pilgrimage shrines.[99] Although deposited outside the house, the concerns, and perhaps even much of the wording itself, were fostered within the home. Requests in the letters for a response by dream vision do locate part of the interaction at home. Within elite households, use by the living of Book of the Dead spells 148 and 190 allowed a direct vision of the deceased and his state, and a general communion with the dead occurred during the "Beautiful Feast of the Valley" when the family gathered at the tomb.[100] Despite reservations raised by both Baines and Sadek,[101] connections between the domestic and funerary spheres were not minimal, but common and multifaceted.

General Protective Measures

A transition between defenses for individual human rites of passage and more general domestic protections is afforded by Papyrus Edwin Smith. The verso of this famed medical papyrus details a series of eight procedures used to protect the home during the lifecycle not of men, but of time itself. During the chaotic "pest of the year" between the old and new years, demonic forces are unleashed upon the world but are deterred by recitations preserved in these Hyksos-era private incantations and much later temple texts.[102] In the first Edwin Smith incantation, a man protects himself by a spell over two vulture feathers which provide "his protection in any place into which he goes." The second incantation is a "recitation by a man while there is a stick of *des*-wood in his hand as he goes outside and he makes a circuit of his house. He cannot die by the pest of the year."[103] The protection of the house is noted again in incantation six, which repels any aggression of Bastet "from the house of a man."[104] While these spells were probably composed and codified in the scriptorium, and are comparable to any in the vast corpus of medical and magical formulae designed to protect an individual, these combine to safeguard the person, the house and household. At Deir el-Medina, any distinction between scriptorium and household texts is effaced by the town's unique circumstances. With no formal priesthood, the exceptionally literate villagers acted as their own clergy and traded among themselves otherwise restricted religious volumes.[105] Here and elsewhere, memorized protective spells and gestures were, of course, employed at all periods.[106]

The link between temple and home is further strengthened at Deir el-Medina by the presence of household altars for state deities, a complementary custom to the altars for personal fertility and ancestor cults already noted. Called "laraires" by Bruyère in reference to Roman practice (*lararium*),[107] these again consist of niches with cornice and jambs, featuring stelae, images, and offering tables. Appearing in the first two rooms, and thus in company with the fertility goddesses Hathor and Taweret, are Amon (of the Good Encounter), Sobek, Ptah and the Syrian Reshef. The primary state deity Amon is not unexpected, but the presence of the crocodile Sobek in this waterless region could be linked to the god's association with male potency.[108] False-door dedications in the second room of most houses honor the deceased Amenhotep I and Queen Ahmose-Nefertari, the official patrons of the settlement otherwise consulted in oracular processions and venerated in tomb paintings and community shrines.[109] Household altars for family cult must have long preceded such Ramesside examples, as offering stands for food and incense were recovered from homes at the Middle Kingdom site of Kahun.[110]

Beyond simple offerings and prayers, any rituals performed at these household altars remain unknown. References to excused absences in Deir el-Medina work rosters do offer some speculative possibilities. Mentions of personal holidays might refer to birthday or other religious devotions spent at home, though these could have been spent in community shrines as well.[111] The same options apply to workers excused for a personal oracular procedure.[112] Correspondence from the same site provides rare attestations of consultations with a female medium or "wise woman."[113] These private "seances" will not have occurred in the male-dominated community shrines. Like their modern counterparts, they will have taken place in the home of seer or client and perhaps entailed preliminary offerings at the domestic altar.

In the kitchen, shrines are found for Meretseger and Renenutet, two linked serpent deities associated with harvest fertility.[114] Inscriptions on the Deir el-Medina shrines praise both Renenutet and Taweret as *nb.t ḥms ḥnw.t grg.t* "Lady of Dwelling, Mistress of Furnishings," titles that have been interpreted to signify "divine patron of marriage."[115] More likely, however, they indicate gods not of any "ritual act" of marriage, but patrons of the quality of "domesticity," guardians of reproduction both human (Taweret) and agricultural (Renenutet). Statues of Renenutet were erected in gardens of the elite,[116] and female fertility figurines found in homes may have acted as protection for the larder as a sort of "corn dolly." One such example was recovered from Roman-era Karanis in the state grain bin C65, and others derive from milling and baking areas of the so-called "Granary Block" at the same site.[117]

At Amarna, household and garden shrines were distinctive, with images of the royal family and the Aton replacing those of traditional deities.[118] Since evidence for household altars long predates the New Kingdom,[119] Amarna represents a shift in focus but probable continuity in basic practice, a conclusion reinforced by the wall paintings noted above and the onsite discovery of figures of Bes, Taweret, and other traditional gods.

For the Egyptian bedroom, various protections have already been discussed, but these are supplemented by a formal ritual for "4 uraei of pure clay with flames in their mouths," placed in each corner of the room in which men and women sleep together.[120] Acting as defensive "nightlights" against nightmares and pests, the serpents are noted in written records from Deir el-Medina and Ptolemaic temples, while actual clay serpents have been excavated throughout Egypt, and related serpent imagery even appears on the legs of beds.[121] Similar protections for sleep are placed on headrests, where Bes (grasping snakes) is depicted to repel night terrors, noxious animals, etc.[122] Bes' patronage of sleep continues into the Greco-Egyptian magical papyri, in which he serves to send and control dreams.[123]

Additional protections against snake and scorpion bite took the form of miniature stelae suspended on household walls. The most widespread of these "phylacteries" or "icons" are the cippi of Horus, which appear in miniature versions as amulets and in larger format as public benefactions.[124] Water poured over the text and depictions absorbed their power and was then drunk by the sufferer.

From public spaces to the bedroom and kitchen, items of domestic cult can be traced throughout the home. It is thus possible to formulate a concept of "household religion" for Ancient Egypt, but that category's many interconnections with broader religious themes make it unlikely to replace current terminological conventions. Family participation in public festivals, community shrines, divine processions, and other religious activities outside of the home has been touched upon only in passing within this discussion, yet those activities are necessary extensions of domestic belief and cult, as are many other features now termed "personal religion." Temple practice is equally related. As noted by Baines for the Middle Kingdom, religious material from houses "includes objects of types that occur in New Kingdom temples and may suggest a continuity of practice between the two spheres and periods."[125] The assembled evidence suggests a far broader continuity, in which for example, similar bedroom rituals are applied in the palace, the temple, and in houses.[126] In Egyptian taxonomy, the state palace and temple are equally considered "homes,"[127] and links between all these households have been amply demonstrated above. For the elite community that we can best document, all Egyptian religious expressions are ultimately "household religion."

Notes

1 U. Luft, "Religion," in *The Oxford Encyclopedia of Egyptology*, ed. D. B. Redford (Oxford: Oxford University Press, 2001), 3: 139–45, which presents only formal, state cult and theology with a brief mention of "personal piety" in closing (p. 144). The *Lexikon der Ägyptologie* treats religion under various headings, particularly "Kult," but no domestic cultic practices are thus highlighted. Personal piety is given an article:

H. Brunner, "Persönliche Frommigkeit," in *Lexikon der Ägyptologie*, ed. W. Helck and E. Otto (Wiesbaden: Otto Harrassowitz, 1982), 4: 951–63.

2 J. Brinks, "Haus," in *Lexikon der Ägyptologie*, ed. W. Helck and E. Otto (Wiesbaden: Otto Harrassowitz, 1977), 2: 1055–62; F. Arnold, "Houses," in *The Oxford Encyclopedia of Egyptology*, ed. D. B. Redford (Oxford: Oxford University Press, 2001), 2: 122–7. Household shrines are noted at Deir el-Medina and Amarna (p. 124).

3 Ibid., p. 123.

4 Ibid., p. 123.

5 Ibid., p. 123.

6 Ibid., p. 124.

7 Ibid., p. 126.

8 S. Allam, "Familie (Struktur)," in *Lexikon der Ägyptologie*, 2: 104–13 (with fuller bibliography).

9 A prominent exception currently under study by the author occurs during the Third Intermediate Period (c. 1100–650 BCE) as the result of intrusive Libyan rulers from tribal backgrounds. For the minimally broader use of "family," see Coffin Text Spell 146 where the term *3b.t* is paralleled by a man's father and mother, children and brethren, loved ones, friends, associates and servants. This is a summary of individuals whose company is desired in the afterlife, not a reference to a societal organizational system. The terms *h3w* and *h(y)nw* primarily mean "those in the vicinity of" the speaker, and so can be family or neighbors. The Egyptian attitude is neatly summarized by a remark in "The Instruction of 'Onchsheshonqy,'" col. 9/12: "Do not dwell in a house with your in-laws" (see R. K. Ritner, "The Instruction of 'Onchsheshonqy,'" in *The Literature of Ancient Egypt*, 3rd edn., ed. W. K. Simpson (New Haven: Yale University Press, 2003), p. 508.

10 R. O. Faulkner, *A Concise Dictionary of Middle Egyptian* (Oxford: Oxford University Press, 1962), p. 66. Note the use of *wḥy.t* for the tribal populations of Mitanni (paralleled by its "cities") in the Gebel Barkal stela (l. 9) of Thutmose III, in W. Helck, *Urkunden der 18. Dynastie* (Berlin: Akademie Verlag, 1955), 17: 1231, l. 7.

11 Examples of the first two terms are too numerous to list, but for references, see the bibliography in Ashraf Sadek, *Popular Religion in Egypt during the New Kingdom* (Hildesheim: Gerstenberg Verlag, 1987) and Helmut Brunner, "Persönliche Frommigkeit," in *Lexikon der Ägyptologie*, 4: 951–63. The expression "religion of the poor" was employed by B. Gunn, "The Religion of the Poor in Ancient Egypt," *Journal of Egyptian Archaeology* 3 (1916): 81–94; and followed by A. R. Schulman, "Ex-votos of the Poor," *Journal of the American Research Center in Egypt* 6 (1967): 153–6. If not simply sculptural trial pieces, the fragments published by Schulman may represent offerings of the lower class, but the individuals at Deir el-Medina surveyed by Gunn were certainly not "poor," see now Jac. J. Janssen, *Commodity Prices from the Ramessid Period* (Leiden: Brill, 1975), pp. 533–8. Popular practices are gathered under the collective title "Surviving Life" in Stephen Quirke, *Ancient Egyptian Religion* (London: The British Museum, 1992), pp. 105–39.

12 Sadek, *Popular Religion in Egypt during the New Kingdom*, 2.

13 Ibid., 3, pp. 76–8 and 82.

14 Ibid., 76. Evidence of religious practice within the village is surveyed in Bernard Bruyère, *Rapport sur les fouilles de Deir el Médineh (1934–35): Le village . . .* (Cairo: Institut Français d'Archéologie Orientale, 1939). "Popular cults" are discussed on pp. 84ff., with material of the "domestic cult" treated specifically on pp. 193–211.

15 John Baines, "Practical Religion and Piety," *The Journal of Egyptian Archaeology* 73 (1987): 79–98. Practical religion is defined on p. 79, and the "model . . . organized around an individual's biography" is discussed on pp. 83ff. For the equation of the terms "popular" and "everyday" religion, see Sadek, *Popular Religion in Egypt during the New Kingdom*, 3. The parallelism between the approach by Baines and myself is otherwise limited, and I would strongly reject his primary analysis of "elite religion" as "repressive" and "bleak," with mankind "far behind" in concern (p. 81; actually listed first in his citation at the bottom of p. 80), the dead relegated to "inequality" (p. 81) and solar ritual pervaded by a "violent, problematic character" (p. 82 n. 12), etc.

16 See Robert K. Ritner, *The Mechanics of Ancient Egyptian Magical Practice* (Chicago: The University of Chicago, 1993), p. 247, following Te Velde. The notion of "practical theology" would apply to both state and popular religion.

17 For a functional definition of "magic" in western and Egyptian concepts, and the critical distinctions between them, see ibid., pp. 3–72.

18 Barry J. Kemp, "How Religious were the Ancient Egyptians?," *Cambridge Archaeological Journal* 5/1 (1995): 32: "domestic cult ('magic')," an equation justified in restricted use regarding clay cobras published by Robert K. Ritner, "O. Gardiner 363: A Spell Against Night Terrors," *Journal of the American Research Center in Egypt* 27 (1990): 25–41. Kemp's discussion treats important features of household religion, but his assessment of Egyptian society as largely secular is based on an irrelevant puritan (p. 29) transactional model requiring exchange of currency (real or votive) and donation on a large scale, signs of material success and attendance at communal worship (p. 25). The idiosyncratic article has gained no following.

19 For discussion and bibliography, see Janet H. Johnson, "Family Law," in *Mistress of the House, Mistress of Heaven*, ed. A. K. Capel and G. E. Markoe (Cincinnati: Cincinnati Art Museum, 1996), pp. 179–85. The expression "spend a happy day" occurs in the most detailed description of a wedding day, found in the tale of Setna I; see Robert K. Ritner, "The Romance of Setna Khaemuas and the Mummies (Setna I)," in *The Literature of Ancient Egypt*, p. 455. The term for marriage is simply "to dwell with" and a spouse is a "dwelling companion"; see W. Erichsen, *Demotisches Glossar* (Copenhagen: Ejnar Munksgaard, 1954), p. 309; and Adolf Erman and Hermann Grapow, *Wörterbuch der ägyptischen Sprache* (Berlin and Leipzig: Akademie-Verlag, 1940–59), 3: 97/12.

20 Contra John Gee, "Notes on Egyptian Marriage: P. BM 10416 Reconsidered," *Bulletin of the Egyptological Seminar* 15 (2001): 17–25, the oath entailed in annuity contracts is exclusively concerned with post-marital property settlements (susbistence, alimony and inheritance rights), and is in no sense critical – or necessary – for the state of marriage itself. Infidelity could be grounds for divorce and financial penalties (as noted by Gee, p. 21), and it is this sort of oath that is noted in P. BM 10416. Cf. U. Kaplony-Heckel, *Die demotischen Tempeleide* (Wiesbaden: Otto Harrassowitz, 1963), 1: 32–50 and 2: 1–12. Such oaths are sworn by both men and women, contra the assertion of Gee (p. 18, n. e) that "oaths have not previously been connected with Egyptian divorce." For the text of P. BM 10416 and its content, see Jac. J. Janssen, "Marriage Problems and Public Reactions," in *Pyramid Studies and Other Essays*, ed. John Baines, T. G. H. James, Anthony Leahy, and A. F. Shore (London: Egypt Exploration Society, 1988), pp. 134–7.

21 Alan B. Lloyd, *Herodotus Book II. Commentary 1–98* (Leiden: Brill, 1976), pp. 351–3.

22 Old Kingdom depictions show women inside the house and men outside; see Sue D'Auria, Peter Lacovara, and Catharine H. Roehrig (eds.), *Mummies and Magic: The Funerary Arts of Ancient Egypt* (Boston: Museum of Fine Arts, Boston, 1988), p. 56; Lloyd, *Herodotus Book II. Commentary 1–98*, pp. 351–2.

23 Edward W. Lane, *An Account of the Manners and Customs of the Modern Egyptians*, 3rd edn. (London: C. Knight and Co., 1842), p. 516.

24 Ibid.

25 This is never shown for private individuals; see the comments of Lloyd, *Herodotus Book II. Commentary 1–98*, p. 352.

26 Thus in his mortuary temple at Medinet Habu, Ramses III is shown plowing and sailing like commoners in vignettes of Book of the Dead Chapter 110, and at Tanis, the tomb of Osorkon II includes a unique scene of private grief within a royal context. Horus cippi of royalty and private individuals are identical; see Keith Seele, "Oriental Institute Museum Notes. Horus on the Crocodiles," *Journal of Near Eastern Studies* 6 (1947): 43–52 (OIM 10738).

27 Baines, "Practical Religion and Piety," pp. 97–8. The continuity between house and temple religious material is noted on p. 93 at n. 75.

28 Geraldine Pinch, *Votive Offerings to Hathor* (Oxford: Griffith Institute, 1993), p. 359, paraphrasing K. Bosse-Griffiths.

29 See the discussion by Pinch, ibid., p. 208. For the royal status of Gurob, see Angela P. Thomas, *Gurob: A New Kingdom Town* (Warminster: Aris & Phillips, 1981). The precise context of the figures within the city is uncertain as the records by Petrie are unclear, though he groups them with other parallels as "funerary" in William F. M. Petrie, *The Funeral Furniture of Egypt* (London: B. Quaritch, 1937), p. 9.

30 Sadek, *Popular Religion in Egypt during the New Kingdom*, 3.

31 For a general summary of relevant practices for birth through adult fertility, see Rosalind M. and Jac. J. Janssen, *Growing up in Ancient Egypt* (London: Rubicon, 1990). As practices to ensure fertility are properly adult, rather than infant, concerns, I have treated them separately below.

32 See the discussion and bibliography in Erik Iversen, "Papyrus Carlsberg No. VIII. With some remarks on the Egyptian origin of some popular birth prognoses," *Historisk-filologiske Meddelelser udgivet af det Kgl. Danske Videnskabernes Selskab* XXVI.5 (1939): 1–31; and Robert K. Ritner, "Cultural Exchanges Between Egyptian and Greek Medicine," in *Foreign Relations and Diplomacy in the Ancient World*, ed. P. Kousoulis and K. Magliveras (Leuven: Peeters, forthcoming).

33 For the most recent translation and text editions, see William K. Simpson, "King Cheops and the Magicians," in *The Literature of Ancient Egypt*, pp. 13–24, passage on p. 21.

34 Elisabeth Staehelin, "Bindung und Entbindung," *Zeitschrift für Ägyptische Sprache und Altertumskunde* 96 (1970): 125–39; Ritner, *The Mechanics of Ancient Egyptian Magical Practice*, p. 144 n. 639.

35 Janssen and Janssen, *Growing up in Ancient Egypt*, pp. 4–8. Overlooked hieroglyphic determinatives showing parturient women with disheveled hair appear in the historical records of Ramses III, in which enemies are described as "spread out" or "prostrate" (as in childbirth); see *The Epigraphic Survey, Later Historical Records of Ramses III (Medinet Habu II)* (Chicago: University of Chicago Press, 1932), plate 82, ll. 23 and 32 (see Figures 10.1–2). Published discussion of the text notes only that the words are "graphically determined to show the distress of the enemy" (W. F. Edgerton and

John A. Wilson, *Historical Records of Ramses III*, SAOC 12 (Chicago: University of Chicago, 1936), 79 no. 23e). While the woman in labor conveys this nuance, the unbound hair indicates not distress but the Egyptian custom of removing constrictions during birth.

36 Josef Wegner, "A decorated birth-brick from South Abydos," *Egyptian Archaeology* 21 (2002): 3–4.

37 See Paul Ghalioungui, *Magical and Medical Science in Ancient Egypt* (London: Hodder and Stoughton, 1963), p. 122. The goddess appears also as a human-headed brick in the vignette for Book of the Dead Spell 125.

38 Janssen and Janssen, *Growing up in Ancient Egypt*, pp. 14–15.

39 Baines, "Practical Religion and Piety," pp. 95–6.

40 I. E. S. Edwards, *Oracular Amuletic Decrees of the Late New Kingdom*, 2 vols., (London: The British Museum, 1960).

41 For an excellent overview, see Carol Andrews, *Amulets of Ancient Egypt* (Austin: University of Texas Press, 1994).

42 Syndey Aufrère, "Le hiéroglyphe du crible à grain et la métaphore désignant le nouveau-né dans l'Égypte ancienne," in *Hommages Fayza Haikal* (Cairo: Institut Français d'Archéologie Orientale, 2003), pp. 17–27 (following early ethnographic reports of Lane and Blackman).

43 See Robert K. Ritner, "Anubis and the Lunar Disc," *The Journal of Egyptian Archaeology* 71 (1986): 149–55 (overlooked in Aufrère, "Le hiéroglyphe du crible . . ."). For a true Coptic descendant of this imagery, see Dom Bede Millard, "St Christopher and the Lunar Disc of Anubis," *The Journal of Egyptian Archaeology* 73 (1987): 237–8.

44 MMA 1944.44.4.4 from Lisht; see William C. Hayes, *The Scepter of Egypt*, 2 vols. (New York: The Metropolitan Museum of Art, 1953), 1: 247; and Florence Friedman, *Gifts of the Nile: Ancient Egyptian Faience* (New York: Thames and Hudson, 1998), pp. 105 and 207.

45 Friedman, *Gifts of the Nile: Ancient Egyptian Faience*, p. 207.

46 Adolf Erman, *Zaubersprüche für Mutter und Kind* (Berlin: Königl. Akademie der Wissenschaften, 1901); and Ritner, *The Mechanics of Ancient Egyptian Magical Practice*, pp. 207 and 231.

47 See Walter Wreszinski, *Bericht über die photographische Expedition von Kairo bis Wadi Halfa* . . . (Halle: Max Niemeyer Verlag, 1927), pl. 36 (amuletic knives misunderstood as bandages by Wreszinski, p. 79); see now Robert K. Ritner, " 'And Each Staff transformed into a Snake': The Serpent Wand in Ancient Egypt," in *Through a Glass Darkly: Magic, Dreams, and Prophecy in Ancient Egypt*, ed. K. Szpakowska (Swansea: University of Wales, Swansea: 2006, p. 212).

48 Hartwig Altenmüller, *Die Apotropaia und die Götter Mittelägyptens* (PhD Dissertation, Ludwig-Maximillians-Universität zu München, 1965); idem, "Apotropaikon," *Lexikon der Ägyptologie*, ed. W. Helck and E. Otto (Wiesbaden: Harrassowitz, 1975), 1: 355–8; idem, "Ein Zaubermesser des Alten Reiches," *Studien zur Altägyptischen Kultur* 13 (1986): 1–27 and pl. 3; William F. Petrie, *Gizeh and Rifeh* (London: Egyptian Research Account, 1907), p. 13 and pl. 12; idem, *Objects of Daily Use* (London: Egyptian Research Account, 1927), p. 40; Janssen and Janssen, *Growing up in Ancient Egypt*, pp. 9–10 (preferring the term "wand"); Robert K. Ritner , "Magical Wand," in *Searching for Ancient Egypt*, ed. D. Silverman (Dallas: Dallas Museum of Art and University of Pennsylvania Museum, 1997), pp. 234–5. These stylized

implements should be considered "weapons" against evil, and as such their forms may approximate (or be conflated with) throwsticks. A similar evolution is perhaps found with serpent wands, cf. the serpent-headed throwstick in the wall painting of Nebamun in Stephen Quirke and J. Spencer, *The British Museum Book of Ancient Egypt* (New York: The British Museum, 1992), p. 153 (at seam); and Wolfgang Decker, "Wurfholz," in *Lexikon der Ägyptologie*, ed. W. Helck and E. Otto (Wiesbaden: Otto Harrassowitz, 1986), 6: 1299–1300.

49 For a Metropolitan Museum example, see Hayes, *The Scepter of Egypt*, 1: 227–8. An example from a private collection appears in Friedman, *Gifts of the Nile: Ancient Egyptian Faience*, pp. 110 and 207. See also Werner Forman and Stephen Quirke, *Hieroglyphs and the Afterlife* (Norman: University of Oklahoma, 1996), p. 103.

50 Robert K. Ritner, " 'And Each Staff transformed into a Snake,' " pp. 205–25.

51 B. Gunn, "A Note on Brit. Mus. 828 (Stela of Simontu)," *The Journal of Egyptian Archaeology* 25 (1939): 218–19; H. G. Fischer, "Notes on the Mo'alla Inscriptions and Some Contemporaneous Texts," *Wiener Zeitschrift für die Kunde des Morgenlandes* 57 (1961): 74–5; Janssen and Janssen, *Growing up in Ancient Egypt*, pp. 37–41.

52 Dominic Montserrat, *Sex and Society in Graeco-Roman Egypt* (London: Kegan Paul International, 1996), pp. 39–41.

53 Despite the hesitation of Janssen and Janssen, *Growing up in Ancient Egypt*, p. 40, terminology and imagery do indicate that "the lock was shaved off at the beginning of puberty, just before circumcision." See the royal images of boys with sidelocks being presented for – but not yet undergoing – circumcision in ibid., p. 92. Later Ramesside fashion allowed longer hair alongside the sidelock. See the depictions of Khaemwaset and Amonherkhepeshef, princes of Ramses III, with and without such hair in their tombs (Valley of the Queens 44 and 55). Certain priestly offices maintained a ceremonial (and artificial) sidelock as part of their formal dress.

54 Dows Dunham, *Naga-ed-Deîr Stelae of the First Intermediate Period* (London: Museum of Fine Arts, Boston, 1937), pp. 103–4 and pl. 32. Contra Dunham, the translation of "circumcised" is not in doubt, nor is the group nature of the ceremony.

55 See further Janssen and Janssen, *Growing up in Ancient Egypt*, pp. 90–8.

56 Rare examples of uncircumcised elite male mummies have been found, with suggestions of hemophilia offered as explanation; see James E. Harris and Kent R. Weeks, *X-Raying the Pharaohs* (New York: Carles Scribner's Sons, 1973), pp. 126–7. Egyptian statuary of nude elite males regularly depicts circumcised phalli.

57 The legal procedures are summarized in Montserrat, *Sex and Society in Graeco-Roman Egypt*, pp. 36–7.

58 T. George Allen, *The Book of The Dead or Going Forth by Day* (Chicago: The University of Chicago, 1974), p. 28 (Spell 17, S10).

59 M. Pillet, "Les scènes de naissance et de circoncision dans le temple nord-est de Mout, à Karnak," *Annales du Service des Antiquités de l'Égypte* 52/1 (1952): 77–104 with plates 1–6, esp. p. 103; Ghalioungui, *Magic and Medical Science in Ancient Egypt*, p. 97.

60 See Robert K. Ritner, "The Victory Stela of Piye," in *The Literature of Ancient Egypt*, p. 385.

61 Robert K. Ritner, "Libyan vs. Nubian as the Ideal Egyptian," in the Festschrift for Leonard Lesko, ed. Stephen E. Thompson (Providence: Brown University, forthcoming).

62 Montserrat, *Sex and Society in Graeco-Roman Egypt*, pp. 41–6.

63 See Barbara Lesko, "Rank, Roles, and Rights," in *Pharaoh's Workers: The Villagers of Deir el Medina*, ed. Leonard Lesko (Ithaca: Cornell University Press, 1994), pp. 26–34.

64 For the *lits clos* or "box-bed," see Bruyère, *Rapport sur les Fouilles de Deir el Médineh (1934–5): Le Village . . .*, pp. 54–64 and pls. 9–10 (for paintings, see p. 50 Fig. 15 and pp. 57–60); Vandier d'Abbadie, "Une fresque civile de Deir el Médineh," *Revue d'Égyptologie* 3 (1938): 27–35; Sadek, *Popular Religion in Egypt during the New Kingdom*, pp. 76–7; Florence Friedman, "Aspects of Domestic Life and Religion," in *Pharaoh's Workers: The Villagers of Deir el Medina*, pp. 95–111 (styled "bed-altars"); and Barry J. Kemp, "How Religious were the Ancient Egyptians?," pp. 30–1. I thank my former University of Pennsylvania graduate student Leslie Warden, whose comments have stimulated my own discussion of these features.

65 Friedman, "Aspects of Domestic Life and Religion," pp. 99–106; Barry J. Kemp, "Wall Paintings from the Workmen's Village at el-'Amarna," *The Journal of Egyptian Archaeology* 65 (1979): 53; and Geraldine Pinch, "Childbirth and Female Figurines at Deir el-Medina and el-'Amarna," *Orientalia* 52 (1983): 407.

66 Janssen and Janssen, *Growing up in Ancient Egypt*, p. 6.

67 Friedman, "Aspects of Domestic Life and Religion," pp. 110–11.

68 T. Eric Peet and C. L. Woolley, *The City of Akhenaten. Part I* (London: Oxford University Press, 1923), pp. 59 and 75–85; Kemp, "Wall Paintings from the Workmen's Village at el-'Amarna," pp. 47–53; and idem, *Amarna Reports III* (London: Egypt Exploration Society, 1986), p. 25.

69 "Wall Paintings from the Workmen's Village at el-'Amarna," p. 49; and Friedman, "Aspects of Domestic Life and Religion," p. 100 (with references).

70 Dominique Valbelle, *"Les ouvriers de la tombe": Deir el-Médineh à l'époque ramesside* (Cairo: Institut Français d'Archéologie Orientale, 1985), pp. 261–2. Cf. Salima Ikram, "Domestic Shrines and the Cult of the Royal Family at el-'Amarna," *Journal of Egyptian Archaeology* 75 (1989): 89–101; and Bernard Bruyère, *Rapport sur les Fouilles de Deir el Médineh (1945–1946 et 1946–1947)* (Cairo: Institut Français d'Archéologie Orientale, 1952), pp. 17–27 (chapels F and G). The Amarna similarities are already signaled by Friedman, "Aspects of Domestic Life and Religion," pp. 110–11.

71 Bruyère, *Rapport sur les Fouilles de Deir el Médineh (1934–35): Le Village . . .*, p. 256.

72 Jaroslav Černý and Alan H. Gardiner, *Hieratic Ostraca* (Oxford: Griffith Institute, 1957), nos. 24/4 and 53/1; Janssen, *Commodity Prices from the Ramessid Period*, pp. 181–2. Hieratic Ostracon 24/4, ll. 2 and 6, notes "protections/amuletic images for the one giving birth."

73 Janssen, *Commodity Prices from the Ramessid Period*, pp. 318–19 (Taweret), pp. 334–5 (Hathor), and cf. the discussion on pp. 93–108; Sadek, *Popular Religion in Egypt during the New Kingdom*, p. 77.

74 William M. F. Petrie, *Illahun, Kahun and Gurob* (London: David Nutt, 1891 [reprinted Warminster: Aris and Phillips, 1974]), p. 11 and pl. VI/9–10; and A. Rosalie David, *The Pyramid Builders of Ancient Egypt* (London: Routledge & Kegan Paul, 1986), p. 134 and Fig. 10. A Bes mask and associated material found in a Kahun house are surely equipment for a community ritual; see David, *Pyramid Builders of Ancient Egypt*, pp. 136–7 and Fig. 9 and cf. the Old Kingdom relief with a Bes figure in Edna R. Russmann, *Eternal Egypt*, (London: The British Museum, 2001), pp. 73–4, no. 7.

75 For an example from a Pan Grave domestic context at Badari, see Guy Brunton, *Qau and Badari III* (London: British School of Archaeology in Egypt, 1930), pp. 4, 7 and pl. 10, no. 5 (broken legs) and for a whole figure, cf. p. 3 and pl. 9, no. 28.

76 Geraldine Pinch, *Votive Offerings to Hathor* (Oxford: Griffith Institute, 1993), pp. 198–234; "Childbirth and Female Figurines at Deir el-Medina and el-'Amarna," pp. 405–14 ; Janssen and Janssen, *Growing up in Ancient Egypt*, pp. 7–8; Christiane Desroches-Noblecourt, "'Concubines du Mort' et mères de famille au Moyen Empire," *Bulletin de l'Institut Français d'Archéologie Orientale* 53 (1953): 7–47; Bruyère, *Rapport sur les Fouilles de Deir el Médineh (1934–35): Le Village . . .*, pp. 109–50; and cf. the "votive beds" unearthed at Medinet Habu and discussed in Uvo Hölscher, *Post-Ramessid Remains: The Excavation of Medinet Habu Vol. V* (Chicago: The University of Chicago, 1954), pp. 11–12. Pinch distinguishes six types: (1) modeled in the round, good workmanship; found in tomb and town, no feet, some with child; (2) nudes modeled in the round, poor quality, spindly legs/feet; (3) like (2) but some seated, pubic triangle incised; (4) molded lying nude women, some from tombs but most from houses at Deir el-Medina, pubic triangle incised; (5) faience or pottery, simplified and elongated molded figures; and (6) women on beds, some with tattoos, some suckling children. Type 6 has three subcategories.

77 Pinch, *Votive Offerings to Hathor*, pp. 198 and 211–25.

78 Robert K. Ritner, "Des preuves de l'existence d'une nécromancie dans l'Égypte ancienne," in *La magie en Égypte*, ed. Yvon Koenig (Paris: Louvre, 2002), pp. 291–2; and idem, "Necromancy in Ancient Egypt," in *Magic and Divination in the Ancient World*, ed. Leda Ciraolo and Jonathan Seidel (Leiden: Brill/Styx, 2002), p. 91 n. 16.

79 Friedman, "Aspects of Domestic Life and Religion," p. 100. Cf. the cautious remarks of Janssen and Janssen, *Growing up in Ancient Egypt*, p. 7.

80 Angela M. J. Tooley, "Child's Toy or Ritual Object," *Göttinger Miszellen* 123 (1991): pp. 101–11.

81 Peet and Wooley, *The City of Akhenaten. Part I*, pp. 24–5 and pl. 12; Kemp, "How Religious were the Ancient Egyptians?," pp. 30–1; and Pinch, "Childbirth and Female Figurines at Deir el-Medina and el-'Amarna," pp. 405–15, esp. p. 414. Two figurines were initially recorded. See Kemp, *Ancient Egypt: Anatomy of a Civilization* (London: Routledge, 1989), pp. 305 and 346 n. 64.

82 See Demotic *ẖrr(y.t)* "space under the stairs" in Erichsen, *Demotisches Glossar*, p. 392. Demotic, Coptic, Aramaic, Greek and Arabic references are gathered in the Chicago Demotic Dictionary under *ẖrr(.t)*. The Coptic term is equated with Greek *hypopession*. Fuller discussion appears in Terry Wilfong, "Menstrual Synchrony and the 'Place of Women' in Ancient Egypt," in *Gold of Praise*, ed. E. Teeter and J. A. Larson (Chicago: The University of Chicago, 1999), pp. 419–34, esp. pp. 429–30. Contra Montserrat, *Sex and Society in Graeco-Roman Egypt*, pp. 47–8, the Egyptian evidence is neither "problematic" nor "flimsy."

83 Peet and Wooley, *The City of Akhenaten. Part I*, p. 24.

84 Benoît Fayolle, *Le Livre du Musée Guimet de Lyon. Égypte: Antiquités Grecques et Romaines* (Lyon: Emanuel Vitte, 1958), p. 81.

85 Ritner, *The Mechanics of Ancient Egyptian Magical Practice*, pp. 112–90.

86 See, inter alia, Emma Brunner-Traut, "Gravidenflasche. Das Salben des Mutterleibes," in *Archaeologie und Altes Testament. Festschrift für Kurt Galling*, ed. A. Kuschke and E. Kutsch (Tübingen: J. C. B. Mohr, 1970), pp. 35–48; Christiane Desroches-

Noblecourt, "Pots anthropomorphes et recettes magico-médicales dans l'Égypte ancienne," *Revue d'Egyptologie* 9 (1952): 49–67; R. K. Ritner, "Magic in Medicine," in *The Oxford Encyclopedia of Ancient Egypt*, ed. Donald B. Redford (Oxford: Oxford University Press, 2001), 2: 328; Janssen and Janssen, *Growing up in Ancient Egypt*, pp. 3–4 and 19–21; U. Hölscher, *Post-Ramessid Remains: The Excavation of Medinet Habu Vol. V*, pp. 12–13 (Fig. 18); Keith C. Seele, "University of Chicago Oriental Institute Nubian Expedition: Excavations Between Abu Simbel and the Sudan Border, Preliminary Report," *Journal of Near Eastern Studies* 33 (1974): 13, Fig. 17; and Edward Brovarski, Susan Doll, and Rita Freed (eds.), *Egypt's Golden Age* (Boston: Museum of Fine Arts, Boston, 1982), pp. 78, 86–7 and 292–4. Female vessels from graves are noted in Janine Bourriau, *Pottery From the Nile Valley Before the Arab Conquest* (Cambridge: Fitzwilliam Museum, 1981), pp. 34–6. More common Hathor and later Bes vessels are discussed in ibid., pp. 37–56. Bes jugs from New Kingdom Kom Rabia (urban Memphis) are noted with a drawing in Janine Bourriau, "All this pottery. What about it?," *Egyptian Archaeology* 26 (2005): 32.

87 R. K. Ritner, "A Uterine Amulet in the Oriental Institute Collection," *Journal of Near Eastern Studies* 43 (1984): 209–21.

88 Pinch, *Votive Offerings to Hathor*, pp. 235–45 and pls. 52–3. For a bibliography and overview of Greco-Roman era terracotta figurines, see G. Nachtergael, "Terre cuites de l'Égypte gréco-romaine," *Chronique d'Égypte* 70 (1995): 254–94.

89 Siegfried Schott, "Die Bitte um ein Kind auf einer Grabfigur des frühen Mittleren Reiches," *The Journal of Egyptian Archaeology* 16 (1930): 23. See further Desroches-Noblecourt, "'Concubines du Mort' et mères de famille au Moyen Empire," pp. 7–47.

90 For a corrective, see Ritner, "Des preuves de l'existence d'une nécromancie dans l'Égypte ancienne," pp. 285–99; and idem, "Necromancy in Ancient Egypt," pp. 89–96.

91 Robert J. Demarée, *The 3ḫ ikr n Rʿ-Stelae. On Ancestor Worship* (Leiden: Nederlands Instituut voor het Nabije Oosten, 1983); Bruyère, *Rapport sur les Fouilles de Deir el Médineh (1934–35): Le Village . . .*, pp. 151–74; Florence Friedman, "On the Meaning of Some Anthropoid Busts from Deir el-Medina," *The Journal of Egyptian Archaeology* 71 (1985): 82–97; and Sadek, *Popular Religion in Egypt during the New Kingdom*, pp. 77–8.

92 For Gurob, see Thomas, *Gurob: A New Kingdom Town*, p. 83 and pl. 55 (nos. 711–12). See also Friedman, "Aspects of Domestic Life and Religion," pp. 114–17.

93 Friedman, "Aspects of Domestic Life and Religion," p. 114, notes that females may be colored red on fertility figurines and related ostraca, but that these instances are exceptional and limited in context.

94 Friedman, "Aspects of Domestic Life and Religion," pp. 115–16.

95 Demarée, *The 3ḫ ikr n Rʿ-Stelae. On Ancestor Worship*; Friedman, "Aspects of Domestic Life and Religion," pp. 111–17.

96 Friedman, "Aspects of Domestic Life and Religion," p. 178 n. 46.

97 Ibid., p. 114.

98 Alan H. Gardiner and Kurt Sethe, *Egyptian Letters to the Dead Mainly from the Old and Middle Kingdoms* (London: Egypt Exploration Society, 1928); with supplementary references in Ritner, *The Mechanics of Ancient Egyptian Magical Practice*, pp. 180–3; Richard Jasnow and Günther Vittmann, "An Abnormal Hieratic Letter to the Dead (P. Brooklyn 37.1799 E)," *Enchoria* 19/20 (1992/93): 23–43; and Baines, "Practical Religion and Piety," pp. 86–7 and 97.

99 For references, see Ritner, "Des preuves de l'existence d'une nécromancie dans l'Égypte ancienne," pp. 285–99; and idem, "Necromancy in Ancient Egypt," pp. 89–96.

100 E. Graefe, "Talfest," in *Lexikon der Ägyptologie*, 6: 187–9; and Friedman, "Aspects of Domestic Life and Religion," p. 95 (with references).

101 Sadek, *Popular Religion in Egypt during the New Kingdom*, p. 3; and Baines, "Practical Religion and Piety," p. 81: "A similar integration of the dead in the society of the living is well attested in other cultures; what is Egyptian is the inequality, to which the apparent lack of reciprocity between living and dead might be related." Given the invariable mention of the dead in the conceptual contexts that Baines is discussing, this "inequality" has no factual basis.

102 James H. Breasted, *The Edwin Smith Surgical Papyrus* (Chicago: The University of Chicago, 1930), pp. 469–87. See further Philippe Germond, *Sekhmet et la Protection du Monde* (Basel and Geneva: Editions de Belles-Lettres, 1981); and idem, *Les invocations à la Bonne Année au temple d'Edfou* (Basel and Geneva: Editions de Belles-Lettres, 1986).

103 Breasted, *The Edwin Smith Surgical Papyrus*, pp. 476 and 478.

104 Ibid., pp. 481–2.

105 See the dockets on P. Geneva MAH 15274, and the case of private owners like Keniherkhepeshef; noted with references in Ritner, *The Mechanics of Ancient Egyptian Magical Practice*, pp. 205–7.

106 Ibid., p. 207 n. 956, and pp. 225–31.

107 Bruyère, *Rapport sur les Fouilles de Deir el Médineh (1934–35): Le Village . . .*, pp. 168–74; and Sadek, *Popular Religion in Egypt during the New Kingdom*, p. 77.

108 Cf. Edward Brovarski, "Sobek," in *Lexikon der Ägyptologie*, ed. W. Helck and E. Otto (Wiesbaden: Otto Harrassowitz, 1984), 5: 998.

109 Friedman, "Aspects of Domestic Life and Religion," p. 111, citing Valbelle, *"Les ouvriers de la tombe": Deir el-Médineh à l'époque ramesside*, pp. 262 and 314.

110 Petrie, *Illahun, Kahun and Gurob*, p. 11 and pl. VI; and David, *The Pyramid Builders of Ancient Egypt*, p. 134.

111 Sadek, *Popular Religion in Egypt during the New Kingdom*, pp. 81–2.

112 Ritner, *The Mechanics of Ancient Egyptian Magical Practice*, p. 215 n. 1000 (*pḥ-nṯr* with lamp).

113 References in Ritner, "Des preuves de l'existence d'une nécromancie dans l'Égypte ancienne," pp. 285–99; idem, "Necromancy in Ancient Egypt," pp. 89–96; and Baines, "Practical Religion and Piety," p. 93.

114 Examples in Bruyère, *Rapport sur les Fouilles de Deir el Médineh (1934–35): Le Village* . . . are summarized in Sadek, *Popular Religion in Egypt during the New Kingdom*, p. 77.

115 J. J. Clère, "Un mot pour 'mariage' en Égyptien de l'époque Ramesside," *Revue d'Égyptologie* 20 (1968): 171–5.

116 Nina de Garis Davies and Norman M. de Garis Davies, "Harvest Rites in a Theban Tomb," *The Journal of Egyptian Archaeology* 25 (1939): 154–6; and Robert K. Ritner, " 'And Each Staff transformed into a Snake': The Serpent Wand in Ancient Egypt," in *Through a Glass Darkly* (p. 215).

117 M. L. Allen, *The Terracotta Figurines From Karanis* (PhD Dissertation, University of Michigan, 1985), 2: 410–13; and Terry G. Wilfong, *Women and Gender in Ancient Egypt* (Ann Arbor: Kelsey Museum of Archaeology, 1997), p. 76 (Kelsey Museum 6483). Examples are third century CE.

118 Ikram, "Domestic Shrines and the Cult of the Royal Family at el-'Amarna."

119 See the remains from Kahun, in Petrie, *Illahun, Kahun and Gurob*, p. 11 and pl. VI/9–10.

120 Robert K. Ritner, "O. Gardiner 363: A Spell Against Night Terrors," pp. 25–41.

121 For clay figures from Amarna and other sites; see Kemp, "How Religious were the Ancient Egyptians?," pp. 31–2; Quirke, *Ancient Egyptian Religion*, pp. 118–19 (Amarna cobra and bed with cobra decoration on legs); Neal Spencer, "The Temples of Kom Firin," *Egyptian Archaeology* 24 (2004): 40; and Kasia Szpakowska, "Playing with Fire: Initial Observations on the Religious Uses of Clay Cobras," *Journal of the American Research Center in Egypt* 40 (2003): 113–22.

122 References in Ritner, " 'And Each Staff transformed into a Snake': The Serpent Wand in Ancient Egypt," p. 219, n. 40.

123 H. D. Betz (ed.), *The Greek Magical Papyri in Translation Including the Demotic Spells*, 2nd edn. (Chicago: The University of Chicago, 1992), pp. 122–3 (PGM VII, 222–49) and 147–8 (PGM VIII, 64–110).

124 See R. K. Ritner, "Horus on the Crocodiles: A Juncture of Religion and Magic in Late Dynastic Egypt," in *Religion and Philosophy in Ancient Egypt*, ed. W. K. Simpson (New Haven: Yale Egyptological Seminar, 1989), pp. 103–16.

125 Baines, "Practical Religion and Piety," p. 93 (correcting the spelling of "new Kingdom").

126 In addition to the examples previously discussed, see Dieter Jankuhn, *Das Buch "Schutz des Hauses" (s3-pr)* (Bonn: R. Habelt, 1972).

127 *Pr-ʿ3* "palace/the great house" (later *pr-Pr-ʿ3* "palace/the house of Pharaoh"), *pr-ny-sw.t* "palace/the house of the king") and *ḥw.t-nṯr* "temple/mansion of god."

11

Household and Domestic Religion in Ancient Egypt

BARBARA S. LESKO

In current Egyptological literature, "domestic religion" is identified as "religious conduct undertaken strictly within the confines of the house," but must we consider only practices *within* the walls of a house when we research ancient "household" religion?[1] Surely rituals and resources that private individuals had to see them through the many threats and challenges they faced throughout life are appropriate to this study. Several dozen religious festivals were held within the walls of one village in ancient Egypt during the year and some featured four solid days of men and women, even children, drinking together.[2] Whether this occurred within homes or in the streets or at a nearby shrine, should we not consider such celebrations part of domestic religion?

Of course much more source material survives from the later centuries than the earlier dynasties to provide evidence of people's personal beliefs and religious practices, but more can be said about earlier indications of these than has been covered so far in this book. And more can be said about women's participation in the private religious life of ancient Egypt. From research undertaken in the past quarter-century, it has become clear that women were *very* much involved in *organized* religion in state-supported temples.[3] We see this already in the Old Kingdom, and not just among a few elite women or royal and court women, but rather among the wives and daughters of skilled workers and managers. Already in the Fourth Dynasty-cemetery of the *workers* at the Great Pyramid, Zahi Hawass has uncovered a small tomb of a construction supervisor and artisan whose wife was a priestess of Hathor.[4] The goddess Hathor was the wife of the supreme god Re, the sun, divine mother of the king of Egypt, and one of the leading deities of ancient Egypt, despite what one might have read in some books on Egyptian religion whose authors try to portray her in more limited terms, quite incorrectly. In her Brandeis doctoral dissertation, Marianne Galvin demonstrated that in the Old Kingdom, beginning with the Fifth Dynasty, *hundreds* of women were priestesses (not just musicians), but *priestesses* and in many cases the heads of cults, of this primary goddess throughout the country.[5]

Although in later periods, most of Hathor's cult places came to be headed by male priests, *elite* women at least remained among her priesthood, as is seen clearly in the Middle Kingdom. Later women seem to have been always among at least the lower echelons of sacred musicians and temple singers even in the greatest temples of the land, such as Karnak, the home of the New Kingdom's supreme deity Amun-Re, while in the Third Intermediate Period, immediately following the New Kingdom and for some centuries after, we again find women holding high priestly positions there.[6] Some women played roles in organized religion, within the inner spaces of sacred temple precincts that were off limits to the vast majority of the Egyptian population, both men and women.

Therefore while women could have public roles in established or organized religion, they surely must have played active parts in household religion. The problem is that most women were illiterate and did not leave us descriptions of themselves, and most males – at least judging from the tomb art produced by male artists – did not go out of their way to portray women's lives. For instance, women's crafts are seldom depicted among the many occupations illustrated in the tomb paintings. However, it is significant that we do have written testimony from Deir el-Medina, as Robert Ritner briefly notes, of wise women who were shamans or clairvoyants and who are not named – perhaps because they were feared as much as they were revered – but who were resorted to by people who wanted to learn the reasons behind tragedies, or wanted help in making decisions, or finding lost items.[7]

It is instructive to peruse the pages of Winifred Blackman's anthropological study of early twentieth-century Egyptian village life to find parallels to ancient evidence. On a number of occasions, she met female as well as male magicians in the humble communities in which she lived with her archaeologist brother.[8] The twentieth-century magician, upon looking at a sick person, could say whether he or she would live or die and produced charms and spells for cures. Besides their spells, village magicians also had many home-made potions that they dispensed to cure eye inflammations and headaches and to help with difficult births and fevers. In New Kingdom Egypt, an inscribed charm obtained from a magician was enclosed in a small case and hung around the neck. A famous example is the published prophylactic spell for the necropolis scribe Kenherkhopshef.[9] This man, who lived during the reign of Ramesses the Great, was surely the best educated and most sophisticated member of his community, but he resorted to an old spell, originally dictated by a magician (two other copies of this are known) which had to be recited four times over a stem of flax which was to be used as an arrow, the papyrus being folded and attached to the arrow. The text, which describes a demon in graphic terms, was meant to keep at bay that obnoxious force meant perhaps to be understood as an illness or a form of possession. I. E. S. Edwards, who published this text and a group of Third Intermediate Period oracular amuletic texts, noted that the majority of the latter were written for women and meant to protect their children. Certainly magic had a central place in daily life in ancient Egypt and was believed (beneficent magic, that is) to be a gift of the gods to humanity.[10]

Harmful magic was still practiced in Egypt in the past century, and the wax figures of an enemy, made to defeat him when they melt in fire, remind one of the wax figures used in an assassination attempt by the royal harem inmates in the reign of Pharaoh Ramesses III in the Twentieth Dynasty and recorded on surviving trial papyri.[11]

The evil eye is still believed in, and children are deemed especially vulnerable. The ability of a stare to harm someone was believed in ancient Egypt to emanate both from live and dead people as well as from gods and demons and snakes. Indeed the evil eye could be understood as an independent force.[12] Stephen Quirke quotes a spell for a girl that specifically stated that it will protect her "from every evil eye, from every evil glare."[13] The text goes on to reveal the many other threats an ancient Egyptian felt existed – everything from falling walls to unpacified deities.

But amulets are and were widely utilized throughout most of Egyptian history (they began to be used at least 1,000 years before the historical period) especially to protect children. This is seen clearly from excavation reports by Guy Brunton, for instance, who excavated Old Kingdom cemeteries at Qau and reported that with the Old Kingdom's Sixth Dynasty already a burgeoning of amulets was noticeable among the burials, but the amulets were surely worn in real life first. Children wore necklaces and bracelets made up of little figures. In the excavator's words: "children and young girls in particular had to be protected as the most valued members of society."[14] In a much later cemetery at Giza, dating to the Late Period, again it was the children's burials which received the most lavish attention and where were found the amulets, especially the *wedjat* eye, and little images of Bes and Hathor (Figure 11.1).[15]

The open hand and the crocodile were especially prevalent among the Old Kingdom amulets in Brunton's report on the Old Kingdom cemetery. Later in the New Kingdom these two images united on one type of common amulet, and such an amulet is mentioned in a written spell to protect a child.[16] Possibly the hand stood for harm from a *human* and the crocodile harm from a *beast* (and certainly the man-eating crocodile lurking where the population had to go to gather water, wash clothes and bathe was particularly feared). There were amulets for the living and amulets placed on the dead person's body. Those for the living could be utilized in jewelry designs. In the New Kingdom tiny images of deities were produced and are found in various materials – gold, semi-precious stones and, most commonly, faience. They can offer indications of favorite deities. Among the most frequently encountered are the hippo goddess Taweret, who helped women in labor, and Bes, the lion-headed dancing dwarf, who guarded children, while male craftsmen looked to Ptah of Memphis as their patron and carried his image while scribes adhered to the ibis or baboon forms of the god Thoth. Most popular amulet of all, however, was the scarab that began to be produced in the Sixth Dynasty and was reproduced hundreds of thousands of times. The scarab beetle was probably associated with the sun and also new life and resurrection, but as R. S. Bianchi suggests, by the

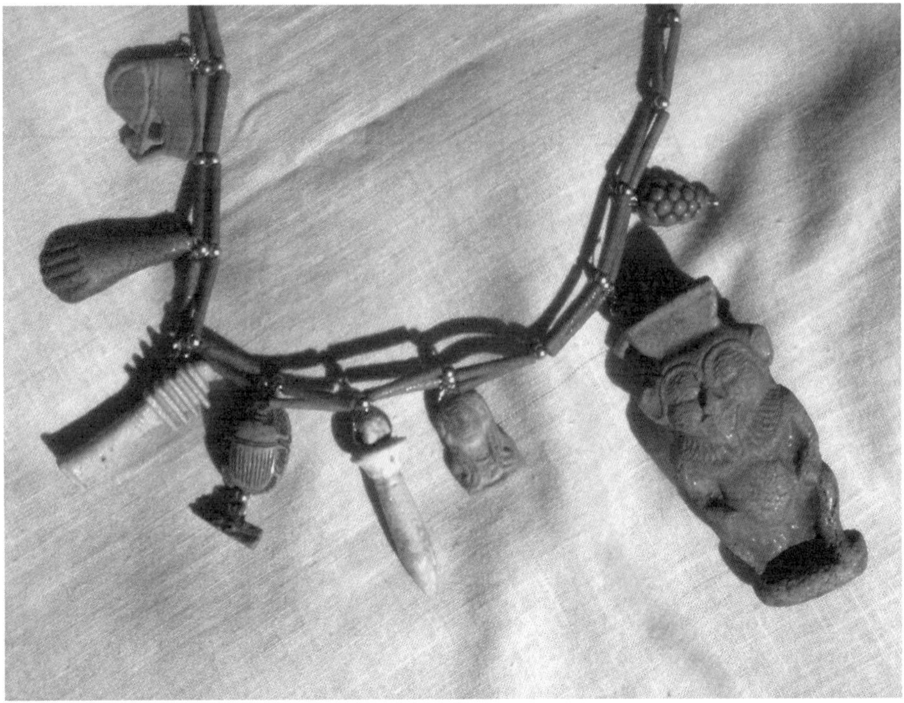

Figure 11.1 Bes figure and assorted Egyptian amulets. Photo by L. H. Lesko

New Kingdom, the vast majority had the purely amuletic purpose of providing protection and attracting good luck.[17]

The village magicians, be they the wise woman or the male scorpion charmer referred to in the ancient texts from the New Kingdom workmen's village,[18] are surely examples of magic on the domestic level, but the housewife and farmer of ancient Egypt also had their religious rituals which are reflected in the traditions of the peasants who lived four thousand years later. Sacrificing the first fruits of a harvest probably goes back to the beginnings of agriculture and the shrine set up in the field for the serpent goddess of the harvest Renenutet illustrates this as does a Middle Kingdom text from the great tomb of Djefai-Hap of Assiut dated to the early Twelfth Dynasty or about 1900 BCE Referring to a ritual for New Year's Day, the text states: "That which he gave to them was one hekat of northern barley for every field of the endowment from the first-fruits of the harvest of the nomarch's estate, just as every common man of Siut gives of the first fruits of his harvest."[19]

Surely household or personal religion should be considered as extending beyond the walls to include the religious activities involved with the daily pursuits of the citizenry, whether farming, herding or any task or craft that ordinary people might engage in. Illustrating religious practice inside the house itself, fortunately, we do have one picture that has survived of a *woman* offering before an ancestor bust

Figure 11.2 Stele showing an offering to an ancestor bust. Reproduced from F. Friedman's chapter in *Pharaoh's Workers, the Villagers of Deir el Medina*, ed. by L. H. Lesko, Copyright Cornell University Press, 1994. Used by permission of the publisher, Cornell University Press

(Figure 11.2).[20] (I know of no comparable scene showing a male doing this). Therefore there is a good chance that the lady of the house, especially in a community like the royal tomb workers' village found at Deir el-Medina whose population was overwhelmingly female most of the week while the men slept in huts near their worksite, played a very active role in household religion.

There is more to religion than magic and ritual, however. What of moral values? Was it not in the home that the moral code, the ethics of the Egyptian way of life, was taught and passed on to the next generation? Apparently Egyptian temple priests did not preach to the people. As Miriam Lichtheim has pointed out, "the gods above were thought of as shepherds of all mankind; shepherds, not teachers."[21]

Values – moral and religious – presumably were taught by parents and even kings and, among the literate, by schoolteachers and professional overseers.[22] The ability to listen to and adhere to wise teachings was praised as a prime achievement and a way to the good life.

We have seen that amulets and magical spells were sought as aids in life and even in the Beyond, but dead family members could also be approached for help during life's crises. The dead were deities; those laid in the town cemetery were called *netjeru*, the word for "deities." But on the other hand, the dead never really left the community of the living and thus could be communicated with. Letters to the dead were written in the house or town and *then* taken to the cemetery to the tomb of a relative who was either interfering with life or was begged to lend support to solve a problem or hinder another person from harming the family. There are letters to the dead written (dictated) by women and there are deceased women who were the recipients of such letters.[23] On the topic of the dead, contrary to Ritner's statement in this volume (his note 25), there is some evidence from Deir el-Medina that poorer people's burials were handled within the family or by their employers.[24] Presumably such people were just wrapped and not mummified, as that lengthy process would have been expensive.

As Ritner correctly states, the temples of Egypt were homes to the deities, not places of communal worship, and the gods daily were awakened, bathed, dressed, and fed amidst liturgical chanting, the burning of incense, and other set ritual. It would not be surprising that certain prayers or rituals were followed within the households of mortals. When we consider religious rites and practices within the household in *modern times*, we all can identify family practices at meal time, such as saying grace before indulging, lighting the Hanukkah candles, teaching bedtime prayers to children, and, among Muslims, cleansing and praying five times a day. The ancestors of contemporary Christians had even more religious observances at home. For instance, consecrations of a new house were once far more common than they are today.

So I am afraid that quite possibly a *vast* amount of knowledge of what ordinary people did in antiquity, and especially what women did in the home connected with religious beliefs, has been lost – rituals in food preparation would be one example. W. Blackman observed that before removing any food from the room in which stores are kept, both Muslims and Copts in early twentieth-century Egypt said: "In the name of God, the Compassionate, the Merciful," and would explain this little ritual as a way of preventing the evil spirits or *afarits* from taking any of the food. She also mentions that women will murmur one or both of these phrases when they begin to mix flour for bread making.[25] Placing bread and salt on the floor alongside a jug of water was meant to keep *afarits* away from the house entirely.[26] These are examples of the type of domestic religious rituals of which, if anything similar was resorted to in antiquity, the knowledge is now lost.

At the end of each ten-day week, someone in an ancient Egyptian family was expected to leave their house and go to the cemetery to leave water and perhaps more in the way of a food offering at deceased relatives' grave sites.[27] At certain religious festivals, like the Feast of the Valley in the Theban area, whole families apparently turned out to gather in the necropolis and spent the night drinking and feasting in a holiday picnic at the burial site of their loved ones.[28] Beer was credited with magical properties, and drunkenness was a significant part of religious observance in ancient Egypt[29] and may have encouraged visions and communications with dead family members. It was doubtless the women who prepared the picnics and food offerings, even though the men of the family prepared the beer, as records from Deir el-Medina indicate.

Anything produced inside the house which was later taken as an offering or votive to a religious site, be it tomb or temple, should be included in our study. Geraldine Pinch has studied a large corpus of small painted cloths dedicated to the goddess Hathor at her cult place, Deir el-Bahri on the west bank at Luxor.[30] These usually depict the donor or donors (female) before the goddess and may well have been created in their homes or village and then taken over to the Deir el-Bahri temple to be given to their favorite goddess, from whom they hoped for some favor, perhaps good marriages for the girls. We have texts (love poems and love charms) that credit the goddess with bringing couples together, and as early at the late Sixth Dynasty the didactic text of Ptahhotep, in his Maxim 12, credits god with providing children to a couple.[31]

The many decorated votive cloths dedicated to Hathor come in a variety of sizes and shapes. Some are decorated with tassels and others have beads within the weaving. Some are actually small shirts, as if baby clothes.[32] The variety is so great that a mass-produced item, sold in a kiosk outside the temple's walls, should perhaps be ruled out in favor of homespun items.

We know that women did weave and sew; we have both pictorial and written documentation from contemporary sources of this.[33] Therefore what we have here in these woven and painted cloths, it seems to me, is an item of religious nature produced in the home but taken to the temple by its owner or a family group as a gift to the goddess in the hope, no doubt, that the deity will in some way intercede for or grant the special requests of the supplicant. Pinch reports that the female donors outnumbered the male by 74 to 10, and many cloths had more than one donor, sometimes whole families or even large groups of unrelated women.[34] Even if a professional painter may have been hired by the women, the smaller expense of the cloth votive (and thus its attraction to women) may be reflected in the fact that three times as many men were donors of votive stone stelae.[35] On the other hand, dozens of stone stelae have been found dedicated by women at another site. T. Duquesne has recently described his research on votive stelae from the site of Assiut, dedicated during the Ramesside period to the local god Wepwawet, and indicates many of the donors were women, and thus it could be that a woven cloth was deemed more appropriate for Hathor, as she was associated with cloth production and received fabric as part of major donations.[36]

Sexual votives, to promote fertility, were also dedicated to this goddess who was thought of as a stimulator of sexuality and fertility. A home-made phallus of stone with inscription by the dedicating scribe (Ramose from the tomb workers community hoping for a family) is a prime example of a man beseeching the goddess of love for an important favor.[37]

Emily Teeter of the University of Chicago has studied the numerous baked clay figurines of females found in ancient Egyptian habitation sites throughout the millennia. Usually these are nude females, sometimes shown on beds and with a baby at their side, but Teeter suggests that, rather than being votives used by women supplicating goddesses, such figurines found in houses and work camps were rather meant to serve as a "good luck charm to ensure the safety of the household," although they would seem specifically to show a hope in the continuance of the family line (Figure 11.3). Similarly, excavated from the ruins of houses come

Figure 11.3 Female figurine from Medinet Habu (OIM 14603). Courtesy of the Oriental Institute, University of Chicago. Third Intermediate Period, baked clay. L: 13.3; W: 8.3; H: 11 cm

numerous small box-like platforms decorated with Hathoric motifs. Teeter suspects these were "kept in the houses to honor the goddess, much like some people today keep religious figures in their homes."[38] However, Professor J. F. Borghouts of Leiden has published a text which shows that clay figures of women were used to increase efficacy of medical arts.[39] Therefore it would be incorrect to assume (as has often been done) that such figurines were always connected with fertility or placed in tombs to stimulate male potency.

Within the house there were certainly altars and amuletic plaques as well as amulets and spells that were worn on the person as Ritner mentions. Indeed, personal amulets have a very long history. In a predynastic Badarian period cemetery, probably fifth millennium BCE, a skeleton was found with the small image of a gazelle tied to his leg, as if to ensure swiftness.[40] By the second millennium, there were tiny healing stelae with the young god Horus surrounded by magical spells and symbols, which were used in the home and whose efficacy could be secured by a person pouring water over the whole and then drinking it.[41] Surely this too is household magic provoked by religious belief.

However, I do not think recent arguments interpreting the enclosed so-called box beds as altars are always convincing. There would be no need for stairs to approach an altar; they would rather be in the way. They only would have been needed if someone needed to get inside, not just ceremonially stand before the structure. Contrary to Ritner's claim, the *lit clos* structures are not "commonly found" at Deir el-Medina. Many houses did not have these enclosed platforms. It makes more sense to me that these structures would have provided a safer environment for the newborn in which possibly the mother could spend her 14 days of purification with her child. Otherwise the baby would have been much closer to a floor that was very likely home to insects, the hedgehogs kept as pets to eat the cockroaches, the occasional scorpions and snakes, and the animal droppings excavators have actually found in these houses. In short, we must be realistic. I have experienced enough cold winters in Luxor to know that no woman is going to spend a very cold night on a roof (much less fourteen days and nights) in an open pavilion with her newborn baby, when she can have an enclosed private warm space in the room of her house. The decoration on these structures' walls point to the protection of women and children. Interestingly, there is – in a job-payments text from Deir el-Medina – reference to "a woman's bed decorated."[42] One has to wonder why some beds would be designated for women and no "man's bed" is found in such texts as well. The person being paid was not a carpenter, but an artist, and the same term for "decorated" was used in this text for work done on coffins and a box. Thus we may see here evidence of the decorating by the professional artist with scenes of protective and fertility-related deities of a box-bed, which the ancients could easily have termed a "woman's bed." Other texts regarding beds mention that they were made of wood but do not usually record the sex of the owner.[43] The box-beds, if used for newborn infants and their nursing, being in the front room of the cramped row house would not always have been in use for that purpose and need not be labeled as "maternity beds," a term Ritner has applied. Because one was found thousands of years later with a statue inside and another with part of a deity's crown does not mean that their *original* purpose was purely religious rather than practical, however. Surely any unused space in these tiny houses could be converted to a storage closet or a shrine if the homeowner deemed it necessary. Also, again it should be noted that it was the women who were at home in this village from which we have our box-bed evidence, and the men who were most of the time not present. Therefore the women were making decisions about their own lives, and there is no indication that childbirth was regarded as so disgusting that women had to risk their health and that of their baby to avoid contaminating the males of the family by living on a cold and windswept roof of their house during the postpartum period. The vine-decorated pavilions on some drawings were probably very *temporary* structures set up to celebrate a birth or be the place where actual delivery could take place in the relative privacy and greater space that a roof could provide the mother and the midwives as opposed to the interior of the small, crowded house. More likely the vine-decorated pavilion was used only for a few hours rather than weeks of postpartum isolation. There is no text associated with the drawings that tells us otherwise, but one text *does* connect the pavilion with the actual process of giving birth.[44] Further, Ritner's inclusion of a place of withdrawal for menstruating women surely has no connection with religion but with hygiene. T. Wilfong, who has studied this subject in ancient Egypt, found no evidence of taboos against women during their periods.[45] Also, the significance of the sidelock of youth begs for further study.[46] There are portrayals from the Ramesside period of mature princes with full heads of hair (or wigs) that still include a sidelock of hair, and there are portrayals of fully clad girls (designating maturity as pre-pubescent children are usually portrayed nude) who have long sidelocks on otherwise shaven heads. Even if hair styles were related to age or a rite of passage does it necessarily follow that *religious* rather than social custom is dictating fashion?

To conclude, we have seen evidence for religious rites, offerings, and beliefs on the domestic level and we have identified activities that do not seem as clearly linked to religious beliefs. We are hindered by a lack of information due to the paucity of existing ancient town sites in Egypt, but we can sometimes find it useful to recall practices among the provincial villages of Egypt in more recent times, where folk traditions and a way of life continue to reflect much earlier society.

This much said, it still troubles me that we know more about the outward evidence of religious practice than its teachings. We have thousands of amulets, stelae, and numerous written texts and graven images, but know little about the way in which Egyptians learned about their religion. How were religious lore and moral standards passed on within a largely illiterate society? Because temples were the houses of deities and were removed from the populace by high walls which protected and sanctified the supernatural powers within, the priests of Egypt may not have played any role in religious teaching of the populace. A very small percentage of the male population attended schools. This should mean, then, that the average household and family were all the more important for the perpetuation of religious beliefs and practices and moral teachings from generation to generation.

Notes

1 From the introduction to a recent publication on the topic: Anna Stevens, "The Material Evidence for Domestic Religion at Amarna and Preliminary Remarks on its Interpretation," *Journal of Egyptian Archaeology* 89 (2003): 143–68.

2 A. G. McDowell, *Village Life in Ancient Egypt: Laundry Lists and Love Songs* (Oxford: University Press, 1999), p. 96.

3 Barbara Lesko, "Ancient Egyptian Religions," *Encyclopedia of Women and World Religion* (New York: Macmillan Reference USA, 1999), p. 32.

4 Zahi Hawass, "The Tombs of the Pyramid Builders – the Tomb of the Artisan Petety and his Curse," in *Egypt, Israel and the Ancient Mediterranean World: Studies in Honor of Donald B. Redford*, ed. Gary H. Knoppers and Antony Hirsch (Leiden: Brill, 2004), p. 29.

5 Marianne Galvin, "The Priestesses of Hathor in the Old Kingdom and the 1st Intermediate Period" (PhD Dissertation, Brandeis University, 1981); and idem, "Addendum," in *Women's Earliest Records from Ancient Egypt and Western Asia*, ed. Barbara S. Lesko (Atlanta: Scholars Press, 1989), pp. 28–30.

6 Saphinaz-Amal Naguib, *Le clergé féminin d'Amon thébain à la 21e Dynastie* (Oslo: Ethnografisk Museum, 1988), pp. 152–321 and Barbara S. Lesko, *The Great Goddesses of Egypt* (Norman: University of Oklahoma Press, 1999), pp. 244–54.

7 Joris F. Borghouts, "Magical Practices Among the Villagers," in *Pharaoh's Workers, the Villagers of Deir el Medina*, ed. Leonard H. Lesko (Ithaca: Cornell University Press, 1994), pp. 129–30.

8 Winifred S. Blackman, *The Fellahin of Upper Egypt* (London: G. G. Harrap & Co. Ltd., 1927).

9 I. E. S. Edwards, "Ḳenhikhopshef's Prophylactic Charm," *Journal of Egyptian Archaeology* 54 (1968): 155–60.

10 Apparently magic was pervasive; see the "Testament of a Heracleopolitan King" for the statement that it was a gift from the gods (Miriam Lichtheim, *Ancient Egyptian Literature Vol. 1: The Old and Middle Kingdoms* [Berkeley: University of California Press, 1973], p. 106).

11 Hans Goedicke, "Was Magic Used in the Harem Conspiracy against Ramesses III?," *Journal of Egyptian Archaeology* 49 (1973): 91–2.

12 Kasia Maria Szpakowska, "The Perception of Dreams and Nightmares in Ancient Egypt: Old Kingdom to Third Intermediate Period" (PhD Dissertation, University of California, Los Angeles, 2000), p. 47.

13 Stephen Quirke, *Ancient Egyptian Religion* (London: British Museum Press, 1992), p. 112.

14 Guy Brunton, *Qau and Badari* (London: British School of Archaeology, 1927), p. 74. For recent studies on amulets, consult Carol A. R. Andrews, "Amulets," in *The Oxford Encyclopedia of Ancient Egypt*, ed. by Donald B. Redford (New York: Oxford University Press, 2000), 1: 75–82 and Andrews' book *Amulets of Ancient Egypt* (Austin: University of Texas Press, 1994).

15 Jessica Kaiser, "Honoring the Dead," *Aeragram: Newsletter of the Ancient Egypt Research Association* 6 (2004): 14.

16 R. B. Parkinson, *Voices from Ancient Egypt: An Anthology of Middle Kingdom Writings* (London: British Museum Press, 1992), pp. 49, 129.

17 Robert S. Bianchi, "Scarabs," in *The Oxford Encyclopedia of Ancient Egypt*, 3: 180.
18 Andrea McDowell, *Village Life*, pp. 115, 117.
19 George A. Reisner, "The Tomb of Hepzefa, Nomarch of Siût," *Journal of Egyptian Archaeology* 5 (1918): 83.
20 Florence D. Friedman, "Aspects of Domestic Life and Religion," in *Pharaoh's Workers*, p. 95 and Fig. 11. Presumably, the wall niches seen in houses at both Amarna and Deir el-Medina could have held such objects. See Stevens, "The Material Evidence for Domestic Religion at Amarna," p. 165, whose article gives evidence of the continuation of reliance upon traditional deities (as well as ancestor cults) among commoners at the heretic pharaoh's new capital city.
21 Miriam Lichtheim, *Moral Values in Ancient Egypt*, Oribis Biblicus et Orientalis 155 (Fribourg: University Press, 1997), p. 95.
22 Edward F. Wente, *Letters from Ancient Egypt* (Atlanta: Scholars Press, 1990), p. 141; Ricardo A. Caminos, *Late-Egyptian Miscellanies* (Oxford: Oxford University Press, 1954), pp. 312–13, 381, 451; and Miriam Lichtheim, *Ancient Egyptian Literature*, 3 vols. (Berkeley: University of California Press, 1973), 1: 99 for the evidence of royal exhortations.
23 Wente, *Letters*, pp. 213–15.
24 Ibid., p. 143.
25 Blackman, *Fellahin*, p. 229.
26 Ibid., p. 237.
27 Koen Donker Van Heel, "Use and Meaning of the Egyptian Term W3h Mw," in *Village Voices*, ed. R. J. Demarée and A. Egberts (Leiden: Leiden University Centre of Non-Western Studies, 1992), pp. 19–30.
28 Norman de Garis Davies and Alan H. Gardiner, *The Tomb of Amenemhet (No. 82)*, The Theban Tomb Series I (London: Egypt Exploration Fund, 1915), p. 96.
29 Joris F. Borghouts *The Magical Texts of Papyrus Leiden I* (Leiden: Brill, 1971), p. 27; Dominic Montserrat, *Sex and Society in Graeco-Roman Egypt* (London: Kegan Paul International, 1996), p. 165.
30 Geraldine Pinch, *Votive Offerings to Hathor* (Oxford: Griffith Institute, Ashmolean Museum, 1993), pp. 103–34.
31 Miriam Lichtheim, *Literature* I, 66, and Andrea McDowell, *Village Life*, pp. 32–3.
32 Pinch, *Votive Offerings*, plates 14–26; 123–34 and see Book of the Dead, Spell 174.
33 Wente, *Letters*, pp. 36, 82, 156: 31 and Gillian M. Vogelsang-Eastwood, "Weaving, Looms, and Textiles," *Oxford Encyclopedia of Ancient Egypt* 3: 490–1.
34 Pinch, *Votive Offerings*, p. 123.
35 Ibid.
36 Terence DuQuesne, "Gender, Class, and Devotion: demographic and social aspects of the Salakhana stelae." *Discussions in Egyptology* 63 (2005): 41–57.
37 John Romer, *Ancient Lives: Daily Life in Egypt of the Pharaohs* (New York: Holt, Rinehart and Winston, 1984), p. 28; and Bernard Bruyère, *Rapport sur les fouilles de Deir el-Médineh, 1927* (Cairo: Institut français archéologique orientale, 1928), pp. 39–40. From Pinch's study it would appear that dedicated phalli were not as rare as Ritner has stated. See her *Votive Offerings*, pp. 235–45.
38 Emily Teeter, "Piety at Medinet Habu," *The Oriental Institute News & Notes* 173 (2002): 1–6.
39 Borghouts, *The Magical Texts of Papyrus Leiden I 348* (Leiden: Brill, 1971), p. 25: "When he places his hand on the belly, his suffering will begin to be healed – to be

recited over a woman's statue of clay." Such female figurines have been reported to be often colored red.

40 Elise J. Baumgartel, *The Culture of Prehistoric Egypt*, 2 vols. (London: Oxford University Press, 1947), 2: 73.

41 Ashraf I. Sadek, *Popular Religion in Egypt during the New Kingdom* (Hildesheim: Gerstenberg Verlag, 1987), p. 285.

42 Kenneth A. Kitchen, *Ramesside Inscriptions Translated and Annotated. Translations* (Oxford: Blackwell, 2003), pp. 4, 115: 153: 11 (or Ostracon Michaelides, recto, p. 13). See Kitchen's transcription of the text in *Ramesside Inscriptions Historical and Biographical* (Oxford: Blackwell, 1990), 4: 153: 4–11 for the word used in all cases.

43 Wente, *Letters*, numbers 256, 280, 283 or pp. 162, 167, 168.

44 Florence D. Friedman considered these structures in depth in her chapter "Aspects of Domestic Life and Religioin," in *Pharaoh's Workers*, pp. 97–111 and Figs. 1–4. See also Emma Brunner-Traut, "Die Wochenlaube," *Mitteilungen des Instituts für Orientforschung* 3 (1955): 11–30, where she posits the booth as the place for delivery but refers to scenes on ostraca showing nursing there without acknowledging that this may have been only the initial nursing of the newborn and not a place for continual use.

45 Terry G. Wilfong, "Menstrual Synchrony and the 'Place of Women' in Ancient Egypt (OIM 13512)," in *Gold of Praise: Studies on Ancient Egypt in Honor of Edward F. Wente*, Studies in Ancient Oriental Civilization 58, ed. Emily Teeter and John A. Larson (Chicago: Oriental Institute, 1999), p. 431.

46 Recent studies have focused on evidence from the Greco-Roman period in Egypt. See, for instance, Salima Ikram, "Barbering the Beardless: a Possible Explanation for the Tufted Hairstyle depicted in the 'Fayum' Portrait of a Young Boy (J. P. Getty 78.AP.262)," *Journal of Egyptian Archaeology* 89 (2003): 247–51; and Dominic Montserrat, "Mallocouria and Therapeuteria: Rituals of Transition in a Mixed Society?" *Bulletin of the American Society of Papyrology* 28 (1991): 45–7.

12

Household Religion in Ancient Greece

Christopher A. Faraone

The family or household religion of the ancient Greeks has not been a burning topic for modern academic discussion, outside of a relatively brief period of interest in the middle of the last century, when a group of scholars with deep interests in comparative folklore – people like H. J. Rose and Martin Nilsson – recognized the ancient Greek house as a special locus of important religious and ritual activities.[1] Their work, dependent on broad cross-cultural comparisons especially within the Indo-European sphere, never really attracted much interest, in part, I think, because at that time scholars were captivated by a more attractive analysis of Greek society that stressed the tension between the worship of the gods by Greek "states" and that performed by "individuals" or between "public" and "private" spheres of religion. This approach, taken up by Festugiere in his 1954 Sather Lectures and by many others since, finds in the development of Greek religion a gradual shift in emphasis from an earlier period of routinized communal ritual to a later period of individual piety and belief.[2] Like so many early studies of ancient religion, this one is flawed by its teleological prejudices – the confessional practices of Christian monotheism always seem to lie at the end of the process – and by its convenient elision of women, children, and slaves on the grounds that the only true individual in the Greek world was the free adult male citizen. Recent treatments of Greek religion are much more nuanced but scholars continue to deny (mainly because of the lack of archaeological evidence) the existence of family and household religion or to discuss it in terms of the individuals who dwell within the house.[3]

One example will suffice to show how complicated it is to distinguish between public and personal religion. Porphyry, a Greek living in the late Roman Empire, reports the story of the simple acts of worship performed by an Arcadian man named Clearchus (Porphyry, *de abstinentia* 2.16):

> Clearchus said that he performed his religious rites and sacrificed earnestly at the appropriate times. Each month at the new moon he cleaned and crowned his Hermes and his Hekate and all the rest of the sacred objects (or "shrines," *hiera*) that his ancestors left behind, and he honored them with offerings of incense, barley cakes (*psaistoi*) and roundcakes (*popanoi*). And each year he performed for himself the public sacrifices (*thusiai demoteleis*), and neglected none of the festivals . . . selecting the gods' portions (*aparchas*) from the available fruits and vegetables, which he got from the land.

Modern scholars (e.g., Rose) sometimes cite this description as evidence for a deep contrast between the piety of an individual and the self-aggrandizing acts of public animal sacrifice at Delphi, which prompts Porphyry's discussion. This approach, however, ignores the fact that Clearchus takes part in both public and private cult and that in the latter case Clearchus' family and household most probably assisted in the ritual renewal of the sacred images in his home or on his property, of which two are singled out for special mention: the image of Hermes, that was most likely the herm that stood before or near the house door, and the image of Hekate, which was most probably the *hekateion*, the doorside altar or aniconic image of the goddess.[4]

In recent years, however, even this popular modern contrast between the public religion of the state and the private religion of the individual has been challenged, a move that even further obscures the religion of the family and household. Christine Sourvinou-Inwood, for instance, has argued that there really is no private religion at all in ancient Greece because, even when animals are sacrificed in the courtyard of a private house, the act "was perceived as part of the *polis* cult and . . . interdependent with the whole system of *polis* religion."[5] Such developments in modern scholarship, in fact, get to the heart of our traditional confusion about the religion of the family or household, which is both "private" in the sense that it is usually screened from the general public, and "communal" in the sense that it almost always involves more than one person and usually assumes a traditional form that is practiced by citizens in other families or households. One aim of this chapter, then, is to push back against the traditional tendency to talk about the head of the Greek household as if he operated alone in domestic cultic matters, and to replace the "individual" with the "household" or "family" as a more important locus of non-civic cult, while at the same time insisting that we somehow distinguish family and household worship as both quantitatively smaller than and qualitatively different from the cult of the city or the neighborhood.

Some Preliminary Definitions: *Oikos* and *Genos*

One way to clear up some of the confusion between these different modes of non-civic cult is to draw a firm distinction between the twinned topics of this volume: the religion of the household and the religion of the family. These two areas of ritual action – the first locative and the second genetic – are, in fact, firmly distinguished in the ancient Greek language. The English words "house" and "household" can both be expressed in Greek by the word *oikos* and it derivatives, which in their primary meaning refer to the building where the nuclear family and household slaves dwell, its inhabitants, and its other valuable contents.[6] The concept of "family," on the other hand, is usually signified by the word *genos* and its derivatives which focus on biological reproduction and genetic relations. These two units, moreover, relate to the rest of Greek society in different but predictable ways: the household (*oikos*), with its focus on place, is firmly planted at the start of a series of increasingly larger geographical units: the neighborhood or county (in Athens it is called a *deme*) and the city-state (*polis*), which in some ways is itself imagined as a huge *oikos*, with its own hearth and dining room for men (*andron* in the house, *prytaneion* in the agora). The family is similarly embedded as the smallest unit of series of larger and larger gentilic groups, which at Athens are called the *phratry* (literally the "brotherhood") and the "tribe." Socrates, in fact, neatly distinguishes household and family cult when he boasts that he has altars and shrines of the household type and the gentilic type (*bomoi kai hiera oikeia kai patrôa*), using the adjective *patroos* ("of or from the father") to mark the cults that connect him through the bloodline to his kin and their shared ancestors.[7]

These twin schemes for setting the family and the household within their larger gentilic and geographical networks were, in Athens at least, crucial to male self-identity and citizenship. Thus when an Athenian (i.e., male) citizen identifies himself formally by his patronymic and then his demotic, he identifies himself in his two roles in the wider matrix of Athenian society, first in his biological family (*genos*), and then in his neighborhood (*deme*). These twin coordinates are even more clearly reflected in the ritually oriented questions that were annually raised during the scrutiny of the incoming executive magistrates (*archons*): "Do you have an Apollo Patroos and a Zeus Herkious? Where are their shrines located?"[8] Thus, in order to show that they were god-fearing citizens and in order to place them precisely on the ritual map of the city, these archon-designates had to assert that they worshiped the most common deity of the gentilic group, Apollo Patroos ("of the Fathers"), as well as Zeus Herkious ("of the Enclosure-Fence) who guarded the periphery of the house and its property. And then they had to name the actual location of these shrines which would reveal where they came from (i.e., the focus of their ancestral worship) and where they now dwelt. Once again, the gentilic and the locative are differentiated and of equal importance.[9]

Household or "oikic-cult" (to coin an awkward but useful term) concerns itself mainly with the preservation and protection of the house itself and the property that it encompasses, as well as its possessions and to some degree the physical bodies of the people that dwell therein. We shall see, moreover, that the sphere of household cult itself was further split according to traditional gender roles: the protection of real estate and human or animal capital from death or destruction seems generally to have been the purview of the men of the family, while health of individual physical bodies seems to have fallen to the ritual work of the females. Family or gentilic-cult, on the other hand, is concerned more with defining and reiterating the relationships that the nuclear family has with outsiders and with how the family wishes to project its image to the outside world. Its three most obvious forms are the annual festivals overseen by the men of these gentilic groups, such as the Apatouria in Athens, in which the family brings forth a son and claims for him adult status within the larger family group, and weddings and funerals overseen by women, which both include processions that parade the wealth and status of a family from the interior of the house, either bearing a family corpse to the graveyard or a family daughter to her new home.[10] Sometimes, these rituals seem to merge one within the other, but slaves are a convenient marker of difference here, for as far as we can tell as family property they are usually included in household rites, as important members of the *oikos*, but excluded from the gentilic ceremonies, since they are not biological members of the *genos*.

In this chapter I shall (as the title suggests) concentrate solely on household religion because it has, at least in the last quarter of a century, been overlooked in comparison to studies that concern themselves with aspects of family cults, especially those overseen by women and those concerned with animal sacrifice that have been dealt with in great detail in recent years.[11] The remainder of my study is roughly divided into two sections. In the first I test the limits of what I believe is a sound traditional argument that household cult – at least in some of its ritual forms – essentially replicates civic cult, albeit in a miniature and more simplified version. We shall see, in fact, that there is a good bit of truth to this idea, as long as we understand the gendered perspective, namely that this pattern is generally limited to those areas of household cult that traditionally fall within the domain of men. In the second section, however, I focus instead on how household cults differ from civic ones, first by discussing the special role of magical ritual in the house and then by addressing the special and important role of women.

Household Cult Overseen by Men

Let me begin, then, with a somewhat old fashioned model for analyzing Greek household religion which stresses the close correspondences between the cult led by the patriarch in his house on behalf of his family and those cults performed by the male leader or leaders of the city on behalf of its citizens. My first example is the Greek scapegoat ritual, during which evil, usually imagined as famine or plague, is symbolically expelled from a community (Plutarch *Moralia* 693f):

> There is a traditional rite of sacrifice (*thusia*), which the *archon* performs at the public hearth (*epi tes koines hestias*) while all the others perform it at home (*ep' oikou*). It is called "Driving out Boulimos (= Famine)." They strike one of the household servants (*oiketon*) with wands of *agnus castus* and drive him out of the doors chanting "Out with Boulimos and in with Wealth (*Plutos*) and Health (*Hygeia*)!"[12]

This is a simple ritual in which a human scapegoat is equated with a famine demon and is chased away from two focal points of human habitation:[13] from the city hearth, by a male civic leader (the *archon*) on behalf of the state, and from the private house, presumably by the patriarch on behalf of the household. In the latter case, all of the participants – including the slave driven out as a scapegoat – are apparently drawn from the household. This ritual is entirely locative in orientation and imagines the city and house as similar kinds of places, each equipped with a hearth and a paternal figure.

Another possible example of household ritual as civic rite in miniature is the Rural Dionysia, a fertility festival performed by the Athenians in the winter. Our earliest and best evidence comes from a fifth-century comic play of Aristophanes entitled the *Acharnians*. When the hero of the play Dicaiopolis returns to his farm after years of enforced wartime residence in the city, the first thing he does is stage a phallic procession and sacrifice in honor of Dionysus (*Acharnians* 245–62):

> *Dicaiopolis*: Speak fair! Speak fair! Will the basket bearer, walk forward a little! Xanthias [a family slave], hold that phallus up straight! Put the basket down, my girl, so we can make the opening sacrifice.
>
> *Daughter*: Mother, hand me the ladle here, so I can pour soup over this beaten-cake.
>
> *Dicaiopolis*: There, that's fine. O Lord Dionysus, may this procession which I hold and this sacrifice [i.e. the offering of the cake] be pleasing to thee, and may I and my householders (*meta ton oiketon*) celebrate with all good fortune the Rural Dionysia, now that I am released from campaigning. And may the thirty years' peace prove a blessing to me. Come now, my pretty girl, be sure to bear your basket prettily, with a savory-eating look . . . Set forward and take great care in the crowd that no-one snaffles your ornaments! And Xanthias, you two must hold the phallus upright behind the basket-bearer! And I'll follow and sing the phallic hymn. And you, missus (*o gunai*, i.e. his wife), watch from the roof. Forward![14]

The text makes it clear that, like the household version of the Chaeronean scapegoat rite, performers and spectators are all drawn from the members of Dicaiopolis' household in order to stage a simple procession at the front of the house: two of his slaves carry the phallus (which apparently serves as the sole image of the god here), his daughter bears the basket containing the offered cake, and the father sings a special hymn to the god, while his wife watches from the roof of the house.

We know from a series of Athenian inscriptions that similar processions and sacrifices were performed by officials of the *deme* that served as the administrative centers of the Attic countryside, and that these festivals likewise often included musical and dramatic performances.[15] They seem, in short, to be bigger and more expensive versions of the celebration at Dicaiopolis' home, at which officials sacrifice animals to the god rather than cakes, and men perform hymns in a chorus rather than in solo voice. These demotic rites are, in turn, smaller than the City Dionysia, the city-wide festival celebrated in similar format a few months later in

Athens in the famous sanctuary of Dionysus at the foot of the Acropolis. We might compare the differing scale of these celebrations as follows:[16]

Level	*Phallic procession?*	*Sacrifice*	*Performance*	*Participants*
Household	yes	cake	monodic	household
Deme	yes	goat	choral and dramatic	demesmen
City	yes	goats	choral and dramatic	Athenian male citizens

My assertion that Dicaiopolis' celebration reflects a standard kind of household rite is not uncontroversial. In recent years, most scholars assume that in Aristophanes' comic presentation Dicaiopolis and his family are actually performing a makeshift private version of the traditionally public *deme*-festival, because there is no one else living in the *deme* at the time on account of the Peloponnesian wars. They argue that, because Dicaiopolis warns his daughter to be careful lest the thieves "in the crowd" steal her jewels (257–8), we must imagine that Dicaiopolis and company are performing a makeshift version of the public demotic procession and do so before their assembled *deme*. This argument, however, suggests paradoxically that the demesmen are unavailable as participants in the procession (as the plot demands), but they are available as spectators. This paradox, moreover, leads to the suggestion that Dicaiopolis simply imagines that there is a big crowd present, as there would or should have been at the *deme* celebration.[17] The mention of "the crowd" can, however, be explained much more economically as a metatheatrical reference to the audience of the play, which does in fact constitute a big crowd and one that Aristophanes is fond of insulting in precisely this manner.[18]

There are, moreover, some significant qualitative differences between the version performed by Dicaiopolis' household and the *deme*-festival: there is, for example, no blood sacrifice in the household version and at least one female (the daughter) is invited to play a key role. Again, scholars suggest that the cake is substituted because the wartime economy does not allow for the usual sheep but, if this is so, we would expect someone on stage to mention it, especially in an anti-war play like this one. And the idea that Dicaiopolis would continue to suffer depredations after he concludes his private piece with the Spartans is not borne out by the rest of play, which reiterates his Rabelaisean enjoyment of pre-war luxuries. It seems a priori more likely that Aristophanes added the detail of the cake without comment, because he knew his audience would be familiar with this family version of the procession. Indeed, that the offering of a cake might be a typical household variant of animal sacrifice is suggested by the fact that Clearchus, the Arcadian man mentioned by Porphyry, also offers sacrifices cakes to his ancestral gods. Musical entertainment provides an additional distinction between the three versions of the Dionysia outlined on the chart: Dicaiopolis sings the phallic hymn solo, while the demotic and civic versions provided much more elaborate choral and dramatic performances. If Dicaiopolis' procession was a comic, makeshift rendition of the demotic festival, we might expect him to lead his household in a group version of the song. Here, too I suggest that Aristophanes preserves a stipulation of the traditional ritual – that only free male adults, those traditional wielders of the phallus, could address the god in song.

Nilsson and Rose suggested similar parallels between household and city cult with regard to the worship of Zeus Ktesios as a protective household spirit. His name, as was mentioned earlier, means "Zeus of the Acquisitions" and we learn from Menander that he was believed to be the guardian of the storehouse and especially effective against thieves.[19] The Athenians seem to have worshiped him with an animal sacrifice in a secluded spot within the household compound (Isaeus 8.15–16):

> When Kiron sacrificed to Zeus Ktesios, a sacrifice about which he was especially serious, he did not admit either slaves or non-family members. He did everything himself, but we (i.e., family members) shared in this sacrifice and joined him in handling and placing the sacrificial victims and doing the other things. He prayed that the god give us health (*hygieia*) and good possession (*ktesis*) and this was only natural because he was our grandfather.

Here we see that the ceremony, apparently a standard kind of animal sacrifice, is restricted to members of the extended family, down to the grandchildren. There is, however, a peculiar tension in this passage between Kiron's allegedly "serious" version of this sacrifice, which excludes slaves and non-family members of the household, and the implied "less serious" version that allows their attendance.[20] We can in either case assume that, in the fourth century at least, slaves regularly did participate in such sacrifices, in households less persnickety than Kiron's. There are, moreover, signs that Iseaus is either tendentious or mistaken here. In the context of a legal trial over a disputed inheritance, he may, for example, have invented this idea of more or less serious versions of the ceremony in the hopes that his audience might confuse the gentilic and oikic rituals, or perhaps even more likely he himself has confused this ceremony with another dedicated to a gentilic form of Zeus, for example Phratrios.[21] The epithet Ktesios, however, is clearly related to the Greek words *ktema* ("property") and *ktesis* ("possession") and, since Isaeus claims that Kiron prayed during the ceremony for "health (*hygieia*) and good possession (*ktesis*)," the epithet seems appropriate. Indeed, the prayer itself recalls the *pharmakos*-cry of the household celebrants at Chaeronea: "Out with hunger and in with health (*hygieia*) and wealth (*ploutos*)!"

Other features of the cult of Zeus Ktesios, however, suggest that it differs qualitatively from the usual sacrificial forms of cult. We know for example, that this same Zeus Ktesios was represented aniconically as an earthenware jar:

> The right way to set up the signs (*semeia*) of Zeus Ktesios is this: Take a new jar with two ears (i.e. handles) and a lid to it and wreath its ears with white wool, and stretch a piece of yellow – anything you can find – from its right shoulder and its forehead, and pour ambrosia into it.[22]

This image of the god of property is, then, an appropriately anthropomorphized storage jar, which is of course one important way in which the ancient household protected its food stores from rodents and insects. Other sources report that images of this god were set up in the storeroom[23] as a good luck charm.[24] The aniconic form and apparent apotropaic function of this image finds a nice parallel in Porphyry's description of Clearchus' pious treatment of his family's herm and *hekateion*, which were also probably aniconic and thought to ward off evil from the home.[25]

Archaeological evidence tells us something that our literary sources do not: Zeus Ktesios could also be worshiped in the form of a snake. We know from literary testimonia, moreover, that in addition to animal sacrifice Zeus Ktesios was sometimes left simple offerings of cake, much like those that Clearchus left for his Hermes and Hecate and like the one that Dicaiopolis's daughter covers with gravy and carries in procession for the phallic Dionysus. Nilsson and Rose – drawing on parallels from the early modern European practice of giving offerings to house snakes – suggested plausibly that Zeus Ktesios was sometimes imagined as a snake that came and ate these offerings. Nilsson also noted the intriguing parallel between this domestic snake god and the popular Athenian belief (attested in Herodotus and Aristophanes) that sacred snakes lived in Athena's temple on the Acropolis and were also offered ritual cakes to eat.[26]

Let's pause for a moment and note some of the similarities and differences between the civic and household forms of the three male-dominated rituals discussed so far. In the case of Plutarch's scapegoat ritual and the celebration of the Rural Dionysia in Athens, the smaller household versions are nearly identical to the public ceremony, although the participation of Dicaiopolis's daughter in the household version of the Dionysia and the lack of animal sacrifice may be significant differences. The worship of Zeus Ktesios, on the other hand, is more varied and therefore more difficult to track. The family sacrifice of animals on a presumably courtyard altar seems identical in form, at least, to civic and demotic sacrifices, but the cakes offered to Zeus Ktesios and the snakes in Athena's temple on the Acropolis offer less compelling parallels because we have no specific evidence that the latter was a public cult offered on behalf of the whole city, although this is not inconceivable. Indeed, it may well be that in popular Athenian imagination Athena had a special snake in her house just as her Athenian worshipers had one in theirs. The use of the aniconic image of Zeus Ktesios as a talisman for the family storeroom, however, has no extant parallels in civic cult, although we saw how in other household rituals the offering of cakes seems to be a common replacement for blood sacrifice.

Women and Magic in the *Oikos*

Now let us turn to the importance of women and magic in household cult. Plato, in fact, closely and tendentiously connects the two when he has a character in the *Laws* named the "Athenian Stranger" recommend that all household religion be banned from the imaginary city of "Magnesia," that he and his companion are contemplating. He begins, however, with the sorcerers alone (*Laws* 909b–c):

> But as to all those . . . who, besides holding that the gods are negligent or open to bribes, despise men, charming the souls of many of the living and claiming that they charm the souls of the dead, and promising to persuade the gods by bewitching them, as it were, with sacrifices, prayers and incantations, and who try thus to wreck utterly not only individuals but even whole families and states for the sake of money, – if any of these men be pronounced guilty, the court shall order him to be imprisoned.[27]

The male gender of these individuals and the mention of monetary payment makes it fairly certain that Plato has professional sorcerers in mind here, although we cannot rule out female sorcerers as well.[28] After a few lines about the incarceration of these men and the treatment of their children, he unexpectedly proposes to do away with household cult as well in order to curb their activities (*Laws* 909d–e):

> For all these offenders (i.e., sorcerers), one general law must be laid down . . . Let no one possess shrines (*hiera*) in their private houses (*en idiais oikiais*). When anyone is moved in spirit to do sacrifice, he shall go to the public places to sacrifice, and he shall hand over his oblations to the priests and priestesses to whom belongs the consecration thereof.

By removing all cultic activity from individual houses and handing it over to priests to be publicly performed, this law would presumably allow the state to monitor and eventually prevent the "impious" activities (mentioned in the previous passage) that were performed secretly in private homes and designed to "wreck" individuals or other families.

Plato, however, in summing up this legislation introduces – almost as an afterthought – a second reason for outlawing household cult (*Laws* 909e–910b):

> This procedure (i.e., the ban on household shrines) shall be observed for the following reasons: – It is no easy task to found temples and gods and to do this rightly (*orthos*) needs much deliberation (*dianoia*); yet it is customary (*ethos*) for all women especially, and for sick folk everywhere, and those in peril or distress (whatever the nature of the distress) . . . to dedicate whatever happens to be at hand at the moment, and to vow sacrifices and promise the founding of shrines to gods and demi-gods and children of the gods; and through terrors caused by waking visions or by dreams . . . they are wont to found altars and shrines, and to fill with them every house and every village, and open spaces too, and every spot which was the scene of such experiences. For all these reasons their action should be governed by the law now stated; and a further reason is

> this – to prevent impious men (*asebountes* = the sorcerers) from acting fraudulently in regard to these matters also, by setting up shrines and altars in private houses (*en idiais oikiais*), thinking to propitiate the gods privily (*lathros*) by sacrifices and vows, . . . so that the whole state reaps the consequences of their impiety.

In the mind of Plato's "Athenian Stranger," then, the proliferation and danger of household shrines is connected with the activities of *two* kinds of people: (1) immoral magicians, who for a price secretly perform at home illicit kinds of ritual or ask the gods for impious things (e.g., curses) that one would not ask at a public shrine; and (2) women or critically ill people, who, because they lack *dianoia* ("intelligence" or "deliberation"), make irrational vows and as a result wrongly multiply their household altars and shrines. Both groups, according to Plato, are involved in an unhealthy privatization of religion which he would prevent by forcing both to pray and sacrifice openly in public shrines.

Plato is not, of course, the ideal source for information about typical Greek beliefs and practices but the views his characters express generally seem to be bound by some degree of plausibility. Thus it seems probable that most Athenians would agree with his description of the numerous votive cults founded in the household by women, or even with the idea that some Athenians performed in their homes magic rites aimed at binding or hurting their neighbors. As it turns out, the two facets of household ritual that Plato dwells upon in this passage – the important roles of women and magic – are, in fact, two areas in which (as we noted earlier) household cult does differ qualitatively from civic religion.

I begin with magic. This pattern is repeated with regard to other rituals as well. An inscription from Cyrene, a wealthy Greek city in North Africa,[29] for example, preserves a series of purification rituals, including one for the removal of an evil spirit or ghost from a private house:

> Visitant sent [by spells] from afar (*hikesios epaktos*).
>
> If a visitant is sent against the household (*oikia*) [and] if he (sc. the house-holder) knows from whom it attacks, he shall name him by proclamation for three days.
>
> If he (sc. the visitant, or perhaps "the sender") is dead and buried in the earth or has in some other manner perished, if he (sc. the householder) knows his name, he shall make a proclamation by name (sc. for three days?).
>
> But if (in either case?) he does not know his name (he shall address him): "O *anthropos*, whether you are a man or a woman," and having made male and female *kolossoi* either from earth or wood he shall entertain them and set beside them a portion of everything. When you have done the customary things take the *kolossoi* and [their] portions and deposit them in an unworked glen.

This ritual is designed to stop the attack of a "hostile visitant," probably a ghost or a demon.[30] Three situations are envisaged, which correspond to the three divisions in the translation given above. The first scenario deals with an attack sent by a living enemy or an angry ghost,[31] while the second directly involves a dead man, probably the uneasy ghost itself operating of its own will from the grave.[32] The ritual in both cases is quite simple if you know the name of the assailant: you simply invoke their name for three days. In the third case, however, we are told that if we do not know the identity of the sender or the ghost, we should make a male-and-female pair of wood or mud statuettes, provide them with a ritual meal, and then deposit them in some uncultivated spot, presumably outside of the city walls. What is most significant here is the fact that the household (*oikia*) is singled out as the object of supernatural attack, and that a single man – presumably the homeowner – is to take charge of the ritual response.

We have no evidence that this particular kind of ghost-banning rite was also performed by the city of Cyrene to rid itself of ghosts, but we do find an interesting civic parallel from Orchomenus that sheds some light on the household rite (Pausanias 9.38.5):

> With regard to Actaeon the Orchomenians say the following: A ghost (*eidolon*) was running amok and ravaging the land. When they inquired at Delphi, the god told them to recover the remains of Actaeon and bury them in the earth. He also commanded them to make a bronze image of the ghost and fasten it to a rock with iron. They also offer chthonic sacrifices (*enagizein*) every year to Actaeon.[33]

The problem in Orchomenus appears to be the same as in Cyrene, but the scale is different. In Cyrene, the ghost attacks a single home but here the ghost of the unburied and violently killed Actaeon "ravages the land," presumably the area in the mountains or foothills near Orchomenus where he was torn apart by his own dogs. In this case, since the ghost is apparently threatening a greater area and number of people, civic action is required: the city sends an inquiry to Delphi in the usual manner and is told what ritual remedy to apply. Both rites, thus, aim at the control and appeasement of dangerous ghosts by manipulating their effigies and by giving them offerings but they differ in one important aspect: the Cyrenean ritual, because it escorts the images away from the house, seems to be a variant of the scapegoat ritual, whereas the binding of the Orchomenian effigy recalls yet another set of popular Greek rituals that show up occasionally in the repertoire of family or household cult: the ritual "binding spells" that the Greeks used to restrain their rivals or enemies.

Such binding spells were apparently quite popular in classical Athens, although once again we run into the problem of distinguishing between individual and household rites. Recent studies of these sorts of binding spells – including my own – assume that they are a form of personal magic used by one individual against his personal opponents.[34] But some curse tablets may, in fact, be aimed by one household against another. Take for example this fourth-century curse from Athens, in which one neighbor seems to curse another (*Defixionum Tabellae Atticae* 87):

> I bind Callias, the tavern-keeper, who is one of my neighbors, and his wife Traitta . . . I bind Sosimenes, his(?) brother, and Carpos his servant, who is the fabric seller . . . and also Agathon, the tavern-keeper, the servant of Sosimenes: all of these I bind the soul, the work, the life, the hands, the feet.

Here the "neighbor" aims his binding curse at a group of individuals, freeborn and servile, that are related both by blood and by trade. Since the text does not hint at the reason for the curse – was the neighbor angry at their loud parties or was he another tavern-keeper jealous over their profits? – we cannot know for sure if this all male group actually represents a household in the strictest sense. Another much briefer curse, however, manages to do precisely this when it aims at binding (*Defixionum Tabellae Atticae* 69) "Dionysius, the helmet-maker, his wife Artemis, the gold-worker, their household (*oikia*), their work, their life . . ." I suggest, moreover, that in these two curse-tablets we see the Greek household in a different light, as an economic unit, a group of workers, related by marriage, blood or (in the case of slaves) by circumstance, who ply the same or related trades probably in or adjacent to the home, which is still the case in many small Mediterranean towns.[35]

Since the authors of these binding curses never sign their names, it is impossible to know precisely who was casting these spells and why, but in these two examples we can I think infer an economic motive and that rival tradesmen stood to gain from the attack. In short: it seems possible that one household is attempting to bind a rival household in order to curtail competition in the same trade, tavern-keepers in the first and metalworkers in the second. That the household might be a common target for curses is, in fact, stated in the passage from Plato's *Laws* quoted earlier, where the Athenian Stranger criticizes those who "persuade the gods by bewitching them, as it were, with sacrifices, prayers and incantations, and who try thus to wreck utterly not only individuals (*idiotai*) but even whole families (*oikiai*) and states (*poleis*)." Thus Plato seems to attribute to the impious sorcerers, who perform rituals at home, the ability to curse others at three different social levels: single individuals, families, and cities. Plato was clearly suspicious that altars and shrines set up in houses could be used for certain kinds of rites that he deems "impious," but it is not clear to me that such hostile magical acts could not be performed on behalf of a city as well as an act of civic cult. Indeed, he himself alludes to this very possibility when he speaks of these sorcerers cursing entire cities. The binding of the effigy of Actaeon's ghost, for example, shows that the ritual creation of magical effigies could be used to bind civic enemies as well, and indeed elsewhere I discuss a number of other cases, especially those that involve the binding of an image of Ares in order to prevent the approach of a hostile army.[36]

Finally, let us turn to Greek women and their roles in household cult, beginning with a brief anecdote: Plutarch, at the very end of his celebrated biography of Pericles, tells us how some friends of the great statesman went to visit him as he lay dying of the plague (*Pericles* 38):

> Certain it is that Theophrastus, in his *Ethics*, querying whether one's character follows the bent of one's fortunes and is forced by bodily sufferings to abandon its high excellence, records this fact, that Pericles, as he lay sick (i.e., of the plague that ended his life) showed one of his friends who had come to see him an amulet (*periapton*) that his womenfolk had hung around his neck, as much as to say that he was very badly off to put up with such folly (*abelteria*) as that.

This final image of Pericles, the pragmatist politician and patron of philosophy, clashes with all assessments (ancient and modern) of his character, and scholars either ignore the incident or follow the lead of Plutarch in interpreting Pericles' gesture to be ironic ("as much as to say . . .").

Plutarch, however, culls this anecdote from a wider philosophic discussion in Theophrastus' *Ethics* about how some people, in fact, lose their philosophic orientation when confronted with bodily sufferings. It seems most likely, then, that Theophrastus recalled this anecdote because he believed that Pericles agreed to wear the amulet only after his illness had clouded his judgment. This inference fits well, in fact, with Plato's assertion (in the passage of the *Laws* that we read earlier) that there were two kinds of people who – because of their lack of *dianoia* – vowed and then established shrines in their houses in connection with healing events: women generally and those who were seriously ill. Pericles' amulet and Plato's votive shrines raise a larger question, then, of the role of women as healers in the ancient Greek household. I suggested in the first section of this chapter that the household cults of Zeus Ktesios, Hermes, and Hecate are apparently initiated and tended by men and were designed to protect perimeters and property (including slaves), and the general health and prosperity of freeborn people who dwell there. Might it be the case, then, that the women of the household performed rituals and founded shrines to improve the health or save the life of sick individuals, whereas men did so to protect the house itself and the people within it?

Conclusion

Let me conclude this chapter briefly by suggesting that the traditional analysis of Greek religion into opposed categories of "public" and "private" or "civic" and "individual" and the more recent efforts to downplay or deny the existence of non-public religion altogether oversimplify and neglect the complex layering of ritual activity in Greek society, which ranges from the largest unit (the city-state) to the smallest and least visible, the household. We have seen how the distinction between public and private cult often confuses the ritual actions of the household with those of the individual man who often performs them on the household's behalf – a confusion that often elides the participation of women, children, and slaves. The model of separate public and private spheres also ignores other intervening levels or layers of communal interaction: the rites of the extended family (in the case of gentilic rituals) and those of the neighborhood or the *deme* (in the case of oikic rituals). This suggests to me that we might think of family or household cult simply as the smallest of a series of nested religious communities. On the other hand, recent arguments that family rites can be called "public" need to be more nuanced, for it might be true in the case of ceremonies performed outside the house at annual gentilic festivals, as well as in the case of wedding and funeral processions which translate family members away from the *oikos*, but this cannot be true for the household rites I have discussed here, at least not as I have defined them. Indeed, if one were to argue for the similarities between these differing levels of household, *deme* and civic ritual, I prefer to use the term "communal," because it conjures up the idea of social groups of varying sizes that at different times see themselves united by common interests and against common enemies: a household worshiping around an open courtyard, a neighborhood at a shared fountain or shrine, or a crowd of male citizens assembled in the agora or on the Acropolis before the public altars and temples of the city.

There are, on the other hand, some important qualitative differences between household and civic cult. We have noted, for instance, the significant role of women, and in many cases we might even say that both household and family religion overlaps in large portion with the religion of Greek women. Thus, for example, the household celebration of the Adonia is discussed in ancient texts as a mysterious female cult that is all but invisible to men. Funerals and weddings, moreover, are also overseen and performed by women and conducted entirely within or from private houses. Recall, too, how the dying Pericles refers to the amulets around his own neck as the work of the women of his household, and how Plato in the *Laws* conflates household votive shrines and female worship. Even in the comic family version of the rural Dionysia, we find the daughter offering a gravy-laden cake to the god, whereas in the county and civic versions men offer animal sacrifice instead. In fact, this replacement of animal sacrifice with a vegetarian one may also be a non-trivial difference, for Porphyry tells us of the pious offerings of cakes and incense to the household herm and elsewhere we learn about the cakes offered to Zeus Ktesios, apparently in the form of a house snake.

Finally, "magical ritual" seems to play an important role in household cult. We have seen how aniconic images seem to proliferate in household worship: the herm and the *hekateion* by the front door, the jug-image of Zeus in the storeroom and the sole focus on the phallus in the family performance of the rural Dionysia. All of these images also seem to be implicated in some way or another with beliefs in the automatic protection of houses or the promotion of their fertility – beliefs that are often discussed by scholars under the rubric of magic. Plato's concern, moreover, that some Greeks used household altars to ask the gods secretly to harm others suggests that cursing rituals might have also been part of the repertoire of household cult. I should stress that the Greeks did indeed use very similar talismans to protect their cities and similar curses to bind their civic enemies but it is curious that in the extant corpus of curse tablets, at least, they seem to do so with less frequency.

My colleague at Chicago, Jonathan Z. Smith, has often remarked that the Greek magical papyri are the best and most useful compendium of cult prescriptions for the late antique world, and he notes how many if not most of these recipes concern rituals that are to be performed within a private home, albeit often under the open sky in a courtyard (as with the sacrifice to Zeus Ktesios) or on a rooftop (as with the Athenian festival of Adonis). Smith argues that much of the household ritual described and recommended in the magical papyri gets there as the result of enormous social change during the Roman Empire, with the collapse of centralized civic cults and their relocation on a smaller scale in homes or house-like edifices, such as early synagogues or early Christian house-churches.[37] And indeed we can find several examples of Egyptian or Greek civic rites that were performed publicly by the state in pre-Roman times, but which appear in the magical papyri in miniature form specially adapted for private use.[38]

In recent years, however, I have been toying with the idea that these magical papyri also preserve recipes for Greek and Egyptian rituals that were from the very beginning staged primarily within the household. We find in the magical papyri, for example, instructions for creating, installing and worshiping a good-luck statue of Hermes, recipes for ghost-banning or manufacturing lead curses like those mentioned earlier, and numerous examples of amulets that in size and shape are probably not very different from those that the women in Pericles' house hung around his neck during the great plague in Athens. In short, I suspect that the history of ancient Greek magic, like the history of the religion of ancient Greek women, also overlaps in some important ways with the history of household religion. This is, I think, clearly how Plato viewed the matter when he describes the nefarious and foolish rites that he wished to ban forever from the ancient Greek household.

Acknowledgments

For Michael H. Jameson, *in memoriam*. I am very grateful to the editors for organizing the excellent conference at which this essay was delivered and to the other participants for their helpful questions and criticisms. I would also like to thank Deborah Boedeker, who read and commented on an earlier written version.

Notes

1 Harald Sjövall, *Zeus im altgriechischen Hauskult* (Lund: H. Ohlsson, 1931); Martin P. Nilsson, "Roman and Greek Domestic Cult," *Opuscula Romana* 1, *Skrifter Utgivna av Svenska Institutet i Rom* 18 (Lund, 1954): 77–85; Herbert Jennings Rose, "The Religion of a Greek Household," *Euphrosyne* 1 (1957): 95–116; and Martin P. Nilsson, *Greek Folk Religion* (New York: Harper, 1961). For a recent reassessment taking into account the evidence of subsequent archaeology, see Michael Jameson, "Private Space and the Greek City," in *The Greek City from Homer to Alexander*, ed. Oswyn Murray and Simon R. F. Price (Oxford: Clarendon Press, 1990), pp. 171–95.

2 Andre Jean Festugière, *Personal Religion among the Greeks* (Berkeley: University of California Press, 1954).

3 Jon D. Mikalson, *Ancient Greek Religion* (Malden MA: Blackwell Publishers, 2005), pp. 133–98, takes a step in the right direction: he closes his description of archaic and classical Greek religion with three chapters: "Religion in the Greek Family and Village," "Religion and the Greek City-State," and "Greek Religion and the Individual," in the first of which he nonetheless atomizes the family into four types of individuals: the father, the mother, the daughter, the son, and the slave. Other assessments are more

pessimistic. Simon R. F. Price, *Religions of the Ancient Greeks* (Cambridge: Cambridge University Press, 1999), pp. 89–90, at the start of his chapter "Girls and Boys, Women and Men," suggests that it is unhelpful to search for the religion of the Greek household, because "Greek houses had no separate room for a household shrine and rarely had permanent altars." Robert Parker, *Polytheism and Society at Athens* (Oxford: Oxford University Press, 2005), p. 9, is more optimistic when he begins his treatment of Athenian religion by noting that "the Athenians did not think in terms of 'the religion of the household' or 'household gods,' " but he admits that members of the household could worship together "within and without the walls of the house." He is tempted, however, to see these gods as "a subset of a larger class of 'ancestral gods' (*patrooi theoi*)," a formulation that obscures the distinction that I make below between gentilic and oikic gods.

4 Rose, "Religion of a Greek Household," pp. 106–7. Christopher A. Faraone, *Talismans and Trojan Horses: Guardian Statues in Ancient Greek Myth and Ritual* (Oxford: Oxford University Press, 1992), pp. 8–10, with notes 40, 49, 51, 56 and 60.

5 Christiane Sourvinou-Inwood, "Further Aspects of Polis Religion," in *Oxford Readings in Greek Religion*, ed. R. Fowler (Oxford: Oxford University Press 2000), pp. 51–4 (quote from p. 54); eadem, "What is Polis Religion?" in *The Greek City from Homer to Alexander*, ed. Oswyn Murray and Simon R. F. Price (Oxford: Clarendon Press, 1990), pp. 295–322; and Robert Parker, *Athenian Religion: A History* (Oxford: Clarendon Press, 1996), pp. 6–7. See also Vincent J. Rosivach, *The System of Public Sacrifice in Fourth-Century Athens*, American Classical Studies 34 (Atlanta: Scholars Press, 1994), pp. 9–11. This recent challenge to the public/private dichotomy is, in fact, part of a general tendency to minimize the differences between sacrificial ritual performed in the public spaces of the city and that performed elsewhere – see Walter Burkert, *Greek Religion* (Cambridge, Mass.: Harvard University Press, 1985), pp. 255–6.

6 If we keep in mind its derivation from Latin *domus*, "house," the range of the English word "domestic" is somewhat similar, which has a locative orientation and can also refer to the things and people within the house, e.g., the older use of "domestic" as a noun to refer to a house servant.

7 Plato, *Euthydemus* 302c. Parker, *Polytheism*, pp. 10–14, confuses family and household cult, I think, when he discusses "household" (= my oikic) gods as a subset of "ancestral gods" (*patrooi theoi*) which to my mind are clearly gentilic. (Indeed, Socrates a little further in the passage just quoted is at pains to stress the fact that Athenians worship Apollo Patrôos, not Zeus Patrôos, because they believe that they, and indeed all Ionians, are descendants of Apollo's son Ion.) I think Parker fails to differentiate between the locative and gentilic because he depends mainly on legal texts and ideas where we indeed find that the son at the death of the father inherits household shrines (along with the house) and is also made responsible for gentilic ones (which are often not located at or near the father's house); thus he sees them both as broadly "ancestral" (i.e., part of his inheritance). This approach, however, confuses legal inheritance and religious obligation and leads to complications, for example, when he discusses the phrase used by Athenian orators to describe a household when the head of the household dies childless: "an *oikos* made empty" (the verb is *eremousthai*). By translating this phrase as "his *oikos* perishes" (p. 11), Parker forces a gentilic notion (lack of an heir) onto what is a clearly a locative idea (i.e., no one will live in the house). Now it may be true that it amounts to the same thing legally, but it is important that the Athenians use the locative expression.

Elsewhere, however, Parker does note that oath takers sometimes pronounced conditional curses "on themselves, their *oikia* and *genos*" (p. 10), an airtight formulation that covers both the locative and the gentilic, and he does stress the locative focus of the adjective *oikeios*, "of the house" when he says that it can refer to both blood relatives and close friends: "One's *oikeioi* were *oikeioi* because they came to one's house to share in the sacrifices."

8 Boedeker in the next chapter treats these questions more thoroughly in connection with her discussion of Zeus Herkious.

9 Sourvinou-Inwood (n. 5), p. 53, resorts to some rather vague formulations when she tries to equate the locative and the gentilic: "the cult of Zeus Herkeious was *in symbolic control* of the *genos*, . . . in which case the altar of Zeus Herkeious *was symbolically dependent* on that of the *genos*" (my emphases). In my view there is no connection, symbolic or otherwise: the people concerned about the cult of Zeus Herkeious were those who lived in or frequented the house where the cult was situated (locative), not the wider blood relations of the inhabitants (gentilic).

10 For funeral and wedding rituals, see Boedeker in this volume.

11 Boedeker in this volume reviews and discusses these rituals in her chapter in this volume, "Family Matters: Domestic Religion in Classical Greece," which by design focuses more on the gentilic rituals.

12 Christopher A. Faraone, "Hipponax Frag. 128W: Epic Parody or Expulsive Incantation?" *Classical Antiquity* 23 (2004): 215.

13 Ibid., pp. 215–17.

14 Alan H. Sommerstein (trans.), *Aristophanes Acharnians* (Warminster: Aris & Phillips, 1980), ad loc., with one minor change for the sake of consistency, "Rural Dionysia" for "Country Dionysia."

15 Jon D. Mikalson, "Religion in the Attic Demes," *American Journal of Philology* 98 (1977): 433–4; and Susan G. Cole, "Procession and Celebration at the Dionysia," in *Theater and Society in the Classical World*, ed. Ruth Scodel (Ann Arbor: University of Michigan Press, 1993), pp. 25–38.

16 Cole, "Procession and Celebration at the Dionysia," compares the *deme* and civic versions.

17 Thus Martha Habash, "Two Complementary Festivals in Aristophanes *Acharnians*," *American Journal of Philology* 116 (1995): 559: "Although Dicaeopolis's procession involves only the members of his household (256) . . . he nevertheless attempts to conduct it as if the *deme* were present: he warns his daughter to beware of thieves in the crowd (257–8) and orders his wife to secure the roof so she can better see the production (260)." See Habash for a review of the earlier scholarship.

18 In his recent commentary, S. Douglas Olson, *Aristophanes: Acharnians* (Oxford: Clarendon Press, 2002), pp. 147–8, suggests that Dicaiopolis is standing in the orchestra when he says this and he gestures to the audience as the possible criminals who might want to pinch his daughter's necklace. There is, however, some obscurity about the place and type of offering. At line 201, Dicaiopolis tells us that he will go inside the house and celebrate the Rural Dionysia (201–2). This suggests that he will celebrate it in the courtyard of his country estate or even within the house itself. But when he returns to the stage at 241 with his daughter and slaves, it is clear that he will perform the procession and the sacrifice with his householders (*meta ton oiketon*) in front of the house. This readjustment could, of course, be dictated entirely by stagecraft or perhaps we are to imagine an interior scene performed outdoors, like the

scene in Aristophanes' *Clouds*, when we apparently see what Socrates' students are doing within the *phrontisterion*.

19 Faraone, *Talismans and Trojan Horses*, pp. 6–7.

20 See Boedeker's treatment in this volume.

21 The fact that elsewhere Ktesios is given cakes, rather than animal sacrifice, may suggest a misattribution to Ktesios in Isaeus 8, but it is hard to imagine that the speaker could have gotten away with such a serious error or misstatement, although later scribes may have.

22 Athenaeus 473b–c; for detailed discussions of the textual problems and other literary references see Arthur Bernard Cook, *Zeus: A Study in Ancient Religion* (Cambridge: The University Press, 1925), 3.1054–7; Jane Ellen Harrison, *Themis: A Study in the Social Origins of Greek Religion*, 2nd edn. (New York: Cambridge University Press, 1927), pp. 297–301; and Faraone, *Talismans and Trojan Horses*, pp. 6–7.

23 Menander, *Ps. Hercules*, frag. 519 K. and Harpocration s.v. "*Ktesiou Dios*" quoting from Hyperides' speech against Apellaios. Cook, *Zeus*, pp. 159–61, and Nilsson, *Greek Folk Religion*, pp. 274–5, discuss Ktesios' incarnation as a snake.

24 E.g., Dio Chrysostom 1.41.3 and 11.76.5 (von Arnim), and the *Suda* s.v. "*Dios koidion*."

25 Faraone, *Talismans and Trojan Horses*, pp. 8–10.

26 Nilsson, *Greek Folk Religion*, pp. 71–2.

27 For this translation, and the two that follow, see R. G. Bury, *Plato: Laws* (Cambridge, MA: Harvard University Press, 1926), loc cit.

28 See Boedeker's discussion in this volume of Medea's shrine to Hekate.

29 *SEG* 9.72.111–21. For full translation, bibliography and commentary, see Robert Parker, *Miasma: Pollution and Purification in Early Greek Religion* (Oxford: Clarendon Press, 1983), pp. 332–51, whose translation is followed except where noted in Faraone, *Talismans and Trojan Horses*, pp. 82–3.

30 Walter Burkert, *Greek Religion* (Cambridge: Harvard University Press, 1985), pp. 68–71 and Parker, *Miasma*, p. 348, who both argued against the prevailing view at the time that the *hikesios* in the passage was a "suppliant." The seemingly contradictory use of the same word *hikesios* to mean both daemonic attacker and suppliant can be paralleled by the puzzling semantic range of *palamnaios*, which can mean murderer, the *daimon* sent by the murder victim against the murderer, and also a suppliant polluted with blood: Parker, *Miasma*, p. 108 n. 13.

31 Xenophon *Cyropaedia* 8.7.18 and Clytemnestra in Aeschylus' *Eumenides* provide examples for murder victims sending out (the verb is *epipempein*) *daimones* from the grave. See also Hesychius s.v. "*antaia*", a word which is glossed as both *hikesios* and *daimon*; he goes on to explain: "and they call Hekate 'Antaia' because she sends out (*epipempein*) these things."

32 For evidence that the angry ghosts themselves came out to do the haunting see, e.g., the bizarre ritual of *maschalismos* (corpse mutilation) which was apparently designed to prevent it (Sophocles, *Electra* 445 and Jebb's note and Appendix ad loc.). See below for a discussion of the angry ghost of Actaeon.

33 See Faraone, *Talismans and Trojan Horses*, p. 83, for this translation and discussion.

34 See, e.g., Christopher A. Faraone, "The Agonistic Context of Early Greek Binding Spells," in *Magika Hiera: Ancient Greek Magic and Religion*, ed. C. A. Faraone and Dirk Obbink (Oxford: Oxford University Press, 1991), pp. 3–32.

35 Jameson, "Private Space and the Greek City," pp. 171–95.

36 Faraone, *Talismans and Trojan Horses*, pp. 74–8.

37 Jonathan Z. Smith, "Trading Places," in *Ancient Magic and Ritual Power*, ed. Marvin W. Meyer and Paul Allen Mirecki (Boston: Brill Academic Publishers, 2001), pp. 13–28.

38 My favorite example is a recipe for prognostication that requires a little table-top shrine for Apollo, which – with its laurel leaves and a miniature tripod – clearly mimics the interior of the god's famous shrine at Delphi. See Christopher A. Faraone, "The Collapse of Celestial and Chthonic Realms in a Late Antique 'Apollonian Invocation' (*PGM* I 262–347)," in *Heavenly Realms and Earthly Realities in Late Antique Religions*, ed. R. Abusch, A. Y. Reed and P. Schäfer (Cambridge: Cambridge University Press, 2004), pp. 213–17.

13

Family Matters: Domestic Religion in Classical Greece

Deborah Boedeker

In what ways was the ancient Greek household or family a locus of religious practices? Christopher Faraone rightly observes in this volume that historians of Greek religion have tended to downplay domestic or private religious rites, viewing the cults of the state, the *polis*, as primary. Christiane Sourvinou-Inwood writes, for example, in an important study:

> The *polis* was the institutional authority that structured the universe and the divine world in a religious system, articulated a pantheon with certain particular configurations of divine personalities, and established a system of cults, particular rituals and sanctuaries, and a sacred calendar . . . [It] assumed the role played in Christianity by the Church – to use one misleading comparison . . . to counteract and destroy alternative, implicit models. It assumed the responsibility and authority to set a religious system into place, to mediate human relationships with the divine world.[1]

Sourvinou-Inwood here expresses very emphatically the *polis*-centered view of Greek religious history, and other experts would agree.[2] This perspective is valid in many respects, including the idea that the classical *polis* "assumed" or *claimed* the authority Sourvinou-Inwood attributes to it.

In a recent introductory book on Greek religion, Jon Mikalson devotes more attention than is usually the case to the ritual practices of family members as such.[3] Even so, Mikalson focuses largely on the religious duties of individuals – varying according to their age, gender, and family role – to their larger communities, rather than on practices centered within the household (*oikos*). The relationship between domestic and civic cults is implicitly presented as unproblematic: the male head of the family offers sacrifices to household gods at home, just as he and his peers honor village gods at the level of the *deme* (township), and the deities of the *polis* at larger civic festivals.[4] In this ideal scheme, every god, every rite, receives its due in proper time, place, and setting, without conflict or competition.

Such a clear hierarchy of religious authority on the one hand, and lack of friction on the other, may well have characterized the lived experience of many Greeks in the classical period: no doubt their household ritual practices generally complemented their cultic responsibilities to larger communities. Nevertheless, a focus on household religion as such indicates that relationships between domestic and civic rituals were more complex and sometimes more fraught with tension than Mikalson's general picture suggests.

This brief chapter will look at a representative sampling of ancient Greek domestic religious practices, whether family (*genos*)- or household (*oikos*)-based, to use Faraone's important distinction,[5] mainly from the classical period, keeping in mind their varying relationships to civic religion. Occasionally family rites conflicted with the cults of larger communities, as we shall see; more often they reflected similar concerns on a smaller scale, in a variety of compatible relationships; and sometimes, domestic rites dealt intimately with matters (such as birth, death, and perhaps also sex) that were excluded from public sanctuaries.

Domestic Cults at Home (and) in the *Polis*

Isaeus, a fourth-century forensic speech-writer in Athens, provides what is perhaps our best-known passage on ancient Greek domestic religion: the account of a family sacrifice to Zeus Ktesios.[6] Here we are told that in his courtyard, in the exclusive presence of close kin, the speaker's grandfather Kiron used to offer animal sacrifices and prayers to this "Zeus of Possessions," aimed at promoting the wealth and health of his family. So restricted was participation in this household cult, Isaeus' client argues, that his inclusion in the sacrifices proves him to be a legitimate member of Kiron's family, with a right to inherit.

This passage is sometimes assumed to illustrate a typical Athenian household rite.[7] Closer examination, however, raises questions about how typical it really was. Did all Athenian families honor Zeus Ktesios with exclusive, strictly-defined kinship groups making sacrifices in the household courtyard? To be sure, we can assume from the context that a rite like Kiron's was plausible, even familiar. What Isaeus says about these sacrifices to Zeus Ktesios depends for its effect on the jurors' recognizing the familial nature of these activities; otherwise, they would have no reason to accept the argument that Kiron did indeed behave like a grandfather to the defendant. Yet we should ask why, if the rite was so widely known, Isaeus goes to such lengths to insist that Kiron's practice was restricted to close kin.

The same kind of evidence (Athenian forensic speeches), moreover, also records less exclusive ways to honor Zeus Ktesios. Antiphon, a speech-writer about two generations earlier than Isaeus, wrote a speech for a young man who was charging his stepmother with the murder of his father.[8] The setting of the homicide involved a sacrifice to Zeus Ktesios. Here, however, this rite included not the immediate family but, as far as Antiphon indicates, only the male celebrant Philoneus, Philoneus' mistress (who participated in the sacrifice), and his close friend, the prosecutor's father. The sacrifice was carried out in Philoneus' (or possibly his mistress') house in Piraeus; it was followed by a dinner that became the scene of the fatality, when the mistress secretly administered to both men what she thought was a love potion (given to her by the stepmother), but which turned out to be a deadly poison: "Gentlemen of the jury, while pouring the libation for the men, who were praying for things that would never be fulfilled, Philoneus' mistress was putting in the poison" (Antiphon 1.19). Here it is to the prosecutor's advantage to emphasize that the murdered man was piously participating in an offering just before his untimely death. Further, the constellation of participants making offerings to Zeus Ktesios, none of them blood relatives, must have been credible to the judges – even if Isaeus' Kiron might not have approved. These two passages combine to show that Zeus Ktesios was clearly a familiar household figure, but his worship was not confined to family members. There was evidently a good deal of flexibility in how, and by whom, this domestic god could be honored.

Dramatic literature from Athens in roughly the same period provides a different perspective on the same figure – and once again, a different set of participants. In Aeschylus' *Agamemnon* (458 BCE), we hear of a shrine of Zeus Ktesios inside Agamemnon's heroic-era palace at Argos. Here, set in the legendary past, the tragedy presents a ritual context less intimate than those we have seen so far. Clytemnestra tells Agamemnon's war-prize Cassandra to go inside the palace and meet with the other slaves at the altar of Zeus Ktesios; actually, she is sending the prophetic princess to her death in the accursed house (*Agam.* 1036–9). For Aeschylus' audience, it might seem appropriate for Cassandra, a new slave in the household, to be directed first to the palace's "Zeus of Possessions," even while they understand that being sent to the altar also foreshadows her imminent "sacrifice" at the hands of Clytemnestra.

These three passages, all produced in Athens within a century of each other, are enough to make it clear that the honors paid to Zeus Ktesios were not all of a stripe, and, most important for our purposes, that they were not necessarily exclusive to the blood-related family or even to members of the same *oikos*. So, too, visual representations of this god also varied considerably. He is shown as a snake in a third-century BCE relief from Thasos, while a passage in Athenaeus (c. 200 CE, but citing a much earlier source)[9] says that the image of Zeus Ktesios should be made of a jug (*kadiskos*) decorated with woolen wreaths and filled with a mixture of water, olive oil, and all kinds of produce (11.473 b–c).[10] In either case, the god's image is quite different from the anthropomorphic images of most gods associated with contemporary *polis* cult. It is clear, further, that rites to Zeus Ktesios were widespread in the Greek world: in addition to Athens and Thasos, he is also attested on Kos (with the Doric dialect variant *Pasios*).[11] Some Greek domestic cults thus transcended geographical boundaries, albeit in heterogeneous forms.

Despite the argument of Isaeus' client that family membership is attested by common worship of Zeus Ktesios, it is actually Zeus Herkeios "of the Courtyard," who turns out to be the more important means for determining familial identity in Athens. We have it on good authority[12] that before taking office, each archon-designate was officially scrutinized to determine whether he was a legitimate citizen and qualified for the task. Among the questions put to him were, "Do you have an Apollo Patroos (Ancestral Apollo) and a Zeus Herkeios?" and "Where are their shrines located?" Evidently, full participation in the *polis* depended on maintaining certain religious practices on the level of the nuclear or extended family.

A domestic shrine of Zeus Herkeios is not just a proof of Athenian identity, but a place that resonates deeply with notions of belonging, protection, security – and not only in Athens. A story set in late sixth-century Sparta also illustrates the sanctity, and the connection with family identity, that centers on this cult. Herodotus tells how the deposed Spartan king Demaratos, charged at a public festival with being illegitimate and therefore not fit to rule, veiled himself, went home, and sacrificed an ox to Zeus. Then Demaratos summoned his mother, and asked her to take the entrails in her hand and swear by Zeus Herkeios to tell him the truth about his paternity (6.67.3–69).[13]

More insight into this god's significance comes to us from epic and tragic poetry. In the *Odyssey*, as the returning hero and his small group of friends are slaughtering the suitors in the palace on Ithaca, Odysseus' household bard Phemios, in fear for his life, considers taking refuge at the altar of Zeus Herkeios:

> He pondered, his mind divided,
> whether he should slip from the hall to the well-built altar of great Zeus
> Herkeios, and sit there, where Laertes and Odysseus
> had burned many thighs of cattle,
> or whether he should rush to Odysseus and beseech him by his knees.
> (*Odyssey* 22.334–7)

Phemios opts for the latter, more direct course of action, but we should not overlook the plan that first entered his mind: the altar of Zeus Herkeios is a natural place to seek sanctuary.

Elsewhere in poetry, however, especially in tragedy, the altar of Zeus Herkeios is a place marked by transgression of those very values of kinship and security. Priam was slain at the altar of Zeus Herkeios as Troy was taken by the Greeks, according to Poseidon in the prologue of Euripides' *Trojan Women* (16–17); so too – by Achilles' son Neoptolemos – in the Cyclic epic *Sack of Ilion* (arg. 2). At the beginning of Euripides' *Herakles*, when the murderous tyrant Lykos forces the hero's sons, his wife Megara, and his father Amphitryon out of their house, they seek refuge outdoors at the altar of Zeus Soter "Savior" (48). Then Herakles returns, dispatches Lykos, and restores his family to their home in safety; all is well until Hera sends the goddess Lyssa, "Frenzy," to madden Herakles. And soon, in a messenger speech, the audience learns that the crazed hero has just slaughtered Megara and the children at an altar of Zeus (not identified by an epithet in the text) in the interior of the house (922–7). Wilamowitz was undoubtedly right when he said that this must refer to a shrine of Zeus Herkeios.[14]

Creon in Sophocles' *Antigone* violates the sanctity of Zeus Herkeios not with a sword but with a terrible threat, which conveys to Sophocles' audience with great economy just how the king disdains and devalues his closest kin, and in so doing, this god of family values:

> Whether she is my sister's child, or closer
> to us than our entire Zeus Herkeios,
> she and her sister will not escape
> a dreadful fate.
>
> (*Antigone* 486–9a)

I do not mean to imply that these passages from epic and tragedy document actual domestic cult places and practices. With due consideration of their genre and context, however, literary passages show us how a given theme could resonate with the intended audience. Therefore I find significant the use of Zeus Herkeios' household altar as a place of expected sanctuary, and conversely of intimate and horrific violation. It is *this* Zeus, domestic god par excellence, that epic and tragic poets find appropriate for such contexts.

Our two household Zeuses, Ktesios and Herkeios, both illustrate a fairly common characteristic of Greek domestic religion, and one of the ways in which it intersects with the practices of larger communities: household cults can be smaller versions of civic cults. It is interesting that not all pre-modern polytheistic systems seem to share the close parallels between larger civic cults and smaller domestic rituals nested or enmeshed within them. For example, the Mayanist Patricia McAnany maintains that domestic rituals in the villages she has studied in northern Belize (dating from c. 1000 BCE to 1000 CE) are quite distinct from the contemporary state rituals: the latter are concerned with structures of power, whereas domestic rituals are concerned with fertility, health, reproduction within the family, in short, with what McAnany describes as household vitality, the power to "endure with exuberance."[15] This difference in the focus of rituals, I postulate, corresponds to the great power differential that existed between the Mayan state and Mayan village households. In contrast, the classical Greek political apparatus was of more modest scope. In Athens, the "government" and "bureaucracy" consisted of ordinary citizens, most of them allotted to year-long offices, after which they would return to private life. In the case of Athens, at least, the operations of *polis* and *oikos* existed within sight of each other, so to speak, and shared many concerns – though of course they dealt with them from different perspectives.

Zeus Ktesios was honored in the Greek household, as we have seen, and also at the level of the *deme*: Pausanias (1.31.4) says he had altars at Phlya and Myrrhinus in Attica, together with Demeter Anesidora ("sender-up of gifts") and other goddesses. Zeus Herkeios, for his part, is listed on the sacrificial calendar of the Attic *deme* Thorikos in an inscription from about 430 BCE, and he even had an altar on the Athenian Acropolis under the sacred olive tree in the Pandroseion sanctuary.[16] This fact supports the notion that the polity of Athens (and other Greek *poleis* as well) was constituted in important ways on the model of an *oikos*. In this instance at least, the priority of the domestic cult seems clear: Zeus Herkeios on the Acropolis is the household Zeus Herkeios writ large.

Many gods besides these two Zeuses were honored in Greek households, too many to discuss in a brief chapter. Of fundamental importance is Hestia, the hearth goddess, an ancient, indeed Indo-European figure, and a member of the Olympian family in Greek myth (cf. Hesiod, *Theogony* 454, where she is listed first among the children of Kronos and Rheia), whose domestic cult was probably the most widespread in the Greek world. General studies of Greek religion tend not to devote much space to Hestia, for she was inconspicuous in *civic* festivals and sanctuaries, and figures in very few myths. In homes, however, she was quite literally the focal point of the family's religious practices.[17] With Hestia all offerings could be said to begin and end; she received the first and last libation at banquets (*Homeric Hymn* 29.4–6). New members of a household – whether bride, newborn, or slave – were ceremoniously presented to Hestia. (See below for a discussion of Hestia's important role after the birth of a baby.)

The hearth was also a place where one could seek asylum, as Odysseus perhaps does when he sits inconspicuously near the fireplace in the Phaeacian palace, a mysterious and needy stranger, before he is able to start on the last leg of his journey home (*Odyssey* 7.153). In Euripides' *Herakles*, Hestia has a prominent place in the discourse of homecoming (523, 599–600), and it is at her altar (like that of Zeus, probably Herkeios, as discussed above) that Herakles' threatened family seeks refuge from the murderous intent of the tyrant Lykos (712–15).[18]

Hestia is another god whose household cult is enmeshed within that of the larger community. While her importance within the individual *oikos* is obvious, cities too had their central hearths, typically in the *prytaneion* or town hall (cf. Pindar, *Nemean* 11.1–7, of Tenedos), where Hestia could be honored as *Prytania*. At a much broader level, it was even possible to speak of the hearth at the panhellenic oracular shrine of Delphi as belonging to all Hellenes (Plutarch, *Aristides* 20.4). Nevertheless, there can be little doubt that for most Greeks, their own hearth at home was the Hestia most often revered.

Greek cities of course had festivals in honor of agricultural gods such as Demeter, events which even in more urban settings maintained their roots in the agricultural year.[19] Parallel to these large-scale rites were prayers and offerings that household members made for success in their farm work – practices that doubtless occurred frequently in the course of the seasons. The Hesiodic didactic poem *Works and Days* provides evidence for household-scale agricultural rites; along with instructions on how to hide the seed from birds while sowing a field, for example, the speaker advises:

> Pray to Zeus Chthonios ("of the earth") and to pure Demeter
> to bring to rich fruition the holy grain of Demeter,
> as you first begin to plough . . .
>
> (*Works and Days* 465–7)

The poet further advises the householder to "make offerings to the immortal gods" according to his ability, with animal sacrifice, libations, or incense "both when you retire and when the holy light returns," so that he will prosper enough to buy someone else's land, rather than the reverse (*Works and Days* 335–41). Further, according to the Hesiodic *Precepts of Cheiron* (a collection of maxims, surviving only in a few quotations by later authors), one should also make "fine offerings" to the gods whenever returning home (for the evening?).[20] The site for all these common pieties is clearly the *oikos*, which seems a far more common locus of religious activity for the Hesiodic farmer than a public sanctuary.[21]

A different kind of household fertility rite takes place in the *Acharnians* of Aristophanes. Here, the comic hero Dicaiopolis orchestrates his own family Dionysia, complete with procession and offerings, at a time when the larger civic community (here represented by the demesmen of Acharnae) was unable to do so because of the constraints of the Peloponnesian War (*Acharnians* 241–79). Faraone proposes that this scene may reflect an actual Attic domestic fertility rite, a Rural Dionysia that was "nested" into similar festivals celebrated by larger cult communities, both *deme* and *polis*. This is a possible inference, but I am less confident than Faraone that Dicaiopolis' phallos-procession represents a festival that was in reality held at the level of the private household. Aristophanes' plot revolves around the fact that Dicaiopolis has just made a private peace treaty with the Spartans, for his own benefit and that of his family. While everyone else in Attica remains at war, he ostentatiously celebrates his little Dionysia in the presence of angry and jealous demesmen. It seems to me more likely that the comic hero here is appropriating for his own *oikos*, in extraordinary circumstances, a rite that "should" be performed by a larger community. In any case, the Acharnians, being unable to afford a celebration of their own because of the war, are outraged and unhappy with Dicaiopolis' rite (*Acharnians* 280–95 and *passim*).

Whether Dicaiopolis' mini-festival reflects a real Athenian domestic rite or is simply a product of comic fantasy, a whole range of household members participates in his little Dionysia. His daughter bears the offering basket, while two male slaves carry the phallos. The role Dicaiopolis assigns his wife is somewhat puzzling; unlike the daughter or slaves, she is told merely to observe from the roof as the procession and offering take place (262). Why is she needed at all? Stephanie Jamison's recent study of Vedic domestic rituals suggests a possible answer. Jamison attributes an important function to the passive but important role of the sacrificer's wife: her mere presence is deemed essential for injecting a necessary sexual energy into the elaborate, orderly sacrifice (admittedly a far cry from Dicaiopolis' celebration). As Jamison explains, in ancient India "women are perceived as the primary locus of active sexuality."[22] Whether as an Indo-European reflex or simply a typological parallel, the presence of female family members may implicitly play a similar role at Greek rituals such as Dicaiopolis' Dionysia, a rite in which the prominent phallos-carrying and remarks about the daughter's incipient sexuality (*Acharnians* 253–60) sufficiently indicate a focus on fertility. Alternatively, the wife's role may simply reflect a tendency of household rites to include all members of the *oikos*, even if their presence at analogous civic festivals (in this case, the City Dionysia) was less conspicuous.

We also hear in Attic Old Comedy of annual civic rites in which families participated qua families. One of these is the spring festival of Diasia, dedicated to Zeus Meilichios ("Kindly"). Another of Aristophanes' comic heroes, Strepsiades in the *Clouds*, recalls the rite as the site of a family barbecue – probably for the extended family (*genos*): "Once at the Diasia . . . while I was roasting a sausage for my relatives [*syngenesin*] . . ." (*Clouds* 408–11). Later, Strepsiades remembers the Diasia again, this time as the festival where he once bought a toy cart for his six-year-old son (*Clouds* 863–4). Here, the family as such went out of the *oikos* to join in, indeed to constitute, a great public rite in honor of the revered civic god Zeus Meilichios.[23]

More controversially, and again largely on the basis of a passage in comedy, Richard Hamilton has argued that the Choes or "Jugs" (new wine) festival, which comprised the second part of the three-day Anthesteria festival at Athens, was celebrated privately as well as publicly. A public contest to determine who could drink an entire *chous* (a large wine pitcher) the fastest appears to be complemented by drinking and dining parties celebrated in private homes, though these were probably restricted to the male head of house and his guests rather than intended for family members as such.[24] Here too Aristophanes' Dicaiopolis is the principal character: he is invited to a private party at the home of the priest of Dionysos (1085–94), and also wins the city's drinking contest (*Acharnians* 1227–32).

The relationships between domestic cults and those celebrated by larger civic communities, then, were varied and nuanced. For the most part, they complemented or at least did not conflict with each other, and in some instances civic cults mirrored domestic ones, suggesting that the city presented itself in some respects as an *oikos* writ large.

Family vs. *Polis* Religion?

One potential source of religious friction between "family" and "state" in classical Athens is competition for religious authority between the increasingly democratic *polis* and certain elite families ("family" here in the sense of *genos*, a group claiming descent from a common ancestor) that had their own venerable cults and religious privileges. Various compromises were found. The elite *genos* of the Eteoboutadai, for example, continued to provide the priestess for the prestigious civic cult of Athena Polias, but the goddess's festivals came to be regulated by state officials according to procedures approved by the citizen body. Priesthoods for new civic cults, moreover, were sometimes determined by democratic processes such as allotment rather than by family membership; this seems to have happened, for example, in the cases of Athena Nike and the Thracian import Bendis, both of them goddesses whose cults were established or expanded in Athens in the second half of the fifth century.[25]

In some notable cases, *genos* identity is associated with the cult of certain gods not shared by the *polis* as a whole. From Herodotus we hear that the (unnamed) family of Isagoras, who was a political rival of the famous reformer Cleisthenes in late sixth-century Athens, sacrificed to Carian Zeus (5.66). The epithet suggests that this god was not Greek, but from Caria in Asia Minor.[26] Herodotus assures us that Isagoras belongs to a distinguished family, but I suspect that the information about Carian Zeus reflects a charge (perhaps leveled by Cleisthenes' own prominent *genos*, the Alkmeonids) that Isagoras lacked an "autochthonous" Athenian pedigree to support his political aspirations.[27]

Another sort of family claim for prominence in religious matters is reflected in the story that shortly after the Persian Wars, in which he had played a leading role, the Athenian general Themistocles (a member of the Lycomid *oikos*) restored his family's initiation sanctuary (*telestêrion*) in the *deme* of Phlya. This cult place was allegedly the home of mystery rites more ancient than those of Demeter at Eleusis.[28] Here, at least according to the much later authors Pausanias and Plutarch, the Lycomid family celebrated private rites (*orgia*) at which they sang songs attributed to the ancient legendary musicians Orpheus and Musaios.[29] With this tradition, a prominent *genos* stakes a claim for religious authority that allegedly predates state cults and religious magistracies. On a more personal level, according to Plutarch (and corroborated by archaeological evidence), Themistocles also built a shrine to Artemis Aristoboule ("of good counsel") in his own *deme* of Melite, alluding with the epithet to his own good counsel during the Persian Wars – and thereby angering his fellow citizens, who were soon to ostracize him (Plutarch, *Life of Themistocles* 22.2–3).[30] This founding or re-establishment of special cults, along with claims to traditional religious privileges, shows how members of certain Athenian families (*genê*) differentiated themselves from the citizen body as a whole.

A negative attitude toward non-civic cults is encountered in Attic dramatic texts as well. In Euripides' *Medea*, the wronged heroine plots revenge on Jason, together with his new bride and her father, the ruler of Corinth. "No one will hurt my heart and go on faring well," Medea threatens, swearing "by Hecate, the mistress I revere most of all and have taken as my ally, dwelling as she does in the inmost part of my hearth" (395–7). Compare with Medea's cult of Hecate the honors paid to the same goddess by Clearchus, the pious male householder celebrated in an essay by Porphyry. At each new moon, Clearchus washed his ancestral images of Hecate and Hermes, decked them with garlands, and gave them simple offerings of incense and cakes (*De Abstinentia* 2.16).[31] Medea's vengeful and subversive hearthside devotion to an occult Hecate doubtless is meant as an extreme example of (from the perspective of the *polis*) deviant domestic religious practice. Nevertheless, the existence of unregulated household cults, especially when managed by females, was a matter of grave concern to some; witness the prohibition from the ideal city that the "Athenian stranger" in Plato's *Laws* would place on *all* household sacrifices and shrines, which he says are typically, and improperly, established by women and those in distress (*Laws* 909 d–e).[32]

It would be a fruitful project, though beyond the scope of this chapter, to trace misgivings about women's religious activities, privately motivated and mostly domestic, throughout Greek tragedy – and comedy as well. I summarize here only how this topic plays out in Aeschylus' magisterial *Oresteia*. The trilogy, whose patriarchal and *polis*-centered ideology has been effectively analyzed by feminist critics,[33] is also very relevant to the relationship between "private" and "public" rituals and the role of gender in them. It includes a shift from household cults under female control to civic cults established by the male-oriented city god par excellence, Athena.

As the *Oresteia* begins, in response to the news that Troy has fallen, Clytemnestra orders sacrifices at all the city's altars (*Agamemnon* 83–103, 261–3, 594–7). She prays to Zeus Teleios "Fulfiller" when Agamemnon, unaware of her plot against him, finally re-enters his palace, treading the crimson carpet (973–4), and she refers ominously to sacrifices for Hestia waiting inside the house (1056–8, cf. 1296–8). Once the deed is done, she calls the murder of Agamemnon and Cassandra her offering to chthonic Zeus (1385–7).

In the second play of the trilogy, Clytemnestra's daughter Electra is instructed by her female servants in how to transform a propitiatory graveside offering to Agamemnon (ordered by Clytemnestra because of ominous dreams) into a virtual raising of his angry ghost (*Choephoroi* 84–123). When Electra's brother Orestes unexpectedly returns from exile and joins the group at the tomb, their familial prayer to the dead king becomes an empowering song that steels the prince to kill his mother and her lover and co-ruler, Aegisthus.

In the third play and magnificent resolution of the trilogy, Clytemnestra and Aegisthus have been killed by her son Orestes, with the support of Electra and the Libation Bearers and another member of the household, the old Nurse of Orestes. Orestes is pursued by the Furies, horrific immortal female avengers, who threaten to torment him eternally for the crime of matricide. Orestes is tried and acquitted for his crime, but the dilemma is not resolved until Athena, civic goddess par excellence, persuades the Furies to change from avengers of crimes against blood relations to fixed local goddesses with a state cult (*Eumenides* 881–995). In exchange for the honors she promises to them, the Furies agree to grant her city fertility, internal harmony, and even military might. This resolution decidedly favors civic religion over female-dominated and subversive domestic practices – even though such practices were also used by Orestes and Electra in overthrowing the rule of Clytemnestra and Aegisthus.

Tragedy, I repeat, is far from providing a snapshot of religious practice or even belief, but it can give us great insight into issues salient to the city that produced it.

The locus of religious authority, including management of supernatural powers within the household, evidently became just such an issue.

With that tension in mind, I turn to a final intersection between domestic and civic religion. We have seen that household gods such as Zeus Herkeios could be appropriated by the *polis* (cf. his altar on the Acropolis). But what happens if a communal ritual is appropriated for private use?

I suggested above that this may be one reason why Dicaiopolis' neighbors are so incensed about his domestic Dionysia festival in Aristophanes' *Acharnians*. The most notorious historical example of a domestic (though not "family") rite is the unauthorized celebrations, or parodies, of the Eleusinian Mysteries that were allegedly held in private houses in Athens, in 415 BCE, just before the city's ultimately disastrous invasion of Sicily (Thucydides 6.28). The travesty led to accusations, trials, and other civic disruptions that reverberated for over a decade.[34] This is an extreme case: the Mysteries of Demeter and her daughter were not only part of a great annual celebration important to the city's well-being, but they were also a solemnly secret rite open to initiates only. The city was appalled by the sacrilege caused by revealing or mocking the Eleusinian Mysteries, and may also have worried about the power harnessed – to what ends? – in the unregulated, privately celebrated rite.[35]

For a lesser example of a private rite dubiously imitating a public one, I turn to an unorthodox use of cephalomancy. Necromantic cult places, such as one at the river Acheron in Thesprotia, where the Corinthian tyrant Periander consulted his dead wife (Herodotus 5.92h [5.92 eta]), or the hero-shrine of Trophonius at Lebadeia, were strewn throughout the Greek world. The special type of necromantic cult in which one consults a dismembered head, however, is attested in classical Greece only for the legendary Orpheus on Lesbos, probably on the coast near Antissa. Consultation of Orpheus' head is depicted on several fifth-century Attic vases; literary attestation comes only much later, in Philostratus' *Heroikos* (third century CE),[36] which tells us that the oracles of Orpheus' head traveled widely, even to the court of Cyrus the Great (*Heroikos* 28.12).

Should an individual set up a cephalomantic shrine in his own house, however, the attitude toward the practice is no longer respect and acceptance as implied by the vase paintings and Philostratus. According to a story set in the late sixth-century BCE but attested only much later, the Spartan king Cleomenes promised his friend Archonides that if he came to power he would always act in concord with Archonides (literally, "do everything with his head"). Becoming king, Cleomenes had Archonides beheaded, preserved his friend's head in a jar of honey, and did indeed consult it in all his decisions (Aelian, *Varia historia* 12.8). The point of this story does not depend on its historicity: it is one of many tales of the madness of Cleomenes, most of them dealing with religious transgressions.[37] Private cephalomancy appears to be another rite that, like the Eleusinian Mysteries on a much greater historical scale, and perhaps like Dicaiopolis' Dionysia in comedy, is desirable on the level of public cult, but inappropriate if conducted at the individual or domestic level.[38]

Household Rites for Birth, Death, and Other Dangers

Stanley Stowers writes in Chapter 2 of this book,

> Birth, death and sexual activity belonged to the house and family [in Greek and Roman cities]. The pollution of these first two events in the life-course of the family severely contaminated the house and anyone who entered. . . . It is easy to think of this as a fixed, almost natural, system of conceptual oppositions embodied in practice, rules, and law.

A number of ad hoc or need-based rites having to do with life transitions and crises, including weddings, births, healing rites, and funerals, though not wholly lacking a public aspect, fell mainly within the competence of the *oikos*, and female family members played leading roles in them. Moreover, as I suggested at the beginning of this chapter, these household rites often had to do with matters that were vigorously excluded from Greek sanctuaries: birth, sex, and death.

About ancient Greek funerary rites a great deal has been written.[39] They were conducted by the family of the deceased and were centered in homes, certainly not in sanctuaries. Female family members traditionally were important agents here, caring for the corpse inside the house, and participating prominently in the procession, public laments, and burial that took place outside it.[40] It appears that Greek (and Roman) practice is in this respect different from that of some other ancient cultures, such as in Mesopotamia (see on Babyon, Nuzi, Emar elsewhere in this volume), where the tendance of ancestors buried within the house was an important aspect of domestic cult. In classical Greece, the dead periodically received honors and offerings from family members, but their burial places were quite separate from the abodes of the living.

As is well known, the participation of women in funerals (and other rites) was legislated, monitored, and restricted by a number of Greek cities. In Athens, apparently from the time of the law-giver Solon in the early sixth century, limits were set on public displays of grief as well as on the time and size of the funeral cortège;[41] we hear of similar restrictions also in other *poleis*, including Iulis (on the island of Keos)[42] and Thasos.[43] A number of cities in the classical period and later even had officials designated to control female behavior at funerals.[44] As scholars have long noted, this arrangement suppresses women's public roles and at the same time limits displays emanating from the family (whether *oikos* or *genos*), and so subordinates family to *polis* – all in keeping with the hierarchy of religious authority described by Sourvinou-Inwood and others.[45]

Families also had to manage the serious pollution (*miasma*) that inevitably affected their household for a certain period, from the moment of death until some days after the burial. Precautions might include providing lustral water to help purify those who came in contact with the house, avoiding sacrifices to household or civic gods, and refraining from food and bathing until after the body was carried out of the house and buried. Practices for dealing with death and its attendant pollution differed somewhat from one community to another; beginning in the fifth century, a number of cities enacted varying regulations to keep the city and sanctuaries pure.[46] Here we see the *polis* defining and directing practices that were in large part carried out at the domestic level. As Robert Parker suggests, it sometimes appears that the political community is legislating against, rather than in accord with, traditional local practices; such is the case with a fifth-century regulation from Iulis on Keos, "Do not put a cup under the bier . . . or take the sweepings to the tomb."[47]

In addition to the management of death, practices connected with marriages and births were essential domestic concerns, dealing with the very continuity of the family. Wedding rites have received a good deal of scholarly attention, though many details remain difficult to ascertain.[48] Greek marriages were arranged between the bridegroom and the bride's father or male guardian in the domestic ceremony called *enguê*, where the dowry was agreed upon and family members (and perhaps others) witnessed the betrothal. Civic deities were not neglected, however, especially in women's preparations for marriage. Brides (typically in their mid-teens) made dedications to a variety of gods at public shrines, such as their maidenly girdle or childhood toys, often to Artemis, and (in fourth-century Athens) a drachma to Aphrodite Ourania.[49]

The wedding, or *gamos*, often took place in the winter month of Gamelion, when the marriage of Zeus and Hera was celebrated. After separate ritual baths for both bride and groom, it focused on the formal transfer (ideally by chariot) of the bride from her natal house to that of her husband, in a procession that typically took place at night. As with funeral rites, no priest or civic official presided at the wedding, which focused on the two households and the journey between them. When the bride and groom arrived at his home, she was welcomed by his mother, and introduced to his household gods (especially Hestia). The couple was pelted with a benign shower of nuts, dried fruits, and other tokens of fertility and prosperity. Overall, the protracted process of betrothal, engagement, and wedding provides another example of enmeshed, mutually reinforcing domestic and civic rites.

The explicit purpose of marriage was to produce legitimate offspring, and the birth of a child, not surprisingly, was marked by a number of rituals within the family. Among these was the formal acceptance of a child by its father, who had to determine whether a baby was to be kept or rejected ("exposed"). In Athens, acceptance was celebrated on (probably) the fifth day of life, in a rite called *amphidromia*, "running around [the hearth]"; this procedure marked the infant as a new member of the family and placed it under the protection of the domestic Hestia. The rite at the family hearth may also have marked the end of the general household pollution incurred during the birth, though the mother's pollution probably lasted longer, perhaps until the *Tesserakosation*, "Fortieth-Day" celebration.[50]

As Robert Garland points out, household members alone conducted the rites pertaining to childbirth; "outside" or "public" religious officials had no role to play in the family matter of accepting a newborn and purifying those affected by the crisis of childbirth. But here too, household rituals were intertwined with cultic duties to the larger community. In Athens, the father introduced a newborn to his phratry, an officially recognized hereditary group used for determining citizenship, at the annual festival of Apaturia. At least in some instances this was done with a sacrifice and a solemn oath that his child was the legitimate child of citizen parents.[51]

There were also public cults that centered on fecundity and successful childbirth: continuity of the community is everyone's concern. Many Greek *poleis* – Athens, Argos, Tegea, Sparta, Olympia, and Delos among them – had a sanctuary dedicated to the birth goddess Eileithyia.[52] Perhaps from one of these, though its provenance is unknown, comes a marble relief dated to the late fifth century.[53] It is usually interpreted as showing Eileithyia, a large female figure, directing her attention to an exhausted woman seated on a stool; the woman has evidently just delivered a tiny baby (with a fine head of hair), which is being held by another woman.[54] The scene is undoubtedly set in the mother's home, and the goddess was undoubtedly invoked there during labor and delivery. Here, the birth that takes place within the house – an action that would be terribly polluting in a public sanctuary – receives public thanks in a shrine located outside the house. In addition to Eileithyia, in Attica and elsewhere Artemis (under many titles, including Eileithyia and Lochia, "Midwife") received dedications from women or couples either seeking children or thanking the goddess for a successful pregnancy.[55]

When women visited general healing shrines, such as the great sanctuary of Asklepios at Epidauros, as far as we can tell the reason usually had to do with childbearing. In one famous case, a certain Kleo, after allegedly being pregnant for five years, made a pilgrimage to Epidauros to undergo the ritual process of incubation in the temple, seeking the god's help. Upon leaving the sanctuary precinct (where birth was prohibited), she promptly delivered a five-year-old son, who washed himself at the fountain and started to walk around with his mother.[56] Other women also went to ask the god for pregnancy – and, if they were wise, for timely delivery as well.[57] Here again, domestic and public practices are enmeshed in a complementary system.

Health and healing were the most frequent topics of dedications in sanctuaries throughout Greece, and corporeal well-being was a great concern at the domestic level as well. Faraone mentions the tradition that Pericles (Plutarch, *Life of Pericles* 38), the great intellectual and rational statesman, when dying of the plague, was seen wearing amulets put around his neck by the women of his household.[58] Children too were protected by amulets and charms, perhaps as early as their formal acceptance into the family in the rite of *amphidromia*.[59] Such domestic practices for gaining supernatural protection seem generally uncontroversial; charms are mentioned as valuable safeguards for children in the *Homeric Hymn to Demeter*, 229–30. Of the hundreds of small painted pitchers (*choes*) associated with the

Athenian festival of Anthesteria, most show very young, naked, crawling boys, and two-thirds of them are wearing a necklace of amulets.[60] Exaggerated attention to apotropaic precautions, however, especially by adult males, could be mocked as superstitious,[61] and we should not forget that Plato's main interlocutor in the *Laws* would like to rid the ideal city of all forms of home-made apotropaics (909d–e).[62] Evidently, household remedies (*pharmaka*) against unseen threats did not always meet with public approval, but I know of no complaints about the use of precautionary amulets for the very young.

Finally, even apart from pregnancy and parturition, there is some material evidence for household shrines concerned with sexuality – a sphere of activity that, along with birth and death, was normally excluded from public sanctuaries. From classical-era Taras in Southern Italy comes a number of terracotta plaques interpreted as the sides of small altars, used for burning incense. Some of the plaques are decorated with what appear to be bridal scenes: in one, a young woman seated on a bed gets help from another woman in removing her shoes, while a small naked Eros flutters toward her.[63] James Redfield imagines such objects being used in women's chambers: a wife could burn an offering of incense to a marriage goddess, and at the same time romantically perfume her bedroom.[64] Whatever their precise function, these domestic altars combine ritual use (incense offerings) with erotic imagery.

Conclusion

While it is obviously correct to see the *polis* as the normal seat of religious authority in the classical Greek world, this does not mean that the rites practiced by good citizens (and others) in their homes were necessarily homogeneous, or that the polity's primacy in religious matters was always uncontested. Domestic gods like Zeus Ktesios were honored in ways that apparently varied with the occasion and with individual preference. Traditional household cults could have great emotional resonance, as in the case of Zeus Herkeios, and also be a gateway to full membership in the political community. Domestic gods could be appropriated by the city, as with the same Zeus Herkeios "writ large" on the Athenian Acropolis, or Hestia in many a city hall.

Some domestic rites, in turn, might mirror civic practices on a small scale (as with prayers to agricultural or healing gods); households might even combine efforts to create a *polis*-wide festival such as the Diasia. A few families, such as the Lycomid *genos* in the Attic *deme* of Phlya, were able to maintain control over sanctuaries their ancestors had founded, perhaps competing to a degree with analogous cults (in this case, the Eleusinian Mysteries) managed by the *polis*. In several respects, household religious practices took care of crucial matters that would be dangerously polluting for civic sanctuaries; they absorbed and dissipated the pollution of birth and death, and in some places may have provided a ritual scenario for sexual activity as well.

The tendency in religious history to exclude, or at best to seclude, domestic religion from civic tends to blind us to these dynamic interactions. *Polis* cult and family cult are not two separate systems, but an interlocking set of practices, asymmetrical though often complementary. What Cynthia Patterson has written in connection with Greek "family (or women's) history," applies equally well to household religion: "The engagement of the long-separated 'private and public spheres' enlarges the historical stage and increases our appreciation of the historical drama."[65] Further work on Greek domestic religion should likewise be wary of segregating it from other forms of religious practice.

Notes

1 Christiane Sourvinou-Inwood, "What Is Polis Religion?" in *Oxford Readings in Greek Religion*, ed. Richard Buxton (Oxford: Oxford University Press, 2000), pp. 19–20.
2 E.g. Robert Parker, *Athenian Religion. A History* (Oxford: Clarendon Press, 1996), 6. See Faraone, this volume, p. 211, for further discussion.
3 Jon D. Mikalson, *Ancient Greek Religion* (Oxford: Blackwell Publishers, 2004).
4 Mikalson, *Ancient Greek Religion*, p. 139. On *deme* religion as falling between "private" and "public," see S. C. Humphreys, *The Strangeness of Gods. Historical Perspectives on the Interpretation of Athenian Religion* (Oxford: Oxford University Press, 2004), pp. 130–96, esp. pp. 130–1.
5 Faraone, this volume, pp. 211f.
6 Isaeus 8.16. Text and translation of Greek literary works cited in this chapter are available in the appropriate volumes of the Loeb Classical Library; the translations used here are my own, except where noted. On this passage see also Faraone, this volume, p. 216.
7 E.g., Mikalson, *Ancient Greek Religion*, p. 134.
8 Antiphon 1.15–19.
9 The Athenaeus item is attributed to the *Exegetikon*, a (probably) Hellenistic-era treatise on ritual practices.
10 See also Faraone, this volume, pp. 216f.
11 Martin P. Nilsson, *Geschichte der griechischen Religion* (Munich: Beck, 1967), p. 1: 403.
12 Aristotle, *Constitution of the Athenians* 55; Demosthenes 57.67.
13 Of course, it is possible that Herodotus or his source inserted into this story the name of the god he deemed appropriate for such a situation. On the disputed identity of Demaratos, see Deborah Boedeker, "The Two Faces of Demaratus," in *Herodotus and the Invention of History*, ed. Deborah Boedeker, *Arethusa* 20 (1987): 185–201; on the oath in particular, see Christopher Faraone, "Curses and Social Control in the Law Courts of Classical Athens," *Dike: Rivista di storia del diritto greco ed ellenistico* 2 (1999): 99–121.
14 Ulrich von Wilamowitz-Moellendorff, *Euripides Herakles*, 2nd edn., vol. 3 (Berlin: Akademie-Verlag, 1959), pp. 206–7; cf. Rush Rehm, *The Play of Space* (Princeton: Princeton University Press, 2002), p. 106, for discussion of how Euripides uses here the holy spaces of hearth and altar. Rehm, like Wilamowitz, seems to imply that Zeus Herkeios is mentioned by name in the text, but this is not the case.

15 In a lecture on Feb. 9, 2005 at Brown University, with special reference to the lowland village K'axob.
16 Thorikos calendar: *Supplementum Epigraphicum Graecum* 33: 147, line 22. Acropolis altar: Philochorus fr. 67 in Felix Jacoby, *Die Fragmente der griechischen Historiker*, Part 3 B (Leiden: Brill, 1964), p. 118. Cf. Nilsson, *Geschichte der griechischen Religion*, 1: 403, who also refers to an inscription locating Zeus Herkeios (with Hermes and Akamas) at a round altar near the Dipylon gate (*Inscriptiones Graecae* II^2 4983).
17 E.g., Walter Burkert, *Greek Religion* (Cambridge, Mass.: Harvard University Press, 1985): 170.
18 See Rehm, *Play of Space*, pp. 104, 106.
19 See Allaire Chandor Brumfield, *The Attic Festivals of Demeter and their Relation to the Agricultural Year* (Salem, New Hampshire: Arno Press, 1981).
20 *Precepts of Cheiron* 1 (= Scholiast on Pindar, *Pythian* 6.19), ed. Hugh G. Evelyn-White, *Hesiod, The Homeric Hymns, and Homerica* (Cambridge, Mass.: Loeb Classical Library, 1964), p. 72.
21 Feasts of the gods (apparently away from home) are mentioned in *Works and Days*, pp. 736 and 742.
22 See Stephanie W. Jamison, *Sacrificed Wife/Sacrificer's Wife. Women, Ritual, and Hospitality in Ancient India* (New York: Oxford University Press, 1996), p. 53.
23 Nilsson, *Geschichte*, pp. 411–12.
24 Richard Hamilton, *Choes and Anthesteria. Athenian Iconography and Ritual* (Ann Arbor: University of Michigan Press, 1991), pp. 12–14, using evidence from Aristophanes' *Acharnians.*
25 Sara B. Aleshire, "The Demos and the Priests: the Selection of Sacred Officials at Athens from Cleisthenes to Augustus," in *Ritual, Finance, Politics: Athenian Democratic Accounts Presented to David Lewis*, ed. Robin Osborne and Simon Hornblower (Oxford: Clarendon Press, 1994), pp. 325–37. See also Deborah Boedeker, "Athenian Religion in the Age of Pericles," in *The Cambridge Companion to the Age of Pericles*, ed. Loren J. Samons II (Cambridge: Cambridge University Press, 2006).
26 On this passage, including the suggestion that "Carian" here might refer not to Caria in Asia Minor but to the citadel of Megara, not far from Athens, see W. W. How and J. Wells, *A Commentary on Herodotus*, 2 vols. (Oxford: Oxford University Press, 1912), 2: p. 32.
27 Athenians in this period sometimes claimed that as a people they had never moved from another land, or displaced earlier inhabitants in Attica, but were literally born from the native soil.
28 Burkert, *Greek Religion*, pp. 278–9.
29 Simonides (fr. 627), from Plutarch *Themistocles* 1.4. On the shrine, its songs and mysteries, see Pausanias 1.22.8; 4.7.5, 7; 9.27.2, 30.12.
30 For the archaeological evidence and a brief historical discussion, see Frank J. Frost, *Plutarch's* Themistocles: *A Historical Commentary* (Princeton: Princeton University Press, 1980), pp. 184–5.
31 On Clearchus, see also Faraone, this volume, pp. 210f., 217.
32 This passage is cited and well discussed by Faraone, this volume, pp. 218f.
33 Most notably, Froma Zeitlin, "The Dynamics of Misogyny: Myth and Mythmaking in the *Oresteia*," *Arethusa* 11 (1978): 149–84.
34 Cf. the speech of Andocides, *On the Mysteries*, dated to 400/399.

35 Profaning the Eleusinian Mysteries becomes a hallmark of serious impiety in Athens; for other examples, see K. J. Dover, "The Freedom of the Intellectual in Greek Society," *Talanta* 7 (1976): 24–54, especially 26–7.

36 On cephalomancy see Daniel Ogden, *Greek and Roman Necromancy* (Princeton: Princeton University Press, 2001), pp. 208–9; J. F. Nagy, "Hierarchy, Heroes, and Heads: Indo-European Structures in Greek Myth," in *Approaches to Greek Myth*, ed. Lowell Edmunds (Baltimore: Johns Hopkins University Press, 1990), pp. 200–38, especially pp. 209–28; Christopher A. Faraone, "Orpheus' Final Performance: Necromancy and a Singing Head on Lesbos," *Studi italiani di filologia classica*, series 4, 2 (2004): 5–27.

37 E.g., Cleomenes tries to get fellow conspirators to swear oaths to him by the water of an Arcadian river called Styx (Herodotus 6.74); the underworld river Styx is said to guarantee the oath of the gods (Hesiod, *Theogony* 784–806).

38 The question of precedence between domestic and public rites is especially complicated in the case of cephalomancy. Faraone, "Orpheus' Final Performance," pp. 15–21, refers to texts explaining how to conduct private necromancy with skulls, attested in first-millennium Mesopotamia and in Greek magical texts from Late Antiquity; such occult private practices may lie behind the head-shrine of Orpheus.

39 E.g., Emily Vermeule, *Aspects of Death in Early Greek Art and Poetry* (Berkeley: University of California Press, 1979); Robert Garland, *The Greek Way of Death* (Ithaca, NY: Cornell University Press, 1985); Christiane Sourvinou-Inwood, *"Reading" Greek Death to the End of the Classical Period* (Oxford: Oxford University Press, 1995); Sarah Iles Johnston, *Restless Dead: Encounters between the Living and the Dead in Ancient Greece* (Berkeley: University of California Press, 1999), especially pp. 37–46.

40 Matthew Dillon, *Girls and Women in Classical Greek Religion* (London: Routledge, 2002), pp. 268–92, provides a good recent summary, including visual evidence and bibliography.

41 Ibid., p. 271. For contrasting views on this provocative topic, see also Ian Morris, "Attitudes toward Death in Classical Greece," *Classical Antiquity* 8 (1989): 296–320; Sourvinou-Inwood, *"Reading" Greek Death*, pp. 413–44.

42 Dillon, *Girls and Women*, pp. 272–3.

43 Robert Parker, "What are Sacred Laws?," in *The Law and the Courts in Ancient Greece*, ed. Edward M. Harris and Lene Rubinstein (London: Duckworth, 2004), pp. 61–2.

44 Monitoring women who participate in public business (usually religious) was the duty of officials called *gynaikonomoi* ("woman-) regulators," who existed in classical Athens and other Greek cities; Plutarch mentions *gynaikonomoi* in his own Thebes (*Solon* 21.5). For funerary restrictions on women, and duties of the *gynaikonomos*, at Gambreion in the Troad, see Parker, "Sacred Laws," p. 61; Dillon, *Girls and Women*, p. 273.

45 See above, p. 229 and n. 1.

46 Robert Parker, *Miasma. Pollution and Purification in Early Greek Religion* (Oxford: Clarendon Press, 1983), pp. 33–42 and *passim* provides a useful survey of traditions and laws.

47 *Inscriptiones Graecae* XII.5.593, quoted in Parker, *Miasma*, p. 35.

48 John H. Oakley and Rebecca H. Sinos, *The Wedding in Ancient Athens* (Madison: University of Wisconsin Press, 1993); Robert Garland, *The Greek Way of Life: From Conception to Old Age* (Ithaca, NY.: Cornell University Press, 1990), pp. 217–25.

49 Garland, *Greek Way of Life*, 219–20; Dillon, *Girls and Women*, pp. 216–17; Mikalson, *Ancient Greek Religion*, pp. 151–3.

50 The family hearth was connected with purity in other ways as well; the Hesiodic *Works and Days* advises men not to expose their "seed-bespattered genitals" to the hearth (733–4). This injunction may reflect the fact that Hestia is, in myth, one of few virgins in the Olympian family (*Homeric Hymn to Aphrodite* 21–32); it may also reflect the common prohibition of sexual activity in a sanctuary, reaffirming the sacral character of the family hearth. On the *amphidromia* see Garland, *The Greek Way of Life*, pp. 93–6.

51 Ibid., p. 121.

52 From Chios come two recently-published inscriptions, which define the fees due to the local priestess of Eileithyia from private as well as public offerings; see Parker, "Sacred Laws," p. 60.

53 New York, The Metropolitan Museum of Art, Fletcher Fund, 1924: MMA 24.97.92; photograph in Nancy Demand, *Birth, Death, and Motherhood in Classical Greece* (Baltimore: Johns Hopkins University Press, 1994), p. 157, Plate 1.

54 For discussion and alternative identification of the divine figure, see ibid., pp. 87–8.

55 Ibid., pp. 88–91.

56 Text A1, in Lynn R. LiDonnici, *The Epidaurian Miracle Inscriptions. Text, Translation and Commentary* (Scholars Press: Atlanta, Georgia, 1995), pp. 84–5.

57 Ibid., pp. 86–7, Text A2: Ithmonika of Pellene appealed to the god to let her conceive; still pregnant three years later, she had to return to Epidauros to ask him to allow her daughter to be born.

58 Noted by Faraone, this volume, pp. 221f.

59 See Garland, *Greek Way of Life*, pp. 94 and 109, Fig. 8.

60 Richard Hamilton, *Choes and Anthesteria: Athenian Iconography and Ritual* (Ann Arbor: University of Michigan Press, 1992), pp. 85, 105–8, Figures 3, 4, 7, 9, 14, and *passim*.

61 See Theophrastus, *Characters* 16 "Superstition," though amulets as such are not mentioned in this negative portrait of one who is "cowardly with respect to the supernatural."

62 On this passage see above, p. 238, and Faraone, this volume, pp. 218f.

63 Pierre Wuilleumier, *Tarante: Des origines à la conquête romaine*, Bibliothèque des écoles françaises d'Athènes et de Rome, fasc. 148 (Paris: de Boccard, 1939), 1: 432–6, 2: Plate XLI 6. Discussed in James Redfield, *The Locrian Maidens. Love and Death in Greek Italy* (Princeton: Princeton University Press, 2003), pp. 364–5.

64 Ibid., p. 365.

65 Cynthia B. Patterson, *The Family in Greek History* (Cambridge, Mass.: Harvard University Press, 1998), p. 226.

14

Cicero's Minerva, *Penates*, and the Mother of the *Lares*: An Outline of Roman Domestic Religion

John Bodel

"Family" and "household" are concepts well known to historians of ancient Rome, whose sources make clear that a Roman *familia* comprised not only a person's kin (or close kin, particularly in the standard nuclear configuration of mother, father, and children) but also, if the person owned property, any slaves or dependents living in the home and any slaves housed elsewhere. Originally and fundamentally, however, a *familia* was a household in that it comprised all those who resided within a single house, the *domus*.[1] Law and custom gave special consideration to slaves living under the same roof as the *paterfamilias*, who was supposed to nurture them, according to the edifying myth, "as if they were his children" (*in loco filiorum*), and whose life they in turn were bound to protect with their own.[2] One Roman conception of the family, in other words, featured a composite household encompassing slaves and freedmen as well as freeborn kin within a complex unit characterized by sharp differentiations in status but (in principle, at least) mutual affective ties and common collective interest. Another construed *familia* more broadly but exclusively as referring to the extended clan. A third conceived of it more narrowly as comprising only the servile property. Our sources use the term variously and at times ambiguously, and it is not always easy to tell, when family religion is concerned, precisely which *familia* is concerned.[3]

Those who lived within a house were not only members of a slave or free family or of a composite household. They were also individuals, and much of the religious behavior manifested in Roman homes – much, that is, of what counts as Roman domestic religion – was more personal and individual than communal and representative in any meaningful sense. In the Roman *domus*, personal piety found expression in familial and household worship through the two standard sets of household gods, the *Lares* (shared by all in the household but a particular focus of attention for the slave staff), and the *Penates* (personal, inherited – and thus familial – images and tokens cultivated by individuals). Roman domestic religion thus had a dual nature, with two distinct but related sets of deities – one generic and collective (the *Lares*), the other pluralistic and individualized in orientation (the *Penates*) – canonically paired and set in juxtaposition with each other. Both types enjoyed a public as well as a private cult, but which influenced which and in what ways over time is unclear and has been much debated. A hundred years ago private religion was seen as a pristine, unfossilized form of popular religion, as yet untainted by institutionalization by the state but scarcely discernible during the historical period. That view predominated for more than half a century, but within the last few decades a new orthodoxy has emerged according to which private religion was so deeply embedded in the cultural identity of the Republican (male) citizen as to have been virtually absorbed by the state apparatus: acts of private worship, particularly those related to the household, provided little evidence of personal devotion but merely reflected engagement with the civic model of religion on which they were modeled.[4] Neither view adequately accounts for the range of behaviors that traversed the porous boundary between Roman civic and familial cult, nor do the conventionally polar modern categories of public and private seem adequately nuanced to characterize the diversity of ways that personal devotion bridged the territory between the two in Roman life.

One recent attempt to skirt the difficulty seeks refuge in ancient Roman definitions but finds those offered by contemporary witnesses to be problematic and incomplete.[5] The second-century compiler Pompeius Festus, for example, categorizes as public "those rites (*sacra*) that are performed at public expense on behalf of the people and for the hills, rural districts, wards, and shrines" of Rome, whereas those "performed on behalf of individual persons, households (*familiae*), and clans (*gentes*)" were private.[6] In determining public and private according to a simple criterion (essentially, who paid), Festus offers a pragmatic and apparently unequivocal means of distinguishing between the two, but he offers no guidance as to how to classify the diverse religious practices sponsored by collective groups other than families, such as the private associations (*collegia*) that played such a prominent role in the social organization of Roman urban life, not only among persons united by extraneous connections but within the slave *familiae* of individual households, nor, in placing "household" between "individual" and "clan" in a spectrum of categories that ranges from a single member to an extended familial network, does he provide any indication where along the scale the nuclear unit that dominates modern conceptions of the family might fall.

Varro's observation that "individual families ought to worship the gods as the state does – communally" points to the common foundation of public and private religion in collective representation but leaves little room for an individual acting individually, not only in civic but in domestic cult.[7] By familial worship Varro refers to the third of Festus's categories of private rites, the gentilicial cults conducted publicly (in a spatial sense: they were financed privately) by representatives of the great families of the Republic on behalf of their individual clans (*gentes*).[8] As clan representation, transmitted only agnatically, died out over the centuries, so too did the gentilicial cults, except those few that were taken over by the state. By the end of the Republic few were actively maintained. Never an important determinant of Roman civic organization or political power, the *gens* waned even in cultural significance during the Empire and was replaced in ideology and practice by the family (*familia*), in the broad sense of blood relations on both the mother's and the father's side.[9] Accordingly, the obligation to perform hereditary gentilicial *sacra*, which remained closely tied in law, as it had always been in principle, to the transmission of property, gave way in practice to the voluntary adoption by individual *familiae* of distinctive customs of dress or adornment.[10] Gentilicial cult as such thus has little relevance for an investigation of Roman household religion: for all its supposed cultural significance, the *gens* always remained more a conception, ill-defined and vague, than a practical social instrument, and the religious rites associated with it, which are occasionally attested during the Republic for particular clans, were even then always performed in public settings outside the house. As conspicuous demonstrations of familial piety, they served to promote the idea of the *gens* in public contexts; as manifestations of "family" religion, they are mere curiosities – relics, at best, during the historical period, more often mere status symbols.

More useful than the *gens* for understanding the nature of Roman domestic cult, paradoxically, is the individual, the third element in Festus's triage of Roman private religion. In discussing the religious conduct of individuals in the second book of his treatise *On Laws*, Cicero defines the boundary between proper and improper practice according to a distinction between gods held separately (*separatim*) and those held privately (*privatim*): "Let no one have gods separately, either new gods or foreign gods, unless publicly adopted. Privately let them worship those gods whom they have received as duly worshiped by their fathers (or ancestors: *patres*)" (*De Legibus* 2.19). In confirming the expected – that gods formally recognized by the state were legitimate objects also of private veneration, whereas certain others were not – Cicero does not explain what distinguishes "separate" from "private," nor does he draw the line between the two quite where we might expect it: "separate" are those rites that are new or foreign, except those that receive public cult; "private" are those handed down by the "fathers." It is unclear whether Cicero is thinking of individual heads of households passing down to their children specific familial deities or of ancestors generally and the gods they collectively worshiped. Left out of his formulation in either case are those foreign cults not handed down by earlier generations but subsequently adopted publicly and therefore no longer separate. These eventually included not only all the traditional civic deities of the Roman pantheon but also various Asiatic and African newcomers (notably Ceres, the Great Mother, Isis, and Serapis), who, once officially recognized, received foreign rites within the formal structures of the state religion. Elsewhere, Cicero showed himself to be sensitive to the argument that Serapis and Isis might well be considered among the ancestral gods on the grounds that they had been accepted by their fathers but, in prescribing the forms of private worship permissible in his ideal state, no space is reserved for them (*De Natura Deorum* 3.47).[11]

In fact, the practices of Roman domestic and household religion were more varied and less clearly demarcated than Cicero or Festus would allow, and the preferences of individuals played a larger role in them than Varro was prepared to concede. The intermingling of deities from outside the traditional Roman pantheon with those sanctioned by the state that Cicero elsewhere brands as an undesirable "confusion of religions" (*De Legibus* 2.25) was in fact characteristic of Roman domestic worship, where personal choices made by individuals stood side by side with collective deities of the household. Modern interpreters, taking their cue from authorities like Cicero, who sanctioned as legitimate only those private cults handed down by the ancestors, have traditionally followed their Roman guides in approaching the subject from the top down – that is, by privileging the idea of collective representation and thus imposing a hierarchical (or perhaps concentric) view of the relation of state to household cult: public acts affected all the people, whereas private ones concerned the progressively narrower circles of clan, family, and household. For scholars of the nineteenth and the first half of the twentieth centuries, who regarded the public state cult as moribund and decadent, the Roman popular religion supposedly already institutionalized and buried by it had necessarily also to appear beyond recovery: if the forms even of public religion were hollow shells, how much more empty must have been the historically visible manifestations of a private religiosity that had long ago been suffocated by it?[12] More recently, with household cult seen as subordinated to and thoroughly embedded within the state religion, the representations in Augustan poetry and household shrines of the early Empire that constitute our primary evidence for it have appeared to be little more than sentimentally contrived fictions evocative of an idealized past.[13]

The undeniable persistence and tenacity of the popular veneration of household gods or of gods in domestic contexts during the period of the Roman Empire has therefore been a consistent embarrassment in modern evaluations of Roman state religion. As an independent object on investigation, household cult has seemed elusive and scarcely able to be disentangled from its public forms. It may appear both less puzzling and less obscure if we abandon the idea of representation and shift our focus from the group (the clan, the family, the household) to the individual – the slave or freedman, the family member, the *paterfamilias* – and personal acts (or attitudes) of religiosity expressed in domestic contexts. If we consider the evidence for personal devotion to deities both public and "foreign" manifested by individuals in the home, we may find it easier to identify the heart of that vibrant polytheistic spirit that eventually, long after the traditional forms of civic public worship had been abandoned, proved so difficult for the more aggressively Christian emperors to eradicate.[14] For an example of this core tradition of private religiosity, we need look no further than to the same treatise of Cicero, *On Laws*, where Cicero recounts an act of personal piety that illustrates well how public and private expressions of devotion not only paralleled but occasionally intersected one another in Roman life, and how the overlap between them might be both observed and exploited.

Cicero's Minerva

Later in the second book *On Laws*, in addressing the subject of "just punishment for the violation of religion," Cicero recalls a personal tragedy that had befallen him a few years previously (in 58 BCE), when a public law carried by his arch enemy P. Clodius banished him from Rome and confiscated his house on the Palatine Hill. "At that time all the laws of religion were violated by the crimes of depraved citizens; my familial *Lares* were assaulted; in their home a temple to Licence was built; and the one who had been driven from their shrines saved them."[15] The "depraved citizens" were Clodius and his flunky Scato, a ghost purchaser of the site; the assault on the *Lares* refers to the destruction of Cicero's house after he had been declared a public enemy (a traditional practice); and the "temple to Licence" alludes to a shrine to Liberty that Clodius had dedicated (and apparently consecrated) on a part of the property, precisely in order to prevent Cicero from reoccupying the site.[16] The final clause refers to Cicero's pious behavior at the time in transporting to the Temple of Jupiter Optimus Maximus on the Capitoline hill a statuette of Minerva that he had cultivated in his home, and in dedicating it there "To Minerva, Guardian of Rome": "I . . . would not allow that guardian of the city to be violated by the wicked, even when my own property was snatched from me and destroyed, but conveyed her from my house to my father's." (*De Legibus* 2.42).[17]

As always, Cicero chose his words, and his gestures, carefully. In dedicating his private Minerva as "Guardian of Rome," a title pointedly reminiscent of the chief civic deity of his beloved Athens, Athena Polias, he cast his personal cult image into a public role, even as he transported her physically from her former to her new "home." At the same time, in describing the Temple of Jupiter Optimus Maximus, the center of the state religion, as "my father's house," he reinscribed both the image and his act of devotion into the world of domestic cult. The gesture, both personal and public, effectively suggested that the fate of the *res publica* was tied to Cicero's own well-being, even as (more conventionally) his personal salvation depended upon the integrity of the *res publica*. More pointedly, Cicero's Minerva, as guardian of the Republic, trumped Clodius's *Libertas*, a symbol of newly won "freedom" (of the site from Cicero's presence and of the state from his tyranny) in a battle of political sloganeering that saw its immediate origins during the period of Cicero's consulship in 63 BCE.[18] By cultivating in his home an image of Palatine Minerva, Cicero did no more than others who combined devotion to a favored divine "protector" with civic-minded allegiance to the chief gods of the state.[19] But by dedicating the same image, salvaged from the shipwreck of his life, in the home of the official Capitoline protector, and by allusively signaling through the inscribed text the nature of the relationship that inspired the dedication ("Custodi Romae"), Cicero succeeded not only in linking his personal fate to that of the *res publica* but in representing himself as simultaneously suppliant and savior.

A skeptic might see here no more than a cynical manipulation of religion for political purposes – Cicero planting the seeds of his eventual rehabilitation and recovery of the property – but the anecdote carried weight as a credible act of personal piety with Plutarch (*Life of Cicero* 31.6) and Cassius Dio (45.17.2–3) more than two hundred years later, and it was taken seriously in Cicero's day. Writing to Q. Cornificius, then governor of Africa, several years later, during the final year of his life (43 BCE), Cicero reports that he had pleaded his case successfully "on Minerva's Day" (the festival of the Quinquatrus, on 19 March) and "with Minerva not unwilling" (*non invita Minerva*, a proverbial phrase) on the very day the senate had passed a decree to set up again the statue of Minerva the Guardian that he had dedicated on the Capitoline fifteen years previously, which had toppled over in a storm (*Letters to his Friends* 12.25.1). On whose authority or by what right Cicero had dedicated his statue on that original occasion we cannot say, but once re-established formally by decree of the senate on the day of her public celebration, Cicero's Minerva became fully inscribed in the official civic cult. At the same time, she continued to serve him also as a personal guardian of his particular interests; rhetorical play aside, she remained, for Cicero, both a public and a private figure: *Minerva nostra, custos urbis.*

From a formal religious perspective, the physical transfer of the statue and the successful establishment of it in a new context could have occurred only with the tacit approval of the goddess herself, whose will (*voluntas*), imagined as embodied in the physical likeness, was felt to express its consent passively by allowing the transfer of the plastic representation. The same conception of divine presence in the image that enabled Cicero to confirm the correctness of his behavior in relocating his Minerva underlay the public Roman practice of *evocatio*, the "calling out" of the statue of a patron deity of a besieged enemy in order to co-opt the deity's support and good will for Rome.[20] According to the jurist Ulpian, writing at the beginning of the third century, when private persons wished to free a *sacrarium* (a storage place for sacred objects) in their home from the bonds of religion, they would "call forth" (*evocare*) the sacred objects housed within it, just as public magistrates "called forth" the cult statues of foreign deities when inviting them to transfer their support to Rome.[21] If the deity did not accept the invitation, it would not allow its statue to be relocated; the image did not so much represent as instantiate the god. The public *Di Penates* once famously manifested their disapproval of an attempt to move them by refusing to depart from their chosen seat. According to legend, after Aeneas had fled from Troy with his ancestral gods and had established them at his new home in Lavinium, his son Ascanius, upon founding a new community at Alba Longa, tried to transfer the figures to this new settlement, but they twice returned of their own accord to Lavinium and were subsequently recognized as having chosen that seat, with the result that Roman magistrates thereafter made annual pilgrimages there to worship them.[22] That the *Penates* are represented as having chosen to remain at the place where their savior guardian had set them up rather than following his offspring to a new location points not only to the importance of place in Roman familial cult but to the personal, individual nature of its orientation.

Cicero in 58 BCE (and again in recounting it a few years later) had greater interest in the beginning of the story, which provided him an opportunity to invest his gesture with potent symbolic significance.[23] Among the objects that Aeneas rescued from Troy, according to some versions of the story, was a small wooden likeness of the armed Athena that had allegedly fallen from the sky and was cultivated by the Trojans as a talisman of their safety. Transferred to Rome, this image, known as the Palladium, was stored along with the *Penates* and other sacred objects in "Vesta's cupboard" (*penus Vestae*) in the shrine of Vesta off the Roman Forum, where its talismanic quality, likewise transferred to Rome, became the subject of edifying stories of sacrifice by individual Romans who jeopardized personal or familial safety to protect it.[24] A silver coin minted in 47 or 46 BCE, a little more than a decade after Cicero's dramatic rescue of his Minerva from the wreckage of his home, by the (then) uncontested master of Rome shows on the reverse, next to the legend CAESAR, an image of Aeneas fleeing Troy with his father Anchises on his left shoulder and the Palladium (represented as a statuette of Minerva) in his right hand (Figure 14.1). When Cicero wrote to Cornificius a few years later

Figure 14.1 Denarius of Julius Caesar, reverse type showing Aeneas carrying Anchises on his shoulder and the Palladium in his right hand. Photo courtesy of The American Numismatic Society (1937.158.262.rev)

to report the official establishment of his Minerva in the Capitoline precinct of Jupiter, he could recall with satisfaction his own enactment of the demonstration of piety evoked by Caesar's coin and his successful deployment of the political symbolism inherent in its iconic image years before the slain Julian dictator asserted, by presumed genealogical right, exclusive claim to association with the legendary founding of Rome.

Divine Menageries

Cultivated at his house on the Palatine, Cicero's Minerva fit comfortably into the category of gods whose private worship, handed down by the ancestors, was fully acceptable. Transported to the public realm, she was equally at home, as a member of the Capitoline triad, enshrined in the house of Jupiter Optimus Maximus on the Capitol. What eased her transition between the two worlds was the common Greco-Roman cultural practice of representing deities in the same guises in public as in private contexts and in conceiving of them in various fluid combinations and groupings more often than separately and individually. This applied not only to the standard Olympian deities but also to those foreign gods whose legitimacy and place in Roman cult were more ambiguous and whose worship "separately" Cicero condemned. In the public precinct of Isis at Pompeii, for example, which had been rebuilt in the name of a six-year-old boy following an earthquake in 62 CE, the boy's father dedicated a small statue of Bacchus in a niche on the outside of the rear wall of the temple building.[25] Such "visiting gods" – votive dedications to deities in the precincts of others – are attested in public temples already in the Greek archaic period, when not only the Olympian gods but also minor gods and mythical figures such as Silenoi and satyrs are found "visiting" the homes of others in the pantheon.[26] In Greek contexts these votive dedications seem normally to have been set up spontaneously by the dedicants, but in the Roman world, characteristically, permission from a local governing body (normally the senate or town council) was normally required, and explicit acknowledgment of the permission received was regularly recorded.[27]

Partly as a consequence of this procedural restriction, evidence of dedications *in situ* to "visiting" gods in Roman public temples is rare. Instead, the intermingling of deities, both insiders and outsiders, is most evident in private contexts, where no formal strictures limited personal religious expression, most notably in the household shrines that formed the locus of cult in Roman domestic worship.[28] These shrines, conventionally known as *lararia* after one of the two principal sets of household gods, the *Lares familiares*, were situated in various places within the house – most often, in the towns around the Bay of Naples buried by Vesuvius in 79 CE (by far our richest source of evidence), in kitchens, but frequently also in *atria* and the small rooms opening off them (*alae*), peristyles, and gardens, less commonly in vestibules, bedrooms, corridors, and rooms of "representation" such as dining rooms and the *tablinum*, where the head of the household conducted business.[29] At Ostia, where most of the evidence belongs to the third and fourth centuries, the most popular locations were courtyards, peristyles, and (in contrast to in the Campanian towns) rooms for receiving and entertaining.[30]

In this, Ostia seems to be more in line with towns elsewhere in Italy and the Germanic provinces, where dining rooms and corporation halls stand out in the meager testimony.[31]

The shrines normally took the form of wall-niches (the most pervasive type) or small aedicular structures or, in Italy (but not, it seems, elsewhere in the western provinces), of painted representations of the canonical pair of dancing *Lares* flanking a figure of the *Genius* (the guardian spirit) of the head of the household in the act of sacrifice (Figure 14.2a and b). Sometimes in the early imperial period an entire room opening off a peristyle was devoted to the cult of the household gods and ancestors; from the second century, at least, small chapels in or opening off of imperial bedrooms served the same purpose; by the later Empire separate *aediculae* large enough to house full-sized statues (an architectural type

Figure 14.2a Drawing of a painted *lararium* from the so-called "House of Pansa" (VI.6.1, Pompeii), a grand house owned by a local magistrate (*duovir* in 55/56 CE) during the last period of the city (c. 60–79 CE), when the fresco was painted. The *lararium* scene is incorporated into the decorative program of the Fourth Style architectural framing, as if it were part of the ornamental design. From Mazois, *Les ruines de Pompéi*, Tab. 45, 2

Figure 14.2b Painted *lararium* scene from the bakery at VII.12.11 (Pompeii). In the upper register Vesta with cornucopia seated on a throne is flanked by a pair of *lares* pouring wine from wine horns (*rhyta*) held high in one hand into pails (*situlae*) and in the other holding an offering dish over an altar (laden with wheat?); an ass emerges from behind. Below, two snakes (representing the procreative power of the *Genius* of the *paterfamilias*) approach offerings on an altar. Vesta as sacrificant in the role normally played by the *Genius* of the *paterfamilias*, along with the ass and wheat, alludes to the cult of Vesta (guardian of the hearth) and particularly to the Vestalia festival on June 9, when matrons offered bread to asses and bakers holidayed. The image illustrates how standardized scenes of *lares* could be tailored to reflect the special interests of the groups they represented. After Fröhlich, *Lararien- und Fassadenbilder*, Taf. 1 (no. L 91), photographed by A. Foglia

common in ornamental gardens already during the early Empire) were sometimes erected in courtyards and other enclosed areas for communal use (Figure 14.5, below p. 261).[32]

Housed within the niches or in the shrines or rooms were small collections of statuettes representing various deities and sometimes (regularly north of the Alps) other small bronze utensils and commemorative tokens (miniature busts, figural bronzes, and the like). Collectively these mixed assemblages, with or without the *Lares*, constituted the other canonical group of Roman household gods, the *Penates*. *Penates*, or *Di Penates* (the word has no singular form), according to both etymology and usage, were gods of the *penus*, the inner "pantry" of the house, where household provisions and food were stored. At Lavinium, they were represented in two forms, as statues in the form of the Dioscuri twins and as aniconic objects (iron and bronze heralds' staffs and a Trojan clay pot, according to the Greek historian Timaeus). At Rome, they were associated with two locations, a shrine on the Velian hill and the *penus Vestae*, the innermost part of the shrine of Vesta in the Forum, where a collection of sacred objects (*sacra*) was preserved along with the Palladium. The precise relationships among these various public manifestations of the public *Penates* at Lavinium and Rome are complex and obscure. For our purposes it is enough that the Roman tradition placing the aniconical *sacra* together with the Palladium in the shrine of Vesta corresponds sufficiently well to the mixed assemblages of small utensils and statuettes found in Roman household shrines to suggest that the latter constituted, collectively, the domestic *Penates*.[33] Like the *Penates*, the *Lares* after a civic reorganization of the city by Augustus in 7 BCE enjoyed a public as well as a private cult, and like them, the *Lares* were somehow associated with dead ancestors (Figure 14.3). Not surprisingly, the two groups were sometimes confused.[34] Fundamentally, however, these two closely related traditions of Roman household religion remained distinct and independent. One was centered on a uniform conception of the familial household gods – the *Lares* – which were represented iconographically in a remarkably consistent way and in paintings were seldom accompanied by depictions of other gods. The other embraced collectively a stylistically heterogeneous and conceptually diverse assortment of aniconic and iconic objects representing individual deities, demi-gods, and heroes.

Of the two strains, only the mixed assemblages of *Penates* are found outside the Italian peninsula, with the anomalous exception of late Republican Delos, an island with close cultural and economic ties to the Campanian region of Italy, where an early example of the later canonical painted representation of a dancing *lar* is found in a private home.[35] North of the Alps, where any native forms of familial or household religion have left little trace in the material record, concentrated finds of small collections of bronze statuettes of divinities and miscellaneous utensils suggest that a Roman-style cult of the *Penates* flourished in Germany and Gaul throughout the first three centuries CE (Figure 14.4).[36] Unlike in Campania, where the chance eruption of Vesuvius preserved many finds *in situ*, most of the collections of statuettes found in the northern European provinces were discovered in deposits

Figure 14.3 Side of the so-called "Belvedere altar" showing Augustus handing statuettes of the *Lares Augusti* to elected block-captains of Rome charged in 7 BCE with cultivating them in their neighborhoods (Rome, Musei Vaticani, inv. 1115) Courtesy of the Deutsches Archäologisches Institut-Rom DAI neg. 75.1290 Rossa

evidently made during times of trauma (*Angstdepots*). The two groups exhibit certain other differences as well, which remind us that Roman household religion was not a static phenomenon in either time or place.[37]

Two features, however, stand out consistently in both groups: the absence from the *lararia* assemblages found in private contexts of any significant evidence of

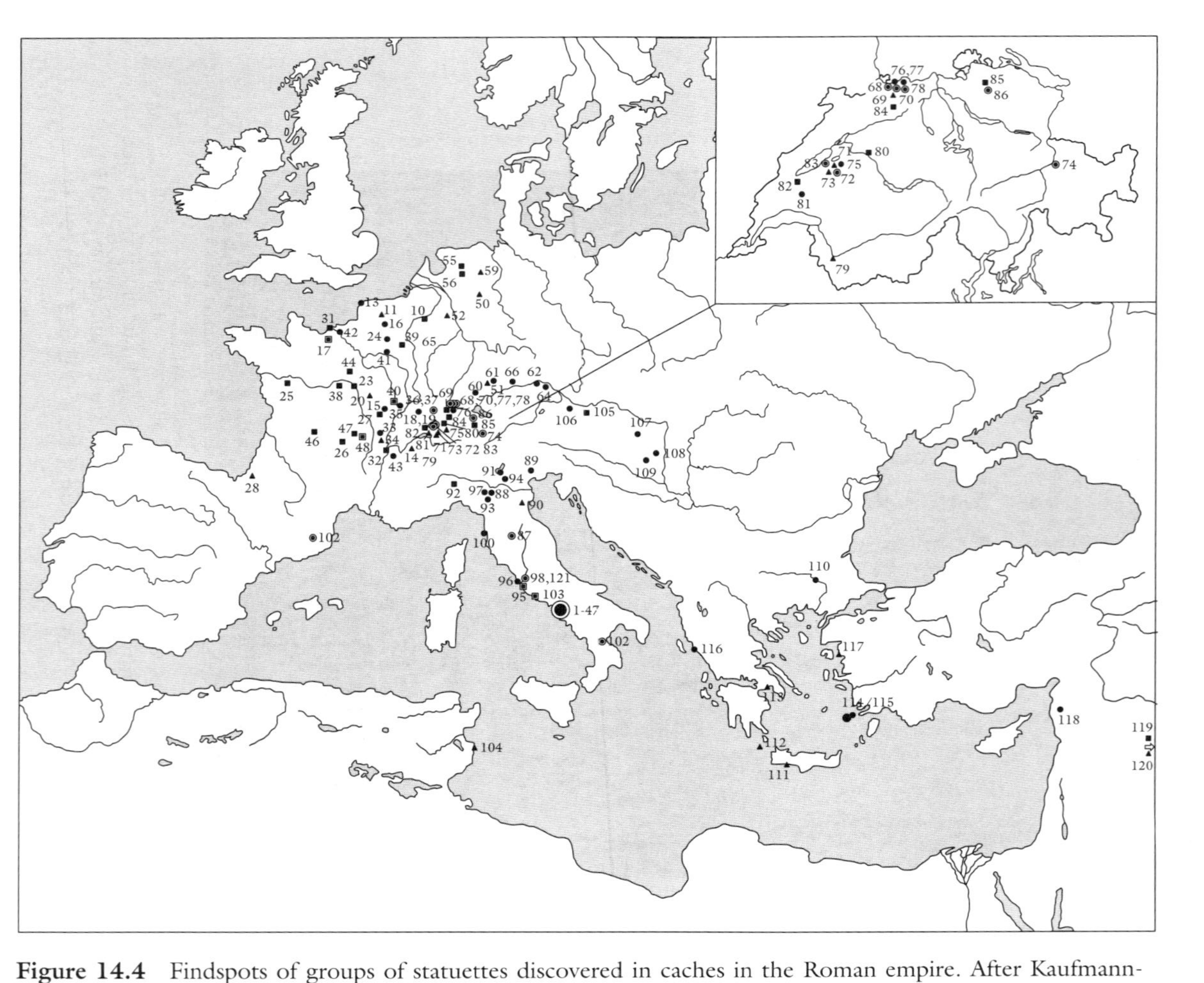

Figure 14.4 Findspots of groups of statuettes discovered in caches in the Roman empire. After Kaufmann-Heinimann, *Götter und Lararien*, p. 207 Abb. 144

votive intentions and the idiosyncratic and eclectic nature of the collections, normally of four to six pieces, which regularly intermingle valuable objects with cheap ones, figurines of a certain scale and workmanship with others of different size and quality, portrait busts with household objects; images of official public deities with those outsiders whose worship "separately" Cicero condemned; and so on. Sometimes the collections include two images of the same divinity; in the northern provinces, statuettes of recognizable Olympian types are sometimes labeled with the names of local deities.[38] All these features suggest the personalized, in some cases individualized character of the collections, in which each object seems to have had intrinsic value, regardless of its representative function: an old and inferior statuette of Mercury was not discarded in place of a new one, for example, because (like the Palladium) each was irreplaceable. We do not know who was responsible for the selections made in these assemblages. The regular and natural assumption that it was the head of the household, perhaps constrained by the inherited choices of earlier heads, is possible but by no means certain. It is in any case often possible to discern, in addition to broad regional trends (such as a relative preponderance of Egyptian deities in Campania or of Mars and Victory in the northern provinces), certain more localized concentrations of interest which seem to reflect the distinctive character of a person or a place.

In the aedicular shrines at Pompeii, for example, along with the *Lares*, we find groupings ranging from a simple pairing of Genius and Venus to more elaborate combinations – some conventional (Mercury, Jupiter, Juno, and Minerva – a Capitoline grouping of which Cicero would have approved), others exotic (Anubis, Isis, Harpocrates, an old man, and a reclining banqueter – probably a deified ancestor or his *genius*), erotic (*Lares*, Venus, Hercules, Priapus, Silenus, and Eros), or eclectic (Jupiter, Minerva, Asculapius, Fortuna, Isis, Harpocrates, and a Bacchant; or a Genius, Jupiter, Isis-Fortuna [two images], Neptune, Helios, and Faunus).[39] In northern Italy and the Alpine provinces, we find a *lararium* deposit with two sets of paired statuettes on individual bases, a Juno and Genius and an Apollo and Sirona (a Gallic deity), Mercury, Amor, Victoria, Fortuna, Luna, and a cornucopia; another comprises Asclepius, Venus, Amor, Priapus, and Epona on horseback; a third includes a Mercury with goat, cock, and tortoise; the foot of a second Mercury; Somnus with mouse; Hercules, and a single Lar (a rarity north of the Alps); and so on.[40] In late antiquity, to judge from both the material and the literary record, the scale of this form of private devotional expression only grew. *Lararia* deposits discovered *in situ* are rare after the early third century, but an elegant *lararium* shrine found intact in the early 1880s in the courtyard of a private house of the late third or early fourth century on the Oppian hill in Rome housed within it, in an apsidal niche at the rear, a nearly life-sized Pentelic marble statue of Isis-Fortuna; a marble statuette and bust of Serapis; a bust of Harpocrates; a "magic" stele of Horus on his crocodiles; statuettes of Zeus, Apollo, Aphrodite, Hecate, and Hercules; and herms of Hercules (two examples) and a Bacchant (Figure 14.5).[41]

When selections of this sort were being made, of a sampling of deities both "approved" and "unapproved" within the terms laid down by Cicero or, beyond

Figure 14.5 Drawing of a *lararium* shrine from the courtyard of a private house on the Esquiline Hill in Rome (c. 300 CE). At the rear of the shrine in an arched niche a statue of Isis-Fortuna (with rudder); to the left (and right, unseen), framed shelving holding portrait busts of ancestors and heroes and statuettes of gods and goddesses. The door to the right of the shrine leads to a stair down to a private Mithraeum. After Visconti, "Del larario," Tav. III

the Italian peninsula, foreign and native, we may assume that the choices were driven by personal preference for or attraction to certain ideas represented by the particular deities selected or by some other talismanic quality embodied in the images themselves, rather than by any formalistic adherence to prescribed norms of practice or belief. This is not a profound observation, but it may help us to locate more accurately than the trivializing caricatures of Tertullian or Jerome where the focus of Roman private devotion lay. In one sense, perhaps, setting up or painting up a pair of *Lares* may have said nothing more than that you believed in the sanctity of house and home – or shop, since "household" shrines are found in many work establishments as well as in houses at both Pompeii and Ostia.[42] But even a token gesture, recognizable as such within the narrow parameters of acceptable private religion, served to demonstrate affirmation of the idea it represented, in the same way that, later, the practice of offering vows for the emperor's safety would prove a litmus test of "Romanness" for imperial authorities hostile to the separatist tendencies of the early Christian community. In a system that privileged orthopraxy over orthodoxy, what you did was more important than what you believed. Observing the correct mode of domestic worship mattered more than which deities or figures you chose, and in practice the traditional architectural setting for the formal domestic cult of the *Lares* provided an increasingly attractive locus for the manifestation and enactment of personal devotion to a variety of alternative, and potentially subversive, deities (or ideas) in a legitimizing context. A bronze statuette in itself was a neutral object, capable of serving a votive or cultic or even a purely ornamental purpose, depending upon its setting. Placing an otherwise commonplace image in a *lararium* invested it with sacrality in a way that placing it in a garden or even, without public authorization to do so, in a temple precinct did not, to the extent that one would feel the need formally to "evoke" it from its setting if it were to be moved. Placing an object in a *lararium*, in other words, was itself an act of domestic worship.

Not every object or deity was considered equally appropriate in a *lararium*, evidently. In the Germanic provinces, the collections of votive statuettes found in sacred hordes from public temples exhibit greater thematic variety and include a greater admixture of native and Roman gods than do the *lararium* deposits. At Pompeii, for reasons that remain obscure, although Bacchus figures prominently in statue dedications in public precincts (such as that of Isis) and is among the deities most commonly depicted in *lararia* (and other) wall paintings, he appears only once among the *lararia* assemblages, in an early terracotta group dating from the first century BCE.[43] Equally clearly, the conventions of display within the private space of the *lararia* shrines were more fluid and experimental than they were in the public realm, and the lines of acceptability were more readily blurred. With time, heroized mortals came to join the divine assemblages in the household shrines, just as divinized emperors joined the state gods in public worship. The imperial biographer Suetonius once obtained a bronze statuette of Augustus as a boy inscribed in iron letters with his boyhood nickname "Thurinus," which he gave to the emperor Hadrian, who cultivated it among the *Lares* in his private chamber (*in cubiculo*). Similar stories aggregated around other emperors, and within the paradigmatic conventions of imperial biography (the emperor's behavior set an *exemplum*; the biographer codified it), became virtually a topos for oblique comment on the parameters of acceptable private belief.[44]

A striking example – fictitious perhaps (the source is notoriously unreliable) but not for that reason less valuable as an indicator of how these shrines could be read as an index of personal spirituality – features the controversial emperor Severus Alexander (222–35 CE). According to his biography in the *Historia Augusta*, on the mornings when he had not slept with his wife on the preceding night, Alexander used to worship (*rem divinam faciebat*) in his *lararium*, in which he kept, along with images of his ancestors, statues of Alexander the Great, a selection of "only the best" deified emperors, certain "more holy" souls (*animae sanctiores*), including the first-century neo-Pythagorean holy man, Apollonius of Tyana, and (on the supposed authority of a contemporary writer), statuettes of Christ, Abraham, Orpheus, and "others of this sort" (Scriptores Historiae Augustae, *Severus Alexander* 29.2).[45] The reference to "more holy souls" (*animae sanctiores*) points to the Christian world of post-Constantinian Rome and the pseudo-biographer's own day, probably the late fourth or early fifth century, but the ecumenical eclecticism of the imaginary *lararium* collection was characteristic of every period.[46] Whatever its plausibility, the mixture of names conjured up by the biographer evokes vividly a particular mentality, characteristic of the times and yet individualized, reflecting both the turbulent ideological winds of late antiquity and the singular preoccupations of a complex man. More than that, the seemingly superfluous detail regarding the circumstances of Alexander's observances at his shrine (only on mornings when he was free of the pollution of sex) suggests that the commitment to this form of worship was meant to be serious, not casual.[47] Whether or not the picture it paints is true, the biographer's decision to breathe spiritual life into it through the device of a collection of cult images housed in a domestic *lararium* lends verisimilitude to the portrait.

Already by the middle of the first century, as the material evidence from Pompeii indicates, domestic shrines housing pairs of *Lares* along with mixed menageries of *Penates* had begun to serve as representational melting pots in which a richly diverse stew of religious belief and practices simmered for more than two centuries before boiling over into a single (and public) ecumenical cult. Along with funerary art, they provide the best window we have into the strong undercurrent of personal devotion that ultimately survived the death blow inflicted to the public state religion by the emperor Theodosius's universal ban on sacrifice in 392 CE. The development of the *lararia* assemblages of the earlier Empire parallels that of the public religion in a general way, but the characteristics of individuality and spiritual eclecticism inherent in them point to a level of personal engagement not found in the public cult; this ultimately provided the key to their longevity and proved essential to their survival.

The Mother of the *Lares*

What then, of the *Lares*? If the *Penates* were fluid and open, the *Lares*, iconographically uniform and in painted depictions seldom accompanied by other deities, were rigid and closed. From Cicero's repeated insistence, not only in private letters and philosophical tracts but in legal argument before the pontiffs, that the seat of his household gods lay in the house on the Palatine he had purchased from the patrician aristocrat Crassus six years before he was banished, we learn that the *Lares*, like the *Penates*, though closely tied to location, were portable. You could move them from one house to another. Unlike the *Penates*, however, which were normally cultivated at a single location within the house, *lararia* might be painted up in more than one location within a single house, suggesting a multiplicity of *foci* of worship. The implication seems to be that *Lares* were more closely tied to the concept of "home" than to "house" and more closely associated with the idea of community than with place. When the jurists needed to define where a man who owned several houses kept his home, they decided it should be "where [he] established his *lar* for marriage" (Ulpian, in *Digest* 25.3.1.2). Thus, when new owners moved into houses at Pompeii, they regularly whitewashed over existing painted *lararia* and had new depictions – often identical in composition to those they replaced – painted over the old ones, which were evidently imagined as having departed with the former owners: it was not the image that changed but the familial group it represented.[48]

Accordingly, when we find, as we often do at the more elegant houses at Pompeii, an architectural *lararium* shrine set up in the public rooms of representation and another more humble *lararium* painted up in the service quarters (always, it seems, painted, never built, and never with *Penates*), we may recognize the physical manifestations of precisely that distinction between our concept of "family" and the Roman *familia* with which we began. The latter, comprising both slaves and kin, is conventionally regarded as sharing household worship together, in one happy group. What the Pompeian evidence suggests instead is a functional division between the ideologically comforting – and legally pragmatic – concept of the unified household and the more socially plausible reality of multiple "households" within the house.[49] Since any slave *familia* of more than a few members could potentially have comprised several different nuclear units, "household" here must be recognized as distinct from "family" not only in being more narrow (slaves but not kin) but in being more broad (including multiple slave "families").[50] What evidently mattered in the articulation of domestic space was the social differentiation of the freeborn kin, with their household gods related somehow to the spirits of ancestors, and the slave household, considered collectively but in fact comprising (at least potentially) elements of multiple slave "families," with its separate but parallel set of household deities.

The question of who was responsible for the secondary depictions of *Lares* remains open, but in some cases, at least, where a painted *lararium* is incorporated into the decorative program of a newly painted wall, it is reasonable to assume that it was the home (and slave) owner rather than any member of the slave family itself who commissioned the work and thus established the location (see Figure 14.2b).[51] Indeed, the more closely one looks at our upper-class literary authorities, the more one begins to notice an insistence on the commonality, but not the conjunction, of the worship of the *Lares* among slave and free "families" within the Roman house. Nor was religious authority distributed equally. According to the elder Cato's influential manual on farming, our oldest complete work of Latin prose, the bailiff's wife must not engage in worship without the orders of the master or mistress; but on the cardinal days of the Roman month, it is she, rather than the bailiff, who must hang a garland over the hearth and pray to the *Lar* of the household (*lar familiaris*) (*De Agricultura* 143.1–2).[52] When Cicero in his treatise on *Laws* prescribes that the worship of the *Lares* "handed down by our ancestors both to masters and to slaves" not be rejected, he does not refer to masters and slaves together but to each separately: *cum dominis tum famulis*.[53] Columella, advising villa owners to accustom their agricultural slaves to take meals "around the household hearth and the master's *Lar*," envisions the master dining frugally in the sight of his slaves (*familia*) but not together with them and only occasionally on holidays bestowing on the most worthy of them the honor of commensality (*Res Rusticae* 11.1.19).

Festus above all is helpful in explaining why woolen balls and effigies were hung at crossroads shrines during the festival of the *Compitalia* in late December or early January: "Because that festival day was believed to belong to the divine ancestors, whom they call *Lares*, on the crossroads shrines as many balls were hung up as there were heads of slaves, and as many statuettes as there were free persons, so that they would spare the living and be content with these balls and likenesses."[54] In explaining the particularities of the ritual, Festus glosses over the question how slaves, who legally and socially had no recognized fathers (slaves were "sons of the soil," *terrae filii*), related to the ancestors. The assumption normally has been, in accordance with the romanticized vision of our late Republican and Augustan literary authorities, that slaves "shared" the ancestors of their masters and that masters took care to include their slaves (at least their household slaves) in their own ancestral rites. Again, the Pompeian evidence suggests otherwise. There, where houses of sufficient size to reveal purpose-built slave quarters are found, and even in many houses lacking segregated quarters for domestic staff, separate, independent household shrines suggest a separate, parallel track of domestic worship among slave and freeborn members of the household. Epigraphy supports this picture of a separate household cult administered by members of an urban slave *familia* and further reveals how multiple slave "families" within a single household could be accommodated by a corporate structure similar to that found in private associations that enabled selected representatives (either elected or appointed) to act on behalf of the group. Thus we find, at Rome and elsewhere throughout the Italian peninsula, household stewards (*dispensatores*) and officers of domestic *collegia* (*magistri*) making donations "to the *Lares* and household" (*Laribus et familiae*) or "to the *Lares* of the household" (*Laribus familiaribus*) on behalf of themselves or their fellow slaves.[55] Beyond corporate dedications to collective deities, individual slaves worshiped personal gods, just as free members of the household did, but expressions of individual identity were systematically discouraged by the institution of slavery, and slaves were denied formal *Penates*: indeed, it was the fear of slaves' "foreign rites" of domestic worship that drove the verdict of severity imposed on the household of the City Prefect in the time of Nero.[56]

Who, then, were the slaves' divine ancestors, their *Lares*? Varro seems to provide an answer in explaining the public celebration of the *Larentalia* on December 23, at the end of the week-long *Saturnalia* festival, when slaves temporarily played the part of free men and, in certain carefully circumscribed social rituals (notably banqueting), behaved as their masters' equals.[57] "This sacrifice [of the *Larentalia*] is made on the Velabrum [a low saddle of land between the Roman Forum and the Cattle Market] at the tomb of Acca Larentia, because near there the priests make sacrifice to the divine spirits of deceased slaves (*diis Manibus servilibus*)" (Varro, *De Lingua Latina* 6.24). Acca Larentia, according to the most authoritative version of the legend, was the nurse of Romulus and thus surrogate mother to the original "son of the soil" washed up in a basket on the banks of the Tiber; when one of Acca's twelve sons died, Romulus offered himself as a surrogate, calling himself and her other sons "Arval Brethren" and thus founding the priestly college revived by Augustus that flourished until well into the third century. In the annual ritual performed by the imperial Arval Brethren at their sanctuary in the Grove of the Dea Dia outside Rome, the priests enacted the same form of sacrifice to deceased ancestors (*parentatio*) to the Mother of the *Lares* as was performed at Acca's tomb during the *Larentalia*, and in the standard sequence of offerings recorded in the Brothers' rites, the *Lares* themselves invariably appear between the "Gods of the Slave Household" (*Dis Famulis*) and the Mother of the *Lares*.[58]

Identification of Acca Larentia with the Mother of the *Lares* seems natural and plausible but is not strictly needed in order to recognize in Varro's aetiology of the *Larentalia* rite a transparent effort to create for the slave population of Rome a public festival honoring their departed forebears collectively at the end of their days of rest, just as the public festival of the *Carisitia* in honor of dead kin immediately followed the collective remembrance of Roman ancestors celebrated by families at their gravesites during the days of the *Parentalia* festival in February.[59] Resistance to the idea that slaves' ancestors could have received formal public commemoration, even collectively, ran strong among nineteenth-century commentators, who sought refuge in presumed textual corruption.[60] The passage is indeed vexed, but no more so than many passages in the battered remnants of Varro's treatise and not at all in the three crucial words, *diis Manibus servilibus*, where the paradosis is clear. Rather than trying to explain away the clear implications of the text, we should perhaps recall the strain of egalitarian ideology that ran through the Roman foundation myth and was particularly associated with Romulus, who opened his asylum to one and all, "without discriminating whether a man were slave or free" and was said thereby to have laid the foundations of Rome's greatness (Livy 1.8.6). More generally we should take more seriously the role of private religion, particularly of the slave household, in shaping public cult and recognize in the *Larentalia* a religious institution of the state designed to sustain the ideology of the *lararia* painted up in Pompeian homes to represent the ancestral hearths of slave *familiae* comprising multiple slave "families" within the household.

Perhaps the most characteristic feature of Roman family and household religion, in the end, is neither its mutual tracking with public cult nor its conceptual focus on ancestors and the hearth, but rather its bipartite nature, which distinguished two related but distinct categories of domestic gods, one open, individualized, and restricted to the biological family, the other standardized, collectively oriented, and centered on the slave household. In ancient Rome "household" religion and "family" religion, like the conditions of slave and free generally, were separate and interdependent, but not equal categories. That the place of personal belief in

Roman domestic worship ended formally with the *Penates* and the freeborn family is merely characteristic of the strategically dehumanizing way that the Roman institution of slavery denied familial ties to the enslaved and channeled any impulses toward individual expression among the slave population into the approved outlets of an archetypal slave ancestor and the immediate head of the household.

Notes

1 For the Roman *familia* and the concept of household, see Richard P. Saller, *Patriarchy, Property, and Death in the Roman Family* (Cambridge: Cambridge University Press, 1994), pp. 74–101. Following the conference at Brown, this essay was improved by stimulating oral discussion at a colloquium on "Epigraphic Texts and Archaeological Contexts in Rome, Italy, and the Western Provinces" at the annual meetings of the American Philological Association and Archaeological Institute of America in Montreal in 2006, and by discerning criticism of a subsequent written draft by Andreas Bendlin, Carlos Galvao Sobrinho, and Zehavi Hussar.

2 The reality was often quite different: when the City Prefect was murdered at home in Rome by one of his slaves in 61 CE, the senate upheld an old custom of executing all the slaves living under the same roof as a master killed by one of them by putting to death four hundred members of his urban household. A proposal that those of his ex-slaves who had lived under the same roof also be deported from Italy did not carry (Tacitus, *Annals* 14.42–5), but in the winning argument for severity put into the mouth of a leading senatorial jurist by the historian Tacitus, a revealing contrast is drawn between former times, when slaves were born on the same estates and in the same houses as their masters, and the current day, when "we have in our households (*in familiis*) entire nations whose rites are different and rituals foreign or nonexistent" (*Annals* 14.44.3; see below, n. 11). Even allowing for rhetorical exaggeration, the nature of whatever is meant by "religion of the household" clearly must accommodate not only multiple religions within the household but change over time.

3 See Saller, *Patriarchy, Property, and Death*, pp. 78–80.

4 For a concise analysis, see Andreas Bendlin, "Looking Beyond the Civic Compromise: Religious Pluralism in Late Republican Rome," in *Religion in Archaic and Republican Rome and Italy: Evidence and Experience*, ed. Edward Bispham and Christopher Smith (Edinburgh: Edinburgh University Press, 2000), pp. 115–25, esp. p. 121.

5 Ittai Gradel, *Emperor Worship and Roman Religion* (Oxford: Clarendon Press, 2002), pp. 8–13.

6 Pompeius Festus, *De Verborum Significatu*, ed. Wallace M. Lindsay (Stuttgart: B. G. Teubner, 1913), p. 284, s.v. *Publica sacra*. Festus's second category of *publica sacra* refers to festivals associated with the topography of Rome, a characteristic of Roman state religion; cf. Georg Wissowa, *Religion und Kultus der Römer*, 2nd edn. (Munich: C. H. Beck, 1912), p. 399 n. 1. The Roman *gens* was properly constituted of those freeborn persons of free ancestry who shared the same family name (*nomen gentilicium*) and who had not suffered a reduction in civil status (*capitis demunitio*) (Cicero, *Topica* 29). Practically, however, the *gens* embraced all those who descended legitimately from a common male ancestor through the male line (agnates). The *gens* rapidly lost importance after Augustus and by the middle of the second century CE had fallen into obscur-

ity (Gaius, *Institutions* 3.17): see Christopher J. Smith, *The Roman Clan* (Cambridge: Cambridge University Press, 2006), pp. 15–64.

7 Varro, in Nonius Marcellus, *De compendiosa doctrina*, ed. Wallace M. Lindsay (Lepizig: B. G. Teubner, 1903), p. 510. Contrast Cato, *De Agri Cultura* 143.1, on the representative nature of domestic worship: "let it be known that the master performs the household rites for the entire household."

8 Like all basic Roman cultural practices, gentilicial rites were given a legendary origin, in the story of Hercules awarding responsibility for an annual sacrifice in his honor at the Great Altar to two clans, the Potitii and the Pinarii (Livy 1.7.12–14). Historically, distinctive cult practices are known for the Nautii, the Claudii, the Julii, the Horatii, and famously, the Fabii, whose exemplary piety during the Gallic sack of the city around 390 BCE in conducting a gentilicial sacrifice on the Quirinal in the face of enemy hostility earned the admiration of later historians (Livy 5.46.2–3): see further Smith, *Roman Clan*, pp. 44–50.

9 The elaborate framework of Latin kinship terminology that supports our picture of Roman familial life and underlies the structural approach to kinship that seems so well suited to analyzing it reflects a narrowly juridical perspective adopted specifically for use in private law but demonstrably at odds with the way families were actually constituted and behaved: See Richard P. Saller, "Roman Kinship: Structure and Sentiment," in *The Roman Family in Italy: Status, Sentiment, Space*, ed. Beryl Rawson and Paul Weaver (Oxford: Clarendon Press, 1997), pp. 7–34.

10 Ostentatious abstention from luxury was a common form: thus the women of the Atilii Serrani avoided linen, the Cornelii Cethegi tunics, the Quinctii gold, the Aelii gold and silver: see Smith, *Roman Clan*, p. 49, for references.

11 See further Andrew R. Dyck, *A Commentary on Cicero, De Legibus* (Ann Arbor: University of Michigan Press, 2004), p. 293. For the specific set of deities that received "foreign rites" (*peregrina sacra*), see Wissowa, *Religion und Kultus*, pp. 89, 348–79, 448. Other alien cults popular in the private sphere, though never publicly accepted, were widely practiced; that of Silvanus, for example, flourished among households of slaves and ex-slaves: see Peter F. Dorcey, *The Cult of Silvanus: A Study in Roman Folk Religion* (Leiden and New York: E. J. Brill, 1992), pp. 105–34.

12 According to Theodor Mommsen, for example, "the Latin religion sank into an incredible insipidity and dullness, and early became shrivelled into an anxious and dreary round of ceremonies": *The History of Rome*, tr. William Purdie Dickson (London: Bentley, 1868) 1: 222. For domestic worship, see Robert Maxwell Ogilvie, *The Romans and their Gods in the Age of Augustus* (New York: Norton, 1970 [c. 1969]), p. 39.

13 Mary Beard, in a paper delivered orally at the conference, argued that Roman household cult as we see it is a product more of nostalgia than of genuine devotion. For a critique of the approach underlying such distinctions, see Bendlin, "Looking Beyond the Civic Compromise," pp. 120–5.

14 A law code promulgated by the emperor Theodosius in 392 CE explicitly prohibited private veneration of the *Lares*, *Penates*, and the *genius* (of the head of the household): *Codex Theodosianus* 16.10.12. For earlier Christian polemic against traditional domestic worship, see, e.g., Tertullian, *Apology*, 13.4; Lactantius, *Divine Institutes*, 2.24.12–13; Jerome, *Against Isiah*, 16.57.7.

15 In his speech *On his house* delivered before the Roman pontiffs at the end of September, 57 BCE, Cicero taxed Clodius with similar language: "Did that darling Liberty of yours drive out my household gods (*deos penates*) and familial *Lares* so that she might establish

herself, as it were, in a captive location?" (*De Domo sua* 108). For the dating of *On Laws* to the late 50s BCE, see Dyck, *Commentary*, pp. 5–7.

16 For details of the affair, see Walter Allen, Jr, "Cicero's House and *Libertas*," *Transactions of the American Philological Association* 75 (1944): 1–9; and Dyck, *Commentary*, pp. 364–67, with further bibliography. The analysis of the episode according to a theory of ritual representation by Anders Lisdorf, "The Conflict Over Cicero's House: An Analysis of the Ritual Element in Cicero's *De Domo Sua*," (*Numen* 52 [2005]: 445–64) sheds little light. For the practice of destroying the houses of public enemies as a form of *damnatio memoriae*, see John Bodel, "Monumental Villas and Villa Monuments," *Journal of Roman Archaeology* 10 (1997): 7–11. Note also Robert G. Nisbet, *M. Tulli Ciceronis, De Domo Sua* (Oxford: Oxford University Press, 1939), pp. 206–9 and 209–12, on the distinction between *dedicatio* and *consecratio*. Strictly *dedicatio* was the voluntary renunciation of ownership or control in favor of a god or gods (the offer), whereas *consecratio* was the delivery of the surrendered property to the divinity (the acceptance), but the concepts were complementary, and in practice the former often implied the latter. Formal *consecratio* could only be undertaken by a public body or its representatives; private individuals had no ability to consecrate: Marcianus, in *Digest* 1.8.6.3.

17 The inscribed dedication is reported (in Greek) by Plutarch, *Life of Cicero* 31.6; cf. Cassius Dio 45.17.2–3. In his speech *On his house*, Cicero invokes Minerva of the Capitoline triad as "guardian of the city, faithful fosterer of my plans, witness of my labors" (*De Domo Sua* 144). For the probable statue-type of Cicero's image, see Henner von Hesberg, "Minerva Custos Urbis – zum Bildschmuck der Porta Romana in Ostia," in *Imperium Romanum. Studien zu Geschichte und Rezeption. Festschrift für Karl Christ zum 75. Geburtstag* (Stuttgart: Franz Steiner, 1998), pp. 370–8.

18 See Allen, "Cicero's House" and Beverly Berg, "Cicero's Palatine House and Clodius' Shrine of Liberty: Alternative Emblems of the Republic in Cicero's *De Domo Sua*," in *Studies in Latin Literature and Roman History*, vol. 8, ed. Carl Deroux (Brussels: Latomus, 1997), pp. 122–43.

19 In his speech *On his consulship*, Cicero seems to have described Minerva as his teacher in the arts (*De Consulatu suo* 1): see Quintilian, *Institutio Oratoria* 11.1.24 with Stephen J. Harrison, "Cicero's 'De Temporibus suis': the Evidence Reconsidered," *Hermes* 118 (1990): 460–2. The satirist Juvenal imagined himself offering incense to his paternal *Lares* and appeasing "his own Jupiter" (*nostrum Iovem*) at home amidst little wax images bedecked with wreaths (12.87–90); see further below, pp. 255–8 on *Penates* and *Lares*.

20 For *evocatio*, see Wissowa, *Religion und Kultus*, pp. 43–50 and A. Blomart, "Die *evocatio* und der Transfer fremder Götter von der Peripherie nach Rom," in *Römische Reichsreligion und Provinzialreligion*, ed. Hubert Cancik and Jörg Rüpke (Tübingen: Mohr Siebeck, 1997), pp. 99–111.

21 Ulpian in *Digest* 1.8.9.2, "A *sacrarium* is a place in which sacred objects are deposited. This can be even in a private building, and those who wish to free that place from *religio* customarily call forth the sacred objects from there."

22 See Valerius Maximus, *Facta et Dicta Memorabilia* 1.8.7 and Dionysius of Halicarnassus, *Roman Antiquities* 1.67, noting that Greek authors rendered "*Penates*" with Greek terms meaning gods of the race, of the family, of the house and property, of the inner house, and of the front court (1.67.3). At Rome, the *Penates* received public

cult in a shrine on the Velian hill and had a "home" in the House of the Vestal Virgins off the Roman Forum: see Annie Doubourdieu, *Les origines et le développement du culte des Pénates à Rome* (Rome: École française de Rome, 1989), pp. 381–451 (Velia), pp. 453–69 (House of the Vestals). For their worship at Lavinium, ibid., pp. 155–80; Yan Thomas, "L'Institution de l'origine: sacra principiorum populi romani," in *Tracés de fondation*, ed. Marcel Detienne (Louvain: Peeters, 1990), pp. 143–70; Clifford Ando, "A Religion for the Empire," in *Roman Religion*, ed. Clifford Ando (Edinburgh: Edinburgh University Press, 2003), pp. 229–34; and below, n. 33.

23 So aptly Allen, "Cicero's House," 8: "Cicero was not the man to be outdone in a contest of phrases and symbols."

24 See, e.g., Ovid, *Fasti* 6.420–54 and Dionysius of Halicarnassus, *Roman Antiquities* 2.66.3–5: the consul L. Caecilius Metellus was blinded by beholding the Palladium directly when rescuing it from a fire in the shrine of Vesta in 241 BCE; Livy 5.40.7–10: when Gauls were sacking the city in 390 BCE, an anonymous plebeian made his wife and family vacate a wagon in order to convey the sacred objects to safety.

25 For the temple and its decorative program, see Hartmut Döhl, "La scultura," in *Pompei 79*, ed. Fausto Zevi (Naples: Gaetano Macchiaeroli, 1984), pp. 182–5. For the rebuilding inscription, see *Corpus Inscriptionum Latinarum* 10.846 [= *Inscriptiones Latinae Selectae* 6367]; further Vincent Tran Tam Tinh, *Essai sur le culte d'Isis à Pompei* (Paris: E De Boccard, 1964), pp. 30–41; Paavo Castrén, *Ordo Populusque Pompeianus. Polity and Society in Roman Pompeii*, 2nd edn. (Rome: Institutum Romanum Finlandiae, 1983), pp. 207–9 on the family (Popidii), rightly dismissing Tran Tam Tinh's arguments against the father's presumed servile origin; and below, n. 43, on the private worship of Bacchus/Dionysius at Pompeii.

26 See Brita Alroth, "Visiting Gods," in *Anathema. Regime delle offerte e vita dei santuari nel Mediterraneo antico*, ed. G. Bartoloni, G. Colonna, and C. Grottanelli (Scienze dell'antichità. Storia, archeologia, antropologia 3–4, 1989–1990) (Rome: Università degli studi di Roma "La Sapienza," 1991), pp. 301–10.

27 At Pompeii, places for private persons to dedicate votive statues within the precinct of Isis were granted by decree of the local senate (*Corpus Inscriptionum Latinarum* 10.849). For the Roman tendency both to require and to announce religious permission, see Arthur Darby Nock, "A Feature of Roman Religion," *Harvard Theological Review* 32 (1939): 83–96.

28 Evidence of any sort for the placement of statuettes and other votive dedications within temple precincts in Italy and the western provinces is rare: see Annemarie Kaufmann-Heinimann, *Götter und Lararien aus Augusta Raurica: Herstellung, Fundzusammenhänge und sakrale Funktion figürlicher Bronzen in einer römischen Stadt* (Augst: Römerstadt Augusta Raurica, 1998), pp. 199–200.

29 The term *lararium* is first attested in the third century in the dedication of a statue in a *lara[rium]* during the reign of the emperor Maximinus (235–8 CE: *Corpus Inscriptionum Latinarum* 9.2125), and in the fourth century, when it was used to describe the miniature temple shrines found in well-to-do houses of the period: see Scriptores Historiae Augustae, *Marcus Aurelius* 3.5; *Severus Alexander* 29.2, 31.5 and below, Figure 14.5). Classical authors refer to "shrines" (*aediculae* or *aedes*) and "seats" (*sedes*) of the *Lares*: see Federica Giacobello, "Lararium (mondo romano)," in *Thesaurus Cultus et Rituum Antiquorum*, vol. 4 (Los Angeles: J. Paul Getty Museum, 2005), pp. 262–4, and, for the Vesuvian towns, Thomas Fröhlich, *Lararien- und Fassadenbilder*

in den Vesuvstädten: Untersuchungen zur "volkstümlichen" pompejanischen Malerei (Mainz: von Zabern, 1991), pp. 28–9, 38; and Pedar W. Foss, "Watchful *Lares*: Roman Household Organization and the Rituals of Cooking and Eating," in *Domestic Space in the Roman World: Pompeii and Beyond*, ed. Ray Laurence and Andrew Wallace-Hadrill (Portsmouth: Journal of Roman Archaeology, 1997), pp. 197–218, who emphasizes the common association of *Lares* with the preparation of food.

30 See Jan Theo Bakker, *Living and Working with the Gods: Studies of Evidence for Private Religion and its Material Environment in the City of Ostia (100–500 AD)* (Amsterdam: J. C. Gieben, 1994), pp. 32–9 (pp. 39–41 on the Campanian finds).

31 See Kaufmann-Heinimann, *Götter und Lararien*, p. 187, with references to evidence for *lararia* in dining rooms at Rome, Vallon, and, probably, Arezzo; in the meeting halls of private associations at Avenches, Homburg-Schwarzenacker, and Chur; and near the kitchen in Vilauba.

32 For more detailed descriptions of the basic types, see George K. Boyce, *Corpus of the Lararia of Pompeii* (Rome: American Academy in Rome, 1937), pp. 10–18; David G. Orr, "Roman Domestic Religion: The Evidence of the Household Shrines," in *Aufstieg und Niedergang der römischen Welt* 2.16.2 (Berlin: De Gruyter, 1978), pp. 84–94, 128–34; Bakker, *Living and Working*, pp. 8–9. For the standard painted representation of the *Lares* and accompanying figures, see Fröhlich, *Lararien- und Fassadenbilder*, pp. 111–29. For representations of the *genius*, Hanne Hänlein Schäfer, "Die Ikonographie des *Genius Augusti* im Kompital- und Hauskult der frühen Kaiserzeit," in *Subject and Ruler: The Cult of the Ruling Power in Classical Antiquity*, ed. Alastair Small (Ann Arbor: Journal of Roman Archaeology, 1996), pp. 73–98 and Hille Kunckel, *Der römische Genius* (Heidelberg: F. H. Kerle Verlag, 1974), pp. 29–33, 42–3, 53–4. For *lararia* in imperial bedrooms (*in cubiculo*), see below n. 44; for the *lararium* museum of the Volusii Saturnini in a room centrally located off the peristyle of their villa at Lucus Feroniae outside Rome, see Bodel, "Monumental Villas," pp. 26–32.

33 Some scholars believe that the *Penates* included the *Lares*, others that they did not. Also uncertain is whether or not the public *Penates* cultivated on the Velian hill in Rome are to be identified, on the basis of a single ambiguous witness (Tacitus, *Annals* 15.41), with the aniconical *sacra* preserved in the shrine of Vesta off the Forum: see Doubourdieu, *Pénates*, pp. 39–44 and Domenico Palombi, "Penates, *aedes*," in *Lexicon Topographicum Urbis Romae IV. P-S*, ed. Eva M. Steinby (Rome: Quasar, 1999), pp. 75–8. For the etymology and meaning of *Penates*, which changed sometime before the first century BCE from an original sense of "gods of the *penus*" to any guardian gods of the house and its occupants, see Georges Dumézil, *Archaic Roman Religion* (Baltimore: Johns Hopkins University Press, 1996), pp. 353–5; Doubourdieu, *Pénates*, pp. 13–120; and above, n. 22.

34 In 7 BCE Augustus transformed the civic cult of the *Lares Compitales* celebrated at neighborhood shrines by substituting for the traditional cult images statuettes of *Lares* associated with his own name (*Augusti*), which he distributed in pairs to newly appointed block-captains: see Figure 14.3 and John Bert Lott, *The Neighborhoods of Augustan Rome* (Cambridge: Cambridge University Press, 2004), pp. 103–6. For the confusion of *Penates* and *Lares*, see G. Piccaluga, "*Penates* e *Lares*," *Studi e Materiali di Storia delle Religioni* 32 (1961): 81–97.

35 U. Bezerra de Meneses and H. Sarian, "Nouvelle peintures liturgiques de Délos," in *Études Déliennes* (Paris: De Boccard, 1973), pp. 93–7.

36 Some one hundred *lararia* assemblages have been discovered throughout the Roman empire, but the evidence is heavily weighted in two locations: central western Italy (principally the Vesuvian cities of Campania) and the Gaulish and Germanic provinces; of the finds, 41 come from Campania, 13 from elsewhere in Italy, 36 from Gaul and Germany, and only 10 from the rest of the empire. That most of the statuettes found in the northern provinces were manufactured in the first century but buried only later in the later second and third centuries suggests that the objects were cultivated for some time before being deposited: see Kaufmann-Heinimann, *Götter und Lararien*, pp. 150–1 Abb. 108.

37 Both terracotta and bronze figurines modeled on Roman prototypes are found in *lararia* north of the Alps, for example, but rarely in the same assemblages, as they regularly are in Campania: Kaufmann-Heinimann, *Götter und Lararien*, p. 159.

38 See Kaufmann-Heinimann, *Götter und Lararien*, p. 201 (objects with votive dedications), p. 194 (renamed deities), with references. From Campania note *Corpus Inscriptionum Latinarum* 4.8426: an appeal to the "holy *Lares*" (*Lares sanctos rogo te ut* [—]) written in carbon on a plaster wall at a crossroads *lararium* at Pompeii next to an altar with remains of a sacrificed chicken found on it, and *L'Année épigraphique* 1977, 219 = 1985, 285, a graffito found near a painted *lararium* in the House of Iulius Polybius (Fröhlich, *Lararien- und Fassadenbilder*, 298 no. L 109) declaring a vow made jointly "at the Lares" by a slave and a free man. Otherwise votive dedications are largely absent from domestic *lararia*.

39 See Fröhlich, *Lararien- und Fassadenbilder*, p. 31 n. 142, with references.

40 See Kaufmann-Heinimann, *Götter und Lararien*, pp. 255–6, GF35 (Malain); 260 GF41 (Marne); 283 GF78 (Kaiseraugst); further the useful tables on pp. 315–18, which indicate at a glance the distribution of all statue types found in the individual assemblages surveyed.

41 See Carlo L. Visconti, "Del larario e del mitrèo scoperti nell'Esquilino presso la chiesa di S. Martino ai Monti," *Bullettino della Commissione Archeologica Comunale di Roma* 13 (1885): 27–36 and, for the sculptural program, S. Ensoli Vittozzi, "Le sculture del 'larario' di S. Martino ai Monti. Un contesto recuperato," *Bullettino della Commissione Archeologica Comunale di Roma* 95 (1993): 221–43. Another similar private *lararium* of the third and fourth centuries has been identified at a house near the start of the Via Latina in Rome as that of the aristocratic Aradii: see Silvio Panciera, "Ancora sulla famiglia senatoria 'Africana' degli *Aradii*" *L'Africa romana* 4.2 (1987): 560–2 [= *Scritti vari* 2.1128–9].

42 See, e.g., Fröhlich, *Lararien- und Fassadenbilder*, pp. 38–40; Bakker, *Living and Working with the Gods*, pp. 65–76, 84–95, both with references.

43 See Kaufmann-Heinimann, *Götter und Lararien*, pp. 204–5 and, for Bacchus at Pompeii, Stefania Adamo-Muscettola, "Osservazioni sulla composizione dei larari con statuette in bronzo di Pompei ed Ercolano," in *Toreutik und figürlichen Bronzen römischer Zeit: Akten der 6. Tagung über antike Bronzen, 13–17 Mai 1980 in Berlin*, ed. G.-M. Faider-Feytmans (Berlin: Staatliche Museen, Antikenmuseum, 1984), pp. 10–11.

44 Suetonius, *Life of Augustus* 7.1. The emperor Domitian (81–96 CE) is said to have kept a statuette of Minerva with his *Lares* (Cassius Dio 67.16.1) and to have had a slave assigned to care for them in his private suite (*in cubiculo*) (Suetonius, *Life of Domitian* 17.2). Galba (68 CE) reportedly cultivated at his villa in Tusculum a statuette of Fortuna that had appeared miraculously at his doorstep in Rome (Suetonius, *Life of Galba* 4.3);

from the time of Antoninus Pius (138–161 CE), a gold statue of Fortuna customarily stood in the emperor's bedroom (Scriptores Historiae Augustae, *Antoninus Pius* 12.5; cf. *Marcus Antoninus* 7.3).

45 This was Alexander's "greater" *lararium* (*lararium maius*); in a secondary shrine he kept busts of Vergil, Cicero, Achilles, and "great men" (*magni viri*): Scriptores Historiae Augustae, *Severus Alexander* 31.4–5. Marcus Aurelius (161–80) was said to have cultivated golden statuettes of his teachers in his *lararium* (*Marcus Antoninus* 3.5).

46 See Johannes Straub, *Heidnische Geschichtsapologetik in der christlichen Spätantike: Untersuchungen über Zeit und Tendenz der Historia Augusta* (Bonn: Habelt, 1963), pp. 166–70, 191. For a soteriological reading of the mixture of gods represented in the Esquiline *lararium* cited above, see Ensoli Vittozzi, "Le sculture."

47 Bendlin, "Looking Beyond the Civic Compromise," pp. 120–35, argues persuasively for the importance of personal belief in the "deregulated religious pluralism" (134) that characterized the religious life of the Roman Empire.

48 See Fausto Zevi, "Die 'volkstümliche Kunst,'" in *Pompejanische Wandmalerei*, ed. Giuseppina Cerulli Irelli, M. Aoyagi, Stefano De Caro, U. Pappalardo (Stuttgart-Zürich: Beiser 1990), p. 278 with Fröhlich, *Lararien- und Fassadenbilder*, p. 200.

49 For slave families within the household, see Marleen B. Flory, "Family in *familia*: Kinship and Community in Slavery," *American Journal of Ancient History* 3 (1978): 78–95.

50 Andrew Wallace-Hadrill, "Houses and Households: Sampling Pompeii and Herculaneum," in *Marriage, Divorce, and Children in Ancient Rome*, ed. Beryl Rawson (Oxford: Oxford University Press, 1991), pp. 220–2, links hearths with *lararia* and suggests that they reflect patterns of habitation.

51 See R. A. Tybout, "Domestic Shrines and 'Popular Painting': Style and Social Context," *Journal of Roman Archaeology* 9 (1991): 367–8.

52 The most famous familial *Lar* in Roman culture, the Prologue speaker of Plautus's *Aulularia*, complains of neglect from the founder's son but rewards the dutiful granddaughter who cultivates him (1–27). In at least four *lararia* paintings from the Vesuvian towns, the principal figure (the sacrificant) is a woman: see Boyce, *Corpus of the Lararia*, pp. 331, 349, 489 and Anna Maria Ragozzino, "Il larario della Casa di C. Giulio Polibio in Pompei (IX, 13, 1–3)," *Rendiconti della Accademia di Archeologia Lettere e Belle Arti di Napoli* n.s. 61 (1987–1988): 81–2, identifying personalized features of the *lararium*. The prevalent assumption that Roman household religion, because overseen by the *dominus*, was exclusively male-oriented does not take account of the importance of women in the maintenance of the *Lar familiaris*.

53 Cicero, *On Laws* 2.27; cf. 2.19.5 with Dyck, *Commentary*, 294–5 ad loc.

54 Paul, the excerptor of Festus, *De Significatu Verborum* 273.7 L. For the *Compitalia*, see Wissowa, *Religion und Kultus*, pp. 167–71, and Howard H. Scullard, *Festivals and Ceremonies of the Roman Republic* (London: Thames and Hudson, 1981), pp. 58–60.

55 See, e.g., *Corpus Inscriptionum Latinarum* 9.2996 = 1^2 1762: our earliest example (c. 100–50 BCE): a slave *mag(ister)* dedicates "a shrine, statuettes, and all the decoration" to the *Lares familiares* in a private house at Anxanum; cf. 9.3434 (Peltuinum Vestinum); 10.773 (Stabiae); 10.8067 (Pompeii); 11.7092 (Perusia); 6.36808 (Rome); *L'Année épigraphique* 1990, 51 (Rome); *AE* 1980, 247 (Herculaneum); *AE* 1996, 677 = 2001, 982 (Aquae Statiellae).

56 For the gods favored by Roman slaves, see Franz Bömer, *Untersuchungen über die Religion der Sklaven in Greichenland und Rom. Erster Teil: Die wichtigsten Kulte und*

Religionen in Rom und im lateinischen Westen, 2nd edn. revised with Peter Herz (Wiesbaden: Franz Steiner Verlag, 1981), pp. 110–79 and above, nn. 2 and 11.

57 For the *Larentalia*, see Wissowa, *Religion und Kultus*, pp. 233–4. For the *Saturnalia*, see Hendrik Versnel, *Transition and Reversal in Myth and Ritual* (Leiden: E. J. Brill, 1993), pp. 136–227; more generally on Roman holidays for slaves, Keith R. Bradley, "Holidays for Slaves," *Symbolae Osloenses* 54 (1979): 111–18.

58 The best source is Aulus Gellius, *Attic Nights* 7.7.5–8, citing the esteemed jurist Masurius Sabinus. See John Scheid, *Romulus et ses frères: Le college des frères Arvales, modèle du culte public dans la Rome des empereurs* (Rome: École française de Rome, 1990), pp. 18–24, 587–98, who remains agnostic concerning the identification of Acca with the Mother of the *Lares*. For the significance of the location of Acca's shrine on the Velabrum, see Filippo Coarelli, *Il Foro Romano * Periodo arcaico*, 3rd edn. (Rome: Edizioni Quasar, 1992), pp. 269–81, esp. p. 280; and, for the tomb (*tarentum Accas Larentinas*), Calvert Watkins, *How to Kill a Dragon: Aspects of Indo-European Poetics* (Oxford: Oxford University Press, 1995), pp. 347–51.

59 For the *Caristia* and the *Parentalia*, see William Warde Fowler, *The Roman Festivals of the Period of the Republic* (London: Macmillan, 1899), pp. 306–10.

60 Theodor Mommsen, *Römische Forschungen*, vol. 2 (Berlin: Weidmann, 1864–79) 2.35: "too little is clear" (*parum constat*); Fowler, *Roman Festivals*, pp. 275–6: "the text is corrupt."

15

Comparative Perspectives

JOHN BODEL AND SAUL M. OLYAN

In this concluding chapter, we move beyond consideration of household and family religion in each of the individual contexts of interest to us. Instead, our focus is Mediterranean and West Asian household and family religion from a comparative perspective. As we mentioned in the introduction to this volume, comparison is valuable because it can raise new questions and lead to fresh insights. It has the potential to help us understand household and family religion better by revealing characteristics common to the cultures of the Mediterranean and West Asia and features specific to a particular cultural setting. We begin with the notion of household and family religion itself, and then treat several salient themes that emerge from our reading of the individual essays in the volume. Though we can only begin to undertake serious comparison in a preliminary way, we hope that our findings will stimulate further comparative research and may provide a cogent demonstration that comparative work is worth the effort.

Naming the phenomenon in question and theorizing it poses interesting challenges in view of differences among the fields in the nature and quantity of the extant evidence and in customary usages within the various disciplines. Albertz, van der Toorn, and Olyan favor family religion as the identifier, mainly because of its flexibility, which allows the scholar to focus on a social unit (the family, however defined) rather than on one particular locus (e.g., the domicile). Given that the domicile, local shrine, and tomb may all potentially play a role in family religion, an ambiguous term such as "family" suits the evidence from second and first millennium West Asia nicely. Others prefer the term "household religion" but place the emphasis variously, on the social nature of the household (Stowers) or on the domicile as the locus for household cult (Ritner, Ackerman). Some find relevance in both conceptual categories and seek only clarity of definition from those who write about the phenomenon (Bodel, Faraone). The classicists share a recognition of the distinction (fundamental in Athenian and Roman culture, owing to the widespread presence in them of domestic slavery, but cogently employed also by Ackerman in the analysis of Israelite society) between the concepts of family and household but differ on how best to approach ritual centered on the house in relation to either group. In the Greek world, Faraone focuses on the more neglected territory of what he terms "oikic cult," the religion of the house (*oikos*), which he distinguishes from the religion of the *genos* (that is, the familial group defined by direct descent, excluding collateral relations). Boedeker on the other hand shows that even so fundamentally localized a household cult as that of Zeus "of the Courtyard" (Herkeios) had important legal and civic implications for familial identity, whereas the domestic worship of Zeus "of Possessions" (Ktesios), the protector of patrimony, might include persons not only from outside the family but from outside the house. Considering the Roman world, Bodel finds evidence for related, parallel tracks of family and household cult within the house, one catering to the individualistic spiritual desires of members of the biological kin group, the other designed to confine and refocus the inclinations of slaves toward personal devotion to deceased kin. Lesko, for her part, struggles with the constraints of the term "domestic religion," standard in the field of Egyptology, stretching it to include devotion at local sanctuaries and in the street – what others might call simply family or even personal religion.

Refining ever more expansive (or restrictive) definitions of non-official religious behavior with the aim of proving this or that activity relevant seems unlikely to advance our understanding. We might better instead recognize that inconcinnities among and even within cultures are inevitable and turn more profitably to the more relevant question of how, in religious terms, within each culture, the semantic territory of the several terms is to be defined. The cult of the dead, for example, in many cultures was (and is) practiced in the house as well as at the tomb, but care for the dead would not be classified by our contributors in all of them as either domestic or household religion. Similarly, household rituals involving shrines and images are closely connected to the family in some cultures, but in others the mode of worship associated with those monuments includes members outside the biological family and is primarily centered on place. Certainly, an interest in the domicile, as a locus, and in the household, as a social group housed within it, is shared by our contributors, but the degree to which the domicile is regarded as the focus of the cultic activity under consideration – whether it is the central location or one among several – and the composition and configuration of the family within the household – whether the nuclear form predominated, as in Egypt and Greece, or whether extended kin groupings were the norm, as in some West Asian contexts – naturally differ from contributor to contributor and from culture to culture.

What all this perhaps suggests is that the boundaries of "household," "familial," and "domestic" cult may need to be drawn differently for different cultures. Within individual cultures, they may also need to be drawn differently in social, political, and legal contexts. Nonetheless, it seems wise in most cases to try to define the boundaries of the phenomenon of interest by indicating the range of behaviors the preferred term is taken to embrace. Indeed, among the more salient results to emerge from a broadly comparative consideration of the phenomena in question may be simply, in the first instance, a clearer recognition of the fundamental (and perhaps obvious) link between the social unit of the family (whether nuclear and biological or composite and socially complex) and the physical spaces in which it was housed, and, secondly, an appreciation of the ways in which carving out the territory of non-official religion within any of the cultures examined impinges on the ways in which the basic units of human society, the biological family (both living and dead) and the household (those who lived together), related to the larger civic or national structures that encompassed them. At a secondary level, how collections of religious behaviors formed themselves around, and indeed helped to shape these various territories, reveals how we construct the religious systems within which the practices had meaning. Comparative study, in other words, provides building blocks for the sociology of religion, as well as for the cultural history of Mediterranean and West Asian antiquity.

Almost inevitably, in view of the range of conceptions of the field offered and the variety of religious behaviors encompassed by them, the area of interest is in some respects most accurately defined by what it is not. Here most of our contributors recognize at least some degree of disjunction between the religion of household and family on the one hand, and state, civic or public cult on the other. This may be significant, as Albertz maintains, arguing that pre-exilic Israelite family religion is for the most part discontinuous with the religion of official cult, or insignificant, as Ritner proposes, contending that Egyptian household cult shares much in common with public devotion. Fleming, like Ritner, emphasizes continuity in his treatment of the evidence from LB Emar. Some contributors to the volume stake out a middle ground, recognizing elements of both continuity and discontinuity in the evidence they consider (Boedeker, Olyan, Schmitt). Others find significance in the ways that public and private religions track each other in both directions (Fleming, Ritner, Faraone, Bodel). Ambiguities arise in part with semantics: "private" in common European and North American usage has two natural opposites: "public," in the sense of official, governmental, and "public" in the sense of out in the open, among the people. In some of the cultures discussed, the same polarities existed and were coincident (that is, behavior enacted in public was invariably official); in others they did not or were not.

Some contributors find diametrically opposed concepts such as public/private and official/personal inappropriate to describe the realities of the cultural worlds they study. Roman society, for example, had clearly demarcated categories of public and private, but religious behavior regularly transgressed their boundaries, and domestic space – the natural locus of household cult – was articulated in ways that blended and blurred the distinctions between the two. The practice of Roman domestic religion is thus better represented by a range of taxonomies with overlapping but not coextensive elements: different elements of the household had different religions in different places within the house. In other cultures, the two categories have clear boundaries and are evidently significant, as, for example, when behavior common to both public and private realms is clearly demarcated according to where it occurs. In several (Israel, Ammon, Ugarit, and some parts of the Greek world), a pattern of non-meat offerings in the domicile sets household worship apart from civic or public cult, where meat sacrifice was the norm. Comparison suggests that we cannot generalize about either the existence or the significance of the continuity or disjunction between household or family and state or public religion in Mediterranean and West Asian antiquity. Clearly, a range of patterns is possible. At the same time, comparison allows us to identify a cross-cultural phenomenon – the avoidance of meat offerings in domestic cult – that invites further comparative investigation and raises a variety of questions.

Although the individual components of household and family religion may differ from context to context, some shared elements emerge from comparison. Devotion to family or household gods is common to household and family religion in a number of contexts (e.g., Greece, Rome, Second Millennium Babylon, Israel). These deities may be approached in domestic shrines or local sanctuaries, depending on the cultural setting, and they may or may not be the same as the major gods of state or civic cult. In some cultures (Emar, Egypt, Rome), the same deities worshiped in state or public shrines figured prominently in household and family religion as well (an element of continuity). In others (Second Millennium Babylon, Greece) distinct household deities who found no place in official cult played a central role in familial devotion in the home. In one (Rome), household worship not only incorporated deities drawn from the public sphere but also provided domestic models for civic versions of private familial rites. Ancestor cults formed a prominent part of familial worship in several cultures, but the locus of devotion varied (e.g., from domicile to sanctuary to tomb, in cases where the tomb was separate from the home), as did the rites and equipment involved.

The use of images and other cult objects to represent family or household gods is common to several cultures, but individual practices varied widely. Not infrequently, household gods, like their counterparts in the public state cult, were figured anthropomorphically: when the same gods were worshiped in household shrines as in the public temples (e.g., Egypt, Rome), it was natural that they be represented similarly. Whether or not they conveyed the same associations in domestic contexts as they did in civic ones, however, is uncertain. In better attested cultures such as ancient Rome, where the richness of the literary record enables us to observe the manipulation of household religion for rhetorical effect, we can see how the private, personal associations of an image cultivated in the house might intersect with and diverge from the deity's public persona in complex ways. In some cultures, specifically ancestral or household gods also appeared in anthropomorphic form (e.g., the Israelite *teraphim* or the Roman *Lares*). In Egypt and Rome, individual ancestors were regularly represented in familial cult by busts. In other cultures, household gods were worshiped in non-anthropomorphic and even aniconic form. In at least one (Rome), a paradigmatic myth established two types of household gods, one an anthropomorphic image (in the recognized type of a public deity: the Palladium), the other an assortment of aniconic household objects (staffs, a jug);

and surviving material evidence shows that both types were intermingled and cultivated together in the household shrines in private practice. In another (Greece), the same household god ("Zeus of Possessions") might be worshiped in different forms in different places (as a snake at Thasos and as a jug at Athens). It should not surprise us that varieties of practice in the expression of devotion to divinities and ancestors might sometimes be evidenced within a single culture: none of the cultures under consideration should be regarded as monolithic; all changed over time, and geographical location, as well as the family's social position within the culture, affected the forms that family and household worship might assume. On this issue, see especially the cautionary remarks of Lewis concerning Ugarit, Faraone and Boedeker on varieties of practice in "Greece," and Bodel on some differences in the manifestations of Roman household religion within and outside Italy.

Several contributors note the difficulty of identifying confidently or even recognizing the material and architectural remains of domestic or other relevant religious activity. As Stowers observes with respect to the Greco-Roman world, "while the remains of temple religion are quite striking, traces of domestic religion are difficult to recognize. A household vessel used for libations is likely to be an ordinary cup, while a temple vessel is one made precisely to display its difference from the ordinary household utensil." At the same time, the use in European provinces of the Roman empire of identical figurines of deities in household shrines for private domestic worship and as votive offerings in public sanctuaries makes it difficult to determine, when hordes of the statuettes are found buried out of context, from which setting a particular set originally derived. The same can be said of the miniature model shrines found in both domestic and sanctuary assemblages in the Levant. In some cases, the purpose of a common household object is unclear and so its potential relevance to family or household religion remains uncertain. So, for example, in Egypt, both the function and the significance of the so-called "pregnancy vases" found in non-utilitarian domestic contexts continue to escape us. Schmitt, noting the ambiguity of much of the material data from Philistine and other West Asian contexts, speaks of the challenges involved in identifying cultic assemblages of any sort in the absence of clear indicators such as the presence of divine figurines, since utilitarian utensils communicate nothing clear in and of themselves.

The potential ambiguity of domestic installations is well captured by examples from several of the cultures under consideration. Ritner and Lesko disagree about the interpretation of the so-called box-beds of Ramesside Deir el-Medina. Ritner argues that these corner platforms approached by steps were household altars linked to childbirth, Lesko that they were places devoted to the initial period of a newborn's nurture (nursery beds). Fleming struggles with the identification of a building called M1, which was occupied by "the diviner of the gods of Emar" and was a repository of a large and important collection of tablets. Was it a domicile or a temple? Though some aspects of the structure suggest a temple, other aspects are inconsistent with such identification. And though Fleming concludes that "the result is more like a house in total composition," he argues nonetheless for a public structure. The architectural and painted shrines in Roman homes that are normally identified as the principal locus of household worship can at times appear as little more than antique furniture, but the objects regularly found with them suggest a vibrant domestic cult. Identifying what material evidence is relevant to an investigation of household or family religion, let alone understanding it, is clearly not an uncomplicated matter in any of the fields of interest to us.

Another category of evidence that may raise difficulties is onomastic data. In certain cultures, personal names incorporating the names of divinities and divine epithets are commonly taken as a sign of family religiosity (so Ritner on Egypt, Lewis on Ugarit, Albertz on Israel). It has even been argued that the absence of onomastic reference to a national religious narrative can indicate that state ideology and cult had little impact on the lives of ordinary persons (Albertz on First Millennium Israelites). Some scholars, however, counsel caution in drawing inferences from personal names, which are not infrequently ambiguous and may follow well-established conventions (e.g., they may simply focus on the personal rather than larger, national concerns, as Olyan points out against Albertz). In some cultures (e.g., Greece) theophoric names are so common that they scarcely convey any originally distinctive religious connotations.

A final theme common to many of the contributions to the volume is a concern with gender. Several contributors identify a central role for women in household or family rites. Indeed, the importance of women as ritual actors in domestic cult in Israel and Greece is marshaled as yet another indication of the disjunction in those cultures between household and family religion on the one hand and public state cult on the other. Albertz, Boedeker, and Faraone all emphasize this contrast in their essays. Lesko, on the other hand, argues from the ritual prominence of women in Egyptian temples for their importance in household cult as well. In her view, the fact that some women had public roles in organized religion suggests a fortiori that women "surely must have" played an important part also in Egyptian household cult. But if women are thought to have been prominent in household and family religion in Greece, Egypt, and Israel, Fleming believes that evidence from Emar points to the consistently central position of leading males both in public cult and in household and family devotion. He does, however, acknowledge the gaps in our knowledge, and suggests that the "household domain of women" might potentially be an exception to this pattern. Van der Toorn, for his part, finds that Second-Millennium family religion in Mesopotamia perpetuates "female dependency on the male" by "creat[ing] and legitimiz[ing] the chain of authority within the extended family." In Rome, where the dominant position of the paterfamilias in familial cult has seemed self-evident and is regularly presumed, the role of women as sacrificants in some domestic *lararium* paintings and the specific monthly cultic obligations to tend the *Lar* of the household imposed on them by prescriptive handbooks suggest that their significance has been underestimated. Within the cultures in which their domestic religious responsibilities are recognized, women played a variety of roles in household and family rites: as healers (Faraone), as preparers and distributors of food (Ackerman), or as tenders of the hearth (Bodel). In other cultures where the domestic tasks of women were similar, preparing food or tending the hearth were activities that had little or no significance for household and family religion (Fleming and van der Toorn). As with the issue of continuity or disjunction between private familial and public state cult, we cannot generalize about gender patterns in household and family religion in Mediterranean and West Asian antiquity, given the diversity of the extant evidence and the variety of ways in which it has been read.

Finally, for all the recognition that family and household religion belongs as much to the horizon of the common person as to that of the social and political elite, few of our contributors have managed entirely to escape the tyranny of the textual, and especially the literary, sources that inevitably bias our picture toward the upper end, where the literate classes of antiquity (a tiny minority in all of the cultures studied) congregated and dominated (Lewis, Ritner). If our literary authorities are themselves merely representing an imaginary ideal, as Beard proposed for Rome, how much further from daily reality does our picture recede if we are forced to reconstruct it primarily from their testimony? Even mundane domestic documents can only provide a slanted view of a world in which few could understand their contents, even if their purposes were evident. Material evidence, as we have seen, presents its own problems, both of identification and of interpretation. The objects and structures of ancient familial and household cult are not always mute, but it is often difficult to understand what language they are speaking or what they say. If progress is to be made, greater hope may lie in the welcome support of the comparative method, which enables us to sift our evidence into different categories, and of theory, which allows us to consider old problems differently and to see the evidence in new ways.

Bibliography

Ackerman, Susan. *Under Every Green Tree: Popular Religion in Sixth-Century Judah*. Harvard Semitic Mongraphs 46. Atlanta: Scholars Press, 1992.

Ackerman, Susan. *Warrior, Dancer, Seductress, Queen: Women in Judges and Biblical Israel*. Anchor Bible Reference Library 17. New York: Doubleday, 1998.

Ackerman, Susan. " 'And the Women Knead Dough': The Worship of the Queen of Heaven in Sixth-Century Judah." In *Gender and Difference in Ancient Israel*. Edited by P. L. Day, pp. 109–24. Minneapolis: Fortress, 1989 (= *Women in the Hebrew Bible: A Reader*. Edited by A. Bach, pp. 21–32. New York and London: Routledge, 1999).

Adamo-Muscettola, Stefania. "Osservazioni sulla composizione dei larari con statuette in bronzo di Pompei ed Ercolano." In *Toreutik und figürlichen Bronzen römischer Zeit: Akten der 6. Tagung über antike Bronzen, 13–17 Mai 1980 in Berlin*. Edited by G.-M. Faider-Feytmans, pp. 9–32. Berlin: Staatliche Museen, Antikenmuseum, 1984.

Adamthwaite, Murray R. *Late Hittite Emar: The Chronology, Synchronisms, and Socio-Political Aspects of a Late Bronze Age Fortress Town*. Louvain: Peeters, 2001.

Aharoni, Yohanan. *Beer-Sheba I: Excavations at Tel Beer-Sheba 1969–1971 Seasons*. Tel Aviv: Institute of Archaeology, 1973.

Aharoni, Yohanan. *Investigations at Lachish: The Sanctuary and the Residency (Lachish V)*. Tel Aviv: Tel Aviv University Institute of Archaeology, 1975.

Albertz, Rainer. *Weltschöpfung und Menschenschöpfung: Untersucht bei Deuterojesaja, Hiob und in den Psalmen*. Calwer Theologische Monographien A 3. Stuttgart: Calwer Verlag, 1974.

Albertz, Rainer. *Persönliche Frömmigkeit und offizielle Religion: Religionsinterner Pluralismus in Israel und Babylon*. Calwer Theologische Monographien A 9. Stuttgart: Calwer Verlag, 1978.

Albertz, Rainer. *A History of Israelite Religion in the Old Testament Period*. 2 vols. The Old Testament Library. Louisville: Westminster/John Knox, 1994.

Albertz, Rainer. "Wieviel Pluralismus kann sich eine Religion leisten? Zum religionsinternen Pluralismus in alten Israel." In *Pluralismus und Identität*. Veröffentlichung der Wissenschaftlichen Gesellschaft für Theologie 8. Edited by Joachim Mehlhausen, pp. 193–213. Gütersloh: Gütersloher Verlagshaus, 1995.

Albertz, Rainer. *Religionsgeschichte Israels in alttestamentlicher Zeit*. 2 vols. Grundrisse zum Alten Testament 8, pp. 1–2. 2nd edn. Göttingen: Vandenhoeck & Ruprecht, 1996–7.

Albertz, Rainer. "Religious Practices of the Individual and Family: Israel." In *Religions of the Ancient World: A Guide*. Edited by Sarah I. Johnston, pp. 429–30. Cambridge, Mass. & London: Belknap Press of Harvard University Press, 2004.

Albertz, Rainer and Schmitt, Rüdiger. *Family Religion in Ancient Israel*. Winona Lake, IN: Eisenbrauns, forthcoming.

Aleshire, Sara B. "The Demos and the Priests: The Selection of Sacred Officials at Athens from Cleisthenes to Augustus." In *Ritual, Finance, Politics: Athenian Democratic*

Accounts Presented to David Lewis. Edited by Robin Osborne and Simon Hornblower, pp. 325–37. Oxford: Clarendon Press, 1994.

Allam, Schafik. "Familie (Struktur)." In *Lexikon der Ägyptologie*. Edited by Wolfgang Helck and Eberhard Otto, 2: 104–13. Wiesbaden: Harrassowitz, 1977.

Allen, M. L. "The Terracotta Figurines from Karanis." 2 vols. PhD dissertation, University of Michigan, 1985.

Allen, T. George. *The Book of The Dead or Going Forth by Day*. Studies in Ancient Oriental Civilization 37. Chicago: The University of Chicago, 1974.

Allen, Jr, Walter. "Cicero's House and *Libertas*." *Transactions of the American Philological Association* 75 (1944): 1–9.

Alroth, Brita. "Visiting Gods." In *Anathema. Regime delle offerte e vita dei santuari nel Mediterraneo antico*. Edited by G. Bartoloni, G. Colonna, and C. Grottanelli (Scienze dell'antichità. Storia, archeologia, antropologia 3–4, 1989–1990), pp. 301–10. Rome: Università degli studi di Roma "La Sapienza," 1991.

Altenmüller, Hartwig. "Die Apotropaia und die Götter Mittelägyptens." 2 vols. PhD dissertation, Ludwig-Maximillians-Universität zu München, 1965.

Altenmüller, Hartwig. "Apotropaikon." In *Lexikon der Ägyptologie*. Edited by Wolfgang Helck and Eberhard Otto, 1: 355–8. Wiesbden: Otto Harrassowitz, 1975.

Altenmüller, Hartwig. "Ein Zaubermesser des Alten Reiches." *Studien zur Altägyptischen Kultur* 13 (1986): 1–27.

Anderson, Gary A. "Sacrifice and Sacrificial Offerings (OT)." In *Anchor Bible Dictionary*. Edited by D. N. Freedman, 5: 870b–886b. New York: Doubleday, 1992.

Ando, Clifford. "A Religion for the Empire." In *Roman Religion*. Edited by Clifford Ando, pp. 220–43. Edinburgh: Edinburgh University Press, 2003.

Andrews, Carol. *Amulets of Ancient Egypt*. Austin: University of Texas Press, 1994.

Andrews, Carol A. R. "Amulets," *Oxford Encyclopedia of Ancient Egypt*. Edited by Donald B. Redford, 1: 75–82. Oxford: Oxford University Press, 2000.

Arnaud, Daniel. *Recherches au pays d'Aštata, Tome 3. Textes sumériens et accadiens*. Paris: Éditions Recherche sur les Civilisations, 1986.

Arnaud, Daniel. "La Syrie du moyen-Euphrate sous le protectorat Hittite: contrats de droit privé." *Aula Orientalis* 5 (1987): 211–42.

Arnaud, Daniel. *Textes syriens de l'âge du Bronze Récent*. Barcelona: Editorial AUSA, 1991.

Arnaud, Daniel. "Tablettes de genres divers du Moyen-Euphrate." *Studi micenei ed egeo-anatolici* 30 (1992): 195–245.

Arnold, D. E. *Ceramic Theory and Cultural Process*. Cambridge: Cambridge University Press, 1985.

Arnold, Felix. "Houses." In *The Oxford Encyclopedia of Egyptology*. Edited by Donald P. Redford, 2: 122–27. Oxford: Oxford University Press, 2001.

Arnold, Patrick M. "Ramah." In *Anchor Bible Dictionary*. Edited by D. N. Freedman, 5: 613b–614b. New York: Doubleday, 1992.

Aufrère, Sydney. "Le hiéroglyphe du crible à grain et la métaphore désignant le nouveau-né dans l'Égypte ancienne." In *Hommages Fayza Haikal*, pp. 17–27. Bulletin de l'Institut Français d'Archéologie Orientale, Cairo 138. Cairo: Institut Français d'Archéologie Orientale, 2003.

Baines, John. "Practical Religion and Piety." *The Journal of Egyptian Archaeology* 73 (1987): 79–98.

Bakker, Jan Theo. *Living and Working with the Gods: Studies of Evidence for Private Religion and its Material Environment in the City of Ostia (100–500 AD)*. Amsterdam: J. C. Gieben, 1994.

Battini-Villard, Laura. *L'Espace domestique en Mésopotamie de la IIIe dynastie d'Ur à l'époque paléo-babylonienne*. BAR International Series 767. Oxford: Archeopress, 1999.

Baumgartel, Elise J. *The Culture of Prehistoric Egypt*. 2 vols. London: Oxford University Press, 1947.

Beckman, Gary M. *Texts from the Vicinity of Emar in the Collection of Jonathan Rosen*. Padua: Sargon srl, 1996.

Beit-Arieh, Itzaq. "A Literary Ostracon from Horvat 'Uza." *Tel Aviv* 20 (1993): 55–65.

Bell, Catherine. *Ritual Theory, Ritual Practice*. New York: Oxford University Press, 1992.

Ben-Barak, Zafrira. "The Legal Status of the Daughter as Heir in Nuzi and Emar." In *Society and Economy in the Eastern Mediterranean*. Edited by Michael Heltzer and Edward Lipinski, pp. 87–97. Leuven: Peeters, 1988.

Bendlin, Andreas. "Looking beyond the Civic Compromise: Religious Pluralism in Late Republican Rome." In *Religion in Archaic and Republican Rome and Italy: Evidence and Experience*. Edited by Edward Bispham and Christopher Smith, pp. 115–35. Edinburgh: Edinburgh University Press, 2000.

Berg, Beverly. "Cicero's Palatine House and Clodius' Shrine of Liberty: Alternative Emblems of the Republic in Cicero's *De Domo Sua*." In *Studies in Latin Literature and Roman History*, vol. 8. Edited by Carl Deroux, pp. 122–43. Brussels: Latomus, 1997.

Berlinerblau, Jacques. "The Israelite Vow: Distress or Daily Life." *Biblica* 72 (1991): 548–55.

Berlinerblau, Jacques. "The 'Popular Religion' Paradigm in the Old Testament Research: A Sociological Critique." *Journal for the Study of the Old Testament* 60 (1993): 3–26.

Berlinerblau, Jacques. *The Vow and the "Popular Religious Groups" of Ancient Israel: A Philological and Sociological Inquiry*. Journal for the Study of the Old Testament Supplement Series 210. Sheffield: Sheffield Academic Press, 1996.

Betz, H. D. (ed.). *The Greek Magical Papyri in Translation Including the Demotic Spells*. 2nd edn. Chicago: The University of Chicago, 1992.

Beyse, K.-M. "'eṣem." In *Theologisches Wörterbuch zum alten Testament*. Ed. G. J. Botterweck and H. Ringgren, 6: 326–32. Stuttgart: W. Kohlhammer, 1989.

Bianchi, Robert Stevens. "Scarabs." In *The Oxford Encyclopedia of Ancient Egypt*. Edited by Donald B. Redford, 3: 179–81. Oxford: Oxford University Press, 2001.

Bird, Phyllis. "The Place of Women in the Israelite Cultus." In *Ancient Israelite Religion: Essays in Honor of Frank Moore Cross*. Edited by P. D. Miller, P. D. Hanson and S. D. McBride, pp. 397–419. Philadelphia: Fortress, 1987.

Bird, Phyllis. "Women's Religion in Ancient Israel." In *Women's Earliest Records from Ancient Egypt and Western Asia*. Brown Judaic Studies 166. Edited by B. S. Lesko, pp. 283–98. Atlanta: Scholars Press, 1989.

Birot, Maurice. *Tablettes économiques et administratives d'époque babylonienne ancienne conservées au musée d'art et d'histoire de Genève*. Paris: Geuthner, 1969.

Blackman, Winifred S. *The Fellahin of Upper Egypt*. London: G. G. Harrap & Co. Ltd., 1927.

Blank, Sheldon H. "The Curse, Blasphemy, the Spell, and the Oath." *Hebrew Union College Annual* 23 (1950/51): 73–95.

Blenkinsopp, Joseph. "The Family in First Temple Israel." In *Families in Ancient Israel: The Family, Religion, and Culture*. Edited by Leo G. Perdue, pp. 48–103. Louisville: Westminster/John Knox Press, 1997.

Bloch, Maurice. *From Blessing to Violence: History and Ideology in the Circumcision Ritual of the Merina of Madagascar*. Cambridge: Cambridge University Press, 1986.

Bloch, Maurice. "The Ritual of the Royal Bath in Madagascar: The Dissolution of Death, Birth and Fertility into Authority." In *Rituals of Royalty: Power and Ceremonial in Traditional Societies*. Edited by David Cannadine and Simon Price, pp. 271–97. Cambridge: Cambridge University Press, 1987.

Bloch-Smith, Elizabeth. *Judahite Burial Practices and Beliefs about the Dead*. Journal for the Study of the Old Testament Supplements 123. Sheffield: Sheffield Academic Press, 1992.

Blomart, A. "Die *evocatio* und der Transfer fremder Götter von der Peripherie nach Rom," in *Römische Reichsreligion und Provinzialreligion*. Edited by Hubert Cancik and Jörg Rüpke, pp. 99–111. Tübingen: Mohr Siebeck, 1997.

Bodel, John. "Monumental Villas and Villa Monuments." *Journal of Roman Archaeology* 10 (1997): 5–35.

Boedeker, Deborah. "The Two Faces of Demaratus." In *Herodotus and the Invention of History*. Edited by Deborah Boedeker. *Arethusa* 20, 1987: 185–201.

Boedeker, Deborah. "Athenian Religion in the Age of Pericles." In *The Cambridge Companion to the Age of Pericles*. Edited by Loren J. Samons II, pp. 46–69. Cambridge: Cambridge University Press, 2006.

Boling, Robert G. *Judges: A New Translation with Introduction and Commentary*. Anchor Bible 6A. Garden City, N.Y.: Doubleday, 1975.

Bömer, Franz. *Untersuchungen über die Religion der Sklaven in Greichenland und Rom. Erster Teil: Die wichtigsten Kulte und Religionen in Rom und im lateinischen Westen*, 2nd edn. revised with Peter Herz. Wiesbaden: Franz Steiner Verlag, 1981.

Borghouts, Joris F. *The Magical Texts of Papyrus Leiden I*. Leiden: Brill, 1971.

Borghouts, Joris F. *Ancient Egyptian Magical Texts*. Leiden: Brill, 1978.

Borghouts, Joris F. "Magical Practices among the Villagers." In *Pharaoh's Workers: the Villagers of Deir el Medina*. Edited by Leonard H. Lesko, pp. 119–30. Ithaca: Cornell University Press, 1994.

Borowski, Oded. "Hezekiah's Reforms and the Revolt against Assyria." *Biblical Archaeologist* 58 (1995): 148–55.

Borowski, Oded. *Daily Life in Biblical Times*. Atlanta: Society of Biblical Literature, 2003.

Bourdieu, Pierre. *An Outline of a Theory of Practice*. Cambridge: Cambridge University Press, 1977.

Bourdieu, Pierre and Wacquant, Loïc J. D. *An Invitation to Reflexive Sociology*. Chicago: The University of Chicago Press, 1992.

Bourriau, Janine. *Pottery from the Nile Valley before the Arab Conquest*. Cambridge: Fitzwilliam Museum, 1981.

Bourriau, Janine. "All this Pottery. What about it?" *Egyptian Archaeology* 26 (2005): 30–3.

Boyce, George K. *Corpus of the Lararia of Pompeii*. Rome: American Academy in Rome, 1937.

Bradley, Keith R. "Holidays for Slaves," *Symbolae Osloenses* 54 (1979): 111–18.

Bradley, Keith R. *Discovering the Roman Family*. New York: Oxford University Press, 1991.

Breasted, James H. *The Edwin Smith Surgical Papyrus*. Oriental Institute Publications 3. Chicago: The University of Chicago, 1930.

Bretschneider, Joachim. *Architekturmodelle in Vorderasien und der östlichen Ägäis vom Neolithikum bis in das 1. Jahrtausend: Phänomene in der Kleinkunst aus Mesopotamien, dem Iran, Anatolien, Syrien, der Levante und dem ägäischen Raum unter besonderer Berücksichtigung der bau- und der religionsgeschichtlichen Aspekte*. Alter Orient und Altes Testament 229. Kevelaer: Butzon & Bercker; Neukirchen-Vluyn: Neukirchener Verlag, 1991.

Brettler, Marc Zvi. "The Book of Judges: Literature as Politics." *Journal of Biblical Literature* 108 (1989): 395–418.

Brettler, Marc Zvi. "Women and Psalms: Toward an Understanding of the Role of Women's Prayer in the Israelite Cult." In *Gender and Law in the Hebrew Bible and the Ancient Near East*. Journal for the Study of the Old Testament Supplement Series 262. Edited by V. H. Matthews, B. M. Levinson, and T. Frymer-Kensky, pp. 25–56. Sheffield: Sheffield Academic Press, 1998.

Brettler, Marc Zvi. "Mother of Psalmist (God's Serving Girl): Pss 22:9–10; 27:10; 35:14; 50:20; 51:5; 71:6; 86:16; 109:14; 116:16; 131:2; 139:13." In *Women in Scripture: A Dictionary of Named and Unnamed Women in the Hebrew Bible, the Apocryphal/*

Deuterocanonical Books, and the New Testament. Edited by C. Meyers, with T. Craven and R. S. Kraemer, pp. 296b–297b. Boston: Houghton Mifflin, 2000.

Brinks, J. "Haus." In *Lexikon der Ägyptologie.* Edited by Wolfgang Helck and Eberhard Otto, 2:1055–62. Wiesbaden: Harrassowitz, 1977.

Brody, Aaron. *"Each Man Cried Out To His God": The Specialized Religion of Canaanite and Phoenician Seafarers.* Atlanta: Scholars Press, 1998.

Brooke, George J. "The Textual, Formal and Historical Significance of Ugaritic Letter RS 34.124 (KTU 2.72)." *Ugarit Forschungen* 11 (1979): 69–87.

Brovarski, Edward, Doll, Susan and Freed, Rita (eds.). *Egypt's Golden Age.* Boston: Museum of Fine Arts, Boston, 1982.

Brovarski, Edward. "Sobek." In *Lexikon der Ägyptologie.* Edited by Wolfgang Helck and Eberhard Otto, 5: 995–1031. Wiesbaden: Harrassowitz, 1984.

Brug, John. F. *A Literary and Archaeological Study of the Philistines.* BAR International Series 265. Oxford: BAR, 1985.

Brumfield, Allaire Chandor. *The Attic Festivals of Demeter and their Relation to the Agricultural Year.* Salem, New Hampshire: Arno Press, 1981.

Brunner, Helmut. "Persönliche Frommigkeit." In *Lexikon der Ägyptologie.* Edited by Wolfgang Helck and Eberhard Otto, 4: 951–63. Wiesbaden: Harrassowitz, 1982.

Brunner-Traut, Emma. "Die Wochenlaube." *Mitteilungen des Instituts für Orientforschung* 3 (1955): 11–30.

Brunner-Traut, Emma. "Gravidenflasche. Das Salben des Mutterleibes." In *Archaeologie und Altes Testament. Festschrift für Kurt Galling.* Edited by A. Kuschke and E. Kutsch, pp. 35–48. Tübingen: J. C. B. Mohr, 1970.

Brunton, Guy. *Qau and Badari.* London: British School of Archaeology, 1927.

Brunton, Guy. *Qau and Badari III.* London: British School of Archaeology in Egypt, 1930.

Bruyère, Bernard. *Rapport sur les Fouilles de Deir el Médineh, 1927.* Fouilles de l'Institut Français d'Archéologie Orientale du Caire 5. Cairo: Institut Français d'Archéologie Orientale, 1928.

Bruyère, Bernard. *Rapport sur les Fouilles de Deir el Médineh (1934–35): Le Village . . .* Fouilles de l'Institut Français d'Archéologie Orientale du Caire 16. Cairo: Institut Français d'Archéologie Orientale, 1939.

Bruyère, Bernard. *Rapport sur les Fouilles de Deir el Médineh (1945–1946 et 1946–1947).* Fouilles de l'Institut Français d'Archéologie Orientale du Caire 21. Cairo: Institut Français d'Archéologie Orientale, 1952.

Buhl, Marie-Louise and Holm-Nielsen, Svend. *Shiloh, The Danish Excavations at Tell Sailun, Palestine, in 1926, 1929, 1932 and 1963.* Copenhagen: National Museum of Denmark, 1969.

Burkert, Walter. *Greek Religion.* Cambridge, Mass.: Harvard University Press, 1985.

Buss, David M. *The Evolution of Desire: Strategies of Human Mating.* New York: Basic Books, 1994.

Callaway, Joseph A. "A Visit with Ahilud." *Biblical Archaeology Review* 9(5) (1983): 42–53.

Callaway, Joseph A. "Ai." In *Anchor Bible Dictionary.* Edited by D. N. Freedman, 1: 125b–130b. New York: Doubleday, 1992.

Callaway, Joseph A. "Ai." In *The New Encyclopedia of Archaeological Excavation in the Holy Land.* Edited by E. Stern, 1: 39–45. Jerusalem: Israel Exploration Society and Carta, 1993.

Callot, Olivier. *Une Maison à Ougarit: Études d'architecture domestique.* Ras Shamra-Ougarit I. Paris: Éditions Recherche sur les Civilisations, 1983.

Callot, Olivier. *La Tranchée "ville sud": Études d'architecture domestique.* Ras Shamra-Ougarit X. Paris: Éditions Recherche sur les Civilisations, 1994.

Callot, Olivier. "A Visit to a Home." *Near Eastern Archaeology* 63(4) (2000): 202–4.

Callot, Olivier and Calvet, Yann. "Le 'Bâtiment au Vase de Pierre' du 'Quartier Residentiel' d'Ougarit (fouille 1966)." In *Études Ougaritiques: I. Travaux 1985–1995.* Ras Shamra-Ougarit XIV. Edited by M. Yon and D. Arnaud, pp. 65–82. Paris: Éditions Recherche sur les Civilisations, 2001.

Caminos, Ricardo A. *Late-Egyptian Miscellanies.* Oxford: Oxford University Press, 1954.

Cassin, Elena. "Tablettes inédites de Nuzi," *Revue d'Assyriologie* 56 (1962): 57–80.

Castel, Corrine. "Naissance et Développement d'une Maison dans la 'Ville Basse' orientale d'Ougarit (fouille 1936)." In *Études Ougaritiques: I. Travaux 1985–1995.* Ras Shamra-Ougarit XIV. Edited by M. Yon and D. Arnaud, pp. 41–64. Paris: Éditions Recherche sur les Civilisations, 2001.

Castrén, Paavo. *Ordo Populusque Pompeianus: Polity and Society in Roman Pompeii*, 2nd edn. Rome: Institutum Romanum Finlandiae, 1983.

Cavigneaux, Antoine and Al-Rawi, Farouk N. H. "Charmes de Sippar et de Nippur." In *Cinquante-deux réflections sur le Proche-Orient ancien offertes en hommage à Léon de Meyer.* Edited by H. Gasche, M. Tanret, C. Janssen and A. Degraeve, pp. 73–89. Leuven: Peeters, 1994.

Černý, Jaroslav and Gardiner, Alan H. *Hieratic Ostraca.* Oxford: Griffith Institute, 1957.

Cetina, Karin Knorr, von Savigny, Eike and Schatzki, Theodore. *The Practice Turn in Contemporary Theory.* London, New York: Routledge, 2001.

Chiera, Edward. *Joint Expedition with the Iraq Museum at Nuzi, V: Mixed Texts.* Publications of the Baghdad School, American Schools of Oriental Research, Texts: Vol. V. Philadelphia: University of Pennsylvania Press, 1934.

Clay, Albert T. *Legal and Commercial Transactions Dated in the Assyrian, Neo-Babylonian and Persian Periods Chiefly from Nippur.* The Babylonian Expedition of the University of Pennsylvania, Series A: Cuneiform Texts VIII/1. Philadelphia: Department of Archaeology, University of Pennsylvania, 1908.

Clemens, David M. *Sources for Ugaritic Ritual and Sacrifice.* Alter Orient und Altes Testament 284. Münster: Ugarit-Verlag, 2001.

Clère, J. J. "Un mot pour 'mariage' en Égyptien de l'époque Ramesside." *Revue d'Égyptologie* 20 (1968): 171–5.

Clines, David J. A. "The Evidence for an Autumnal New Year in Pre-Exilic Israel Reconsidered." *Journal of Biblical Literature* 93 (1974): 22–40.

Coarelli, Filippo. *Il Foro Romano * Periodo arcaico,* 3rd edn. Rome: Edizioni Quasar, 1992.

Cohen, Mark E. *The Cultic Calendars of the Ancient Near East.* Bethesda, Md.: CDL, 1993.

Cohen, Yoram. "Feet of Clay at Emar: A Happy End?" (forthcoming).

Cole, Susan Guettel. "Procession and Celebration at the Dionysia." In *Theater and Society in the Classical World.* Edited by Ruth Scodel, pp. 25–38, Ann Arbor: University of Michigan Press, 1993.

Cole, Susan Guettel. *Landscape, Gender, and Ritual Space: The Ancient Greek Experience.* Berkeley: University of California Press, 2004.

Cook, Arthur Bernard. *Zeus: A Study in Ancient Religion.* 3 vols. Cambridge: Cambridge University Press, 1925.

Courtois, Jacques-Claude. "L'Architecture domestique à Ugarit au bronze récent." *Ugarit Forschungen* 11 (1979): 105–34.

Crawford, Michael. *Roman Republican Coinage.* Cambridge: Cambridge University Press, 1974.

Cross, Frank Moore. *Canaanite Myth and Hebrew Epic.* Cambridge, Mass.: Harvard University Press, 1973.

Cross, Frank Moore and Freedman, David Noel. "The Song of Miriam." *Journal of Near Eastern Studies* 14 (1955): 237–50.

Cuneiform Texts from Babylonian Tablets in the British Museum. London: Trustees of the British Museum, 1896–.

d'Abbadie, J. Vandier. "Une fresque civile de Deir el Médineh." *Revue d'Égyptologie* 3 (1938): 27–35.

Dalley, Stephanie, Walker, C. B. F. and Hawkins, J. D. *The Old Babylonian Tablets from Tell al Rimah.* London: British School of Archaeology in Iraq, 1976.

D'Auria, Sue, Lacovara, Peter, Roehrig, Catharine H. (eds.). *Mummies and Magic: The Funerary Arts of Ancient Egypt.* Boston: Museum of Fine Arts, 1988.

Daviau, Paulette M. Michèle. "The Fifth Season of Excavations at Tall Jawa (1994): A Preliminary Report." *Annual of the Department of Antiquities of Jordan* 40 (1996): 83–100.

Daviau, Paulette M. Michèle. "Family Religion: Evidence for the Paraphernalia of the Domestic Cult." In *The World of the Aramaeans II. Studies in History and Archaeology.* Journal for the Study of the Old Testament Supplement Series 325. Edited by P. M. Michèle Daviau, John W. Wevers, and Michael Weigl, pp. 199–229. Sheffield: Sheffield Academic Press, 2001.

Daviau, Paulette M. Michèle. *Excavations at Tall Jawa, Jordan.* 2 vols. Culture and History of the Ancient Near East 11. Vol. 1: *The Iron Age Town*, Leiden and Boston: E. J. Brill, 2003. Vol. 2: *The Iron Age Artifacts*, Leiden and Boston: E. J. Brill, 2002.

David, A. Rosalie. *The Pyramid Builders of Ancient Egypt.* London: Routledge & Kegan Paul, 1986.

Davies, Nina de Garis and de Garis Davies, Norman M. "Harvest Rites in a Theban Tomb." *The Journal of Egyptian Archaeology* 25 (1939): 154–6.

Davies, Norman de Garis and Gardiner, Alan H. (eds.). *The Tomb of Amenemhet (No. 82).* The Theban Tomb Series I. London: Egypt Exploration Fund, 1915.

Day, Peggy. "Anat: Ugarit's 'Mistress of Animals.'" *Journal of Near Eastern Studies* 51 (1992): 181–90.

de Polignac, Francois. *Cults, Territory, and the Origins of the Greek City-State.* Chicago: The University of Chicago, 1995.

de Tarragon, Jean-Michel. *Le culte à Ugarit.* Paris: J. Gabalda, 1980.

de Vaux, Roland. *Ancient Israel.* New York: McGraw-Hill, 1961.

Decker, Wolfgang. "Wurfholz." In *Lexikon der Ägyptologie.* Edited by Wolfgang Helck and Eberhard Otto, 6: 1299–1300. Wiesbaden: Harrassowitz, 1986.

del Olmo Lete, Gregorio. *Canaanite Religion According to the Liturgical Texts of Ugarit.* Bethesda, Md.: CDL Press, 2004.

Deller, Karlheinz. "Die Hausgötter der Familie Shukrija S. Huja." In *Studies on the Civilization and Culture of Nuzi and the Hurrians in Honor of Ernest R. Lacheman.* Studies on the Civilization and Culture of Nuzi and the Hurrians 1. Edited by Martha A. Morrison and David I. Owen, pp. 47–76. Winona Lake: Eisenbrauns, 1981.

Demand, Nancy. *Birth, Death, and Motherhood in Classical Greece.* Baltimore: Johns Hopkins Press, 1994.

Demarée, Robert J. *The 3ḫ ikr n Rʿ-Stelae. On Ancestor Worship.* Egyptologische uitgaven 3. Leiden: Nederlands Instituut voor het Nabije Oosten, 1983.

Desroches-Noblecourt, Christiane. "Pots anthropomorphes et recettes magico-médicales dans l'Égypte ancienne." *Revue d'Egyptologie* 9 (1952): 49–67.

Desroches-Noblecourt, Christiane. "'Concubines du Mort' et mères de famille au Moyen Empire." *Bulletin de l'Institut Français d'Archéologie Orientale* 53 (1953): 7–47.

Dever, William G. *Recent Archaeological Discoveries and Biblical Research.* Seattle and London: University of Washington Press, 1990.

Dever, William G. "Women's Popular Religion, Suppressed in the Bible, Now Revealed in Archaeology." *Biblical Archaeology Review* 17 (1991): 64–5.

Dever, William G. *What Did the Biblical Writers Know and When Did They Know It? What Archaeology Can Tell Us about the Reality of Ancient Israel.* Grand Rapids and Cambridge: Eerdmans, 2002.

Dever, William G. *Who Were the Early Israelites and Where Did They Come From?* Grand Rapids and Cambridge: Eerdmans, 2003.

Dever, William G. *Did God Have a Wife? Archaeology and Folk Religion in Ancient Israel.* Grand Rapids and Cambridge: Eerdmans, 2005.

Dietrich, Manfried, Loretz, Oswald and SanMartin, Joaquin. *Die Keilalphabetischen Texte aus Ugarit.* Alter Orient und Altes Testament 24. Kevelaer: Butzon & Bercker; Neukirchen-Vluyn: Neukirchener, 1976.

Dijkstra, Meindert. "The List of *qdšm* in KTU 4.412 +ii 8ff." *Aula Orientalis* 17–18 (1999–2000): 81–9.

Dijkstra, Meindert. "Women and Religion in the Old Testament." In *Only One God? Monotheism in Ancient Religion and the Veneration of the Goddess Asherah.* Biblical Seminar 77. Edited by Bob Becking, idem, Marjo C. A. Korpel, and Karel J. H. Vriezen, pp. 164–88. Sheffield: Continuum, 2001.

Dillon, Matthew. *Girls and Women in Classical Greek Religion.* London: Routledge, 2002.

Dixon, Suzanne. *The Roman Family.* Baltimore: Johns Hopkins University Press, 1992.

Döhl, Hartmut. "La scultura." In *Pompei 79*, pp. 177–89. Edited by Fausto Zevi. Naples: Gaetano Macchiaeroli, 1984.

Dohmen, C. "*massekah.*" In *Theological Dictionary of the Old Testament.* Edited by G. J. Botterweck, H. Ringgren, and H.-J. Fabry, 8: 431–7. Grand Rapids and Cambridge: Eerdmans, 1997.

Donker Van Heel, Koen. "Use and Meaning of the Egyptian Term *W3h Mw.*" In *Village Voices.* Edited by R. J. Demarée and A. Egberts, pp. 19–30. Leiden: Leiden University Centre of Non-Western Studies, 1992.

Dorcey, Peter F. *The Cult of Silvanus: A Study in Roman Folk Religion.* Leiden and New York: E. J. Brill, 1992.

Dothan, Moshe. *Ashdod II/III: The Second and Third Season of Excavations, 1963, 1965, Soundings in 1967.* ATIQOT IX/X. Jerusalem: Central Press, 1971.

Dothan, Moshe. "Ashdod". In *The New Encyclopedia of Archaeological Excavations in the Holy Land.* Edited by Ephraim Stern, 1: 93–102. Jerusalem: Israel Exploration Society, 1993.

Dothan, Moshe and Dothan, Trude. *People of the Sea: The Search of the Philistines.* New York: Maxmillan, 1992.

Dothan, Moshe and Freedman, David Noel. *Ashdod I: The First Season of Excavations.* ATIQOT VII. Jerusalem: Central Press, 1967.

Dothan, Moshe and Porath, Yosef. *Ashdod IV: The Fourth Season of Excavations.* ATIQOT XV. Jerusalem: Israel Antiquities Authority, 1982.

Dothan, Moshe and Porath, Yosef. *Ashdod V: The Fourth–Sixth Seasons of Excavations 1968–1970.* ATIQOT XIII. Jerusalem: Israel Antiquities Authority, 1993.

Dothan, Trude. *The Philistines and their Material Culture.* New Haven: Yale University Press, 1982.

Doubourdieu, Annie. *Les origines et le développement du culte des Pénates à Rome.* Rome: École française de Rome, 1989.

Dover, K. J. "The Freedom of the Intellectual in Greek Society." *Talanta* 7 (1976): 24–54.

Dumézil, Georges. *Archaic Roman Religion*, 2 vols., translated by Philip Krapp. Baltimore: Johns Hopkins University Press, 1996.

Dunham, Dows. *Naga-ed-Deîr Stelae of the First Intermediate Period.* London: Museum of Fine Arts, Boston, 1937.

DuQuesne, Terence. "Gender, Class and Devotion: demographic and social aspects of the Salakhana Stelae." *Discussions in Egyptology* 63 (2005): 41–57.

Durand, Jean-Marie. "Tombes familiales et culte des ancêtres à Emar." *Nouvelles assyriologiques brèves et utilitaires* (1989): 112.

Durand, Jean-Marie. Review of D. Arnaud, *Recherches au Pays d'Aštata, Emar VI. Revue d'Assyriologie et d'Archaeologie Orientale* 84 (1990): 49–85.

Durand, Jean-Marie and Marti, Lionel. "Chroniques du Moyen-Euphrate.2. Relecture de documents d'Ekalte, Émar, et Tuttul." *Revue d'Assyriologie* 97 (2003): 141–80.

Dyck, Andrew R. *A Commentary on Cicero, De Legibus.* Ann Arbor: University of Michigan Press, 2004.

Ebertz, Michael N. and Schultheis, Frank (eds.). *Volksfrömmigkeit in Europa: Beiträge zur Soziologie populärer Religiosität in 14 Ländern.* Religion–Wissen–Kultur: Studien und Texte zur Religionssoziologie 2. München: Kaiser, 1986.

Edgerton, William F. and Wilson, John A. *Historical Records of Ramses III* (SAOC 12). Chicago: The University of Chicago Press, 1936.

Edwards, I. E. S. *Oracular Amuletic Decrees of the Late New Kingdom.* Hieratic Papyri in the British Museum 4. 2 vols. London: The British Museum, 1960.

Edwards, I. E. S. "Ḳenhikhopshef's Prophylactic Charm." *Journal of Egyptian Archaeology* 54 (1968): 155–60.

Eißfeldt, Otto. "'Mein Gott' im Alten Testament." *Zeitschrift für die alttestamentliche Wissenschaft* 61 (1945–8): 3–16.

Epigraphic Survey, The. *Later Historical Records of Ramses III (Medinet Habu II).* Chicago: The University of Chicago Press, 1932.

Erichsen, W. *Demotisches Glossar.* Copenhagen: Ejnar Munksgaard, 1954.

Erman, Adolf. *Zaubersprüche für Mutter und Kind.* Berlin: Königl. Akademie der Wissenschaften, 1901.

Erman, Adolf and Grapow, Hermann. *Wörterbuch der ägyptischen Sprache.* 5 vols. Berlin and Leipzig: Akademie-Verlag, 1940–59.

Evelyn-White, Hugh G. (ed.). *Hesiod, The Homeric Hymns, and Homerica.* Loeb Classical Library. Cambridge, Mass.: Harvard University Press, 1964.

Exum, J. Cheryl. "Promise and Fulfillment: Narrative Art in Judges 13." *Journal of Biblical Literature* 99 (1980): 43–59.

Exum, J. Cheryl. "'Mother in Israel': A Familiar Figure Reconsidered." In *Feminist Interpretation of the Bible.* Edited by L. M. Russell, pp. 73–85. Philadelphia: Westminster, 1985.

Exum, J. Cheryl. *Fragmented Women: Feminist (Sub)versions of Biblical Narratives.* Valley Forge: Trinity Press International, 1993.

Exum, J. Cheryl. "Feminist Criticism: Whose Interests are Being Served?" In *Judges and Method: New Approaches in Biblical Studies.* Edited by G. A. Yee, pp. 65–90. Minneapolis: Fortress, 1995.

Faraone, Christopher A. "An Accusation of Magic in Classical Athens (Ar. Wasps 946–48)." *Transactions of the American Philological Association* 119 (1989): 149–60.

Faraone, Christopher A. "The Agonistic Context of Early Greek Binding Spells." In *Magika Hiera: Ancient Greek Magic and Religion.* Edited by Christopher A. Faraone and Dirk Obbink, pp. 3–32. New York: Oxford University Press, 1991.

Faraone, Christopher A. *Talismans and Trojan Horses: Guardian Statues in Ancient Greek Myth and Ritual.* Oxford: Oxford University Press, 1992.

Faraone, Christopher A. "Curses and Social Control in the Law Courts of Classical Athens," *Dike: Rivista di storia del diritto greco ed ellenistico* 2 (1999): 99–121.

Faraone, Christopher A. "Hipponax Frag. 128W: Epic Parody or Expulsive Incantation?" *Classical Antiquity* 23 (2004): 209–45.

Faraone, Christopher A. "Orpheus' Final Performance: Necromancy and a Singing Head on Lesbos." *Studi italiani di filologia classica*, series 4, 2 (2004): 5–27.

Faraone, Christopher A., Garnand, B., and López-Ruiz, C. "Micah's Mother (Judg. 17:1–4) and a Curse from Carthage (*KAI* 89): Canaanite Precedents for Greek and Latin Curses against Thieves?" *Journal of Near Eastern Studies* 64 (2005): 161–86.

Farber, Walter. “Zur älteren akkadischen Beschwörungsliteratur,” *Zeitschrift für Assyriologie* 71 (1981): 51–72.

Farber, Walter. *Schlaf! Schlaf, Kindchen, Schlaf! Mesopotamische Baby-Beschwörungen und -Rituale*. Winona Lake: Eisenbrauns, 1989.

Faulkner, Raymond O. *A Concise Dictionary of Middle Egyptian*. Oxford: Oxford University Press, 1962.

Fayolle, Benoît. *Le Livre du Musée Guimet de Lyon. Égypte. Anitquités Grecques et Romaines.* Lyon: Emanuel Vitte, 1958.

Feliu, Lluís. *The God Dagan in Bronze Age Syria*. Translated by Wilfrid G. E. Watson. Leiden: E. J. Brill, 2003.

Festugière, Andre Jean. *Personal Religion among the Greeks.* Berkeley: University of California Press, 1954.

Fincke, Andrew. *The Samuel Scroll from Qumran: 4QSam^{a} Restored and Compared to the Septuagint and 4QSam^{c}*. Leiden, Boston, Köln: Brill, 2001.

Finkbeiner, Uwe, Attoura, Hala, Faist, Betina, König, Uta, Saka, Ferhan and Starke, Frank. “Emar 1999 – Bericht über die 3. Kampagne der syrisch-deutschen Ausgrabungen.” *Baghdader Mitteilungen* 32 (2001): 42–110 and charts.

Finkbeiner, Uwe. “Emar 2001 – Bericht über die 4. Kampagne der syrisch-deutschen Ausgrabungen.” *Baghdader Mitteilungen* 33 (2002): 109–46 and charts.

Finkbeiner, Uwe and Sakal, Ferhan. “Emar 2002 – Bericht über die 5. Kampagne der syrisch-deutschen Ausgrabungen.” *Baghdader Mitteilungen* 34 (2003): 10–100 and charts.

Finkelstein, Israel. “The History and Archaeology of Shiloh from the Middle Bronze Age II to Iron Age II.” In *Shiloh: The Archaeology of a Biblical Site*. Edited by I. Finkelstein, pp. 371–93. Tel Aviv: Monograph Series of Tel Aviv University, 1993.

Fischer, Henry G. “Notes on the Mo’alla Inscriptions and Some Contemporaneous Texts.” *Wiener Zeitschrift für die Kunde des Morgenlandes* 57 (1961): 74–5.

Fleming, Daniel E. “The Voice of the Ugaritic Incantation Priest.” *Ugarit Forschungen* 23 (1991): 141–54.

Fleming, Daniel E. *The Installation of Baal’s High Priestess at Emar: A Window on Ancient Syrian Religion*. Atlanta: Scholars Press, 1992.

Fleming, Daniel E. *Time at Emar: The Cultic Calendar and the Rituals from the Diviner’s Archive*. Winona Lake: Eisenbrauns, 2000.

Fleming, Daniel E. “Schloen’s Patrimonial Pyramid: Explaining Bronze Age Society.” *Bulletin of the American Schools of Oriental Research* 328 (2002): 73–80.

Fleming, Daniel E. *Democracy’s Ancient Ancestors: Mari and Early Collective Governance.* Cambridge: Cambridge University Press, 2004.

Fleming, Daniel E. “Review of Regine Pruzsinszky, *Die Personennamen der Texte aus Emar*.” In the *Journal of the American Oriental Society* 124 (2004): 595–99.

Flory, Marleen B. “Family in *familia*: Kinship and Community in Slavery.” *American Journal of Ancient History* 3 (1978): 78–95.

Forman, Werner and Quirke, Stephen. *Hieroglyphs and the Afterlife*. Norman: University of Oklahoma, 1996.

Foss, Pedar W. “Watchful *Lares*: Roman Household Organization and the Rituals of Cooking and Eating.” In *Domestic Space in the Roman World: Pompeii and Beyond*. Edited by Ray Laurence and Andrew Wallace-Hadrill, pp. 197–218. Portsmouth: Journal of Roman Archaeology, 1997.

Fowler, Jeaneane D. *Theophoric Personal Names in Ancient Hebrew: A Comparative Study.* Journal for the Study of the Old Testament Supplement Series 49. Sheffield: Sheffield Academic Press, 1988.

Fox, Bonnie J. *Family Patterns, Gender Relations.* 2nd edn. New York: Oxford University Press, 2001.

Freedman, Sally M. *If a City is Set on a Height: The Akkadian Omen Series Shumma Alu ina Mele Shakin. Vol. 1: Tablets 1–21.* Occasional Publications of the Samuel Noah Kramer Fund 17. Philadelphia: The University of Pennsylvania Museum, 1998.

Friedman, Florence. "On the Meaning of Some Anthropoid Busts from Deir el-Medina." *The Journal of Egyptian Archaeology* 71 (1985): 82–97.

Friedman, Florence D. "Aspects of Domestic Life and Religion." In *Pharaoh's Workers: The Villagers of Deir el Medina.* Edited by Leonard H. Lesko, pp. 95–117. Ithaca: Cornell University Press, 1994.

Friedman, Florence. *Gifts of the Nile: Ancient Egyptian Faience.* New York: Thames and Hudson, 1998.

Fritz, Volkmar and Kempinski, Aharon. *Ergebnisse der Ausgrabungen auf der Hirbet el-Masos (Tel Masos), 1972–1975*, 3 volumes. Wiesbaden: Harrassowitz, 1983.

Fröhlich, Thomas. *Lararien- und Fassadenbilder in den Vesuvstädten: Untersuchungen zur 'volkstümlichen' pompejanischen Malerei.* Mainz: von Zabern, 1991.

Frost, Frank J. *Plutarch's* Themistocles. *A Historical Commentary.* Princeton: Princeton University Press, 1980.

Frost, Honor. "Anchors Sacred and Profane." In *Arts et Industries de la Pierre.* Ras Shamra-Ougarit VI. Edited by Marguerite Yon and Annie Caubet, pp. 355–410. Paris: Éditions Recherche sur les Civilisations, 1991.

Galvin, Marianne. "The Priestesses of Hathor in the Old Kingdom and the 1st Intermediate Period." PhD dissertation, Brandeis University, 1981. Galvin, Marianne. "Addendum." In *Women's Earliest Records from Ancient Egypt and Western Asia.* Edited by Barbara S. Lesko, pp. 28–30. Atlanta: Scholars Press, 1989.

Gardiner, Alan H. and Sethe, Kurt. *Egyptian Letters to the Dead Mainly from the Old and Middle Kingdoms.* London: Egypt Exploration Society, 1928.

Garland, Robert. *The Greek Way of Death.* Ithaca: Cornell University Press, 1985.

Garland, Robert. *The Greek Way of Life: From Conception to Old Age.* Ithaca: Cornell University Press, 1990.

Gee, John. "Notes on Egyptian Marriage: P. BM 10416 Reconsidered." *Bulletin of the Egyptological Seminar* 15 (2001): 17–25.

Gelb, Ignace et al. (eds.). *Chicago Assyrian Dictionary.* Chicago: Oriental Institute, 1956–2007.

George, Andrew R. "Ninurta-paqidat's Dog Bite, and Notes on Other Comic Tales." *Iraq* 55 (1993): 63–75.

George, Andrew R. *The Babylonian Gilgamesh Epic: Introduction, Critical Edition and Cuneiform Texts.* 2 vols. Oxford: Oxford University Press, 2003.

Germond, Philippe. *Sekhmet et la Protection du Monde.* Ægyptiaca Helvetica 9. Basel and Geneva: Editions de Belles-Lettres, 1981.

Germond, Philippe. *Les invocations à la Bonne Année au temple d'Edfou.* Ægyptiaca Helvetica 11. Basel and Geneva: Editions de Belles-Lettres, 1986.

Gerstenberger, Erhard S. *Der bittende Mensch: Bittritual und Klagelied des Einzelnen im Alten Testament.* Wissenschaftliche Monographien zum Alten und Neuen Testament 51. Neukirchen-Vluyn: Neukirchener Verlag, 1980.

Gerstenberger, Erhard. *Theologien im Alten Testament. Pluralität und Synkretismus alttestamentlichen Gottesglaubens.* Stuttgart, Berlin and Köln: Kohlhammer, 2001.

Ghalioungui, Paul. *Magic and Medical Science in Ancient Egypt.* London: Hodder and Stoughton, 1963.

Giacobello, Federica. "Lararium (mondo romano)." In *Thesaurus Cultus et Rituum Antiquorum*, vol. 4, pp. 262–64. Los Angeles: J. Paul Getty Museum, 2005.

Gitin, Seymour. "Ekron of the Philistines Part II: Olive-Oil Suppliers to the World." *Biblical Archaeology Review XVI, 2* (1990): 33–42; 59.

Gitin, Seymour. "Seventh Century BCE. Cultic Elements at Ekron." In *Biblical Archaeology Today 1990: Proceedings of the Second International Congress on Biblical Archaeology, Jerusalem, June–July 1990.* Edited by Avraham Biran and Joseph Aviram, pp. 248–54. Jerusalem: Israel Exploration Society, 1993.

Gitin, Seymour, Dothan, Trude, and Naveh, Joseph. "A Royal Dedicatory Inscription from Ekron." *Israel Exploration Journal* 47 (1997): 1–16.

Gitin, Seymour. "The Four-Horned Altar and Sacred Space: An Archaeological Perspective." In *Sacred Time, Sacred Place: Archaeology and the Religion of Israel.* Edited by Barry M. Gittlen, pp. 95–123. Winona Lake: Eisenbrauns, 2002.

Gitin, Seymour. "Israelite and Philistine Cult and the Archaeological Record in Iron Age II: The 'Smoking Gun' Phenomenon." In *Symbiosis, Symbolism, and the Power of Past: Canaan, Ancient Israel, and Their Neighbors from the Late Bronze Age through Roman Palestine: Proceedings of the Centennial Symposium W. F. Albright Institute of Archaeological Research and American Schools of Oriental Research Jerusalem, May 29–May 31, 2000.* Edited by William G. Dever and Seymour Gitin, pp. 279–95. Winona Lake: Eisenbrauns, 2003.

Goedicke, Hans. "Was Magic Used in the Harem Conspiracy against Ramesses III?" *Journal of Egyptian Archaeology* 49 (1973): 91–2.

Gradel, Ittai. *Emperor Worship and Roman Religion.* Oxford: Clarendon Press, 2002.

Graeber, David. *Toward an Anthropological Theory of Value.* New York: Palgrave, 2001.

Graefe, E. "Talfest." In *Lexikon der Ägyptologie.* Edited by Wolfgang Helck and Eberhard Otto, 6: 187–9. Wiesbaden: Harrassowitz, 1986.

Granqvist, Hilma. *Child Problems among the Arabs.* Helsingfors, Söderström, 1950.

Greenstein, Edward L. "Kirta." In *Ugaritic Narrative Poetry.* Edited by S. B. Parker, pp. 9–48. Atlanta: Scholars Press, 1997.

Groneberg, Brigitte R. M. "Eine Einführungsszene in der altbabylonischen Literatur: Bemerkungen zum persönlichen Gott." In *Keilschriftliche Literaturen: Ausgewählte Vorträge der XXXII. Recontre Assyriologique Internationale.* Berliner Beiträge zum Vorderen Orient 6. Edited by Karl Hecker and Walther Sommerfeld, pp. 93–108. Münster: Dietrich Reimer, 1986.

Groneberg, Brigitte R. M. *Lob der Ishtar: Gebet und Ritual an die altbabylonische Venusgöttin.* Cuneiform Monographs 8. Groningen: Styx, 1997.

Grosz, Katarzyna. "Daughters Adopted as Sons at Nuzi and Emar." In *La femme dans le Proche-Orient antique.* Edited by Jean-Marie Durand, pp. 81–6. Paris: Editions Recherche sur les Civilisations, 1987.

Gruber, Mayer I. *The Motherhood of God and Other Studies.* South Florida Studies in the History of Judaism 57. Atlanta: Scholars Press, 1992.

Gunn, Battiscombe. "The Religion of the Poor in Ancient Egypt." *Journal of Egyptian Archaeology* 3 (1916): 81–94.

Gunn, Battiscombe. "A Note on Brit. Mus. 828 (Stela of Simontu)." *The Journal of Egyptian Archaeology* 25 (1939): 218–19.

Gunn, David M. *Judges.* Blackwell Bible Commentaries. Oxford: Blackwell Publishing, 2005.

Guthrie, Stewart. *Faces in the Clouds: A New Theory of Religion.* New York: Oxford, 1993.

Habash, Martha. "Two Complementary Festivals in Aristophanes *Acharnians.*" *American Journal of Philology* 116 (1995): 559–77.

Hachlili, Rahel. "Figurines and Kernoi." In Moshe Dothan. *Ashdod II/III: The Second and Third Season of Excavations, 1963, 1965, Soundings in 1967*, pp. 125–35. ATIQOT IX/X. Jerusalem: Central Press, 1971.

Hallo, William W. "Two Letter-Prayers to Amurru." In *Boundaries of the Ancient Near Eastern World: A Tribute to Cyrus H. Gordon.* JSOT Supplement Series 273. Edited by Meir Lubetski, Claire Gottlieb and Sharon Keller, pp. 397–410. Sheffield: Sheffield Academic Press, 1998.

Hamilton, Richard. *Choes and Anthesteria. Athenian Iconography and Ritual.* Ann Arbor: University of Michigan Press, 1991.
Hänlein Schäfer, Hanne. "Die Ikonographie des *Genius Augusti* im Kompital- und Hauskult der frühen Kaiserzeit." In *Subject and Ruler: The Cult of the Ruling Power in Classical Antiquity.* Edited by Alastair Small, pp. 73–98. Ann Arbor: Journal of Roman Archaeology, 1996.
Haran, Menahem. "Zebaḥ Hayyamim," *Vetus Testamentum* 19 (1969): 11–22.
Haran, Menahem. *Temples and Temple Service in Ancient Israel.* Oxford: Clarendon, 1978.
Harris, James E. and Kent R. Weeks. *X-Raying the Pharaohs.* New York: Charles Scribner's Sons, 1973.
Harrison, Jane Ellen. *Themis: A Study in the Social Origins of Greek Religion.* 2nd edn. New York: Cambridge University Press, 1927.
Harrison, Stephen J. "Cicero's 'De Temporibus suis': the Evidence Reconsidered," *Hermes* 118 (1990): 460–2.
Hawass, Zahi. "The Tombs of the Pyramid Builders – The Tomb of the Artisan Petety and his Curse." In *Egypt, Israel and the Ancient Mediterranean World: Studies in Honor of Donald B. Redford.* Edited by Gary H. Knoppers and Antony Hirsch, 21–40. Leiden: E. J. Brill, 2004.
Hayes, William C. *The Scepter of Egypt.* 2 vols. New York: The Metropolitan Museum of Art, 1953.
Heinrich, Ernst and Ursula Seidl. "Grundrisszeichnungen aus dem Alten Orient." *Mitteilungen der Deutschen Orient-Gesellschaft* 98 (1967): 24–45.
Helck, Wolfgang. *Urkunden der 18: Dynastie.* Heft 17. Berlin: Akademie-Verlag, 1955.
Heltzer, Michael. *The Rural Community in Ancient Ugarit.* Wiesbaden: Reichert, 1976.
Heltzer, Michael. *The Internal Organization of the Kingdom of Ugarit.* Wiesbaden: Reicher Verlag, 1982.
Heltzer, Michael. "The Late Bronze Age Service System and Its Decline." In *Society and Economy in the Eastern Mediterranean.* Edited by M. Heltzer and E. Lipiński, pp. 7–18. Leuven: Peeters, 1988.
Heltzer, Michael. "The Economy of Ugarit." In *Handbook of Ugaritic Studies.* Edited by W. G. E. Watson and N. Wyatt, pp. 423–54. Leiden: E. J. Brill, 1999.
Herrmann, Christian. *Ägyptische Amulette aus Palästina/Israel: Mit einem Ausblick auf ihre Rezeption durch das Alte Testament.* Orbis Biblicus et Orientalis 138. Fribourg: Universitätsverlag; Göttingen: Vandenhoeck & Ruprecht, 1994.
Hess, Richard. "The Onomastics of Ugarit." In *Handbook of Ugaritic Studies.* Edited by W. G. E. Watson and N. Wyatt, pp. 499–528. Leiden: E. J. Brill, 1999.
Hestrin, Ruth, and Dayagi-Mendels, Michal. *Inscribed Seals: First Temple Period, Hebrew, Ammonite, Moabite, and Aramaic.* Jerusalem: Israel Museum, 1979.
Hoffner, Harry A. "Second Millennium Antecedents to the Hebrew *'ob.*" *Journal of Biblical Literature* 86 (1976): 385–401.
Hoffner, Harry A. "Name, Namengebung. C. Bei den Hethitern." *Reallexikon der Assyriologie.* Edited by Erich Ebeling and Bruno Meissner, 9: 116 21. Berlin: De Gruyter, 1998.
Holladay, John S., Jr. "Religion in Israel and Judah Under the Monarchy: An Explicitly Archaeological Approach." In *Ancient Israelite Religion: Essays in Honor of Frank Moore Cross.* Edited by Patrick D. Miller Jr., Paul D. Hanson, and S. Dean McBride, pp. 249–99. Philadelphia: Fortress Press, 1987.
Hölscher, Uvo. *Post-Ramessid Remains: The Excavation of Medinet Habu Vol. V.* Oriental Institute Publications 66. Chicago: The University of Chicago, 1954.
Hopkins, Keith. *Conquerors and Slaves.* Cambridge: Cambridge University Press, 1978.
Horton, Robyn. *Patterns of Thought in Africa and the West.* Cambridge: Cambridge University Press, 1993.

How, W. W. and Wells, J. *A Commentary on Herodotus*, 2 vols. Oxford: Oxford University Press, 1912.

Humphreys, S. C. *The Strangeness of Gods: Historical Perspectives on the Interpretation of Athenian Religion*. Oxford: Oxford University Press, 2004.

Hutter, Manfred (ed.). *Offizielle Religion, locale Kulte und individuelle Religiosität: Akten des religionsgeschichtlichen Symposiums "Kleinasien und angrenzende Gebiete vom Beginn des 2. bis zur Mitte des 1. Jahrtausends v. Chr.": (Bonn, 20.–22. Februar 2003)*. Alter Orient und Altes Testament 318. Münster: Ugarit-Verlag, 2004.

Ikram, Salima. "Domestic Shrines and the Cult of the Royal Family at el-'Amarna." *Journal of Egyptian Archaeology* 75 (1989): 89–101.

Ikram, Salima. "Barbering the Beardless: A Possible Explanation for the Tufted Hairstyle Depicted in the 'Fayum' Portrait of a Young Boy (J. P. Getty 78.AP.262)." *Journal of Egyptian Archaeology* 89 (2003): 247–51.

Iversen, Erik. "Papyrus Carlsberg No. VIII. With some remarks on the Egyptian Origin of Some Popular Birth Prognoses." *Historisk-filologiske Meddelelser udgivet af det Kgl. Danske Videnskabernes Selskab* XXVI.5 (1939): 1–31.

Jacobs, Paul F. and Borowski, Oded. "Tell Halif 1992." *Israel Exploration Journal* 43 (1993): 66–70.

Jacobsen, Thorkild. *The Treasures of Darkness: A History of Mesopotamian Religion*. New Haven: Yale University Press, 1976.

Jacoby, Felix. *Die Fragmente der griechischen Historiker*, Part 3 B. Leiden: Brill, 1964.

Jameson, Michael. "Private Space and the Greek City." In *The Greek City from Homer to Alexander*. Edited by Oswyn Murray and S. R. F. Price, pp. 171–95. Oxford: Clarendon Press, 1990.

Jamison, Stephanie W. *Sacrificed Wife/Sacrificer's Wife. Women, Ritual, and Hospitality in Ancient India*. New York: Oxford University Press, 1996.

Jankuhn, Dieter. *Das Buch "Schutz des Hauses" (s3-pr)*. Bonn: R. Habelt, 1972.

Janssen, Jac. J. *Commodity Prices from the Ramesside Period*. Leiden: Brill, 1975.

Janssen, Jac. J. "Marriage Problems and Public Reactions." In *Pyramid Studies and Other Essays*. Edited by J. Baines, T. G. H. James, Anthony Leahy, and A. F. Shore. London: Egypt Exploration Society, 1988, pp. 134–7.

Janssen, Rosalind M. and Janssen, Jac. J. *Growing up in Ancient Egypt*. London: Rubicon, 1990.

Jasnow, Richard and Vittmann, Günther. "An Abnormal Hieratic Letter to the Dead (P. Brooklyn 37.1799 E)." *Enchoria* 19/20 (1992/93): 23–43.

Jean, Charles-F. *Contrats de Larsa*. Textes cuneiforms du Louvre 11. Paris: Geuthner, 1926.

Jebb, Richard Claverhouse, trans. *The Rhetoric of Aristotle*. Cambridge: Cambridge University Press, 1909.

Jirku, Anton. *Materialien zur Volksreligion Israels*. Leipzig: A. Deichert'sche Verlagsbuchhandlung, 1914.

Johnson, Janet H. "Family Law." In *Mistress of the House, Mistress of Heaven*. Edited by A. K. Capel and G. E. Markoe, pp. 179–85. Cincinnati: Cincinnati Art Museum, 1996.

Johnston, Sarah Iles. *Restless Dead: Encounters between the Living and the Dead in Ancient Greece*. Berkeley: University of California Press, 1999.

Johnston, Sarah Iles (ed.). *Religions of the Ancient World: A Guide*. Cambridge and London: Harvard University Press, 2004.

Kaiser, Jessica. "Honoring the Dead." *Aeragram: Newsletter of the Ancient Egypt Research Association* 6 (2004): 10–14.

Kalla, Gábor. "Das altbabylonische Wohnhaus und seine Struktur nach philologischen Quellen." In *Houses and Households in Ancient Mesopotamia: Papers Read at the 40e Rencontre Assyriologique Internationale*. Edited by Klaas R. Veenhof, pp. 247–56. Istanbul: Nederlands Historisch-Archaeologische Instituut, 1996.

Kaplony-Heckel, Ursula. *Die demotischen Tempeleide.* 2 vols. Wiesbaden: Harrassowitz, 1963.

Kaufmann-Heinimann, Annemarie. *Götter und Lararien aus Augusta Raurica: Herstellung, Fundzusammenhänge und sakrale Funktion figürlicher Bronzen in einer römischen Stadt* (Forschungenr in Augst 26). Augst: Römerstadt Augusta Raurica, 1998.

Keel, Othmar and Uehlinger, Christoph. *Gods, Goddesses, and Images of God in Ancient Israel.* Minneapolis: Fortress, 1998.

Keel, Othmar and Uehlinger, Christoph. *Göttinnen, Götter und Gottessymbole: Neue Erkenntnisse zur Religionsgeschichte Kanaans und Israels aufgrund bislang unerschlossener ikonographischer Quellen.* 4th edn. Quaestiones Disputatae 134. Freiburg & Basel & Wien: Herder, 1999.

Keith, Kathryn Elizabeth. "Cities, Neighborhoods, and Houses: Urban Spatial Organization in Old Babylonian Mesopotamia." PhD dissertation, University of Michigan, 1999. UMI Microfilm 9938459.

Kemp, Barry J. "Wall Paintings from the Workmen's Village at el-'Amarna." *The Journal of Egyptian Archaeology* 65 (1979): 47–53.

Kemp, Barry J. *Amarna Reports III.* London: Egypt Exploration Society, 1986.

Kemp, Barry J. *Ancient Egypt: Anatomy of a Civilization.* London: Routledge, 1989.

Kemp, Barry J. "How Religious were the Ancient Egyptians?" *Cambridge Archaeological Journal* 5(1) (1995): 25–54.

Kempinski, Aharon and Ronny Reich (eds.). *The Architecture of Ancient Israel: From the Prehistoric to the Persian Periods, in Memory of Immanuel (Munya) Dunayevsky.* Jerusalem: Israel Exploration Society, 1992.

King, Leonard W. *The Letters and Inscriptions of Hammurabi.* London: Luzac, 1900.

King, Leonard W. *The Seven Tablets of Creation.* London: Luzac, 1902.

King, Philip J. and Stager, Lawrence E. *Life in Biblical Israel.* Library of Ancient Israel. Louisville and London: Westminster/John Knox, 2001.

Kitchen, Kenneth A. *Ramesside Inscriptions Historical and Biographical.* Vol. IV. Oxford: Blackwell, 1990.

Kitchen, Kenneth A. *Ramesside Inscriptions Translated and Annotated. Translations.* Vol. IV. Oxford: Blackwell, 2003.

Klein, Lillian. *The Triumph of Irony in the Book of Judges.* Journal for the Study of the Old Testament Supplement Series 68. Bible and Literature Series 14. Sheffield: Almond, 1988.

Kletter, Raz. *The Judean Pillar-Figurines and the Archaeology of Asherah.* Biblical Archaeology Review International Series 636. Oxford: Hadrian Books, 1996.

Koehler, Josef and Arthur Ungnad. *Hammurabi's Gesetz.* Leipzig: Pfeiffer, 1909.

Korpel, Marjo C. A. *A Rift in the Clouds.* Münster: Ugarit-Verlag, 1990.

Kottsieper, Ingo. "El – ferner oder naher Gott?" In *Religion und Gesellschaft.* Alter Orient und Altes Testament 248. Edited by Rainer Albertz, pp. 25–74. Münster: Ugarit Verlag, 1997.

Kottsieper, Ingo. "Eine Tempelbauinschrift aus Ekron." In *Texte aus der Umwelt des Alten Testaments Ergänzungslieferung.* Edited by Otto Kaiser, pp. 189–90. Gutersloh: Gütersloher Verlagshaus, 2001.

Krafeld-Daugherty, Maria. *Wohnen im Alten Orient: Eine Untersuchung zur Verwendung von Räumen in altorientalischen Wohnhäusern.* Altertumskunde des Vorderen Orients 3. Münster: Ugarit-Verlag, 1994.

Kraus, Fritz Rudolf (ed.). *Altbabylonische Briefe in Umschrift und Übersetzung.* Leiden: Brill, 1964–.

Kunckel, Hille. *Der römische Genius.* Heidelberg: F. H. Kerle Verlag, 1974.

Lacheman, Ernest R. *Excavations at Nuzi, 5: Miscellaneous Texts from Nuzi, 2: The Palace and Temple Archives.* Harvard Semitic Studies 14. Cambridge, Mass.: Harvard University Press, 1950.

Lacheman, Ernest R. *Excavations at Nuzi, 8: Family Law Documents.* Harvard Semitic Studies 19. Cambridge, Mass.: Harvard University Press, 1962.

Lacheman, Ernest R. and Owen, David I. "Texts from Arrapha and from Nuzi in the Yale Babylonian Collection." In *Studies on the Civilization and Culture of Nuzi and the Hurrians in Honor of Ernest R. Lacheman.* Studies on the Civilization and Culture of Nuzi and the Hurrians 1. Edited by Martha A. Morrison and David I. Owen, pp. 377–432. Winona Lake: Eisenbrauns, 1981.

Lanczkowski, Günter. *Begegnung und Wandel der Religionen.* Darmstadt: Wissenschaftliche Buchgesellschaft, 1981.

Landsberger, Benno. *The Series HAR-ra "hubullu", Tablets I–IV.* Materials for the Sumerian Lexicon 5. Rome: Pontificium Institutum Biblicum, 1957.

Lane, Edward W. *An Account of the Manners and Customs of the Modern Egyptians.* 3rd edn. London: C. Knight and Co., 1842.

Lang, Bernhard. "Persönlicher Gott und Ortsgott: Über Elementarformen der Frömmigkeit im Alten Israel." In *Fontes atque Pontes: Festschrift Helmut Brunner.* Ägypten und Altes Testament 45. Edited by Manfred Görg, pp. 271–301. Wiesbaden: Harrassowitz, 1983.

Lang, Bernhard. *Jahwe, der biblische Gott: Ein Porträt.* Darmstadt: Wissenschaftliche Buchgesellschaft, 2002.

Lesko, Barbara S. (ed.). *Women's Earliest Records.* Brown Judaic Studies 166. Atlanta: Scholars Press, 1989.

Lesko, Barbara. "Rank, Roles, and Rights." In *Pharaoh's Workers: The Villagers of Deir el-Medina.* Edited by L. Lesko, pp. 26–34. Ithaca: Cornell University Press, 1994.

Lesko, Barbara S. "Ancient Egyptian Religions." *Encyclopedia of Women and World Religion,* pp. 32–5. New York: Macmillan Reference USA, 1999.

Lesko, Barbara S. *The Great Goddesses of Egypt.* Norman: University of Oklahoma Press, 1999.

Lesko, Leonard H. (ed.). *Pharaoh's Workers: The Villagers of Deir el-Medina.* Ithaca: Cornell University Press, 1994.

Levy, Thomas (ed.). *The Archaeology of Society in the Holy Land.* New York: Facts on File, 1995.

Lewis, Theodore J. *Cults of the Dead in Ancient Israel and Ugarit.* Harvard Semitic Monographs 39. Atlanta: Scholars Press, 1989.

Lewis, Theodore J. "How Far Can Texts Take Us? Evaluating Textual Sources for Reconstructing Ancient Israelite Beliefs about the Dead." In *Sacred Time, Sacred Space: Archaeology and the Religion of Israel.* Edited by B. M. Gittlen, pp. 169–217. Winona Lake: Eisenbrauns, 2002.

Lewis, Theodore J. "Syro-Palestinian Iconography and Divine Images." In *Cult Image and Divine Representation in the Ancient Near East.* Edited by N. H. Walls, pp. 69–107. Boston: American Schools of Oriental Research, 2005.

Lichtheim, Miriam. *Ancient Egyptian Literature.* 3 vols. Berkeley: University of California Press, 1973.

Lichtheim, Miriam. *Moral Values in Ancient Egypt.* Orbis Biblicus et Orientalis 155. Fribourg: Universitätsverlag, 1997.

LiDonnici, Lynn R. *The Epidaurian Miracle Inscriptions: Text, Translation and Commentary.* Atlanta: Scholars Press, 1995.

Lipiński, Edward. "The Socio-Economic Condition of the Clergy in the Kingdom of Ugarit." In *Society and Economy in the Eastern Mediterranean.* Edited by M. Heltzer and E. Lipiński, pp. 125–50. Leuven: Peeters, 1988.

Lisdorf, Anders. "The Conflict over Cicero's House: An Analysis of the Ritual Element in Cicero's *De Domo Sua,*" *Numen* 52 (2005): 445–64.

Liverani, Mario. "Ras Shamra, histoire." In *Supplément au Dictionnaire de la Bible,* vol. 9. Edited by H. Cazelles and A. Feuillet, pp. 1298–1345. Paris: Letouzey & Ané, 1979.

Lloyd, Alan B. *Herodotus Book II. Commentary 1–98.* Leiden: E. J. Brill, 1976.
Lott, J. Bert. *The Neighborhoods of Augustan Rome.* Cambridge: Cambridge University Press, 2004.
Luft, Ulrich. "Religion." In *The Oxford Encyclopedia of Egyptology.* Edited by Donald B. Redford, 3: 139–45. Oxford: Oxford University Press, 2001.
Mack, Burton. "On Redescribing Christian Origins." *Method and Theory in the Study of Religion* 8 (1996): 247–69.
Mallet, Joel and Matoïan, Valerie. "Une Maison au Sud du "Temple aux Rhytons" (fouilles 1979–1999)." In *Études Ougaritiques: I. Travaux 1985–1995.* Ras Shamra-Ougarit XIV. Edited by M. Yon and D. Arnaud, pp. 83–190. Paris: Éditions Recherche sur les Civilisations, 2001.
Marchegay, Sophie. "The Tombs." *Near Eastern Archaeology* 63 (2000): 208–9.
Margueron, Jean-Claude. "Architecture et urbanisme." In *Meskéné-Emar: Dix ans de travaux, 1972–1982.* Edited by Dominique Beyer, pp. 23–39. Paris: Éditions Recherche sur les Civilisations, 1982.
Marquet-Krause, Judith. *Les fouilles de ʿAy (et-Tell), 1933–35.* Bibliothèque archéologique et historique 45. Paris: Geuthner, 1949.
Martin, Dale B. "The Construction of the Ancient Family: Methodological Considerations." *Journal of Roman Studies* 86 (1996): 40–60.
Martin, Dale B. "Slave Families and Slaves in Families." In *Early Christian Families in Context.* Edited by David L. Balch and Carolyn Osiek, pp. 207–30. Grand Rapids: Eerdmans, 2003.
Martin, James D. *The Book of Judges.* Cambridge Biblical Commentary. Cambridge: Cambridge University Press, 1975.
Martin, Luther H. "Comparison." In *Guide to the Study of Religion.* Edited by Willi Braun and Russell T. McCuthcheon, pp. 45–56. London: Cassell, 2000.
Matoush, Lubor. "Les contrats de partage provenant des archives d'Iddin-Amurru." In *Symbolae ad studia orientis pertinentes Frederico Hrozny dedicatae.* Archiv Orientální 17/2. Edited by V. Eihar, J. Klima, and L. Matoush, pp. 142–73 and Pls. I–II. Prague: Czechoslovak Oriental Institute, 1949.
Matthews, Victor H. *Judges and Ruth.* New Cambridge Biblical Commentary. Cambridge: Cambridge University Press, 2004.
Mau, August and Kelsey, Francis W. *Pompeii. Its Life and Art,* 2nd edn. London: Macmillan, 1902.
Mazar, Amihai. *Excavations at Tell Qasile I.* QEDEM 12. Jerusalem: Institute of Archaeology, Hebrew University of Jerusalem, 1980.
Mazar, Amihai. "The 'Bull Site' – An Iron Age I Open Cult Place." *Bulletin of the American Schools of Oriental Research* 247 (1982): 27–42.
Mazar, Amihai. "Excavations at Tell Qasile 1982–1984, Preliminary Report." *Israel Exploration Journal* 36 (1986): 1–15.
Mazois, Charles François. *Les ruines de Pompéi.* Vol. II. Paris: F. Didot, 1812.
McAnany, Patricia A. *Living with the Ancestors: Kinship and Kingship in Ancient Maya Society.* Austin: University of Texas Press, 1995.
McAnany, Patricia A. (ed.). *K'axob: Ritual, Work, and Family in an Ancient Maya Village.* Monumenta Archaeologica 22. Los Angeles: The Cotsen Institute of Archaeology at UCLA, 2004.
McCarter, P. Kyle. *I Samuel: A New Translation with Introduction and Commentary.* Anchor Bible 8. Garden City, N.Y.: Doubleday, 1980.
McClellan, Thomas L. "Houses and Households in North Syria during the Late Bronze Age." In *Les maisons dans la Syrie antique du IIIe millénaire aux débuts de l'Islam.* Edited by Corinne Castel, Michel al-Maqdissi and François Villeneuve, pp. 29–60. Beirut: Institut Français d'Archéologie du Proche-Orient, 1997.

McDowell, Andrea G. *Village Life in Ancient Egypt: Laundry Lists and Love Songs.* Oxford: Oxford University Press, 1999.

McGeough, Kevin M. "Locating the Marziḥu Archaeologically." *Ugarit Forschungen* 35 (2003): 407–20.

McGeough, Kevin M. "Exchange Relationships at Ugarit: A Study of the Economic Texts." PhD dissertation. University of Pennsylvania, 2005.

McKinnon, Susan. *Neo-Liberal Genetics: The Limits and Moral Tales of Evolutionary Psychology.* Chicago: Prickly Paradigm, 2005.

McLaughlin, John. *The Marzeaḥ in the Prophetic Literature.* Leiden: E. J. Brill, 2001.

McNutt, Paula. *Reconstructing the Society of Ancient Israel.* Library of Ancient Israel. Louisville: Westminster/John Knox; London: SPCK, 1999.

Merlo, Paolo and Paolo Xella. "The Ugaritic Cultic Texts." In *Handbook of Ugaritic Studies.* Ed. W. G. E. Watson and N. Wyatt, pp. 287–358. Leiden: E. J. Brill, 1999.

Meshel, Ze'ev. *Kuntillet ʿAjrud: A Religious Center from the Time of the Judean Monarchy on the Border of Sinai.* Jerusalem: The Israel Museum, 1978.

Meyer, Eduard. *Der Papyrusfund von Elephantine: Dokumente einer jüdischen Gemeinde aus der Perserzeit und das älteste erhaltene Buch der Weltliteratur.* 3rd edn. Leipzig: J. C. Hinrichs'sche Buchhandlung, 1912.

Meyers, Carol. *Discovering Eve: Ancient Israelite Women in Context.* New York and Oxford: Oxford University Press, 1988.

Meyers, Carol. "Ephod." In *Anchor Bible Dictionary.* Edited by D. N. Freedman, 2: 550a–b. New York: Doubleday, 1992.

Meyers, Carol. "The Hannah Narrative in Feminist Perspective." In *Go to the Land I Will Show You: Studies in Honor of Dwight W. Young.* Edited by J. Coleson and V. Matthews, pp. 117–26. Winona Lake: Eisenbrauns, 1996 (= "Hannah and her Sacrifice: Reclaiming Female Agency." In *A Feminist Companion to Samuel and Kings.* The Feminist Companion to the Bible 5. Edited by A. Brenner, pp. 93–104. Sheffield: Sheffield Academic Press, 1994.

Meyers, Carol. "An Ethnoarchaeological Analysis of Hannah's Sacrifice." In *Pomegranates and Golden Bells: Studies in Biblical, Jewish, and Near Eastern Ritual, Law, and Literature in Honor of Jacob Milgrom.* Edited by D. P. Wright, D. N. Freedman, and A. Hurvitz, pp. 77–91. Winona Lake: Eisenbrauns, 1995.

Meyers, Carol. "The Family in Early Israel." In *Families in Ancient Israel.* Edited by Leo G. Perdue, Joseph Blenkinsopp, John J. Collins, and Carol Meyers, pp. 1–47. Louisville: Westminster/John Knox, 1997.

Meyers, Carol. "Everyday Life: Women in the Period of the Hebrew Bible." In *The Women's Bible Commentary, Expanded Edition, with the Apocrypha.* Edited by C. A. Newsom and S. Ringe, pp. 251–9. London: SPCK; Louisville: Westminster/John Knox, 1998.

Meyers, Carol. "Judg 17:1–4, Mother of Micah." In *Women in Scripture: A Dictionary of Named and Unnamed Women in the Hebrew Bible, the Apocryphal/Deuterocanonical Books, and the New Testament.* Edited by C. Meyers, with T. Craven and R. S. Kraemer, pp. 248a–b. Boston: Houghton Mifflin, 2000.

Meyers, Carol L. "From Household to House of Yahweh: Women's Religious Culture in Ancient Israel." In *Congress Volume Basel 2001.* Vetus Testamentum Supplement 92. Edited by André Lemaire, pp. 277–303. Leiden and Boston: E. J. Brill, 2002.

Meyers, Carol. "Engendering Syro-Palestinian Archaeology: Reasons and Resources." *Near Eastern Archaeology* 66 (2003): 185–97.

Meyers, Carol. "Material Remains and Social Relations: Women's Culture in Agrarian Households of the Iron Age." In *Symbiosis, Symbolism, and the Power of the Past: Canaan, Ancient Israel, and Their Neighbors from the Late Bronze Age through Roman Palaestina. Proceedings of the Centennial Symposium, W. F. Albright Institute of Archaeological*

Research and American Schools of Oriental Research, Jerusalem, May 29 – May 31, 2000. Edited by W. G. Dever and S. Gitin, pp. 425–44. Winona Lake: Eisenbrauns, 2003.

Meyers, Eric. "Secondary Burials in Palestine." *Biblical Archaeologist* 33 (1970): 2–29.

Michalowski, Piotr. "Incantation and Literary Letter Incipits." *Nouvelles Assyriologiques Brèves et Utilitaires* (1991): 48.

Mikalson, Jon D. "Religion in the Attic Demes" *American Journal of Philology* 98 (1977): 424–35.

Mikalson, Jon D. *Ancient Greek Religion.* Oxford: Blackwell, 2004.

Millard, Dom Bede. "St Christopher and the Lunar Disc of Anubis." *The Journal of Egyptian Archaeology* 73 (1987): 237–8.

Miller, Patrick D. "Things Too Wonderful: Prayers of Women in the Old Testament." In *Biblische Theologie und gesellschaftlicher Wandel: Für Norbert Lohfink SJ.* Edited by G. Braulik, W. Gross, and S. McEvenue, pp. 237–51. Freiburg, Basel, and Wien: Herder, 1993.

Miller, Patrick D. *They Cried to the Lord: The Form and Theology of Biblical Prayer.* Minneapolis: Fortress, 1994.

Miller, Patrick D. *The Religion of Ancient Israel.* Library of Ancient Israel. London: SPCK; Louisville: Westminster/John Knox, 2000.

Miller, Stephen R. "Ramah." In *Eerdman's Dictionary of the Bible.* Edited by D. N. Freedman, 1108a–b. Grand Rapids: Eerdmans, 2000.

Mommsen, Theodor. *The History of Rome.* Translated by William Purdie Dickson. London: Bentley, 1868.

Montserrat, Dominic. "Mallocouria and Therapeuteria: Rituals of Transition in a Mixed Society?" *Bulletin of the American Society of Papyrology* 28 (1991): 45–9.

Montserrat, Dominic. *Sex and Society in Graeco-Roman Egypt.* London: Kegan Paul International, 1996.

Moore, George F. *A Critical and Exegetical Commentary on Judges.* 2nd edn. International Critical Commentary. Edinburgh: T. & T. Clark, 1903.

Morris, Ian. *Burial and Ancient Society: The Rise of the Greek City-State.* Cambridge: Cambridge University Press, 1987.

Morris, Ian. "Attitudes toward Death in Classical Greece." *Classical Antiquity* 8 (1989): 296–320.

Mueller, E. Aydeet. *The Micah Story: A Morality Tale in the Book of Judges.* Studies in Biblical Literature 34. New York: Peter Lang, 2001.

Murray, Oswyn and Price, S. R. F. (eds.). *The Greek City from Homer to Alexander.* Oxford: Clarendon Press, 1990.

Nachtergael, G. "Terre cuites de l'Égypte gréco-romaine." *Chronique d'Égypte* 70 (1995): 254–94.

Naguib, Saphinaz-Amal. *Le clergé féminin d'Amon thébain à la 21e Dynastie.* Oslo: Ethnografisk Museum, 1988.

Nagy, J. F. "Hierarchy, Heroes, and Heads: Indo-European Structures in Greek Myth." In *Approaches to Greek Myth.* Edited by Lowell Edmunds, pp. 200–38. Baltimore: Johns Hopkins University Press, 1990.

Nakhai, Beth Alpert. *Archaeology and the Religions of Canaan and Israel.* Boston: American Schools of Oriental Research, 2001.

Nashef, Khaled. "Zur Frage des Schutzgottes der Frau." *Wiener Zeitschrift für die Kunde des Morgenlandes* 67 (1975): 29–30.

Negbi, Ora. *Canaanite Gods in Metal: An Archaeological Study of Ancient Syro-Palestinian Figurines.* Tel Aviv: Tel Aviv University Institute of Archaeology, 1976.

Negbi, Ora. "Israelite Cult Elements in Secular Contexts of 10th Century BCE." In *Biblical Archaeology Today 1990: Proceedings of the Second International Congress on Biblical*

Archaeology, Jerusalem, June–July 1990. Edited by Avraham Biran and Joseph Aviram, pp. 221–30. Jerusalem: Israel Exploration Society, 1993.

Nilsson, Martin P. "Roman and Greek Domestic Cult." *Opuscula Romana* 1, *Skrifter Utgivna av Svenska Institutet i Rom* 18 (Lund 1954): 77–85.

Nilsson, Martin P. *Greek Folk Religion*. New York: Harper, 1961.

Nilsson, Martin P. *Geschichte der griechischen Religion*. 2 vols. Munich: Beck, 1967.

Nisbet, Robert G. *M. Tulli Ciceronis, De Domo Sua*. Oxford: Oxford University Press, 1939.

Nock, Arthur Darby. "A Feature of Roman Religion," *Harvard Theological Review* 32 (1939): 83–96.

Noegel, Scott B., Walker, Joel, and Wheeler, Brannon (eds.). *Prayer, Magic, and the Stars in the Ancient and Late Antique World*. Magic in History 8. University Park: Pennsylvania State University Press, 2003.

Noth, Martin. *Die israelitischen Personennamen im Rahmen der gemeinsemitischen Namengebung*. Beiträge zur Wissenschaft vom Alten und Neuen Testament 46. Stuttgart: Kohlhammer, 1928.

Oakley, John H. and. Sinos, Rebecca H. *The Wedding in Ancient Athens*. Madison: University of Wisconsin Press, 1993.

O'Connor, Michael P. "Northwest Semitic Designations for Elective Social Affinities." *Journal of the Ancient Near Eastern Society* 18 (1986): 67–80.

O'Connor, Michael P. "The Onomastic Evidence for Bronze-Age West Semitic." *Journal of the American Oriental Society* 124 (2004): 439–70.

Ogden, Daniel. *Greek and Roman Necromancy*. Princeton: Princeton University Press, 2001.

Olson, S. Douglas. *Aristophanes: Acharnians*. Oxford: Clarendon Press, 2002.

Olyan, Saul M. *Asherah and the Cult of Yhwh in Israel*. Society of Biblical Literature Monograph Series 34. Atlanta: Scholars Press, 1988.

Olyan, Saul M. *Biblical Mourning: Ritual and Social Dimensions*. Oxford: Oxford University Press, 2004.

Onians, Richard B. *The Origins of European Thought about the Body, the Mind, the Soul, the World, Time, and Fate*, 2nd edn. Cambridge: Cambridge University Press, 1954.

Oppenheim, A. Leo. *Ancient Mesopotamia: Portrait of a Dead Civilization*, rev. edn. Chicago and London: The University of Chicago Press, 1977.

Orr, David G. "Roman Domestic Religion: The Evidence of the Household Shrines." In *Aufstieg und Niedergang der römischen Welt* 2.16.2, pp. 1557–91. Berlin, De Gruyter, 1978.

Palombi, Domenico. "Penates, *aedes*." In *Lexicon Topographicum Urbis Romae* IV *P-S*, 75–8. Edited by Eva Maragareta Steinby. Rome: Quasar, 1999.

Pals, Daniel L. *Eight Theories of Religion*. 2nd edn. New York: Oxford University Press, 2006.

Panciera, Silvio. "Ancora sulla famiglia senatoria 'Africana' degli *Aradii*," *L'Africa romana* 4.2 (1987): 547–72 [= *Epigrafi, epigrafia, epigrafisti. Scritti vari editi e inediti (1956–2005) con note complementari e indici*. Rome: Quasar, 2006: 2.1119–36].

Pardee, Dennis. "*Marziḥu*, *Kispu* and the Ugaritic Funerary Cult: A Minimalist View." In *Ugarit, Religion and Culture*. Edited by N. Wyatt, W. G. E. Watson, and J. Lloyd, pp. 273–87. Münster: Ugarit-Verlag, 1996.

Pardee, Dennis. "The 'Aqhatu Legend." In *The Context of Scripture, Vol. I. Canonical Compositions from the Biblical World*. Edited by W. W. Hallo and K. L. Younger, pp. 343–56. Leiden: E. J. Brill, 1997.

Pardee, Dennis. "The Ba'lu Myth." In *The Context of Scripture, Vol. I. Canonical Compositions from the Biblical World*. Edited by W. W. Hallo and K. L. Younger, pp. 241–74. Leiden: E. J. Brill, 1997.

Pardee, Dennis. "The Kirta Epic." In *The Context of Scripture, Vol. I. Canonical Compositions from the Biblical World*. Edited by W. W. Hallo and K. L. Younger, pp. 333–43. Leiden: E. J. Brill, 1997.

Pardee, Dennis. "Kosharoth." In *Dictionary of Deities and Demons in the Bible.* 2nd edition. Edited by K. van der Toorn, B. Becking and P. W. van der Horst, pp. 491–2. Leiden: E. J. Brill, 1999.

Pardee, Dennis. *Les textes rituels.* Ras Shamra-Ougarit XII. Paris: Éditions Recherche sur les Civilisations, 2000.

Pardee, Dennis. "'Anantēnu to His Master Ḫiḏmiratu." In *The Context of Scripture, Vol. III. Archival Documents from the Biblical World.* Edited by W. W. Hallo and K. L. Younger, pp. 112–13. Leiden: Brill, 2002.

Pardee, Dennis. "Double Letter, from 'Azzī'iltu to his Parents, From Same to his Sister." In *The Context of Scripture, Vol. III. Archival Documents from the Biblical World.* Edited by W. W. Hallo and K. L. Younger, p. 112. Leiden: E. J. Brill, 2002.

Pardee, Dennis. *Ritual and Cult at Ugarit.* Writings from the Ancient World 10. Atlanta: Society of Biblical Literature, 2002.

Pardee, Dennis and Bordreuil, Pierre. "Ugarit: Texts and Literature." In *The Anchor Bible Dictionary*, Vol. VI. Edited by D. N. Freedman, pp. 706–21. New York: Doubleday, 1992.

Parker, Robert. *Miasma: Pollution and Purification in Early Greek Religion.* Oxford: Clarendon, 1983.

Parker, Robert. *Athenian Religion: A History.* Oxford: Clarendon Press, 1996.

Parker, Robert. "What Are Sacred Laws?" In *The Law and the Courts in Ancient Greece.* Edited by Edward M. Harris and Lene Rubinstein, pp. 57–70. London: Duckworth, 2004.

Parker, Simon B. *The Pre-Biblical Narrative Tradition: Essays on the Ugaritic Poems Keret and Aqhat.* Atlanta: Scholars Press, 1989.

Parker, Simon (ed.). *Ugaritic Narrative Poetry.* Atlanta: Scholars Press, 1997.

Parkinson, R. B. *Voices from Ancient Egypt: An Anthology of Middle Kingdom Writings.* London: British Museum Press, 1992.

Parpola, Simo and Watanabe, Kazuko. *Neo-Assyrian Treaties and Loyalty Oaths.* State Archives of Assyria 2. Helsinki: Helsinki University Press, 1988.

Patterson, Cynthia B. *The Family in Greek History.* Cambridge, Mass.: Harvard University Press, 1998.

Peet, T. Eric and Woolley, C. L. *The City of Akhenaten. Part I.* London: Oxford University Press, 1923.

Penner, Hans. "You Don't Read a Myth for Information." In *Radical Interpretation in Religion.* Edited by Nancy Frankenberry, pp. 161–70. Cambridge: Cambridge University Press, 2002.

Perdue, Leo G. "The Israelite and Early Jewish Family: Summary and Conclusions." In *Families in Ancient Israel: The Family, Religion, and Culture.* Edited by idem, pp. 163–222. Louisville: Westminster, 1997.

Petrie, William F. M. *Illahun, Kahun and Gurob.* London: David Nutt, 1891 [reprinted Warminster: Aris and Phillips, 1974.]

Petrie, William F. M. *Gizeh and Rifeh.* British School of Archaeology in Egypt Publication 13. London. Egyptian Research Account, 1907.

Petrie, William F. M. *Objects of Daily Use.* British School of Archaeology in Egypt Publication 42. London: Egyptian Research Account, 1927.

Petrie, William F. M. *The Funeral Furniture of Egypt.* British School of Archaeology Publication 59. London: B. Quaritch, 1937.

Piccaluga, G. "*Penates* e *Lares*," *Studi e Materiali di Storia delle Religioni* 32 (1961): 81–97.

Pillet, M. "Les scènes de naissance et de circoncision dans le temple nord-est de Mout, à Karnak." *Annales du Service des Antiquités de l'Égypte* 52/1 (1952): 77–104.

Pinch, Geraldine. "Childbirth and Female Figurines at Deir el-Medina and el-'Amarna." *Orientalia* 52 (1983): 405–14.

Pinch, Geraldine. *Votive Offerings to Hathor.* Oxford: Griffith Institute, 1993.

Pitard, Wayne. "Care of the Dead at Emar." In *Emar: The History, Religion, and Culture of a Syrian Town in the Late Bronze Age*. Edited by Mark W. Chavalas, pp. 123–40. Bethesda, Md.: CDL, 1996.

Plunket, P. (ed.). *Domestic Ritual in Ancient Mesoamerica*, Monograph 46. Los Angeles: Cotsen Institute of Archaeology at UCLA, 2002.

Pluralismus in Israel und Babylon. Calwer Theologische Monographien A9. Stuttgart: Calwer, 1978.

Poebel, Arno. *Babylonian Legal and Business Documents from the Time of the First Dynasty of Babylon Chiefly from Nippur*. The Babylonian Expedition of the University of Pennsylvania 6/2. Philadelphia: University Museum, 1909.

Poole, Fritz John Porter. "Metaphors and Maps: Toward Comparison in the Anthropology of Religion." *Journal of the American Academy of Religion* 54 (1986): 411–57.

Prang, Erwin. "Das Archiv des Imgûa." *Zeitschrift für Assyriologie* 66 (1976): 1–44.

Prang, Erwin. "Das Archiv des Bitûa." *Zeitschrift für Assyriologie* 67 (1977): 217–34.

Pritchard, James B. *The Ancient Near East in Pictures Relating to the Old Testament*. 2nd edn., with supplement. Princeton: Princeton University Press, 1969.

Pritchard, James B. *Tell es-Sa'idiyeh: Excavations on the Tell, 1964–1966*. University Museum Monograph 60. Philadelphia: University of Pennsylvania, 1985.

Pruzsinszky, Regine. *Die Personennamen der Texte aus Emar*. Bethesda: CDL, 2003.

Quirke, Stephen. *Ancient Egyptian Religion*. London: British Museum Press, 1992.

Quirke, Stephen and Spencer, J. *The British Museum Book of Ancient Egypt*. New York: The British Museum, 1992.

Rainey, Anson. "The Social Stratification of Ugarit." PhD dissertation. Brandeis University, 1962.

Rainey, Anson. "Family Relationships at Ugarit." *Orientalia* 34 (1965): 10–22.

Rast, Walter. *Taanach I: Studies in the Iron Age Pottery, Excavation Reports*. Cambridge, MA: American Schools of Oriental Research, 1978.

Rechenmacher, Hans. *Personennamen als theologische Aussagen: Die syntaktischen und semantischen Strukturen der satzhaften theophoren Personennamen in der hebräischen Bibel*. Münchener Universitätsschriften 50. St Ottilien: Eos Verlag, 1997.

Redfield, James M. *The Locrian Maidens: Love and Death in Greek Italy*. Princeton: Princeton University Press, 2003.

Rehm, Rush. *The Play of Space*. Princeton: Princeton University Press, 2002.

Reiner, Erica. "Plague Amulets and House Blessings." *Journal of Near Eastern Studies* 19 (1960): 148–55.

Reinhartz, Adele. "Samson's Mother: An Unnamed Protagonist." *Journal for the Study of the Old Testament* 55 (1992): 25–37.

Reinhartz, Adele. *"Why Ask My Name?" Anonymity and Identity in Biblical Narrative*. New York and Oxford: Oxford University Press, 1998.

Reisner, George A. "The Tomb of Hepzefa, Nomarch of Siût." *Journal of Egyptian Archaeology* 5 (1918): 79–98.

Renger, Johannes. "Untersuchungen zum Priestertum in der altbabylonischen Zeit, 2. Teil." *Zeitschrift für Assyriologie* 59 (1969): 104–230.

Renz, Johannes, and Röllig, Wolfgang. *Handbuch der Althebräischen Epigraphik, I/1: Die althebräischen Inschriften: Text und Kommentar*. Darmstadt: Wissenschaftliche Buchgesellschaft, 1995.

Richter, Thomas. "Die Lesung des Goetternamens AN.AN.MAR.TU." In *General Studies and Excavations at Nuzi 10/2*. Studies on the Civilization and Culture of Nuzi and the Hurrians 9. Edited by David I. Owen and Gernot Wilhelm, pp. 135–7. Bethesda: CDL Press, 1998.

Ringgren, Helmer. *Israelitische Religion*. Religionen der Menschheit 26. Stuttgart: Kohlhammer, 1982.

Ritner, Robert K. "A Uterine Amulet in the Oriental Institute Collection." *Journal of Near Eastern Studies* 43 (1984): 209–21.

Ritner, Robert K. "Anubis and the Lunar Disc." *The Journal of Egyptian Archaeology* 71 (1986): 149–55.

Ritner, Robert K. "Horus on the Crocodiles: A Juncture of Religion and Magic in Late Dynastic Egypt." In *Religion and Philosophy in Ancient Egypt*. Yale Egyptological Studies 3. Edited by W. K. Simpson, pp. 103–16. New Haven: Yale Egyptological Seminar, 1989.

Ritner, Robert K. "O. Gardiner 363: A Spell against Night Terrors." *Journal of the American Research Center in Egypt* 27 (1990): 25–41.

Ritner, Robert K. *The Mechanics of Ancient Egyptian Magical Practice*. Studies in Ancient Oriental Civilization 54. Chicago: The University of Chicago, 1993.

Ritner, Robert K. "Magical Wand." In *Searching for Ancient Egypt*. Edited by David P. Silverman, pp. 234–35. Dallas: Dallas Museum of Art and University of Pennsylvania Museum, 1997.

Ritner, Robert K. "Magic in Medicine." In *The Oxford Encyclopedia of Ancient Egypt*. Edited by Donald B. Redford, 2: 326–9. Oxford: Oxford University Press, 2001.

Ritner, Robert K. "Necromancy in Ancient Egypt." In *Magic and Divination in the Ancient World*. Edited by Leda Ciraolo and Jonathan Seidel, pp. 89–96. Leiden: Brill/Styx, 2002.

Ritner, Robert K. "Des preuves de l'existence d'une nécromancie dans l'Égypte ancienne." In *La magie en Égypte*. Edited by Y. Koenig, pp. 285–99. Paris: Louvre, 2002.

Ritner, Robert K. "The Instruction of 'Onchsheshonqy.'" In *The Literature of Ancient Egypt*. 3rd edn. Edited by W. K. Simpson, pp. 497–529. New Haven: Yale University Press, 2003.

Ritner, Robert K. "The Romance of Setna Khaemuas and the Mummies (Setna I)." In *The Literature of Ancient Egypt*. 3rd edn. Edited by W. K. Simpson, pp. 453–69. New Haven: Yale University Press, 2003.

Ritner, Robert K. "The Victory Stela of Piye." In *The Literature of Ancient Egypt*. 3rd edn. Edited by W. K. Simpson, pp. 367–85. New Haven: Yale University Press, 2003.

Ritner, Robert K. " 'And Each Staff transformed into a Snake': The Serpent Wand in Ancient Egypt." In *Through a Glass Darkly: Magic, Dreams, and Prophecy in Ancient Egypt*. Edited by Kasia Szpakowska, pp. 205–25. Swansea: University of Wales, 2006.

Ritner, Robert K. "Cultural Exchanges between Egyptian and Greek Medicine." In *Foreign Relations and Diplomacy in the Ancient World*. Edited by P. Kousoulis and K. Magliveras. Leuven: Peeters, forthcoming.

Ritner, Robert K. "Libyan vs. Nubian as the Ideal Egyptian." In the Festschrift for Leonard Lesko. Edited by Stephen E. Thompson. Providence: Brown University, forthcoming.

Robertson, John F. "The Internal Political and Economic Structure of Old Babylonian Nippur: The Guennakum and His 'House.' " *Journal of Cuneiform Studies* 36 (1984): 145–90.

Röemer, Willem H. Ph. "Miscellanea Sumerologica, V: Bittbrief einer Gelähmten um Genesung an die Göttin Nintinugga." In *Literatur, Politik und Recht in Mesopotamien: Festschrift für Claus Wilcke*. Orientalia Biblica et Christiana 14. Edited by Walther Sallaberger, Konrad Volk and Annette Zgoll, pp. 237–49. Wiesbaden: Harrassowitz, 2003.

Romer, John. *Ancient Lives: Daily Life in Egypt of the Pharaohs*. New York: Holt, Rinehart and Winston, 1984.

Rose, Herbert Jennings. "The Religion of a Greek Household." *Euphrosyne* 1 (1957): 95–116.

Rose, Martin. *Der Ausschließlichkeitsanspruch Jahwes: Deuteronomische Schultheologie und Volksfrömmigkeit in der späten Königszeit*. Beiträge zur Wissenschaft vom Alten und Neuen Testament 106. Stuttgart: Kohlhammer, 1975.

Rosivach, Vincent J. *The System of Public Sacrifice in Fourth-Century Athens*. American Classical Studies 34. Atlanta: Scholars Press, 1994.

Rost, Leonard. "Weidewechsel und alttestamentlicher Festkalender." In idem, *Das kleine Credo und andere Studien zum Alten Testament*, pp. 101–12. Heidelberg: Quelle und Meyer, 1965.

Russmann, Edna R. *Eternal Egypt*. London: The British Museum, 2001.

Sadek, Ashraf Iskander. *Popular Religion in Egypt during the New Kingdom*. Hildesheimer ägyptologische Beiträge 27. Hildesheim: Gerstenberg Verlag, 1987.

Sallaberger, Walther. "Zu einer Urkunde aus Ekalte über die Rückgabe der Hausgötter." *Ugarit Forschungen* 33 (2001): 495–9.

Saller, Richard P. *Patriarchy, Property, and Death in the Roman Family*. Cambridge: Cambridge University Press, 1994.

Saller, Richard P. "Roman Kinship: Structure and Sentiment." In *The Roman Family in Italy: Status, Sentiment, Space*. Edited by Beryl Rawson and Paul Weaver: 7–34. Oxford: Clarendon Press, 1997.

Saller, Richard and Garnsey, Peter. *The Roman Empire: Economy, Society and Culture*. Berkeley: University of California Press, 1987.

Scharbert, Josef. "*'alah*." In *Theological Dictionary of the Old Testament*. Edited by G. J. Botterweck and H. Ringgren, 1: 261–6. Grand Rapids: Eerdmans, 1974.

Schatzki, Theodore. *Social Practices: A Wittgensteinian Approach to Human Activity and the Social*. New York: Cambridge University Press, 1996.

Schatzki, Theodore. *The Site of the Social: A Philosophical Account of the Constitution of Social Life and Change*. University Park, Pennsylvania: University of Pennsylvania Press, 2002.

Scheid, John. *Romulus et ses frères. Le college des frères Arvales, modèle du culte public dans la Rome des empereurs*. Rome: École française de Rome, 1990.

Schloen, J. David. *The House of the Father as Fact and Symbol: Patrimonialism in Ugarit and the Ancient Near East*. Studies in the Archaeology and History of the Levant 2. Winona Lake: Eisenbrauns, 2001.

Schmitt, Rüdiger. "Philistäische Terrakottafigurinen." *Ugarit-Forschungen 31* (1999): 576–676.

Schorr, Moses. *Urkunden des altbabylonischen Zivil- und Prozessrechts*. Vorderasiatische Bibliothek 5. Leipzig: J. C. Hinrichs, 1913.

Schott, Siegfried. "Die Bitte um ein Kind auf einer Grabfigur des frühen Mittleren Reiches." *The Journal of Egyptian Archaeology* 16 (1930): 23.

Schulman, Alan R. "Ex-votos of the Poor." *Journal of the American Research Center in Egypt* 6 (1967): 153–6.

Schwemer, Daniel. *Die Wettergottgestalten Mesopotamiens und Nordsyriens im Zeitalter der Keilschriftkulturen*. Wiesbaden: Harrassowitz, 2001.

Scullard, Howard H. *Festivals and Ceremonies of the Roman Republic*. London: Thames and Hudson, 1981.

Scurlock, JoAnn. "Soul Emplacements in Ancient Mesopotamian Funerary Rituals." In *Magic and Divination in the Ancient World*. Ancient Magic and Divination 2. Edited by Leda Ciraolo and Jonathan Seidl, pp. 1–6. Leiden: Brill/Styx, 2002.

Scurlock, JoAnn. "Ancient Mesopotamian House Gods." *Journal of Ancient Near Eastern Religions (JANER)* 3 (2003): 99–106.

Seele, Keith C. "Oriental Institute Museum Notes: Horus on the Crocodiles." *Journal of Near Eastern Studies* 6 (1947): 43–52.

Seele, Keith C. "University of Chicago Oriental Institute Nubian Expedition: Excavations between Abu Simbel and the Sudan Border, Preliminary Report." *Journal of Near Eastern Studies* 33 (1974): 1–43.

Segal, Judah B. "Popular Religion in Ancient Israel." *Journal of Semitic Studies* 27 (1976): 1–22.

Seow, C. L. *Myth, Drama, and the Politics of David's Dance.* Harvard Semitic Monographs 44. Atlanta: Scholars Press, 1989.

Shiloh, Yigael. "Iron Age Sanctuaries and Cult Elements in Palestine." In *Symposia Celebrating the Seventy-Fifth Anniversary of the Founding of the American Schools of Oriental Research (1900–1975).* Edited by F. M. Cross, pp. 147–57. Cambridge, Mass.: American Schools of Oriental Research, 1979.

Simpson, William K. "King Cheops and the Magicians." In *The Literature of Ancient Egypt.* 3rd edit. Edited by William K. Simpson, pp. 13–24. New Haven: Yale University, 2003.

Sjövall, Harald. *Zeus im altgriechischen Hauskult.* Lund: H. Ohlsson, 1931.

Smelik, Klaas A. D. *Writings from Ancient Israel: A Handbook of Historical and Religious Documents.* Louisville: Westminster/John Knox, 1991.

Smith, C. J. *The Roman Clan: The* Gens *from Ancient Ideology to Modern Anthropology.* Cambridge: Cambridge University Press, 2006.

Smith, Jonathan Z. *Imagining Religion: From Babylon to Jonestown.* Chicago: The University of Chicago Press, 1982.

Smith, Jonathan Z. *To Take Place: Toward Theory in Ritual.* Chicago: The University of Chicago, 1987.

Smith, Jonathan Z. *Drudgery Divine: On the Comparison of Early Christianities and the Religions of Late Antiquity.* Chicago: The University of Chicago, 1990.

Smith, Jonathan Z. "Classification." In *Guide to the Study of Religion.* Edited by Willi Braun and Russell T. McCuthcheon, pp. 35–44. London: Cassell, 2000.

Smith, Jonathan Z. "The End of Comparison: Redescription and Rectification." *A Magic Still Dwells.* Edited by Kimberley Patton and Benjamin Ray, pp. 237–42. Berkeley: University of California Press, 2000.

Smith, Jonathan Z. "Trading Places." In *Ancient Magic and Ritual Power.* Edited by Marvin W. Meyer and Paul Allen Mirecki, pp. 13–28. Boston: Brill Academic Publishers, 2001.

Smith, Jonathan Z. "Here, There and Anywhere." In *Prayer, Magic and the Stars in the Ancient and Late Antique World.* Magic in History 8. Edited by Scott B. Noegel, Joel Walker, and Brannon M. Wheeler, pp. 21–36. University Park: Pennsylvania State University Press, 2003.

Smith, Jonathan Z. *Relating Religion: Essays in the Study of Religion.* Chicago and London: The University of Chicago Press, 2004.

Smith, Mark S. *The Early History of God: Yahweh and the Other Deities in Ancient Israel.* New York: HarperCollins, 1990.

Smith, Mark. *The Origins of Biblical Monotheism.* Oxford: Oxford University Press, 2001.

Soden, Wolfram von. *Akkadisches Handwörterbuch.* 3 vols. Wiesbaden: Harrassowitz, 1965.

Sommerfeld, Walther. *Der Aufstieg Marduks.* Alter Orient und Altes Testament 213. Kevelaer: Butzon & Bercker; Neukirchen-Vluyn: Neukirchener Verlag, 1982.

Sommerstein, Alan H., trans. *Aristophanes Acharnians.* Warminster: Aris & Phillips, 1980.

Sourvinou-Inwood, Christiane. "Further Aspects of Polis Religion." *Annali Istituto Orientale de Napoli: Archaeologia e Storia Antica* 10 (1988): 259–74.

Sourvinou-Inwood, Christiane. "What is Polis Religion?" In *The Greek City from Homer to Alexander.* Edited by Oswyn Murray and S. R. F. Price, pp. 295–322. Oxford: Clarendon Press, 1990.

Sourvinou-Inwood, Christiane. *"Reading" Greek Death to the End of the Classical Period.* Oxford: Oxford University Press, 1995.

Spaey, Johanna. "Emblems in Rituals in the Old Babylonian Period." In *Ritual and Sacrifice in the Ancient Near East: Proceedings of the International Conference organized by the Katholieke Universiteit Leuven from the 17th to the 20th of April 1991.* Orientalia lovaniensia analecta 55. Edited by Jan Quaegebeur, pp. 411–20. Leuven: Peeters, 1993.

Spencer, Neal. "The Temples of Kom Firin." *Egyptian Archaeology* 24 (2004): 38–40.

Spiro, Melford. "Religion: Problems of Definition and Explanation." *Anthropological Approaches to the Study of Religion.* Edited by Michael Banton, pp. 85–126. London: Tavistock, 1966.

Staehelin, Elisabeth. "Bindung und Entbindung." *Zeitschrift für Ägyptische Sprache und Altertumskunde* 96 (1970): 125–39.

Stager, Lawrence E. "The Archaeology of the Family in Ancient Israel." *Bulletin of the American Schools of Oriental Research* 260 (1985): 1–35.

Stamm, Johannes J. "Hebräische Ersatznamen." In *Studies in Honor of Benno Landsberger on His Seventy-Fifth Birthday, April 1965*, pp. 413–24. Assyrological Studies 16. Chicago: The University of Chicago Press 1965 = Idem. *Beiträge zur Hebräischen und Altorientalischen Namenkunde*, pp. 59–79. Orbis Biblicus and Orientalis 3. Fribourg: Universitätsverlag; Göttingen: Vandenhoeck & Ruprecht, 1980.

Steinkeller, Piotr. "The Eblaite Preposition *qidimay* 'Before'." *Oriens Antiquus* 23 (1984): 33–7.

Steinkeller, Piotr. "Early Semitic Literature and Third Millennium Seals with Mythological Motifs." In *Literature and Literary Language at Ebla.* Quaderni di Semitistica 18. Edited by Pelio Fronzaroli, pp. 243–83. Florence: University of Florence, Department of Linguistics, 1992.

Stevens, Anna. "The Material Evidence for Domestic Religion at Amarna and Preliminary Remarks on its Interpretation," *Journal of Egyptian Archaeology* 89 (2003): 143–68.

Stol, Marten. "Das Heiligtum einer Familie." In *Literatur, Politik und Recht in Mesopotamien: Festschrift Claus Wilcke.* Orientalia Biblica et Christiana 14. Edited by Walther Sallaberger, Konrad Volk, and Annette Zgoll, pp. 293–300. Wiesbaden: Harrassowitz, 2003.

Stol, Marten. "Wirtschaft und Gesellschaft in altbabylonischer Zeit." In *Mesopotamien: Die altbabylonische Zeit.* Orbis Biblicus et Orientalis 160/4. Edited by Dominique Charpin, Dietz Otto Edzard, and Marten Stol, 643–975. Fribourg: Academic Press; Göttingen: Vandenhoeck & Ruprecht, 2004.

Stowers, Stanley. "Greeks Who Sacrifice and Those Who Do Not: Toward an Anthropology of Greek Religion." In *The First Christians and Their Social World: Studies in Honor of Wayne A. Meeks.* Edited by L. Michael White and Larry O. Yarbrough, pp. 293–333. Philadelphia: Fortress Press, 1995.

Stowers, Stanley. "What is Pauline Participation in Christ?" In *Redefining First-Century Jewish and Christian Identities: Essays in Honor of Ed P. Sanders.* Edited by Mark Chancey, Susannah Heschel, Gregory Tatum, and Fabian Udoh. Notre Dame: University of Notre Dame Press, forthcoming.

Streck, Maximilian (ed.). *Assurbanipal und die letzten assyrischen Könige bis zum Untergange Nineveh's.* 3 vols. Leipzig: J. C. Hinrichs, 1916.

Streck, Michael P. *Das amurritische Onomastikon der altbabylonische Zeit. Band 1: Die Amurriter; Die onomastische Forschung; Orthographie und Phonologie; Nominalmorphologie.* Alter Orient und Altes Testament 271/1. Münster: Ugarit-Verlag, 2000.

Streck, Michael P. "Die Klage 'Ishtar Bagdad.'" In *Literatur, Politik und Recht in Mesopotamien: Festschrift fuer Claus Wilcke.* Orientalia Biblica et Christiana 14. Edited by Walther Sallaberger, Konrad Volk and Annette Zgoll, pp. 301–12. Wiesbaden: Harrassowitz, 2003.

Streck, Michael P., and Weninger, Stefan (eds.). *Altorientalische und semitische Onomastik.* Alter Orient und Altes Testament 296. Münster: Ugarit Verlag, 2002.

Supplementum epigraphicum graecum. Vol. 33. Edited by H. W. Pleket and R. S. Stroud. Amsterdam: Gieben, 1983 (1986).

Sweet, Ronald F. G. "An Akkadian Incantation Text." In *Essays on the Ancient Semitic World.* Edited by John W. Wevers and Donald B. Redford, pp. 6–11. Toronto and Buffalo: University of Toronto Press, 1970.

Syme, Ronald. *Historia Augusta Papers.* Oxford: Oxford University Press, 1983.

Szpakowska, Kasia Maria. "The Perception of Dreams and Nightmares in Ancient Egypt: Old Kingdom to Third Intermediate Period." PhD dissertation, University of California, Los Angeles, 2000.

Szpakowska, Kasia."Playing with Fire: Initial Observations on the Religious Uses of Clay Cobras." *Journal of the American Research Center in Egypt* 40 (2003): 113–22.

Teeter, Emily. "Piety at Medinet Habu." *The Oriental Institute News & Notes* 173 (2002): 1–6.

Teeter, Emily. *Baked Clay Figurines and Votive Beds from Medinet Habu.* Chicago: The Oriental Institute of the University of Chicago, 2007.

Thomas, Angela P. *Gurob: A New Kingdom Town.* Warminster: Aris & Phillips, 1981.

Tigay, Jeffrey. *You Shall Have No Other Gods: Israelite Religion in the Light of Hebrew Inscriptions.* Harvard Semitic Studies 31. Atlanta: Scholars Press, 1986.

Tigay, Jeffrey. "Israelite Religion: The Onomastic and Epigraphic Evidence." In *Ancient Israelite Religion: Essays in Honor of Frank Moore Cross.* Edited by Patrick D. Miller Jr, Paul D. Hanson, and S. Dean McBride, pp. 157–94. Philadelphia: Fortress Press, 1987.

Tita, Hubert. *Gelübde als Bekenntnis: Eine Studie zu den Gelübden im Alten Testament,* Orbis Biblicus and Orientalis 181. Fribourg: Universitätsverlag; Göttingen: Vandenhoeck & Ruprecht, 2001.

Tooley, Angela M. J. "Child's Toy or Ritual Object." *Göttinger Miszellen* 123 (1991): 101–11.

Toorn, Karel van der. "The Nature of the Biblical Teraphim in the Light of the Cuneiform Evidence." *Catholic Biblical Quarterly* 52 (1990): 203–23.

Toorn, Karel van der. "Ilib and the 'God of the Father.'" *Ugarit Forschungen* 25 (1993): 379–87.

Toorn, Karel van der. "Gods and Ancestors in Emar and Nuzi." *Zeitschrift für Assyriologie* 84 (1994): 38–59.

Toorn, Karel van der. "The Domestic Cult at Emar." *Journal of Cuneiform Studies* 47 (1995): 35–49.

Toorn, Karel van der. "Migration and the Spread of Local Cults." In *Immigration and Emigration within the Ancient Near East: Festschrift E. Lipinski.* Orientalia lovaniensia analecta 65. Edited by Karel Van Lerberghe and Anton Schoors, pp. 365–77. Leuven: Peeters, 1995.

Toorn, Karel van der. "Ancestors and Anthroponyms: Kinship Terms as Theophoric Elements in Hebrew Names." *Zeitschrift für die alttestamentliche Wissenschaft* 108 (1996): 1–11.

Toorn, Karel van der. *Family Religion in Babylonia, Syria and Israel: Continuity and Change in the Forms of Religious Life.* Studies in the History and Culture of the Ancient Near East 7. Leiden, New York and Köln: E. J. Brill, 1996.

Toorn, Karel van der. "Israelite Figurines: A View from the Texts." In *Sacred Time, Sacred Place. Archaeology and the Religion of Israel.* Edited by Barry M. Gittlen, pp. 45–62. Winona Lake: Eisenbrauns, 2002.

Toorn, Karel van der. "Nine Months among the Peasants in the Palestinian Highlands: An Anthropological Perspective on Local Religion in the Early Iron Age." In *Symbiosis, Symbolism, and the Power of Past: Canaan, Ancient Israel, and Their Neighbors from the Late Bronze Age through Roman Palestine: Proceedings of the Centennial Symposium W. F. Albright Institute of Archaeological Research and American Schools of Oriental Research Jerusalem, May 29–May 31, 2000.* Edited by William G. Dever and Seymour Gitin, pp. 393–410. Winona Lake: Eisenbrauns 2003.

Toorn, Karel van der. "Religious Practices of the Individual and Family: Introduction." In *Religions of the Ancient World: A Guide.* Edited by Sarah Iles Johnston, pp. 423–4. Cambridge and London: Harvard University Press, 2004.

Toorn, Karel van der. "Religious Practices of the Individual and Family: Syria-Canaan." In *Religions of the Ancient World: A Guide.* Edited by Sarah Iles Johnston, pp. 427–29. Cambridge and London: Harvard University Press, 2004.

Toorn, Karel van der and Houtman, Cees. "David and the Ark." *Journal of Biblical Literature* 113 (1994): 209–31.

Toorn, Karel van der and Lewis, Theodore J. "Terapim." In *Theologisches Wörterbuch zum Alten Testament.* 10 vols. Edited by G. J. Botterweck & Helmer Ringgren, 8: 765–78. Stuttgart: Kohlhammer, 1995.

Tran Tam Tinh, Vincent. *Essai sur le culte d'Isis à Pompei.* Paris: E De Boccard, 1964.

Tran Tam Tinh, Vincent. "Lar, Lares." In *Lexicon Iconographicum Mythologiae Classicae* 6.1, pp. 205–12. Zurich: Artemis, 1992.

Trible, Phyllis. "A Meditation . Mourning: The Sacrifice of the Daughter of Jephthah," *Union Seminary Quarterly Review* 36 (1981): 59–73.

Trible, Phyllis. *Texts of Terror: Literary-Feminist Readings of Biblical Narratives.* Overtures to Biblical Theology 13. Philadelphia: Fortress, 1984.

Trible, Phyllis. "A Daughter's Death: Feminism, Literary Criticism, and the Bible." In *Backgrounds for the Bible.* Edited by M. P. O'Connor and D. N. Freedman, 1–14. Winona Lake: Eisenbrauns, 1987.

Trible, Phyllis. "Bringing Miriam out of the Shadows." *Bible Review* 5(1) (February 1989): 14–25, 34.

Tropper, Josef. *Ugaritische Grammatik.* Münster: Ugarit-Verlag, 2000.

Tsevat, Matitiahu. "Traces of Hittite at the Beginning of the Ugaritic Epic of AQHT." *Ugarit-Forschungen* 3 (1971): 351–2.

Tsukimoto, Akio. *Untersuchungen zur Totenpflege (kispum) im alten Mesopotamien.* Alter Orient und Altes Testament 216. Kevelaer: Butzon & Bercker; Neukirchen-Vluyn: Neukirchener Verlag, 1985.

Tybout, R. A. "Domestic Shrines and 'Popular Painting': Style and Social Context." *Journal of Roman Archaeology* 9 (1991): 358–74.

Uehlinger, Christoph. "Anthropomorphic Cult Statuary in Iron Age Palestine and the Search for Yahweh's Cult Images." In *The Image and the Book: Iconic Cults, Aniconism, and the Rise of Book Religion in Israel and the Ancient Near East.* Edited by Karel van der Toorn, pp. 97–155. Leuven: Peeters, 1997.

Ussishkin, David. "Schumacher's Shrine in Bulding 338 at Megiddo," *Israel Exploration Journal* 39 (1989): 149–72.

Valbelle, Dominique. *"Les ouvriers de la tombe": Deir el-Médineh à l'époque ramesside.* Cairo: Institut Français d'Archéologie Orientale, 1985.

van der Leeuw, S. E. "Towards a Study of the Economy of Pottery Making." In *Ex Horreo.* Edited by B. L. van Beek, R. W. Brandt, and W. Groenman-van Waateringe, pp. 68–76. Amsterdam: Universiteit van Amsterdam, 1977.

van Selms, Adrianus. *Marriage and Family Life in Ugaritic Literature.* London: Luzac, 1954.

van Soldt, Wilfred H. "'Atn Prln, ''Attā/ēnu the Diviner'," *Ugarit Forschungen* 21 (1989): 365–8.

van Soldt, Wilfred H. "Babylonian Lexical, Religious and Literary Texts and Scribal Education at Ugarit and its Implications for the Alphabetic Literary Texts." In *Ugarit: Ein ostmediterranes Kulturzentrum im Alten Orient.* Edited by M. Dietrich and O. Loretz, pp. 171–212. Münster: Ugarit-Verlag, 1995.

van Soldt, Wilfred H. "Ugarit: A Second Millennium Kingdom on the Mediterranean Coast." In *Civilizations of the Ancient Near East.* Vol. 2. Edited by J. M. Sasson, pp. 1255–66. New York: Scribner's, 1995.

van Soldt, Wilfred H. *The Topography of the City-State of Ugarit.* Münster: Ugarit-Verlag, 2005.

Vargyas, Peter. "Stratification Sociale à Ugarit." In *Society and Economy in the Eastern Mediterranean.* Edited by M. Heltzer and E. Lipiński, pp. 111–23. Leuven: Peeters, 1988.

Vermeule, Emily. *Aspects of Death in Early Greek Art and Poetry.* Berkeley: University of California Press, 1979.

Versnel, Hendrik. *Transition and Reversal in Myth and Ritual.* Leiden: E. J. Brill, 1993.

Visconti, Carlo L. "Del larario e del mitrèo scoperti nell'Esquilino presso la chiesa di S. Martino ai Monti," *Bullettino della Commissione Archeologica Comunale di Roma* 13 (1885): 27–38.

Vita, Juan-Pablo. "The Society of Ugarit." In *Handbook of Ugaritic Studies.* Edited by W. G. E. Watson and N. Wyatt, pp. 455–98. Leiden: E. J. Brill, 1999.

Vogelsang-Eastwood, Gillian. "Weaving, Looms, and Textiles." In *The Oxford Encyclopedia of Ancient Egypt.* Edited by Donald B. Redford, 3: 490–1. Oxford: Oxford University Press, 2001.

von Hesberg, Henner. "Minerva Custos Urbis – zum Bildschmuck der Porta Romana in Ostia." In *Imperium Romanum. Studien zu Geschichte und Rezeption. Festschrift für Karl Christ zum 75. Geburtstag.* Edited by Peter Kneissel and Volker Losemann, pp. 370–8. Stuttgart: Franz Steiner, 1998.

Vorländer, Hermann. *Mein Gott: Vorstellungen vom persönlichen Gott im Alten Testament und im Alten Orient.* Alter Orient und Altes Testament 23. Kevalaer: Butzon & Bercker; Neukirchen-Vluyn: Neukirchener Verlag, 1975.

Vrijhof, Pieter H. and Waardenburg, Jacques (eds.). *Official and Popular Religion: Analysis of a Theme for Religious Studies.* Religion and Society 19. The Hague: Mouton, 1979.

Wallace-Hadrill, Andrew. "Houses and Households: Sampling Pompeii and Herculaneum." In *Marriage, Divorce, and Children in Ancient Rome.* Edited by Beryl Rawson, pp. 191–227. Oxford: Oxford University Press, 1991.

Wallace-Hadrill, Andrew. *Houses and Society in Pompeii and Herculaneum.* Princeton: Princeton University Press, 1994.

Wallace-Hadrill, Andrew. "*Domus* and *Insulae* in Rome: Families and Housefuls." In *Early Christian Families in Context.* Edited by David L. Balch and Carolyn Osiek, pp. 3–18. Grand Rapids: Eerdmans, 2003.

Walls, Neal H. *The Goddess Anat in Ugaritic Myth.* SBL Dissertation Series 135. Atlanta: Scholars Press, 1992.

Walters, Stanley D. "Hannah and Anna: The Greek and Hebrew Texts of 1 Samuel 1." *Journal of Biblical Literature* 107 (1988): 385–412.

Warde Fowler, William. *The Roman Festivals of the Period of the Republic.* London: Macmillan, 1899.

Watkins, Calvert. *How to Kill a Dragon: Aspects of Indo-European Poetics.* Oxford: Oxford University Press, 1995.

Watkins, Leslie (based on material submitted by Israel Finkelstein). "Shiloh." In *The Oxford Encyclopedia of Archaeology in the Near East.* Edited by E. M. Meyers, 5: 28b–29b. New York and Oxford: Oxford University Press, 1997.

Watson, Wyatt G. E. "Daily Life in Ancient Ugarit (Syria)." In *Life and Culture in the Ancient Near East.* Edited by R. E. Averbeck, M. W. Chavalas, and D. B. Weisberg, pp. 121–52. Bethesda: CDL Press, 2003.

Wegner, Josef. "A decorated birth-brick from South Abydos." *Egyptian Archaeology* 21 (2002): 3–4.

Weinberg, Saul S. "A Moabite Shrine Group." *Muse* 12 (1978): 30–48.

Weippert, Manfred. "Synkretismus und Monotheismus: Religionsinterne Konfliktbewältigung im Alten Israel." In *Kultur und Konflikt.* Edited by Jan Assmann, pp. 143–79. Frankfurt am Main: Suhrkamp, 1990 = Idem. *Jahwe und die anderen Götter: Studien zur Religionsgeschichte des antiken Israel in ihrem syrisch-palästinischen Kontext*, pp. 1–33. Forschungen zum Alten Testament 18. Tübingen: Mohr Siebeck, 1997.

Wellhausen, Julius. *Der Text der Bücher Samuelis untersucht.* Göttingen: Vandenhoeck & Ruprecht, 1871.

Wente, Edward F. *Letters from Ancient Egypt.* Society of Biblical Literature Writings from the Ancient World 1. Atlanta: Scholars Press, 1990.

Wiggermann, Frans A. M. *Mesopotamian Protective Spirits: The Ritual Texts.* Cuneiform Monographs 1. Groningen: Styx & PP Publications, 1992.

Wiggermann, Frans A. M. "Ninshubur." *Reallexikon der Assyriologie.* Edited by Erich Ebeling and Bruno Meissner, 9: 490–500. Berlin: De Gruyter, 2001.

Wiggins, Steve. *A Reassessment of "Asherah": A Study According to the Textual Sources of the First Two Millennia* BCE. Alter Orient und Altes Testament 235. Kevelaer: Butzon & Bercker; Neukirchen-Vluyn: Neukirchener Verlag, 1993.

Wilamowitz-Moellendorff, Ulrich von. *Euripides Herakles,* 2nd edn., Vol. 3. Berlin: Akademie-Verlag, 1959.

Wilcke, Claus. "Nachlese zu A. Poebels Babylonian Legal and Business Documents From the Time of the First Dynasty of Babylon Chiefly from Nippur (BE 6/2), Teil 1." *Zeitschrift für Assyriologie* 73 (1983): 48–66.

Wilfong, Terry G. *Women and Gender in Ancient Egypt.* Ann Arbor: Kelsey Museum of Archaeology, 1997.

Wilfong, Terry G. "Menstrual Synchrony and the 'Place of Women' in Ancient Egypt (OIM 13512)." In *Gold of Praise: Studies on Ancient Egypt in Honor of Edward F. Wente.* Studies in Ancient Oriental Civilization 58. Edited by Emily Teeter and John A. Larson, pp. 419–34. Chicago: The Oriental Institute, 1999.

Willett, Elizabeth A. "Women and Household Shrines in Ancient Israel." PhD dissertation, University of Arizona, 1999.

Winter, Urs. *Frau und Göttin.* Orbis Biblicus et Orientalis 53. Fribourg: Universitätsverlag; Göttingen: Vandenhoeck & Ruprecht, 1983.

Wissowa, Georg. *Religion und Kultus der Römer,* 2nd edn. Munich: C. H. Beck, 1912.

Wolff, Hans W. *Anthropology of the Old Testament.* Philadelphia: Fortress, 1974.

Wood, Bryant G. *The Sociology of Pottery in Ancient Palestine: The Ceramic Industry and the Diffusion of Ceramic Style in the Bronze and Iron Ages.* Journal for the Study of the Old Testament Supplement Series 103. Sheffield: JSOT Press, 1990.

Wreszinski, Walter. *Bericht über die photographische Expedition von Kairo bis Wadi Halfa. Zwecks Abschluss der Materialsammlung für meinen Atlas zur Altägyptischen kulturgeschichte.* Halle: Max Niemeyer Verlag, 1927.

Wuilleumier, Pierre. *Tarante: Des origines à la conquête romaine.* Bibliothèque des écoles françaises d'Athènes et de Rome, fasc. 148, 2 vols. Paris: de Boccard, 1939.

Wyatt, Nicolas. *Religious Texts from Ugarit: The Words of Ilimilku and his Colleagues.* Sheffield: Sheffield Academic Press, 1998.

Wyatt, Nicolas. "The Religion of Ugarit: An Overview." In *Handbook of Ugaritic Studies.* Edited by W. G. E. Watson and N. Wyatt, pp. 529–85. Leiden: E. J. Brill, 1999.

Yon, Marguerite, P. Lombard, and M. Reniso. "L'organisation de l'Habitat: Les Maisons A, B, et E." In *Le Centre de la ville, 38–44e (1978–1984).* Ras Shamra-Ougarit III. Edited by M. Yon et al., 11–128. Paris: Éditions Recherche de la Civilisation, 1987.

Yon, Marguerite. "Ugarit: History and Archaeology." In *The Anchor Bible Dictionary.* Vol. VI. Edited by D. N. Freedman, pp. 695–706. New York: Doubleday, 1992.

Yon, Marguerite. "Ugarit: The Urban Habitat – The Present State of the Archaeological Picture." *Bulletin of the American Schools of Oriental Research* 286 (1992): 19–34.

Yon, Marguerite. "The Temple of the Rhytons at Ugarit." In *Ugarit, Religion and Culture.* Edited by N. Wyatt, W. G. E. Watson, and J. Lloyd, pp. 405–22. Münster: Ugarit-Verlag, 1996.

Yon, Marguerite. *La cité d'Ougarit sur le tell de Ras Shamra.* Paris: Éditions Recherche sur les Civilisations, 1997.

Yon, Marguerite. "Ugarit." In *The Oxford Encyclopedia of Archaeology in the Near East.* Vol. 5. Edited by E. M. Meyers, pp. 255–62. New York: Oxford University Press, 1997.

Yon, Marguerite. *The City of Ugarit at Tell Ras Shamra.* Winona Lake: Eisenbrauns, 2006.

Zaccagnini, Carlos. "Feet of Clay at Emar and Elsewhere." *Orientalia* 63 (1994): 1–4.

Zeitlin, Froma. "The Dynamics of Misogyny: Myth and Mythmaking in the *Oresteia*." *Arethusa* 11 (1978): 149–84.

Zevi, Fausto. "Die 'volkstümliche Kunst'." In *Pompejanische Wandmalerei*. Edited by Giuseppina Cerulli Irelli, M. Aoyagi, Stefano De Caro and U. Pappalardo, pp. 273–80. Stuttgart-Zürich: Beiser 1990.

Zevit, Ziony. *The Religions of Ancient Israel: A Synthesis of Parallactic Approaches*. London & New York: Continuum, 2001.

Zimmern, Heinrich. *Beiträge zur Kenntnis der babylonischen Religion*. Leipzig: J. C. Hinrichs, 1896.

Zwickel, Wolfgang. *Räucherkult und Räuchergeräte: Exegetische und archäologische Studien zum Räucheropfer im Alten Testament*. Orbis Biblicus et Orientalis 97. Fribourg: Universitätsverlag; Göttingen: Vandenhoeck & Ruprecht, 1990.

Zwickel, Wolfgang. *Der Tempelkult in Kanaan und Israel: Studien zur Kultgeschichte Palästinas von der Mittelbronzezeit bis zum Untergang Judas*. Forschungen zum Alten Testament 10. Tübingen: Mohr Siebeck, 1994.

Zwickel, Wolfgang. "Religionsgeschichte Israels: Einführung in den gegenwärtigen Forschungsstand in den deutschsprachigen Ländern." In *Religionsgeschichte Israels: Formale und materiale Aspekte*. Veröffentlichungen der wissenschaftlichen Gesellschaft für Theologie 15. Edited by Bernd Janowski and Matthias Köckert, pp. 9–56. Gütersloh: Bertelsmann, 1999.

Index